CORPORATE CONTROLLER'S

HANDBOOK OF

FINANCIAL MANAGEMENT

SECOND EDITION

D1299549

CORPORATE CONTROLLER'S
HANDBOOK OF
FINANCIAL MANAGEMENT

SECOND EDITION

Joel G. Siegel, Ph.D., CPA
Jae K. Shim, Ph.D.
Nicky A. Dauber, MS, CPA

PRENTICE HALL

Library of Congress Cataloging-in-Publication Data

(Revised for Suppl.)
Shim, Jae K.
    Corporate controller's handbook of financial management / Jae K.
Shim, Joel G. Siegel, Nicky A. Dauber.—2nd ed.
      p. cm.
    Siegel's name appears first on the earlier edition.
    Includes Index.
    1. Corporations—Finance. 2. Managerial accounting. I. Siegel,
Joel G. II. Dauber, Nicky A. III. Title.
HG4026.S486 1997   97-17048
658.15—dc21   CIP
ISBN 0-13-042372-6

© 2002 by Prentice Hall

Printed in the United States of America

10 9 8 7 6 5 4 3 2 1

This publication is designed to provide accurate and authoritative information in regard to the subject matter covered. It is sold with the understanding that the publisher is not engaged in rendering legal, accounting, or other professional service. If legal advice or other expert assistance is required, the services of a competent professional person should be sought.
—*From the Declaration of Principles jointly adopted by a Committee of the American Bar Association and a Committee of Publishers and Associations*

ISBN 0-13-042372-6

ATTENTION: CORPORATIONS AND SCHOOLS
Prentice Hall books are available at quantity discounts with bulk purchase for educational, business, or sales promotional use. For information, please write to: Prentice Hall Special Sales, 240 Frisch Court, Paramus, New Jersey 07652. Please supply: title of book, ISBN, quantity, how the book will be used, date needed.

PRENTICE HALL
Paramus, NJ 07652

On the World Wide Web at http://www.phdirect.com

DEDICATION

TODD B. PORTELLO

*The Best Chef in the World
and a Dear Friend*

WHAT THIS SUPPLEMENT WILL DO FOR YOU

This supplement updates the main volume of *Corporate Controller's Handbook of Financial Management, Second Edition.* It includes current developments in financial management, accounting, and taxes. These developments take the form of recent trends in finance, new technology or software applications, and new authoritative accounting requirements. The following are some of the areas that have been updated:

- New pronouncements of the Financial Accounting Standards Board in the areas of income statements, balance sheets, accounting and disclosures, and divestiture.
- Updates to leases, pensions, profit sharing plans, accounting for income taxes, derivative products, and accounts receivable management.
- Updates for payroll taxes.
- Cost-volume-profit analysis and leverage.
- The use of capital budgeting in decision making.
- International finance.

The following new chapters take into account recent developments and/or provide for comprehensive coverage of corporate finance:

- The Corporate Controller and Database Management Systems
- The Corporate Controller and the Client/Server Environment
- The Corporate Controller and Artificial Intelligence Applications
- Accounting Software Packages
- Financial Management Information Systems and Software Packages
- Business Law
- Accounting for Multinational Operations

- Avoiding Financial Distress: Key Financial Ratios and Metrics for Nonprofits
- Total Quality Management (TQM) and Quality Costs
- Risk Management and Analysis
- Reengineering and Outsourcing the Business
- Forecasting and Financial Planning
- Financial and Earnings Forecasting
- Cash Flow Forecasting
- Interest Rate Forecasting
- Forecasting Foreign Exchange Rates
- Evaluation of Forecasts
- Forecasting Tools and Software
- The Use of Computer Software in Managerial Accounting
- Corporate Valuations
- Management Analysis of Operations
- Economic Feasibility Study for an Information Technology (IT) Investment
- Legal and Regulatory Environment of the Firm
- Financial Derivative Products and Financial Reengineering
- Forensic Accounting

Like the main volume, the contents of this supplement are clear, concise, and to the point. Use the cumulative index at the back of this work to locate topics covered in this work or the main volume. Use the two works as your handy "how-to" reference tool.

SUPPLEMENT CONTENTS

THE CORPORATE CONTROLLER AND DATABASE MANAGEMENT SYSTEMS

The corporate controller needs to access a database because it includes accumulated interrelated records of different types and files. The stored information is used by the financial manager to have enough data to make an informed decision. Use should be made of clustering the database in which there is a logical order to the stored information. For example, revenue and cost data may be kept and retrieved in sequential order in department and division order. In database concurrency, there is simultaneous accessing of the database by more than one financial person or application. In looking at the database file, the financial manager sees an accumulation of related records explaining a subject by using a field set.

A database management system refers to software managing and controlling the database. Typically, the database is on a server. Financial managers can define, create, modify, and maintain the database. The standard query language (SQL) is usually used to create and maintain the relational databases, including their access and updating.

A systems catalog lists the data contained in a database. The data may be kept in a text file or a dictionary-like document. The financial manager should be concerned with administering financial information such as managing information resources; developing, designing, planning, and keeping standards; and maintaining policies and procedures.

A network database model is one comprised of interrelated records and data items. The database should furnish a wide range of data to users. It should range from easy questioning to report writing based on different desired specifications to very complex solutions related to decision support systems. A network database model fosters many relationships such as the association between a vendor's database and the stocking of particular merchandise. The merchandise may be bought from different vendors, and each vendor can sell many different types of merchandise.

The financial manager should schedule in sequential order database functions or transactions to accomplish a task in the most efficient way. In sequential access, the financial manager selects all records of a particular type.

In a leap file, financial records are in the identical order of insertion. Database files may be subdivided (fragmented) over a number of documents. In replication, there is a duplicating of key elements of the database in different locations and assuring that copies of the information are updated simultaneously.

In a computer-aided manufacturing database we store manufacturing-related data—for example, *as* data for the production of goods such as appliances.

We can use sensitivity analysis to determine how output is affected by inputs. Input variables may be modified at the same time to see the impact on outcome. Sensitivity analysis allows us to determine the relative importance of the various inputs. A model may be constructed to forecast multiple variables. An experimentation with different combinations of input variables may lead to better overall results. Further, the financial manager should rank variables in the order of importance.

It is possible that data on a particular topic of interest is obtained from different sources. In such cases, the controller should be careful that erroneous conclusions are not drawn when the various sources present similar data in different manners. If data are missing, the controller must be careful if he or she decides to guess at the data left out or use mean, median, or common value figures.

Data conversion tool software extracts information from heterogeneous sources and transfers the source information to target data and then derives the programming codes to process it. Data must be carefully checked for consistency to ensure successful processing.

The financial manager should split the database into segments of similar financial records. An example is sales territories having a particular range of sales. In segmentation, the corporate controller may want to break down a larger project into smaller ones for analysis purposes.

In hypothesis testing, the financial manager attempts to prove or disprove an assumption. The hypothesis is proved or not by evaluating information via observation and testing.

This chapter discusses database security, classification of data, object databases, distributed databases, hierarchical databases, multidimensional databases, multimedia databases, meta-data, data warehousing, data marts, data modeling, link analysis, knowledge-based systems, market basket analysis, memory-based reasoning, data mining, fuzzy searches, neural networks, online analytical processing, online transaction processing, genetic algorithms, decision trees, and personal information agents.

DATABASE SECURITY

Kerberos is one centralized server having secured user names and passwords for all information and resources on the network. Kerberos servers have such security features as login database access and authorization codes. The Kerberos server identifies and validates a user.

It may be advisable to have a secure single login in which users log into the network rather than to each specific server or application. Access is permitted only to authorized resources.

Security of the database may be aided by referential integrity checks, which compare data among tables for appropriateness and logical relationship order. For security, we should match the database to the transaction log file. A transaction log is a listing of database transactions including updates for managing and control purposes.

The security analyzer tool for analyzing networks (SATAN) reviews the network to spot security weak points. System fault tolerances are networking aspects that safeguard the network from faults. An analytical report is prepared indicating problem areas and possible solutions.

The financial manager should hide sensitive financial information in the database so it is not revealed to unauthorized individuals. To access a database, proper identification such as a password is required. In a database lock, database data cannot be accessed or altered until a transaction has been finalized. A shared lock is a database lock that allows users to read data but not update it.

A time bomb is a virus activated at a particular date or time. Antivirus software must be used.

To assure staff are familiar with the security procedures and policies to be adhered to in a database management system, a control plan should exist. Control-related statements should provide detailed directions to conduct procedures and explain the needs for the security system. Any policy statements should not be subject to short-term modifications. The control plan should be distributed and consistent throughout the company. The plan should have some flexibility so it may be successfully adapted to different parts of the entity that may differ to some degree from one another. The control plan should be periodically reviewed to insure that any changes in the company's circumstances or improvements in technologies are responded to.

Databases containing sensitive information must be restricted only to authorized individuals. Database access should be assigned different levels of confidentiality and security such as generally accessible data (unrestricted), internal use only, and top secret. Confidential information should not be displayed on computer screens without the appropriate access codes. Employee compliance should be periodically reviewed to insure that individuals are honoring the controls that have been established. Each database function (e.g., payroll) should require its own password so that employees only have access to the areas that they have been approved and authorized for. Segregation of duties should also exist. For example, a programer who modifies or patches a program should not have access to the computer database area or library to assure the prevention of data manipulation. Thus, segregation of duties should exist between programers, installation librarians, operators, data processing personnel, users, and control employees.

The Information Technology Internal Auditor should be concerned with the following areas when reviewing the company's database system:

- Monitoring and appraising the company's computer policy and security standards applying to the database and network.
- Supporting internal auditing functions during operational and compliance audits.

In auditing a typical database system, the IT auditor will review and analyze the following areas of the company's information system:

- Personnel practices applying to the installation.
- Contingency planning and disaster recovery.
- Data center structure.
- Backup controls of the data center.
- Effectiveness and efficiency of operating and administrative procedures.
- Standards of developing the installation.
- Specific control practices.
- Control procedures of the database information library.

The Information Technology auditor is responsible to assure that the company's database system controls are in place and properly functioning. To achieve this, the following specific control functions should be watched and appraised by the IT auditor:

- Errors and omissions are identified and corrected. However, the emphasis should be on preventing these problems in the first place.
- Assurance that jobs are performed in a timely manner.
- Transactions are properly approved and authorized by the appropriate level of management.
- Transactions are correctly processed.
- Functions should be reviewed periodically with incompatible activities being segregated.

Transaction trails should exist of additions, deletions, or modifications of data processed by the database. Audit trails should be created or made available to provide the IT auditor information regarding (1) the date and time of the transactions, (2) who processed the transactions, and (3) where the transaction was initiated (e.g., terminal). Most database software has the ability to track database transactions.

CLASSIFICATION

Data may be classified from the population in similar groups. The classification may be based on a training model. The classes of information are periodically appraised and updated. For example, we can classify potential clients as low, medium, or high risk. In some cases, the financial manager may start with a training set and build a predictor model on the grouping of new records. For example, credit card customers may be segmented into predefined classes to ascertain whom to send promotional mailings.

OBJECT DATABASES

In an object database management system, objects are stored in a multiuser client/server form. We can have concurrent access to objects. Objects can be protected from threats and transactions can be safeguarded. The object database management system adds to the traditional database management system the functions of questioning, concurrency, locking, and protection.

DISTRIBUTED DATABASE MANAGEMENT SYSTEMS

A distributed database is a collection of tables spread over at least two servers in the company at different locations. With distributed transactions, one transaction gives a sequence of database requests to different remote database servers. This allows for database update on various servers. A transaction consists of SQL statements, each allowing for the access of data at different locations. In distributed transactions processing, transactions are processed over multiple distributed linked computers in multiple geographically situated locations.

HIERARCHICAL DATABASES

In a hierarchical database, there is a family tree of related record types. Lower-level records are subordinate to higher-level ones.

MULTIMEDIA DATABASES

In a multimedia database we have abstract unstructured data such as audio, graphics, video, animation, hypertext, and hypermedia.

MULTIDIMENSIONAL DATABASES

With multidimensional databases, we handle multiple dimensions that include product, service, geographic locality, customer, client, guest, order, salesperson, and time period. A multidimensional database for a company's products may include time, territory, sales volume, customer, price, vendor, store, and total sales. Data may be appraised using alternative dimensions.

DATA WAREHOUSING

A data warehouse enhances productivity within the controller's department. It provides timely and accurate financial information. The data warehouse organizes and classifies information.

In data warehousing, there is a voluminous database of summarized and detailed interrelated information that may be extracted and analyzed in making financial management decisions. Detailed information may relate to sales, purchases, payables, and receivables. There is a vast accumulation of past and current data. It is updated continuously because data are reliable for a specified time period. This updating may be via planned batch processing to foster comparative analysis. (However, in some cases, a data warehouse may not be designed to update data immediately and repetitively.) The database is subject-oriented and timely. Complex, analytical, and investigative questioning of the data warehouse may solve financial problems. Data warehousing includes data regarding payroll, accounting, finance, marketing, and management. Information stored is usually classified by type such as by product/service line, department, division, sales territory, marketing survey data, suppliers, customers, orders, transactions, physical resource, personnel, or financial resource. A major purpose of a data warehouse is to question a database spread over a multinational company.

The data warehouse allows the company to integrate its cumulative operational information into an accessible means so that forecasts, trends, and strategic decisions may be derived.

The financial data of all departments of the company are put into a database that can be managed, controlled, and evaluated.

In data warehousing, there should be integration of extraction, retrieval, cleansing, questioning, and summarizing. For this purpose, meta-data integration software is available.

The Corporate Controller and Database Management Systems

Data transformation from the data sources to the data warehouse should be well documented. Data going into the data warehouse are from numerous operational databases inside and outside the company. Thus, information is accumulated from sources in different locations. The financial manager should be abreast of where information came from and how it was modified and transformed. Merged information should be put into a standardized and consistent format to enhance decision making and support. Therefore, there should be a derived commonality in data definition, structure, and relationships. Errors and inconsistencies in the data must be rectified to assure information quality. A data warehouse may be used for training purposes.

Data warehousing may be used in internal audits by providing information and analysis to appraise corporate activities and control operations. It fosters an examination of the company's efficiency. Inefficiencies may be indicated by comparing estimated to actual amounts. Areas of fraud, irregularities, and errors may readily be identified. Areas of sensitivity are highlighted.

Marketers may use a customer or guest database to profile individuals who are apt to respond to special incentives. Further, the company may accumulate information regarding buying patterns of their major customers to stimulate purchases by them.

Problems with the quality of goods may be identified by looking at the trend in product returns or allowances due to defective merchandise. An analysis may also be made of buying schedules to ascertain the appropriate times to buy merchandise to take advantage of lower prices and quantity discounts.

Data warehousing can be used by insurance companies to ascertain prospective policyholders who may be underwriting risks.

Divisions doing poorly may be identified. Then either corrective action may be taken or those divisions may be liquidated or sold.

Applications of data warehousing include:

- Measuring the impact of changing prices on product demand
- Detailing credit standing of a new customer
- Pricing based on inventory patterns and demand
- Detecting insurance and warranty claims fraud

Meta-data describe data included in the data warehouse including where they came from, content, and importance. Information flow in and out of the data warehouse is indicated. Therefore, the history of any data may be reconstructed. Meta-data reveal what data are available in the system and their location. As such, meta-data enable financial managers to comprehend the logical data model of the data warehouse. Meta-data enable us to track the data components of the data warehouse, data content, integration and transformation of data, and from where the data were derived. Meta-data involve a review and analysis of where information was extracted, indexing process, statistical analysis, data aggregations, and patterns. For control purposes, meta-data should be well defined, updated, secured, integrated, comprehendible, and documented. Retrieval policies should be specified.

DATA MARTS

A data mart is a data file consisting of logical records. It is an element of a data warehouse furnishing summarized information that can be used in decision making by a department or division manager. The data mart may be either tied to or separated from the entity's centralized data warehouse. Because data marts have much less data than a data warehouse, a data mart is simpler to understand and utilize.

Data marts service the data requirements of particular departments within the organization. Data marts are of benefit and use to specific departments. A data mart is a subset of a data warehouse that accumulates the information required by a particular department or other responsibility unit such as a product or service line. Also, a given data mart might be used solely by two or more departments on a shared basis for common requirements.

Information for the data mart is directly obtained from the data warehouse of the overall company. (However, it is possible to construct a data mart as an independent unit with departmental information accumulated just for it.) With a data mart, information may be available more quickly because of substantially less transaction volume. Further, the information may be better customized to meet the department's needs. Another benefit of a data mart is that its cost is much lower than that of a data warehouse.

Data marts may be transportable personal warehouses on a laptop to be used by internal auditing staff when auditing branches.

DATA MODELING

A data model involves designing and planning a database. In an entity's data model there is shown important financial information, key relationships between financial data, and the impact of the information on the firm. The financial manager should make use of a data model in explaining information, their interrelations, and limitations. The financial manager wants to fully understand the database. Noted are cases in which data are shared.

In modeling, an output(s) is derived from inputs. In a time series model, we see the effect of a factor over time, such as the market price of the company's stock based on various changes associated with the company's financial health. In a clustering model, financial records are grouped in terms of similarity. An example is finding what similar financial characteristics divisions of the company have in common. In a classification model, we classify a record based on some predetermined criteria. New classifications may emerge in addition to old classifications. A prediction model forecasts future results based on past and current information. The correctness of the model as a predictor should be assessed by comparing what is expected to what actually happens. What is the degree of deviation? The model should be tested over time. Any changes should be incorporated as needed.

LINK ANALYSIS

The financial manager should engage in link analysis, looking at the relationship between fields such as relating departmental profit to departmental assets. In link appraisal, the financial manager looks at how financial records are related to see what patterns exist. For example, the financial manager may want to know the likelihood that merchandise or services will be purchased together. Also, how are vendors associated and what effect will that have on the company if there is a shortage of raw material? What is the link between customers, lenders, and employee unions?

In link analysis, the corporate controller may find new characteristics associated with financial data. However, the controller should note that link analysis is not as reliable with large data sets as with smaller ones.

KNOWLEDGE DISCOVERY

Knowledge discovery does not involve prior assumptions. The financial manager searches database information so as to draw new views or management conclusions. A knowledge base is a set of information to answer queries and solve business problems. What patterns are evident? There is an emphasis on finding meaningful information. Data are chosen, refined, and put into a useful form. The data are then evaluated to see what should be investigated further. Based on the results, management will undertake steps to control a problem situation or eliminate a problem. For example, is there a way to attract additional business? Special attention should be given to unusual associations. However, when files are marked "secure," they may not be transferred.

Knowledge discovery helps us determine who is apt to purchase certain kinds of merchandise.

MARKET BASKET ANALYSIS

The market basket analysis (MBA) method classifies item groupings that take place together in a transaction. MBA is particularly appropriate for numeric and categorical data. The financial manager should examine the likelihood of different goods or services being bought together in some logical order. Thus, we can use MBA to examine multiple buys by a customer or a sales catalog of numerous types of merchandise. Guidelines for this process should be enumerated. Why do customers purchase certain products? Which customers buy multiple products simultaneously and why? MBA also aids in establishing a good advertising and promotion plan.

With MBA, we can better compare sales derived from different geographic areas like urban versus suburban. Seasonal differences may be taken into account.

If there is an unexpected combination of insurance claims over a short time period, it may point to fraud.

MEMORY-BASED REASONING

Under memory-based reasoning (MBR), we use cases of known events or occurrences to predict unknown events or instances. We look at similar events (neighbors) in prior years to predict what will happen now. The number of neighbors to use for analysis depends on information distribution and the nature of the problem being evaluated. What was an insurance company's historical experience with the types of claims being submitted now? Did fraud occur in prior years? Were the claims legitimate and immediately paid? MBR can also be used to predict how customers will react to a particular advertisement.

The degree of similarity or dissimilarity between the historical records and current records must be ascertained. What is the distance between the two? The less distance, the more reliable will be the conclusions drawn.

The training set is the historical records that enable us to find the nearest neighbors to an unknown (current) record. For useful results to occur, an adequate amount of records by category is necessary. The more the neighbors used, the more accurate will be the conclusions.

The training set should include a sufficient number of occurrences for all possible classifications. We should also include for analytical purposes rare instances such as fraud so we have a good balance of usual and unusual occurrences for all categories. Better results are achieved when the training set is voluminous and representative.

DATA MINING

Data mining involves software examining a database to identify patterns, relationships, and trends to assist in financial management decision making. We extract past and current information from a voluminous database for analysis. Are there any problem areas requiring corrective action? To be effective, data mining relies on the source data to be accurate, consistent, and integrated. Data mining looks both to confirm anticipated patterns and to uncover new patterns. Anything unusual, hidden, or unexpected should be investigated.

Data mining allows financial managers to evaluate integrated consistent information for future strategic decisions. However, over time, data mining results may change due to, say, changing economic and political factors. Data mining results should be reviewed by the controller for common sense and reasonableness. The controller may be able to come up with new ideas, guidelines, yardsticks, and rules. Data mining assists in improving corporate operations and the resulting bottom line.

A data warehouse stores data while data mining extracts, cleanses, and appraises the information for management decision making. Data mining provides intelligence to a database.

In deciding on the appropriate data mining method suitable in a given situation, the corporate controller should take into account the circumstances, tasks to be performed, nature of input in terms of quality and amount, reliability required, type of output, importance, training desired, available software and data, scalability, and accuracy and understandability of the model.

In data mining, we go through large databases to search for useful patterns, relationships, and trends. Some of the results ensuing will be expected, others will be unexpected. The corporate controller will continually question the database until a complete financial picture emerges. Any unanticipated patterns should be verified through repeated questioning and evaluation. The controller can refine his or her search by only extracting key information. In actuality, data mining is most advantageous when there is a vast amount of sophisticated and complex information.

We may use artificial intelligence or statistical methods when searching and evaluating the data warehouse or data marts. Data mining involves clusters, segmentation, grouping, linking, predicting, explaining, and highlighting variances between expected and actual financial figures.

Managerial and financial applications for which data mining may be applied include determining whether a bank should grant a loan to a particular borrower (and, if so, how much), spotting insurance fraud, noting fraudulent warranty claims and credit card fraud, creating advertising and promotional efforts to maximize sales (including gauging which prospective customers will react best to a specified promotion, or which products or services are most favored by customers in a particular geographic area), evaluating and selecting vendors, financial statement analysis including the appraisal of profitability and liquidity, customer profiling based on such factors as buying behavior, selection of stocks and bonds in portfolio management, establishing a credit rating for a loan applicant or customer, pricing of products and/or services, ascertaining risk level for a new project or proposal, predicting sales, inventory control, production management, detecting questionable patterns of internal funds transfers, ascertaining the degree of customer confidence and commitment, customer service, determining which products or services to cross-sell, marketing research and planning, and finding the reasons why products or services sell better in certain markets or to certain customer types.

Other applications include appraising seasonality issues, deciding on which products to push and when, arranging merchandise in a branch store or sales catalog to generate the most orders, deciding how to best package merchandise, profiling clients and hotel guests, uncovering forgeries in documents, quality control including identifying defective goods bought from a supplier, determining products a particular class of customer is likely to buy (e.g., young people are more apt to buy sporting merchandise than older individuals), predicting future prices in commodities, forecasting foreign currency exchange rates, direct marketing, predicting employee theft, deriving optimal selling techniques, credit approval, employee or customer development and retention, deciding on whether to offer discounts for certain products to promote sales, planning store layout to promote business, assessing the possibility of a product or service line failing, determining the merchandise mix in a retail store, projecting profit of a new product or service, forecasting expected profit from a new customer, predicting trading patterns of securities, estimating which hotel guests are likely to return, grouping and classifying customers, picking the best location for a new store, improving product design, determining customer retention, appraising suppliers, deciding which customers should receive incentives so they do not switch to competitors, efficiently allocating resources, deciding on advertising approaches to maximize orders, determining the best piggyback products, risk reduction, and demographic analysis.

Numeric variables are good for data mining purposes because they may be totaled and sorted in mathematical computations. An example is costs.

There are many considerations to take into account when selecting data mining software. These include how many data records exist, database access, reporting aspects and requirements, network functioning, simplicity, documentation, graphic support, operating systems, data compatibility, scalability in product and users, technical support, interfaces supported, and organizational fit.

FUZZY SEARCH

In a fuzzy search, user direction is absent or minimal. If–then rules may also be derived. The controller may in fact not know beforehand what he or she is looking for. As far as the search process is concerned, in market basket analysis, the controller tries to identify patterns where the occurrence of something implies something else will happen. In a sequential search, there is a chronological time order to events or patterns. In a search cluster, the controller looks to classify items in homogeneous groupings.

NEURAL NETWORKS

In neural networks (NN), the financial manager must identify input and output factors. A range from 0 to 1 must exist after inputs and outputs have been modified. It is crucial to select the "right" input data and the appropriate examples. Multiple inputs should be used. The neural network can be used to derive outputs for unknown inputs.

A training set is the basis to teach the NN. Based on the findings of the examples in a training set, learning occurs. NNs imitate the human mind. NNs uncover patterns in information and express the extent of a relationship between two variables. Combinations of variables are considered. Actual results are compared to expectations. The training process has been completed once the training set has gone through a maximum number of times or there is no or minimal change in the weights. At that time, the NN is the working model.

The training set should have a full assortment of all the factors the network will experience. The training variables must be representative. The neural network learns from past patterns. It must be updated for current developments.

Prediction is enhanced through the use of training examples. Training examples should exist for each weight in the network. Each weight should have about 20 training examples. Internal weights are improved to aid prediction. However, the number of training examples per output should be approximately the same. Both good and bad examples should be used. After all, you want the NN to identify problem situations. For example, if we are trying to spot a rare occurrence (e.g., credit card fraud), the training set should have a sufficient number of instances of the rare occurrences.

Once the neural network has learned from the training set, a new set of examples should be used. How well has the neural network been instructed? Is further training required?

The time required to train the NN partly depends on the number of inputs involved. The more variables, the longer the time period to train. Further, if the number of input factors grows too large, less reliable solutions may be forthcoming. The discarding of unimportant variables will improve prediction accuracy.

In feed-forward networks, the financial manager should take into account activation (how units react and merge), topology (how units are connected), and back propagation (how the network learns to recognize patterns).

Two advantages of the NN are that many different types of problem areas are solved and canned software is available. A disadvantage of NNs is the inability to explain results.

ONLINE ANALYTICAL PROCESSING

Online analytical processing (OLAP) assists financial executives in gaining a clear and consistent perspective on financial information so as to facilitate decision making. OLAP enables controllers to gain perception of information quickly and consistently in an interactive way. What patterns and trends are evident in the financial data?

Information can be modified depending on need. The controller may use OLAP for data reporting purposes.

OLAP techniques are used in accessing voluminous databases, including data stored in a centralized data warehouse, operational system, or virtual distributed warehouse. OLAP extracts information from a data warehouse that is relevant, understandable, important, correct, and timely. Many OLAP tools have drill-down capabilities into the initial database. The controller is able to get interactive access to a large variety of data views.

OLAP is an approach to original and condensed historical multidimensional data to assist corporate controllers in better understanding the information and reaching sound decisions. As the financial environment changes, an updating of the information will be necessary. The result will be comprehensive, current, and reliable data.

In OLAP, why and what-if questions can be asked and answered to improve financial decision making. For instance, the financial manager may wish to find out how the entity's new products have affected its sales over the past three years by major geographic region. There are significant analytical attributes. Data may be evaluated by some predetermined criteria. Further, OLAP gives financial managers the opportunity to probe and appraise corporate data in bits and pieces.

OLAP is mostly a decision support technique with such beneficial characteristics as links, dimensions, and formulas. The specifics of each feature are evaluated. With OLAP, the controller is provided with the records answering his queries as well as with scenario settings.

There are several factors that need to be considered in choosing a suitable OLAP tool for a given application. Factors include type of software used, conformity to the company's environment, future needs, scalability, questioning capabilities and evaluative techniques, operations to be conducted, performance, and ability to add, delete, or modify data.

In OLAP, we have multidimensional aggregate data providing fast access to key financial information so it can be properly appraised by the corporate controller. In most cases, corporate controllers examine financial information by product or service line, scenario, geographic area, and time. It is essential that financial executives can appraise data by dimension, function, or aggregation level. Multidimensional online analytical processing is suitable for financial applications where detailed computations are needed for different products, services, business segments, responsibility units, divisions, and departments of the company. With multidimensional information, financial executives may obtain budgeted compared to actual amounts as well as summarized financial data by product/service line, time, and organization. Sales may be noted by time, product, service, sales price, geographic area, distribution channel, and customer. A typical query in OLAP is, "What are the sales by product, service, customer, quarter, and store?" OLAP can go across various domains—for example, presenting sales in stores and credit card charges.

Financial applications of OLAP include financial forecasting (e.g., sales), retrieval of relevant financial information for decision making from large data sets, budgeting, operating performance analysis, financial modeling, and activity-based costing. In production, OLAP assists in manufacturing planning and uncovering assembly line problem areas. In marketing, OLAP assists with marketing research, market segmentation, customer appraisal, and advertising and promotion.

In evaluating the company compared to competitors, OLAP can be helpful to financial managers by looking at the percentage growth in accounts such as revenue, costs, and assets. We can model complex and sophisticated relationships.

Advantages of OLAP include fast computation and response time, flexibility, interactivity, and easy application. Also, it considers multidimensional data, supplies timely information, and is sound in analyzing time series. Unfortunately, continuous variables are not handled well.

ONLINE TRANSACTION PROCESSING

With online transaction processing (OLTP), transactions are immediately entered. Information has to be accurate and consistent. The nature of processing is repetitive with continual updates. Database integrity should have proper controls. Numerous applications exist such as inventory control, management control, and collections. OLTP is mostly structured for transactional, repetitive processing instead of unstructured investigative processing. By using OLTP, the financial manager can optimize his or her transaction processing capability associated with such applications as manufacturing, accounting, marketing, and sales. OLTP is application and event driven. Data in OLTP are changing and volatile.

In OLTP, the nature of questioning involves day-to-day operations such as the updating of inventory for buys and sells. At a certain inventory level, a reorder occurs.

GENETIC ALGORITHMS

Genetic algorithms (GAs) may be used in scheduling physical and human resources subject to limitations (e.g., budget). There is an allocation of limited resources, taking into account relationships among resources and users.

GAs can help find optimal values such as the best selling price, optimal number of units to produce, and correct number of staff to service customer/client needs. Disadvantages of GAs involve encoding and high cost.

DECISION TREES

A decision tree breaks down records into subsets. They are easy to understand because the flow of the financial decision process is shown such as:

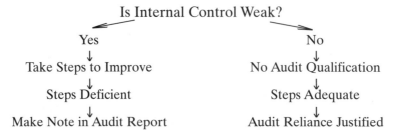

A decision tree asks questions in sequential order. This method is feasible when you can derive comprehendible and explainable rules.

Decision trees can prioritize inputs by importance. The features that are higher on the decision tree have superior predictive ability.

Benefits of using the decision tree approach are better understanding of the logical sequence of events, a presentation of the importance of factors, and a facilitation of the derivation of rules.

PERSONAL INFORMATION AGENTS

Personal information agents are mobile applications on data warehouses to perform questioning or uncover data patterns. Many agents are rule-based, such as "if A occurs, do Y." Agents should be able to note unexpected occurrences or events within a data warehouse. The typical personal information agent can specify the particular subject or event based on a specified time frame. Any changes in the subject area are updated.

THE CORPORATE CONTROLLER AND THE CLIENT/SERVER ENVIRONMENT

The corporate controller should have some basic familiarity with the client/server environment. There should be a list of authorized users with specified identifications to access certain equipment or information files. Different layers of authorization should exist depending on the activities to be performed.

A network should be designed to meet corporate goals and purposes. In a client/server arrangement, computers are connected by a network in which some computers (clients) process applications while other computers (servers) provide services (e.g., Internet hosting, file storage) to the clients. Depending on need, it is possible to combine various clients and servers. In-process servers execute in the same processing space as clients.

In a client/server environment, the corporate controller is primarily concerned with issues of functioning, decision making, and security.

FUNCTIONING

Does transparency exist, and if so, to what extent? Transparency is the ability of distributed processing systems to merge clients and servers of different operating systems and protocols into a logical framework that processes distributed applications.

Middleware is the software layer enabling the communication and accessing of information between servers and clients. If differences or irregularities are found, they should be reconciled.

Network traffic may be appraised with a network analyzer. An example is the decoding of data packets. A work flow manager facilitates and monitors multistep data movement through the network. Transaction processing (TP) monitors and polices client/server traffic. It manages transactions from the initiation point, typically on the client, across servers, and then back to the initiating client. TP monitors can run transactions, route and execute transactions, and restart them after failure. If a network management issue needs to be resolved, point products software may be written.

On a periodic basis, equipment and software should be checked as to their proper functioning, including making comparisons to norms. To safeguard the system, one server should substitute for another one that has malfunctioned.

The financial manager may want to make use of a remote procedure call allowing software running on the client to use the services of a program running on the server.

A network management platform (framework) enables integration between a shared database and modules to which alerts and warnings are stored.

There should be global services in which the network operating system can locate a particular user, resource, or server regardless of location.

With a peer-to-peer network any computer on the network can act as a server. Local area networks (LANs) accommodate network activities for departments and divisions. To access shared network services and resources, use LAN resource management software.

Point-to-point protocol clients are remote clients that are linked to servers operating in different network operating systems.

Financial managers should make use of groupware so staff can communicate and work together in electronic form so as to enhance productivity regardless of location or time.

For the distribution of code and data across clients and servers we use mobile agents.

DECISION MAKING

An executive information system furnishes data on how the entity is presently conducting its financial and operating functions. It gives management up-to-date information to make better decisions.

The financial manager should be aware of performance metrics, which compare actual performance to established standards. A significant variance is examined for corrective action.

The financial manager should engage in what-if analysis, which is a simulation approach predicting the outcome of changing inputs relative to alternative network scenarios. What-if analysis is undertaken to derive optimal solutions. To look at what-if possibilities associated with the network we can use network simulation and modeling software. Decision support system software allows managers to derive better decisions based on available information. Customization of reports occurs.

In packetizing, we add management information to raw data so it is properly delivered.

Personal information agents represent mobile applications on the data warehouse. Questions are asked to uncover patterns and unexpected events. Agents are usually rule-based. Agents warn if something unusual occurs. A financial manager may use personal information management software to maximize his or her productivity.

SECURITY CONCERNS

The financial manager should be assured that protective steps have been taken to protect the computer system such as financial database files. We can restrict access to information on the network by having a nonprivileged mode.

Encryption equipment can be used to assure proper security during transmission. Encryption safeguards a message so it cannot be comprehended except if the receiver has a "key" to decipher it. A private key is a shared confidential key used to encrypt or decrypt a message or transmission. In encryption, we begin with an initial uncoded message and scramble the plain text with an algorithm that has a key to derive unintelligible ciphertext. Further, checksums should be used to provide confidence that data have not been improperly changed while being processed over the network.

There should be a security server keeping security data such as names and passwords. A password authentication protocol repeatedly transmits user identifications and passwords for authentication reasons. A digital signature (electronic identification) assures the author's authenticity and the integrity of the communication or message. A digital signature is attached to documents being transferred electronically for security to guarantee that a sender is actually who he or she purports to be. The signature gives assurance that the document has not been changed improperly. Digital signature encryption is public key encryption in reverse. Further, security can be enhanced by using network auditing tools that highlight which users accessed which network files.

Before a server acts on an important client request, the server should substantiate the appropriateness of the request.

There is network filtering software that examines source and destination addresses to determine access. Internal firewalls are filters on the network to ascertain if corporate transmissions on the internal network are authorized. Filter tables list those individuals authorized to proceed through the firewall server into the entity's network. Filter tables may have different levels of access to different file types. With application-level filters, there is additional security by evaluating the whole data request rather than just the source and destination addresses.

There should be workstation-based security software. To monitor suspicious behavior of employees and outside users we can use intrusion detection software. The financial manager should make use of performance monitoring software in which limits are set for which an overage over such limits indicates a problem to be appraised and corrected for. There is usually an audit trail.

The financial manager should note the proper values applicable to various data fields. We may use and allow decoy files to be infected so as to identify, monitor, and control viruses. In preemptive monitoring, there is a problem run on a recurring basis to diagnostically test network traffic to alert the financial manager if a malfunction is detected. We must be on guard against polymorphic viruses, which are viruses that change their appearance each time infected software is run to make detection more difficult. A Trojan horse is a virus hidden in a legitimate program. We can identify unknown viruses via running an emulation program. Antivirus software must be used to safeguard data files and programs.

Any out-of-the-ordinary occurrences should be investigated. We can use event detection software to identify and filter data for such unexpected events.

Security penetration/vulnerability analysis should be conducted periodically to uncover any possible problems. Penetration tools, such as the Security Analysis Tool for Auditing Networks (SATAN), should be used to try to break into a system to uncover weaknesses in the firewall and router configurations. Automated tools exist to audit the computer system and report potential security weaknesses. Vulnerabilities are identified such as poor passwords or failure to update software with security patches. Vulnerability testing tools search for potential weaknesses that may allow an attacker to gain unauthorized access.

Vulnerability tests may audit the system or launch a mock attack. Vulnerability testing programs may be classified according to scope. Their focus may be narrow and they may examine just a single vulnerability or their emphasis may be broad and they may appraise the whole system.

Access controls should exist to use a specific terminal or application. Data and time constraints along with file usage should be enumerated. Unauthorized use should deactivate or lock a terminal.

The Corporate Controller and Artificial Intelligence Applications

The purpose of artificial intelligence (AI) is to replicate human reasoning and brain activity. AI aids in distributing expertise to nonexpert staff. A "shell" is a collection of software packages and tools used to design, develop, implement, and maintain AI expert systems for a company.

EXPERT SYSTEMS

An expert system is a set of computer programs conducting a task at the level of a human expert. A good candidate for an expert system is an application requiring the use of expert knowledge, judgment, and experience. Expert systems can explain the reasoning behind a conclusion, and this capability is critical in validating the results. In fact, the expert system can ultimately become more knowledgeable over time. The expert system keeps learning and applies that knowledge to formulate better decisions.

A series of logical sequential questions is asked of the user by the expert system. Follow-up questions are based on the answers to the prior questions. After all questions have been asked and answered, conclusions are drawn by the expert system.

There are six key elements in an expert system comprised of:

- Knowledge database of rules, cases, and criteria in making decisions.
- Domain database of suitable information in the particular area of interest.

- Database management system to control the input and management of the above two databases.

- Inference engine (processing system) consisting of the interface strategies and controls used by experts in using and manipulating the first two databases. It acts as the brain of the expert system. It receives the request from the user interface and carries out reasoning in the knowledge base. The inference engine assists in problem solving by processing and scheduling rules. It asks for further data from the user, makes assumptions about the information, and formulates conclusions and recommendations. The inference engine may also determine the degree to which a recommendation is qualified and, in the case of multiple solutions, rank them.

- User interfaces are the explanatory features, online assistance, and debugging tools assisting the user in comprehending and properly using the expert system.

- Knowledge acquisition facility enables interactive processing between the user and the system. It allows the system to obtain appropriate knowledge and experience of the human.

Figure 1 presents expert system relationships.

The knowledge is comprised of two kinds of knowledge representations: rule-based and case-based. The rule base of an expert system contains

Figure 1   Expert System Relationships

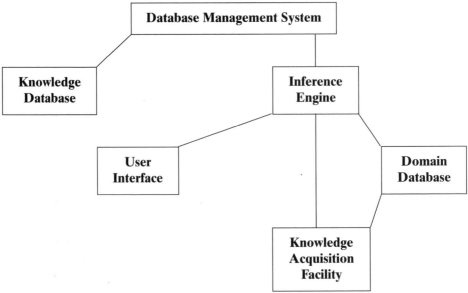

a set of production rules. Each rule has an "if-then" clause. Expert system users furnish facts or statements so that production rules are triggered and conclusions forthcoming. In a case-based expert system, an inductive method is used to perform expert system reasoning. A case base is used comprised of many "historical" cases having different results. Cases consist of information regarding a situation, the solution, results of using that solution, and major attributes. The expert inference engine searches through the case base and finds the appropriate historical case, which matches the facts of the present problem to be resolved. After there is a match, the solution of the matched historical case will be modified and used as the new suggestions for the current problem.

Expert systems provide decision models for planning and control. Applications of expert systems include:

- Financial analysis
- Preparing and conducting audits
- Preparation of accounts and reports
- Evaluate creditworthiness of customers
- Planning to reduce costs
- Planning to enhance productivity and quality of products and services
- Appraisal of internal controls
- Claim authorization and processing
- Competitive analysis
- Manufacturing and capacity planning and scheduling
- Analysis of revenue (by price, volume, and product/service mix)
- Cost analysis (by category and type)
- Inventory analysis
- Resource planning
- Preparation of budgets and forecasts
- Credit authorization
- Appraisal of risk
- Bankruptcy prediction
- Ascertaining sufficiency of expense provisions and revenue sources
- Appraisal of mergers and acquisitions
- Compliance reporting
- Aging of accounts (e.g., customers)
- Deciding whether to refinance debt
- Improve productivity

In auditing, expert systems can reduce the cost and time in making audit decisions and in improving the audit plan and substantive testing. Expert systems can choose or develop an audit program, perform an analytical review, appraise source information and evidence, select a sample and test data, compute and analyze error rate, plan and watch over the audit engagement, identify relationships between accounts that do not make sense, appraise assets and liabilities, evaluate internal control and risk level, and ascertain disclosure compliance.

Business Foundations' Internal Operations Risk Analysis software appraises a company's areas of risk and internal control structure. It highlights strengths and weaknesses in business operations. A risk rating is assigned to risk categories. It recommends corrective steps for problem areas.

In managerial accounting, expert systems assist in capital budgeting decision making such as buying the "right" asset, having the most advantageous product and service mix, keeping or selling a business segment, and buying or leasing. Expert systems aid in optimally allocating resources based on such factors as cost, time availability, risk, and demand patterns. Financial Advisor developed at MIT's Sloan School of Management evaluates capital investments in property, plant, and equipment. It also provides advice on projects, products, and acquisitions. Arthur D. Little's expert system conducts variance analysis and explains the reasons for significant variances.

In taxation, expert systems are used in tax preparation and planning, and in facilitating compliance with tax rules and procedures.

The expert system can decide if a loan should be made and if so, the amount of credit to be given. It takes into account profitability, risk, economic factors, and management's policy. The expert system can approve the loan based on predetermined criteria and subject to specified restrictions and limitations. The expert system may decide on the appropriate interest rate, credit line, collateral requirements, and repayment schedule. Questionable loans are highlighted for careful attention.

In investment analysis, expert systems can recommend suitable investments, taking into account such considerations as return/risk preferences, tax rate, dividend yield, portfolio mix, liquidity, and economic conditions. Expert systems aid in the best timing of purchases and sales of stocks because they integrate and consider real-time multiple internal/external data sources. Watchdog Investment Monitoring System is used in investment analysis and management, including financial statement analysis and financial forecasting.

A "rule generator" expert system notes information patterns and formulates trading recommendations. A "critic" expert system evaluates and reviews system-suggested trades coupled with the explanation of doing so. An expert system can provide 24-hour trading programs so as to optimally take advantage of domestic and international market conditions such as changes in foreign exchange rates. Expert systems can identify and evaluate arbitrage opportunities and trigger transactions.

An insurance company may use expert systems to appraise and prcoess claims including those of a questionable nature. Escape is used for claim authorization and processing.

The knowledge base of the expert system for marketing purposes includes market structure, customer characteristics, and competition. Expert systems may be used in market planning, marketing decision making, product/service introduction, new product development and enhancement, product features and options, marketing mix decisions, price formulation, return policy, warranty service planning, appraisal of product quality, discount formulation policy, setting credit terms, and advertising and promotion.

Applied Expert Systems' Plan Power is a financial planning expert system that takes into account a financial situation, then matches needs with the most suitable financial products and services. Additionally, the system will run scenario spreadsheets showing the income tax situation, cash flows, net worth, and other key factors based on alternative decisions.

NEURAL NETWORKS

Neural network software simulates human intelligence and learns from experience. For example, each time neural network software makes the correct decision (predetermined by a human expert) on recognizing sequential patterns of information, the programmer reinforces the program with a stored confirmation message. However, if there is an incorrect decision a negative message is reinforced. Hence, over time experimental knowledge is built in a subject.

Financial managers may use neural networks to aid in decision making, to provide early warning signs of problems, and to confirm assessments. In developing a neural network, the network should be furnished with sufficient information to recognize a pattern. It needs to be trained. The neural network should be part of other software to have a user interface. The companies regularly retrain the network and update the software at all locations. Finally, the companies conduct follow-up and monitor the performance of the neural network. In planning the neural network, there should be a clear and precise definition of what the network should achieve, when the network should accomplish the task, and how the results are to be communicated.

A neural network may be used in portfolio management and investment selection. Neural network software may be used to predict changes in stock and bond prices, predict movements in currency exchange rates, and spot undervalued securities.

Training the neural network can be done in one of two ways—a massive set (all securities in a class or market segment) or a simplified set (a representative sample of securities within a class or market segment). With regard to a massive set, the neural network requires significantly more time to train because training involves examining the information hundreds of thousands of times. Thus, if the number of observations is large (tens of thousands or millions), the training iterations become millions or billions. The risk associated with smaller training sets revolves on the possibility that the neural network will memorize the actual training data and then be unable to make predictions about other securities in the market segment when tracking the broader data set. In any event, part of the training includes a holdout sample to test the trained network. This test gives assurance concerning the ability of the neural network to reliably predict the behavior of securities in the market segment appraised.

After the neural network is trained, the trained network can be integrated with other decision support systems to monitor movements in various capital markets. The neural network then recommends whether to buy, sell, or hold securities. By tracking changes in the marketplace, the neural network can predict upswings and downswings in the market, signaling buy and sell decisions.

Over time, conditions change and the patterns of various securities and markets also change. With additional experience, the neural network can be retrained by adding new experience to the training set. The neural network can be retrained on a monthly or quarterly basis to incorporate the most current changes in conditions. Some financial managers, however, may opt to delete the oldest data set and replace it with the newest experience. The drawback of doing this is that the financial manager loses experience gained before using the neural network.

Financial managers using neural networks should try to ascertain how well the neural networks predict the behavior of individual securities and the overall market. If the neural network is just retrained annually or semiannually, and the selected securities fluctuate differently from predictions of the neural network during any month or quarter, the follow-up should indicate that retraining should take place immediately.

Neural networks can be used to select those securities that optimize the position of the investment portfolio. Neural networks can be used to identify specific securities from among a set that yield the highest return. The neural network highlights those securities that will best achieve the objectives of the portfolio.

The planning and design of the neural network depends on the financial manager's objectives. If the monitoring applies to particular securities or specific markets or market segments, the software may involve a series of neural networks, one for each security. The financial manager may need some up-front processing of information to accumulate and consolidate market or market segment data before running a series of neural networks, one for each market or market segment. Further, software to communicate the results of the neural network prediction to the financial manager or a real-time basis must link to the neural networks. Most financial managers embed neural networks in their online or e-commerce software that accounts for marketable securities.

The financial manager locates data sources to provide the information necessary to achieve the objectives of buying and selling decisions for marketable securities in the company's portfolio. The data sources vary depending on the company, but usually are a combination of databases from subscription services, internal databases, and direct feed from the various stock exchanges. The plan should identify the needed result of the neural network and what information is to be gathered. If the financial manager is evaluating individual securities, outcomes of prior assessments furnish the best way to train the neural network to ascertain if particular stocks should be purchased or sold in the future.

Data Mind offers neural network-based software to conduct time series analysis of stock and commodity trading.

Math Works offers Datafeed Toolbox, which connects with Bloomberg's financial information services to download data to MATLAB, which includes neural network, time series, and statistical functions for evaluating securities.

Stock 100, Incorporated uses neural network-based proprietary software to advise financial managers on investments. The company offers online monitoring and trading in conjunction with CyBerCorporation to provide ongoing, real-time securities prediction services.

Ward Systems' (Frederick, Maryland) Neuro Shell Trader is a neural network software package to identify buy and sell clusters of securities within a market.

BioComp Systems' (Redman, WA) Profit 2000 is a neural network software package to assist the financial manager in timing securities trading decisions to optimize profitability by accurately predicting stock prices.

The AND Corporation has advanced neural network-based software for derivative/commodity forecasting, currency trading, and other financial market predictions.

NeuroDimensions' (Gainesville, Florida) Trading Solutions is a neural network software package used in forecasting stock prices.

Applied Analytic Systems (Pittsburgh, Pennsylvania) provides corporate consulting services in developing neural network-based financial market prediction software.

Lester Inger Research (Chicago, Illinois) provides consulting services to companies engaged in the commodities futures trading markets.

State Stree Bank filed a patent on a portfolio construction system developed by State Street Global Advisors around a neural network. The software aids in predicting stock price movements.

A financial manager may also use neural networks to identify potential customers who may be poor credit risks. Further, neural network software can be used to identify credit card fraud by recognizing suspicious activity based on the pattern of charges.

A financial manager may use neural networks in the control and valuation of inventory. Neural networks provide inventory control by recognizing patterns indicating processing inefficiencies, cover-up of inventory theft, and fraudulent reporting. Neural networks furnish an efficient method to predict changes in inventory prices and inventory movement, to aid in determining inventory obsolescence and identifying items for consideration of lower of cost or market adjustments. The neural network watches over inventory transactions to spot potential errors and frauds in the transactions that take place in the automated inventory system.

The information used by the firm to develop neural networks may include a number of observations including prior transactions for a given inventory item, size of each transaction, frequency of transactions, customer characteristics (for inventory sales transactions), supplier characteristics (for purchase transactions), and employee activity data. The financial manager should retain information from individual inventory accounts that have been subjected to fraud or errors with similar information for good transactions. Companies use as much data as possible for this type of neural network, usually two to five years of history.

A neural network may be developed to monitor employee expense reimbursement claims to uncover potential fraudulent claims and provide the company an opportunity to cease authorization of payment or flag those claims requiring further investigation. The claim data from false claims usually has some pattern. The database for the neural network may include prior employee reimbursement expense claims for a particular activity, size of each claim transaction, frequency of reimbursement claim transactions, and employee characteristics. The company should use information from expense accounts that have been fraudulently submitted with similar valid employee reimbursement claims data. Two to five years of information should be collected.

Neural networks aid the financial manager in detecting excess hedging in the budgetary process so realistic budget figures may be used. Neural networks can provide online prescreening of accounts and details for various budgetary units.

Neural networks assist in assessing internal control, making potential fraud assessments, gathering evidence, and providing support for audits. Neural networks can recognize patterns of internal control and make a recommendation on the establishment of control risk to be used in audit planning. Neural networks can identify the control risk level associated with different levels of internal control components.

Nester Incorporated's PRISM Card Alert is a neural network fraud risk management system.

Neural networks may also be used in operational auditing. Neural networks can identify clusters of operations with high or low potential for improvements in either effectiveness or efficiency. Some operational auditors use neural networks successfully to provide rapid identification of the best opportunities for improvement from a large group of operations.

Other applications of neural networks include:

- Appraising spending patterns
- Predicting bankruptcy
- Evaluating customer behavior patterns
- Working capital management

Examples of popular neural network software are:

- AI Ware, 11000 Cedar Avenue, Cleveland, Ohio 44106. Telephone number (216) 421–2380.
- California Scientific Software, 10024 Newtown Road, Nevada City, California 95959. Telephone number (800) 284–8112.
- Neural Systems, Inc. 2827 West 43rd Avenue, Vancouver, British Columbia V6N3HG. Telephone number (604) 263–3667.
- Neural Ware, Inc., Penn Center West, Building IV, Suite 227, Pittsburgh, Pennsylvania 15276. Telephone number (412) 787–8222.
- Scientific Consultant Services, 20 Stagecoach Road, Selden, New York 11784. Telephone number (516) 696–3333.

Network Security

Communication security over the network may be in the form of:

- **Access control.** Guards against improper use of the network. For example, KEYBEROS is commercial authentication software that is added to an existing security system to verify a user's existence to assure the person is not an imposter. KEYBEROS accomplishes this by encrypting passwords transmitted around networks. Passwords control and use user authentication devices such as Security Dynamics' Secur ID (800-SECURID). Review all dial-up terminal users.
- **Data confidentiality.** There is in place protection of confidential information during transmission.

- **Routing control.** Inhibits data flow to insecure network elements such as identified unsecured relays, links, or subnetworks.
- **Identification.** Identifies the origin of a communication within the network by digital signals or notarization.
- **Authentication.** Substantiates the identity of an originating or user entity within the network. Examples of security controls are time stamping, passwords, synchnronized checks, nonrepudiation, and multiple-way handshakes. Biometric authentication methods measure body characteristics with the use of equipment attached to the workstation. Keystroke dynamics is another form of identification.
- **Digital signature.** Messages are signed with a private key.
- **Traffic padding.** A traffic analysis of data for reasonableness.
- **Data integrity.** Steps exist to guard against unauthorized changes of information at the receiving and sending points.

Security should exist in different layers. Security needs to be provided over networking facilities and telecommunication elements. Controls must be placed over both host computers and subnetworks.

Network traffic may be over many subnetworks, each having its own security levels, depending on confidentiality and importance. Hence, different security controls may be needed.

A firewall is used to control access between two networks. Its objective is to restrict unauthorized traffic. A firewall performs the following two functions:

- restricts or blocks certain traffic.
- permits certain traffic.

Firewalls provide logging and auditing functions for security purposes. For example, security data may be gathered about the number of login attempts and password failures.

Digital signatures can be used when the content of the message is not secret, but the sender wants to authenticate his or her identity and confirm that he or she wrote the message.

ACCOUNTING SOFTWARE PACKAGES

This chapter discusses several software applications of particular interest to accountants. The discussion includes the major players in the area and some important features to look for when considering a particular type of software.

There are many factors that must be weighed when selecting a computer software package. Besides determining the software features currently needed and required in the future, the buyer must have a thorough understanding of the firm's existing system and know whether proposed software will integrate with all areas of that system and business.

Some of the basic considerations include: features and capabilities, compatibility and integration, ease of customization, ease of use, written documentation and technical support, price, and vendor's reputation and stability.

In the DOS world, vendors tried to top each other by constantly enhancing features. With the advent of Windows, they are competing by concentrating on improving integration and customization. With Windows interfaces, data can more easily be linked and exchanged with all types of applications, such as spreadsheets, databases, and even e-mail. Thus, compatibility with existing systems and data is an extremely important consideration when selecting new software. Likewise, customization of input screens and reports to conform to a firm's needs can more easily be done, and capabilities vary between packages.

Although the price of a system is an important consideration, it should never be the deciding factor. Often the cost of software is relatively insignificant when compared to the costs of implementation, training, ongoing maintenance, and support. Training costs can be reduced if the program has good context-sensitive online help. Installation will be much simpler if the program has a checklist or "wizard" that actually walks the user through the installation procedure.

Before buying any package, try calling the customer support department of the vendor. Customer support can give you detailed information about the features of a package. Vendors typically offer a demo or a free or low-cost trial of their computer software products. You might also get information about specials or discounts available to professionals such as practicing accountants.

Benefits of Windows Interface

Accountants have been slow to migrate to the Windows interface. However, that movement has been accelerating and a growing number of vendors offer software with a Windows interface. In fact, most new software packages are Windows-based and provide a graphical representation of documents such as the check, purchase order, invoice, and reports in a WYSIWYG (what you see is what you get) format.

The Windows environment makes it easy to format reports exactly as the user wants them to look. An important advantage of the Windows interface is the ability to perform "event-driven" inputting. In a typical DOS system one must navigate through an inflexible menu system, and before entering into another operation, one must back out of the old operation. In Windows, you can freely and much more efficiently move among activities as needed, thus inputting is "event-driven."

With Windows, one can have several applications, as well as documents, open on the desktop and active at the same time. Thus you can transport or move data among them much more readily. As indicated, the ability to easily transfer data between applications has increased the need to make sure that a software purchase is compatible, and can integrate, with your current programs and applications.

Practically a standard feature in a Windows-based product is the ability to drill down to the detail level of on-screen reports. Using a mouse, you can click on an item or amount in a report. This opens up (called drilling down) the underlying source document for this report. For even further detail, you can further drill down on this report. This process can be continued until you reach the bottom-level transaction. For example, in an accounts receivable aging schedule, you can click or drill down to get a list of customers whose accounts are more than 90 days old. You can then further click on a specific customer and find other information, such as the customer's credit limit and information about other outstanding invoices and transactions.

ACCOUNTING SOFTWARE

The fundamental task of accounting software is to automate the routine chore of entering and posting accounting transactions. This information is organized in an electronic format so as to produce financial statements and can be accessed immediately to assist in the management of the firm.

An accounting software package consists of a series of highly integrated modules. Each module corresponds to a specific accounting function (e.g., payroll, accounts receivable, and accounts payable). In an integrated system, after the details of the transaction are entered in one of the modules, the chart of accounts from the general ledger is "read." The transaction is then automatically posted to the accounts in the general ledger. For example, when a sale on account is entered in the accounts receivable module, a debit is automatically made to the accounts receivable account in the general ledger and an offsetting credit is made to the general ledger sales account.

Synex Systems' F9 software does financial reporting including variance and ratio analysis. Activity Financial's Activity package also prepares financial statements.

In Peachtree Accounting, the user also has the ability to enter data or perform tasks within a module by use of navigation aids. These aids, which are a graphical representation of the task flow of a module, can appear on the bottom of each screen. For example, in the navigation aid for payables, the user can directly enter purchases or record payments, print checks, and maintain vendor information and the general ledger.

Module Descriptions

The basic modules typically required by a firm and often integrated in an accounting software package include the following: general ledger, accounts receivable and invoicing, accounts payable and purchase order processing, inventory, payroll, job costing, and fixed assets.

General Ledger

The general ledger is the heart of the accounting system. It contains the chart of accounts of the business. A general ledger module should contain a sample chart of accounts which can be customized to a particular business. In addition, it should contain predefined reports that support budget data and prior year comparisons which can be tailored to a firm's specific needs. Other essential features include the capability to generate automatic reversing and recurring journal entries, having at least 13 periods open at one time, and the ability to make prior period adjustments or post entries to another year without closing the current year.

Accounts Receivable and Invoicing

The accounts receivable and invoicing functions are often combined in the same module. This module allows you to enter sales data and permits extensive sales analysis. It provides customer receivables management by tracking customers' balances, and generates invoices and/or monthly statements, as well as aging reports. It should allow for setting up credit limits for each customer, provide for flexible billing options, and provide the ability to apply partial payments to specific invoices or to the oldest balance. For faster processing, online inquiry should show the complete customer record at a glance including balances and unpaid invoices, and should allow you to make changes "on the fly."

Accounts Payable and Purchase Order Processing

Accounts payable and purchase order processing can also be combined in a single module. The module tracks obligations to vendors and determines a best payments schedule, prints checks, and provides for the distribution to accounts. It should allow for enhanced management of order processing by tracking orders from the start to the receipt of goods. It should be able to detect supply problems and thus permit early planning for alternate sources. To analyze vendor performance, it must track the complete purchase and delivery history of vendors and allow for easy access to this information.

Inventory

This module automatically tracks inventory as purchases or sales are made, and maintains cost and price data for each inventory item. In an integrated system, the inventory main file, which stores the product's number, is checked when a sales invoice is created in the accounts receivable module. If sufficient inventory is on hand, the amount of the sale is reduced from the balance. Likewise, when inventory is purchased, the inventory quantity is automatically increased. The module should help improve inventory management by alerting the user when to reorder, identifying slow-moving items, and analyzing performance by item and category.

Payroll

The payroll module maintains default information for each employee (e.g., rate of pay and income tax withholding information). The module calculates the wages to be paid, prints checks, and keeps track of deductions, sick and vacation days, and other such information. It maintains information for government reporting (e.g., 941, W–2, unemployment and state tax forms). For cost control, it should be able to provide for expense distribution or integrate with a costing module.

Job Costing

A job costing module allows you to track and report on the costs, income, and profitability of individual jobs or projects. This is done by assigning a job ID number to purchases, sales, and employee hours. A job cost module should provide for an accurate audit trail, detailed income, expenses, and committed costs, as well as the tracking of other user-defined categories. For example, Maxwell Business Systems' JAMIS is a job costing accounting package that tracks costs by project, contract, or organization over multiple years.

Fixed Assets

Fixed assets usually represent a significant investment by a firm, thus it is essential to keep track of them, but extremely tedious to do so. Tracking fixed assets and the repetitive calculation of depreciation is well suited for the computer. Most accounting software packages include a fixed asset module or capabilities to control fixed assets. It is also possible to purchase dedicated, stand-alone fixed asset packages.

Fixed asset software can handle large amounts of data and a variety of depreciation methods for financial accounting and tax purposes. It should be able to maintain detailed information about each asset, including a description of the asset, its location, date placed in service, and estimated useful life. It should also be able to track additions and disposals, as well as basis adjustments. An example of a fixed asset package is Decision Support Technology's BASSETS Fixed Asset System.

Before purchasing an accounting package, check if it has a fixed asset module, or capabilities sufficient for your needs. If not, ask if the vendor produces a stand-alone version, or would recommend a third-party vendor. Before purchasing a stand-alone fixed asset software package, make sure that it allows for easy sharing of information with your general ledger, tax packages, and other data repositories.

Market Leaders

There are a number of accounting software products. They can conveniently be categorized as (a) low-end, (b) mid-level, and (c) high-end packages.

In a May 1996 article in the *Journal of Accountancy,* the best low-end packages were reviewed. Not too long ago, if an accounting package cost less than a few thousand dollars, it would have very few features and would not be recommended to a client. However, the market has changed significantly. Figure 1 contains four low-end products reviewed in the May 1996 article.

Figure 1 Accounting Software

Low-End

DacEasy
800-322-3279

Mind Your Own Business
   Accounting
BEST!WARE
800-322-6962

Mid-Level

American Business Systems
800-356-4034

AccountMate Premiere
SourceMate
800-877-8896

Peachtree Accounting for Windows
Peachtree Software
800-228-0068

Profit
Great Plains
800-926-8962

QuickBooks for Windows
Intuit
800-624-8742

Accounting Visdion/32
Intellisoft
800-933-4889

ACCPAC 2000
Computer Associates
408-432-1764

ACCPAC Plus
Computer Associates
408-432-1764

Avista
Avista Software
404-564-8000

One-Write Plus
NEBS Software
800-388-8000

Simply Accounting
4 Home Productions
800-733-5445

BusinessWorks for Windows
State of the Art
800-854-3415

CYMA Professional Accounting
   Series
CYMA Software
800-292-2962

Great Plains Accounting
Great Plains Software
800-456-0025

Great Plains Dynamics
Great Plains Software
800-456-0025

LIBRA Accounting
Libra Software
800-453-3827

Maeola
Maeola Software
800-468-0834

MAS 90
State of the Art
800-854-9415

Open Systems
Open Systems Software
800-328-2276

Figure 1 *Continued*

Mid-Level, continued

Platinum	Solomon III Btrieve
Platinum Software	Solomon Software
800-999-1809	800-476-5666
RealWorld	Solomon IV
RealWorld Software	Solomon Software
800-678-6336	800-476-5666
SBT Professional	SouthWare
SBT	SouthWare Software
800-944-1000	800-547-4179

High-End

R/3 System	Oracle Applications	PeopleSoft
SAP America	Oracle	PeopleSoft
610-725-4500	800-ORACLE1	800-947-7743

They all cost about $250 or less, are all Windows-based, and have significant features and power.

Each year CIS, Inc. evaluates accounting software packages which have proven themselves to be popular, versatile, in widespread use, and have solid vendor support. Listed in Figure 1 are the systems which were reviewed in the Fall 1995 edition. They can be considered mid-level packages.

The February 1996 issue of *CFO* magazine contains a discussion of high-end accounting software. This category is extremely young and the marketplace is very chaotic, thus only the top three products are listed in Figure 1. R/3 from SAP A.G. of Walldorf, Germany is the most dominant player in the marketplace. The next two players are far behind. The price range for each of these products is over $1 million.

WRITE-UP SOFTWARE

With the development of easy-to-use and inexpensive accounting software, many companies who previously relied on CPAs to keep their books are doing it themselves. CPA firms can counter this trend with dedicated write-up software which is easy-to-use and provides more features so as to add value to their write-up services.

Write-up software should allow you to do more than just record transactions. One of the biggest features to look for is the ability to easily

Figure 2 Write-Up Software

Datawrite Client Accounting SCS/Compute 800-326-1040	Write-Up Plus UniLink 800-456-8321
Peachtree Client Write-Up Peachtree Software 800-228-0068	Write-Up Solutions II Creative Solutions 800-968-8900
PDS Client Accounting Professional Design Systems, Inc. 800-628-9802	

create an array of printouts and reports that a client might need. This includes being able to link and transfer data from other software packages and applications.

Another important feature is the ability to customize the input screen, so that it is consistent with the layout of the client's source documents, thereby reducing unneeded keystrokes. Easy setup is another means to reduce the cost of write-up service. The package should contain sample company data, and the ability to copy common information and make changes to default information included in the setup "on the fly."

Major Players

A large number of products are available in the write-up area. Recently eight write-up products were reviewed by *Accounting Today* and sixteen were reviewed by *Accounting Technology*. Figure 2 lists five products included in both reviews. Most products in this area are DOS-based. It can be argued that a DOS system is better than a Windows system for write-up—a very intensive data entry application. Due to all the features of a Windows product, repetitive data entry can be slower as compared to a DOS product. However, there's no telling what will happen in the future, and most development money is being spent in the Windows environment.

TAX PREPARATION SOFTWARE

Computer technology has had a significant impact on the way tax returns are prepared. Computerized tax return preparation lets the user prepare a return quickly and accurately, and allows the user to quickly analyze different tax planning strategies. Some software packages have built-in tools for tax research and permit for the electronic filing of tax returns. This software also lets the user easily do "what-if" planning and then quickly makes all the necessary changes. Furthermore, data can be imported directly from accounting packages or electronic spreadsheets into tax preparation software.

While tax preparation software can help with tax planning, one should consider a dedicated tax research package for serious tax research. Most Compact disc (CD)-based tax services can effectively replace the printed version of tax services. A major advantage of using CD-based tax services is having the ability to do electronic keyword searches. This can greatly facilitate the tax research process and make it much more efficient. In addition, it is easier to maintain and store all this information on a CD, thereby saving a good deal of library storage space.

The industry is going through rapid and significant changes in terms of features and key players in the marketplace. As with other software, improvements are continuously being made. One of the major improvements in the last few years has been the introduction of Windows versions of products. The switch to Windows seems to have been resisted and has been slow to get started. However, as more people upgrade their hardware, the switch to Windows will accelerate further and Windows will inevitably become the platform of choice.

The tax software industry is fiercely competitive and continues to go through consolidations and shakeouts. Thus it makes sense to deal with the larger, better-known vendors whose products are more likely to be supported in the future.

Market Leaders

The leading tax software packages can be categorized into segments:

Lower-Cost Alternatives. The price in this category is generally under $1,000. In spite of the low price, their features compare favorably with those of the higher-priced products. The five products included in this category are listed in Figure 3.

Mainstream. These packages are suitable for mainstream tax practices. They are generally easy to use and learn, but are not intended to handle every situation that may arise. The packages in this category are generally more powerful than those in the lower-cost category.

High-End. This group is marketed for use by multistate regional and national firms. These packages are able to handle the most complex returns and track their progress through large offices.

Figure 3 Tax Software

Lower-Cost-Alternatives

ProSeries
Intuit
800-934-1040

TAX$IMPLE
TAX$IMPLE
800-323-2662

Tax/Pack Professional
Alpine Data Inc.
800-525-1040

Veritax
Cold River Software
800-837-4829

Tax Relief
Micro Vision Software
800-829-7354

Mainstream

CPASoftware
CPA Software
904-434-2685

Professional Tax System
Tax and Accounting Software Corp.
   (TAASC)
918-493-6500

Digitax
Cold River Software Inc.
800-432-1065

RAM
RAM Software Inc.
800-888-6217

Lacerte Software Corporation
800-765-7777

TaxWorks
Laser Systems

LMS/Tax
SCS/Compute Inc.
800-488-0779

Nax Machine
SCS/Compute Inc.

Package EX
ExacTax Inc.
800-352-3638

Ultra Tax
Creative Solutions Inc.
800-968-8900

Pencil Pushers Tax Software
Damirus Corp.
800-370-2500

High-End

A-Plus-Tax	Go System & EasyGo	Prosystem fx
Arthur Andersen	CLR/Fast-Tax	CCH Inc.
800-872-1040	800-327-8829	800-457-7639

AUDIT SOFTWARE

Audit software is used by accountants to perform audits efficiently and effectively. Software audit tools include automated workpapers, data extraction software, and trial balance software.

Products such as APG (Audit Program Generator) by the American Institute of Certified Public Accountants (AICPA) and the optional add-on modules allow you to prepare customized audit programs. It eliminates the photocopying, cutting, and pasting usually required when creating the audit program and guides users through the engagement.

Data extraction software such as IDEA (Interactive Data Extraction and Analysis), also by the AICPA, allows auditors to access clients' files for audit testing. The auditor can either access the client's live data or obtain a copy of the company's data files on tape or disk. Data extraction software allows the auditor to audit "through the computer." The auditor can, for example, select a sample of accounts receivables for confirmations, or perform analytical reviews and do ratio analysis. Transactions may be compared to predetermined criteria. Linton Shafer's Audit Sampling Software package selects random numbers and dates. It handles multiple ranges and evaluates results. It performs compliance and substantive testing.

Trial balance software, such as the AICPA's ATB (Accountant's Trial Balance), helps the auditor organize a client's general ledger balances into a working trial balance. The auditor can then perform adjustments and update account balances. The calculation of financial ratios is extremely simple with trial balance software. This type of software aids in the preparation of financial statements. While trial balance software is designed primarily for audits, it can be used instead of write-up software for compilation and review services.

Price Waterhouse Researcher is an accounting, auditing, and reporting research system on a single CD-ROM disc. Equivalent to a 100,000 page library, PW Researcher includes generally accepted accounting principles (GAAP), generally accepted auditing standards (GAAS), Securities and Exchange Commission (SEC) regulations, and U.S. Cost Accounting Standards. The information on the CD includes American Institute of CPAs (AICPA), Financial Accounting Standards Board (FASB), SEC, and Emerging Issues Task Force (EITF) publications, along with Price Waterhouse guidance, analysis, and interpretations. The CD is updated quarterly and also includes international accounting and auditing standards. The easy-to-use database may be searched using a key word or phrase. Users may make personal notes and markers. The authors highly recommend this excellent product.

Price Waterhouse TeamMate is an electronic working paper system that helps automate the working paper preparation, review, reporting, and storage process. It includes standard and free-form schedule templates, an automatic tick mark system, and a powerful cross-referencing capability. PW TeamMate also integrates popular spreadsheet, word processing, and imaging software. There are hypertext links between documents and applications enabling the auditor to jump backward through related numbers in reports or spreadsheets to the original data. The search, cross-referencing, and retrieval capabilities allow the auditor to automatically correct errors in all affected documents. The working paper review features include automatic exception reporting, a working paper navigation system, and text and voice annotation. For example, the auditor can obtain a directory of all review notes pertaining to a document. The reporting features include key audit point summarization, report drafting, audit status reports, and time summaries. Financial data is quickly accessed by the sorting and filtering tools. A standard index provides a branch and node system for all papers. There is a simultaneous multiuser feature so auditors/reviewers can work with the same document set even if they are working in various locations. PW TeamMate improves the quality, productivity, and effectiveness of the auditor's work.

Price Waterhouse Controls facilitates the documentation, evaluation, and testing of internal controls. The software expedites the collection and summarization of controls in place, appraises their effectiveness, and identifies areas of risk exposure. PW Controls can be used by auditors to document particular business processes. Control weaknesses are identified with resultant recommendations for improvement. The auditor can view control effectiveness at different levels within the company (e.g., by activity, by business unit). A comparison and analysis may be made of the relative control performance of different operating units.

Price Waterhouse Chekhov is a software package that automates the completion of checklists.

Figure 4   Audit Software

ACE for Windows CLR Professional Software 800-241-3306	CA-PanAudit Plus/PC Computer Associates 800-225-5224
ACL ACL Software 604-669-4225	GuideWare PPC 800-323-8724
APG AICPA 800-862-4272	IDEA AICPA 800-862-4272
ATB AICPA 800-862-4272	Perfect Balance PPC 800-323-8724
AuditVision Peer Software 800-613-2331	Workpapers Plus Cogent Technologies 717-283-2257

Figure 4 contains a number of audit software packages. They contain one or more features previously discussed.

SPREADSHEETS

More than any other product, the electronic spreadsheet has done more to make the capabilities of microcomputers evident to the business community. An electronic spreadsheet allows the user to work with data in a huge number of rows and columns. The user works with this data in a columnar spreadsheet, a format familiar to accountants. A big advantage of the spreadsheet is that it eliminates the need to perform manual calculations and can perform powerful computer-aided operations.

The spreadsheet has become a valuable tool in business planning, since it permits the user to perform "what-if" scenarios. Inputs can be continuously changed, and the results will automatically be recalculated throughout the spreadsheet. Thus, the effect of alternative decisions is easily determined and planning greatly facilitated. The use of templates is another important feature of spreadsheets. Templates provide the format and contain the formulas which are used to repeatedly solve various business applications. Since one doesn't have to be a programmer to construct a template, all firms could now more easily use the vast power of the computer to help make better decisions in the management of a firm.

Major Players and Selection Considerations

The chief players in the spreadsheet field have been reduced to three:

Lotus 1–2–3
IBM Corp.

Microsoft's Excel
Microsoft Corp.

QuattroPro
Corel

In actuality, all the players have the same basic features. Although a particular feature may currently be lacking in a specific spreadsheet, that feature may very well be included in the next upgrade of that product. Therefore the decision of which product to buy should not be based primarily on features. More importantly, be certain the planned spreadsheet supports and is compatible with the major applications of your business. Thus, make sure that the spreadsheet can directly access your databases and that any macros or templates that have already been developed are compatible with the proposed acquisition.

Managing Risk Using Fuzzy Analysis

A unique spreadsheet, FuziCalc, takes the computational complexity out of fuzzy arithmetic. This spreadsheet allows us to easily incorporate ranges or intervals in our analysis, and assign the ranges different weights. Implicit in any type of decision analysis is the assumption that judgmental inputs can be accurately represented by a single precise number. However, it generally is not possible to quantify judgment with such precision. Most of the traditional tools for decision analysis are crisp. By crisp we mean that the tools require precise inputs. In contrast, most of the problems facing managers are fuzzy, vague, or imprecise. Traditionally, managers have incorporated imprecision in their analysis through probability theory. An alternate framework, based on the fuzzy set theory, allows imprecision in data analysis. It allows the decision maker to benefit from the structure of quantitative decision analysis, without forcing the user to provide very precise numerical inputs.

From a practical perspective, fuzzy analysis is easy to do using the FuziCalc spreadsheet. There are no new techniques to learn. Anyone familiar with a conventional spreadsheet can quickly adapt to the FuziCalc spreadsheet. All fuzzy data can be represented by "belief graphs." Belief graphs are the heart of the FuziCalc spreadsheet. Fuzzy data inputs are made using belief graphs. The simplest way to represent a fuzzy number is to use a triangular shape. You need a minimum of three points to represent any fuzzy number. A triangular fuzzy number has many practical applications. To construct a triangular fuzzy number of sales price, we need to determine the highest, the most likely, and the lowest sales price. Let's assume our estimates for the highest, the most likely, and the lowest sales prices are $35, $25, and $20, respectively. A belief graph of this fuzzy triangular number can then be constructed as shown in Figure 5.

Let's contrast the fuzzy number in Figure 5 with the crisp number 25 in Figure 6. A crisp number does not have a range of values; its belief graph is a straight line.

Figure 5   Fuzzy Number

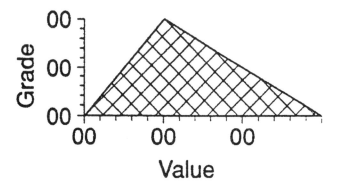

Figure 6 Crisp Number

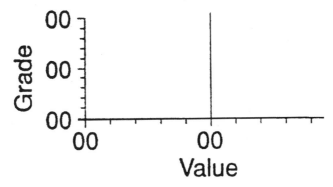

FuziCalc provides five common shapes to represent fuzzy data. The five shapes from FuziCalc's Gallery are shown in Figure 7.

The triangular shape was discussed earlier; its use is appropriate when the user has a single best estimate of the most likely value and can specify the endpoints of the range. Sometimes it is not possible for the user to give one best estimate of the most likely value. A trapezoidal fuzzy number would be most appropriate when only a range of most likely values can be given. The user may select the multipeaked shape to represent fuzzy numbers where the low and high values are more likely than the middle values. The tent shape is most appropriate where all of the values in the range have a high possibility of occurring. The rocket shape might be used when the user believes a wide range exists, but a narrow range within it has a much better possibility. The five shapes will be sufficient for the needs of most users. However, FuziCalc allows users to easily alter the shape to represent any fuzzy number.

It is possible to add, subtract, multiply, and divide fuzzy numbers just like regular or "crisp" numbers. The advantage of using the FuziCalc spreadsheet is that users don't need to concern themselves with the complex underlying computations.

FuziCalc's primary strength is in modeling under uncertainty. Beyond that, FuziCalc offers little to spreadsheet users. As a spreadsheet, FuziCalc

Figure 7 Shape

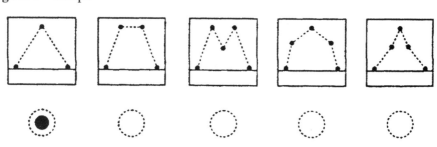

offers only the very basic features. Users of conventional spreadsheets might even find working in FuziCalc a little frustrating. Many of the features that one is accustomed to in conventional spreadsheets are missing in FuziCalc. Thus it would be used to supplement, rather than to replace, a conventional spreadsheet.

FuziCalc is sold by:

FuziWare, Inc.
800–472–6183

ABC SOFTWARE

An Activity-Based Costing (ABC) system accumulates costs on the basis of production or service activities at a firm. Basically it assigns costs by activity and links them to specific products. It is argued that the resulting cost data is much more realistic and precise as compared to the data obtained from a traditional costing system. Aided by computer software designed for ABC, the management accountant can more easily and accurately accumulate cost information and perform "what-if" testing. With this data, management is in a better position to evaluate and make decisions regarding its operations and products. There is a good deal of software that the management accountant can use to aid in accumulating cost data. Some software programs are actually spreadsheet applications; others are modules of mainframe packages. The Winter 1994 issue of the *Journal of Cost Management* reviewed nine cost management software packages. All these packages are for use on a personal computer and most were designed for activity-based costing or activity-based management. Figure 8 separates these packages into two categories: those developed by independent vendors, and those supported or developed by a Big-Five CPA firm. It should be noted that some products include consulting support as part of the overall package.

Price Waterhouse's ACTIVA is a comprehensive activity-based costing (ABC), profitability, and performance management software tool. Its features and capabilities include budgeting and planning, product costing and pricing, cost management and analysis, decision support, process improvement, activity-based management, and variance determination and evaluation. Developed using state-of-the art client/server technology, its additional features include capital investment analysis, production sourcing, distribution logistics, and foreign currency appraisal. ACTIVA aids in measuring the profitability by customer, product, service, market, process, and distribution channel. ACTIVA can support many users conducting diverse applications in multiple locations worldwide. The software contain sophisticated security features.

Figure 8   ABC Software

Independent Vendors

NetProphet
Sapling Software
416-678-1661

QUOTE-A-PROFIT
Manufacturing Management Systems,
   Inc.

CMS-PC
ICMS

Big-Five CPA Firm

TR/ACM
Deloitte & Touche
617-261-8615

The Profit Manager Series
KPMG Peat Marwick
313-983-0321

ACTIVA
Price Waterhouse
314-425-0500

ABCost Manager
Coopers & Lybrand
312-701-5783

Lead Software's Activity Analyzer assigns activities to cost objects and calculates by activity costs and profitability. Profitability may be determined by product, service, customer, and territory. Armstrong Laing's Hyper ABC is a multidimensional, multiperiod activity-based management system. Sapling Software's NetProphet combines activity-based costing and management, process view analysis, budgeting, capacity planning, and constraint checking.

ABC helps in determining what a product or process should cost, areas of possible cost reduction, and value-added versus nonvalue-added aspects. Activity-based costing is beneficial in appraising value-chain functions. Further, costs are a function of their consumption factors such as number of employees, units produced, labor hours, etc.

FINANCIAL MANAGEMENT INFORMATION SYSTEMS AND SOFTWARE PACKAGES

Finance has been an important functional area for virtually all types of organizations. The finance area monitors cash flow and profitability. Well-conceived financial information systems are capable of providing financial managers with timely information, which is vital to success in today's competitive global economy. History has witnessed the results of poor financial decisions. Banks and savings institutions have gone into bankruptcy because of bad decisions and unfavorable economic conditions. Companies with too much debt and leverage have also gone bankrupt. On the contrary, good financial decisions have resulted in growing and prosperous organizations. A financial management information system provides financial information to all financial managers within an organization. Specifically, the financial MIS assists the financial manager in performing his/her responsibilities which include the following:

- *Financial analysis and planning*—analyzing historical and current financial activity and determining the proper amount of funds to employ in the firm; that is, designating the size of the firm and its rate of growth.
- *Investment decisions*—allocating funds to specific assets (things owned). The financial manager makes decisions regarding the mix and type of assets acquired, as well as modification or replacement of assets.
- *Financing and capital structure decisions*—projecting future financial needs and raising funds on favorable terms; that is, determining the nature of the company's liabilities (obligations). For instance, should funds be obtained from short-term or long-term sources?

Figure 1   Overview of a Financial MIS

Inputs	Subsystems	Outputs
Strategic goals Transaction processing system Internal auditing External sources	Financial forecasting Financial data from departments (profit/loss and costing) Financial intelligence	Financial forecasts Funds management Financial budget planning and control

    • *Management of financial resources*—monitoring and controlling the use of funds over time and managing cash, receivables, and inventory to accomplish higher returns without undue risk.

Figure 1 shows the inputs, function-specific subsystems, and outputs of a financial MIS.

INPUTS TO THE FINANCIAL MANAGEMENT INFORMATION SYSTEM

Decisions supported by the financial MIS require diverse information needs. The sources, both internal and external, are briefly discussed below.

1. *Corporate strategic goals and policies.* The strategic plan covers major financial goals and targets. Earnings growth, loan ratios, and expected returns are some of the measures that can be incorporated in the strategic plan. The plan often projects financial needs three to five years down the road. More specific information needs, such as expected financing needs, the return on investment (ROI) for various projects, and desired debt-to-equity ratios, evolve directly from the strategic plan.

2. *The transaction processing system.* Important financial information is captured by a number of internal accounting systems. One is the *order entry system*, which enters the orders into the accounting system. Another is the *billing system*, which sends bills or invoices to customers. A third is the *account receivable system*, which collects the funds. Other key financial information is also collected from almost every transaction processing application—payroll, inventory control, accounts

payable, and general ledger. Many financial reports are based on payroll costs, the investment in inventory, total sales over time, the amount of money paid to suppliers, the total amount owed to the company from customers, and detailed accounting data.

3. *External sources.* Information from and about the competition can be critical to financial decision making. Annual reports and financial statements from competitors and general news items and reports can be incorporated into MIS reports to provide units of measure or as a basis of comparison. Government agencies also provide important economic and financial information. Inflation, consumer price indexes, new housing starts, and leading economic indicators can help a company plan for future economic conditions. In addition, important tax laws and financial reporting requirements can also be reflected in the financial MIS.

FINANCIAL MIS SUBSYSTEMS AND OUTPUTS

Financial decisions are typically based on information generated from the accounting system. Depending on the organization and its needs, the financial MIS can include both internal and external systems that assist in acquiring, using, and controlling cash, funds, and other financial resources. The financial subsystems, discussed below, include financial forecasting, profit/loss and costing, and financial intelligence systems. Each subsystem interacts with the transaction processing system in a specialized, functionally oriented way, and has informational outputs that assist financial managers in making better decisions. The outputs are financial forecasts, management of funds reports, financial budgets, and performance reports such as variance analysis used for control purposes.

FINANCIAL FORECASTING

Financial forecasting, the process of making predictions on the future growth of products or the organization as a whole, is based on projected business activity. For example, expected sales of goods and services can be converted into expected revenues and costs. The sales price per unit and production cost factors can be multiplied by the number of units expected to be sold in order to arrive at a forecasted value for revenues and costs. Fixed costs, such as insurance, rent, and office overhead, are estimated and used to determine expected net profits on a monthly, quarterly, or yearly basis. These estimates are then incorporated into the financial MIS. The financial forecasting subsystem relies on input from another functional subsystem (namely, the marketing forecasting system) to determine projected revenues.

Having an estimate of future cash flows can be one of the first steps for sound financial management. Financial managers and executives use this valuable information to project future cash needs. For instance, an organization's managers will know in advance that in some months, additional cash might be required, while in other months excess cash will have to be invested. Improperly managed cash flow is one of the major causes of business failure and bankruptcy. Financial forecasting can help financial executives avoid cash-flow problems by predicting cash-flow needs.

PROFIT/LOSS AND COST SYSTEMS

Two specialized financial functional systems are profit/loss and cost systems. Revenue and expense data for various departments is captured by the transaction processing system (TPS) and becomes a primary internal source of financial information. Many departments within an organization are profit centers, which means they track total expenses, revenues, and net profits. An investment division of a large insurance or credit card company is an example of a profit center. Other departments may be revenue centers, which are divisions within the company that primarily track sales or revenues, such as a marketing or sales department. Still other departments may be cost centers, which are divisions within a company that do not directly generate revenue, such as manufacturing or research and development. These units incur costs with little or no revenues. Data on profit, revenue, and cost centers is gathered (mostly through the TPS but sometimes through other channels as well), summarized, and reported by the financial MIS.

FINANCIAL INTELLIGENCE

Financial intelligence is responsible for gathering data and information from stockholders, the financial community, and the government. Since the financial function controls the money flow through the firm, information is needed to expedite this flow. The day-to-day flow of money from customers and to vendors is controlled by the internal accounting subsystem. The financial intelligence subsystem is concerned with flows other than those involved in daily operations. This system seeks to identify the best sources of additional capital and the best investments of surplus funds.

Most of the information flows from the firm to the stockholders in the form of annual and quarterly reports. Stockholders have an opportunity to communicate information (complaints, suggestions, ideas, etc.) to the firm through the stockholder relations department. Also, once a year an annual stockholders meeting is held where stockholders can learn firsthand what the firm is doing. Very often, stockholders use these meetings as an opportunity to communicate directly with top management. Information gathered informally from stockholders is seldom entered into the computerized system, but it is disseminated by verbal communication and written memo to key executives in the firm.

The relationship between the firm and the financial community also receives attention from financial management. There should be a balanced flow of money through the firm, but this equilibrium is not always achieved. At times additional funds are needed or investments of surplus funds are desired. It is the responsibility of the financial intelligence subsystem to compile information on sources of funds and investment opportunities. An important indirect environmental effect influences this money flow through the firm. The federal government controls the money market of the country through the Federal Reserve System. There are various means of releasing the controls to expedite the money flow and of tightening the controls to reduce the flow.

The firm therefore must gather information from both financial institutions and the Federal Reserve System. This information permits the firm to remain current on national monetary policies and trends and possibly to anticipate future changes. A variety of publications can be used for this purpose. They are prepared by both the financial institutions and the government. Two examples are the *Monthly Economic Letter* prepared by the City Bank of New York and the *Federal Reserve Bulletin* prepared by the Federal Reserve System.

In addition to the need to acquire funds, the firm frequently must invest surplus funds on either a short- or long-term basis. These funds can be invested in a number of different ways in United States Treasury securities, commercial paper, or certificates of deposit (CDs). Since the terms and rates of return for some of these vary over time, it is necessary to monitor these investment opportunities continually so that the optimum ones can be used when needed.

Gathering information from the financial environment is the responsibility of the financial intelligence subsystem. As with the other two functional intelligence subsystems, the information is usually handled outside the computer system. This subsystem is one area where computer use could improve.

Two major financial dailies are worth mentioning as a great source of financial intelligence: the *Wall Street Journal (WSJ)* and *Investor's Business Daily (IBD)*. The *WSJ* contains news of happenings throughout the business community. It provides especially informative descriptions of the economic environment in which businesses operate. Simply by reading a periodical such as the *WSJ,* you can keep up with many of the important environmental influences that shape a manager's decision strategy.

Each day the front page contains a "What's News" section in columns 2 and 3. The "Business and Finance" column offers a distillation of the day's major corporate, industrial, and economic news. The "World-Wide" column captures the day's domestic and international news developments. "Special Reports" appears in column 5 each day. On Monday, "The Outlook" provides an economic overview, analyzing the economy from every conceivable angle. On Tuesday, the "Labor Letter" addresses work news of all kinds—government, portfolio, management, unions, labor relations, and personnel. Wednesday brings the "Tax Report," which alerts readers to new tax trends. The "Business Bulletin" appears each Thursday and tries to spot emerging trends. The idea is to make information available while managers can still act on it. Finally, every Friday brings the "Washington Wire," providing an interpretation of government policy and its possible impact on business.

Published by William O'Neil & Co., Inc., *Investor's Business Daily* reports daily coverage of: (1) The Top Story—The most important news event of the day, (2) The Economy—Sophisticated analysis of current economic topics and government economic reports, (3) National Issue/Business—A major national and business issue of our time, (4) Leaders & Success—Profiles of successful people and companies, (5) Investor's Corner—Coverage of a wide variety of personal finance topics including investment ideas, and (6) Today's News Digest—35 to 40 brief but important news items of the day.

FUNDS MANAGEMENT

Funds management is another critical function of the financial MIS. Companies that do not manage and use funds effectively produce lower profits or face possible bankruptcy. Outputs from the funds management subsystem, when combined with other aspects of the financial MIS, can locate serious cash-flow problems and help the company increase returns. Internal uses of funds include additional inventory, new plants and equipment, the acquisition of other companies, new computer systems, marketing and advertising, raw materials, and investments in new products. External uses of funds are typically investment-related. On occasion, a company might have excess cash from sales that is placed into an external investment. Current profitability is only one important factor in predicting corporate success; current and future cash flows are also essential. In fact, it is possible for a profitable company to have a cash crisis; for example, a company with significant credit sales but a very long collection period may show a profit without actually having the cash from those sales.

Financial managers are responsible for planning how and when cash will be used and obtained. When planned expenditures require more cash than planned activities are likely to produce, financial managers must decide what to do. They may decide to obtain debt or equity funds or to dispose of some fixed assets or a whole business segment. Alternatively, they may decide to cut back on planned activities by modifying operational plans, such as ending a special advertising campaign or delaying new acquisitions, or to revise planned payments to financing sources, such as bondholders or stockholders. Whatever is decided, the financial manager's goal is to balance the cash available and the needs for cash over both the short and the long term.

Evaluating the statement of cash flows is essential if you are to appraise accurately an entity's cash flows from operating, investing, and financing activities and its liquidity and solvency positions. Inadequacy in cash flow has possible serious implications, including declining profitability, greater financial risk, and even possible bankruptcy.

Financial management also involves decisions relating to source of financing for, and use of financial resources within, an organization. Virtually all activities and decisions within an organization are reflected in financial information. One useful application of a real-time system to financial information involves inquiry processing. An on-line financial information system enables immediate response to inquiries concerning comparisons of current expenditure with budgeted expenditure, up-to-date calculations of profit center contribution, or information required for audit investigation.

The fund management subsystem can prepare a report showing cash flow for the next twelve-month period. The report can be printed by a mathematical model that uses the sales forecast plus expense projections as the basis for the calculation.

Another application of real-time systems to financial management which has great potential is the area of computer models for financial planning, which is discussed later.

FINANCIAL BUDGETING, PLANNING, AND CONTROL

More and more companies are developing computer-based models for financial planning and budgeting, using powerful, yet easy-to-use, financial modeling languages such as Up Your Cash Flow and Comshare's Interactive Financial Planning System (IFPS) (to be discussed and illustrated in a later chapter). The models help not only to build a budget for profit planning but to answer a variety of "what-if" scenarios. The resultant calculations provide a basis for choice among alternatives under conditions of uncertainty. Furthermore, budget modeling can also be accomplished using spreadsheet programs such as Microsoft's Excel.

In this section we will illustrate the use of spreadsheet software such as Excel and stand-alone packages such as Up Your Cash Flow to develop a financial model. For illustrative purposes, we will present:

1. three examples of projecting an income statement
2. forecasting financial distress with Z score
3. forecasting external financing needs—the percent-of-sales method

Figure 2 Projected Income Statement

	1	2	3	4	5	6	7	8	9	10	11	12	Total	Percent
Sales	$60,000	$63,000	$66,150	$69,458	$72,930	$76,577	$80,406	$84,426	$88,647	$93,080	$97,734	$102,620	$955,028	100%
Less: VC														
Cost of sales	$25,200	$26,460	$27,783	$29,172	$30,631	$32,162	$33,770	$35,459	$37,232	$39,093	$41,048	$43,101	$401,112	42%
Operating ex.	$3,000	$3,150	$3,308	$3,473	$3,647	$3,829	$4,020	$4,221	$4,432	$4,654	$4,887	$5,131	$47,751	5%
CM	$31,800	$33,390	$35,060	$36,812	$38,653	$40,586	$42,615	$44,746	$46,983	$49,332	$51,799	$54,389	$506,165	53%
Less: FC														
Op. expenses	$10,000	$10,000	$10,000	$10,000	$10,000	$10,000	$10,000	$10,000	$10,000	$10,000	$10,000	$10,000	$120,000	13%
Net income	$21,800	$23,390	$25,060	$26,812	$28,653	$30,586	$32,615	$34,746	$36,983	$39,332	$41,799	$44,389	$386,165	40%
Less: Tax	$6,540	$7,017	$7,518	$8,044	$8,596	$9,176	$9,785	$10,424	$11,095	$11,800	$12,540	$13,317	$115,849	12%
NI after tax	$15,260	$16,373	$17,542	$18,769	$20,057	$21,410	$22,831	$24,322	$25,888	$27,533	$29,259	$31,072	$270,315	28%

Figure 3 Projecting Income Statement

	1	2	3	4	5	6	7	8	9	10	11	12	Total	Percent
Sales	$60,000	$66,000	$72,600	$79,860	$87,846	$96,631	$106,294	$116,923	$128,615	$141,477	$155,625	$171,187	$1,283,057	134%
Less: VC														
Cost of sales	$25,200	$27,720	$30,492	$33,541	$36,895	$40,585	$44,643	$49,108	$54,018	$59,420	$65,362	$71,899	$538,884	56%
Operating ex.	$6,000	$6,600	$7,260	$7,986	$8,785	$9,663	$10,629	$11,692	$12,862	$14,148	$15,562	$17,119	$64,153	7%
CM	$28,800	$31,680	$34,848	$38,333	$42,166	$46,383	$51,021	$56,123	$61,735	$67,909	$74,700	$82,170	$615,867	64%
Less: FC														
Op. expenses	$10,000	$10,000	$10,000	$10,000	$10,000	$10,000	$10,000	$10,000	$10,000	$10,000	$10,000	$10,000	$120,000	13%
Net income	$18,800	$21,680	$24,848	$28,333	$32,166	$36,383	$41,021	$46,123	$51,735	$57,909	$64,700	$72,170	$495,867	52%
Less: Tax	$5,640	$6,504	$7,454	$8,500	$9,650	$10,915	$12,306	$13,837	$15,521	$17,373	$19,410	$21,651	$148,760	16%
NI after tax	$13,160	$15,176	$17,394	$19,833	$22,516	$25,468	$28,715	$32,286	$36,215	$40,536	$45,290	$50,519	$347,107	36%

Example 1. Given:

    Sales for 1st month = $60,000
    Cost of sales = 42% of sales, all variable
    Operating expenses = $10,000 fixed plus 5% of sales
    Taxes = 30% of net income
    Sales increase by 5% each month

(a) Based on this information, Figure 2 presents a spreadsheet for the contribution

(b) Figure 3 shows the same in (1) assuming that sales increase by 10% and operating expenses = $10,000 plus 10% of sales. This is an example of a "what-if" scenario.

Example 2. Delta Gamma Company wishes to prepare a three-year projection of net income using the following information:

1. 2000 base year amounts are as follows:

Sales revenues	$4,500,000
Cost of sales	2,900,000
Selling and administrative expenses	800,000
Net income before taxes	800,000

2. Use the following assumptions:

   - Sales revenues increase by 6% in 2001, 7% in 2002, and 8% in 2003.
   - Cost of sales increase by 5% each year.
   - Selling and administrative expenses increase only 1% in 2001 and will remain at the 2001 level thereafter.
   - The income tax rate = 46%.

Figure 4 presents a spreadsheet for the income statement for the next three years.

Figure 4 Delta Gamma Company
        Three-Year Income Projections (2000–2003)

	2000	*2001*	*2002*	*2003*
Sales	$4,500,000	$4,770,000	$5,103,900	$5,512,212
Cost of sales	$2,900,000	$3,045,000	$3,197,250	$3,357,113
Gross margin	$1,600,000	$1,725,000	$1,906,650	$2,155,100
Selling & adm. exp.	$800,000	$808,000	$808,000	$808,000
Earnings before tax	$800,000	$917,000	$1,098,650	$1,347,100
Tax	$368,000	$421,820	$505,379	$619,666
Earnings after tax	$432,000	$495,180	$593,271	$727,434

        Financial Management Information Systems and Software Packages

Example 3. Based on specific assumptions (see Figure 5), develop a budget using Up Your Cash Flow (Figure 6).

Figure 5

Category	Assumptions

Sales: alternative 1 from Book Up Your cash flow

Cost of goods sold: use 45% of sales

Advertising: 5% of sales

Automobile: Company has 4 auto @ 1500 ea.
4 × 1500 = 6000 ÷ 12 = 500 per month

Bad debts: maintain @ 2% of sales – I hope!

Business promotion: Prior year was 65000. 10% increase equals $71500 ÷ 12

Collection costs: use 1000 per month

Continuing education: $1000 per month

Depreciation: $84000 per year – use 7000 per month

Donations: $10,000 per year = ÷ 12

Insurance—general: agent said $24000; use 2000 per month

Insurance—group: 15 employees @ 1500 ea = 22500 ÷ 12 = monthly #.

Insurance—life: 600 per month

Interest: expect to borrow 250M @ 15% = 37,500 ÷ 12 = 3125 per month + other borrowings.

Office supplies: 2% of sales – and keep it that please!

Rent: 4000 per month

Repairs and maintenance: use 400 per month

Salaries: schedule the payroll per month

Taxes and license: Prior years was 1.5% of sales use same this year.

Taxes, payroll: 20% of monthly payroll

Telephone—utilities: $29000 last year. Use 33000 ÷ 12
Travel – use $1000 per month.

Figure 6

	Jan.	Feb.	Mar.	Apr.	May	Jun.	Jul.	Aug.	Sep.	Oct.	Nov.	Dec.	Total
Sales	$129,030	$129,030	$129,030	$129,030	$192,610	$192,610	$162,610	$129,030	$192,610	$129,030	$162,690	$192,690	$1,870,000
Cost of Sales @ 45%	58,063	58,063	58,063	58,063	86,675	86,675	73,211	58,063	86,675	58,063	73,211	86,675	841,500
Gross profit	70,967	70,967	70,967	70,967	105,935	105,935	89,479	70,967	105,935	70,967	89,479	105,935	1,028,500
Advertising @ 5%	6,450	6,450	6,450	6,450	9,600	9,600	8,100	6,450	9,600	6,450	8,100	10,050	93,750
Automobile	500	500	500	500	500	500	500	500	500	500	500	500	6,000
Bad debts @ 2%	2,580	2,580	2,580	2,580	3,840	3,840	3,240	2,580	3,840	2,580	3,240	3,920	37,400
Business promotion	5,958	5,958	5,958	5,958	5,958	5,958	5,958	5,958	5,958	5,958	5,958	5,962	71,500
Collection costs	1,000	1,000	1,000	1,000	1,000	1,000	1,000	1,000	1,000	1,000	1,000	1,000	12,000
Continuing education	1,000	1,000	1,000	1,000	1,000	1,000	1,000	1,000	1,000	1,000	1,000	1,000	12,000
Depreciation	7,000	7,000	7,000	7,000	7,000	7,000	7,000	7,000	7,000	7,000	7,000	7,000	84,000
Donations	833	833	833	833	833	833	833	833	833	833	833	837	10,000
Dues & subscriptions	833	833	833	833	833	833	833	833	833	833	833	837	10,000
Insurance—general	2,000	2,000	2,000	2,000	2,000	2,000	2,000	2,000	2,000	2,000	2,000	2,000	24,000
Insurance—group	1,875	1,875	1,875	1,875	1,875	1,875	1,875	1,875	1,875	1,875	1,875	1,875	22,500
Insurance—life	600	600	600	600	600	600	600	600	600	600	600	600	7,200
Interest	3,125	3,125	3,125	3,125	4,375	4,375	4,375	4,450	4,450	4,450	4,450	4,450	47,875
Legal & accounting	1,000	1,000	1,000	1,000	1,000	1,000	1,000	1,000	1,000	1,000	1,000	1,000	12,000
Office supplies @ 2%	2,580	2,580	2,580	2,580	3,840	3,840	3,240	2,580	3,840	2,580	3,240	3,920	37,400
Rent	4,000	4,000	4,000	4,000	4,000	4,000	4,000	4,000	4,000	4,000	4,000	4,000	48,000
Repairs	400	400	400	400	400	400	400	400	400	400	400	400	4,800
Salaries	21,000	21,000	21,000	21,000	21,000	21,000	24,833	24,833	24,833	24,833	24,833	24,835	275,000
Taxes & license @ 1.5%	1,935	1,935	1,935	1,935	2,880	2,880	2,430	1,935	2,880	1,935	2,430	2,890	28,000
Taxes, payroll	4,200	4,200	4,200	4,200	4,200	4,200	4,966	4,966	4,966	4,966	4,966	4,970	55,000
Telephone—utilities	2,750	2,750	2,750	2,750	2,750	2,750	2,750	2,750	2,750	2,750	2,750	2,750	33,000
Travel	1,000	1,000	1,000	1,000	1,000	1,000	1,000	1,000	1,000	1,000	1,000	1,000	12,000
Profit	$(1,652)	$(1,652)	$(1,652)	$(1,652)	$25,451	$25,451	$7,546	$(7,576)	$20,777	$(7,576)	$7,471	$20,139	$85,075

A budget is a tool for both planning and control. At the beginning of the period, the budget is a plan or standard; at the end of the period it serves as a control device to help management measure its performance against the plan so that future performance may be improved. Each month, each manager with budget responsibilities receives a report showing actual expenditures compared with the budget figures and appropriate variances, so that unusual variances need to be addressed and properly rewarded or penalized.

In addition to the budget, the financial control system generates a number of *performance measures* or *ratios* that enable managers on all levels to compare their performance with benchmarks such as standards or targets. There are quite a few financial or operational ratios. A couple of ratios are given as an example. One popular ratio is the *current ratio,* which measures a firm's ability to pay short-term bills:

$$\text{Current ratio} = \left(\frac{\text{Current assets}}{\text{Current liabilities}} \right)$$

Another popular ratio is the *debt ratio,* which reveals the amount of money a company owes to its creditors. Excessive debt means greater risk to the company. The debt ratio is:

$$\text{Debt ratio} = \left(\frac{\text{Total liabilities}}{\text{Total assets}} \right)$$

FORECASTING FINANCIAL DISTRESS WITH Z-SCORE

There has recently been an increasing number of bankruptcies. Will your company go bankrupt? Will your major customers or suppliers go bankrupt? What warning signs exist and what can be done to avoid corporate failure?

Prediction models can help in a number of ways: In merger analysis, they can help to identify potential problems with a merger candidate. Bankers and other business concerns can use them to determine whether or not to give a new loan (credit) or extend the old one. Investors can use them to screen out stocks of companies which are potentially risky. Internal auditors can use such models to assess the financial health of the company. Those investing in or extending credit to a company may sue for losses incurred. The model can help as evidence in a lawsuit.

Financial managers, investment bankers, financial analysts, security analysts, and auditors have been using early-warning systems to detect the likelihood of bankruptcy. But their system is primarily based on financial ratios of one type or the other as an indication of financial strength of a company. Each ratio (or set of ratios) is examined independent of others. Plus, it is up to the professional judgment of a financial analyst to decide what the ratios are really indicating.

To overcome the shortcomings of financial ratio analysis, it is necessary to combine mutually exclusive ratios into a group to develop a meaningful predictive model. Regression analysis and multiple discriminant analysis (MDA) are two statistical techniques that have been used thus far.

Z-SCORE MODEL

This section describes the Z-score predictive model which uses a combination of several financial ratios to predict the likelihood of future bankruptcy. Altman developed a bankruptcy prediction model that produces a Z-score as follows:

$$Z = 1.2*X1 + 1.4*X2 + 3.3*X3 + 0.6*X4 + 0.999*X5$$

where

$X1$ = Working capital/Total assets

$X2$ = Retained earnings/Total assets

$X3$ = Earnings before interest and taxes (EBIT)/Total assets

$X4$ = Market value of equity/Book value of debt
(Net worth for privately-held firms)

$X5$ = Sales/Total assets

Altman established the following guideline for classifying firms:

Z score	Probability of failure
1.8 or less	Very high
3.0 or higher	Unlikely
1.81–2.99	Not sure

The Z-score is known to be about 90 percent accurate in forecasting business failure one year in the future and about 80 percent accurate in forecasting it two years in the future. There are more updated versions of Altman's model.

Example 4. Navistar International (formerly International Harvester) continues to struggle in the heavy and medium truck industry, and is selected for illustrative purposes. Figure 7 shows the 20-year financial history and the Z-scores of Navistar. Figure 8 presents the corresponding graph.

Financial Management Information Systems and Software Packages

Figure 7

	Balance Sheet						Income Statement		Stock Data	Calculations					
Year	Current Assets (CA)	Total Assets (TA)	Current Liability (CL)	Total Liability (TL)	Retained Earnings (RE)	Working Capital (WC)	SALES	EBIT	Market Value or Net worth (MKT-NW)	WC/TA (X1)	RE/TA (X2)	EBIT/TA (X3)	MKT-NW/TL (X4)	SALES/TA (X5)	Z Score
1979	3266	5247	1873	3048	1505	1393	8426	719	1122	0.2655	0.2868	0.1370	0.3681	1.6059	3.00
1980	3427	5843	2433	3947	1024	994	6000	-402	1147	0.1701	0.1753	-0.0688	0.2906	1.0269	1.42
1981	2672	5346	1808	3864	600	864	7018	-16	376	0.1616	0.1122	-0.0030	0.0973	1.3128	1.71
1982	1656	3699	1135	3665	-1078	521	4322	-1274	151	0.1408	-0.2914	-0.3444	0.0412	1.1684	-0.18
1983	1388	3362	1367	3119	-1487	21	3600	-231	835	0.0062	-0.4423	-0.0687	0.2677	1.0708	0.39
1984	1412	3249	1257	2947	-1537	155	4861	120	575	0.0477	-0.4731	0.0369	0.1951	1.4962	1.13
1985	1101	2406	988	2364	-1894	113	3508	247	570	0.0470	-0.7872	0.1027	0.2411	1.4580	0.89
1986	698	1925	797	1809	-1889	-99	3357	163	441	-0.0514	-0.9813	0.0847	0.2438	1.7439	0.73
1987	785	1902	836	1259	-1743	-51	3530	219	1011	-0.0268	-0.9164	0.1151	0.8030	1.8559	1.40
1988	1280	4037	1126	1580	150	154	4082	451	1016	0.0381	0.0372	0.1117	0.6430	1.0111	1.86
1989	986	3609	761	1257	175	225	4241	303	1269	0.0623	0.0485	0.0840	1.0095	1.1751	2.20
1990	2663	3795	1579	2980	81	1084	3854	111	563	0.2856	0.0213	0.0292	0.1889	1.0155	1.60
1991	2286	3443	1145	2866	332	1141	3259	232	667	0.3314	0.0964	0.0674	0.2326	0.9466	1.84
1992	2472	3627	1152	3289	93	1320	3875	-145	572	0.3639	0.0256	-0.0400	0.1738	1.0684	1.51
1993	2672	5060	1338	4285	-1588	1334	4696	-441	1765	0.2636	-0.3138	-0.0872	0.4119	0.9281	0.76
1994	2870	5056	1810	4239	-1538	1060	5337	158	1469	0.2097	-0.3042	0.0313	0.3466	1.0556	1.19
1995	3310	5566	1111	4696	-1478	2199	6342	262	966	0.3951	-0.2655	0.0471	0.2057	1.1394	1.52
1996	2999	5326	820	4410	-1431	2179	5754	105	738	0.4091	-0.2687	0.0197	0.1673	1.0804	1.36
1997	3203	5516	2416	4496	-1301	787	6371	242	1374	0.1427	-0.2359	0.0439	0.3055	1.1550	1.32
1998	3715	6178	3395	5409	-1160	320	7885	410	1995	0.0518	-0.1878	0.0664	0.3688	1.2763	1.51

Note: (1) To calculate Z-score for private firms, enter Net Worth in the MKT-NW column. (For publicly held companies, enter Market Value of Equity).
(2) EBIT = Earnings before Interest and Taxes

63

Figure 8 Z-Score Graph (Navistar International)

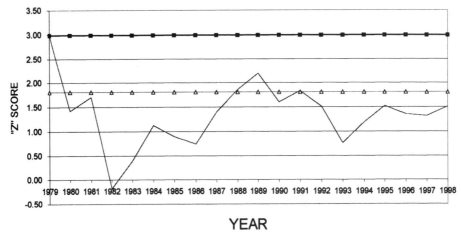

The graph shows that Navistar International performed at the edge of the ignorance zone ("unsure area") for the year 1979. Since 1980, though, the company started signaling a sign of failure. However, by selling stock and assets, the firm managed to survive. Since 1983, the company showed an improvement in its Z-scores, although the firm continually scored in the danger zone. Note that the 1994 Z-score of 1.19 is in the high probability range of <1.81. The 1995 to 1998 Z-scores appear to be on the rise. This indicates that Navistar is improving its financial position and becoming a more viable business.

MORE APPLICATIONS OF THE Z-SCORE

Various groups of businesspeople can take advantage of this tool for their own purposes. For example,

1. *Merger analysis.* The Z-score can help identify potential problems with a merger candidate.
2. *Loan credit analysis.* Bankers and lenders can use it to determine if they should extend a loan. Other creditors such as vendors have used it to determine whether to extend credit.
3. *Investment analysis.* The Z-score model can help an investor in selecting stocks of potentially troubled companies.
4. *Auditing analysis.* Internal auditors are able to use this technique to assess whether the company will continue as a going concern.

5. *Legal analysis.* Those investing or giving credit to your company may sue for losses incurred. The Z-score can help in your company's defense.

WORDS OF CAUTION

The Z-score offers an excellent measure for predicting a firm's insolvency. But, like any other tool, one must use it with care and skill. The Z-score of a firm should be looked upon not for just one or two years but for a number of years. Also, it should not be used as a sole basis of evaluation.

The Z-score can also be used to compare the economic health of different firms. Here again, extreme care should be exercised. Firms to be compared must belong to the same market. Also, Z-scores of the same periods are to be compared.

FORECASTING EXTERNAL FINANCING NEEDS— THE PERCENT-OF-SALES METHOD

Percentage of sales is the most widely used method for projecting the company's financing needs. Financial officers need to determine the next year's fund requirements, and the portion of which has to be raised externally. This way they can have a head start for arranging a least-cost financing plan.

This method involves estimating the various expenses, assets, and liabilities for a future period as a percent of the sales forecast and then using these percentages, together with the projected sales, to construct pro forma balance sheets.

Basically, forecasts of future sales and their related expenses provide the firm with the information needed to project its future needs for financing.

The basic steps in projecting financing needs are:

1. Project the firm's sales. The sales forecast is the initial most important step. Most other forecasts (budgets) follow the sales forecast.
2. Project additional variables such as expenses.
3. Estimate the level of investment in current and fixed assets that is required to support the projected sales.
4. Calculate the firm's financing needs.

The following example illustrates how to develop a pro forma balance sheet and determine the amount of external financing needed.

Figure 9 Pro Forma Balance Sheet (in Millions of Dollars)

	Present (20X0)	% of Sales (20X0 Sales=$20)	Projected (20X1 Sales=$24)	
Assets				
Current assets	2	10	2.4	
Fixed assets	4	20	4.8	
Total assets	6		7.2	
Liabilities and Stockholders' Equity				
Current liabilities	2	10	2.4	
Long-term debt	2.5	n.a.	2.5	
Total liabilities	4.5		4.9	
Common stock	0.1	n.a.	0.1	
Paid-in-Capital	0.2	n.a.	0.2	
Retained earnings	1.2		1.92[a]	
Total equity	1.5		2.22	
Total liabilities and stockholders' equity	6		7.12	Total financing needed
			0.08[b]	
			7.2	Total

[a]20X2 retained earnings = 20X1 retained earnings + projected net income – cash dividends paid

$$= \$1.2 + 5\%(\$24) - 40\%[5\%(\$24)]$$
$$= \$1.2 + \$1.2 - \$0.48 = \$2.4 - \$0.48 = \$1.92$$

[b]External financing needed = projected total assets – (projected total liabilities + projected equity)

$$= \$7.2 - (\$4.9 + \$2.22) = \$7.2 - \$7.12 = \$0.08$$

Example 5. Assume that sales for 20X0 = $20, projected sales for 20X1 = $24, net income = 5% of sales, and the dividend payout ratio = 40%. The steps for the computations are outlined as follows:

Step 1. Express those balance sheet items that vary directly with sales as a percentage of sales. Any item such as long-term debt that does not vary directly with sales is designated "n.a.," or "not applicable."

Step 2. Multiply these percentages by the 20X1 projected sales = $2.4 to obtain the projected amounts as shown in the last column.

Step 3. Simply insert figures for long-term debt, common stock, and paid-in-capital from the 20X0 balance sheet.

Step 4. Compute 20X1 retained earnings as shown in (b).

Step 5. Sum the asset accounts, obtaining a total projected assets of $7.2, and also add the projected liabilities and equity to obtain $7.12, the total financing provided. Since liabilities and equity must total $7.2, but only $7.12 is projected, we have a shortfall of $0.08 "external financing needed."

Figure 9 presents the projected balance sheet.

The major advantage of the percent-of-sales method of financial forecasting is that it is simple and inexpensive to use. To obtain a more precise projection of the firm's future financing needs, however, the preparation of a cash budget is required. One important assumption behind the use of the method is that the firm is operating at full capacity. This means that the company has no sufficient productive capacity to absorb a projected increase in sales and thus requires additional investment in assets.

FINANCIAL MODELING LANGUAGES

Remember that financial models are essentially used to generate pro forma financial statements and financial ratios. These are the basic tools for budgeting and profit planning. Also, the financial model is a technique for risk analysis and "what-if" experiments. The financial model is also needed for day-to-day operational and tactical decisions for immediate planning problems. For these purposes, the use of computers is essential. In recent years, spreadsheet software and computer-based financial modeling software have been developed and utilized for budgeting and planning in an effort to speed up the budgeting process and allow CFOs to investigate the effects of changes in budget assumptions and scenarios.

These languages do not require any knowledge of computer programming on the part of financial officers. They are all English-like languages. Among the well-known system packages are: IFPS, SIMPLAN, EXPRESS, Encore! Plus, Venture, Cashe, and MicroFCS.

FINANCIAL ANALYSIS WITH SPREADSHEETS

Companies large or small, whether profit-oriented or nonprofit, employing one hundred or ten thousand, etc., live or die by the extent of their powers in financial planning. There are other important contributing factors to success in business, but nothing can send a company into the abyss of Chapter

11 bankruptcy faster than a few major ill-fated financial decisions. Financial analysis is employed in an effort to be a bit more scientific about coming to a good financial decision. Questions must be asked about the company and accurate answers found to gain insight that will assist in determining the most prudent use of precious resources for some period in the future. The questions stem from numerous aspects of the business. Some are straightforward and easily answered: Are profits greater this year than last? Other questions are not as easily answered: Will an increase in advertising expenditures lead to increased profits? Would a price cut be more appropriate? Would some combination of the two be best?

Spreadsheet programs are ideally suited for performing financial analyses because they possess the capacity to hold and process complex formulas and functions while at the same time making modification and manipulation of one or more variables or functions an easy operation. With a micro, software, and some training and practice, you can master rather complex financial analysis techniques.

FINANCIAL RATIO ANALYSIS

Financial ratio analysis is a means of determining how well the business is performing. Problem spots can be identified, and groundwork is established for predictions and projections of future performance. The types of questions addressed include:

- How well is the business doing?
- Where are its strengths?
- What are its weaknesses?
- How does the firm rate vis-a-vis other similar firms in the industry?

A checklist of relevant factors for consideration in critiquing the performance of the firm follows:

- Profitability ratios
- Liquidity ratios
- Valuation ratios
- Efficiency of asset use
- Growth ratios
- Use of debt capital

These ratios are not necessarily useful in and of themselves. To give them relevance, the financial manager should calculate these same ratios for several different periods so they can be compared and trends can be identified. They can also be compared to industry norms to see how the firm measures up.

The numbers with which these ratios are calculated come from the balance sheet and income statement for a given period. Simple formulas are entered onto the spreadsheet, which accesses the two financial statements (assuming that they, too, are on the spreadsheet) to obtain the pertinent figures, perform the necessary computations, and come up with the appropriate ratios. If the financial statements of the period for which ratios are being prepared are not contained on the spreadsheet, the pertinent figures can be manually entered to the appropriate spreadsheet cells with relative ease. If ratios are desired for a number of past periods for which only hard copies of the financial statements exist, the financial manager enters the figures for a period in the aforementioned manner, has the spreadsheet calculate the results, and then prints the results to obtain a hard copy for later comparison. You then move on to the financial statements of the next period to be analyzed, entering those figures to the spreadsheet for computation.

MAXIMUM VERSUS MINIMUM PROFITS

Accounting systems are the creations of humans, and although they are usually thought of as cold and objective, they can be manipulated to arrive at different results for different purposes and based on different philosophies. The most obvious example is accounting used on one hand to increase and maximize profits in order to look good to outsiders, while on the other hand accounting is used to minimize profits for tax purposes. It is not uncommon for a company to maintain two (sometimes even more) sets of accounting records, one for each purpose. Spreadsheets can perform many functions to assist in determination of the two different bottom lines. This includes the actual production of the two opposing income statements. Basically, any calculation you might perform on paper in arriving at the two figures can be set up and performed on the spreadsheet. Also, certain calculation routines on the spreadsheet can obtain required figures from cells on the spreadsheet that contain the results of other calculations, thus avoiding repetitive entries. All of these numbers and computations should interact and funnel down to their appropriate final positions in the different income statements.

CHOICE OF DEPRECIATION METHOD

Whenever a company purchases a depreciable asset, it must decide which depreciation method will be used to write off the value of the asset over its useful life. The method chosen depends on the objective of management: Is it the greatest possible tax relief in the current period, or the largest bottom-line profit possible? The lowest possible tax liability in the near term is the most common objective when choosing a depreciation method for tax purposes.

Checklist of Depreciation Methods
- Straight-line depreciation
- Accelerated depreciation
- Modified Accelerated Cost Recovery System (MACRS)
- Production basis depreciation

It is up to the firm to determine its motives and establish objectives in deciding on a depreciation method. Whatever they are, the spreadsheet can play an important and useful role in the decision process, a role that will not be altered by the motives. The idea is to determine which method best produces the results. The following are required:

- Cost of the asset
- Estimation of the asset's post-useful life salvage value
- IRS guidelines on the asset's useful life (found in IRS publication number 534)
- IRS guidelines on MACRS

The spreadsheet is used to compute projections for certain elements of the income statement and income tax return. Based on these projections, the appropriate depreciation method can be determined.

Checklist of Projection Results Desired
- Depreciation expense
- Income before taxes
- Income tax
- Net income

PLANNING AND FORECASTING

Once you enter the realm of the future for the business through forecasting and planning, the power of a spreadsheet or integrated program can really pay off. Performing repeated "what-if" calculations is the essence of forecasting and the electronic worksheet's specialty.

Checklist of Possible Planning and Forecasting Questions
- What will the projected profit and cash flows be, based on current operational plans?
- If the financial manager proceeds with present plans, how will it affect the company's current and fixed assets?

- What levels of expenditures are needed to increase current and fixed assets?
- What will be the additional cash requirements of the business if present plans are followed?
- What is the break-even point?
- In what areas is the firm strong and how can such strengths be maximized?
- Where is the company weak and what can be done to improve?
- What are "what-if" scenarios and their impact on profit, break-even point, cash flow, assets required, return on assets, funding required, working capital, etc?

In performing ratio analysis, you scrutinize historical data to gain insight into things that have already occurred. In forecasting and planning, on the other hand, you are creating a picture of future events if present plans are followed; you predict how future financial statements will appear.

Before embarking on this process, work with the staff to develop the best guesses possible about future market conditions, market share, net sales, and so forth. These predictions are combined with present conditions to create a model on the spreadsheet for future company performance. The methods are rather straightforward and easy to master. For example, one part of the spreadsheet would multiply current net sales by the estimated percentage of market sales increase (or decrease) to arrive at next year's projected net sales. Running the program again at this point would yield projected net sales for year 2 of the forecast (or perhaps the formula could be set up to automatically provide projected net sales in year 5 immediately, etc.); changes in the firm's market share would also be programmed in if they were anticipated. You can continue from this modest beginning until you have created a forecast tool that can be saved on diskette for the future. But for now, once all the data have been entered, the program can be run and the results obtained. It is at this point that the fun begins—the experimentation with "what-if" scenarios. If you change one or more figures, percentages, and so forth, the spreadsheet will provide new results for all items affected.

SHORT-TERM DECISIONS

The short-term decisions that businesses make are usually more or less involved with working capital. The types of issues addressed include:

- What is a safe minimum cash balance for the firm?
- How much does the cash flow fluctuate seasonally?
- When do these seasonal fluctuations occur?

- What are the temporary, seasonal working-capital borrowing requirements versus borrowing for more permanent items?
- How much should your company borrow to increase inventory?
- When is the best time for this borrowing to occur?
- When would it benefit most to pay it back?
- What is the cost of capital?
- What would be the effect on revenues and profit of a change in the firm's credit terms?
- What is the amount lost if the company does not avail itself of all discounts offered by suppliers for expeditious payment?

The following financial ratios are useful in determining the status of the firm, and in rating the financial manager's working capital decisions:

- Current ratio
- Quick ratio
- Net working capital
- Accounts receivable turnover
- Inventory turnover
- Sales to working capital
- Sales to fixed assets

The computations of these ratios are easily set up and performed on a spreadsheet program. A spreadsheet can also be used to generate a cash budget for determining the requirements, timing, and character of cash sought; and for analyzing the effects of credit terms as a component of the marketing mix through analysis of the following factors:

- Present sales
- Change in sales attributable to changes in credit terms
- Gross margin
- Potential effect on bad debts
- Credit terms on increase in sales
- Cost of short-term borrowing

Spreadsheets are also ideal for calculating interest received or extended in any of various credit situations, such as past due accounts receivable and missed discounts.

LONG-TERM ASSET DECISIONS

Long-term asset decisions by their very nature are encountered less frequently than the types of working capital decisions previously discussed. Issues encountered include:

- Does this particular fixed-asset purchase decision make sense and seem appropriate?
- Which of several proposals seem the most advantageous?
- Should the firm buy this item at all, or would it be better to make it?
- Based on several proposals, which should be the priority purchase if funds are limited?

Spreadsheet programs can be very helpful in answering these types of questions. One of their most useful abilities in this particular area is that of calculating present values (or the time value of money). They all have the net present value (NPV) function built in for convenience and efficiency. By calculating the NPV of two or more long-term fixed-asset options, the more advantageous option becomes evident: The highest NPV is the most profitable. Thus, use of a spreadsheet program for calculating NPV can render fixed-asset decision making a more straightforward and less difficult process.

LONG-TERM FINANCING DECISIONS

The third major financial decision type is that of long-term financing. The types of issues addressed include:

- The lease or buy decision
- Debt versus equity as a means of raising capital
- Safe debt limitations and sources of financing

The lease-or-buy decision can involve the following:

- Production equipment
- Motor vehicles
- Buildings
- Office equipment
- Computers
- Tools

A spreadsheet can be used to determine the net cash outflow associated with leasing versus buying a given item. This can help in making the best decision, since the lower present value of net cash outflow of the two given options is the cheaper one. When deciding on the use of debt versus equity financing, the financial manager can set up formulas in the spreadsheet to show the effects of each option on the following:

- Cash flow
- Net income
- Degree of company solvency
- Company value
- Debt capacity

This is accomplished by projecting certain elements of the balance sheet and income statement, as well as certain financial ratios for each alternative. By analyzing the results and determining which alternative yields the highest earnings per share and considering other factors such as whether the debt ratio is acceptable, you arrive at the optimum alternative.

OTHER FINANCIAL MANAGEMENT SOFTWARE

More and more financial software—client/server and Windows-based—is clouding the market. A few popular ones are summarized below.

Commander FDC and Commander Budget

Comshare's integrated suite of Windows-based, client/server financial and managerial applications for statutory consolidations, enterprise budgeting, and management reporting is built around a central financial database and shares the same core technology. Commander FDC and Commander Budget provide specialized application interfaces to the financial database, which holds historic, actual, budget, and forecast data. Commander FDC is designed for use by finance professionals involved in the monthly closing process. Commander Budget is designed to meet the needs of all business professionals involved in the budgeting process, from cost center managers to budget administrators. With either application, anyone familiar with Excel or Lotus 1–2–3 can easily do reporting and data entry. Additional modules for what-if analysis, exception detection, and executive reporting from the financial database round out Comshare's financial managerial applications.

Cashe

Cashe by Business Matters Incorporated is a new approach to financial forecasting and business modeling for people who make decisions that have an impact on the overall financial positions of their organizations. Cashe gives you a disciplined way of capturing and modifying your business assumptions so that financial forecasts can be reviewed, updated, and compared easily. Cashe's power comes from its built-in content and knowledge, which allow you to forecast your business's financial performance accurately without having to worry about formulas or accounting rules. Working on the business information you provide, Cashe's self-adjusting model ensures accuracy by automatically reflecting any changes you make throughout the entire model. Cashe is not intended to replace your spreadsheet but to work with it, allowing you to import and export all your financial models. The result is that with Cashe, you forecast more accurately, more comprehensively, and more often.

QL Financials

QL Financials by Microcompass Systems, Ltd., delivers true client/server financial management with many advanced features in a full Windows environment. It is a fully integrated suite of functionally rich modules, including general ledger, budget management, cash book/treasury management, accounts payable, accounts receivable, sales ordering/invoicing, fixed assets, requisitioning/purchase ordering, inventory management, and system integration. QL is written in Uniface Version 6, the world's leading 4GL development environment, and has been designed to meet the needs of both public and private sectors at departmental and corporate levels. Written to full TICKIT standards, QL offers multicurrency and multilingual functionality in a complete desktop environment.

POPULAR BUDGETING AND PLANNING SOFTWARE

In addition to the specialized budgeting and financial modeling software discussed previously, there are a variety of computer programs designed specifically for budgeting and *Decision Support Systems (DSS)* software. Some are *stand-alone* packages, others are *templates*, and still others are spreadsheet *add-ins*.

1. Budget Express

Budget Express "understands" the structure of financial worksheets and concepts such as months, quarters, years, totals, and subtotals, speeding up budget and forecast preparation. The program creates column headers for months, automatically totals columns and rows, and calculates quarterly and yearly summaries. And for sophisticated what-if analyses, just specify your goal and Budget Express displays your current and target values as you make changes. (Add-in)

2. ProPlans

ProPlans creates your financial plan automatically and accurately—and slices months from your annual planning and reporting process. You just enter your forecast data and assumptions into easy-to-follow, comprehensive data-entry screens, and ProPlans automatically creates the detailed financials you need to run your business for the next year—your income statement, balance sheet, cash flow statement, receipts and disbursements cash flow statements, and ratio reports. (Template)

3. Profit Planner

Profit Planner provides titles and amounts for revenues, cost of sales, expenses, assets, liabilities, and equity in a ready-to-use 1–2–3 template. Financial tables are automatically generated on-screen. It presents results in 13 different table formats, including a pro forma earnings statement, balance sheet, and cash flow statements. Profit Planner even compares your earnings statement, balance sheet, and ratios against industry averages, so you're not working in a vacuum. (Template)

4. Up Your Cash Flow

The program generates cash flow and profit or loss forecasts; detailed sales by product/product line and payroll by employee forecasts; monthly balance sheets; bar graphs; ratio and break-even analyses, and more. (Stand-alone)

5. Cash Collector

The program assists you in reviewing and aging receivables. You always know who owes what; nothing "falls through the cracks." What happens when collection action is required? Simply click through menu-driven screens to automatically generate letters and other professionally-written collection documents (all included) that are proven to pull in the payments. (Stand-alone)

6. Cash Flow Analysis

This software provides projections of cash inflow and cash outflow. You input data into eight categories: sales, cost of sales, general and administrative expense, long-term debt, other cash receipts, inventory build-up/reduction, capital expenditures (acquisition of long-term assets such as store furniture), and income tax. The program allows changes in assumptions and scenarios and provides a complete array of reports. (Stand-alone)

7. Quicken

This is a fast, easy to use, inexpensive accounting and budgeting program that can help you manage your business, particularly your cash flow. You record bills as postdated transactions when they arrive; the program's *Billminder* feature automatically reminds you when bills are due. Then, you can print checks for due bills with a few keystrokes. Similarly, you can record invoices and track aged receivables. Together, these features help you maximize cash on hand. (Stand-alone)

8. CapPLANS

This program evaluates profitability based on Net Preset Value (NPV), Internal Rate of Return (IRR), and payout period. Choose among five depreciation methods, including Modified Accelerated Cost Recovery System (MACRS). Run up to four sensitivity analyses. Project profitability over a 15-year horizon. In addition to a complete report of your analysis, CapPLANS generates a concise, four-page executive summary—great for expediting approval. Add ready-made graphs to illustrate profitability clearly, at a glance. (Template)

9. Project Evaluation Toolkit

The program calculates the dollar value of your project based on six valuation methods, including discounted cash flow and impact on the corporate balance sheet. Assess intangibles such as impact on corporate strategy, investors, or labor relations. Use scenario planning to show the effects of changing start dates, sales forecasts, and other critical variables. (Template)

10. @Risk

How will a new competitor affect your market share? @RISK calculates the likelihood of changes and events that affect your bottom line. First use @Risk's familiar @ functions to define the risk in your worksheet. Then let @Risk run thousands of what-if tests using one of two proven statistical sampling techniques—Monte Carlo or Latin Hypercube. You get a clear, colorful graph that tells you the likelihood of every possible bottom-line value. At a glance, you'll know if your risk is acceptable or if you need to make a contingency plan. (Add-in)

11. CFO Spreadsheet Applications

These ready-to-use spreadsheet templates offer easy ways to make many financial decisions. They are divided into four modules: cash management, tax strategies, capital budgeting, and advanced topics. (Template)

12. What's Best!

If you have limited resources—for example, people, inventory, materials, time, or cash—then What's Best! can tell you how to allocate these resources in order to maximize or minimize a given objective, such as profit or cost. What's Best! uses a proven method—linear programming (LP)—to help you achieve your goals. This product can solve a variety of business problems that cut across every industry at every level of decision making. (Stand-alone)

13. Inventory Analyst

Inventory Analyst tells precisely how much inventory to order, and when to order it. Choose from four carefully explained ordering methods: economic order quantity (EOQ), fixed order quantity, fixed months requirements, and level load by workdays. Inventory Analyst ensures that you'll always have enough stock to get you through your ordering period.

Just load up to 48 months worth of inventory history, and Inventory Analyst makes the forecast based on one of three forecasting methods: time series, exponential smoothing, or moving averages. It explains which method is best for you. Inventory Analyst will adjust your forecast for seasonality. (Template)

BUSINESS LAW

CONTRACTS

While the corporate controller is not ordinarily trained in legal matters, he or she is often relied upon to recognize situations requiring the need for legal counsel. When contracts are drawn, the controller is often consulted on accounting and other business matters. The area of contracts therefore represents an area with which the controller needs some basic familiarity.

By definition, a contract is a legally enforceable agreement, and is governed by (1) Article 2 of the Uniform Commercial Code (UCC) if the contract pertains to the sale of tangible personal property (i.e., goods), and (2) common law if the subject matter covered by the contract is real estate, services, or intangibles.

Types of Contracts

Essentially, there are nine types of contracts:

1. An *executory* contract is based on conditions that have not yet been fully performed by both parties to the contract.
2. An *executed* contract is created when both parties have fully performed the conditions required by the contract.
3. An *express* contract involves an agreement expressed in words, whether spoken or written.
4. An *implied* contract is a contract that is inferred as a result of the acts or conduct of the parties involved.
5. A *bilateral* contract arises when one promise is given in exchange for another.

6. A *unilateral* contract involves an offer of a promise and an act that is committed as a result of reliance on the promise.

7. A *quasi*-contract represents an obligation created by law in order to prevent unjust enrichment.

8. A *void* contract is a contract without any legal obligations on the part of each party.

9. A *voidable* contact is a contract that may be avoided or ratified by one or more of the parties.

Elements of Contracts

The four elements required for a contract are agreement, consideration, legality, and capacity of the parties.

Agreement involves an offer and acceptance. The terms of an offer must be definite and must demonstrate an intent to incur a legal obligation. To be valid, an offer must be communicated to the offeree by the offeror (or his or her agent) and is deemed to be effective when the offeree receives it. The offeree may accept an offer until it is terminated. In general, an offer will terminate if (1) the offer has expired (i.e., it is not accepted within the time specified or within a reasonable period of time, if no time is stipulated), (2) the offer is revoked at any time prior to acceptance, (3) the offer is rejected, (4) a counteroffer is made, (5) either party dies or becomes disabled, (6) the subject matter of the offer is destroyed, or (7) the subject matter of the offer subsequently becomes illegal. In connection with point 2, it should be noted that certain offers are irrevocable. An option contract, which is irrevocable, involves an offer supported by consideration; therefore, it cannot be withdrawn prior to the expiration of the stated period of time, or a reasonable period of time if no time is specified. A firm offer, which is also irrevocable, involves a merchant who makes a written offer to buy or sell goods and specifies that the offer will remain open for a specified period. Finally, in a unilateral contract, even though the act necessary to accept the offer has not been completed, performance has begun, and the offer becomes irrevocable.

Acceptance of the offer must be unequivocal. Accordingly, the offeree cannot alter or qualify the provisions of the offer. Acceptance may be effected by any reasonable means of communication, unless a specific means of acceptance is stipulated by the offeror. Acceptance is generally effective upon dispatch (e.g., when mailed).

As noted, consideration is a necessary element of a contract. As such, both parties to the contract must give consideration. For consideration to exist, there must be legal sufficiency (i.e., something of value) and a bargained-for exchange. It should be noted, however, that some types of transactions do not require consideration for enforcement. For example, promissory estoppel, also known as the doctrine of detrimental reliance, prevents the promisor from pleading lack of consideration for his or her promise where he or she has induced the promisee to make a substantial change of position in reliance thereon. In addition, no consideration is necessary in order to modify contracts for the sale of goods.

The subject matter of a contract must be legal. An agreement will be illegal and unenforceable when formation or performance of an agreement is criminal, tortious, or otherwise opposed to public policy. In these circumstances, the contract is void.

Capacity of the parties is also necessary for a contract to be valid. While a contract made by a minor is voidable at his or her election, it may be ratified upon reaching majority. Further, a contract made by a legally insane person is generally voidable. Where one has been legally declared insane, attempted contracts are void. Last, with respect to an intoxicated individual, a contract is voidable if the degree of intoxication was such that the individual did not realize he or she was entering into a contract.

The Statute of Frauds

Pursuant to the statute of frauds, to be enforceable, certain executory contracts must be in writing and signed by the party to be charged with performance. The written contract may be formal or informal and may be set forth in one or more documents, but must clearly indicate the parties, specify the subject matter and essential terms, and include the signature of the party against whom enforcement is sought. The contracts covered by the statute of frauds include, but are not limited to:

1. Contracts involving the sale of goods with a price of at least $500.
2. Contracts involving the sale of investment securities.
3. Contracts conveying an interest in real property.
4. Contracts that cannot be performed within one year after the contract is made.
5. Contracts of guaranty.

Needless to say, there are exceptions to the statute of frauds. For example, with respect to sales of real property, under the doctrine of part performance, an oral contract is enforceable if the buyer makes full or partial payment, and either (1) the buyer takes possession of the property (with the seller's approval), or (2) valuable and permanent improvements have been made to the property by the buyer. With respect to the sale of goods, an oral contract will fall outside the statute of frauds if the contract covers specially manufactured goods. A written contract is also unnecessary with respect to goods that have been accepted or for which payment has been made. Finally, it should be obvious that the statute of frauds is not applicable when a party admits in court that a contract was in fact made.

The Parol Evidence Rule

Any written or oral evidence that is not contained in the written contract is known as parol evidence. The parol evidence rule stipulates that no parol evidence of any prior or contemporaneous agreement will be allowed to change or otherwise modify any of the terms or provisions of an existing written agreement. The parol evidence rule, however, is sometimes inapplicable. For example, the rule does not apply (1) to contracts that are partly written and partly verbal, (2) to an obvious clerical or typographical error, or (3) when it is necessary to explain terms that are ambiguous.

Conclusion

The controller should be able to recognize when a contract exists. Accordingly, he or she must understand the basic elements of a contract. Further, the controller needs to be cognizant of the statute of frauds and the parol evidence rule. Not being a legal expert, the controller should contact the appropriate legal counsel if he or she perceives that (1) a contract has been breached, (2) a contract is not valid, or (3) a modification to a contract is being attempted.

SALES

Generally accepted accounting principles require that a sale be afforded accounting recognition upon its execution.

In general, the concepts of contract law are applicable to sales. It should be obvious that the seller is required to deliver the full agreed-upon quantity to the buyer. Unless otherwise stipulated, if a carrier is involved, the seller's delivery obligation depends on the pertinent shipment terms (i.e., F.O.B. shipping point or F.O.B. destination point). The place of delivery is deemed to be the seller's place of business, however, if no carrier is involved. The buyer is of course entitled to full delivery and has the right to reject delivery of a partial or excess quantity. Upon acceptance, however, the buyer will be responsible for those items accepted. In general, the buyer has the right to examine goods prior to accepting them or paying for them. However, with respect to Collect on Delivery (C.O.D.) sales, payment by the buyer is necessary before inspection. Said payment does not constitute acceptance and any nonconforming goods may be rejected.

Remedies for Breach

The various remedies for breach of a sales contract are dependent upon which party caused the breach.

Seller. If the buyer causes the breach, the seller may generally withhold delivery. If a down-payment was received by the seller, and a liquidating damages clause is not included in the contract, then the seller is entitled to keep the smaller of 20% of the purchase price or $500. The excess down-payment must therefore be returned to the buyer.

A breach on the part of the buyer also entitles the seller to stop delivery of goods in transit or in possession of a third party.

Further, the seller may reclaim goods if demand is made within ten days of receipt by an insolvent buyer.

In situations where the seller has attempted to deliver nonconforming goods, the seller has the right to notify the buyer of an intent to cure and deliver conforming goods within the time limits specified in the original contract.

With respect to manufactured goods, the seller is permitted to complete manufacture of unfinished goods, identify them to the contract, and sell them, or cease their manufacture and sell the remainder for scrap. In any event the seller is entitled to recover the difference between the contract and selling prices.

Finally, in certain instances, the seller may either cancel the contract or sue for the contract price and/or damages. Legal counsel should of course be consulted if a lawsuit is contemplated.

Buyer. If the seller effectuates the breach, the buyer may reject the goods if they are nonconforming. The seller must be given notice, and if the buyer is a merchant, the buyer is required to follow the seller's reasonable instructions pertaining to the rejected goods.

When goods are not in conformity with the contract, and the nonconformity decreases the value of the goods, the buyer may generally revoke acceptance.

Alternatively, the remedy of "cover" may be available. In situations where the buyer procures the same or similar goods from another vendor, the buyer may be entitled to recover the difference between the cost of cover and the contract price, increased by any incidental damages, but reduced by any expenses saved as a result of the seller's breach.

In lieu of suing for cover, the buyer may be entitled to sue for damages. In these instances, the measure of damages is the difference between the market price at the time the buyer learned of the breach and the contract price, increased by any incidental damages, but reduced by any expenses saved as a result of the seller's breach.

INVESTMENT SECURITIES

There are two types of investment securities: those that are "certificated," and those that are "uncertificated." Only certificated securities are negotiable.

To be certificated, an investment security must be registered to a specific party or be in bearer form. A registered security states the name of the party entitled to the security or the rights it represents. Accordingly, the issuer must maintain books to record its transfer.

To be a bona fide purchase of an investment security, the purchase must be made (1) for value, (2) in good faith, and (3) without notice of any adverse claim. Investment securities should be carefully safeguarded because stolen securities that are properly endorsed may actually be transferred to a bona fide purchaser who takes them free of the prior party's title claim.

The transfer of a certificated security to a purchaser for value carries with it the implied warranties that the transfer is effective and rightful, the security is genuine and has not been materially altered, and the transferor is unaware of any facts that might impair the security's validity.

Endorsement of a security, by itself, does not constitute a transfer; delivery of the security on which the endorsement appears must take place for a transfer to be consummated.

The controller should also be aware that the statute of frauds is applicable to contracts involving the sale of securities; accordingly, the contract must generally be in writing.

Sometimes, no matter how tight controls are, investment securities may be lost, stolen, or accidentally destroyed. In these instances, the owner is entitled to a replacement certificate provided that (1) a request for a replacement is made before the issuer becomes aware that the security has been transferred to a bona fide purchaser, (2) a sufficient indemnity bond is filed with the issuer, and (3) all reasonable requirements of the issuer are met.

EMPLOYMENT REGULATIONS

This section is intended to expand on the business law concepts briefly mentioned on pages 703 and 704 of the main text. An awareness of the provisions contained in this section will enable the controller to interface with responsible individuals in the personnel department.

The Federal Occupational and Safety Health Act (OSHA)

The Occupational and Health Administration of the Department of Labor is authorized to administer and enforce the Act. Its objective is to promote safety in the work environment.

The Act, while not applicable to federal, state, and local governments, applies to virtually all private employers.

Under the Act, a general duty is imposed on employers to furnish a work environment that is "free from recognized hazards that are causing or are likely to cause death or serious physical harm" to employees. It should be noted, however, that an employer's liability under the Act arises only where the employer actually knew or should have known of danger. In addition to complying with the general standards of the Act, employers must also comply with certain industry-specific OSHA standards.

Workplace inspections, which are conducted without prior notification, represent the Act's simple means of enforcing compliance. To be legal, however, inspections are generally subject to employer permission. Alternatively, where the government has probable cause, a search warrant may be secured.

Employers are subject to both civil and criminal penalties for violations of the Act's provisions. Civil penalties as high as $1,000 per violation may be imposed; a $10,000 penalty may be imposed for repeated violations. An employer deemed to be a willful violator may be fined up to $10,000 and/or imprisoned for up to six months.

Finally, it is illegal to fire an employee who reveals an OSHA violation.

The Federal Fair Labor Standards Act (FLSA)

FSLA requires that employers pay a minimum hourly wage; further, employers must generally pay an overtime rate equal to time-and-a-half for work in excess of 40 hours per week. The Act, however, exempts professionals, administrative employees, executives, and outside sales workers from the minimum wage and overtime provisions.

In addition, the Act regulates the employment of children in non-agricultural positions. Under the Act, children under the age of 14 may generally not be employed. However, they may be employed for newspaper delivery, acting, and working for their parents. Children between the ages of 14 and 15 may be employed to a limited extent outside of school hours in nonhazardous work. Finally, a child who is either 16 or 17 years old may be employed to perform nonhazardous tasks.

The Equal Pay Act

The Equal Pay Act makes it illegal for an employer to discriminate on the basis of gender by paying different wages for substantially equal work. The Act does, however, permit payment of different wages based on seniority, merit, quantity or quality of work, or any other factor not relating to gender. Should an employer violate the Act, it may be directed to discontinue its illegal pay structure and it may be required to provide back pay to any injured employees.

The Civil Rights Act of 1964 (CRA)

CRA makes it illegal for an employer to discriminate on the basis of race, color, religion, gender, or national origin. The Act also prohibits sexual harassment but not discrimination based on sexual preference. The Act is applicable to entities that employ 15 or more employees for 20 weeks in the current or preceding year. After enactment, the Act was modified to include The *Pregnancy Discrimination Act Amendment,* which forbids employment discrimination based on pregnancy, childbirth, or related medical conditions. It should be noted that employment discrimination based on gender, religion, and national origin (but not race) is allowable if the employer can show it to be a bona fide occupational qualification. Employment practices dependent on seniority systems and work-related merit are also permitted. Violations of CRA may entitle victims to up to two years' back pay in additional to recovery of reasonable legal fees. Reinstatement, injunctive relief, and affirmative action represent possible equitable remedies.

Age Discrimination in Employment Act (ADEA)

The Act, which is applicable to nonfederal employers with 20 or more employees, forbids employment discrimination based solely on age. ADEA is applicable to all employees at least 40 years old; the Act also contains a prohibition against mandatory retirement of nonmanagerial employees based on age. Subsequent to enactment, the ADEA was amended to ban age discrimination with respect to employee benefits. The Act does, however, allow age discrimination where justified by a bona fide seniority system, a bona fide occupational qualification, or a bona fide employee benefit plan. Injured individuals may seek injunctive relief, affirmative action, and back pay.

Rehabilitation Act of 1973

The Rehabilitation Act of 1973 was enacted to prevent discrimination on the basis of handicap by any employer that is the recipient of federal assistance or contracts. While employers subject to the Act are required to make reasonable efforts to accommodate the handicapped, they are not required to hire or promote handicapped persons who are unable to perform the job after reasonable accommodations are made. Persons with physical and mental handicaps are covered by the Act, while persons with alcohol or drug abuse problems are not.

Americans with Disabilities Act (ADA)

ADA, which is applicable to entities employing 15 or more individuals, prevents an employer from employment discrimination against qualified individuals with disabilities. A qualified individual with a disability is an individual who is able to perform the essential job function, with or without reasonable accommodation. A disabled person is an individual with or without a history of a physical or mental impairment that substantially limits one or more major life activities. In this connection, ADA affords protection to persons afflicted with cancer and HIV infections; recovering alcoholics and drug addicts are also protected. The Act bars employers from asking job applicants about disabilities but does allow inquiry about the applicant's ability to perform job-related tasks. Prospective employees are also protected by the Act's prohibition of pre-employment medical exams. However, if such exams are required of all other job applicants, the employer is not barred. The Act does afford protection to an employer as well. Accordingly, an employer may refuse to hire or promote a disabled person in situations where (1) accommodation would present an undue hardship, (2) the disabled person cannot fulfill job-related criteria that cannot be reasonably accommodated, and (3) the disabled person would represent a direct threat to the health of other individuals.

Comprehensive Omnibus Budget Reconciliation Act of 1985 (COBRA)

COBRA mandates that employers allow voluntarily or involuntarily terminated (and certain disabled) employees to continue their group health insurance coverage for a period not to exceed to 18 (if disabled, up to 29) months following termination. The terminated employee must, however, bear the expense of the premiums. COBRA applies to nongovernmental entities (1) employing at least 20 individuals and (2) offering an employer-sponsored health plan to employees. An employee's spouse and minor children must also be given the right to continue their group health coverage.

Worker Adjustment and Retraining Notification Act (WARN)

WARN, which is applicable to employers of more than 100 employees, requires that employees be given 60 days notice of plant closures or mass layoffs. A plant closing is defined as the permanent or temporary closing of a single plant or parts of a plant but only if at least 50 employees will lose their jobs within a specified 30-day period. A mass layoff arises when the jobs of at least 500 employees are terminated during a 30-day period, or the jobs of at least one-third of the employees are terminated at a given site, if that one-third equals at least 50 employees.

The Family and Medical Leave Act (FMLA)

FMLA, which is applicable to entities with at least 50 employees, requires an employer to provide 12 weeks unpaid leave each year for medical or family reasons. While on leave, an employee is entitled to continued medical benefits, and upon return, an employee is entitled to the same or an equivalent job.

SECURED TRANSACTIONS

A secured transaction is defined as any transaction that is aimed at creating a security interest in personal property or fixtures. When an agreement between a debtor and creditor has been reached, whereby the creditor shall have a security interest, a security agreement results. The security agreement must be in writing, must be signed by the debtor, and must delineate any collateral, if the agreement pertains to a nonpossessory interest.

When an interest in personal property or fixtures that secures payment or performance of an obligation exists, by definition, a security interest is created. Security interests may be either possessory or nonpossessory. Attachment must occur in order for rights of a secured party to be enforceable against the debtor. Perfection is necessary in order to make the security interest effective against most third parties.

In order for attachment to occur, (1) the secured party must have collateral pursuant to an agreement with the debtor (or the debtor must have signed a security agreement delineating collateral), (2) the creditor gives value, which may be any consideration that would support a simple contract, and (3) the debtor is afforded property rights in collateral.

Once the security interest has attached, perfection is said to have occurred. In general, the filing of a financing statement with the appropriate public official accomplishes perfection. The content of the financing statement is usually governed by state law, but generally includes, at a minimum, the names and addresses of the secured party and debtor, specification of the collateral, and the signature of the debtor.

Perfection may also be accomplished by attachment alone, without filing, through the use of a purchase money security interest (PMSI) in consumer goods. This form of perfection provides protection against a debtor's other creditors and a debtor's trustee in bankruptcy.

Finally, perfection is achieved when the creditor is in possession of the collateral. This means of perfection is useful for a security interest in goods, instruments, negotiable documents, and letters of credit. In the case of negotiable instruments, this is the only acceptable means of perfection.

It should be understood that there are two types of secured transactions; namely, a secured credit sale and a secured loan transaction. The former concerns a sales transaction in which the creditor is involved either as a seller or a money lender. The creditor takes a purchase money security interest (PMSI). Possession and risk of loss pass to the buyer, but the creditor retains a security interest in the goods until he or she has been paid in full. In the case of the latter, there is no sale of goods. Rather, the creditor lends money while simultaneously accepting a debtor-pledged security interest in collateral.

Essentially, there are four types of collateral; i.e., goods, negotiable instruments, intangibles, and fixtures.

Goods include consumer goods, inventory and equipment. Consumer goods consist of items that are used or purchased for use primarily for personal, family, or household purposes. Inventory, on the other hand, includes goods held for sale or lease, including unfinished goods. A security interest in inventory may result in a "floating lien," whereby the lien attaches to inventory in the hands of the dealer as it is received by the dealer. Equipment, it should noted, may also be subject to a "floating lien."

Negotiable instruments include commercial paper, documents of title, and investment securities.

Intangibles include both accounts receivable and contract rights.

Perfecting a Security Interest

As previously noted, to accomplish perfection, a financing statement must be filed with an appropriate public official. In instances where conflicting interests exist, the order of perfection is crucial and will decide priority, regardless of attachment. The first security interest to attach is afforded priority in cases where none of the conflicting security interests have been perfected.

If, within a ten-day period before or after the debtor takes possession of the collateral, a purchase money security interest in noninventory collateral is filed, the creditor will be protected as of the day on which the security interest was created (i.e., the day on which the debtor takes possession of the collateral) against any nonpurchase money security interest previously filed during the ten-day period. Creditor protection also applies to previously filed floating liens. In the event that the security interest is perfected after the ten-day period, the secured party will be afforded protection as of the date of filing but will not be able to secure protection against previously perfected non-PMSI.

A PMSI in inventory takes priority over conflicting security interests (i.e., previously perfected non-PMSI) but only if both (1) the PMSI-holder perfected the interest in the inventory on or before the date the inventory was received by the debtor and (2) the PMSI-holder furnished written notice (before the debtor takes possession of the inventory) indicating the acquisition of the interest and describing the secured inventory to all holders of conflicting security interests that previously filed a financing statement pertaining to the same type of inventory.

A filing will be necessary to protect against an innocent, nonmerchant purchaser from the consumer/debtor, even though no filing is required in order to perfect a purchase money security interest in consumer goods.

The written financing statement needed to perfect a security interest must generally include the names and addresses of both the debtor and the creditor. Only the debtor must sign the statement. The financing statement must also describe the collateral covered, and is effective for a five-year period commencing on the date filed. In order to extend the original five-year period for another five years, a continuation statement, signed by the secured party, is necessary and must be filed by the secured party within the six-month period prior to the original statement's expiration date.

Rights of Parties upon Default

The secured party may, upon default by the buyer/debtor, have the right to repossess the goods without going through legal channels. Alternatively, the secured party may sell the goods and apply the proceeds to any outstanding debt.

The secured party generally will be protected against subsequent creditors and most other third parties if a security interest has been perfected. However, holders in due course will defeat the claims of any and all secured parties. Furthermore, a buyer in the ordinary course of business is not controlled by a seller-created security interest, even in instances where the security interest was perfected and the buyer was conscious of it. This is quite prevalent where inventory has been pledged as collateral.

Upon default, the secured party may exercise a privilege to notify the obligor on accounts receivable, contract rights, instruments, etc., to directly remit remuneration.

While the debtor has the right to redeem collateral prior to disposition, the creditor has the right to retain goods. However, unless the debtor had relinquished rights after default, the creditor must give the debtor written notice about his or her intention(s). Furthermore, except in cases involving consumer goods, the creditor must send this notice to all other interested secured parties. If the creditor receives an objection to his or her retention within a 21-day period following the sending of this notice, then the creditor is required to dispose of the property.

If the debtor has satisfied at least 60% of the obligation, and the collateral consists of consumer goods with a PMSI, then the creditor is forced to sell the collateral within 90 days of the collateral's repossession, unless the debtor has relinquished his or her rights after default. Any excess debt owed, plus repossession costs, must be returned by the secured party to the debtor.

When, for value and without knowledge of any defects in the sale, a good-faith purchaser acquires collateral that was disposed of after default, the acquisition is free of any subordinate (but not superior) security interests. Finally, the debtor has no right to redeem collateral sold to a good-faith purchaser.

SURETYSHIP AND CREDITOR'S RIGHTS

Suretyship involves situations where one party agrees to be unconditionally liable for the debt or default of another party.

The parties involved in suretyship include the surety or guarantor (i.e., the party, whether compensated or not, who is responsible for the debt or obligation of another), the creditor (i.e., the party who is owed the debt or obligation), and the debtor or principal debtor (i.e., the party whose obligation it is). It should be noted that co-sureties may exist. If this is the case, more than one surety is obligated for the same debt, although each co-surety may not be liable for the same amount nor may they be aware of each other's existence.

Since guaranty of collection imposes only a secondary liability upon the guarantor, the creditor must initially attempt collection from the debtor before attempting collection from the guarantor. It should be noted that, except in instances where collection is subject to some condition, guaranty and suretyship are synonymous terms.

Under the statute of frauds discussed earlier, a promise of guaranty must be set forth in writing and signed by the guarantor in order to be enforceable. On the other hand, a surety agreement does not have to be set forth in writing.

While the surety/guarantor need not receive consideration, consideration is needed to support the surety/guarantor's promise, and is usually represented by the creditor's granting of the loan.

Surety's Rights against Debtor or Co-Sureties

Once payment is made by the surety to the creditor, the surety is entitled to seek indemnification or reimbursement from the debtor.

In situations involving co-sureties, once the surety has made payment to the creditor, one co-surety may seek a proportionate share from any other co-sureties.

A co-surety's share of the principal debt is calculated by multiplying the amount of principal debt by a fraction, the numerator of which is the amount for which the co-surety is liable and the denominator of which is the total amount of liabilities for all co-sureties.

In the event that a co-surety is released by a creditor, any remaining co-sureties will be liable, but only to the extent of their proportionate shares.

After the creditor is paid by the surety, the surety stands in the shoes of the creditor; this is known as subrogation.

If the debtor defaults, the surety may seek relief from the courts. The courts may order the debtor to pay the creditor. A surety may seek similar relief against co-sureties. This equitable right of the surety against the debtor is known as exoneration.

Defenses of a Surety

In general, a surety may raise any defense that may be raised by a party to an ordinary contract. As such, a surety may claim mutual mistake, lack of consideration, undue influence, and creditor fraud.

On the other hand, a surety may not claim such defenses as death, insolvency, or bankruptcy of the debtor. The statute of limitations is similarly barred as a defense.

Another possible defense arises when the surety is not advised by the creditor about matters material to the risk when the creditor reasonably believes that the surety does not possess knowledge of such matters.

A defense also arises if the surety does not consent to material modification of the original contract. There is, however, a difference between a noncompensated surety and a compensated surety. The former is completely discharged automatically. The latter is discharged only to the extent that the material modification results in the surety sustaining a loss.

The release of the debtor by the creditor without the surety's consent may also be claimed as a defense. However, if the creditor specifically reserves his or her rights as against the surety, the reservation of rights will be effective and the surety shall remain liable pursuant to the original promise.

When the security is released or its value is impaired by the creditor, the surety is discharged but only to the extent of the security released or impaired.

Finally, the debtor's tender of payment to the creditor may be used as a defense.

Rights of the Creditor

The rights of the creditor, like the defenses of the surety, depend on the facts and circumstances of the events giving rise to the suretyship.

When improvements are made to real property and the provider is not paid for labor or materials, the creditor has the right to place a mechanic's lien on the property.

Pursuant to writ of execution, which is a postjudgment remedy, a court directs the sheriff to (1) seize and sell a debtor's nonexempt property and (2) apply the proceeds to the costs of execution and the creditor's judgment.

A writ of attachment, on the other hand, is a prejudgment remedy whereby the sheriff is directed to seize the debtor's nonexempt property. The seized property is then sold to pay the judgment, but only if a judgment against the debtor is secured. This remedy is not obtained easily and requires the creditor to post a bond sufficient to cover court costs and damages for a possible wrongful attachment action by the debtor.

Alternatively, a creditor may wish to secure a writ of garnishment. This course of action may be a prejudgment or postjudgment remedy. The writ of garnishment is aimed at a third party, such as a bank or employer, holding debtor-owned funds. The third party is directed to pay a regular portion of those funds to the creditor. The federal government's desire to prevent abusive and excessive garnishment resulted in enactment of the Consumer Credit Protection Act. Under the Act, a debtor may retain the larger of 75 percent of the weekly disposable earnings, or an amount equal to 30 hours of work at the federal minimum wage rate.

An assignment for the benefit of creditors is also a viable option. Under this option, a debtor voluntarily transfers property to a trustee, who then sells the property and applies the sale proceeds on a pro rata basis to the creditors of the debtor.

It should be noted that a homestead exemption is afforded to a debtor in bankruptcy. Accordingly, the debtor is permitted to retain a family home, or a portion of the proceeds from the sale of a family home, free from the claims of unsecured creditors and trustees. However, the protection of the homestead exemption is not available to tax liens, liens for labor or materials pertinent to real property improvements, and contract obligations for the purchase of real property.

Finally, if a debtor transfers property to a third party with the intent of defrauding the debtor's creditors, and the property becomes unavailable to the debtor's creditors, a fraudulent conveyance has taken place, and is voidable at the option of the debtor's creditors.

Federally-Enacted Statutes

The federal government passed the Truth-in-Lending Act (TLA) to require that creditors disclose finance charges and credit extension charges. TLA also sets limit on garnishment proceedings. Further, a consumer who uses his or her principal residence as security for credit purposes is given the right to cancel the transaction within three business days of the credit transaction date, or the date the creditor provided the debtor with a required notice of the right to cancel, whichever is later. In general, TLA applies to consumer credit purchases up to $25,000. The $25,000 limit is not applicable, however, where the creditor maintains a security interest in the principal dwelling of the debtor.

TLA was later amended to include the Consumer Leasing Act (CLA) to expand its disclosure requirements to leases of consumer goods of up to $25,000. The provisions of CLA, however, are not applicable to real estate leases or leases between consumers.

Another amendment to TLA is the Fair Credit and Charge Card Disclosure Act, which requires disclosure of credit terms on credit and charge card solicitations and applications.

In an effort to ensure that there is no discrimination in the extension of credit, the Equal Credit Opportunity Act was enacted. Under the Act, it is illegal to discriminate on the basis of race, color, national origin, religion, age, gender, marital status, or receipt of income from public assistance programs.

By virtue of the Fair Credit Billing Act (FCBA), payment may be withheld by a credit card customer for supposedly defective products. FCBA regulates credit billing and establishes a mechanism enabling consumers to challenge and correct billing errors.

Finally, the Fair Debt Collection Practices Act may be useful as it affords protection to consumer-debtors from abusive, deceptive, and unfair practices by debt collectors.

DOCUMENTS OF TITLE

The controller should have a basic knowledge of documents of title because they indicate ownership of goods and emanate from shipment or storage of goods. Documents of title may be sold, transferred, or even pledged as collateral, and include bills of lading issued by a carrier to evidence the receipt of shipment and warehouse receipts used to evidence receipt of goods by persons hired to store goods.

It should be understood that there is a difference between a negotiable document and a nonnegotiable document. In the case of the former, the document states that goods are to be delivered to "bearer" or to the "order of" a named person. Accordingly, the goods are required to be delivered to the holder of the document. A negotiable document of title is not, however, payable in money, as commercial paper is. In the case of the latter, goods are consigned to a specified person, and therefore delivery must be made to the specified person. A nonnegotiable document, also known as a straight bill of lading, represents a receipt for the goods rather than a document of title.

Transfer or Negotiation

Transfer of nonnegotiable documents is in essence an assignment, whereby the assignee is effectively subject to all defenses that are available against the assignor.

The rules applicable to negotiable documents are much more complex and depend on whether the document is order paper or bearer paper.

With respect to order paper, which is negotiable by endorsement and delivery, a transferee of an order document which was not endorsed has a right to obtain such endorsement. It should be noted that the endorsement of a document of title does not render the endorser liable for any default by the bailee or by previous endorsers.

An endorser does, however, warrant to the immediate purchaser (1) the genuineness of the document, (2) that the transferor has no knowledge of any fact that would impair the validity of the document, and (3) that the transferor's negotiation is rightful and fully effective with respect to the document's title and the goods represented by the document.

Bearer paper, on the other hand, is negotiable by delivery alone.

To be "duly negotiated," a document must be properly negotiated to a holder who, in the regular course of business or financing and not in settlement or payment of a money obligation, has purchased the document in good faith, for value, and without notice of defenses.

To secure proper negotiation of order paper, the transferor must obtain a document with proper consent of the owner, and with the owner's endorsement.

Warehouse Obligations

Goods should only be delivered to the person possessing the negotiable document, which is required to be surrendered for cancellation.

Further, a warehouse has the right to refuse delivery of the goods until payment for the goods has been made.

Finally, a completed warehouse receipt, issued with blanks and purchased in good faith, entitles the purchaser to recover from the warehouse that issued the incomplete document.

CORPORATIONS

By definition, a corporation is a separate legal entity that possesses certain powers stipulated in its charter or by governing statutes.

Classification of Corporations

There are eight classifications of corporations: public, private, domestic, foreign, closely held, publicly held, professional, and S corporation.

A *public corporation* is a corporation that is formed for governmental purposes.

A *private corporation* essentially includes all other corporations, whether publicly held or not.

A *domestic corporation* is a corporation organized under the laws of a particular state.

A *foreign corporation* is a corporation deemed to be "foreign" with respect to every state other than the state of incorporation.

A *closely held corporation* is a corporation, the stock of which is owned by a small number of persons, who are quite commonly related to each other.

A *publicly held corporation* is a corporation, the stock of which (1) is owned by a large number of persons, and (2) is widely traded through one of the stock exchanges.

A *professional corporation* is a corporation enabling professionals, including certified public accountants, to operate utilizing the corporate form.

An *S corporation,* as discussed in Chapter 42, is a corporation that (1) has satisfied certain IRS requirements, and (2) is electing to be taxed essentially like a partnership.

Parties to a Corporation

If the decision is made to form a publicly held corporation, the services of a promoter are usually necessary. The promoter is responsible for developing ideas pertinent to the corporation, securing stock subscribers, and entering into contracts on behalf of the corporation to be established. While corporations are generally not legally bound by contracts until a preincorporation contract is assumed by the formed corporation, promoters are generally deemed to be personally liable on contracts.

An incorporator is an important party as well, since he or she is the individual charged with devising the formal application needed to create the corporation. Corporate existence only begins upon the state's issuance of the certificate of incorporation.

The stockholders are the owners of the corporation's stock. They are empowered to elect directors who will manage the entity, vote on important issues, inspect books and records, and receive financial statements. Since stockholders, as owners, share in the corporation's profits, they are entitled to receive dividends declared at the discretion of the board of directors. Stockholders may force the board to make dividend payments only when directors are found to have abused their judgment regarding dividend declaration. It should be noted that a dividend received by a stockholder during the period of a company's insolvency must be returned to the corporation.

One of the greatest advantages of the corporate form, from the stockholders' point of view, is that stockholders are generally not liable beyond their investment. The courts may, however, "pierce the corporate veil," and hold the stockholders liable if, among other circumstances, the courts determine that the corporation (1) was established in order to perpetrate a fraud, or (2) is undercapitalized.

Directors, elected by the stockholders, are charged with establishing the corporation's essential policies and electing corporate officers. Since directors are employed in a fiduciary capacity, they are liable for negligence but not errors in judgment. Stockholders may commence a derivative action to cure any damage done by the directors. Directors acting in a representative capacity, however, are entitled to corporate indemnification with respect to acts performed on behalf of the corporation. While directors have the discretion to declare dividends, they will be held to be personally liable for illegal dividends; i.e., dividend payments made during the corporation's period of insolvency, or dividend payments that force the corporation into insolvency, or dividend payments made from an unauthorized account.

The corporate officers are responsible for managing the daily operations of the corporation, and their rights and powers are governed by agency law and are limited by the corporation's charter and bylaws. Corporate officers, appointed by the board of directors, while liable for negligent acts, are entitled to indemnification for acts performed within the scope of their authority, so long as they acted in good faith.

Powers and Rights of a Corporation

A corporation's sources of power include the corporation's charter and bylaws as well as relevant statutes. A corporation is normally empowered to borrow and lend money, enter into contracts, acquire and dispose of property, have perpetual existence, and have exclusive use of its legal corporate name.

Dissolution or Termination of Corporations

While a corporation normally is afforded perpetual existence, there are circumstances that enable a corporation to terminate its existence. Termination may be accomplished by voluntary or involuntary dissolution.

In order to dissolve voluntarily, the board of directors must approve a corporate resolution. Approval generally requires a majority vote on the part of stockholders possessing stock with voting rights. A special shareholders' meeting is needed and all shareholders must be provided written notice of the purpose, time, date, and location of the special meeting.

Involuntary dissolution, on the other hand, may result from an administrative hearing on the part of the secretary of state, or from a judicial proceeding prompted by either a shareholder or corporate creditor.

To force an involuntary dissolution based on an administrative hearing, the secretary of state must prove that the corporation has failed to comply with state laws. Accordingly, the corporation's failure to file required annual reports or pay taxes may result in an involuntary dissolution.

A court may also force a corporation to dissolve. To do so, it must prove that the corporation fraudulently obtained its charter, the corporation was involved in ultra vires acts (i.e., those abusing or in excess of its authority), the board of directors was involved in an illegal or fraudulent act, or the assets of the corporation are being wasted or misapplied. A court-forced dissolution may also result when either (1) the shareholders are deadlocked and have failed to elect directors for at least two consecutive annual meetings, or (2) the directors are deadlocked, the shareholders cannot break the deadlock, and irreparable damage is threatened or being suffered by the corporation.

Consolidation or Merger

From a legal standpoint, a consolidation involves joining two or more corporations in order to form a new entity with the assets and liabilities of the old corporations. A merger, on the other hand, occurs when one corporation absorbs another. The corporation absorbed is accordingly terminated, while the other corporation (i.e., the survivor) continues its existence. The survivor logically assumes the liabilities of the corporation absorbed in the merger.

In order to effectuate a consolidation or merger, the board of directors of each corporation must ratify a formal plan, which must then be submitted to the stockholders of each corporation for their approval. Approval constitutes the consent of a majority of each corporation's voting shareholders, following due notice of a special shareholders' meeting. Furthermore, each voting shareholder must be given a copy of the merger or consolidation plan.

Any dissenting shareholders must be provided an appraisal remedy; i.e., they must be given the value of the shares immediately prior to the action to which the dissenter objects plus accrued interest, if any. In order to obtain an appraisal remedy, a dissenting shareholder must (1) file a written notice of dissent with the corporation prior to the vote of the shareholders,

(2) vote against the proposed transaction, and (3) demand in writing that an appraisal remedy be made after the shareholders' vote of approval.

Finally, articles of consolidation or merger must be filed with the absorbing corporation's state of incorporation. The merger or consolidation is effective only when this document is filed.

It should be noted that a short-form merger is often permitted when a merger of a subsidiary into a parent corporation is desired. To qualify, a parent corporation must own at least 90 percent of the outstanding shares of each class of stock in a subsidiary. It is interesting to note that only the approval of the parent corporation's board of directors is necessary. It is not necessary to secure the approval of either the shareholders of each corporation or the board of directors of the subsidiary corporation. Additionally, only the shareholders of the subsidiary corporation need be given an appraisal remedy.

BANKRUPTCY

A knowledge of bankruptcy law is essential, given today's economic conditions and competitive markets. This section is designed to update and expand on the material contained on pages 989 and 990 in the main text. From a legal standpoint, the primary basis for bankruptcy is insolvency in the equity sense as opposed to balance sheet insolvency. Accordingly, the entity must be unable to pay debts as they become due as opposed to merely having an excess of liabilities over assets.

Bankruptcy Reform Act of 1994

The Bankruptcy Reform Act of 1994 essentially contains two chapters applicable to corporations.

Chapter 7 permits the voluntary or involuntary liquidation of a debtor's nonexempt assets, the distribution of the proceeds to creditors, and the discharge of the remaining business and/or personal debt of the debtor. While Chapter 7 relief is available to corporations, a discharge of indebtedness is not available if the debtor is a corporation, since the limited liability of shareholders would preclude the need for a discharge. Under Chapter 7, it should be apparent that the business no longer continues to operate.

Chapter 11, on the other hand, is quite different. Chapter 11 relief, which is generally available if the entity is eligible for relief under Chapter 7, enables reorganization by the entity's business debtors, in order to keep the financially troubled business in operation. Fraud, incompetence, or gross mismanagement, however, will prevent the desired continuity.

A petition under Chapter 11 may be voluntary or involuntary, and insolvency in the balance sheet sense is not a condition precedent. The filing of a voluntary petition by an eligible debtor operates as an order for relief, effectively eliminating the need for a formal hearing.

Appointment of a committee of unsecured creditors follows an order of relief. The parties holding the seven largest unsecured claims against the debtor usually sit on the committee.

Under Chapter 11, the debtor usually remains in possession and control of the business. However, a trustee may be appointed by the Court for cause, which includes, but is not limited to, fraud on the part of the debtor or incompetence of the debtor.

The right to file a reorganization plan during the first 120 days following the order for relief rests with the debtor, unless the court has appointed a trustee. If the creditors do not accept a timely filed plan, then no other party is permitted to file a plan for reorganization during the first 180 days after the order for relief. Thereafter, however, a plan for reorganization may be filed by one or more interested parties.

In order to be effective, each class of creditors must accept the proposed plan for reorganization. Confirmation by the Bankruptcy Court is then required. Acceptance by a class of creditors requires approval by creditors holding at least two-thirds of the debt owed to that class of creditors and holding more than one-half of the allowed claims for that class.

Upon confirmation by the court, a final decree is entered, resulting in the discharge of the debtor from most preconfirmation debts.

An expedited reorganization process is available to a qualified small business, which is defined as a business whose aggregate noncontingent liquidated secured and unsecured debts are less than $2 million. The expedited process enables elimination of creditor committees and affords the debtor the exclusive right to file a reorganization plan within 100 days.

Bankruptcy Petitions

A bankruptcy petition must be filed in order to begin bankruptcy proceedings. If the debtor files the petition, it is said to be a voluntary petition. A voluntary petition generally lists the entity's creditors, exempt property, and a description of financial condition. Upon filing a voluntary petition, an order for relief is entered.

If the creditors of the entity file the petition, it is referred to as an involuntary petition. The debtor, of course, has the right to contest the petition in court. An order for relief, however, is entered only after a court hearing.

Three petitioning creditors are required when the debtor has 12 or more creditors; only one creditor is required if the debtor has less than 12 creditors. In either situation, the petition must allege unsecured debts of at least $10,000 owed by the debtor to the petitioning creditors.

If the petition is opposed by the debtor, the court may enter an order of relief only if (1) the debtor is not paying debts as they mature, or (2) within 120 days before the petition is filed, to enforce a lien against the property, a receiver took possession of substantially all of the debtor's property.

A successful contest of an involuntary bankruptcy petition by the debtor may result in the court granting a judgment for (1) costs, (2) reasonable attorney's fees, and (3) compensatory damages. The debtor may also be awarded punitive damages should the court determine that the petition was filed in bad faith.

Priority of Claims

The priority of a claim depends on whether it is a secured claim or an unsecured claim. A creditor with a perfected secured claim against specific property of the debtor is afforded first priority to the proceeds from that property. To the extent that the proceeds of the sale of the secured asset are not sufficient to fully discharge the claim of the secured party, the creditor is considered to be an unsecured creditor.

After secured claims are satisfied, unsecured creditors are entitled to any remaining assets. Since some unsecured claims are given priority, they must be paid in full before payment is made to subordinate claims. In the event that a debtor's assets are not sufficient to fully pay unsecured creditors with the same priority, payments must be made on a pro rata basis.

The general order of priority applicable to nonsecured claims is (1) administrative expenses, (2) debt obligations incurred after commencement of an involuntary bankruptcy case, but before the order for relief or appointment of a trustee, (3) unsecured claims for wages earned within 90 days before the filing of a bankruptcy petition or cessation of business, whichever is first, limited to $4,000 for each employee, (4) contributions to employee benefit plans based on services rendered within 180 days before the filing of the bankruptcy petition, but limited to $4,000 per employee, (5) deposits with the debtor to the extent of $1,800 per individual for the purchase, rental, or lease of property or personal services, for family or household use, (6) taxes, and (7) general creditor claims.

Discharge of Debt

While a discharge in bankruptcy generally discharges debt, certain obligations are not discharged. Some of the more common debts that are not discharged include taxes in general; unlisted debts and debts where the creditor notice did not stipulate the debtor's name, address, and taxpayer identification number; debts for fraud, embezzlement, or larceny; liability for injury that was willful and malicious; fines and penalties; debts surviving an earlier bankruptcy proceeding; and loans used to pay federal taxes.

Discharge of debt will be denied if the debtor, within a one-year period before the petition is filed, or during the hearing of the case, (1) directly or indirectly transferred, destroyed, or concealed property, (2) concealed, destroyed, falsified, or failed to preserve any records necessary for determining financial condition, (3) committed fraud, refused to testify, or attempted bribery in connection with the bankruptcy, (4) failed to explain satisfactorily any loss or deficiency of assets, (5) refused to obey a lawful court order, (6) has been granted a discharge in a case commenced within six years before the date of the filing of the petition, or (7) executed a court-approved written waiver of discharge after the order for relief.

It should be noted that under certain conditions, a debtor and a creditor may agree to honor a discharged debt. The agreement is known as a reaffirmation agreement.

ENVIRONMENTAL LAW

Violation of environmental law may subject the corporation to stiff criminal and civil fines and penalties. As a valued member of management, the controller should possess some basic knowledge of relevant federal statutes pertinent to environmental law.

Federal statutes have been enacted to extend common law liability for nuisance (i.e., unreasonable interference with use and enjoyment of another's land) and trespass (i.e., the intentional and unlawful entry upon another's land).

The Environmental Protection Agency (EPA) is a federal administrative agency that is charged with administering federal laws designed to protect the environment.

The National Environmental Policy Act (NEPA) requires the federal government to consider the "adverse impact" of proposed legislation, rule-making, or other federal government action on the environment before the action is set in motion. Under the law, an environmental impact statement must be prepared in connection with all proposed federal legislation or major federal action that significantly impacts the quality of the human environment.

The Clean Air Act, which regulates air quality, specifically addresses (1) national ambient air quality standards, (2) stationary sources of air pollution, (3) mobile sources of air pollution, and (4) toxic air pollutants.

The Clean Water Act enables the EPA to establish water quality criteria in order to regulate the concentrations of permissible pollutants in a body of water and limit the amounts of pollutants that are discharged from a particular source. Enforcement of the Act is delegated to individual states.

The Noise Control Act enables the EPA to establish noise standards for new products. Under the Act, the EPA (with the Federal Aeronautics Administration) is empowered to establish noise limits for new aircraft and to regulate, with the assistance of the Department of Transportation, noise emissions from trucks.

The Resource Conservation and Recovery Act (RCRA) authorizes the EPA to identify hazardous wastes. Further, the Act authorizes the EPA to regulate entities that generate, treat, store, and dispose of wastes deemed to be hazardous.

Finally, the Comprehensive Environmental Response, Compensation, and Liability Act (CERCLA), often referred to as the "Superfund" law, mandates that the EPA identify hazardous waste sites. The EPA must rank the identified sites according to the severity of the environmental risk they pose.

Should the EPA have to clean up a hazardous site, it may recover the cost of the cleanup from one or more responsible parties.

FINANCIAL STATEMENT REPORTING: THE INCOME STATEMENT

FINANCIAL ACCOUNTING STANDARDS BOARD STATEMENT NUMBER 130

FASB Statement Number 130 (Reporting Comprehensive Income) requires companies to report comprehensive income and its elements in a full set of financial statements. FASB Statement Number 130 keeps the current reporting requirements for net income, but it considers net income a major element of comprehensive income. A restatement of previous years' financial statements is needed when presented for comparative purposes.

Comprehensive income applies to the change in equity (net assets) arising from either transactions or other occurrences with nonowners. Excluded are investments and withdrawals by nonowners. Comprehensive income is comprised of two components: net income and other comprehensive income. Other comprehensive income relates to all items of comprehensive income excluding net income. Thus, net income plus other comprehensive income equals total comprehensive income. Other comprehensive income includes the following:

- Foreign currency items including translation gains and losses, and gains and losses on foreign currency transactions designated as hedges of a net investment in a foreign entity.
- Unrealized losses or gains on available-for-sale securities.

- Minimum pension liability adjustments applying to the amount by which the additional pension liability exceeds the unrecognized prior service cost.
- Changes in market value of a futures contract that is a hedge of an asset reported at fair value.

FASB Statement Number 130 provides flexibility on how comprehensive income may be shown in the financial statements. There are three allowable options for reporting other comprehensive income and its components, as follows:

1. Below the net income figure in the income statement, or
2. In a separate statement of comprehensive income beginning with net income, or
3. In a statement of changes in equity as long as such statement is presented as a primary financial statement. It cannot appear only in the footnotes.

Options 1 and 2 are income-statement-type formats, while option 3 is a statement-of-changes-in-equity format. Options 1 and 2 are preferred.

A sample presentation under option 1 within the income statement follows:

Statement of Income and Comprehensive Income

Net Income		$600,000
Other Comprehensive Income:		
Foreign currency translation loss	($50,000)	
Unrealized gain on available-for-sale securities	70,000	
Minimum pension liability adjustment	(10,000)	
Total Other Comprehensive Income		10,000
Total Comprehensive Income		$610,000

Under the second option, a separate statement of comprehensive income is presented. The reporting follows:

Income Statement

Net Income	$600,000

Statement of Comprehensive Income

Net Income		$600,000
Other Comprehensive Income:		
Foreign currency translation loss	($50,000)	
Unrealized gain on available-for-sale securities	70,000	
Minimum pension liability adjustment	(10,000)	
Total Other Comprehensive Income		10,000
Total Comprehensive Income		$610,000

Under the third option, comprehensive income and its components are presented in the comprehensive income column as part of the statement of changes in equity. An illustrative format of the comprehensive income column follows:

Comprehensive Income:

Net Income		$600,000
Other Comprehensive Income:		
Foreign currency items	($50,000)	
Unrealized loss or gain on available-for-sale securities	70,000	
Minimum pension liability adjustment	(10,000)	
Total Other Comprehensive Income		10,000
Total Comprehensive Income		$610,000

In the stockholders' equity section, "accumulated other comprehensive income" is presented as one amount for all items and listed for each component separately.

The components of other comprehensive income for the period may be presented on a before-tax basis with one amount for the tax impact of all the items of other comprehensive income.

A reclassification adjustment may be required so as not to double-count items reported in net income for the current period which have also been considered as part of other comprehensive income in a prior period. An example is the realized gain on an available-for-sale security sold in the current year when a holding gain was also included in other comprehensive income in a prior year. Reclassification adjustments may also apply to foreign currency translation. The reclassification adjustment applicable to a foreign exchange translation only applies to translation gains and losses realized from the sale or liquidation of an investment in a foreign entity.

Reclassification adjustments may be presented with other comprehensive income or in a footnote. The reclassification adjustment may be shown on a gross or net basis (except that the minimum pension liability adjustment must be presented on a net basis).

Example 1. On January 1, 20X1, a company purchased 1,000 shares of available-for-sale securities having a market price per share of $100. On December 31, 20X1, the available-for-sale securities had a market price of $150 per share. On January 1, 20X2, the securities were sold at a market price of $130 per share. The tax rate is 30%.

The unrealized gain or loss included in other comprehensive income is determined below:

	Before Tax	Tax Effect at 30%	Net of Tax
20X1 (1,000 × $50*)	$50,000	$15,000	$35,000
20X2 (1,000 × $20**)	(20,000)	(6,000)	(14,000)
Total gain	$30,000	$9,000	$21,000

*$150 – $100 = $50
**$150 – $130 = $20

The presentation in the income statement for 20X1 and 20X2 follows:

	20X1	20X2
Net Income:		
Gross realized gain on available-for-sale securities		$30,000
Tax expense		9,000
Net realized gain		$21,000
Other Comprehensive Income:		
Unrealized gain or loss after tax	$30,000	$(9,000)
Reclassification adjustment net of tax		(21,000)
Net gain included in other comprehensive income	$30,000	$(30,000)
Total effect on comprehensive income	$30,000	$(9,000)

In interim financial statements issued to the public, FASB Statement Number 130 requires a business to present total comprehensive income. However, it is not required for interim reporting to present the individual components of other comprehensive income.

DISCLOSURES ASSOCIATED WITH OPERATIONS

Disclosure should be made of a company's major products and services including principal markets by geographic area. The information enables a proper evaluation of the entity's nature of operations. Further, AICPA Statement of Position (SOP) Number 94-6 mandates disclosure of major risks and uncertainties facing the entity. The SOP also requires disclosure in the significant accounting policies footnote that the financial information presented is based on management's estimates and assumptions. Reference should be made that actual results may differ from such estimates.

SERVICE SALES REVENUE

A transaction often involves the sale of both a product and a service. It is thus necessary to determine if the transaction should be classified primarily as a product transaction or a service transaction, or a combination of both.

For transactions having both a product and service element, the following applies:

- A transaction should be classified as primarily a service transaction if the inclusion or exclusion of the product would not change the total price of the transaction.
- If the inclusion or exclusion of the service would not alter the total transaction price, then the transaction should be classified as primarily a product transaction.
- If the inclusion or exclusion of the service or product would change the total transaction price, then the transaction should be split and the product component should be accounted for separately from the service element.

The following four methods should be used to recognize revenue from service activities:

- The specific performance method is used when performance involves a single action and the revenue is recognized when that action occurs.
- The proportional performance method is used when performance relates to a series of actions. If the transaction involves an unspecified number of actions over a stated time period, an equal amount of revenue should be recognized at fixed intervals. If the transaction relates to a specified number of similar actions, an equal amount of revenue should be recorded when each action is completed. If the transaction relates to a given number of dissimilar or unique actions, revenue

should be recognized based upon the following ratio: direct costs involved in a single action ÷ total estimated direct costs of the transaction × total revenue for the entire transaction.

- The completed performance method is used to recognize revenue when completing the final action is so critical that the entire transaction should be considered incomplete without it.

- The collection method is used to recognize revenue when there is significant uncertainty with regard to the collection of revenue. Revenue is not recognized until cash is received.

The three major cost categories that arise from service transactions are:

- Initial direct costs are incurred to negotiate and obtain a service agreement. They include commissions, credit investigation, legal fees, and processing fees.

- Direct costs arise from rendering the service, such as labor charges and the cost of materials.

- Indirect costs are all the costs needed to perform the service, but cannot be classified as either initial direct costs or direct costs. Indirect costs include rent, depreciation, selling and administrative costs, allowance for bad debts, and the costs to negotiate transactions that are not consummated.

Indirect costs are expensed as incurred. Initial direct costs and direct costs are expensed only when the related revenue is recognized, using either the specific performance or completed performance method. In other words, initial direct costs and direct costs should be recorded as prepaid assets and expensed once the service has been rendered. The same accounting treatment is used to expense initial direct costs under the proportional performance method; that is, initial direct costs are recorded as prepaid assets and expensed when the revenue is recognized. On the other hand, direct costs should be expensed as incurred when the proportional performance method is used. This is done because of the close relationship between the direct costs incurred and the completion of the service. If the collection method is used, both initial direct costs and direct costs are expensed as incurred.

A loss may be incurred in a service transaction. A loss should be recognized when initial direct costs and estimated total direct costs exceed the estimated revenue. The loss is first applied to reduce the prepaid asset and any remaining loss is charged against the estimated liability account.

A service transaction may involve initiation and/or installation fees. The fees are usually nonrefundable. If one can objectively determine the value of the right or privilege granted by the initiation fees, then the fees should be recognized as revenue and the associated direct costs should be expensed on the initiation date. On the contrary, if the value cannot be determined, the fees should initially be deemed unearned revenue, a liability account. Revenue should be recognized from such initiation fees using one of the service revenue recognition methods.

The accounting afforded to equipment installation fees depends upon whether the customer can buy the equipment independent of the installation. If equipment may be bought independent of installation, then the transaction is considered a product transaction and installation fees are treated as part of the product transaction. On the contrary, if both the equipment and installation are essential for service and the customer cannot buy the equipment separately, then the installation fees should be treated as unearned revenue. Unearned revenue should be recognized and the cost of installation and equipment should be amortized over the estimated service period.

CONTRACT TYPES

There are various types of construction contracts including time and materials, unit price, fixed-price, and cost-type. Time and materials contracts reimburse the contractor for direct labor and direct material costs. Unit price contracts provide payment to the contractor based on the amount of units completed. Fixed-price contracts are not usually subject to adjustment such as due to increasing construction costs. Cost-type contracts may be either cost without a fee or cost plus a fee. The fee is usually based on a profit margin. However, the fee may be based on some other factor such as total expected costs, uncertainty in estimating costs, project risk, economic conditions, etc. The contract cost should never be more than its net realizable value, otherwise the contract would not be financially feasible. A loss is recognized when accumulated cost exceeds net realizable value.

Contracts which are very similar may be grouped for accounting purposes. Similarity may be indicated by a similar project management, single customer, conducted sequentially or concurrently, interrelated, and negotiated as a package deal. The segmenting of a contract is segregating the larger unit into smaller ones for accounting purposes. By breaking up a unit, revenues are associated with different components or phases. In consequence, different profitability margins may apply to each different unit or phase. Segmenting of a project may be indicated when all of the following criteria are satisfied:

- The project may be segregated into its components.
- A contract bid price exists for the entire project and its major components.
- Customer approval is received.

Even if all of these conditions are not met, the project may still be segmented if all of the following exist:

- Segregation is logical and consistent.
- Risk differences are explainable.
- Each segment is negotiated.
- Cost savings arise.
- Stability exists.
- Similarity exists in services and prices.
- Contractor has a track record.

An addition or modification made to an existing contact arising from an option clause is accounted for as a separate contract if any of the following applies:

- Price of the new product or service is distinct.
- Product or service is similar to that in the original contract but differences do exist in contract pricing and cost.
- Product or service is materially different than the product or service provided for in the initial contract.

A claim is an amount above the contract price that a contractor wants customers to pay because of customer errors in specifications, customer delays, or other unanticipated causes resulting in higher costs to the contractor. The contractor may recognize additional revenue because of these claims if justification exists and the amount is determinable. The revenue is recognized only to the extent that contract costs related to the claim have been incurred. As per AICPA Statement of Position 81-1, the following benchmarks exist to establish the ability to record the additional revenue:

- Additional costs incurred were not initially expected when the contract was signed.
- The claim has a legal basis.
- The claim is verifiable and objective.
- Costs are determinable.

If the above conditions are not met, a contingent asset should be disclosed.

CONTRACT COSTS

Costs incurred to date on a contract include pre-contract costs and costs incurred after the contract date. Pre-contract costs include learning costs for a new process, design fees, and any other expenditures likely to be recouped after the contract is signed. After the contract, the pre-contract costs are considered contract costs to date.

Some pre-contract costs, such as for materials and supplies, may be deferred to an asset called Deferred Contract Costs in anticipation of a specific contract as long as recoverability is probable. If recoverability is not probable, the pre-contract costs must be immediately expensed. If excess goods are produced in anticipation of future orders, related costs may be deferred to inventory if the costs are considered recoverable.

After the status of a contract bid has been determined (accepted or rejected) a review should be conducted of the pre-contract costs. If the contract has been approved, the deferred pre-contract costs are included in contract costs. If the contract is rejected, the pre-contract costs are immediately expensed unless there are other related contracts pending that might recoup these costs.

Back charges are billable costs for work performed by one party that should have been performed by the party billed. Such an agreement is usually stipulated in the contract. Back charges are accounted for by the contractor as a receivable from the subcontractor with a corresponding reduction in contract costs. The subcontractor accounts for the back charge as contract costs and as a payable.

GOVERNMENT CONTRACTS

On cost-plus-fixed-fee government contracts, fees should typically be accrued as billable. If an advance payment is received, it should not offset receivables unless the payment is for work-in-process. If any amounts are offset, disclosure is required.

If a government contract is subject to renegotiation, a renegotiation claim to which the contractor is accountable for should be charged to sales and credited to a current liability. Disclosure must be provided of the basis used to compute the anticipated refund.

If the government terminates a contract, contract costs included in inventory should be transferred to receivables. The claim against the government should be shown under current assets unless a long delay in payment is anticipated. A termination claim should be accounted for as a sale. A subcontractor's claim arising from the termination should be included in the contractor's claim against the government. Assume a contractor has a termination claim receivable of $800,000 of which $200,000 applies to the contractor's obligation to the subcontractor. In this situation, a liability should be accrued for $200,000. The termination claim is reduced by any inventory applying to the contract that the contractor is retaining. Disclosure should be provided of the terms of terminated contracts.

Direct costs are included in contract costs such as material, labor, and subcontracting costs. Indirect costs are allocated to contracts on an appropriate basis. Allocable costs include quality control, insurance, contract supervision, repairs and maintenance, tools, and inspection. Learning and startup costs should be charged to existing contracts. The entry for an expected loss on a contract is to make a loss provision.

REVENUE RECOGNITION WHEN A RIGHT OF RETURN EXISTS

A reasonable estimate of returned merchandise may be impaired if the products are not similar, there is a lack of previous experience in estimating returns because the product is new or circumstances have changed, a long time period exists for returns, and the product has a high degree of obsolescence.

Example 2. On March 1, 20X5, product sales of $1,000,000 were made. The cost of the goods is $600,000. A 60-day return privilege exists. The anticipated return rate of goods is 10%. On April 15, 20X5, a customer returns goods having a selling price of $80,000. The criteria to recognize revenue when the right of return exists have been satisfied. The journal entries follow:

March 1, 20X5

Accounts Receivable	1,000,000	
Sales		1,000,000
Cost of Sales	600,000	
Inventory		600,000
Sales Returns	100,000	
Allowance for Sales Returns		100,000

$1,000,000 × 10% = $100,000

Inventory	40,000	
Cost of Sales		40,000

$100,000 × 40% (gross profit rate) = $40,000

April 15, 20X5

Allowance for Sales Returns	80,000	
Accounts Receivable		80,000

Cost of Sales	8,000	
Inventory		8,000*
*Inventory assumed returned ($100,000 × 40%)		$40,000
Less: Amount returned ($80,000 × 40%)		32,000
Adjustment to inventory		$ 4,000

SOFTWARE REVENUE RECOGNITION

As per AICPA Statement of Position 97-2, revenue should be recorded when the software contract does not involve major production, change, or customization as long as the following conditions exist:

1. The contract is enforceable.
2. The software has been delivered.
3. Receipt of payment is probable.
4. The selling price is fixed or known.

Separate accounting is required for the service aspect of a software transaction if the following conditions exist:

1. The services are required for the software transaction.
2. A separate provision exists in the contract covering services so a price for such services is provided for.

A software contract may include more than one component, such as up-grade, customer support subsequent to sale, add-ons, and return or exchange provision. The total selling price of the software transaction should be allocated to the contractual components based on their fair values. If fair value is not ascertainable, revenue should be deferred until it is determinable or when all components of the transaction have been delivered. *Note:* The four revenue criteria stipulated above must be met before any allocation of the fee to the contractual elements may be made. Additionally, the fee for a contractual component is ascertainable if the element is sold separately.

WARRANTY AND MAINTENANCE REVENUE

Extended warranty and product maintenance contracts are often provided by retailers as separately priced services in addition to the sale of their products. Any warranty or maintenance agreements that are not separately priced should be accounted for as contingencies. Services under contracts may be provided at fixed intervals, a certain number of times, or as required to keep the product operational.

Revenues and incremental direct cost from separately priced extended warranty and product maintenance contracts should be initially deferred. Revenue should be recorded on a straight-line basis over the contract period. The associated incremental direct costs should be expensed proportionately to the revenue recognized. Incremental direct costs arise from obtaining the contract. Other costs, such as the cost of services rendered, general and administrative costs, and the costs of contracts not consummated, should be expensed as incurred.

Losses from these contracts should be recognized when the anticipated costs of rendering the service plus the unamortized portion of acquisition cost exceeds the corresponding deferred revenue. To ascertain loss, contracts should be grouped in a consistent manner. Losses are not recognized on individual contracts but instead apply to a grouping of similar contracts. Loss is recognized by initially reducing unamortized acquisition costs. If this is insufficient, a liability is recorded.

CONTRIBUTIONS

FASB Statement Number 116 applies to the accounting and reporting for contributions received and contributions made. Cash, other monetary and nonmonetary assets, services, or unconditional promises to give assets or services qualify as contributions. Contributions may involve either donor-imposed restrictions or donor-imposed conditions. If the donor restricts the way a contribution is to be used (such as to build a research laboratory), it is considered a restriction and the revenue from such a contribution and any associated costs are recognized immediately. However, if the donor imposes a condition, such as the donee must obtain matching funds, that condition must be met before revenue may be recognized.

A donor may make an unconditional or conditional promise. An unconditional promise exists if the donor has no right to take back the donated asset and the contribution would be available after some stated time period or on demand. Unconditional promises to give contributions are recognized immediately. A conditional promise is contingent upon the happening of a future occurrence. If that event does not take place, the donor is not obligated by the promise. A vague promise is considered conditional. Conditional promises are recorded only when their terms are met. A conditional promise may be treated as an unconditional promise if the possibility that the condition will not be satisfied is remote.

There must be supporting evidence to substantiate that a promise has been made. Such evidence includes information about the donor (e.g., donor's name and address), the amount the donor commits to give such as in a public announcement, when the amount promised will be given, and to whom the promise to give was made. The donor may have taken certain actions relying on the promise. The donor may have made partial payments. A recorded promise should be at the fair market value of the consideration. If the amount will be collected beyond one year, a discounted cash flow calculation may be made. If discounting is done, the interest is accounted for as contribution income, not interest income.

Contributed services should be recognized if specialized skills are rendered by the donor and those skills would have been purchased by the donee if they were not donated. Contributions received should be recorded at fair value by debiting the asset and crediting revenue. Quoted market prices or market prices for similar assets, appraisal by independent experts, or valuation techniques such as discounted cash flows should be used to compute fair value. The value of contributed services should be based on quoted market prices for those services.

Disclosures are required in the financial statements of recipients of contributions. For unconditional promises to give, the amount of receivables due within one year, in one to five years, and in more than five years should be disclosed along with the amount expected to be uncollected. For conditional promises to give, disclosure is required of promised amounts along with a description of the promise. Promises with similar characteristics may be grouped. Disclosure should be made of the nature and degree of contributed services, limitations or conditions set by the donor, and the programs or activities benefiting from contributed services. Companies are encouraged to disclose the fair value of services received but not recorded as revenue.

The donor should record an expense and a corresponding decrease in assets, or an increase in liabilities, at fair value, in the year in which the contribution is made. If fair value differs from carrying value, a loss or gain on disposition is recorded.

ADVERTISING COSTS

American Institute of CPAs' Statement of Position 93-7 (Reporting on Advertising Costs) requires the expensing of advertising as incurred when the advertising program first occurs. However, the cost of direct-response advertising may be deferred if the major purpose of the promotion is to elicit sales to customers who respond specifically to the advertising and for which future benefit exists. For example, the former condition is satisfied if the response card is specially coded. The latter condition is met if the resulting future revenues exceed the future costs to be incurred. The deferred advertising is amortized over the expected benefit period using the revenue method (current year revenue to total revenue). The cost of a billboard should also be capitalized and amortized. Advertising expenditures incurred after revenue is recognized should be accrued. These advertising costs should be expensed when the related revenues are recognized.

RESTRUCTURING CHARGES

Securities and Exchange Commission Staff Accounting Bulletin Number 67 requires restructuring charges to be expensed and presented as a component in computing income from operations.

In general, an expense and liability should be accrued for employee termination benefits in a restructuring. Disclosure should be made of the group and number of workers laid off.

An exit plan requires the recognition of a liability for the restructuring changes incurred if there is no future benefit to continuing operations. The expense for the estimated costs should be made on the commitment date of the exit plan. Expected gains from assets to be sold in connection with the exit plan should be recorded in the year realized. These gains are not allowed to offset the accrued liability for exit costs. Exit costs incurred are presented as a separate item as part of income from continuing operations. Disclosures associated with an exit plan include the terms of the exit plan, description and amount of exit costs incurred, activities to be exited from, method of disposition, expected completion date, and liability adjustments.

ORGANIZATION COSTS

Organization costs (e.g., legal and accounting fees to start a business) must be expensed as incurred.

Start-Up Costs

Under SOP 98-5, start-up (preoperating, preopening) costs must be expensed as incurred. Start-up costs include the one-time costs of opening a new business, introducing a new product or service, conducting business in a new territory, or having business with a new class of customer.

Costs to Develop or Obtain Computer Software for Internal Use

AICPA Statement of Position 98-1 (Accounting for the Costs of Computer Software Developed or Obtained for Internal Use) deals with software development or purchase for internal (not external) use. The company has no plan to sell the software.

The three stages of computer development are:

1. *Preliminary project stage.* This stage may involve such activities as structuring an assembly team, appraising vendor proposals, and think-

ing about reengineering efforts. A software development strategy or vendor has not yet been decided upon. During this stage, all costs should be expensed as incurred without separate presentation in the income statement.

2. *Application development stage.* A determination has been made as to how the software development work will be carried out. Costs incurred during this stage are capitalized provided it is probable the project will be completed successfully. Typical costs that should be capitalized include direct material and/or services contributing to the project, payroll costs, and any interest costs incurred during the development process, testing, and installation. General and administrative costs, overhead, and training costs are not deferred.

3. *Postimplementation/operation stage.* The stage begins when the internal use software is put in service. Capitalized costs should be amortized on a straight-line basis over the estimated useful life of the internally-used software. Because the estimated life is typically short, it should be reappraised periodically. Capitalized costs of any existing software that is to be replaced by newly developed software should be expensed when the new software is ready for use.

Costs for upgrades or enhancements should only be capitalized if they result in additional functionality beyond the original software.

Manual data conversion costs should be expensed. However, costs to develop bridging software should be capitalized.

If internally developed computer software is used in R&D activities, it should be accounted for under FASB Statement Number 2 (Accounting for Research and Development Costs). The software development costs included as R&D expenditures are (1) software acquired to be used in R&D activities where the software has no alternative future use, and (2) software applicable to a specific pilot R&D project.

In the event it is later decided to sell computer software initially developed for internal use, the sales proceeds (in excess of direct incremental costs) should be netted against the book value of the deferred software costs. When book value is reduced to zero, profit is recognized on the excess amount. Under EITF Issue 97-13 (Accounting for Costs Incurred in Connection with a Consulting Contract or an Internal Project That Combines Business Process Reengineering and Information Technology Transformation), business process reengineering costs are expensed irrespective of whether such reengineering efforts are performed as a separate project or as an element of a larger project encompassing software development.

EARNINGS PER SHARE

FASB Statement Number 128 (Earnings per Share) covers the computation, reporting, and disclosures associated with earnings per share. The pronouncement makes some major changes in the computation of earnings per share as previously existed under APB Opinion Number 15. Presentation of both basic and diluted earnings per share is mandated.

Basic earnings per share takes into consideration only the actual number of outstanding common shares during the period (and those contingently issuable in certain cases).

Diluted earnings per share includes the effect of common shares actually outstanding and the effect of convertible securities, stock options, stock warrants, and their equivalents. Diluted earnings per share should not assume the conversion, exercise, or contingent issuance of securities having an antidilutive effect (increasing earnings per share or decreasing loss per share) because it violates conservatism.

BASIC EARNINGS PER SHARE

Basic earnings per share equals net income available to common stockholders divided by the weighted average number of common shares outstanding. Common stock equivalents are no longer presented in this computation. When a prior period adjustment occurs that causes a restatement of previous years' earnings, basic EPS should be restated.

Example 3. The following data are presented for a company:

Preferred stock, $10 par, 6% cumulative, 30,000 shares issued and outstanding	$300,000
Common stock, $5 par, 100,000 shares issued and outstanding	$500,000
Net income	$400,000

The cash dividend on the preferred stock is $18,000 (6% × $300,000).

Basic EPS equals $3.82 as computed below.

Earnings available to common stockholders:

Net income	$400,000
Less: Preferred dividends	(18,000)
Earnings available to common stockholders	$382,000

Basic EPS = $382,000/100,000 shares = $3.82

Example 4. On January 1, 20X3, David Company had the following shares outstanding:

6% Cumulative preferred stock, $100 par value 150,000 shares

Common stock, $5 par value   500,000 shares

During the year, the following took place:

- On April 1, 20X3, the company issued 100,000 shares of common stock.
- On September 1, 20X3, the company declared and issued a 10% stock dividend.
- For the year ended December 31, 20X3, the net income was $2,200,000.

Basic earnings per share for 20X3 equals $2.06 ($1,300,000/632,500 shares) computed below.

Earnings available to common stockholders:

Net income	$2,200,000
Less: Preferred dividend (150,000 shares x $6)	(900,000)
Earnings available to common stockholders	$1,300,000

Weighted-average number of outstanding common shares is determined as follows:

1/1/20X3 - 3/31/20X3 (500,000 x 3/12 x 110%)	137,500
4/1/20X3 - 8/31/20X3 (600,000 x 5/12 x 110%)	275,000
9/1/20X3 - 12/31/20X3 (660,000 x 4/12)	220,000
Weighted average outstanding common shares	632,500

DILUTED EARNINGS PER SHARE

If potentially dilutive securities exist that are outstanding, such as convertible debt, convertible preferred stock, stock options, or stock warrants, then both basic and diluted earnings per share must be shown.

FASB Statement Number 128 retains the "if converted method" to account for convertible securities in earnings per share determination. The pronouncement also retains the "treasury stock method" to account for stock options and warrants.

If options are granted as part of a stock-based compensation agreement, the assumed proceeds from the exercise of the options under the treasury stock method include deferred compensation and the ensuing tax benefit that would be credited to paid-in capital arising from the exercise of the options.

The denominator of diluted earnings per share equals the weighted average outstanding common shares for the period plus the assumed issue of common shares arising from convertible securities plus the assumed shares issued because of the exercise of stock options or stock warrants, or their equivalent.

Table 1 shows in summary form the earnings per share fractions.

Table 1 Earnings Per Share Fractions

BASIC EARNINGS PER SHARE = Net Income Available to Common Stockholders/Weighted Average Number of Common Shares Outstanding

DILUTED EARNINGS PER SHARE = Net Income Available to Common Stockholders + Net of Tax Interest and/or Dividend Savings on Convertible Securities/Weighted Average Number of Common Shares Outstanding + Effect of Convertible Securities + Net Effect of Stock Options

---

Example 5. Assume the same information as in the prior example dealing with basic earnings per share for David Company. Assume further that potentially diluted securities outstanding include 5% convertible bonds (each $1,000 bond is convertible into 25 shares of common stock) having a face value of $5,000,000. There are options to buy 50,000 shares of common stock at $10 per share. The average market price for common shares is $25 per share for 20X3. The tax rate is 30%. Diluted earnings per share for 20X3 is $1.87 ($1,475,000/787,500 shares) as computed below.

Income for diluted earnings per share:		
Earnings available to common stockholders		$1,300,000
Interest expense on convertible bonds		
($5,000,000 × .05)	$250,000	
Less: Tax savings ($250,000 × .30)	(75,000)	
Interest expense (net of tax)		175,000
Income for diluted earnings per share		$1,475,000
Shares outstanding for diluted earnings per share:		
Weighted average outstanding common shares		632,500
Assumed issued common shares for convertible bonds		
(5,000 bonds × 25 shares)		125,000
Assumed issued common shares from exercise of option	50,000	
Less: Assumed repurchase of treasury shares		
(50,000 × $10 = $500,000/$25)	(20,000)	30,000
Shares outstanding for diluted earnings per share		787,500

Basic earnings per share and diluted earnings per share (if required) must be disclosed on the face of the income statement. A reconciliation is required of the numerators and denominators for basic and diluted earnings per share.

FINANCIAL STATEMENT REPORTING: THE BALANCE SHEET

LOANS RECEIVABLE

FASB Statement Number 91 (Accounting for Nonrefundable Fees and Costs Associated with Originating or Acquiring Loans and Initial Direct Costs of Leases) applies to both the incremental direct costs of originating a loan and internally incurred costs directly related to loan activity. Loan origination fees are netted with the related loan origination costs and are accounted for in the following manner:

- For loans held for resale, the net cost is capitalized and recognized at the time the loan is sold.
- For loans held for investment, the net cost is capitalized and amortized over the loan period using the interest method.

Loan commitment fees are initially deferred and recognized in earnings as follows:

- If the commitment is exercised, the fee is recognized over the loan period by the interest method.
- If the commitment expires, the fee is recognized at the expiration date.
- If, based upon previous experience, exercise of the commitment is remote, amortize the fee over the commitment period using the straight-line method.

IMPAIRMENT OF LOANS

FASB Statement Number 114 (Accounting by Creditors for Impairment of a Loan) provides that a loan is a contractual obligation to receive money either on demand or at a fixed or determinable date. Loans include accounts receivable and notes if their maturity dates exceed one year. If it is probable that some or all of the principal or interest is uncollectible, the loan is deemed impaired. A loss on an impaired loan is recorded immediately by debiting bad debt expense and crediting a valuation allowance.

Determining the Value of an Impaired Loan

The loss on an impaired loan is the difference between the investment in loan and the discounted value of future cash flows using the effective interest rate on the original loan. In general, the investment in loan is the principal plus accrued interest. In practical terms, the value of a loan may be based on its market price, if available. The loan value may also be based on the fair value of the collateral, less estimated selling costs, if the loan is collateralized and the security is expected to be the only basis of repayment.

Example 1. On December 31, 2000, Debtor Inc. issues a five-year, $100,000 note at an annual interest rate of 10% payable to Creditor Inc. The market interest rate for the loan is 12%. The discounted value of the principal is $56,742 (based on a principal of $100,000 discounted at 12% for 5 years). The discounted value of the interest payments is $36,048 (based on annual interest of $10,000 for 5 years discounted at 12%). Thus, the discounted value of the loan is $92,790 ($56,742 plus $36,048). Discount on Notes Receivable is $7,210 ($100,000 less $92,790). The discount will be amortized using the effective interest method. Creditor Inc. records the note as follows:

Notes Receivable	100,000	
Discount on Notes Receivable		7,210
Cash		92,790

On December 31, 2002, Creditor Inc. determines that it is probable that Debtor Inc. will only be able to repay interest of $8,000 per year (rather than $10,000 per year) and $70,000 (rather than $100,000) of face value at maturity. This loan impairment requires the immediate recognition of a loss. The discounted value of future cash flows discounted for 3 years at 12% for $70,000 is $49,824, and for $8,000 is $19,215. Therefore, the total present value of future cash flows is $69,039 ($49,824 plus $19,215). On 12/31/02, the carrying value of the investment in loan is $95,196. As a result, the impairment loss is $26,157 ($95,196 less $69,039). The journal entry to record the loss is:

| Bad Debts | 26,157 | |
| Allowance for Bad Debts | | 26,157 |

Interest income from an impaired loan may be recognized using several methods, including cash basis, cost recovery, or a combination.

If the creditor's charging off of some part of the loan results in recording an investment in an impaired loan below its present value of future cash flows, no additional impairment is to be recorded.

In determining the collectibility of a loan, consideration should be given to the following:

- Financial problems of borrower
- Borrower in an unstable or unhealthy industry
- Regulatory reports
- Compliance exception reports
- Amount of loan
- Prior loss experience
- Lack of marketability of collateral

A loan is not considered impaired when the delay in collecting is insignificant.

Disclosures

The following should be disclosed either in the body of the financial statements or in the footnotes:

- The creditor's policy of recognizing interest income on impaired loans, including the recording of cash receipts.
- The average recorded investment in impaired loans, the related interest revenue recognized while the loans were impaired, and the amount of interest revenue recognized using the cash basis while the loans were impaired.
- The total investment in impaired loans including (1) the amount of investments for which a related valuation allowance exists, and (2) the amount of investments for which a valuation allowance does not exist.

PATENTS

The legal life of patents is 20 years.

DONATION OF FIXED ASSETS

FASB Statement Number 116 (Accounting for Contributions Received and Contributions Made) requires a donated fixed asset to be recorded at its fair market value by debiting the fixed asset and crediting contribution revenue.

According to FASB Statement 116, the company donating a nonmonetary asset recognizes an expense for the fair value of the donated asset. The difference between the carrying value and the fair value of the donated asset is a gain or loss.

Example 2. Hartman Company donates land costing $100,000 with a fair value of $130,000. The journal entry is:

Contribution Expense	130,000	
Land		100,000
Gain on Disposal of Land		30,000

If a company pledges unconditionally to give an asset in the future, accrue contribution expense and a payable. However, if the pledge is conditional, an entry is not made until the asset is transferred.

IMPAIRMENT OF FIXED ASSETS

FASB Statement Number 121 (Accounting for the Impairment of Long-Lived Assets and for Long-Lived Assets to be Disposed Of) states that a noncurrent asset is considered impaired if the total of (undiscounted) expected future cash flows from using it is below its carrying value. (In ascertaining whether asset impairment has occurred, its carrying value should include any associated goodwill.) If this recoverability test for asset impairment is satisfied, an impairment loss must be computed as the excess of the asset's book value over its fair value. Fair value is the amount at which the asset could be purchased or sold between willing participants; fair value is not based on a forced or liquidation sale. Possible methods to determine fair market value include the market price in an active market, price of similar assets, or value based on a valuation technique (e.g., present value of future cash flows, options pricing model).

If the fair market value is not determinable and the discounted value of future cash flows is used, the asset should be grouped at the lowest level at which the cash flows are separately identifiable.

An impairment loss is charged against earnings with a similar reduction in the recorded value of the impaired fixed asset. After impairment, the reduced carrying value becomes the new cost basis for the fixed asset. Thus, the fixed asset cannot be written up for a subsequent recovery in market value. Therefore, the impaired loss cannot be restored. Depreciation is based on the new cost basis.

In the event that the impaired asset is to be disposed of instead of being kept in service, the impaired asset should be recorded at the lower of cost or net realizable value.

An impairment may arise from a major change in how the asset is used, a decline in market value, continued expected losses from the asset, excess construction costs over expected amounts, adverse business conditions, or legal problems.

Example 3. A company has a fixed asset with a cost of $1,000,000 and accumulated depreciation of $200,000. In applying the recoverability test to ascertain if an impairment has taken place, it is determined that the total of (undiscounted) expected future net cash flows is $840,000. No impairment exists because the undiscounted future expected net cash flows ($840,000) is more than the carrying value of the asset ($800,000).

Example 4. Assume the same data as in the prior example except that the total of (undiscounted) future net cash flows is $700,000. The recoverability test now shows an impairment loss because the total (undiscounted) cash flow ($700,000) is less than the book value ($800,000) of the fixed asset. Assuming the fixed asset has a fair market value of $680,000, the impairment loss equals $120,000 (book value of $800,000 less fair market value of $680,000). The journal entry to record the impairment is:

Loss on Impairment of Fixed Asset	120,000	
Accumulated Depreciation		120,000

The following must be footnoted in connection with impaired fixed assets:

- Identification of the asset impaired
- Amount of loss
- Method used to determine fair market value
- Cause of impairment
- Business segment experiencing the impairment in asset value

If an impaired asset is to be disposed of instead of used, the impaired asset is presented at the lower of cost or net realizable value (fair value less cost to sell). The selling costs include brokerage commissions and transfer fees. However, insurance, security services, utility expenses, and costs to protect or maintain the asset are usually not deemed selling costs in determining net realizable value. The present value of costs to sell may be used when the fair value of the asset is based on the discounted cash flows and the sale is expected to take place after one year.

If the asset is to be disposed of shortly, the net realizable value is a better measure of the cash flows that one can expect to receive from the impaired asset. Assets held for disposal are not depreciated. Conceptually, these assets are more like inventory because they are expected to be sold in the near term.

BARTER TRANSACTIONS

A barter transaction may relate to an exchange of goods or services or barter credits. With respect to the latter, for example, the asset inventory may be exchanged for barter credits. (FASB Emerging Issues Task Force [EITF] Issue Number 93–11, Accounting for Barter Transactions Involving Barter Credits)

EITF Issue Number 93–11 stipulates that APB Opinion Number 29 (Accounting for Nonmonetary Transactions) should be applied to an exchange of a nonmonetary asset for barter credits. With respect to barter credits, it is assumed that the fair market value of the asset exchanged is more clearly evident than the fair market value of the barter credits received. As a result, the barter credits received should be recorded at the fair market value of the asset exchanged. In ascertaining the fair market value of the asset surrendered, it is assumed that the fair market value of the asset does not exceed its book value.

In the event that the fair market value of the asset surrendered is below its book value, an impairment should be recorded before making the entry for the exchange. As an example, inventory being exchanged in a barter transaction should be reflected at the lower of cost or market value before recording the barter transaction.

At year-end, the recorded amount of barter credits should be appraised for impairment. We recognize an impairment loss when the fair market value of any remaining barter credits is below its book value, or in the event that it is probable that what is left of the barter credits will not be used.

STOCK-BASED COMPENSATION

FASB Statement Number 123 (Accounting for Stock-Based Compensation) applies to stock option plans, nonvested stock, employee stock purchase plans, and stock compensation awards that are to be settled by cash payment.

Stock Option Plans

Employers may account for stock option plans using either the "intrinsic value" method or the "fair value" method.

The intrinsic value method is the one in place before FASB Statement Number 123. It is already discussed in the main volume. The fair value method under FASB Statement Number 123 is discussed in this supplement.

Under the fair value method, fair value is computed by using an option-pricing model that takes into account several factors. A popular option pricing model is Black and Scholes. It is used to compute the equilibrium value of an option. The model provides insight into the valuation of debt relative to equity. This model may be programmed into computer spreadsheets and some pocket calculators. The Black-Scholes model makes it possible to determine the present value of hypothetical financial instruments. Some assumptions of this model are that (1) the stock options are freely traded and (2) the total return rate (considering the change in price plus dividends) may be determined based on a continuous compounding over the life of the option. Under FASB Statement Number 123, the option life is the expected time period until the option is exercised, rather than the contractual term. By reducing the option's life, its value is reduced. It is a random variable derived from a normal bell curve distribution. The Black-Scholes model was developed based on European-style options exercisable only at expiration. However, most employee stock options are American-style and are exercisable at any time during the option life once vesting has taken place. The Black-Scholes model uses the volatility expected for the option's life. *Note:* Difficulties arise in determining option values when there is an early option exercise and variability in stock price and dividends. The Black-Scholes model may also be used in valuing put options by modifying computations. See the chapter on Financial Derivatives Products and Financial Engineering for more information on Black-Scholes.

Other models may be used for option pricing such as the more complicated binomial model.

Before the current value of an option may be computed, consideration must be given to its expiration value.

Compensation expense is based on the fair value of the award at the grant date, and is recognized over the period between the grant date and the vesting date, in a way similar to the intrinsic value method.

Under the fair value method, the stock option is accounted for in a similar way as the journal entries under the intrinsic value method, except the fair value of the option would be recognized as deferred compensation and amortized over the period from the grant date to the date the option is initially exercisable.

Note: Noncompensatory stock option plans may also exist. Such plans are characterized by having stock offered to employees on some basis (e.g., equally, percent of salary), participation by full-time employees, a reasonable time period for the exercise of the options, and the discount to employees to buy the stock is not better than that afforded to company stockholders. If any of these criteria are not satisfied, then the plan is compensatory in nature. The objective of a noncompensatory plan is to obtain funds and to have greater widespread ownership in the company among employees. It is not primarily designed to provide compensation for services performed. Therefore, no compensation expense is recognized.

Nonvested Stock

Nonvested stock is stock that cannot be sold currently because the employee who was granted the shares has not yet satisfied the vesting requirements to earn the right to the shares. The fair value of a share of nonvested stock awarded to an employee is measured at the market price per share of non-restricted stock on the grant date unless a restriction will be imposed after the employee has a vested right to it, in which case the fair value is approximated considering the restriction.

Employee Stock Purchase Plans

An employee stock purchase plan allows employees to buy stock at a discount. It is noncompensatory if the discount is minor (5% or less), most full-time employees may participate, and the plan has no option features.

Stock Compensation Awards Required to Be Settled by Paying Cash

Some stock-based compensation plans require an employer to pay an employee, either on demand or at a particular date, a cash amount based on the appreciation in the market price of the employer's stock. A ceiling stock price may be established depending on the plan. The compensation cost applicable to the award is the amount of change in stock price.

Disclosures

The following should be disclosed regarding the fair value method to account for stock options as well as for stock-based compensation plans in general:

- Weighted-average grant date fair value of options and/or other equity instruments granted during the year.
- A description of the method and assumptions used to estimate fair value of options.
- Major changes in the terms of stock-based compensation plans.
- Amendments to outstanding awards.

Tax Aspects

Compensation expense is deductible for tax reporting when paid but deducted for financial reporting when accrued. This results in interperiod income tax allocation involving a deferred income tax credit. If for some reason reversal of the temporary difference does not occur, a permanent difference exists which does not impact profit. The difference should adjust paid-in-capital in the year the accrual occurs.

ACCOUNTING AND DISCLOSURES

SEGMENTAL DISCLOSURES

FASB Statement Number 131 (Disclosures About Segments of an Enterprise and Related Information) requires that the amount reported for each segment item should be based on what is used by the "chief operating decision maker" in formulating a determination as to how much resources to assign to a segment and how to appraise the performance of that segment. The term "chief operating decision maker" may apply to the chief executive officer or chief operating officer or to a group of executives. *Note:* The reference of "chief operating decision maker" may apply to a function and not necessarily to a specific person(s).

Revenue, gains, expenses, losses, and assets should only be allocated to a segment if the chief operating decision maker considers it in measuring a segment's earnings for purposes of making a financial or operating decision. The same is true with regard to allocating to segments eliminations and adjustments applying to the company's general purpose financial statements. Any allocation of financial items to a segment should be rationally based.

In measuring a segment's earnings or assets, the following should be disclosed for explanatory purposes:

- Measurement or valuation basis used.
- Differences in measurements used for the general-purpose financial statements relative to the financial information of the segment.

- A change in measurement method relative to prior years.
- A symmetrical allocation, meaning an allocation of depreciation or amortization to a segment without a related allocation to the associated asset.

Segmental information is required in annual financial statements. Some segmental disclosures are required in interim financial statements.

Segmental Attributes

An operating segment is a distinct revenue-producing component of the business for which internal financial data are produced. Expenses are recognized as incurred in that segment. *Note:* A start-up operation would qualify as an operating segment even though revenue is not being earned. An operating segment is periodically reviewed by the chief operating decision maker to evaluate performance and to determine what and how much resources to allocate to the segment.

A reportable segment requiring disclosure is one which is both an operating segment and meets certain percentage tests discussed in the next section.

An aggregation may be made of operating segments if they are similar in terms of products or services, customer class, manufacturing processes, distribution channels, legal entity, and regulatory control.

Percentage Tests

A reportable segment satisfies one of the following criteria:

- Revenue including unaffiliated and intersegment sales or transfers is 10% or more of total (combined) revenue of all operating segments.
- Operating profit or loss is 10% or more of total operating profit of all operating segments.
- Assets are 10% or more of total assets of all operating segments.

After the 10% tests have been made, additional segments may be reported on if they do not satisfy the 10% tests until at least 75% (constituting a substantial portion) of total revenue of all operating segments have been included. As a practical matter, no more than 10 segments (upper limit) should be reported because to do otherwise would result in too cumbersome or detailed reporting. In this case, combined reporting should be of those operating segments most closely related.

If a segment does not meet the 10% test for reportability in the current year but met the 10% test in prior years and is expected to be reportable in future years, it should still be reported in the current year.

If a segment passes the 10% test in the current year because of some unusual and rare occurrence, it should be excluded from reporting in the current year.

Reconciliation

A company does not have to use the same accounting principles for segmental purposes as that used to prepare the consolidated financial statements. There must be a reconciliation between segmental financial data and general purpose financial statements. The reconciliation is for revenue, operating profit or loss, and assets. Any differences in measurement approaches between the company as a whole and its segments should be explained. If measurement practices have changed over the years regarding the operating segments, that fact should be disclosed and explained. The business must describe its reasoning and methods in deriving the composition of its operating segments.

Restatement

If the business structure changes, this may require a restatement of segmental information presented in prior years to aid in comparability. If restatement occurs, appropriate footnote disclosure should be made.

Disclosures

Disclosure should be provided of major sources of foreign revenue constituting 10% or more of total revenue. Further, disclosure is necessary if a foreign area constitutes 10% or more of total operating profit or loss, or of total assets. The foreign area and the percentage derived therein should be disclosed.

Disclosure should exist of the dollar sales to major customers comprising 10% or more of total revenue. A single customer may refer to more than one customer if under common control (e.g., subsidiaries of a parent). A single customer may also be defined as government agencies.

Information about foreign geographic areas and customers is required even if this information is not used by the business in formulating operating decisions.

Disclosure should be made of major contracts to other entities and governments.

Disclosure should be made of how reporting segments were determined (e.g., customer class, products or services, geographic areas). Disclosure should be given identifying those operating segments that have been aggregated. The following should be disclosed for each reportable segment:

- Types of products and services.
- Revenue to outside customers as well as intersegment revenue.
- Operating profit or loss.
- Total assets.
- Capital expenditures.
- Depreciation, depletion, and amortization.
- Major noncash revenues and expenses excluding those immediately above.
- Interest revenue and interest expense.
- Extraordinary and unusual items.
- Equity in earnings of investee.
- Tax effects.

Example 1. A company reports the following information for its reportable segments:

Segment	Total Revenue	Operating Profit	Identifiable Assets
1	$500	$50	$200
2	250	10	150
3	3,500	200	1,950
4	1,500	100	900
Total	$5,750	$360	$3,200

The revenue test is 10% × $5,750 = $575. Segments 3 and 4 satisfy this test.

The operating profit (loss) test is 10% × $360 = $36. Segments 1, 3 and 4 satisfy this test.

The identifiable assets test is 10% × $3,200 = $320. Segments 3 and 4 satisfy this test.

Therefore, the reportable segments are 1,3 and 4.

DISCLOSURE OF CAPITAL STRUCTURE INFORMATION

FASB Statement Number 129 (Disclosure of Information About Capital Structure) requires footnote disclosure regarding the rights and privileges of common and preferred stockholders such as dividend preferences, participation privileges, conversion terms, unusual voting rights, sinking fund requirements, and terms for additional issuances. In a liquidation situation, footnote information must be made of liquidation preferences such as dividend arrearages and liquidation values for preferred stock. In the case of redeemable stock, disclosure must be made of redemption requirements for each of the next five years.

RELATED PARTY DISCLOSURES

FASB Statement Number 57 deals with disclosures for related party transactions. Such transactions occur when a transacting party can significantly influence or exercise control of another transaction party because of a financial, common ownership, or familial relationship. It may also arise when a nontransacting party can significantly impact the policies of two other transacting parties. Related party transactions include those involving:

- Joint ventures.
- Activities between a subsidiary and parent.
- Activities between affiliates of the same parent company.
- Relationships between the company and its principal owners, management, or their immediate families.

Related party transactions often occur in the ordinary course of business and may include such activities as granting loans or incurring debt, sales, purchases, services performed or received, guarantees, allocating common costs as the basis for billings, compensating balance requirements, property transfers, rentals, and filing of consolidated tax returns.

Related party transactions are presumed not to be at arm's length. They are usually not derived from competitive, free-market dealings. Some possible examples follow:

- A "shell" company (with no economic substance) purchases merchandise at inflated prices.
- A lease at "bargain" or excessive prices.
- Unusual guarantees or pledges.
- A loan at an unusually low or high interest rate.
- Payments for services at inflated prices.

Related party disclosures include the following:

- Nature and substance of the relationship.
- Amount of transaction.

- Terms of transaction.
- Year-end balances due or owed.
- Any control relationships that exist.

DISCLOSURES FOR DERIVATIVES

The Securities and Exchange Commission requires certain disclosures for the accounting and reporting for derivatives, including financial instruments and commodities. Derivative commodity instruments include futures, forwards, options, and swaps. These disclosures include:

- The types and nature of derivative instruments to be accounted for.
- The accounting method used for derivatives, such as the fair value method, accrual method, and deferral method. Disclosure should be made where gains and losses associated with derivatives are reported.
- The risks associated with the derivatives.
- Distinguishment of derivatives used for trading or nontrading purposes.
- Derivatives used for hedging purposes including explanation.

INFLATION INFORMATION

FASB Statement Number 89 (Financial Reporting and Changing Prices) permits an entity to voluntarily disclose inflation information so management and financial statement readers can better evaluate the impact of inflation on the business. Selected summarized financial information should be presented based on current costs and adjusted for inflation (in constant purchasing power) for a five-year period. The Consumer Price Index for All Urban Consumers may be used. Inflation disclosures include those for sales and operating revenue stated in constant purchasing power, income from continuing operations (including per-share amounts) on a current cost basis, cash dividends per share in constant purchasing power, market price per share restated in constant purchasing power, purchasing power gain or loss on net monetary items, inflation-adjusted inventory, restated fixed assets, foreign currency translation based on current cost, net assets based on current cost, and the Consumer Price Index used.

ENVIRONMENTAL REPORTING AND DISCLOSURES

Companies are faced with federal and local compliance requirements regarding environmental issues. Environmental laws provide rigorous specifications with which companies must comply. The costs of compliance could significantly increase a company's expected cost of projects and processes. Failure to abide by environmental dictates could result in substantial costs and risks including civil and criminal prosecution and fines. The company must police itself to avoid legal defense fees and penalties. An effective compliance program, such as having preventive and detective controls, is crucial in minimizing environmental risks. The corporate manager must be assured that appropriate accounting, reporting, and disclosures for environmental issues are being practiced by the firm.

Legislation

The Environmental Protection Agency (EPA) enforces Federal laws regulating pollution, sold waste disposal, water supply, pesticide and radiation control, and ocean dumping. EPA regulations require adherence to specific pollution detection procedures, such as leak testing, and installation of corrosion protection and leak detection systems applicable to underground storage tanks.

The Clean Air Act of 1963 concentrates on issues such as acid rain, urban smog, airborne toxins, ozone-depleting chemicals, and other air pollution problems. The Clean Water Act established controls of water pollution and wetlands preservation.

The Environmental Response Compensation and Liability Act (Superfund) relates to uncontrolled or abandoned hazardous waste disposal sites. Companies must disclose emergency planning, spills or accidents of hazardous materials, and when chemicals are released into surrounding areas. The chemicals must be disclosed to prospective buyers, employees, and tenants.

To go from a reactive position (the company just complies with regulations) to a proactive policy (the company envelops environmental concerns into its daily business practices), the entity must formulate financial information to complement technical and scientific data. Further, environmental expenditures have to be segregated so as to improve decision making and accountability for environmental responsibilities. There should be an appraisal model for setting priorities as the basis for resource allocations.

Accounting and Reporting

Securities and Exchange Commission Staff Accounting Bulletin Number 92 deals with how environmental liabilities are determined, future contingencies, "key" environmental factors, and disclosures of environmental problems. Depending on the circumstances, a liability and/or footnote disclosure would be required. Examples are:

- Information on site remediation projects such as current and future costs and remediation trends. Site remediation includes hazard waste sites.
- Contamination due to environmental health and safety problems.
- Legal and regulatory compliance issues such as with regard to cleanup responsibility.
- Water or air pollution.

Environmental problems should be addressed immediately to avoid significant future costs including additional cleanup costs, penalties, and legal fees.

Environmental costs should be compared to budgeted amounts, and variances may be computed and tracked. Forecasted information should be changed as new information is available. Internal controls must be established over the firm's environmental responsibility, including internal checks, safeguarding of assets, and segregation of duties.

A financial analysis of environmental costs should be conducted by analyzing cost trends over the years within the company, comparisons to competing companies, and comparisons to industry averages. Additionally, comparisons should be made between projects within the company.

Environmental costs should be allocated across departments, products, and services. Environmental cost information is useful in product and service mix decisions, pricing policies, selecting production inputs, appraising pollution prevention programs, and evaluating waste management policies.

KEY FINANCIAL ACCOUNTING AREAS

LEASES

Transfer of Lease Receivable

The lessor may transfer a lease receivable. The gain on sale equals the cash received less both the portion of the gross investment sold and unearned income related to the minimum lease payments.

Example 1. A lessor has on its books a lease receivable with an unguaranteed residual value. Unlike guaranteed residual value, unguaranteed residual value does not qualify as a financial asset. The lessor sells an 80% interest in the minimum lease payments for $100,000. The lessor keeps a 20% interest in the minimum lease payments and a 100% interest in the unguaranteed residual value. Other information follows:

Minimum lease payments		$110,000
Unearned income in minimum lease payments		75,000
Gross investment in minimum lease payments		185,000
Add: Unguaranteed residual value	7,000	
Unguaranteed income in residual value	13,000	
Gross investment in residual value		20,000
Gross investment in lease receivable		$205,000

The journal entry for the sale of the lease receivable is:

Cash	100,000	
Unearned income ($75,000 × 80%)	60,000	
Lease receivable ($185,000 × 80%)		148,000
Gain		12,000

Related Parties

In a related-party lease where substantial influence exists, the lease should be accounted for based on its economic substance rather than its legal form. If substantial influence is absent, the related-party lease should be classified and accounted for as if the participants were unrelated.

FASB Statement Number 13 requires that a parent must consolidate a subsidiary whose principal business operation is leasing property from a parent or other affiliates.

A related-party lease agreement involving significant influence may require consolidation accounting for the lessor and lessee if all of the following conditions are present:

- Most of the lessor's activities apply to leasing assets to one specific lessee.

- The lessee incurs the risks and rewards applicable with rented property along with any related debt. This may occur if the lease agreement gives the lessee control and management over the leased property, the lessee guarantees the lessor's debt or residual value of the leased item, and the lessee has the right to purchase the property at a lower than fair value price.

- The lessor's owners do not have a significant residual equity capital investment at risk.

If the consolidation conditions are not met, combined financial statements instead of consolidated financial statements may be appropriate.

FASB Statement Number 57 requires disclosure of the nature and degree of leasing transactions among related parties.

Money-Over-Money Lease

A money-over-money lease occurs when an entity manufactures or purchases an asset, leases it to the lessee, and receives nonrecourse financing exceeding the cost of the asset. The collateral for the borrowing is the leased asset and any future rental derived therefrom. The lessor is prohibited from offsetting the asset (in an operating lease) or the lease receivable

Key Financial Accounting Areas

(in other than an operating lease) and the nonrecourse obligation unless a legal right of setoff exists. The leasing and borrowing are considered separate transactions.

Business Combinations

A business combination by itself has no bearing on lease classification. In a purchase transaction, the acquirer may assign a new value to a capitalized lease because of the allocation of acquisition price to the net assets of the acquired entity. However, provided the lease terms are not modified, the lease should be accounted for using the original terms and classification. A similar treatment is afforded under the pooling-of-interest method in that the new lease would retain its classification.

With respect to a leveraged lease when the purchase method is used the following guidelines are followed:

- The classification continues as a leveraged lease.
- The net investment in the leveraged lease should be recorded at fair market value including tax effects.
- The usual accounting for a leveraged lease should be practiced.

Disposal of a Business Segment

The expected costs directly associated with a disposal of a business segment decision includes future rental payments less amounts to be received from subleases. The difference between the unamortized cost of the leased property and the discounted value of the minimum lease payments to be received from the sublease is recognized as a gain or loss.

PENSION PLANS

Employers Having More Than One Defined Benefit Plan

If an employer has more than one pension plan, it has to prepare separate calculations of pension expense, fair value of plan assets, and liabilities for each plan.

The employer is prohibited from offsetting assets or liabilities of different pension plans unless a legal right exists to use the assets of one plan to pay the debt or benefits of another plan.

Disclosures may be combined for all pension plans kept by the employer with the following exceptions:

- U.S. pension plans may not be aggregated with foreign pension plans unless there exist similar assumptions.
- A minimum pension asset of one plan may not be used to offset a minimum pension liability of another, and vice versa.

Multiemployer Plans

A multiemployer plan typically includes participation of two or more unrelated employers. It often arises from a collective-bargaining contract with the union. The plan is typically administered by a Board of Trustees. In this instance, plan assets contributed by one employer may be used to pay employee benefits of another participating employer. Hence, the assets are combined for all employers and are available and unrestricted to pay benefits to all employees irrespective of whom they are employed by. In other words, there is no segregation of assets in a particular employer's account or any restrictions placed on that employer's assets. An example is a plan contributed to by all employers employing the members of a particular union regardless of whom the employees work for. Retirees of different employers receive payment from the same combined fund. An example is the Teamsters' union.

In a multiemployer plan, the employer's pension expense equals its contribution to the plan for the year. If a contribution is accrued, the employer must record a liability.

If an employer withdraws from the multiemployer plan, it may incur a liability for its share of the unfunded benefit obligation of the plan. If an employer would probably incur a liability if it withdraws from the plan and the amount is reasonably ascertainable, a loss must be accrued with a concurrent liability. However, if the loss is reasonably possible, only footnote disclosure is needed.

Footnote disclosures for employers involved with a multiemployer plan include:

- A description of the plan including employees covered.
- The benefits to be provided.
- Nature of matters affecting the comparability of information for the years presented.
- Pension expense for the period.

Multiple-Employer Plans

These plans have similarities to multiemployer plans. They also consist of two or more unrelated employers. However, multiple-employer plans are in effect aggregated single-employer plans that are combined so that assets of all may be totaled so as to lower administrative costs. The assets are merged so as to improve the overall rate of return from investing them. In many instances, participating employers may use different benefit formulas for their respective pension contributions. Each employer in the plan accounts for its particular interest separately. An example of such an arrangement is when businesses in an industry have their trade group handle the plans of all the companies. Each company retains its responsibilities only for its own workers. Multiple-employer plans are typically not associated with collective-bargaining agreements.

Annuity Contracts

An employer may sign a valid and irrevocable insurance contract to pay benefit obligations arising from a defined benefit plan. Annuity contracts are used to transfer the risk of providing employee benefits from the employer to the insurance company.

If the annuity contracts are the basis to fund the pension plan and to pay plan obligations, the employer's insurance premium is the pension expense for the period covering all currently earned benefits. In this instance, the company and plan do not report plan assets, accumulated benefit obligation, or a projected benefit obligation. On the contrary, if the annuity contracts only cover part of the benefit obligation, the employer is liable for the uncovered obligation.

In a participating annuity contract, the insurer pays the employer part of the income earned from investing the insurance premiums. In most instances, income earned (e.g., interest, dividends) reduces pension expense. A disadvantage to the employer of a participating contract is that it costs more than one which is nonparticipating due to the participation privilege. This additional cost applicable to the participation right should be recognized as a pension plan asset. Therefore, except for the cost of participation rights, pension plan assets exclude the cost of annuity contracts. In later years, fair value should be used in valuing the participation right included in plan assets. In the event that fair value may not be reasonably determined, the asset should be recorded at cost with amortization based on the dividend period stipulated in the contract. However, unamortized cost cannot exceed the net realizable value of the participation right. If the terms of the participating annuity contract are such that the employer retains all or most of the risk applicable to the benefit obligation, the purchase of this contract does not constitute a settlement of the employer's obligations under the pension plan.

Insurance contracts other than annuity contracts are considered investments. They are reported as pension plan assets and reported at fair value. Fair value may be in terms of conversion value, contract value, cash surrender value, etc., depending on the circumstances.

The definition of an annuity contract is *not* met if one or more of the following exist:

- There exists uncertainty as to whether the insurance company will be able to pay its debts due to financial difficulties.
- There is a captive insurance company, meaning that the insurance entity has as its major client the employer or any of its associated parties.

An employer has to record a loss when it assumes the obligation to pay retirees because the insurance company is financially unable to do so. The loss is recorded at the lower of any gain associated with the original insurance contract or the amount of benefit assumed. An unrecognized additional loss should be treated as an amendment to the pension plan.

Employee Retirement Income Security Act (ERISA)

The Act generally provides for full vesting of pension benefits if an employee has worked for 15 years. Past service costs must be funded over a period of not more than 40 years.

Employer's Accounting for Postemployment Benefits

FASB Statement Number 112 provides authoritative guidance in accounting and reporting for postemployment benefits. The pronouncement relates to benefits to former or inactive employees, their beneficiaries, and dependents after employment, but before retirement. Former or inactive employees include individuals on disability and those who have been laid off. However, individuals on vacation or holiday or who are ill are not considered inactive.

Postemployment benefits are different from postretirement benefits. Postemployment benefits may be in cash or in kind and include salary continuation benefits, supplemental unemployment benefits, severance benefits, disability related benefits, job training and counseling benefits, life insurance benefits, and health care benefits.

An accrual is made for postemployment benefits if the following conditions are met:

- The amount of benefits is reasonably determinable.
- Benefits apply for services already rendered.
- Payment of benefits is probable.
- Benefit obligations vest or accumulate.

146

PROFIT SHARING PLANS

A profit sharing plan may be discretionary (contributions are at the discretion of the Board of Directors) or nondiscretionary (contributions are based on a predetermined formula and depend on attaining a specified earnings level). In a discretionary plan, an accrual of expense is made when set by the Board. The entry is to debit profit sharing expense and credit accrued profit sharing liability. In a nondiscretionary arrangement, an accrual is made when required under the plan terms.

INCOME TAX ACCOUNTING

Multiple Tax Jurisdictions

The determination for federal reporting purposes may differ from that of local reporting requirements. As a result, temporary differences, permanent differences, and loss carrybacks or carryforwards may differ between federal and state and/or city reporting. If temporary differences are significant, separate deferred tax computations and recording will be required.

Tax Status Changes

The impact of any change in tax status affecting a business requires an immediate adjustment to deferred tax liabilities (or assets) and to income tax expense. An example of a tax status change requiring an adjustment on the accounts is a company opting for C corporation status. There should be a footnote describing the nature of the status change and its impact on the accounts.

Business Combinations

In a business combination accounted for under the purchase method, the costs assigned to the acquired entity's net assets may differ from the valuation of those net assets on the tax return. This may cause a temporary difference arising in either a deferred tax liability or deferred tax asset reported on the acquirer's consolidated financial statements.

The amortization of goodwill for tax purposes is over a mandatory 15-year period, while for books goodwill may be amortized over a 40-year period. This gives rise to a temporary difference. Negative goodwill may also result in a temporary difference arising from the difference in depreciation expense for book and tax purposes.

A company may have unrecognized tax benefits applicable to operating losses or tax credits arising from a purchase business combination. This may give rise to other similar tax advantages after the combination date. The tax benefits realized should be apportioned for book reporting between pre- and post-acquisition tax benefits.

Under the pooling-of-interests method, if the combined entity will be able to use an operating loss or tax credit carryforward, the deferred tax benefits should be recognized when the previous year's financial statements are restated.

In some cases, a pooling-of-interests is taxable, requiring a step-up of the net assets of a combining company for tax reporting. The difference between the stepped-up basis and the book value of net assets on the books constitutes a temporary difference.

Separate Financial Statements of a Subsidiary

If separate financial statements are prepared, the consolidated income tax expense should be allocated to each of the subsidiaries.

Employee Stock Ownership Plans

Retained earnings is increased for the tax benefit arising from deductible dividends paid on unallocated shares held by an ESOP. However, dividends paid on allocated shares are includable in income tax expense.

Quasi-Reorganization

The tax benefits applicable to deductible temporary differences and carry-forwards on the date of a quasi-reorganization should usually be recorded as an increase in paid-in-capital if the tax benefits will occur in later years.

DERIVATIVE PRODUCTS

FASB Statement Number 133 (Accounting for Derivative Investments and Hedging Activities) deals with the accounting and reporting requirements for derivative instruments and for hedging activities. Derivatives are rights and obligations and must be presented in the financial statements. Financial instruments must be reported at fair value.

FASB Statement Number 133 defines a derivative as a financial instrument or contract having the following three components:

1. Underlying Price or Rate on an Asset or Liability. It is not the asset or liability itself. Examples of an underlying might be stock or commodity

price, index of prices, interest rate, and foreign exchange rate. Further, there is either a notational amount (number of shares, pounds, or currency units stipulated in the contract) or payment provisions (fixed or determinable amount required to settle the underlying instrument, such as interest rate).

2. A required or allowable net settlement exists.

3. There exists no net investment or a smaller initial net investment than would be anticipated for a contract with similar terms linked to changing market conditions.

There are many examples of derivatives, including futures contracts, forward contracts, interest rate swaps, and stock option contracts.

A company must report derivatives at fair value as either assets or liabilities. Depending on the circumstances, a derivative must be a hedge of exposure to either:

1. Changes in the fair value of a recognized asset or liability or an unrecognized firm commitment.

2. Variable cash flows applicable to a forecasted transaction.

3. Foreign currency risk of a net investment in a foreign operation, foreign-currency denominated forecasted transaction, available-for-sale security, or an unrecognized firm commitment.

How the change in fair value of a derivative (gain or loss) is accounted for varies with the planned use of the derivative as follows:

- A derivative designed to hedge vulnerability to changes in the fair value of a recognized asset or liability or firm commitment will have the gain or loss included in net income in the year of change coupled with the offsetting loss or gain on the hedged item associated with the hedged risk. The net impact of this accounting is to include in net income the degree to which the hedge is not effective in offsetting changes in fair value.

- A derivative hedging exposure to variable cash flows of a forecasted transaction (cash flow hedge) will have the effective part of the derivatives gain or loss initially presented as an element of other comprehensive income (outside of earnings) and later reclassified into earnings when the forecasted transaction impacts earnings. The ineffective part of the gain or loss is immediately presented in earnings. If a cash flow hedge is discontinued because it is probable that the initial forecasted transaction will not take place, the net gain or loss in accumulated other comprehensive income shall be immediately reclassified into earnings.

- A derivative whose purpose is to hedge foreign currency exposure of a net investment in a foreign activity will have the gain or loss presented under other comprehensive income as an element of the cumulative translation adjustment. The hedge of the foreign currency exposure may apply to an unrecognized firm commitment or an available-for-sale security.

Note: If a derivative is not to hedge an instrument, the gain or loss is included in net income in the period of change.

A company opting to use hedge accounting must disclose the method it will use to evaluate the success of the hedging derivative and the measurement means to ascertain the ineffective part of the hedge. The methods chosen must conform to the company's risk management policy.

Accounting for the change in fair value (gain or loss) of a derivative depends on whether or not it qualifies as part of a hedging arrangement and, if such is the case, the purpose of holding the derivative. Either all or a proportion of a derivative may be considered a hedging instrument. The proportion must be stated as a percentage of the whole derivative so that the risk in the hedging part of the derivative is the same as the entire derivative.

Two or more derivatives, or parts thereof, may be considered in combination and jointly designated as a hedging instrument.

If an impairment loss is recorded on an asset or liability associated with a hedged forecasted transaction, any offsetting net gain associated with that transaction in accumulated other comprehensive income should be reclassified immediately into net income of the period. In a similar manner, a recovery of the asset or liability resulting in a reduction of the net loss should be shown in earnings.

Required disclosures include identifying derivatives, time period for intended hedging, risk management policies of the company, where net gain or loss associated with derivatives are presented in the financial statements, and description of transactions or other events that will result in reclassification into earnings of gain and loss reported in accumulated other comprehensive income.

ACCOUNTING FOR MULTINATIONAL OPERATIONS

INTRODUCTION: ACCOUNTING DIMENSIONS OF INTERNATIONAL BUSINESS

Today, the world economy is truly internationalized and globalized. Advances in information technology, communications, and transportation have enabled businesses to service a world market. Many U.S. companies, both large and small, are now heavily engaged in international trade. The foreign operations of many large U.S. multinational corporations now account for a significant percentage (10% to 50%) of their sales and/or net income.

The basic business functions (i.e., finance/accounting, production, management, marketing) take on a new perspective when conducted in a foreign environment. There are different laws, economic policies, political frameworks, and social/cultural factors which all have an effect on how business is to be conducted in that foreign country. From an accounting standpoint, global business activities are faced with three realities:

1. Accounting standards and practices differ from country to country. Accounting is a product of its own economic, legal, political, and sociocultural environment. Since this environment changes from country to country, the accounting system of each country is unique and different from all others.

2. Each country has a strong "accounting nationalism": It requires business companies operating within its borders to follow its own accounting standards and practices. Consequently, a foreign company

operating within its borders must maintain its books and records and prepare its financial statements in the local language, using the local currency as a unit of measure, and in accordance with local accounting standards and procedures. In addition, the foreign company must comply with the local tax laws and government regulations.

3. Cross-border business transactions often involve receivables and payables denominated in foreign currencies. During the year, these foreign currencies must be translated (converted) into the local currencies for recording in the books and records. At year-end, the foreign currency financial statements must be translated (restated) into the parent's reporting currency for purposes of consolidation. Both the recording of foreign currency transactions and the translation of financial statements require the knowledge of the exchange rates to be used and the accounting treatment of the resulting translation gains and losses.

The biggest mistake a company can make in international accounting is to not be aware of, or even worse, to ignore these realities. It should know that differences in accounting standards, tax laws, and government regulations do exist; and that these differences need to be an integral part of formulating its international business plan.

FOREIGN CURRENCY EXCHANGE RATES

Exchanges rates are used to convert one currency into another currency. An exchange rate is the price of one currency in terms of another currency, i.e., the amount of one currency that must be given to buy one unit of another currency. Because U.S. firms have to prepare their financial statements in U.S. dollars, we shall focus on foreign currency exchange rates in terms of U.S. dollars.

Foreign currency exchange rates are quoted daily in the financial press. Two different rates are quoted for each day:

- A direct quote, which is the amount in U.S. dollars of one unit of foreign currency:

  1 British pound = US$ 1.5505

- An indirect quote, which is the amount of foreign currency equivalent to 1 U.S. dollar:

  US$ 1 = .6450 British pound

The above quotes are called spot rates, which are rates quoted for transactions to be settled within two business days. For some major currencies, forward rates are also quoted for future delivery (30-day, 60-day, 180-day forward) of the foreign currency.

Currencies are bought and sold like other goods. Under the current system of floating exchange rates, foreign exchange rates (like stock prices) are constantly fluctuating, depending on the forces of supply and demand. Because current exchange rates are both volatile and unpredictable, international business transactions are subject to the additional risk of exchange rate fluctuations.

ACCOUNTING FOR FOREIGN CURRENCY TRANSACTIONS

International business transactions are cross-border transactions, therefore two national currencies are usually involved: the currency of the buyer and the currency of the seller. For example, when a United States corporation sells to a corporation in Germany, the transaction can be settled in U.S. dollars (the seller's currency) or in German marks (the buyer's currency).

TRANSACTIONS DENOMINATED IN U.S. CURRENCY

When the foreign transaction is settled in U.S. dollars, no measurement problems occur for the U.S. corporation. As long as the U.S. corporation receives U.S. dollars, the transaction can be recorded in the same way as a domestic transaction.

Example 1. A U.S. firm sells on account equipment worth $100,000 to a German company. If the German company will pay the U.S. firm in U.S. dollars, no foreign currency is involved and the transaction is recorded as usual:

Accounts Receivable	100,000	
Sales		100,000

To record sales to German company.

TRANSACTIONS DENOMINATED IN FOREIGN CURRENCY

However, if the transaction above is settled in German marks, the U.S. corporation will receive foreign currency (German marks) which must be translated into U.S. dollars for purposes of recording on the U.S. company's books. Thus, a foreign currency transaction exists when the transaction is settled in a currency other than the company's home currency.

A foreign currency transaction must be recorded in the books of accounts when it is begun (date of transaction), then perhaps at interim reporting dates (reporting date), and finally when it is settled (settlement date). On each of these three dates, the foreign currency transaction must be recorded in U.S. dollars, using the spot rate on that date for translation.

Accounting at Transaction Date

Before any foreign currency transaction can be recorded, it must first be translated into the domestic currency, using the spot rate on that day. For the U.S. company, this means that any receivable and payable denominated in a foreign currency must be recorded in U.S. dollars.

Example 2. Assume a U.S. firm purchases merchandise on account from a French company on December 1, 20X1. The cost is 50,000 French francs, to be paid in 60 days. The exchange rate for French francs on December 1 is $.20. Using the exchange rate on December 1, the U.S. firm translates the FFr 50,000 into $10,000 and records the following entry:

Dec. 1	Purchases	10,000	
	Accounts Payable		10,000
	To record purchase of merchandise on account (FFr 50,000 x $.20 = $10,000).		

Accounting at Interim Reporting Date

Foreign currency receivables and payables that are not settled at the balance sheet date are adjusted to reflect the exchange rate at that date. Such adjustments will give rise to foreign exchange gains and losses which are to be recognized in the period when exchange rates change.

Example 3. Assume that on December 31, 20X1, the exchange rate for the French franc is $0.22. The U.S. firm will make the following adjusting entry:

Dec. 31	Foreign Exchange Loss	1,000	
	Accounts Payable		1,000
	To adjust accounts payable to current exchange rate (FFr 50,000 x $0.22 = $11,000; $11,000 – $10,000 = $1,000).		

Accounting at Settlement Date

When the transaction is settled, if the exchange rate changes again, the domestic value of the foreign currency paid on the settlement date will be different from that recorded on the books. This difference gives rise to translation gains and losses which must be recognized in the financial statements.

Example 4. To continue our example, assume that on February 1, 20X2, the exchange rate for the French franc is $0.21. The settlement will be recorded as follows:

Feb. 1	Accounts Payable	11,000	
	Cash		10,500
	Foreign Exchange Gain		500

To record payment of accounts payable
(FFr 50,000 x $0.21 = $10,500) and foreign exchange gain.

To summarize: In recording foreign currency transactions, SFAS 52 adopted the two-transaction approach. Under this approach, the foreign currency transaction has two components: the purchase/sale of the asset, and the financing of this purchase/sale. Each component will be treated separately and not netted with the other. The purchase/sale is recorded at the exchange rate on the day of the transaction and is not adjusted for subsequent changes in that rate. Subsequent fluctuations in exchange rates will give rise to foreign exchange gains and losses. They are considered as financing income or expense and are recognized separately in the income statement in the period the foreign exchange fluctuations happen. Thus, exchange gains and losses arising from foreign currency transactions have a direct effect on net income.

TRANSLATION OF FOREIGN CURRENCY FINANCIAL STATEMENTS

When the U.S. firm owns a controlling interest (more than 50%) in another firm in a foreign country, special consolidation problems arise. The subsidiary's financial statements are usually prepared in the language and currency of the country in which it is located, and in accordance with the local accounting principles. Before these foreign currency financial statements can be consolidated with the U.S. parent's financial statements, they must first be adjusted to conform with U.S. GAAP, and then translated into U.S. dollars.

Two different procedures may be used to translate foreign financial statements into U.S. dollars: (1) translation procedures and (2) remeasurement procedures. Which one of these two procedures is to be used depends on the determination of the functional currency for the subsidiary.

THE FUNCTIONAL CURRENCY

SFAS 52 defines the functional currency of the subsidiary as the currency of the primary economic environment in which the subsidiary operates. It is the currency in which the subsidiary realizes its cash flows and conducts its operations. To help management determine the functional currency of its subsidiary, SFAS 52 provides a list of six salient economic indicators regarding cash flows, sales price, sales market, expenses, financing, and intercompany transactions. Depending on the circumstances:

- The functional currency can be the local currency. For example, a Japanese subsidiary manufactures and sells its own products in the local market. Its cash flows, revenues, and expenses are primarily in Japanese yen. Thus its functional currency is the local currency (Japanese yen).

- The functional currency is the U.S. dollar. For foreign subsidiaries which are operated as an extension of the parent and integrated with it, the functional currency is that of the parent. For example, if the Japanese subsidiary is set up as a sales outlet for its U.S. parent, i.e., it takes orders, bills and collects the invoice price, and remits its cash flows primarily to the parent, then its functional currency would be the U.S. dollar.

The functional currency is also the U.S. dollar for foreign subsidiaries operating in highly inflationary economies (defined as having a cumulative inflation rate of more than 100% over a three-year period). The U.S. dollar is deemed the functional currency for translation purposes because it is more stable than the local currency.

Once the functional currency is determined, the specific conversion procedures are selected as follows:

- Foreign currency is the functional currency—use translation procedures.

- U.S. dollar is the functional currency—use remeasurement procedures.

Translation Procedures

If the local currency is the functional currency, the subsidiary's financial statements are translated using the current rate method. Under this method:

- All assets and liabilities accounts are translated at the current rate (the rate in effect at the financial statement date).

- Capital stock accounts are translated using the historical rate (the rate in effect at the time the stock was issued).
- The income statement is translated using the average rate for the year.
- All translation gains and losses are reported on the balance sheet, in an account called "Cumulative Translation Adjustments" in the stockholders' equity section.

The purpose of these translation procedures is to retain, in the translated financial statements, the financial results and relationships among assets and liabilities that were created by the subsidiary's operations in its foreign environment.

Example 5. To illustrate, suppose that the following trial balance, expressed in the local currency (LC) is received from a foreign subsidiary, XYZ Company. The year-end exchange rate is 1 LC = $1.50, and the average exchange rate for the year is 1 LC = $1.25. Under the current rate method, XYZ Company's trial balance would be translated as shown in Figure 1.

Figure 1 shows the translation procedures applied to XYZ Company's trial balance. Note that the translation adjustment is reflected as an adjustment of stockholders' equity in U.S. dollars.

Remeasurement Procedures

If the U.S. dollar is considered to be the functional currency, the subsidiary's financial statements are then remeasured into the U.S. dollar by using the temporal method. Under this method:

- Monetary accounts such as cash, receivable, and liabilities are remeasured at the current rate on the date of the balance sheet.
- Non-monetary accounts such as inventory, fixed assets, and capital stock are remeasured using the historical rates.
- Revenues and expenses are remeasured using the average rate, except for cost of sales and depreciation expenses which are remeasured using the historical exchange rates for the related assets.
- All remeasurement gains and losses are recognized immediately in the income statement.

The objective of these remeasurement procedures is to produce the same U.S. dollar financial statements as if the foreign entity's accounting records had been initially maintained in the U.S. dollar. Figure 2 shows these re-measurement procedures applied to XYZ Company's trial balance. Note that the translation gain/loss is included in the income statement.

Figure 1 Translation Procedures XYZ Company Trial Balance 12/31/01

	Local Currency		Exchange Rate	U.S. Dollars	
	Debit	Credit		Debit	Credit
Cash	LC 5,000		(1 LC = $1.50)	$7,500	
Inventory	15,000		"	22,500	
Fixed Assets	30,000		"	45,000	
Payables		LC 40,000	"		$60,000
Capital Stock		4,000	Historical rate		5,000
Retained Earnings		6,000	to balance		10,000
Sales		300,000	(1 LC = $1.25)		375,000
Cost of Goods Sold	210,000		"	262,500	
Depreciation Expense	5,000		"	6,250	
Other Expenses	85,000		"	106,250	
	LC 350,000	LC 350,000		$450,000	$450,000

Figure 2   Remeasurement Procedures XYZ Company Trial Balance 12/31/01

	Local Currency		Exchange Rate	U.S. Dollars	
	Debit	Credit		Debit	Credit
Cash	LC 5,000		(1 LC = $1.50)	$7,500	
Inventory	15,000		(1 LC = $1.30)	19,500	
Fixed Assets	30,000		(1 LC = $0.95)	28,500	
Payables		LC 40,000	(1 LC = $1.50)		$60,000
Capital Stock		4,000	–		5,000
Retained Earnings		6,000			7,000
Sales		300,000	(1 LC = $1.25)		375,000
Cost of Goods Sold	210,000		(1 LC = $1.30)	273,000	
Depreciation Expense	5,000		(1 LC = $0.95)	4,750	
Other Expenses	85,000		(1 LC = $1.25)	106,250	
				439,500	447,000
Translation Gain/Loss				7,500	
	LC 350,000	LC 350,000		447,000	447,000

INTERPRETATION OF FOREIGN FINANCIAL STATEMENTS

To evaluate a foreign corporation, we usually analyze the financial statements of the foreign corporation. However, the analysis of foreign financial statements needs special considerations:

1. We often have the tendency of looking at the foreign financial data from a home country perspective. For example, a U.S. businessman has the tendency of using U.S. Generally Accepted Accounting Principles (GAAP) to evaluate the foreign financial statements. However, U.S. GAAP are not universally recognized and many differences exist between U.S. GAAP and the accounting principles of other countries (industrialized or nonindustrialized).

2. Because of the diversity of accounting principles worldwide, we have to overcome the tendency of using our home country GAAP to evaluate foreign financial statements. Instead, we should try to become familiar with the foreign GAAP used in the preparation of these financial statements and apply them in our financial analysis.

3. Business practices are culturally based. Often they are different from country to country and have a significant impact on accounting measurement and disclosure practices. Therefore, local economic conditions and business practices should be taken into consideration to correctly analyze foreign financial statements.

HARMONIZATION OF ACCOUNTING STANDARDS

The diversity of accounting systems is an obstacle in the development of international trade and business and the efficiency of the global capital markets. Many concerted efforts have been made to reduce this diversity through the harmonization of accounting standards. Also, as international business expands, there is a great need for international accounting standards which can help investors make decisions on an international scale. The agencies working toward the harmonization of accounting standards are:

A. The International Accounting Standards Committee (IASC)

The IASC was founded in 1973. At that time, its members consisted of the accountancy bodies of Australia, Canada, France, Japan, Mexico, the Netherlands, the United Kingdom, Ireland, the United States, and West Germany. Since its founding, membership has grown to around 116 accountancy bodies from approximately 85 countries.

IASC's fundamental goal is the development of international accounting standards. It is also working towards the improvement and harmonization of accounting standards and procedures relating to the presentation and comparability of financial statements (or at least through enhanced disclosure, if differences are present). To date, it has developed a conceptual framework and issued a total of 32 International Accounting Standards (IAS) covering a wide range of accounting issues. It is currently working on a project concerned with the core standards in consultation with other international groups, especially the International Organization of Securities Commissions (IOSCO), to develop worldwide standards for all corporations to facilitate multi-listing of foreign corporations on various stock exchanges.

B. The International Federation of Accountants (IFAC)

IFAC was founded in 1977 by 63 accountancy bodies representing 49 countries. By 1990, IFAC membership had grown to 105 accountancy bodies from 78 different countries. Its purpose is to develop "a coordinated worldwide accountancy profession with harmonized standards." It concentrated on establishing auditing guidelines to help promote uniform auditing practices throughout the world. It also promoted general standards for ethics, education, and accounting management.

In addition to the IASC and IFAC, there are a growing number of regional organizations involved in accounting harmonization at the regional level. These organizations included, among others, the Inter-American Accounting Association (established in 1949), the ASEAN Federation of Accountants (AFA) (established in 1977), and the Federation des Experts Comptables Europeens (FEE), created by the merger in 1986 of the former Union Europeenne des Experts Comptables Economiques et Financiers (UEC) and the Groupe d'Etude (GE).

C. The European Economic Community (EEC)

The EEC, although not an accounting body, has made great strides in harmonizing the accounting standards of its member countries. During the 1970s, it began the slow process of issuing EEC directives to harmonize the national accounting legislation of its member countries. The directives must go through a three-step process before they are finalized. First, they are proposed by the EEC Commission and presented to the national representatives of the EEC members. Second, if the proposal is satisfactory to the nations, it is adopted by the Commission. Finally, it must be issued by the Council of Ministers of the EEC before it can be enforced on the members.

The most important directives in the harmonization of accounting standards among EEC members are:

- *The Fourth Directive* (1978) regarding the layout and content of annual accounts, valuation methods, annual report, publicity and audit of public and private company accounts.
- *The Seventh Directive* (1983) regarding the consolidation of accounts for certain groups of enterprises.
- *The Eighth Directive* (1984) regarding the training, qualification, and independence of statutory auditors.

COST-VOLUME-PROFIT ANALYSIS AND LEVERAGE

BREAK-EVEN AND COST-VOLUME-REVENUE ANALYSIS FOR NONPROFIT ORGANIZATIONS

By definition, the goal of a nonprofit entity is *not* to earn a profit. The non-profit organization's objective is to render as much suitable service as possible with as little human and physical services, as needed. Ideally, the performance in a nonprofit organization is to break even. This means that, by and large and on a short-term basis, revenues should equal costs. If you generate a surplus, a possibility is that you may not receive the same amount from the funding agency as last year. On the other hand, if you produce a deficit, you may run into insolvency, a danger for survival. Further, chances are that you may not be able to borrow money from the bank, as not-for-profit entities often can, because of your weak financial stance. One thing is clear; over the long run, nonprofit entities cannot survive without reserves and cannot sustain persistent deficits.

Cost-volume-revenue (CVR) analysis, together with cost behavior information, helps nonprofit managers perform many useful analyses. CVR analysis deals with how revenue and costs change with a change in the service level. More specifically, it looks at the effects on revenues of changes in such factors as variable costs, fixed costs, prices, service level, and mix of services offered. By studying the relationships of costs, service volume, and revenue, nonprofit management is better able to cope with many planning decisions.

Break-even analysis, a branch of CVR analysis, determines the break-even service level. The break-even point—the financial crossover point where revenues exactly match costs—does not show up in financial reports, but nonprofit financial managers find it an extremely useful measurement in a variety of ways. It reveals which programs are self-supporting and which are subsidized.

Questions Answered by CVR Analysis

CVR analysis tries to answer the following questions:

(a) What service level is (or what units of service are) required to break even?

(b) How would changes in price, variable costs, fixed costs, and service volume affect a surplus?

(c) How do changes in program levels and mix affect aggregate surplus/deficit?

(d) What alternative break-even strategies are available?

Analysis of Revenues. Revenues for nonprofit entities are typically classified into the following categories:

- Grants from governments.
- Grants from private sources.
- Cost reimbursements and sales.
- Membership fees.
- Public contributions received directly or indirectly.
- Legacies and memorials.
- Other revenues such as investment income (e.g., interest, dividends).

For managerial purposes, however, each type of revenue is grouped into its fixed and variable parts. Fixed revenues are those that remain unchanged regardless of the level of service, such as gifts, grants, and contracts. In colleges, for example, donations, gifts, and grants have no relationship to enrollment. Variable revenues are the ones that vary in proportion to the volume of activity. Examples are cost reimbursements and membership fees. In colleges, tuition and fees are variable in relation to the number of students. Different nonprofit entities may have different sources of revenue: variable revenue only, fixed revenue only, or a combination of both. In this chapter, we will cover all three cases in treating break-even and CVR questions.

Analysis of Cost Behavior. For external reporting purposes, costs are classified by managerial function (such as payroll, occupancy, and office), and also by programs and supporting services. A model functional classification is *IRS Form 990 Part II—Statement of Functional Expenses,* an excerpt from which is shown below:

IRS Form 990 Line No.	*Functional expense category*
26	Salaries and wages
27	Pension plan contributions
28	Other employee benefits
29	Payroll taxes
30	Professional fund-raising fees
31	Accounting fees
32	Legal fees
33	Supplies
34	Telephone
35	Postage and shipping
36	Occupancy
37	Equipment rental and maintenance
38	Printing and publications
39	Travel
40	Conferences, conventions, meetings
41	Interest
42	Depreciation, depletion, etc.
43	Other expenses (itemize)

For managerial purposes (such as planning, control, and decision making), further classification of costs is desirable. One such classification is by behavior. Depending on how a cost will react or respond to changes in the level of activity, costs may be viewed as variable or fixed. This classification is made within a specified range of activity, called the relevant range. The relevant range is the volume zone within which the behavior of variable costs, fixed costs, and prices can be predicted with reasonable accuracy.

Typical activity measures are summarized as follows:

Measures of the Service Level

Nonprofit Types	Units of Service
Hospital or health care	Bed-days, patient contact hours, patient-days, service hours
Educational	Number of enrollments, class size, full-time equivalent (FTE) hours
Social clubs	Number of members served

Variable Costs. Variable costs vary in total with changes in volume or level of activity. Examples of variable costs include supplies, printing and publications, telephone, and postage and shipping.

Fixed Costs. Fixed costs do not change in total regardless of the volume or level of activity. Examples include salaries, accounting and consulting fees, and depreciation.

The following table shows the fixed–variable breakdown of IRS Form 990 functional expenses.

IRS Form 990 Line No.	Expense Category
	FIXED COSTS
26	Salaries and wages
27	Pension plan
28	Other benefits
29	Payroll taxes
30	Fund-raising fees
31	Accounting fees
32	Legal fees
36	Occupancy
37	Equipment rental/maintenance
41	Interest
42	Depreciation
43	Other
	VARIABLE COSTS
33	Supplies
34	Telephone
35	Postage and shipping

38	Printing and publications
39	Travel
40	Conferences, meetings
43	Other

Types of Fixed Costs—Program-Specific or Common. Fixed costs of nonprofit entities are subdivided into two groups. Direct or program-specific fixed costs are those that can be directly identified with individual programs. These costs are avoidable or escapable if the program is dropped. Examples include the salaries of the staff whose services can be used only in a given program, and depreciation of equipment used exclusively for the program. Common fixed costs would continue even if an individual program were discontinued.

CVR Analysis with Variable Revenue Only

For accurate CVR analysis, a distinction must be made between costs as either variable or fixed. In order to compute the break-even point and perform various CVR analyses, note the following important concepts.

Contribution Margin (CM). The contribution margin is the excess of revenue(R) over the variable costs (VC) of the service. It is the amount of money available to cover fixed costs (FC) and to generate surplus. Symbolically, CM = R – VC.

Unit CM. The unit CM is the excess of the unit price (P) over the unit variable cost (V). Symbolically, unit CM = P – V.

CM Ratio. The CM ratio is the contribution margin as a percentage of revenue, i.e.,

$$\text{CM ratio} = \frac{\text{CM}}{\text{R}} = \frac{\text{R} - \text{VC}}{\text{R}} = 1 - \frac{\text{VC}}{\text{R}}$$

The CM ratio can also be computed using per-unit data as follows:

$$\text{CM ratio} = \frac{\text{Unit CM}}{\text{P}} = \frac{\text{P} - \text{V}}{\text{P}} = 1 - \frac{\text{V}}{\text{P}}$$

Note that the CM ratio is 1 minus the variable cost ratio. For example, if variable costs are 40 percent of revenue, then the variable cost ratio is 40 percent and the CM ratio is 60 percent.

Example 1. To illustrate the various concepts of CM, assume that Los Altos Community Hospital has an average revenue of $250 per patient day. Variable costs are $50 per patient day. Total fixed costs per year are $650,000. Expected number of patient days is 4,000. The projected statement of revenue and expenditures follows:

	Total	Per Unit	Percentage
Revenue (4,000 days)	$1,000,000	$250	100%
Less: Variable costs	200,000	50	20
Contribution margin	$ 800,000	$200	80%
Less: Fixed costs	650,000		
Net income	$ 150,000		

From the data listed above, CM, unit CM, and the CM ratio are computed as:

$$CM = R - VC = \$1,000,000 - \$200,000 = \$800,000$$
$$\text{Unit CM} = P - V = \$250 - \$50 = \$200$$

$$\text{CM ratio} = \frac{CM}{R} = \frac{\$ 800,000}{\$1,000,000} = 1 - \frac{\$ 200,000}{\$1,000,000}$$
$$= 0.8 = 80\%$$

$$\text{or} = \frac{\text{Unit CM}}{P} = \frac{\$200}{\$250} = 0.8 = 80\%$$

Break-Even Analysis

The break-even point represents the level of revenue that equals the total of the variable and the fixed costs for a given volume of output service at a particular capacity use rate. Generally, the lower the break-even point, the higher the surplus and the less the operating risk, other things being equal. The break-even point also provides nonprofit managers with insights into surplus/deficit planning. To develop the formula for the break-even units of service, use the following variables:

R = Total revenue

P = Price or average revenue per unit

U = Units of service

VC = Total variable costs

V = Unit variable cost

FC = Total fixed costs

To break even means: Total revenue − total costs = 0

$$R - VC - FC = 0 \text{ or } PU - VU - FC = 0$$

To solve, factor U out to get $(P - V)U - FC = 0$
Rearrange as $(P - V)U = FC$ and divide by $(P - V)$ to isolate U.

$$U = \frac{FC}{(P - V)}$$

In other words,

$$\text{Break-even point in units} = \frac{\text{Fixed costs}}{\text{Unit CM}}$$

If you want break-even point in dollars, use

$$\text{Break-even point in dollars} = \frac{\text{Fixed Costs}}{\text{CM ratio}}$$

Example 2. Using the same data as given in Example 1, where unit CM = $250 − $50 = $200 and CM ratio = 80%, we get:

Break-even point in units = $650,000/$200 = 3,250 patient days
Break-even point in dollars = $650,000/0.8 = $812,500

Or, alternatively,

3,250 patient days × $250 = $812,500. The hospital needs 3,250 patient days to break even.

Graphical Approach in a Spreadsheet Format. The graphical approach to obtaining the break-even point is based on the so-called *break-even (B-E) chart* as shown in Figure 1. Sales revenue, variable costs, and fixed costs are plotted on the vertical axis while volume, x, is plotted on the horizontal axis. The break-even point is the point where the total revenue line intersects the total cost line. The chart can effectively report surplus potentials over a wide range of activity and therefore can be used as a tool for discussion and presentation.

The *surplus-volume (S-V) chart,* as shown in Figure 2, focuses on how surplus varies with changes in volume. Surplus is plotted on the vertical axis, while units of output are shown on the horizontal axis. The S-V chart provides a quick, condensed comparison of how alternatives on pricing, variable costs, or fixed costs may affect surplus (or deficit) as volume changes. The

S-V chart can be easily constructed from the B-E chart. Note that the slope of the chart is the unit CM.

Determination of Target Surplus Volume. Besides determining the break-even point, CVR analysis determines the volume to attain a particular level of surplus. The formula is:

$$\text{Target surplus level} = \frac{\text{Fixed costs plus target surplus}}{\text{Unit CM}}$$

Example 3. Using the same data as given in Example 1, assume the hospital wishes to accumulate a surplus of $250,000 per year. Then, the target surplus service level would be:

$$\frac{\$650,000 + \$250,000}{\$250 - \$50} = \frac{\$900,000}{\$200} = 4,500 \text{ patient days}$$

Figure 1 Break-Even Chart

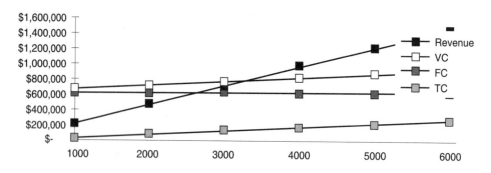

Figure 2 Surplus-Volume (S-V) Chart

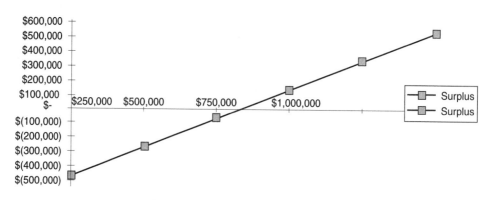

Cost-Volume-Profit Analysis and Leverage

Margin of Safety. The margin of safety is a measure of the difference between the actual level of service and the break-even service level. It is the amount by which revenue may drop before deficits begin, and is expressed as a percentage of expected service level:

$$\text{Margin of safety} = \frac{\text{Expected level} - \text{Break-even level}}{\text{Expected level}}$$

The margin of safety is used as a measure of operating risk. The larger the ratio, the safer the situation, since there is less risk of reaching the break-even point.

Example 4. Assume that Los Altos Hospital projects 4,000 patient days with a break-even level of 3,250. The projected margin of safety is

$$\frac{4,000 - 3,250}{4,000} = 18.75\%$$

Example 5. A nonprofit college offers a program in management for executives. The program has been experiencing financial difficulties. Operating data for the most recent year are shown below.

Tuition revenue (40 participants @$7,000)	$280,000
Less variable expenses (@$4,000)	160,000
Contribution margin	$120,000
Less fixed expenses	150,000
Operating deficit	$(30,000)

The break-even point is $150,000/($7,000 – $4,000) = 50 participants.

Example 6. In Example 5, the dean of the school is convinced that the class size can be increased to more economical levels without lowering the quality. He is prepared to spend $15,000 per year in additional promotional and other support expenses. If that is the case, the new break-even point is 55 participants ($165,000/($7,000 – $4,000).

To generate a surplus of $30,000, the school must get 60 participants [$150,000 + $30,000)/$3,000].

Some Applications of CVR Analysis and What-If Analysis. The concepts of contribution margin and the contribution income statement have many applications in surplus/deficit planning and short-term decision making. Many "what-if" scenarios can be evaluated using them as planning tools, especially utilizing a spreadsheet program such as Microsoft Excel or Lotus 1-2-3. Some applications are illustrated below, using the same data as in Examples 1 and 5.

Example 7. Recall from Example 1 that Los Altos Hospital has unit CM = $250 − $50 = $200, CM ratio = 80%, and fixed costs of $650,000. Assume that the hospital expects revenues to go up by $250,000 for the next period. How much will surplus increase?

Using the CM concepts, we can quickly compute the impact of a change in the service level on surplus or deficit. The formula for computing the impact is:

$$\text{Change in surplus} = \text{Dollar change in revenue} \times \text{CM ratio}$$

Thus:

$$\text{Increase in surplus} = \$250,000 \times 80\% = \$200,000$$

Therefore, the income will go up by $200,000, assuming there is no change in fixed costs. If we are given a change in service units (e.g., patient days) instead of dollars, then the formula becomes:

$$\text{Change in surplus} = \text{Change in units} \times \text{Unit CM}$$

Example 8. Assume that the hospital expects patient days to go up by 500 units. How much will surplus increase? From Example 1, the hospital's unit CM is $200. Again, assuming there is no change in fixed costs, the surplus will increase by $100,000, as computed below:

$$500 \text{ additional patient days} \times \$200 \text{ CM per day} = \$100,000$$

Example 9. Referring back to Example 5, another alternative under consideration is to hold the present program without any change in the regular campus facilities instead of in rented outside facilities that are better located. If adopted, this proposal will reduce fixed costs by $60,000. The variable costs will decrease by $100 per participant. Is the move to campus facilities advisable if it leads to a decline in the number of participants by 5?

		Present		Proposed
S(40 × $7,000)		$280,000	(35 × $7,000)	$245,000
VC(40 × $4,000)		160,000	(35 × $3,900)	136,500
CM		$120,000		$108,500
FC		150,000		90,000
Surplus		$(30,000)		$ 18,500

The answer is yes, since the move will turn into a surplus.

Cost-Volume-Profit Analysis and Leverage

CVR Analysis with Variable and Fixed Revenues. Many nonprofit organizations derive two types of revenue: fixed and variable. In this situation, the formulas developed previously need to be modified. The following example illustrates this.

Example 10. ACM, Inc., a mental rehabilitation provider, has a $1,200,000 lump-sum annual budget appropriation to help rehabilitate mentally ill clients. The agency charges each client $600 a month for board and care. All the appropriation must be spent. The variable costs for rehabilitation activity average $700 per patient per month. The agency's annual fixed costs are $800,000. The agency manager wishes to know how many patients can be served.

Let U = units of service = number of clients to be served.

We set up: Total revenue – Total expenses = 0

$$\text{Lump sum appropriation} + R - VC - FC = 0$$
$$\text{Lump sum appropriation} + PU - VU - FC = 0$$
$$\$1,200,000 + \$7,200\,U - \$8,400\,U - \$800,000 = 0$$
$$(\$7,200 - \$8,400)U = \$800,000 - \$1,200,000$$
$$-\$1,200\,U = -\$400,000$$
$$U = \$400,000/\$1,200$$
$$U = 333 \text{ clients}$$

Alternatively, you may use the following formula:

$$\text{Break-even point in units} = \frac{\text{Fixed costs} - \text{Fixed revenue}}{\text{Unit CM}}$$

Thus,

$$\text{Break-even number of patients} = \frac{\$800,000 - \$1,200,000}{-\$1,200}$$
$$= \$400,000/\$1,200 = 333 \text{ clients}$$

We will investigate the following two "what-if" scenarios:

Example 11. In Example 10, suppose the manager of the agency is concerned that the total budget for the coming year will be cut by 10 percent to $1,080,000. All other things remain unchanged. The manager wants to know how this budget cut affects the next year's service level. Using the formula yields:

$$\text{Break-even number of clients} = \frac{\$800,000 - \$1,080,000}{-\$1,200}$$
$$U = -\$280,000/-\$1,200$$
$$U = 233 \text{ clients}$$

Example 12. In Example 10, the manager does not reduce the number of patients served despite a budget cut of 10 percent. All other things remain unchanged. How much more does he or she have to charge clients for board and care? We let V = board and care charge per year and set up:

$$\$1,200,000 + \$7,200\,U - \$8,400\,U - \$800,000 = 0$$
$$(\$7,200 - \$8,400)U = \$800,000 - \$1,200,000$$
$$-\$1,200\,U = -\$400,000$$
$$U = \$400,000/\$1,200$$
$$U = 333 \text{ clients}$$
$$\$1,080,000 + 333V - \$8,400\,(333) - \$800,000 = 0$$
$$333V = \$2,797,200 + \$800,000 - \$1,080,000$$
$$333V = \$2,517,200$$
$$V = \$2,517,200/333 \text{ clients}$$
$$V = \$7,559$$

Thus, the monthly board and care charge must be increased to $630 (7,559/12 months).

Use of Spreadsheet Software. "What-if" scenarios can easily be analyzed using popular spreadsheet software such as Microsoft Excel, Lotus 1-2-3, or QuattroPro. Examples 11 and 12 can be solved using the GoalSeek command. For example, in Excel, you find this command under Tools Bar.

CVR Analysis with Fixed Revenue Only. Some nonprofit entities may have only one source of revenue, typically a government budget appropriation. In this case, the break-even formula becomes:

$$\text{Break-even points in units} = \frac{\text{Fixed revenue} - \text{Fixed costs}}{\text{Unit variable cost}}$$

Example 13. A social service agency has a government budget appropriation of $750,000. The agency's main mission is to assist disabled people who are unable to seek or hold jobs. On the average, the agency supplements each individual's income by $6,000 annually. The agency's fixed costs are

$150,000. The agency CEO wishes to know how many people could be served in a given year. The break-even point can be computed as follows:

$$\frac{\$750,000 - \$150,000}{\$6,000} = 100$$

Example 14. In Example 13, assume that the CEO is concerned that the total budget for the year will be reduced by 10 percent to a new amount of 90%($750,000) = $675,000. The new break-even point is:

$$\frac{\$675,000 - \$150,000}{\$6,000} = 88 \text{ (rounded)}$$

The CEO has the option of cutting the budget in one or more of three ways: (1) Cut the service level, as computed above, (2) reduce the variable cost, the supplement per person, and (3) seek to cut down on the total fixed costs.

Program Mix Analysis

Previously, our main concern was to determine program-specific break-even volume. But as we are aware, most nonprofit companies are involved in multiservice, multiprogram activities. One major concern is how to plan aggregate break-even volume, surplus, and deficits. Break-even analysis and cost-volume-revenue analysis require additional computations and assumptions when an organization offers more than one program. In multiprogram organizations, program mix is an important factor in calculating an overall break-even point. Different rates and different variable costs result in different unit CMs. As a result, break-even points and cost-volume-revenue relationships vary with the relative proportions of the programs offered, called the *program mix.*

When the product is defined as a package, the multiprogram problem is converted into a single-program problem. The first step is to determine the number of packages that need to be served to break even. The following example illustrates a multiprogram, multiservice situation.

Example 15. The Cypress Counseling Services is a nonprofit agency offering two programs: psychological counseling (PC) and alcohol addiction control (AAC). The agency charges individual clients an average of $10 per hour of counseling provided under the PC program. The local Chamber of Commerce reimburses the company at the rate of $20 per hour of direct service provided under the AAC. The nonprofit agency believes that this billing variable rate is low enough to be affordable for most clients and also high enough to derive clients' commitment to the program objectives. Costs of administering the two programs are given below.

	PC	AAC
Variable costs	$4.6	$11.5
Direct fixed costs	$120,000	$180,000

There are other fixed costs that are common to the two programs, including general and administrative and fund raising, of $255,100 per year. The projected surplus for the coming year, segmented by programs, follows:

	PC	AAC	Total
Revenue	$500,000	$800,000	$1,300,000
Program mix in hours	(50,000)	(40,000)	
Less: VC	(230,000)	(460,000)	(690,000)
Contribution margin	$270,000	$340,000	$610,000
Less: Direct FC	(120,000)	(180,000)	(300,000)
Program margin	$150,000	$160,000	$310,000
Less: Common FC			(255,100)
Surplus			$54,900

First, based on program-specific data on the rates, the variable costs, and the program mix, we can compute the package (aggregate) value as follows:

Program	P	V	Unit CM	Mix*	Package CM
PC	$10	$4.6	$5.4	5	$27
AAC	20	11.5	8.5	4	34
Package total					$61

*The mix ratio is 5:4 (50,000 hours for PC and 40,000 hours for AAC).

We know that the total fixed costs for the agency are $555,100. Thus, the package (aggregate) break-even point is

$$\frac{\$555,100}{\$61} = 9,100 \text{ packages}$$

The agency must provide 45,500 hours of PC (5 × 9,100) and 36,400 hours of AAC (4 × 9,100) to avoid a deficit. To prove:

Cost-Volume-Profit Analysis and Leverage

	PC	AAC	Total
Revenue	$455,000 (a)	$728,000 (b)	$1,183,000
Program mix in hours	(45,500)	(36,400)	
Less: VC	(209,300) (c)	(418,600)(d)	(627,900)
Contribution margin	$245,700	$309,400	$ 555,100
Less: Direct FC	(120,000)	(180,000)	(300,000)
Program margin	$125,700	$129,400	$ 255,100
Less: Common FC			(255,100)
Surplus			$ 0

(a) 45,500 × $10   (c) 45,500 × $4.60
(b) 36,400 × $20   (d) 36,400 × $11.50

Example 16. Assume in Example 15 that 56,000 hours of PC services are budgeted for the next period. The agency wants to know how many hours of AAC services are necessary during that period to avoid an overall deficit. The answer is 29,729 hours, as shown below.

Directions: Set surplus = 0 and PC units of service = $56,000 and let Goal Seeking determine ACC units of service.

Input Data	PC	AAC
Rates	$ 10	$ 20
Units of service (Hours)	56,000	29,729
Variable cost per unit	$ 4.6	$ 11.5

Contribution Statement of Surplus or Deficit

	PC	AAC	Total
Revenue	$560,000	$594,588	$1,154,588
Less: Variable Costs	257,600	341,888	(599,488)
Contribution margin	$302,400	$252,700	$ 555,100
Less: Direct fixed costs	120,000	180,000	(300,000)
Program margin	$182,400	$ 72,700	$ 255,100
Less: Common fixed costs			(255,100)
Surplus			$ (0)

Management Options

Cost-volume-revenue analysis is useful as a frame of reference, as a vehicle for expressing overall managerial performance, and as a planning device via break-even techniques and "what-if" scenarios. In many practical situations, management will have to resort to a combination of approaches to reverse a deficit, including:

1. Selected changes in volume of activity.
2. Planned savings in fixed costs at all levels.
3. Some savings in variable costs.
4. Additional fund drives or grant seeking.
5. Upward adjustments in pricing.
6. Cost reimbursement contracts.

All these approaches will have to be mixed to form a feasible planning package. Many nonprofit managements fail to develop such analytical approaches to the economics of their operations. Further, the accounting system is not designed to provide information to investigate cost-volume-revenue relations.

Cost-Volume-Profit Analysis and Leverage

The Use of Capital Budgeting in Decision Making

COMPARING PROJECTS WITH UNEQUAL LIVES

A replacement decision typically involves two mutually exclusive projects. When these two mutually exclusive projects have significantly different lives, an adjustment would be necessary. We discuss two approaches: (1) the replacement chain (common life) approach and (2) the equivalent annual annuity approach.

The Replacement Chain (Common Life) Approach

This procedure extends one or both projects until an equal life is achieved. For example, Project A has a 6-year life, while Project B has a 3-year life. Under this approach, the projects would be extended to a common life of 6 years. Project B would have an adjusted NPV equal to the NPV_B plus the NPV_B discounted for 3 years at the project's cost of capital. Then the project with the higher NPV would be chosen.

Example 1. Sims Industries, Inc. is considering two machines to replace an old machine. Machine A has a life of 10 years, will cost $24,500, and will produce net cash savings of $4,800 per year. Machine B has an expected life of 5 years, will cost $20,000, and will produce net cash savings in operating costs of $6,000 per year. The company's cost of capital is 14 percent. Project A's NPV is:

$NPV_A = PV - I = \$4,800 \; PVIFA_{10,14} - \$24,500$

$\quad = \$4,800(5.2161) - \$24,500 = \$25,037.28 - \$24,500$

$\quad = \$537.28$

Project B's extended time line can be set up as follows:

0	1	2	3	4	5	6	7	8	9	10
−200	60	60	60	60	60	60	60	60	60	60
						−200				(in hundredths)

$\text{Adjusted } NPV_B = PV - I = \$6,000 \; PVIFA_{10,14} - \$20,000 \; PVIF_{5,14} - \$20,000$

$\quad = \$6,000(5.2161) - \$20,000(0.5194) - \$20,000$

$\quad = \$31,296.60 - \$10,388.00 - \$20,000$

$\quad = \$908.60$

Or, alternatively,

$NPV_B = PV - I = \$6,000 \; PVIFA_{5,14} - \$20,000$

$\quad = \$6,000(3.4331) - \$20,000$

$\quad = \$20,598.60 - \$20,000$

$\quad = \$598.60$

$\text{Adjusted } NPV_B = NPV_B + NPV_B \text{ discounted for 5 years}$

$\quad = \$598.60 + \$598.60 \; PVIF_{5,14}$

$\quad = \$598.60 + \$598.60(0.5194)$

$\quad = \$598.60 + \$310.91$

$\quad = \$909.51 \text{ (due to rounding errors)}$

The Equivalent Annual Annuity (EAA) Approach. It is often cumbersome to compare projects with different lives. For example, one project might have a 4-year life versus a 10-year life for the other. This would require a replacement chain analysis over 20 years, the lowest common denominator of the two lives. In such a case, it is often simpler to use an alternative approach, the *equivalent annual annuity method.*

This procedure involves three steps:

1. Determine each project's NPV over its original life.
2. Find the constant annuity cash flow or EAA, using:

$$\frac{\text{NPV of each project}}{PVIFA_{n,i}}$$

The Use of Capital Budgeting in Decision Making

3. Assuming infinite replacement, find the infinite horizon (or perpetuity) NPV of each project, using:

$$\frac{\text{EAA of each}}{\text{cost of capital}}$$

Example 2. From Example 1, $NPV_A = \$537.28$ and $NPV_B = \$598.60$. To obtain the constant annuity cash flow or EAA, we do the following:

$$EAA_A = \$537.28/PVIFA_{10,14} = \$537.28/5.2161 = \$103.00$$
$$EAA_B = \$598.60/PVIFA_{5,14} = \$598.60/3.4331 = \$174.36$$

Thus, the infinite horizon NPVs are as follows:

Infinite horizon $NPV_A = \$103.00/0.14 = \$735.71$
Infinite horizon $NPV_B = \$174.36/0.14 = \$1,245.43$

The Concept of Abandonment Value

The notion of abandonment value recognizes that abandonment of a project before the end of its physical life can have a significant impact on the project's return and risk. This distinguishes between the project's economic life and physical life. Two types of abandonment can occur:

1. Abandonment of an unprofitable asset.
2. Sale of the asset to some other party who can extract more value than the original owner.

Example 3. ABC Company is considering a project with an initial cost of $5,000 and net cash flows of $2,000 for next three years. The expected abandonment cash flows for years 0,1,2, and 3 are $5,000, $3,000, $2,500, and $0. The firm's cost of capital is 10 percent. We will compute NPVs in three cases.

Case 1. NPV of the project if kept for 3 years.
$$NPV = PV - I = \$2,000 \; PVIFA_{10,3} = \$2,000(2.4869) - \$5,000$$
$$= -\$26.20$$

Case 2. NPV of the project if abandoned after Year 1
$$NPV = PV - I = \$2,000 \; PVIF_{10,1} + \$3,000 \; PVIF_{10,2} - \$5,000$$
$$= \$2,000(0.9091) + \$3,000(0.9091) - \$5,000$$
$$= \$1,818.20 + \$2,727.30 - \$5,000 = -\$454.50$$

Case 3. NPV of the project if abandoned after Year 2

$$\begin{aligned}
\text{NPV} &= \text{PV} - \text{I} = \$2,000 \text{ PVIF}_{10,1} + \$2,000 \text{ PVIF}_{10,2} + \$2,500 \text{ PVIF}_{10,2} - \$5,000 \\
&= \$2,000(0.9091) + \$2,000(0.8264) + \$2,500(0.8264) - \$5,000 \\
&= \$1,818.20 + \$1,652.80 + \$2,066.00 - \$5,000 = \$537
\end{aligned}$$

The company should abandon the project after Year 2.

HOW INCOME TAXES AFFECT INVESTMENT DECISIONS

Income taxes make a difference in many capital budgeting decisions. The project which is attractive on a before-tax basis may have to be rejected on an after-tax basis, and vice versa. Income taxes typically affect both the amount and the timing of cash flows. Since net income, not cash inflows, is subject to tax, after-tax cash inflows are not usually the same as after-tax net income.

How to Calculate After-Tax Cash Flows

Let us define:

S = Sales

E = Cash operating expenses

d = Depreciation

t = Tax rate

Then, before-tax cash inflows (or cash savings) = S – E and net income = S – E – d

By definition,

After-tax cash inflows = Before-tax cash inflows – Taxes = (S – E) – (S – E – d) (t)

Rearranging gives the short-cut formula:

$$\begin{aligned}
\text{After-tax cash inflows} &= (S - E)(1 - t) + (d)(t) \text{ or} \\
&= (S - E - d)(1 - t) + d
\end{aligned}$$

As can be seen, the deductibility of depreciation from sales in arriving at taxable net income reduces income tax payments and thus serves as a *tax shield*.

Tax shield = Tax savings on depreciation = (d)(t)

Example 4. Assume:

S = $12,000

E = $10,000

d = $500 per year using the straight-line method

t = 30%

The Use of Capital Budgeting in Decision Making

Then,

$$\text{After-tax cash inflow} = (\$12{,}000 - \$10{,}000)\,(1 - .3) + (\$500)(.3)$$
$$= (\$2{,}000)(.7) + (\$500)(.3)$$
$$= \$1{,}400 + \$150 = \$1{,}550$$

$$\text{Note that a tax shield} = \text{tax savings on depreciation} = (d)(t)$$
$$= (\$500)(.3) = \$150$$

Since the tax shield is dt, the higher the depreciation deduction, the higher the tax savings on depreciation. Therefore, an accelerated depreciation method (such as double-declining balance) produces higher tax savings than the straight-line method. Accelerated methods produce higher present values for the tax savings, which may make a given investment more attractive.

Example 5. The Navistar Company estimates that it can save $2,500 a year in cash operating costs for the next ten years if it buys a special-purpose machine at a cost of $10,000. No residual value is expected. Depreciation is by straight-line. Assume that the income tax rate is 30%, and the after-tax cost of capital (minimum required rate of return) is 10%. After-tax cash savings can be calculated as follows:

Note that depreciation by straight-line is $10,000/10 = $1,000 per year. Thus,

$$\text{After-tax cash savings} = (S - E)\,(1 - t) + (d)(t)$$
$$= \$2{,}500(1 - .3) + \$1{,}000(.3)$$
$$= \$1{,}750 + \$300 = \$2{,}050$$

To see if this machine should be purchased, the net present value can be calculated.

$$PV = \$2{,}050\ T4(10\%,\ 10\ \text{years}) = \$2{,}050\ (6.145) = \$12{,}597.25$$

Thus, $NPV = PV - I = \$12{,}597.25 - \$10{,}000 = \$2{,}597.25$

Since NPV is positive, the machine should be bought.

Capital Budgeting Decisions and the Modified Accelerated Cost Recovery System (MACRS)

Although the traditional depreciation methods still can be used for computing depreciation for book purposes, 1981 saw a new way of computing depreciation deductions for tax purposes. The current rule is called the

Modified Accelerated Cost Recovery System (MACRS) rule, as enacted by Congress in 1981 and then modified somewhat in 1986 under the Tax Reform Act of 1986. This rule is characterized as follows:

1. It abandons the concept of useful life and accelerates depreciation deductions by placing all depreciable assets into one of eight age property classes. It calculates deductions, based on an allowable percentage of the asset's original cost (see Tables 1 and 2).

   With a shorter asset tax life than useful life, the company would be able to deduct depreciation more quickly and save more in income taxes in the earlier years, thereby making an investment more attractive. The rationale behind the system is that this way, the government encourages the company to invest in facilities and increase its productive capacity and efficiency. (Remember that the higher d, the larger the tax shield (d)(t)).

2. Since the allowable percentages in Table 1 add up to 100%, there is no need to consider the salvage value of an asset in computing depreciation.

3. The company may elect the straight-line method. The straight-line convention must follow what is called the *half-year convention*. This means that the company can deduct only half of the regular straight-line depreciation amount in the first year. The reason for electing to use the MACRS optional straight-line method is that some firms may prefer to stretch out depreciation deductions using the straight-line method rather than to accelerate them. Those firms are the ones that have just started out or have little or no income and wish to show more income on their income statements.

Example 6. Assume that a machine falls under a 3-year property class and costs $3,000 initially. The straight-line option under MACRS differs from the traditional straight-line method in that under this method, the company would deduct only $500 depreciation in the first year and the fourth year ($3,000/3 years = $1,000; $1,000/2 = $500). The table below compares the straight-line with half-year convention with the MACRS rule.

Year	Straight-Line (half-year) Depreciation	Cost		MACRS %	MACRS deduction
1	$ 500	$3,000	×	33.3%	$ 999
2	1,000	3,000	×	44.5	1,335
3	1,000	3,000	×	14.8	444
4	500	3,000	×	7.4	222
	$3,000				$3,000

Example 7. A machine costs $10,000. Annual cash inflows are expected to be $5,000. The machine will be depreciated using the MACRS rule and will fall under the 3-year property class. The cost of capital after taxes is 10%. The estimated life of the machine is 4 years. The salvage value of the machine at the end of the fourth year is expected to be $1,200. The tax rate is 30%.

The formula for computation of after-tax cash inflows $(S - E)(1 - t) + (d)(t)$ needs to be computed separately. The NPV analysis can be performed as follows:

	Present value factor @ 10%	Present value
Initial investment: $10,000	1.000	$(10,000.00)
$(S - E)(1 - t)$:		
$5,000 (1 - .3) = $3,500 for 4 years	3.170(a)	$11,095.00
$(d)(t)$:		

Year	Cost		MACRS %	d	$(d)(t)$		
1	$10,000	×	33.3%	$3,330	$ 999	.909(b)	908.09
2	$10,000	×	44.5	4,450	1,335	.826(b)	1,102.71
3	$10,000	×	14.8	1,480	444	.751(b)	333.44
4	$10,000	×	7.4	740	222	.683(b)	151.63

Salvage value:		
$1,200 in year 4: $1,200 (1 - .3) =		
840(c)	.683(b)	573.72
Net present value (NPV)		$4,164.59

(a) Present value of an annuity of $1 = 3.170 (from Table A-4 in the Appendix).
(b) Present values of $1 obtained (from Table A-3 in the Appendix).
(c) Any salvage value received under the MACRS rules is a *taxable gain* (the excess of the selling price over book value, $1,200 in this example), since the book value will be zero at the end of the life of the machine.

Since NPV = PV – I = $4,164.59 is positive, the machine should be bought.

Example 8. A firm is considering the purchase of an automatic machine for $6,200. The machine has an installation cost of $800 and zero salvage value at the end of its expected life of 5 years. Depreciation is by the straight-line method with the *half-year convention*. The machine is considered 5-year property. Expected cash savings before tax is $1,800 per year over the five years. The firm is in the 40 percent tax bracket. The firm has determined the cost of capital (or minimum required rate of return) of 10 percent after taxes.

	Year(s) Having Cash Flows	Amount of Cash Flows	10% PV Factor	PV
Initial investment	Now	$(7,000)	1.000	$(7,000)
Annual cash inflows:				
$1,800				
× 60%				
$1,080	1-5	1,080	3.791	4,094

Depreciation deductions:

Year	Depreciation	Tax Shield at 40%				
1	$700	$280	1	280	0.909	255
2	1,400	560	2	560	0.826	463
3	1,400	560	3	560	0.751	421
4	1,400	560	4	560	0.683	382
5	1,400	560	5	560	0.621	348
6	700	280	6	280	0.564	158
Net Present Value						$(879)

The firm should not buy the automatic machine since its NPV is negative.

Example 9. The Wessels Corporation is considering installing a new conveyor for materials handling in a warehouse. The conveyor will have an initial cost of $75,000 and an installation cost of $5,000. Expected benefits of the conveyor are: (a) Annual labor cost will be reduced by $16,500, and (b) breakage and other damages from handling will be reduced by $400 per month. Some of the firm's costs are expected to increase as follows: (a) Electricity cost will rise by $100 per month, and (b) annual repair and maintenance of the conveyor will amount to $900.

Assume the firm uses the MACRS rules for depreciation in the 5-year property class. No salvage value will be recognized for tax purposes. The conveyor has an expected useful life of 8 years and a projected salvage value of $5,000. The tax rate is 40 percent. We will determine the project's NPV at 10 percent. Should the firm buy the conveyor?

Annual cash inflows are computed as follows:

$16,500	Reduction in labor cost
4,800	Reduction in breakage
−1,200	Increase in electricity costs
−900	Increase in repair and maintenance cost
$19,200	

The Use of Capital Budgeting in Decision Making

Initial amount of investment is:

$75,000 + $5,000 = $80,000

		Year(s) Having Cash Flows	Amount of Cash Flows	10% PV Factor	PV
Initial investment		Now	$(80,000)	1.000	$(80,000)
Annual cash inflow:					
	$19,200				
	× 60%				
After-tax cash inflow:	$11,520	1-8	11,520	5.335	61,459.20
Depreciation deduction:					

Year	Cost	MACRS	Depreciation	Tax Shield				
1	$80,000	20%	$16,000	$ 6,400	1	6,400	0.909	5,817.60
2	80,000	32	25,600	10,240	2	10,240	0.826	8,458.24
3	80,000	19.2	15,360	6,144	3	6,144	0.751	4,614.14
4	80,000	11.5	9,200	3,680	4	3,680	0.683	2,513.44
5	80,000	11.5	9,200	3,680	5	3,680	0.621	2,285.28
6	80,000	5.8	4,640	1,856	6	1,856	0.564	1,046.78
								$24,735.48

Salvage value will be fully taxable since book value will be zero:

$5,000				
× 60%				
$3,000	8	3,000	0.467	1,401.00
Net present value				$7,595.68

The Wessels Corporation should buy and install the conveyor since it brings a positive NPV.

Table 1 Modified Accelerated Cost Recovery System Classification of Assets

Property class

Year	3-year	5-year	7-year	10-year	15-year	20-year
1	33.3%	20.0%	14.3%	10.0%	5.0%	3.8%
2	44.5	32.0	24.5	18.0	9.5	7.2
3	14.8a	19.2	17.5	14.4	8.6	6.7
4	7.4	11.5a	12.5	11.5	7.7	6.2
5		11.5	8.9a	9.2	6.9	5.7
6		5.8	8.9	7.4	6.2	5.3
7			8.9	6.6a	5.9a	4.9
8			4.5	6.6	5.9	4.5a
9				6.5	5.9	4.5
10				6.5	5.9	4.5
11				3.3	5.9	4.5
12					5.9	4.5
13					5.9	4.5
14					5.9	4.5
15					5.9	4.5
16					3.0	4.4
17						4.4
18						4.4
19						4.4
20						4.4
21						2.2
Total	100%	100%	100%	100%	100%	100%

a Denotes the year of changeover to straight-line depreciation.

Table 2   MACRS Tables by Property Class

MACRS Property Class & Depreciation Method	Useful Life (ADR Midpoint Life) "a"	Examples of Assets
3-year property 200% declining balance	4 years or less	Most small tools are included; the law specifically excludes autos and light trucks from this property class.
5-year property 200% declining balance	More than 4 years to less than 10 years	Autos and light trucks, computers, typewriters, copiers, duplicating equipment, heavy general-purpose trucks, and research and experimentation equipment are included.
7-year property 200% declining balance	10 years or more to less than 16 years	Office furniture and fixtures and most items of machinery and equipment used in production are included.
10-year property 200% declining balance	16 years or more to less than 20 years	Various machinery and equipment, such as that used in petroleum distilling and refining and in the milling of grain, are included.
15-year property 150% declining balance	20 years or more to less than 25 years	Sewage treatment plants, telephone and electrical distribution facilities, and land improvements are included.
20-year property 150% declining balance	25 years or more	Service stations and other real property with an ADR midpoint life of less than 27.5 years are included.
27.5-year property Straight-line	Not applicable	All residential rental property is included.
31.5-year property Straight-line	Not applicable	All nonresidential real property is included.

"a" The term ADR midpoint life means the "useful life" of an asset in a business sense; the appropriate ADR midpoint lives for assets are designated in the Tax Regulations.

Avoiding Financial Distress: Key Financial Ratios and Metrics for Nonprofits

Financial statement analysis reveals how well a nonprofit organization (NPO) did in meeting its targets. Interrelated ratios reveal the financial standing and areas of financial trouble. Each ratio should be compared over the years for a trend, to an industry norm (e.g., health care standard ratio), and to comparable NPOs to obtain a relative standing. Ratios vary depending on the service provided, complexity of operations, funding sources, and donor restrictions. A cost/benefit analysis should be undertaken for new programs. Risk/return analysis is also essential.

When evaluating the service efforts of an NPO, look to see how much of every dollar goes to the primary mission as opposed to the fund-raiser's commissions and the executive director's salary. Carefully monitor the relationship of supporting services to program services expenses.

Financial statement analysis is undertaken by those working within the NPO, such as managers, and by outsiders evaluating the NPO's financial statements. Financial statement preparers are provided with "red flags" as to impending financial problems that need to be identified and corrected. Areas of strength are also identified and taken further advantage of. Financial statement users include resource providers such as contributors and grantors. They want to know how well their funds are being spent for the purposes solicited. Financial statements reveal this fiduciary trust. Further, donors do not want to pour money into a sinking ship. Suppliers and loan officers analyze the financial statements to determine whether to give credit, and if so, how much and for what time period. Companies and government (federal and local) agencies awarding contracts appraise financial statements as to whether contractual provisions are being adhered to. Government regulators (watchdogs) evaluate the financial statements to ascertain if compliance is being achieved with prescribed regulations and limitations. An NPO serves the public, so concerned citizens may want to analyze the financial statements to determine if service goals are being met.

The primary objectives of this chapter are twofold. First, the chapter focuses on ways NPOs can assess the progress and health of their businesses. It takes you through step-by-step procedures in performing financial statement analysis. The procedures involve the following:

- Appraise the balance sheet for financial position and flexibility.
- Analyze the Statement of Activities for operating performance.
- Evaluate the Statement of Cash Flows for cash position.
- Refer to footnote information.
- Evaluate the auditor's opinion.
- Review internal documents related to financial health.
- Review budgets to determine if plans are practical and for future directions.

The chapter discusses some key financial ratios that are critical for assessing the financial health of NPOs. Second, it introduces some key financial metrics for NPOs. Also, as a giver or donor, you need know how to distinguish among NPOs in the same field. You want to address questions such as:

How do you figure out who does the most with the contributions and who spends inordinate sums, however well intentioned, on raising the money and on excessive overhead? Several indexes would be helpful to answer those questions: charity commitment, fund-raising efficiency, and donor dependency.

A case study, presented at the end of the paper, analyzes a nonprofit organization, including trend analysis, ratio computations, and analytical evaluation.

TREND ANALYSIS

A trend (horizontal) analysis is a time series analysis of financial statements of the NPO, covering more than one accounting period. It looks at the percentage change in an account or category over time. The percentage change equals the change over the prior year. For example, if salaries expense increased from $140,000 to $165,000 from 20X1 to 20X2, the percentage increase is 18 percent ($25,000 + $140,000). The reason (or reasons) for such an increase should be determined. Does the increase indicate more staff was needed because operations improved, or does it indicate a lack of cost control, or is there some other cause? Is the situation an unfavorable one requiring management attention? By evaluating the magnitude of direction of a financial statement item over the years, the analyst can appraise its reasonableness.

Example 1. Membership fee revenue declined from $100,000 to $80,000 over the last year. The percentage decline equals:

$$\frac{\text{Amount of Change}}{\text{Base Year Amount}} = \frac{\$20,000}{\$100,000} = 20\%$$

Why such a significant decline in membership fees? Is this a problem peculiar just to this NPO, or does it affect all NPOs in the industry? Is the problem controllable or uncontrollable by management? Is the decline due to dissatisfaction among members of the NPO, who object to its policies, or was it caused by overall poor economic conditions? Trend analysis reveals direction, positive or negative, requiring further study of the causes. The decline may indicate a problem requiring corrective action.

ANALYSIS OF THE BALANCE SHEET

An evaluation of the balance sheet considers the NPO's liquidity, asset utilization, solvency, financial flexibility, and capital structure. Assets, liabilities, and fund balance must be scrutinized. Beside looking at book values for ratio computations, market values may also be used to express current values.

LIQUIDITY ANALYSIS

FASB 117 requires NPOs to present information about their liquidity. Liquidity is the ability of the NPO to pay current debts as they come due. Liquidity is how fast the NPO's assets turn into cash. A liquid asset has less risk than an illiquid one. In evaluating liquidity, exclude restricted funds because they are unavailable for use.

Liquidity considers the seasonality of cash flows. Wide fluctuations in cash flows may result in a liquidity problem.

Working Capital. Working capital equals current assets less current liabilities. The higher the working capital amount, the better the liquidity.

Current Ratio.   The current ratio is a measure of liquidity equal to:

Current Ratio = Current Assets/Current Liabilities

Current assets are those assets to be converted to cash within one year or the normal operating cycle of the NPO, whichever is greater. Current liabilities are due within one year.

In general, the current ratio should be a minimum of 2:1. A low ratio means poor liquidity.

An excessively high ratio may also be a negative sign because it may indicate too much money is being tied up in current assets rather than invested in noncurrent assets for a higher return.

A limitation of the current ratio is that not all current assets have the same degree of liquidity. For example, accounts receivable is more liquid than inventories of suppliers. Prepaid expenses are not redeemable for cash but rather a prepayment for future benefit (e.g., prepaid advertising).

Current unrestricted assets include cash and cash equivalents (marketable securities), accounts receivable, investment income receivable, inventories of supplies, and prepaid expenses. Current unrestricted liabilities include accounts payable, prepaid services, and the current portion of mortgage payable.

Current Ratio for Unrestricted Current Assets and Current Liabilities =
Current Unrestricted Assets/Current Unrestricted Liabilities

Temporarily restricted assets should also be considered. An example is Pledges Receivable arising from gifts to finance operating activities. However, another type of Pledges Receivable exists, namely unconditional and unrestricted Pledges Receivable. Another temporarily restricted asset is Grants Receivable.

With respect to temporarily restricted net assets, determine when the resources will be available. For example, if temporarily restricted net assets include term endowments and annuities, it may be best to consider them permanently restricted.

Current Ratio for Unrestricted and Temporarily Restricted =
Current Unrestricted Assets + Current Temporarily Restricted Assets for Operations/Current Unrestricted Liabilities

A determination should be made as to the nature of the restrictions on pledges receivable.

Acid-Test (Quick) Ratio.   The quick unrestricted assets are the most liquid assets. Excluded are inventories of supplies and prepaid expenses. The quick unrestricted assets include cash and cash equivalents, accounts receivable, and investment income receivable.

Quick Ratio = Quick Unrestricted Assets/Current Unrestricted Liabilities

A higher ratio is better. It should be at least 1:1.

Accounts Receivable Ratios. Useful ratios are turnover and the collection period.

Accounts Receivable Turnover = Fees for Services on Credit/Average Net Accounts Receivable

Net Accounts Receivable = Accounts Receivable less Allowance for Uncollectible Accounts

The ratio shows the number of times average net accounts receivable turn over relative to fees generated. The more the turnover the better.

Days to Collect on Receivables = 365/Turnover

The ratio indicates the amounts owed the NPO as well as its accounts receivable management success. A lower ratio is better because it takes fewer days to collect on receivables. Cash received earlier can be reinvested for a return. A high ratio is bad because money is being tied up in receivables that could be invested elsewhere. Further, the longer receivables are held the greater is the chance of uncollectibility. Perhaps billing is deficient. Receivables must be kept under control.

In looking at the collection period, consider terms of sale, account profile, service mix, collection policies, and the collection period of comparable NPOs.

An aging of receivable balances should be prepared, broken down by current, past due (0–30 days), past due (31–60 days), past due (61–90 days), and past due (91 days–120 days). The aging listing should be in both alphabetical order and by magnitude of receivable balances outstanding. The older the receivables are, the less the chance of collection. A determination should be made of both time distribution and size distribution. For how many billing periods has a particular account been unpaid?

A determination should be made of what percent receivables are to total assets equal to:

Total Accounts Receivable/Total Assets

A high ratio is a problem, especially if most of the accounts receivable are from a few sources.

Pledges Receivable and Turnover. The turnover ratio for pledges receivable is similar to that of accounts receivable.

Turnover = Net Contributions from Pledges/Average Net Pledges
Receivable

A lower turnover for pledges receivables means a longer collection period.

Collection Period = 365/Turnover

Is the collection period for pledges less than expected? If so, is it because of inadequate collection efforts? Compare to industry averages. Determine the reasonableness of the provision for uncollectible pledges. Analyze pledges receivable in terms of time and size diversification.

The turnover and age of grants receivable should be determined in a similar way.

Inventory. Inventory may have a low turnover because it is too costly, of poor quality, or lacks appeal.

Days in Cash. The ratio equals:

Days = (Cash + Cash Equivalents) x 365/Operating
Expenses – Depreciation

The days' cash is the number of days the NPO can continue in operation if cash inflow stops. It is the number of days of average cash payments the NPO can manage without cash inflow. The more days, the better.

Example 2. An NPO expends $30,000 daily on average in a one-year period. If it has $900,000 of cash and cash equivalents on hand, it has 30 days' cash.

Cash Flow to Total Debt. The ratio equals:

Net Income + Depreciation/Total Liabilities

The ratio indicates how much of internally generated cash is available to pay debt. A higher ratio is better because there is better liquidity, in that cash flow from operations is being generated.

Days Purchases Unpaid. The ratio equals:

Accounts Payable/Daily Purchases

Daily Purchases = (Purchases/360)

The ratio is used to evaluate trade credit. It shows how long (how many days) trade credit remains unpaid.

It the suppliers' payment terms are 30 days and the NPO pays in 90 days on average, it may mean there are liquidity problems.

Current Liability Coverage.   The ratio equals:

Cash + Marketable Securities (unrestricted)/Current Liabilities

The ratio reveals how much of current liabilities can be paid from cash and short-term investments if cash inflows cease.

FINANCIAL FLEXIBILITY

The greater the amount of unrestricted net assets, the greater the amount of financial flexibility. NPOs with huge, permanently restricted endowments and minimal unrestricted net assets may not enjoy much flexibility. Can the NPO respond and adapt to financial adversity and unexpected needs and opportunities? Which resources are available when needed?

ASSET UTILIZATION

Asset utilization applies to the efficiency with which the assets are used in the operating activities of the NPO. For example, a higher ratio of revenue to assets indicates more efficiency of assets in generating profit. What assets are excessive relative to the optimal level?

The efficiency usage of supplies may be determined as follows:

Turnover of Supplies = Annual Total Supplies Expense/Average Total Inventory of Supplies

A low turnover is a negative sign because it means supplies are excessive and not being used efficiently.

The available days of supplies use equals 360/Turnover. What is the rate of supplies usage? How fast would the current usage level deplete supplies inventory?

Average Daily Total Supplies Expense equals:

Annual Total Supplies Expense/Average Number of Days of Supplies' Use

The ratio shows how often supplies are used, such as in a particular program.

ANALYSIS OF
FIXED ASSETS

In the long run, buying assets is cheaper than renting. The NPO also has more control by buying because it doesn't have to concern itself with lessors unexpectedly raising rental rates or demanding certain prohibitions on using the property.

The average accounting age of equipment (e.g., computers) may be determined as follows:

Accumulated Depreciation/Depreciation Expense

The ratio reveals how old the equipment is. It shows the rate at which equipment is being used and replaced. A lower ratio is better.

The ratio is of particular interest to hospitals because it must buy expensive, up-to-date technological medical equipment and keep facilities in good working order for the best patient care.

A low depreciation charge may indicate the NPO is making significant use of rentals.

Does a reduction in fixed assets mean there is less capacity and utilization?

ANALYSIS OF
LIABILITIES

Short-term borrowing may be used to fill the gap resulting from the temporary shortfall in contributions or other sources of cash inflow.

If long-term debt is used to finance fixed assets, the NPO has greater financial leverage risk. The NPO must be able to pay principal and interest.

Analyze the long-term indebtedness of the NPO, including:

- Interest rate being charged.
- Excessiveness of debt.
- Reason for borrowings. How is the money to be used?
- Maturity dates of debt. Are debt payments staggered? Can the debt be repaid?
- Lines of credit.
- Loan restrictions such as collateral requirements. Are such restrictions tying the hands of the manager?
- Understated liabilities such as the liability for severance payments or for earned but unused vacation time.

APPRAISAL OF SOLVENCY, CAPITAL STRUCTURE, AND FUND BALANCE

A healthy capital structure will help assure the NPO's ability to engage in its daily activities. High leverage (debt to fund balance) means risk. The debt ratio will increase if the NPO must finance fixed asset expansion with borrowed funds.

The ratio of long-term debt to total unrestricted fund balance reveals the NPO's long-term credit commitments to its ability to pay the debt. It relates borrowed funds to owned funds. A ratio over 1 may indicate a problem in handling additional debt. Can the NPO pay existing interest and principal payments?

Analysis of the fund balance depends on the facts and circumstances. A surplus indicates better financial health than a deficit. An increasing trend in the surplus is a favorable sign. Surpluses provide savings for financing the future and the ability to pay off debt.

EVALUATION OF THE STATEMENT OF ACTIVITIES

An NPO should communicate to the users of the financial statements which specific revenues and expenses are included in the operating measure. If the NPO's use of the term *operating* is not clear from the details on the face of the statement, FASB 117 requires a footnote describing the nature of the measure of operating performance. The financial analyst should carefully review the NPO's definition of the operating measure. A comparison should be made with similar NPOs and the definition should be consistently applied. Generally, the operating income measure is a subtotal in arriving at the net change in unrestricted net assets.

In analyzing the Statement of Activities, determine:

- Whether the entity is self-sustaining and operating well.
- If service efforts are being successful.
- Whether management has discharged its stewardship responsibilities.

In the long run, if an NPO does not spend all of its revenues, it is not funding as much service as possible to the public. On the other hand, if it keeps spending more than its revenues, it will go bankrupt.

In analyzing an NPO, consider "operating capital maintenance," which means whether the NPO is maintaining its capital by having its revenues at least equal to its expenses. Why did a surplus or deficit occur?

An NPO should not report a profit consistently each year. If it always shows a profit, the NPO may not be accomplishing its objective of providing as much service as possible with available resources. It should either provide more service and thereby increase its costs, or reduce prices it charges for services. The objective of an NPO's financial policy should be to break-even.

An NPO (such as a membership organization) may have a policy of having an operating excess one year but a deficit in another year, which balances out. For example, member dues may be increased only once each three years. In the year of the dues increase, an operating surplus may arise. In the second year, there may be a break-even, and in the third year a deficit may exist. Dues are then increased again.

In a similar vein, an NPO may want an operating excess in one year to eliminate a deficit from the previous year.

An operating surplus may also be desired to have adequate funding for expansion, to subsidize programs, or as a result of a lawsuit. A surplus may be desired as a contingency for unexpected problems, and to replace assets.

An NPO may want to operate at a deficit in one year to reduce an accumulated surplus or to meet a special need.

In conclusion, an NPO does not have to break even each year. It may have a surplus in one year(s) and a deficit in another year(s) to meet its unique circumstances, as long as it balances out over a number of years.

REVENUE

The revenue base should be diversified to reduce risk. For example, overdependence on one revenue source may be dangerous (e.g., grants).

A decline in revenue may indicate ineffectiveness. For example, a decline in college tuition may mean problems in attracting students at a college. How does actual revenue compare to expected revenue?

Total revenue needed daily on average equals:

Total Revenue (prior year)/365

COSTS

Expenses should be analyzed in terms of program and object of expense. Variances between actual and budgeted expenses should be investigated.

Determine the reason for a sizable increase or decrease in an expense. For example, a significant increase to a specific expense may not be due to a change in organizational plan but may reflect contributed services instead.

A determination should be made of the cost per unit of service. A lower rate means better cost containment. When costs need to be reduced, the first things to cut are lower-priority programs least accomplishing the NPO's goals. However, consider how changes in program activities would affect donor contributions and volunteer support. Identify controllable and uncontrollable costs. Ask these questions:

- Can costs be reduced by replacing obsolete and/or inactive equipment?
- Can costs be reduced by improved technology?
- Will an improved repairs and maintenance program lower costs?
- Can staff improvements be made to lower costs?
- Can energy costs be reduced thorough improved traffic management?
- Can productivity be improved?

Ratios include:

Operating Expenses/Total Revenue

A lower ratio indicates better cost control.

Fund-Raising Costs/Total Donations

The ratio evaluates the effectiveness of fund-raising efforts. Is fund-raising cost excessive for funds obtained?

The Statement of Functional Expenses is required of voluntary and health organizations. The Statement is helpful to the financial analyst because it provides a detailed breakdown of expenses by program. It is analogous to segment reporting in business enterprises.

PROFITABILITY

Profitability is needed for NPOs that are trying to expand or enter new areas, that are unstable, and that are ever-changing. Profitability measures include:

Profit Margin = (Revenue – Expenses)/Revenue

A higher ratio shows better operational performance (profit).

Operating Margin = (Operating Revenue – Operating Expenses)/Operating Revenue

Operating revenue excludes nonoperating sources such as fund-raising revenue, dividends, and extraordinary items. The operating profit is derived solely from operating activities without having to rely on contributors. A higher ratio is better.

Return on Fund Balance (Net Assets) =
(Total Revenue – Total Expenses)/Average Net Assets

The ratio shows how efficiently the fund balance has created the year's profit.

Ratios of investment performance include:

Interest and/or Dividend Income/Investments at Cost

Interest and/or Dividend Income/Investments at Market Value

Higher ratios indicate better returns on investments.

DISCLOSURES

In examining footnote disclosures, identify contingencies, including positive and negative developments affecting the NPO. Disclosure of possible future funding problems is a "red light." An example is changing political policies directed toward reducing government funding.

A lawsuit against the NPO is a negative sign, particularly if it is reasonable possible that the NPO will lose.

PERFORMANCE METRICS

We have to examine the quality of the services and programs offered by the NPO, beside just looking at dollars. The NPO's objective is to render an amount and quality of services. For example, measures of performance (or metrics) for a college include number of courses and ratio of faculty to students. Some general performance measures to keep in mind include:

- Capital per unit of service.
- Number of patients treated daily by a doctor.
- Number of welfare cases handled by a social worker.
- Input/output relationships such as what was the cost and time of performing a service and what was the quality and quantity of service provided.
- Number of complaints.

How do you figure out who does the most with the contributions and who spends inordinate sums, however well intentioned, on raising the money and excessive overhead? Several indexes would be helpful to answer those questions: charity commitment, fund-raising efficiency, and donor dependency.

Charity Commitment

Charity commitment percentage =

$$\frac{\text{Charitable expense (program support or program service expense)}}{\text{Total expenses}}$$

Essentially, the resulting figure excludes such overhead as management and fund-raising.

Fund-Raising Efficiency

This measures how much of the money raised from private sources remains after accounting for fund-raising. This is computed by taking the total funds raised from the public through direct contributions, indirect contributions (such as from United Way), and proceeds from one-time special events, subtracting fund-raising costs, then expressing the result as a percentage of the total amount from the public (private support).

Donor Dependency

This index tries to measure how badly a charity needs your contribution— as opposed to money raised from selling products or tickets or reaping in-

Table 1 Charitable Commitment, Fund-Raising Efficiency, and Donor Dependency

Alzheimer's Disease & Related Disorders Association
(Alzheimer's disease research) Chicago IL (**www.alz.org**)

FY ending 6/30/98
All figures in $mil except where otherwise noted

Private support	Gvt support	Total support	Other income	Total revenue
97	0	97	17	114

	Program service expenses	Mgmt & gen'l	Fund-raising	Total expenses
	84	9	16	109

Surplus (Loss)	Net Assets	Charitable commitment[1]	Fund-raising efficiency[2]	Donor dependency[3]
5		77.1%	83.5%	94.8%

[1] 77.1% = 84/109

[2] 83.5% = (97 – 16)/97

[3] 94.8% = (97 – 5)/97

SOURCES: IRS Form 990; annual reports, statements of individual charities; **www.guidestar.org**.

vestment gains—to fund its current operations. We figure this by subtracting a charity's annual surplus (excess of revenue over expenses) from public donations (private support), then dividing this figure by the public donations (private support). A percentage at or above 100% means that the nonprofit is totally dependent on donations and is not salting away funds for a rainy day. A *negative* index number means surpluses exceeding all donations for the reporting year.

Table 1 presents these indexes for a selected charity organization

FUND-RAISING ABILITY

Creditors evaluate the NPO's fund-raising ability as a major source of debt repayment for non-revenue-generating projects. Donated funds are important to consider when appraising the NPO's creditworthiness. Refunding is issuing new debt to replace existing debt and may occur if (1) market interest rates have decreased, (2) excessive restrictions exist in current debt, or (3) there is a desire to lengthen debt maturity.

ANALYSIS OF PLEDGES

In appraising pledges, consider:

- Are pledges decreasing among a particular category of donors or all donors?
- Does poor economic activity result in fewer pledges?
- Have new tax laws made gift giving less advisable?
- Do donors feel the objectives of the NPO no longer match with their views?

Creditors may not assign a value to pledges receivable when analyzing the NPO because donors are not legally bound to honor their dollar pledge or time promised. For example, if the donor goes bankrupt, although unlikely, the promise will not be kept. The donor may change his or her mind in giving because of a change in circumstances. However, the creditor should examine who the donors are, their past history of giving, their current financial status, and their reliability. If the donor's profile indicates a high probability of giving the amount promised, creditors will give loans based on security or the pledges receivable. For example, pledges may be used to secure debt service or construction loans.

The analyst considers pledges due within one year of higher quality than pledges due in five years. Thus, the shorter the time period associated with the pledge, the less risk involved.

ANALYSIS OF CONTRIBUTIONS

A potential cash problem is indicated when actual contributions significantly fall short of expectations. Restricted contributions are unavailable for operating purposes and to pay short-term debt. How much funds are available and when? What are the restrictions (e.g., scholarship fund, building fund)? Are the restrictions very specific or excessive? It is better to have a higher ratio of unrestricted contributions to total contributions, because unrestricted contributions are available to be used by the NPO in its regular activities. Restricted contributions do little to improve the NPO's liquidity unless the terms of the donor allow for the transfer of funds for operating purposes.

NPOs with substantial contributed services need special attention. The footnote on contributed services should be closely read because it describes the program or activities that use volunteer services, the nature and extent of contributed services in monetary and nonmonetary terms, and the amount of contributed services recognized as revenue for the year.

LOOKING AT ENDOWMENTS

An endowment represents long-term investments. Investment income from the endowment may be unrestricted and available to finance operating activities, or restricted as to use. Donors want financial feedback as to whether the NPO has expended resources received, if expenditures are in accord with promises made, if services and activities provided are of high quality, and the remaining balance of resources. Constraints and commitments made to donors regarding fund use are disclosed in the financial statements, including status thereto. Are legal requirements being met?

A decrease in endowments is a negative sign because it may indicate less interest in or dissatisfaction with the NPO. However, poor economic conditions may be the reason.

Answer these questions about the portfolio in which endowment funds are invested:

- How much fluctuation exists in the securities portfolio?
- Is diversification of the portfolio adequate?
- Are the securities negatively or positively correlated?

Total return on endowment investments may be estimated by computing it as a percentage of the average balance of endowment investments.

Example 3. The return on an endowment portfolio is $60,000. The beginning and ending balances are $1,000,000 and $1,200,000, respectively.

$$\text{Return Rate} = \frac{\text{Return}}{\text{Average Balance}} = \frac{\$60,000}{\$1,100,000} = 5.5\%$$

A lower return rate is a negative sign.

The return on the endowment investment should be higher as the risk of the investment increases.

EVALUATION OF GRANTS

In analyzing grants, answer the following questions:

- Has there been a sufficient attempt to obtain public and private grants?
- Was reference made to suitable sources such as the Foundation Directory?
- Do the Foundation's objectives match the grant proposal?
- Are matching funds required to receive the grant?
- Was the proposal completely done (e.g., detailed information, clear discussion of how funds will be used)?
- Were due date filings met?

RISK/RETURN ANALYSIS

Is the return sufficient to justify the risk? The greater the risk, the greater should be the return. Risk means the probability of an activity accomplishing its objective. For example, there may be a high degree of risk associated with a new specialized academic program in a university or a new medical procedure at a hospital. There is always risk in allocating human and financial resources to new programs.

Ways to control or reduce risk include:

- Use agents and representatives including volunteers.
- Carry adequate insurance protection. For example, insurance should be sufficient relative to the value of the insured property.
- Carefully hire qualified staff to avoid damages and injuries to others.
- Have written policies and communicate them carefully through the organization.

Avoiding Financial Distress: Key Financial Ratios and Metrics for Nonprofits

- Have proper supervision over new hires.
- Have protective provisions in contracts to limit the NPO's liability for contractor malfeasance.
- Have proper security over assets to guard against theft or destruction.
- Diversify operations.
- Avoid dealings with selected groups that may result in legal liability problems, such as dealing with young children or dealing with hazardous items.

AUDIT RELIABILITY

Many state and local governments require audits to be conducted of NPOs. Have the NPO's financial statements been subject to an audit, review, or compilation? A big difference exists between these processes in terms of the reliability of the NPO's financial statements. The highest level of reliability and testing is in an audit. In a review, no testing exists but a determination is made of whether the financial statements make sense. A compilation, the least reliable, involves just collecting and reformatting financial records.

In looking at the audit opinion, an "except for" qualification or a disclaimer may indicate a problem. An unqualified opinion is best.

SOFTWARE

Software exists for analyzing NPOs. For example, The Functional Cost Analysis Program develops credit union income and cost information along functional lines and gives comparisons of data among credit unions and banks.

SPOTTING POTENTIAL BANKRUPTCY AND AVOIDING FINANCIAL PROBLEMS

A negative fund balance (total liabilities exceed total assets) indicates a worrisome deficit position that is an indicator of potential bankruptcy. Cash forecasts showing expected cash outflows that exceed expected cash inflows may point to financial distress. If cash is a problem, timely steps may be needed to improve cash flow and solve problems. How long will the current cash position last if all cash inflows were to cease?

A balanced budget, using conservative revenue estimates, is one way to avoid financial ruin. A balanced budget requires difficult choices, such as curtailment or elimination of certain services or programs.

Answer the following questions in gauging the probability of potential failure:

- Is there adequate insurance?
- Does excessive legal exposure exist? What is the nature of pending lawsuits? Is the NPO abreast of all current laws and regulations affecting it?
- What government adjustments are expected regarding rate charges and reimbursements?
- Is there inadequate control over expenditures?
- Is there deferred maintenance, which can no longer be postponed?
- Are loan restrictions excessive?
- What effect will contractual violations have?
- Are costs skyrocketing? Why?
- Are bills past due?
- Is debt excessive?
- Are debt repayment schedules staggered?
- Should maturity dates be extended?
- Is the public or government criticizing the NPO?
- Is there a decreasing trend in donor interest?
- To what extent are donor contributions restricted? Restricted donations cannot be used to pay current expenses unless the restriction is satisfied or lifted.
- Is there less community interest in the NPO (e.g., fewer members, patients)?
- Are fewer volunteers available?
- Are more grant applications being rejected?
- Is there a cash shortage?
- Is the NPO anticipating future trends (e.g., social, political, technological)?
- Does the NPO have sufficient expertise in the areas it is involved in?
- Is there a buildup in assets (e.g., receivables)?
- Is a hedging approach used to finance assets by matching them against the maturity dates of liabilities?
- Are long-term fixed-fee contracts hurting the NPO?
- Is there a sharp increase in the number of employees per unit of service?
- Are there open lines of credit?
- Does a lack of communication exist?

Avoiding Financial Distress: Key Financial Ratios and Metrics for Nonprofits

Ways to avoid financial problems include:

- Merge with another financially stronger, similar NPO. Will a merger aid in financing, lower overall operating costs, increase synergy and efficiency, and promote program expansion?
- Restructure the organization.
- Sell off unproductive assets.
- Defer paying bills.
- Discard programs and activities no longer financially viable.
- Implement a cost reduction program including layoffs and attrition. Will this eliminate programs that will be hard to start up again? Are we getting rid of scarce talents? These are referred to as irreversible reductions, which in the long run may not be wise.
- Increase service fees.
- Increase fund-raising efforts and contributions.
- Apply for grants.
- Stimulate contracts.

Example 4. A nonprofit organization provides the following financial information:

Summary of Income, Expenses, and Cash Balances

	20X1	20X2	Percentage Change
Income			
Membership and program fees	$125,000	$130,000	4%
Contributions	126,000	130,000	3
Other	13,000	35,000	169
Total income	$254,000	$295,000	12
Expenses			
Salaries	$100,000	160,000	60
Rent	40,000	70,000	43
Insurance	10,000	20,000	100
Supplies	20,000	40,000	100
Total expenses	$170,000	$290,000	71
Excess of income over expenses	94,000	$5,000	95
Cash balance, beginning of year	50,000	144,000	
Cash balance, end of year	$144,000	$149,000	

From 20X1 to 20X2, total expenses have increased 71% while total revenue has increased only 12%. This is a very negative sign. It may mean the failure to control costs, declining fees for services possibly due to membership dissatisfaction, etc. Why have contributions only increased by 3%. Are donors upset with the NPO's policies, objectives, or management?

It is particularly alarming that profitability has declined by a stunning 95%. The sharp increase in each expense category must be closely scrutinized for cause and corrective action immediately taken. Unless something is done to correct this unfavorable trend, the NPO is in serious trouble!

CASE STUDY IN FINANCIAL STATEMENT ANALYSIS: FAMILY SERVICE AGENCY OF UTOPIA

This case study is based on a sample NPO provided by the Internal Revenue Service in Form 990. The sample completed tax return as prepared by the IRS for illustrative purposes is also presented.

Trend Analysis (All line references are to Form 990)

	12/31/93	12/31/94	Percent change
Total Cash (Lines 45 and 46)	$248,700	$228,500	–8.1%
Pledges Receivable (Line 48c)	$46,000	$58,900	28.0%
Grants Receivable (Line 49)	$4,600	$5,800	26.1%
Inventories (Line 52)	$6,100	$7,000	14.8%
Fixed Assets (Line 57c)	$168,500	$174,800	3.7%
Total Assets (Line 59)	$916,000	$964,800	5.3%
Total Liabilities (Line 66)	$111,200	$112,300	1.0%
Current Unrestricted Fund (Line 67a)	$446,300	$485,100	8.7%
Current Restricted Fund (Line 67b)	$10,000	$6,400	–36.0%
Land, Buildings, and Equipment (Line 68)	$156,800	$116,200	–25.9%
Endowment Fund (Line 69)	$191,700	$194,800	1.6%
Total Fund Balances (Net Assets) (Line 74)	$804,800	$852,500	5.9%

	For the Year Ended		Percent change
	1993	1994	
Contributions, Gifts, and Similar Amounts (1994 from Line 1: 1993 from Schedule A, Line 15)	$742,300	$710,800	–4.2%
Membership Dues (1994 from Line 3; 1993 from Schedule A, Line 16)	$1,100	$1,600	45.5%

An analysis of the trends from 1993 to 1994 reveals the following:

- The cash position declined, having a negative affect on liquidity.
- Pledges and grants receivable have both significantly increased, reflecting success in obtaining pledges and grants to the NPO, which is a favorable sign. However, it may be that there is a problem in collecting the pledges and grants due to higher receivable balances.
- The build-up in inventories may mean greater realization risk.
- Fixed assets were fairly constant.
- The increase in total assets is a favorable indicator.
- Total liabilities were about the same.
- While the balance in current unrestricted funds increased, a favorable sign, there was a decline in the current restricted fund. However, the dollar amount of the decline is small even though it's a higher percentage.
- More funds are available for fixed asset expansion.
- The NPO has been successful in generating more endowment funds.
- The increase in total fund balances (net assets) of about 6% is a positive sign.
- Contributions, gifts, grants, and similar items decreased about 5%. The reasons for the decrease should be determined. Is there less interest in the NPO among donors? If so, why?
- The membership revenue almost doubled, reflecting greater interest in the NPO's policies as indicated by more enrollments or an increase in per-member fees. Perhaps there was a successful membership drive.

LIQUIDITY ANALYSIS

$$\frac{\text{Total Current Assets (Balance Sheet (BS)—12/31/94)}}{\text{Total Assets (BS)}} = \frac{\$315,600}{\$964,800} = .33$$

Each $1 of total assets is comprised of $.33 of current assets.

$$\text{Current Ratio} = \frac{\text{Current Assets (BS)}}{\text{Current Liabilities (BS)}} = \frac{\$315,600}{\$98,900} = 3.2$$

The high ratio means good liquidity.

Current Ratio for Unrestricted Current Assets
and Current Unrestricted Liabilities =

$$\frac{\text{Current Unrestricted Assets (BS)}}{\text{Current Unrestricted Liabilities (BS)}} = \frac{\$304,400}{\$98,900} = 3.1$$

The high ratio further indicates good liquidity.

$$\text{Quick Ratio} = \frac{\text{Quick Unrestricted Current Assets* (BS)}}{\text{Current Unrestricted Liabilities (BS)}}$$

$$= \frac{\$283,600}{\$98,900} = 2.87$$

Because the quick ratio (2.87) exceeds the norm of 1.0, good liquidity is evident.

Accounts Receivable Turnover =

$$\frac{\text{Program Service Revenue (Form 990, Line 2)}}{\text{Average Net Accounts Receivable (Form 990, Line 47c)}} = \frac{\$2,600}{\$1,700} = 1.5$$

Receivables turn over 1.5 times per year relative to fees generated. The low turnover rate indicates less liquidity. Perhaps there is risk in collecting.

$$\text{Days to Collect on Receivables} = \frac{365}{\text{Turnover}} = \frac{365}{1.5} = 243 \text{ days}$$

It takes 243 days to collect on receivables, indicating a possible collection problem.

$$\frac{\text{Total Accounts Receivable (Form 990, Line 47c)}}{\text{Total Assets (Form 990, Line 59)}} = \frac{\$1,600}{\$964,800} = .2\%$$

---

*Quick Unrestricted Current Assets = Total Current Assets – Inventories – Prepaid Expenses
= $304,400 – $7,000 – $13,800 = $283,600

Avoiding Financial Distress: Key Financial Ratios and Metrics for Nonprofits

The very low ratio means receivables are insignificant relative to total assets.

Pledges Turnover =

Net Contributions from Pledges (From Statement of Revenue, Expenses, and Changes in Fund Balance (SRECF)

Average Net Pledges Receivable (Form 990, Line 48c)

$$= \frac{\$473,700}{\$52,450} = 9 \text{ times}$$

The high turnover rate means faster collection on pledges, which is a favorable liquidity indicator.

$$\text{Collection Period on Pledges} = \frac{365}{\text{Turnover}} = \frac{365}{9} = 40.6 \text{ days}$$

It takes about 41 days to collect on pledges. This is favorable.

$$\text{Cash Flow to Total Debt} = \frac{\text{Net Income} + \text{Depreciation}}{\text{Total Liabilities}}$$

$$= \frac{\text{Form 990, Line 18} + \text{Line 42}}{\text{Form 990, Line 66}}$$

$$= \frac{\$47,700 + \$5,200}{\$112,300} = .47$$

This computation indicates that $.47 of internally generated cash is available to pay $1 of debt.

Current Liability Coverage =

$$\frac{\text{Cash} + \text{Marketable Securities (Unrestricted) (BS)}}{\text{Total Current Liabilities (BS)}} = \frac{\$221,100}{\$98,900} = 2.2$$

For each $1 in current liabilities, there is $2.20 of cash and short-term investments available to pay it.

$$\frac{\text{Total Current Liabilities (BS)}}{\text{Total Liabilities (BS)}} = \frac{\$98,900}{\$112,300} = .88$$

Current debt is a high proportion of total liabilities. This is an unfavorable liquidity indicator.

ANALYSIS OF SOLVENCY

$$\frac{\text{Total Assets (Form 990, Line 59)}}{\text{Total Liabilities (Form 990, Line 66)}} = \frac{\$964,800}{\$112,300} = 8.6$$

There are $8.60 in assets for each $1 in liabilities, indicating a good solvency position.

$$\frac{\text{Total Liabilities (Form 990, Line 66)}}{\text{Total Fund Balance (Net Assets) (Form 990, Line 74)}} = \frac{\$112,300}{\$852,500} = .13$$

The low ratio of debt to fund balance is a favorable indicator of the ability of the NPO to meet its obligations. It indicates less risk.

$$\frac{\text{Long-term Debt (BS)}}{\text{Total Unrestricted Fund Balance (BS)}} = \frac{\$13,400}{\$485,100} = 2.8\%$$

This ratio is a further indication of a solid solvency position. The NPO is able to fulfill its long-term debt commitments.

ANALYSIS OF THE STATEMENT OF ACTIVITIES

$$\text{Daily Revenue (2000)} = \frac{\text{Total Revenue for Current Year}}{365}$$

$$= \frac{\text{Form 990, Line 12}}{365} = \frac{\$760,300}{365} = \$2,083$$

$$\text{Daily Revenue (1999)} = \frac{\text{Total Revenue for Prior Year}}{365}$$

$$= \frac{\text{Form 990, Schedule A, Line 23}}{365} = \frac{\$800,600}{365} = \$2,193$$

The declining revenue per day from 1999 to 2000 is a negative sign for operating performance.

$$\frac{\text{Total Expenses (Form 990, Line 17)}}{\text{Total Revenue (Form 990, Line 12)}} = \frac{\$712,600}{\$760,300} = 93.7\%$$

Total expenses are a high percentage of total revenue, cutting into surplus.

$$\frac{\text{Fund-raising Costs (Form 990, Line 15)}}{\text{Total Donations (SRECF)}} = \frac{\$65,400}{\$473,700} = 13.8\%$$

Fund-raising costs as a percentage of contributions are reasonable, indicating an effective fund-raising campaign.

$$\text{Profit Margin} = \frac{\text{Excess of Revenue over Expenses}}{\text{Total Revenue}}$$

$$\frac{\text{Form 990, Line 18}}{\text{Form 990, Line 12}} = \frac{\$47,700}{\$760,300} = 6.3\%$$

The profit margin should be compared to other similar NPOs. If it is lower, it indicates less operational performance.

$$\text{Return on Fund Balance (Net Assets)} =$$

$$\frac{\text{Excess of Revenue over Expenses (Form 990, Line 18)}}{\text{Average Net Assets (Form 990, Line 59)}} = \frac{\$47,700}{\$940,400} = 5.1\%$$

This ratio reflects reasonable efficiency of the fund balance in generating yearly surplus for the year.

$$\text{Dividends and Interest from Securities} = \frac{\text{Form 990, Line 5}}{\text{Investments Form 990, Line 54}}$$

$$= \frac{\$16,400}{\$474,400} = 3.5\%$$

The rate of return earned on the investment portfolio is low.

$$\text{Return Rate on Endowment Funds} =$$

$$\frac{\text{Total Revenue on Endowment Fund}}{\text{Total Assets in Endowment Fund}} = \frac{\text{SRECF}}{\text{BS}} = \frac{\$3,100}{\$194,800} = 1.6\%$$

The return rate on endowment funds is very low.

Table 2 summarizes financial statement analysis covered throughout the chapter.

Table 2 Financial Ratio Analysis

	12/31/93	12/31/94
Assets		
Total Cash (Lines 45 and 46)	$248,700	$228,500
Accounts Receivable (Line 47c)	$1,800	$1,600
Pledges Receivable (Line 48c)	$46,000	$58,900
Grants Receivable (Line 49)	$4,600	$5,800
Other Receivables (Line 50)	$-	$-
Other Notes and Loans Receivable (Line 51c)	$-	$-
Inventories (Line 52)	$6,100	$7,000
Prepaid Expenses and Deferred Charges (Line 53)	$9,600	$13,800
Total Current Assets (Line 45 through 53)	$316,800	$315,600
Investments—Securities (Line 54)	$430,700	$474,400
Investments—Land, Buildings (Line 55c)	$-	$-
Fixed Assets (Line 57c)	$168,500	$174,800
Other Fixed Assets (Line 58)	$-	$-
Total Assets (Line 59)	$916,000	$964,800
Liabilities		
Accounts Payable and Accrued Expenses (Line 60)	$46,000	$39,300
Grants Payable (Line 61)	$-	$-
Support and Revenue Designed for Future Periods (Line 62)	$61,600	$59,600
Loans from Officers (Line 63)	$-	$-
Total Current Liabilities (Line 60 through Line 63)	$107,600	$98,900
Tax-exempt Bond (Line 64a)	$-	$-
Mortgages (Line 64b)	$3,600	$3,200
Other Liabilities (Line 65)	$-	$10,200
Total Liabilities (Line 66)	$111,200	$112,300
Fund Balances or Net Assets		
Current Unrestricted Fund (Line 67a)	$446,300	$485,100
Current Restricted Fund (Line 67b)	$10,000	$6,400
Land, Buildings, and Equipment (Line 68)	$156,800	$166,200
Endowment Fund (Line 69)	$191,700	$194,800
Other Funds (Line 70)	$-	$-
Capital Stock (Line 71)		

Continued

Table 2 *Continued*

Fund Balances or Net Assets (cont.)
Paid-In Capital (Line 72)
Retained Earnings (Line 73) $- $-
Total Fund Balances (Net Assets)
  (Line 74) $804,800 $852,500
Total Liabilities and Fund Balances
(Line 75 = Line 66 + Line 74) $916,000 $964,800

	For the Year Ended	
	1993	1994
Program Service Revenue (Line 2)		$2,600
Dividends and Interest from Securities (Line 5)		$16,400
Total Revenue (Line 12 and Line 23, Schedule A)	$800,600	$760,300
Fund-Raising Costs (Line 15)		$65,400
Total Expenses (Line 17)		$712,600
Excess or (Deficit) (Line 18)		$47,700
Depreciation (Line 42)		$5,200

Liquidity Analysis
(1) Total Current Assets/Total Assets   0.33
(2) Current Ratio = Current Assets/Current Liabilities   3.2
(3) *Accounts Receivable Turnover =*
     Program Service Revenue/Accounts Receivable   1.5
(4) *Days to Collect on Receivables =*
     365 days/Accounts Receivable Turnover   239
(5) *Total Accounts Receivable/Total Assets*   0.2%
(6) *Cash Flow to Total Debt*
     = (Net Income + Depreciation)/Total Liabilities   0.47
(7) Total Current Liabilities/Total Liabilities   0.88

Analysis of Solvency
(8) Total Assets/Total Liabilities   8.6
(9) Total Liabilities/Total Fund Balance (Net Assets)   0.13
(10) Long-Term Debt/Total Unrestricted Fund Balance   2.8%

Analysis of the Statement of Activities
(11) *Daily Revenue* = Total Revenue/365 days   2193   2083
(12) Total Expenses/Total Revenue   93.7%
(13) *Profit Margin =*
     Excess of Revenue over Expenses/Total Revenue   6.3%
(14) *Return on Fund Balances =*
     Excess of Revenue over Expenses/Net Assets   5.1%
(15) Dividends and Interest from Securities/Investments   3.5%

CONCLUSION

The NPO's liquidity is favorable, meaning it is able to pay its short-term obligations. Its solvency is also favorable, meaning it can satisfy its long-term debt when due. The NPO is having difficulty in its operating performance as indicated by declining daily revenue, high expenses to revenue, and low investment return. However, fund-raising costs are being controlled, resulting in successful fund-raising efforts. Profit margin and return on fund balance appear reasonable. There is more interest in the NPO as indicated by the increasing membership base.

OMB No. 1545-0047

Form 990

Return of Organization Exempt From Income Tax

Under section 501(c) of the Internal Revenue Code (except black lung benefit trust or private foundation) or section 4947(a)(1) nonexempt charitable trust

Note: *The organization may have to use a copy of this return to satisfy state reporting requirements.*

1994

This Form is Open to Public Inspection

Department of the Treasury
Internal Revenue Service

A For the 1994 calendar year, OR tax year period beginning _____, 1994, and ending _____, 19___

B Check if:
- ☐ Change of address
- ☐ Initial return
- ☐ Final return
- ☐ Amended return (required also for State reporting)

Please use IRS label or print or type. See Specific Instructions.

C Name of organization
Family Service Agency of Utopia, Inc.

Number and street (or P.O. box if mail is not delivered to street address) Room/suite
1414 West Ash Drive

City, town, or post office, state, and ZIP code
Utopia, PA 11111

D Employer identification number
12 3456789

E State registration number
567890

F Check ▶ ☐ if exemption application is pending

G Type of organization—▶ ☒ Exempt under section 501(c)(**3**) ◀ (insert number) OR ▶ ☐ section 4947(a)(1) nonexempt charitable trust

Note: *Section 501(c)(3) exempt organizations and 4947(a)(1) nonexempt charitable trusts MUST attach a completed Schedule A (Form 990).*

H(a) Is this a group return filed for affiliates? . . . . . . ☐ Yes ☒ No

(b) If "Yes," enter the number of affiliates for which this return is filed:. ▶ _____

(c) Is this a separate return filed by an organization covered by a group ruling? ☐ Yes ☒ No

I If either box in H is checked "Yes," enter four-digit group exemption number (GEN) ▶ ....

J Accounting method: ☐ Cash ☒ Accrual
☐ Other (specify) ▶

K Check here ▶ ☐ if the organization's gross receipts are normally not more than $25,000. The organization need not file a return with the IRS; but if it received a Form 990 Package in the mail, it should file a return without financial data. Some states require a complete return.

Note: *Form 990-EZ may be used by organizations with gross receipts less than $100,000 and total assets less than $250,000 at end of year.*

Part I   Statement of Revenue, Expenses, and Changes in Net Assets or Fund Balances

1	Contributions, gifts, grants, and similar amounts received:			
a	Direct public support	1a	$483,300	
b	Indirect public support	1b	227,500	
c	Government contributions (grants)	1c		
d	Total (add lines 1a through 1c) (attach schedule—see instructions) (cash $ 710,800 noncash $ _____) . . .	1d		$710,800
2	Program service revenue including government fees and contracts (from Part VII, line 93)	2		2,600
3	Membership dues and assessments (see instructions)	3		1,600
4	Interest on savings and temporary cash investments	4		14,800
5	Dividends and interest from securities	5		16,400
6a	Gross rents	6a		
b	Less: rental expenses	6b		
c	Net rental income or (loss) (subtract line 6b from line 6a) . . .	6c		
7	Other investment income (describe ▶)	7		
8a	Gross amount from sale of assets other than inventory . . . . . . (A) Securities 24,200 / (B) Other 8a	8a		
b	Less: cost or other basis and sales expenses. 23,700	8b		
c	Gain or (loss) (attach schedule) 500	8c		
d	Net gain or (loss) (combine line 8c, columns (A) and (B)) . . .	8d		500
9	Special events and activities (attach schedule—see instructions):			
a	Gross revenue (not including $ -0- of contributions reported on line 1a) . . .	9a	28,400	
b	Less: direct expenses other than fundraising expenses	9b	18,000	
c	Net income or (loss) from special events (subtract line 9b from line 9a) . . .	9c		10,400
10a	Gross sales of inventory, less returns and allowances . .	10a	1,400	
b	Less: cost of goods sold	10b	1,000	
c	Gross profit or (loss) from sales of inventory (attach schedule) (subtract line 10b from line 10a) .	10c		400
11	Other revenue (from Part VII, line 103)	11		2,800
12	Total revenue (add lines 1d, 2, 3, 4, 5, 6c, 7, 8d, 9c, 10c, and 11)	12		$760,300
13	Program services (from line 44, column (B)—see instructions)	13		$577,400
14	Management and general (from line 44, column (C)—see instructions)	14		57,400
15	Fundraising (from line 44, column (D)—see instructions)	15		65,400
16	Payments to affiliates (attach schedule—see instructions)	16		12,400
17	Total expenses (add lines 16 and 44, column (A))	17		$712,600
18	Excess or (deficit) for the year (subtract line 17 from line 12) . . .	18		$ 47,700
19	Net assets or fund balances at beginning of year (from line 74, column (A)) . . .	19		804,800
20	Other changes in net assets or fund balances (attach explanation) . . .	20		-0-
21	Net assets or fund balances at end of year (combine lines 18, 19, and 20)	21		$852,500

For Paperwork Reduction Act Notice, see page 1 of the separate instructions.   Cat. No. 11282Y   Form **990** (1994)

Part II Statement of Functional Expenses All organizations must complete column (A). Columns (B), (C), and (D) are required for section 501(c)(3) and (4) organizations and section 4947(a)(1) nonexempt charitable trusts but optional for others. (See instructions.)

Do not include amounts reported on line 6b, 8b, 9b, 10b, or 16 of Part I.		(A) Total	(B) Program services	(C) Management and general	(D) Fundraising
22 Grants and allocations (attach schedule) . (cash $ 35,900 noncash $)	22	$ 35,900	$ 35,900		
23 Specific assistance to individuals (attach schedule)	23	45,800	45,800		
24 Benefits paid to or for members (attach schedule)	24				
25 Compensation of officers, directors, etc. . .	25	62,800	46,600	$ 8,800	$ 7,400
26 Other salaries and wages	26	184,700	131,000	24,300	29,400
27 Pension plan contributions	27	300	200	100	
28 Other employee benefits	28	13,000	9,400	2,100	1,500
29 Payroll taxes	29	23,800	17,700	3,000	3,100
30 Professional fundraising fees	30				
31 Accounting fees	31				
32 Legal fees	32				
33 Supplies	33	30,000	26,500	1,800	1,700
34 Telephone	34	15,400	11,600	1,500	2,300
35 Postage and shipping	35	23,100	13,100	1,000	9,000
36 Occupancy	36	37,750	34,900	1,500	1,350
37 Equipment rental and maintenance . . .	37	8,750	5,900	1,500	1,350
38 Printing and publications	38	14,100	12,200	300	1,600
39 Travel	39	22,000	16,700	2,300	3,000
40 Conferences, conventions, and meetings .	40	17,700	12,800	4,500	400
41 Interest	41	900	100	800	
42 Depreciation, depletion, etc. (attach schedule)	42	5,200	4,200	600	400
43 Other expenses (itemize): a _Dues_	43a	500	500		
b _Professional Fees_	43b	127,900	124,500	2,600	800
c _Insurance_	43c	26,300	25,650	600	50
d _Miscellaneous_	43d	4,300	2,150	100	2,050
e	43e				
44 Total functional expenses (add lines 22 through 43) Organizations completing columns (B)-(D), carry these totals to lines 13-15	44	$700,200	$577,400	$57,400	$65,400

Reporting of Joint Costs.—Did you report in column (B) (Program services) any joint costs from a combined educational campaign and fundraising solicitation? . . . . ▶ ☒ Yes ☐ No
If "Yes," enter (i) the aggregate amount of these joint costs $ 9,600 ; (ii) the amount allocated to Program services $ 2,800 ; (iii) the amount allocated to Management and general $ 700 ; and (iv) the amount allocated to Fundraising $ 6,000

Part III Statement of Program Service Accomplishments (See instructions.)

What is the organization's primary exempt purpose? ▶ _Family counseling_

All organizations must describe their exempt purpose achievements. State the number of clients served, publications issued, etc. Discuss achievements that are not measurable. (Section 501(c)(3) and (4) organizations and 4947(a)(1) nonexempt charitable trusts must also enter the amount of grants and allocations to others.)

	Program Service Expenses (Required for 501(c)(3) and (4) orgs., and 4947(a)(1) trusts; but optional for others.)
a Counseling – The organization provided 5,954 hours of counseling to individuals and families. A total of 635 cases were assisted involving 2,426 individuals. The agency also made a grant to its national affiliate for a research project. (Grants and allocations $ 3,000)	$257,000
b Adoption Services - The agency placed 50 children in adoptive families. This included counseling for 189 birth parents. Five adoptions involved children from foreign countries. There were 65 home studies completed during this year. (This program was assisted (Grants and allocations $)	
c by $8,000 of donated services in 1994.) Under the Adoption Services program, the agency made grants to three organizations for related services. (Grants and allocations $ 21,000)	187,800
d Foster Care - The agency placed 28 children in 16 foster homes. The agency also made grants to two other organizations providing foster home care for hard-to-place children. (Grants and allocations $ 11,900)	131,800
e Other program services (attach schedule) (Grants and allocations $)	
f Total of Program Service Expenses (should equal line 44, column (B), Program services) . . . . ▶	$577,400

Part IV   Balance Sheets

Note: *Where required, attached schedules and amounts within the description column should be for end-of-year amounts only.*			(A) Beginning of year		(B) End of year
	Assets				
45	Cash—non-interest-bearing		$ 4,000	45	$ 6,400
46	Savings and temporary cash investments		244,700	46	222,100
47a	Accounts receivable	47a	$ 1,800			
b	Less: allowance for doubtful accounts . . .	47b	200	1,800	47c	1,600
48a	Pledges receivable	48a	70,100			
b	Less: allowance for doubtful accounts . . .	48b	11,200	46,800	48c	58,900
49	Grants receivable			4,600	49	5,800
50	Receivables due from officers, directors, trustees, and key employees (attach schedule)				50	
51a	Other notes and loans receivable (attach schedule)	51a				
b	Less: allowance for doubtful accounts . . .	51b			51c	
52	Inventories for sale or use			6,100	52	7,000
53	Prepaid expenses and deferred charges			9,600	53	13,800
54	Investments—securities (attach schedule) . . .			430,700	54	474,400
55a	Investments—land, buildings, and equipment: basis	55a				
b	Less: accumulated depreciation (attach schedule)	55b			55c	
56	Investments—other (attach schedule)				56	
57a	Land, buildings, and equipment: basis . . .	57a	188,000			
b	Less: accumulated depreciation (attach schedule)	57b	13,200	168,500	57c	174,800
58	Other assets (describe ▶ _____)				58	
59	Total assets (add lines 45 through 58) (must equal line 75)			$916,000	59	$964,800
	Liabilities				
60	Accounts payable and accrued expenses			$ 46,000	60	$ 39,300
61	Grants payable				61	
62	Support and revenue designated for future periods (attach schedule) . .			61,600	62	59,600
63	Loans from officers, directors, trustees, and key employees (attach schedule)				63	
64a	Tax-exempt bond liabilities (attach schedule)				64a	
b	Mortgages and other notes payable (attach schedule)			3,600	64b	3,200
65	Other liabilities (describe ▶ Payable under capital lease)				65	10,200
66	Total liabilities (add lines 60 through 65)			$111,200	66	$112,300
	Fund Balances or Net Assets				
Organizations that use fund accounting, check here ▶ ☒ and complete lines 67 through 70 and lines 74 and 75 (see instructions).					
67a	Current unrestricted fund			$446,300	67a	$485,100
b	Current restricted fund			10,000	67b	6,400
68	Land, buildings, and equipment fund			156,800	68	166,200
69	Endowment fund			191,700	69	194,800
70	Other funds (describe ▶ _____)			-0-	70	-0-
Organizations that do not use fund accounting, check here ▶ ☐ and complete lines 71 through 75 (see instructions).					
71	Capital stock or trust principal				71	
72	Paid-in or capital surplus				72	
73	Retained earnings or accumulated income				73	
74	Total fund balances or net assets (add lines 67a through 70 OR lines 71 through 73; column (A) must equal line 19 and column (B) must equal line 21)			$804,800	74	$852,500
75	Total liabilities and fund balances/net assets (add lines 66 and 74) . .			$916,000	75	$964,800

Form 990 is available for public inspection and, for some people, serves as the primary or sole source of information about a particular organization. How the public perceives an organization in such cases may be determined by the information presented on its return. Therefore, please make sure the return is complete and accurate and fully describes the organization's programs and accomplishments.

Part IV　Reason for Non-Private Foundation Status (See instructions for definitions.)

The organization is not a private foundation because it is (please check only ONE applicable box):

5　☐　A church, convention of churches, or association of churches. Section 170(b)(1)(A)(i).

6　☐　A school. Section 170(b)(1)(A)(ii). (Also complete Part V, page 3.)

7　☐　A hospital or a cooperative hospital service organization. Section 170(b)(1)(A)(iii).

8　☐　A Federal, state, or local government or governmental unit. Section 170(b)(1)(A)(v).

9　☐　A medical research organization operated in conjunction with a hospital. Section 170(b)(1)(A)(iii). Enter the hospital's name, city, and state ▶ ....

10　☐　An organization operated for the benefit of a college or university owned or operated by a governmental unit. Section 170(b)(1)(A)(iv). (Also complete the Support Schedule below.)

11a　☒　An organization that normally receives a substantial part of its support from a governmental unit or from the general public. Section 170(b)(1)(A)(vi). (Also complete the Support Schedule below.)

11b　☐　A community trust. Section 170(b)(1)(A)(vi). (Also complete the Support Schedule below.)

12　☐　An organization that normally receives: (a) no more than 33⅓% of its support from gross investment income and unrelated business taxable income (less section 511 tax) from businesses acquired by the organization after June 30, 1975, and (b) more than 33⅓% of its support from contributions, membership fees, and gross receipts from activities related to its charitable, etc., functions—subject to certain exceptions. See section 509(a)(2). (Also complete the Support Schedule below.)

13　☐　An organization that is not controlled by any disqualified persons (other than foundation managers) and supports organizations described in: (1) lines 5 through 12 above; or (2) section 501(c)(4), (5), or (6), if they meet the test of section 509(a)(2). (See section 509(a)(3).)

Provide the following information about the supported organizations. (See instructions for Part IV, line 13.)

(a) Name(s) of supported organization(s)	(b) Line number from above

14　☐　An organization organized and operated to test for public safety. Section 509(a)(4). (See instructions.)

Support Schedule (Complete only if you checked a box on line 10, 11, or 12 above.) *Use cash method of accounting.*
Note: *You may use the worksheet in the instructions for converting from the accrual to the cash method of accounting.*

Calendar year (or fiscal year beginning in) ▶	(a) 1993	(b) 1992	(c) 1991	(d) 1990	(e) Total
15　Gifts, grants, and contributions received. (Do not include unusual grants. See line 28.) . .	$742,300	$696,800	$640,600	$594,300	$2,674,000
16　Membership fees received	1,100	1,500	1,500	1,400	5,500
17　Gross receipts from admissions, merchandise sold or services performed, or furnishing of facilities in any activity that is not a business unrelated to the organization's charitable, etc., purpose	31,200	26,400	30,600	24,900	113,100
18　Gross income from interest, dividends, amounts received from payments on securities loans (section 512(a)(5)), rents, royalties, and unrelated business taxable income (less section 511 taxes) from businesses acquired by the organization after June 30, 1975 .	26,000	27,700	22,100	20,400	96,200
19　Net income from unrelated business activities not included in line 18					
20　Tax revenues levied for the organization's benefit and either paid to it or expended on its behalf .					
21　The value of services or facilities furnished to the organization by a governmental unit without charge. Do not include the value of services or facilities generally furnished to the public without charge .					
22　Other income. Attach a schedule. Do not include gain or (loss) from sale of capital assets					
23　Total of lines 15 through 22	$800,600	$752,400	$694,800	$641,000	$2,888,800
24　Line 23 minus line 17	$769,400	$726,000	$664,200	$616,100	$2,775,700
25　Enter 1% of line 23	$　8,006	$　7,524	$　6,948	$　6,410	
26　Organizations described in lines 10 or 11:					
a　Enter 2% of amount in column (e), line 24 . . . . ▶					$　55,514
b　Attach a list (which is not open to public inspection) showing the name of and amount contributed by each person (other than a governmental unit or publicly supported organization) whose total gifts for 1990 through 1993 exceeded the amount shown in line 26a. Enter the sum of all these excess amounts here . . . . . . ▶					-0-

(Support Schedule continued on page 3)

TOTAL QUALITY MANAGEMENT (TQM) AND QUALITY COSTS*

TOTAL QUALITY MANAGEMENT

In order to be globally competitive in today's world-class manufacturing environment, firms place an increased emphasis on quality and productivity. *Total quality management (TQM)* is an effort in this direction. Simply put, it is a system for creating competitive advantage by focusing the organization on what is important to the customer. Total quality management can be broken down into: "Total": that is the whole organization is involved and understands that customer satisfaction is everyone's job. "Quality": the extent to which products and services satisfy the requirements of internal and external customers. "Management": the leadership, infrastructure, and resources that support employees as they meet the needs of those customers.

TQM is essentially an endless quest for perfect quality. It is a *zero-defects* approach. It views the optimal level of quality costs as the level where zero defects are produced. This approach to quality is opposed to the traditional belief, called *acceptable quality level (AQL),* which allows a predetermined level of defective units to be produced and sold. AQL is the level where the number of defects allowed minimizes total quality costs. The rationale behind the traditional view is that there is a trade-off between prevention and appraisal costs and failure costs. Quality experts maintain that the optimal quality level should be about 2.5% of sales.

---

* This chapter was coauthored by Anique Qureshi, Ph.D., CPA, CIA, associate professor of accounting at Queens College, and an accounting professional.

Principles of TQM

Making a product right the first time is one of the principal objectives of TQM. Implementing a successful TQM program will in fact reduce costs rather than increase them. There is no question that better quality will result in better productivity. This is based on the principle that when less time is spent on rework or repair, more time is available for manufacturing, which will increase productivity.

When an organization maintains accurate records of its cost of quality, TQM will demonstrate that effective quality assurance geared towards prevention versus correction will pay for itself. A good example of this is the situation where it is possible to eliminate 100% inspection with a good statistical process control (SPC) program. Elimination of high reject rates results in fewer products being repaired, reworked, or scrapped, with the obvious reductions in cost.

Tying the cost of quality to TQM is necessary in order to motivate management, who are cost-motivated in both industry and government. In a TQM environment, management will start utilizing the cost data to measure the success of the program. The corporate financial planner can determine that overall product costs are being reduced by the TQM program. Given this success in the prevention of defects, the following failure costs will be reduced or eliminated:

1. Rework or repair
2. Inspection of rework
3. Testing of rework
4. Warranty costs
5. Returned material
6. Discounts, adjustments, and allowances

It is quite obvious that the cost of prevention in TQM is minor when taken against the above-listed failure costs.

A checklist of TQM features are as follows:

- A systematic way to improve products and services
- A structured approach in identifying and solving problems
- Long-term
- Conveyed by management's actions
- Supported by statistical quality control
- Practiced by everyone

Elements of TQM

The principal elements of TQM are straightforward and embrace a common-sense approach to management. However, each of the individual elements must be integrated into a structured whole to succeed. The elements are as follows:

1. *A Focus on the Customer*

   Every functional unit has a customer, whether it be an external consumer or an internal unit. TQM advocates that managers and employees become so customer-focused that they continually find new ways to meet or exceed customers' expectations. We must accept the concept that quality is defined by the customer and meeting the customer's needs and expectations is the strategic goal of TQM.

2. *A Long-Term Commitment*

   Experience in the U.S. and abroad shows that substantial gains come only after management makes a long-term commitment, usually five years or more, in improving quality. Customer focus must be constantly renewed to keep that goal foremost.

3. *Top Management Support and Direction*

   Top management must be the driving force behind TQM. Senior managers must exhibit personal support by using quality improvement concepts in their management style, incorporating quality in their strategic planning process, and providing financial and staff support.

4. *Employee Involvement*

   Full employee participation is also an integral part of the process. Each employee must be a partner in achieving quality goals. Teamwork involves managers, supervisors, and employees in improving service delivery, solving systemic problems, and correcting errors in all parts of work processes.

5. *Effective and Renewed Communications*

   The power of internal communication, both vertical and horizontal, is central to employee involvement. Regular and meaningful communication from all levels must occur. This will allow an agency to adjust its ways of operating and reinforce the commitment of TQM at the same time.

6. *Reliance on Standards and Measures*

   Measurement is the springboard to involvement, allowing the organization to initiate corrective action, set priorities, and evaluate progress. Standards and measures should reflect customer requirements and changes that need to be introduced in the internal business of providing those requirements. The emphasis is on "doing the right thing right the first time."

7. *Commitment to Training*

Training is absolutely vital to the success of TQM. The process usually begins with awareness training for teams of top-level managers. This is followed by courses for teams of mid-level managers, and finally by courses for non-managers. Awareness training is followed by an identification of areas of concentration, or of functional areas where TQM will first be introduced. Implementing TQM requires additional skills training, which is also conducted in teams.

8. *Importance of Rewards and Recognition*

Most companies practicing TQM have given wide latitude to managers in issuing rewards and recognition. Here, a common theme is that individual financial rewards are not as appropriate as awards to groups or team members, since most successes are group achievements.

QUALITY COSTS

Costs of quality are costs that occur because poor quality may exist or actually does exist. More specifically, quality costs are the total of the costs incurred by (1) investing in the prevention of nonconformances to requirements; (2) appraising a product or service for conformance to requirements; and (3) failure to meet requirements.

Quality costs are classified into three broad categories: prevention, appraisal, and failure costs. *Prevention costs* are those incurred to prevent defects. Amounts spent on quality training programs, researching customer needs, quality circles, and improved production equipment are considered in prevention costs. Expenditures made for prevention will minimize the costs that will be incurred for appraisal and failure. *Appraisal costs* are costs incurred for monitoring or inspection; these costs compensate for mistakes not eliminated through prevention. *Failure costs* may be internal (such as scrap and rework costs and reinspection) or external (such as product returns due to quality problems, warranty costs, lost sales due to poor product performance, and complaint department costs). Market shares of many U.S. firms have eroded because foreign firms have been able to sell higher-quality products at lower prices.

Studies indicate that costs of quality for American companies are typically 20 to 30% of sales. Quality experts maintain that the optimal quality level should be about 2.5% of sales.

Two Different Views Concerning Optimal Quality Costs

There are two views concerning optimal quality costs:

1. the traditional view that uses an acceptable quality level
2. the world-class view that uses total quality control

Optimal Distribution of Quality Costs: Traditional View. The traditional approach uses an *acceptable quality level (AQL)* that permits a predetermined level of defective units to be produced and sold. AQL is the level where the number of defects allowed minimizes total quality costs. The reasoning of the traditional approach is that there is a trade-off between failure costs and prevention and appraisal costs. As prevention and appraisal costs increase, internal and external failure costs are expected to decrease. As long as the decrease in failure costs is greater than the corresponding increase in prevention and failure costs, a company should continue increasing its efforts to prevent or detect defective units.

Optimal Distribution of Quality Costs: World-Class View. The world-class view uses total quality control and views the optimal level of quality costs as the level where zero defects are produced. The zero-defects approach uses a quality performance standard that requires:

1. all products to be produced according to specifications
2. all services to be provided according to requirements

Zero defects reflect a total quality control philosophy used in just-in-time (JIT) manufacturing. Figure 1 illustrates the relationship between these two cost components under two different views.

QUALITY COST AND PERFORMANCE REPORTS

The principal objective of reporting quality costs is to improve and facilitate managerial planning, control, and decision making. Potential uses of quality cost information include:

(a) quality program implementation decisions
(b) evaluation of the effectiveness of quality programs
(c) strategic pricing decisions (For example, a reduction in quality costs might enable a firm to reduce its selling price, improve its competitive position, and increase market share.)

Figure 1

Traditional View

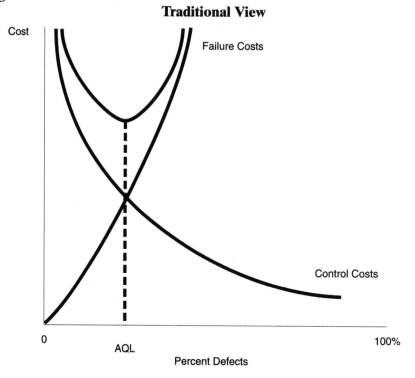

World-Class View

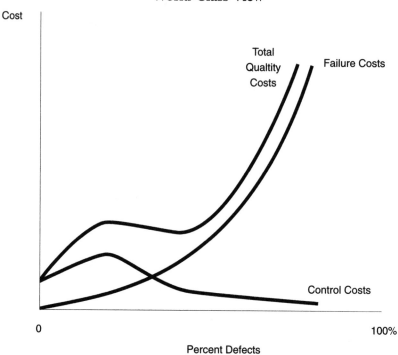

Total Quality Management (TQM) and Quality Costs

The control process involves comparing actual performance with quality standards. This comparison provides feedback that can be used to take corrective action if necessary. The first step in a quality cost reporting system is to prepare a detailed listing of actual quality costs by category. Furthermore, each category of quality costs is expressed as a percentage of sales. This serves two purposes: (a) It permits managers to assess the financial impact of quality costs, and (b) it reveals the relative emphasis currently placed on each category.

Figure 2 Quality Costs—General Description

Prevention Costs

The costs of all activities specifically designed to prevent poor quality in products or services. Examples are the costs of new product review, quality planning, supplier capability surveys, process capability evaluations, quality improvement team meetings, quality improvement projects, quality education and training.

Appraisal Costs

The costs associated with measuring, evaluating, or auditing products or services to assure conformance to quality standards and performance requirements. These include the costs of incoming and source inspection/test of purchased material, in-process and final inspection/test, product, process, or service audits, calibration of measuring and test equipment, and the costs of associated supplies and materials.

Failure Costs

The costs resulting from products or services not conforming to requirements or customer/user needs. Failure costs are divided into internal and external failure cost categories.

Internal Failure Costs

Failure costs occurring prior to delivery or shipment of the product, or the furnishing of a service, to the customer. Examples are the costs of scrap, rework, reinspection, retesting, material review, and downgrading.

External Failure Costs

Failure costs occurring after delivery or shipment of the product, and during or after furnishing of a service, to the customer. Examples are the costs of processing customer complaints, customer returns, warranty claims, and product recalls.

Total Quality Costs

The sum of the above costs. It represents the difference between the actual cost of a product or service, and what the reduced cost would be if there were no possibility of substandard service, failure of products, or defects in their manufacture.

Quality cost reports (Figure 3) can be used to point out the strengths and weaknesses of a quality system. Improvement teams can use them to describe the monetary benefits and ramifications of proposed changes. Return-on-investment (ROI) models and other financial analyses can be constructed directly from quality cost data to justify proposals to management. In practice, quality costs can define activities of quality program and quality improvement efforts in a language that management can understand and act on—dollars.

The negative effect on profits resulting from product or service of less than acceptable quality or from ineffective quality management is almost always dynamic. Once started, it continues to mushroom until ultimately the company finds itself in serious financial difficulties due to the two-pronged impact of an unheeded increase in quality costs coupled with a declining performance image. Management that clearly understands this understands the economics of quality.

In the quality cost report, quality costs are grouped into one of four categories:

1. prevention costs
2. appraisal costs
3. internal failure costs
4. external failure costs

In addition, each category of quality costs is expressed as a percentage of sales. There are four types of performance reports to measure a company's quality improvement. They are:

1. *Interim quality performance report.* It measures the progress achieved within the period relative to the planned level of progress for the period (see Figure 4).

2. *One-year quality trend report.* It compares the current year's quality cost ratio with the previous year's ratio. More specifically, it compares the current year's variable quality cost ratio with the previous year's variable quality cost ratio, and the current year's actual fixed quality costs with the previous year's actual fixed quality costs (see Figure 5).

3. *Long-range quality performance report.* It compares the current year's actual quality costs with the firm's intended long-range quality goal (see Figure 6).

Activity-Based Management and Optimal Quality Costs

Activity-based management supports the zero-defect view of quality costs.

Activity-based management classifies activities as: (1) value-added activities and (2) non-value-added activities.

Quality-related activities (internal and external failure activities, prevention activities, and appraisal activities) can be classified as value-added and non-value-added.

Internal and external failure activities and their associated costs are non-value-added and should be eliminated.

Prevention activities that are performed efficiently are value-added. (Costs caused by inefficiency in prevention activities are non-value-added costs.)

Appraisal activities may be value-added or non-value-added depending upon the activity. For example, quality audits may serve a value-added objective.

Once the quality-related activities are identified for each category, resource drivers can be used to improve cost assignments to individual activities. Root or process drivers can also be identified and used to help managers understand what is causing the cost of the activities.

Using Quality Cost Information

The principal objective of reporting quality costs is to improve and facilitate managerial planning, control, and decision making.

Potential uses of quality cost information include:

1. quality program implementation decisions
2. evaluation of the effectiveness of quality programs
3. strategic pricing decisions (For example, improved reporting of quality costs might be used by managers to target specific quality costs for reductions. A reduction in quality costs might enable a firm to reduce its selling price, improve its competitive position, and increase market share.)
4. inclusion of quality costs in cost-volume-profit analysis (For example, overlooking quality cost savings results in a higher break-even and possible rejection of a profitable project.)

The control process involves comparing actual performance with quality standards. This comparison provides feedback that can be used to take corrective action if necessary.

Figure 3

Allison Products
Quality Cost Report
For the Year Ended March 31, 2xxx

	Quality Costs		Percentage of Sale(a)
Prevention costs:			
Quality training	$30,000		
Reliability engineering	79,000	$109,000	3.73%
Appraisal costs:			
Materials inspection	$19,000		
Product acceptance	10,000		
Process acceptance	35,000	$64,000	2.19%
Internal failure costs:			
Scrap	$40,000		
Rework	34,000	$74,000	2.53%
External failure costs:			
Customer complaints	$24,000		
Warranty	24,000		
Repair	15,000	$63,000	2.16%
Total quality costs		$310,000	10.62% (b)

(a) Actual sales of $2,920,000
(b) $310,000/$2,920,000 = 10.62 percent. Difference is rounding error.

Figure 4

Allison Products
Interim Standard Performance Report
For the Year Ended March 31, 2xxx

	Actual Costs	Budgeted Costs(a)	Variance
Prevention costs:			
Quality training	$30,000	$30,000	$0
Reliability engineering	79,000	80,000	1,000 F
Total prevention	$109,000	$110,000	$1,000 F
Appraisal costs:			
Materials inspection	$19,000	$28,000	$9,000 F
Product acceptance	10,000	15,000	5,000 F
Process acceptance	35,000	35,000	0
Total appraisal	$64,000	$78,000	$14,000 F

Total Quality Management (TQM) and Quality Costs

Internal failure costs:			
Scrap	$40,000	$44,000	$4,000 F
Rework	34,000	36,500	2,500 F
Total internal failure	$74,000	$80,500	$6,500 F
External failure costs:			
Fixed:			
Customer complaints	$24,000	$25,000	$1,000 F
Variable:			
Warranty	24,000	20,000	(4,000) U
Repair	15,000	17,500	2,500 F
Total external failure	$63,000	$62,500	($500) U
Total quality costs	$310,000	$331,000	$21,000 F
Percentage of actual sales	10.62%	11.34%	0.72% F

(a) Based on actual sales
(b) Actual sales of $2,920,000

Figure 5

Allison Products
Quality Cost, One-Year Trend
For the Year Ended March 31, 2xxx

	Actual Costs 20X2(a)	Budgeted Costs 20X1	Variance
Prevention costs:			
Quality training	$30,000	$36,000	$6,000 F
Reliability engineering	79,000	120,000	41,000 F
Total prevention	$109,000	$156,000	$47,000 F
Appraisal costs:			
Materials inspection	$19,000	$33,600	$14,600 F
Product acceptance	10,000	16,800	6,800 F
Process acceptance	35,000	39,200	4,200 F
Total appraisal	$64,000	$89,600	$25,600 F
Internal failure costs:			
Scrap	$40,000	$48,000	$8,000 F
Rework	34,000	40,000	6,000 F
Total internal failure	$74,000	$88,000	$14,000 F
External failure costs:			
Fixed:			
Customer complaints	$24,000	$33,000	$9,000 F

Variable:			
Warranty	24,000	23,000	(1,000) U
Repair	15,000	16,400	1,400 F
Total external failure	$63,000	$72,400	$9,400 F
Total quality costs	$310,000	$406,000	$96,000 F
Percentage of actual sales	10.62%	13.90%	3.29% F

(a) Based on actual sales = $2,920,000

Figure 6

Allison Products
Long-Range Performance Report
For the Year Ended March 31, 2xxx

	Actual Costs	Target Costs(a)	Variance
Prevention costs:			
Quality training	$30,000	$14,000	($16,000) U
Reliability engineering	79,000	39,000	(40,000) U
Total prevention	$109,000	$53,000	($56,000) U
Appraisal costs:			
Materials inspection	$19,000	$7,900	($11,100) U
Product acceptance	10,000	0	(10,000) U
Process acceptance	35,000	12,000	(23,000) U
Total appraisal	$64,000	$19,900	($44,100) U
Internal failure costs:			
Scrap	$40,000	$0	($40,000) U
Rework	34,000	0	(34,000) U
Total internal failure	$74,000	$0	($74,000) U
External failure costs:			
Fixed:			
Customer complaints	$24,000	$0	($24,000) U
Variable:			
Warranty	24,000	0	(24,000) U
Repair	15,000	0	(15,000) U
Total external failure	$63,000	$0	($63,000) U
Total quality costs	$310,000	$72,900	($237,100) U
Percentage of actual sales	10.62%	2.50%	–8.12% U

(a) Based on actual sales of $2,920,000. These costs are value-added costs.

RISK MANAGEMENT AND ANALYSIS

Risk management involves identifying risk exposure, analyzing risk, measuring potential loss, determining the best insurance strategy (or whether to self-insure), cost projections and control, volatility of operations, timing of adverse events, claims adjustment, proper cost allocation, and the use of risk management software.

Risks facing a business may negatively affect its reputation, bottomline, cost and availability of financing, credit rating, market price of stock, regulatory or legislative changes, and elimination of barriers to entry.

An evaluation must be made of the trade-off between risk and return. A higher risk mandates a higher rate of return to justify taking the extra risk.

A risk program must be in place. The program must have built-in flexibility to adjust, as conditions require. The program must conform to the goals, objectives, and policies of the business.

The company must have a workable contingency plan such as a recovery plan. Employees must be instructed what to do in such eventualities. Test runs should be practiced. Contingency plans must be updated periodically to incorporate new technologies, changing staff, and new areas of business activity.

Areas of risk must be identified and corrective action taken to reduce those risks. Unusually high risk will not only have negative effects on earnings but might also place in question the continuity of the operation.

Models and quantitative approaches including actuarial techniques may be used to appraise potential catastrophic losses, product/service liability, intellectual property losses, and business interruption. Probability distributions should be arrived at of expected losses based on the model or quantitative technique used.

APPRAISAL OF RISK

The "red flags" of undue risk must be identified and controlled. "Red flags" include poor employee training and performance, inadequate planning, fragmentation, poor communication, lateness, improper focus, failure to observe government regulations or laws (e.g., the federal Comprehensive Environmental Response, Compensation and Liability Act covering the release and disposal of hazardous substances and wastes), overconfidence, and "hostile" attitudes.

When appraising a particular situation, evaluate the risk profile, financial status, and acceptable risk exposure. What is the entity's risk tolerance level? To what extent does the risk of a situation exceed predetermined maximum risk levels? Has management received proper approval to undertake the high-risk level? Has proper planning been performed to take into account the adverse effects on the business if things do not work out? For example, if losses are incurred that significantly exceed the entity's traditional insurance program, the company might be permanently crippled. Examples include a business interruption resulting from a terrorist bombing, loss of a major vendor, misinterpretation of law, or a product recall.

In appraising risk, consideration must be given to the company's liquidity and solvency position to withstand loss. A determination must be made of the costs associated with various risks.

Risk should be evaluated and minimized. Risk may be reduced through the following means:

- Vertically integrate to reduce the price and supply risk of raw materials.
- Take out sufficient insurance coverage for possible asset and operating losses (including foreign risk protection). A lower trend in insurance expense to the asset insured may indicate inadequate coverage.
- Diversify activities, product/service line, market segments, customer bases, geographic areas, and investments.
- Sell to diversified industries to protect against cyclical turns in the economy.
- Sign a forward contract to take delivery of raw materials at fixed prices at a specified future date so the entity insulates itself from price increases.
- Enter into foreign currency futures contracts to lock in a fixed rate.
- Participate in joint ventures and partnerships with other companies. In so doing, obligations of the parties must be taken into account. For example, questions to be asked are: *Which company is to absorb most of the losses? What are our company's duties and exposure under the agreement?*

- Sell low-priced products as well as more expensive ones to protect against inflationary and recessionary periods.
- Change suppliers who prove unreliable.
- Take steps so the company is less susceptible to business cycles (e.g., inelastic demand products, negatively correlated products/services).
- Add products/services having different seasonal attractiveness and demand.
- Emphasize a piggyback product base (similar merchandise associated with the basic business).
- Balance the company's financing mix.

In analyzing the company's product/service line, determine:

- Extent of correlation between products. Positive correlation means high risk because the demand for all the products goes in the same direction. Negative correlation minimizes the risk. No correlation means indifference between products.
- Product demand elasticity equal to the percentage change in quantity relative to the percentage change in price. Elastic demand means that a minor change in price has a significant impact on quantity demanded. This indicates higher risk. Inelastic product demand minimizes risk because a change in price will have little effect on quantity demanded.

In analyzing the risk associated with multinational companies, compute:

- Total assets in high-risk foreign countries to total assets.
- High-risk foreign revenue to total revenue. High-risk revenue is based on risk ratings of companies in published sources (e.g., International Country Risk Guide).
- High-risk foreign revenue to net income.
- Percentage of earnings associated with foreign government contracts.
- Fluctuation in foreign exchange rates.

When evaluating risk, a number of questions must be answered:

- What is the internal process in place to reduce risk?
- What appraisal is being made of control aspects?
- Are controls effective?
- Do controls function as planned?
- Who is responsible for risk management?

- Is risk being managed properly to prevent fraud?
- What are the specific areas of risk vulnerability?
- Is financial and operational information being reported correctly?

TYPES OF RISK

The corporate financial manager needs to take into account the various types of risk the entity faces. For example, corporate risk may be in the form of overrelying on a few key executives or the underinsurance of assets. Industry risk may be the high technological environment, or an industry scrutinized under the "public eye," or a capital-intensive business. Moving toward a variable cost-oriented business may minimize industry risk. Economic risk includes susceptibility to the business cycle. This risk may be reduced by having a low-priced substitute for a high-priced one.

Social risk occurs when a company experiences customer boycott or discrimination cases. A way to reduce this risk is to be engaged in community involvement and sensitivity training.

A company must properly instruct its personnel not to intrude with electronic mail, slander others, or commit libel. The company must carefully train and monitor staff to guard against possible infractions causing employee lawsuits or federal/local government investigation.

Political risk applies to relations with U.S. and local government agencies, and with foreign governments when operations are carried out overseas. This risk may be reduced through lobbying efforts and by avoiding activities or placing assets in high-risk foreign areas.

Environmental risk includes product lines and services susceptible to changes in the weather. Having counterseasonal goods and services or moving to another geographic location may reduce this risk. Multinational entities are susceptible to environmental risk, particularly in the former Iron Curtain countries. There are often problems with land and resource use, including pollution and hazardous waste. The acquiring company must be cautious of not only the cleanup costs, but also associated penalties and fines. Prior to acquisition, the acquirer must be assured that there is a contract under which the seller will be responsible for all or part of the environmental obligations. A high-risk premium applies to corporate investments in countries with environmental problems. Insurance companies, for example, should reject potential clients that are not environmentally certified or fail to meet particular environmental norms. Banks need to be concerned with the collectibility of loans to companies with major environmental exposure. If a company is "dirty," it may have difficulty obtaining adequate insurance or loans. Further, the effect of impending government environmental laws on the business must be considered. Environmental problems and disasters may significantly hurt earnings.

Terrorism is also of concern to certain types of businesses. Security measures must be in place to guard against bombing.

A determination must be made as to how the risks facing a business interact. A model must consider alternative scenarios.

RISK ANALYSIS AND MANAGEMENT SOFTWARE

Software is available to assess, evaluate, and control the risks facing a company. A risk management information system (RMIS) includes hardware and software components. However, we consider here software availability, implications, benefits, and applications. The software selected should be that which offers a proper "fit" with the environment and circumstances of the company.

In deciding on the "right" software, the financial manager should consider the company's requirements and expectations, corporate culture, report preparation needs, regulatory reporting mandates, product/service line, nature of operations, claims processing and administration, government compliance laws, business policies and procedures, insurance coverage, technological resources, employee background and experience, levels of communication, legal liability aspects, organizational structure, and work flow. The risk management and analysis software should include the ability to manipulate data into risk patterns.

Are the "right" managers being provided with the appropriate information on a timely basis? A determination must also be made of the communication and distribution features of the software. The software should be flexible so that reports may be customized depending on the data needed and for whom. For example, a factory supervisor or manager wants to know how many employee injuries occurred and of what nature. On the other hand, the accounting department manager wants to know the negative financial effects the accidents have on the company's financial position and operating performance.

Software may be used to evaluate safety statistical data by division, department, responsibility unit, geographic location, and manager. Potential difficulties may be highlighted. An example of a risk management software application is providing a report on how many employee injuries took place by department, operation, and activity. Is the client's incidence rate above or below expected ranges? How does the client injury rate compare to competitors and industry averages? There should be a software feature, such as an expert system, on how to correct the problem of a high rate of employee accidents and offer other relevant recommendations.

If a company is exchanging risk information with others (e.g., insurance company, investment banker, and government agencies), then software compatibility is needed. Further, there should exist appropriate operating systems and network support. A company may use its intranet to expand risk management throughout the company. It is important that there be proper user interfaces.

RISK CONTROL

Risk control includes environmental compliance, periodic inspections, and alarm systems. Loss prevention and control must consider physical and human aspects. For example, "safer" machines may be used to prevent worker injury. Appropriate sprinklers may be installed to prevent fires. Consultants may be retained in specialized areas such as industrial hygiene. Product labeling should be appraised as to appropriateness and representation. Any consumer complaints should be immediately investigated to avoid possible government action or litigation.

The financial manager must determine the best kind, term, and amount of insurance to carry to guard against losses. Insurance coverage may be taken out for losses to plant, property, and equipment, product/service deficiencies, and employee conduct. The financial manager should consider insuring areas not typically insured against, such as industrial espionage, loss of intellectual property, or employee theft. An example of the latter is employment practice liability insurance (EPLI). This policy is available from many insurance companies, such as Chubb and Lexington. Unfortunately even this type of policy often excludes coverage for bodily injury, workers' compensation, and infractions under ERISA. It is not unusual for an employee to sue because of an employer's promotion and hiring policies. The insurance premium may be lowered by increasing the deductible or changing to less expensive insurance carriers.

The financial manager must carefully monitor the entity's fiduciary responsibilities, working conditions, contractual commitments, and employment practices. Systems such as fire alarm devices must be checked on an ongoing basis for defects in functioning. The company must be certain that its employee policies are fair and in conformity with federal and local laws.

Risk control includes provisions against terrorist acts related to loss of life, product losses, and property damage. Security procedures including access controls must be strong in high-risk areas, such as in a foreign country with extremist groups. Employees must be instructed to use safety precautions.

RISK SOFTWARE PACKAGES AND PRODUCTS

There are many risk management software packages available to financial managers. Some useful packages are described below.

Decision Support Systems' The Expert Business Impact Analysis System provides risk appraisal factors and protection strategy recommendations. It has a database of global threats, vulnerability assessments, comparative analysis, and reporting capabilities (including by location). It contains threat probabilities with documented statistical sources, outage durations, and regional segmentation. It has interactive "what-if" analysis features for scenario planning to evaluate the benefits of alternative solutions and to perform comparisons with the current and historical background. (For information, telephone: (800) 788-6447, e-mail: BIAsys@aol.com, or write to Decision Support Systems, 380 S. State Road 434, Suite 1004-117, Altamonte Springs, FL 32714.)

Strohl Systems offers contingency planning software products to plan for unexpected disruptions in the company's operations. It is better to anticipate interruptions before they turn into major problems. BIA Professional is a business impact analysis tool allowing the company to quickly and easily define the effects of disaster and help target critical functions for contingency planning. Living Disaster Recovery Planning Systems (LDRPS) is continuity (recovery) planning software including a question-and-answer feature, sample documents and diagrams, graphics, report writer, recovery strategies and contingency planning, and presentation of recovery activities in the form of Program Evaluation and Review Technique (PERT) and Gantt charts. Plans and procedures cover emergency response, crisis management, notification, facilities relocation, security, asset management and retrieval, vital records, contamination, safety, and health. (For information, write: Strohl Systems, 500 North Gulph Road, King of Prussia, PA 19406, telephone: (610) 768-4120, fax: (610) 768-4138, or Web: http://www.strohl-systems.com.)

CSCI's Recovery PAC is business recovery planning software including comprehensive business impact analysis and risk assessment. It identifies critical business functions and applications and sets priorities for recovery. It also identifies risk exposures that can potentially turn into a disaster. (For information, telephone: (800) 925-CSCI.)

Business Foundations' Internal Operations Risk Analysis software evaluates a company's areas of risk and internal control structure. It is an expert system developed around 180 interview questions. Based on the answers to the questions, the software prepares a management report highlighting the strengths and weaknesses in the operations of the business. A risk rating (high, medium, or low) is assigned to categories of risk. Relevant management and analytical reports are generated. Operational areas evaluated by the software include working environment, objects, planning, and personnel. It has database capabilities. It recommends corrective steps for problem areas. There is an upgrade for industry-specific components.

Price Waterhouse's Controls assists in risk analysis by documenting, evaluating, and testing the company's internal controls. Areas of risk exposure are identified. Control weaknesses are highlighted with resultant recommendations for improvement. Control effectiveness may be evaluated at different levels within the company (e.g., by activity, by business unit). A comparison and analysis may be made of the relative control performance of different operating units. (For information, fax: (201) 292-3800, or Web: http://www.pw.com.)

Pleier and Associates' ADM Plus performs risk management, planning, and analysis.

Corporate Systems' CS EDGE Series offers a risk-management information system providing claim processing and evaluation, accident analysis, management of fixed assets, and risk reporting and appraisal. (For information, telephone: (800) 9-CS-EDGE, or Web: http://www.csedge.com.)

American International Group (AIG)'s IntelliRisk is a risk management information system providing claims information, asset management, risk reduction strategies, account information, payment history, report preparation, searches and sorting, and communication online features with underwriters, brokers, and adjusters. (For information, telephone: Alan Louison, Director of Risk Management Information Services at (800) 767-2524, or write: American International Group, Department A, 70 Pine Street, New York, NY 10270.)

Dorn Technology Group's RISK MASTER/WIN integration package has many features, including incident reporting, claim adjustments and reporting, policy management, workers' compensation, actuarial reporting, and reserve analysis. (For information, telephone: (800) 587-1440 or (313) 462-5800, fax: (313) 462-5809, or Web: http://dorn.com.)

Health Management Technologies' RETURN is software for workers' compensation, disability, and group health plans. It manages cases, channels information to network providers, monitors both work status and return to work, and documents activity and case outcome. It offers an electronic Rolodex of providers, treatment centers, resources, and contacts. The package evaluates provider performance and results in cost savings. The features include a standard letter generator, report writer, accounts receivable for case management, bill repricing, and job analysis. (For information, telephone: (800) 647-7007, or write: Health Management Technologies, 1150 Moraga Way, Suite 150, Moraga, CA 94556.)

California Interactive Computer's Claims and Risk Management Systems has modules for workers' compensation, group medical, property and casualty, disability management, and general risk management. The software can be customized for your particular needs by the vendor. (For information, telephone: (805) 294-1300, fax: (805) 294-1310, write: California Interactive Computing, 25572 Avenue Stanford, Valencia, CA 91355, or Web: http://calinteractive.com.)

Conway Computer Group's Pabblo and Paccasso are Windows-based client/server solutions for workers' compensation and property/casualty insurance administration. (For information, telephone: (601) 957-7400, write: Conway Computer Group, P.O. Box 12801, Jackson, MS 39211, or Web: http://www.ccg.com.)

PC Solutions' Certifitra keeps track of insurance certificates, aids in insurance auditing, and prepares reports of insurance status (e.g., coverage, expiration dates). (For information, telephone: (704) 525-9330, fax: (704) 525-9539, or e-mail: pcsoln@vnet.net.)

CCH Incorporated's Safety Compliance Assistant is interactive software to comply with the U.S. Occupational Safety and Health Administration (OSHA) General Industry Standards. It provides inspection and training checklists, detects OSHA compliance violations, maintains required documents, and corrects violations. (For information, telephone: (800) 228-8353.)

CIC Incorporated's Back Track software verifies employees' background for hiring purposes. (For information, telephone: (800) 321-HIRE extension 126, or fax: (813) 559-0232.)

QA Systems QASYS is innovative, flexible risk-management software for insurance companies. (For information, telephone: (800) 946-1717 or (212) 599-1717, or write: QA Systems, 220 E. 42nd St., New York, NY 10017.)

RISK MODELING SOFTWARE APPLICATIONS

Risk modeling is a decision-making aid to the financial manager. Models may be used in analyzing risks while financial models can evaluate the financial consequences arising from accidents or other adverse developments. Risk models may be developed for measuring the financial impact due to catastrophes (fire, flood, earthquake, nuclear). The probable loss arising from the accident, disaster, or other event may be estimated. The model may also determine the probable effects on business activities as well as possible competitive reactions. A contingency model may help in planning an appropriate strategy and response. A "what-if" scenario analysis may be formulated to see the end-result effects of changing input variables and factors. An example of a scenario modeling analysis is to simulate the possible operating and financial consequences to the company from various possibilities arising from a hurricane. The company's risk vulnerability from such an event may be "mapped" and appraised. The "best-case," "worst-case," and "likely" scenarios may be depicted and reviewed. The model simulation has the benefit of aiding the company in determining beforehand how to best minimize the damage operationally and financially and how to provide proper protective measures.

The software enables the company to determine the areas, types, and degrees of risk facing the business. A minimum-maximum range of loss figures may be derived.

Risk modeling may be used to identify and define the type and amount of risks related to various exposures. A priority ranking based on risk and uncertainty may also be prepared and studied. Risk problem areas may be analyzed along with a set of appropriate alternative responses.

RISK MANAGEMENT INFORMATION SYSTEMS (RMIS) TESTING LABORATORY

Deloitte and Touche, CPAs has started the first independent risk management systems testing laboratory that tests software, develops systems solutions, evaluates software usefulness, provides benchmarking information, and customizes applications. Deloitte and Touche, CPAs will compare software products, compare reporting and application features, and appraise their effectiveness in meeting your needs. (For information, contact David Duden, RMIS/Lab Director at telephone: (860) 543-7341, e-mail: dduden@ dttus.com, or Web: http://www.rmislab.com.)

ONLINE RISK-MANAGEMENT DATABASE SERVICES

There are many online services available providing important risk-management information. For example, the National Council on Compensation Insurance (NCCI) Inc. provides an online InsNet Workers' Compensation Characteristic Series containing claims data useful in having a cost-effective workers' compensation system. The service aids in evaluating risks, determining and appraising workers' compensation costs including frequency data, specifying injury claim characteristics, providing demographic and body claim characteristics, and specifying benefit type information. (For information about NCCI's InsNet online service, telephone: (800) 622-4123, access the Web site: http://www.ncci.com, or write to: National Council on Compensation Insurance, 750 Park of Commerce Drive, Boca Raton, FL 33487.)

REENGINEERING AND OUTSOURCING THE BUSINESS

Reengineering includes downsizing and restructuring. It should be properly balanced. Outsourcing is contracting out production or service functions performed by the company to save on costs or to establish efficiencies. The financial manager must identify problems within the organization and recommend solutions. The financial manager must therefore understand what reengineering and outsourcing are about, how they affect the business, and how they may be implemented correctly. The financial manager needs to analyze, evaluate, offer suggestions, and comment on the company's existing or possible efforts to reengineer, downsize, restructure, and outsource the business.

REENGINEERING

A strategy is the implementation of a company's plans and tactics. A company may downsize or right-size to its "core" to create value. Reengineering is defined as a multidisciplinary approach to making fundamental changes in how operations, activities, functions, and procedures are conducted within a business. The objective of such change is to improve performance, productivity, and profitability. Reengineering should be undertaken if the benefit exceeds the cost of doing so, considering money and time. There should be a "road map" of the steps in the reengineering process. Reengineering may be done for the company as a whole, for one or more business units, or for particular geographic locations. There is a risk in reengineering of making not enough or too much change. For reengineering to succeed, the following should be present: employee understanding and cooperation, good project planning and management, timely assessment, benchmarks, and realistic expectations. Reengineering may take different forms of approach, including business process redesign (redesigning processes to achieve efficiencies and enhance service quality) and process innovation (making fundamental changes to improve the importance of processes). Reengineering attempts to effect continual improvement in business procedures.

In reengineering, the focus should be on the current and potential customer and then on corporate structure and processes designed accordingly—in other words, reengineering from the outside in. Managers must monitor and track the current and emerging satisfaction needs of customers and formulate the products and services they demand. New product innovation and creativity may be required. Reengineering must create "real value" for the customer. In so doing, consider whether the current product/service line helps in keeping present customers and expanding the customer base.

Objectives for cost reduction should be established, such as time for each job (task, operation, activity), expected maintenance, and compatibility.

Employees must understand the why of reengineering so their support, contribution, and continued morale may be obtained. Cultural differences have to be taken into account. Disproportionate downsizing is a mistake. The company must be restructured logically and practically. Proper planning is required to avoid any surprises.

Reengineering may aid in developing new products and/or services, improving product distribution, and achieving growth. A successful strategy can include joint ventures and franchising. The purposes of reengineering include:

- Cost control and reduction (e.g., employee costs)
- Revenue, profit, and rate of return maximization
- Growth and capacity therefore
- Reduction in risk
- Appreciation in stock and bond price
- Improvement in bond rating
- Lowering the cost of financing
- Inventory reduction
- Improved market share
- Remaining competitive
- Reduction in headcount
- Change in corporate culture
- Additional flexibility
- Spinoff of a segment or operation

- Improved quality
- Improved integration
- Streamlining production and distribution
- Keeping up-to-date with the latest technology
- Improved productivity
- Improved interaction and communication
- Improved product delivery and service
- Change in the product/service mix

In reengineering, consideration should be given to the cost and time of doing so, new ideas, developing products and services, managing operations and projects, portfolio management, retraining, acquisitions and mergers, joint ventures, automation, amount of restructuring needed, change to equipment, employee training, inspection requirements, infrastructure, risk profile, whether fundamental or incremental change is needed, reassignment (if any) of displaced employees, and legal and contractual provisions and limitations.

The right resources must be at the right places at the right time. Processes may be redesigned to improve service quality and promote efficiencies. Continuous improvement in processes and procedures, job descriptions, and work flow mandate commitment and follow-through. However, be careful not to make inappropriate or incorrect changes to the system or process. The effect of current changes on the future must be taken into account. A manager does not want to make a change that will have an immediate benefit but will have a long-term negative effect. An example is laying off experienced supervisors who will be needed to train employees when business picks up in the future. Questions to be answered in reengineering follow:

- Should the reengineering effort be centralized or decentralized? If decentralized, how will integration be accomplished?
- Where does reengineering begin and end?
- What expectations are there to be achieved?
- What is the role of technology in the reengineering effort?
- What are the logistics throughout the project's life?
- What effect do reengineering efforts have on the environmental program of the business?
- How much value does the reengineering plan achieve?
- What uncertainties and risks does reengineering have and what steps have been undertaken to reduce such risks? The risks associated

with reengineering include financial, technological, operational, and political.

- What legal issues and contract commitments are raised because of the reengineering program?
- Will outside consultants be involved? If so, to what extent?
- When and how will periodic reviews (reports) take place?
- Is reengineering proceeding as scheduled? If not, what is the problem and how may it be rectified?
- Who will be assigned to the reengineering effort, and why? What are their qualifications and time commitment?

Before full-scale reengineering takes place at the entire company, a pilot program and prototyping should be conducted to identify problems, learn from mistakes, and formulate sound strategies and approaches based on experience. By developing solutions to expected problems before full-scale implementation, the company may save in cost and time as well as reduce risks. It is best to complete one reengineering project before proceeding to the next, because the manager becomes more focused and learns from experience.

Scenario analysis should be undertaken, looking at high, low, and average situations. Probabilities, weights, and rankings may be assigned to alternative scenario situations as part of the evaluative process. There is a link between scenario planning and business reengineering. Scenario analysis considers uncertainties, range of possibilities (outcomes), what is critical and what is not, controllable and uncontrollable factors, the effect on other areas of implementing a strategy in one area, contingent possibilities (a course of action is valuable only in particular scenario settings). Scenario analysis considers advisable steps to take now or in the future, or if a particular change in circumstance occurs. It is similar to a simulation to determine what will happen in the "real world." "Red flags" should be recognized and corrective action taken. What are the positive and negative outcomes from implementing a particular procedure or strategy? Scenario analysis assists in reducing risk and focusing on reengineering efforts. The scenario program provides "visions" as to the future. Its results suggest what activities should be emphasized or deemphasized, and what actions should be eliminated. Scenario analysis looks at the alternative possibilities available and aids in timely implementation. A priority ranking of alternatives may be established.

Reengineering in the plant may take the form of automating operations, updating manufacturing approaches, and accomplishing greater flexibility. It may involve reorganizing the human resource function to achieve

Reengineering and Outsourcing the Business

economies and eliminate duplication. Internal organizational processes and product/service deliveries may be redesigned.

One must be careful that reengineering does not result in "dumb-sizing," whereby the entity's long-term financial position and operating results are adversely impacted. Does the reengineering program lay off experienced personnel, cut vital services, increase risk, result in legal liability, cause conflicts with vendors or customers, result in worker mistrust, cause injuries or malfunctioning of equipment, or cause other negative aspects that outweigh any benefits achieved? The authors are aware of instances when in fact a reengineering program that was improperly administered was counterproductive.

The reengineering team should consist of those who are representative of those to be affected within the department by the ultimate outcome of the proposed reengineering. The group should be a cross section of individuals within the company. In other words, there should be organizational diversity. Determine who is responsible for what and how, and how often performance will be measured. If individuals are trying to sabotage the reengineering effort, take necessary steps to remove the roadblock, such as dismissing uncooperative employees.

OUTSOURCING AND INSOURCING

A corporate policy must be established regarding outsourcing. Outsourcing is contracting to others work that was formerly done within the company. It includes buying goods and services from vendors. As a general rule, outsourcing is more appropriate for "core" activities than "noncore" operations. Companies more suitable for outsourcing are those that are decentralized, are engaged in restructuring (e.g., downsizing), and are out-of-date.

There are many outsourcing service providers in areas such as finance, administration, engineering, manufacturing, buying, human resources, customer service, real estate management, computer systems, marketing and sales, investment management, maintenance, product procurement, distribution (e.g., shipping) and logistics, technology, and transportation. For example, information technology services are provided by Integrated Systems Solutions of White Plains, NY. Xerox Corporation offers many business services related to office work and duplication functions.

Before outsourcing, consideration should be given to whether it makes sense in light of expectations, company objectives and needs, business plans, major sources of revenue, cost (including conversion costs), risk (including business uncertainties), contract period, legal liability, availability, security, confidentiality, time constraints (including time to implement and schedule), capacity limitations, employee expertise and proficiency, employee morale, time concerns, nature of item (e.g., critical importance), compatibility, corporate culture, degree of control sought, innovation and creativity, logistics, and cost of redeployment and relocation. A company may be able to outsource an aspect of its operations for less than it costs to train and manage employees to conduct the same function within the business. If a function is "mission critical," it probably should not be outsourced because management would want to retain control over it. An activity that gives the company a significant competitive advantage (differentiation) should most likely stay within the company.

Outsourcing allows a business to be more efficient and effective, engage in subcontracting legacy systems, reduce costs (e.g., staff), reduce risk, streamline and simplify operations, improve quality, focus on core activities and competencies, free up capital and human resources, improve existing processes, improve delivery of activities, generate efficiencies and effectiveness, enhance flexibility, obtain a competitive advantage, redeploy staff and assets, achieve economies, enhance productivity, convert fixed costs to variable costs, and obtain improved up-to-date technology.

In selecting an outsourcing vendor, consider reputation, contacts, references, reliability, experience, specialty and focus, fees, flexibility, stability, expertise (specialized skills), cost, quality of service, creativity and innovation, upgrade potential, communications, commitment, contract provisions and restrictions (e.g., penalty and cancellation clauses), and "fit."

Ask the outsource vendor for a "trial period" to see how things are going before entering into a regular contract. However, avoid long-term contracts, especially those that are rigid in their terms. You want flexibility and do not want to be locked in for the long term. We recommend renewable, short-term contracts. The contract should be updated as the environment and circumstances change.

Insist that outsourcing contracts contain provisions regarding performance expectations (e.g., service-level goals) and measurement guidelines. Undertake periodic performance appraisals. Customer satisfaction with the outsourcer's services is crucial, so surveys should be conducted periodically.

Insourcing is the self-manufacture of goods or services. Instead of buying the items from outside, the company produces the product or renders the service in an attempt to lower costs, improve quality, hasten availability, and be less reliant on outsiders. The costs and benefits of insourcing must be carefully evaluated.

FORECASTING AND FINANCIAL PLANNING

Financial management in private organizations typically operates under conditions of uncertainty or risk. Probably the most important function of business is forecasting. A forecast is a starting point for planning. The objective of forecasting is to reduce risk in decision making. In business, forecasts are the basis for capacity planning, production and inventory planning, personnel planning, planning for sales and market share, financial planning and budgeting, planning for research and development, and top management's strategic planning. Sales forecasts are especially crucial aspects of many financial management activities, including budgets, profit planning, capital expenditure analysis, and acquisition and merger analysis.

Figure 1 illustrates how sales forecasts relate to various managerial functions of business.

WHO USES FORECASTS?

Forecasts are needed for marketing, production, purchasing, personnel, and financial planning. Further, top management needs forecasts for planning and implementing long-term strategic objectives and planning for capital expenditures. More specifically, marketing managers use sales forecasts to 1) determine optimal sales force allocations, 2) set sales goals, and 3) plan promotions and advertising. Other forecasts such as market share, prices, and trends in new product development are required.

Production planners need forecasts in order to:

- Schedule production activities.
- Order materials.

Figure 1 Sales Forecasts and Managerial Functions

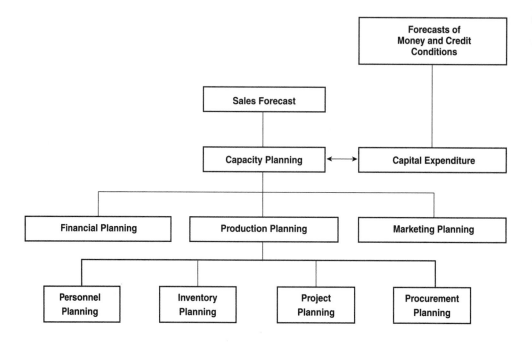

- Establish inventory levels.
- Plan shipments.

Some other areas which need forecasts include material requirements (purchasing and procurement), labor scheduling, equipment purchases, maintenance requirements, and plant capacity planning.

As shown in Figure 1, as soon as the company makes sure that it has enough capacity, the production plan is developed. If the company does not have enough capacity, it will require planning and budgeting decisions for capital spending for capacity expansion.

On this basis, the financial manager must estimate the future cash inflow and outflow, and must plan cash and borrowing needs for the company's future operations. Forecasts of cash flows and the rates of expenses and revenues are needed to maintain corporate liquidity and operating efficiency. In planning for capital investments, predictions about future economic activity are required so that returns or cash inflows accruing from the investment may be estimated.

Forecasts must also be made of money and credit conditions and interest rates so that the cash needs of the firm may be met at the lowest possible cost. The finance and accounting functions must also forecast interest rates to support the acquisition of new capital, the collection of accounts receivable to help in planning working capital needs, and capital equipment expenditure rates to help balance the flow of funds in the organization. Sound predictions of foreign exchange rates are increasingly important to financial managers of multinational companies (MNCs).

Long-term forecasts are needed for the planning of changes in the company's capital structure. Decisions as to whether to issue stock or debt in order to maintain the desired financial structure of the firm require forecasts of money and credit conditions.

The personnel department requires a number of forecasts in planning for human resources in the business. Workers must be hired and trained, and there must be benefits provided that are competitive with those available in the firm's labor market. Also, trends that affect such variables as labor turnover, retirement age, absenteeism, and tardiness need to be forecast as input for planning and decision making in this function.

The service sector today accounts for two-thirds of the U.S. gross domestic product (GDP), including banks, insurance companies, restaurants, and cruise ships. All need various projections for their operational and long-term strategic planning. For example, a bank has to forecast demands of various loans and deposits, as well as money and credit conditions so that it can determine the cost of money it lends.

TYPES OF FORECASTS

The types of forecasts used by businesses and other organizations may be classified in several categories, depending on the objective and the situation for which a forecast is to be used. Four types are discussed below.

Sales Forecasts

As discussed in the previous section, the sales forecast gives the expected level of sales for the company's goods or services throughout some future period and is instrumental in the company's planning and budgeting functions. It is the key to other forecasts and plans.

Financial Forecasts

Although the sales forecast is the primary input to many financial decisions, some financial forecasts need to be made independently of sales forecasts. This include forecasts of financial variables such as the amount of external financing needed, earnings, cash flows, and prediction of corporate bankruptcy.

Economic Forecasts

Economic forecasts, or statements of expected future business conditions, are published by governmental agencies and private economic forecasting firms. Businesses can use these forecasts and develop their own forecasts about the external business outlook that will affect their product demand. Economic forecasts cover a variety of topics including GDP, levels of employment, interest rates, and foreign exchange rates.

Technological Forecasts

A technological forecast is an estimate of rates of technological progress. Certainly, software makers are interested in the rates of technological advancement in computer hardware and its peripheral equipment. Technological changes will provide many businesses with new products and materials to offer for sale, while other companies will encounter competition from other businesses. Technological forecasting is probably best performed by experts in the particular technology.

FORECASTING METHODS

There is a wide range of forecasting techniques which the company may choose from. There are basically two approaches to forecasting: qualitative and quantitative. They are as follows:

1. Qualitative approach—forecasts based on judgment and opinion:
   - Executive opinions
   - Delphi technique
   - Sales force polling
   - Consumer surveys
   - Techniques for eliciting experts' opinions—PERT-derived
2. Quantitative approach
   a) Forecasts based on historical data:
      - Naive methods
      - Moving averages
      - Exponential smoothing
      - Trend analysis
      - Decomposition of time series
      - Box-Jenkins

b) Associative (causal) forecasts:
  - Simple regression
  - Multiple regression
  - Econometric modeling
c) Forecast based on consumer behavior:
  Markov approach
d) Indirect methods:
  - Market surveys
  - Input-output analysis
  - Economic indicators

Figure 2 summarizes the forecasting methods.

Quantitative models work superbly as long as little or no systematic change in the environment takes place. When patterns or relationships do change, by themselves, the objective models are of little use. It is here where the qualitative approach based on human judgment is indispensable. Because judgmental forecasting methods also base forecasts on observation of existing trends, they too are subject to a number of

Figure 2 Forecasting Methods

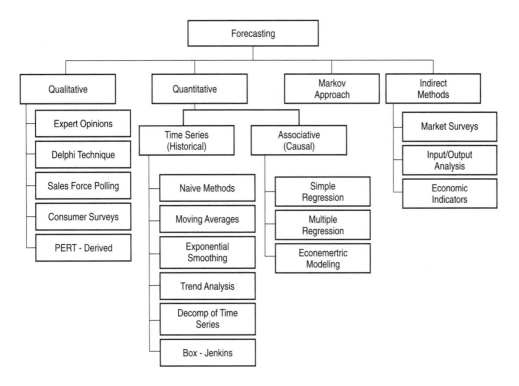

shortcomings. The advantage, however, is that they can identify systematic change more quickly and interpret better the effect of such change on the future.

We will discuss the qualitative method here in this chapter, while various quantitative methods along with their illustrations will be taken up in subsequent chapters.

SELECTION OF FORECASTING METHOD

The choice of a forecasting technique is significantly influenced by the stage of the product life cycle, and sometimes by the firm or industry for which a decision is being made.

In the beginning of the product life cycle, relatively small expenditures are made for research and market investigation. During the first phase of product introduction, these expenditures start to increase. In the rapid growth stage, considerable amounts of money are involved in the decisions; therefore a high level of accuracy is desirable. After the product has entered the maturity stage, the decisions are more routine, involving marketing and manufacturing. These are important considerations when determining the appropriate sales forecast technique.

After evaluating the particular stages of the product, and firm and industry life cycles, a further probe is necessary. Instead of selecting a forecasting technique by using whatever seems applicable, decision makers should determine what is appropriate. Some of the techniques are quite simple and rather inexpensive to develop and use, whereas others are extremely complex, require significant amounts of time to develop, and may be quite expensive. Some are best suited for short-term projections, whereas others are better prepared for intermediate- or long-term forecasts.

What technique or techniques to select depends on the following criteria:

1. What is the cost associated with developing the forecasting model compared with potential gains resulting from its use? The choice is one of benefit-cost trade-off.
2. How complicated are the relationships that are being forecasted?
3. Is it for short-run or long-run purposes?
4. How much accuracy is desired?
5. Is there a minimum tolerance level of errors?
6. How much data are available? Techniques vary in the amount of data they require.

THE QUALITATIVE APPROACH

The qualitative (or judgmental) approach can be useful in formulating short-term forecasts and can also supplement the projections based on the use of any of the quantitative methods. Four of the better-known qualitative forecasting methods are Executive Opinions, the Delphi Method, Sales Force Polling, and Consumer Surveys.

Executive Opinions

The subjective views of executives or experts from sales, production, finance, purchasing, and administration are averaged to generate a forecast about future sales. Usually this method is used in conjunction with some quantitative method such as trend extrapolation. The management team modifies the resulting forecast based on their expectations.

The advantage of this approach is that the forecasting is done quickly and easily, without need of elaborate statistics. Also, the jury of executive opinions may be the only feasible means of forecasting in the absence of adequate data. The disadvantage, however, is that of "groupthink." This is a set of problems inherent to those who meet as a group. Foremost among these problems are high cohesiveness, strong leadership, and insulation of the group. With high cohesiveness, the group becomes increasingly conforming through group pressure, which helps stifle dissension and critical thought. Strong leadership fosters group pressure for unanimous opinion. Insulation of the group tends to separate the group from outside opinions, if given.

The Delphi Method

This is a group technique in which a panel of experts are individually questioned about their perceptions of future events. The experts do not meet as a group, in order to reduce the possibility that consensus is reached because of dominant personality factors. Instead, the forecasts and accompanying arguments are summarized by an outside party and returned to the experts along with further questions. This continues until a consensus is reached by the group, especially after only a few rounds. This type of method is useful and quite effective for long-range forecasting.

The technique is done by questionnaire format and thus eliminates the disadvantages of groupthink. There is no committee or debate. The experts are not influenced by peer pressure to forecast a certain way, as the answer is not intended to be reached by consensus or unanimity. Low reliability is cited as the main disadvantage of the Delphi Method, as well as lack of consensus from the returns.

Figure 3 An Example of the Use of the Delphi Method

1 Population (in Millions)	2 Midpoint	3 Number of Panelists	4 Probability Distribution of Panelists	5 Weighted Average (2×4)
30 and above	00	0	.00	0
20-30	25	1	.05	1.25
15-19	17	2	.10	1.70
10-14	12	2	.10	1.20
5-9	7	7	.35	2.45
2-4	3	8	.40	1.20
Less than 2	1	0	.00	0
Total		20	1.00	7.80

Case example: "In 1982, a panel of 20 representatives, with college educations, from different parts of the U.S.A., were asked to estimate the population of Bombay, India. None of the panelists had been to India since World War I.

"The population was estimated to be 7.8 million, which is very close to the actual population."

Source: Singhvi, Surendra. "Financial Forecast: Why and How?" *Managerial Planning.* March/April, 1984.

Sales Force Polling

Some companies use as a forecast source salespeople who have continual contacts with customers. They believe that the sales force, who are closest to the ultimate customers, may have significant insights regarding the state of the future market. Forecasts based on sales force polling may be averaged to develop a future forecast, or they may be used to modify other quantitative and/or qualitative forecasts that have been generated internally in the company. The advantages to this method of forecasting are (1) it is simple to use and understand, (2) it uses the specialized knowledge of those closest to the action, (3) it can place responsibility for attaining the forecast in the hands of those who most affect the actual results, and (4) the information can be easily broken down by territory, product, customer, or salesperson.

The disadvantages include salespeople being overly optimistic or pessimistic regarding their predictions, and inaccuracies due to broader economic events that are largely beyond their control.

Consumer Surveys

Some companies conduct their own market surveys regarding specific consumer purchases. Surveys may consist of telephone contacts, personal interviews, or questionnaires as a means of obtaining data. Extensive statistical analysis is usually applied to survey results in order to test hypotheses regarding consumer behavior.

PERT-Derived Forecasts

A technique known as PERT (Program Evaluation and Review Technique) has been useful in producing estimates based on subjective opinions such as executive opinions or sales force polling. The PERT methodology requires that the expert provide three estimates: (1) pessimistic [a], (2) the most likely [m], and (3) optimistic [b]. The theory suggests that these estimates combine to form an expected value, or forecast, as follows:

$$EV = (a + 4m + b)/6$$

with a standard deviation of

$$\sigma = (b - a)/6$$

where

EV = expected value (mean) of the forecast

σ = standard deviation of the forecast

For example, suppose that management of a company believes that if the economy is in recession, the next year's sales will be $300,000, and if the economy is in prosperity sales will be $330,000. Their most likely estimate is $310,000. The PERT method generates an expected value of sales as follows:

$$EV = (\$300,000 + 4(\$310,000) + \$330,000)/6 = \$311,667$$

with a standard deviation of

$$\sigma = (\$330,000 - \$300,000)/6 = \$5,000$$

Advantages:

1. It is often easier and more realistic for the expert to give optimistic, pessimistic, and most likely estimates than a specific forecast value.

2. The PERT method includes a measure of dispersion (the standard deviation), which makes it possible to develop probabilistic statements regarding the forecast. In the above example, the forecaster is 95 percent confident that the true value of the forecasted sales lies between plus or minus two standard deviations from the mean ($311,667). That is, the true value can be expected to be between $211,667 and $411,667.

A Word of Caution

It is also important to realize that forecasting is not an exact science, like mathematics; it is an art. The quality of forecasts tends to improve over time as the forecaster gains more experience. Evidence shows, however, that forecasts using qualitative techniques are not as accurate as those using quantitative techniques:

> Humans possess unique knowledge and inside information not available to quantitative methods. Surprisingly, however, empirical studies and laboratory experiments have shown that their forecasts are not more accurate than those of quantitative methods. Humans tend to be optimistic and underestimate the future uncertainty. In addition, the cost of forecasting with judgmental methods is often considerably higher than when quantitative methods are used.[1]

Therefore, a forecaster must use both qualitative as well as quantitative techniques to create a reasonable forecast.

COMMON FEATURES AND ASSUMPTIONS INHERENT IN FORECASTING

As pointed out, forecasting techniques are quite different from each other. But there are certain features and assumptions that underlie the business of forecasting. They are:

1. Forecasting techniques generally assume that the same underlying causal relationship that existed in the past will continue to prevail in the future. In other words, most of our techniques are based on historical data.

---

[1] "Science of Forecasting," *International Journal of Forecasting,* Vol. 2, 1986, p. 17.

2. Forecasts are very rarely perfect. Therefore, for planning purposes, allowances should be made for inaccuracies. For example, the company should always maintain a safety stock in anticipation of stockouts.

3. Forecast accuracy decreases as the time period covered by the forecast (that is, the time horizon) increases. Generally speaking, a long-term forecast tends to be more inaccurate than a short-term forecast because of the greater uncertainty.

4. Forecasts for groups of items tend to be more accurate than forecasts for individual items, since forecasting errors among items in a group tend to cancel each other out. For example, industry forecasting is more accurate than individual firm forecasting.

STEPS IN THE FORECASTING PROCESS

There are five basic steps in the forecasting process. They are:

1. Determine the what and why of the forecast and what will be needed. This will indicate the level of detail required in the forecast (for example, forecast by region, forecast by product, etc.), the amount of resources (for example, computer hardware and software, manpower, etc.) that can be justified, and the level of accuracy desired.

2. Establish a time horizon, short-term or long-term. More specifically, project for the next year or next five years, etc.

3. Select a forecasting technique. Refer to the criteria discussed before.

4. Gather the data and develop a forecast.

5. Identify any assumptions that had to be made in preparing the forecast and using it.

6. Monitor the forecast to see if it is performing in a manner desired. Develop an evaluation system for this purpose. If not, go to step 1.

Figure 4 The Forecasting Process

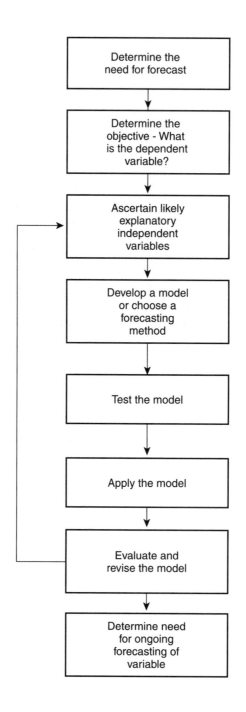

FINANCIAL AND EARNINGS FORECASTING

Financial forecasting, an essential element of planning, is the basis for *budgeting* activities. It is also needed when estimating future financing requirements. The company may look either internally or externally for financing. Internal financing refers to cash flow generated by the company's normal operating activities. External financing refers to capital provided by parties external to the company. You need to analyze how to estimate *external* financing requirements. Basically, forecasts of future sales and related expenses provide the firm with the information to project future external financing needs. This chapter discusses (1) the *percent-of-sales method* to determine the amount of external financing needed, (2) the CPA's involvement in prospective financial statements, and (3) earnings forecast.

THE PERCENT-OF-SALES METHOD

Percentage of sales is the most widely used method for projecting the company's financing needs. This method involves estimating the various expenses, assets, and liabilities for a future period as a percent of the sales forecast and then using these percentages, together with the projected sales, to construct pro forma balance sheets.

Basically, forecasts of future sales and their related expenses provide the firm with the information needed to project its future needs for financing. The basic steps in projecting financing needs are:

1. Project the firm's sales. The sales forecast is the initial most important step. Most other forecasts (budgets) follow the sales forecast.

2. Project additional variables such as expenses.

3. Estimate the level of investment in current and fixed assets required to support the projected sales.
4. Calculate the firm's financing needs.

The following examples illustrate how to develop a pro forma balance sheet and determine the amount of external financing needed.

Example 1. Assume that sales for 20X1 = $20, projected sales for 20X2 = $24, net income = 5% of sales, and the dividend payout ratio = 40%. Figure 1 illustrates the method, step by step. All dollar amounts are in millions.

Figure 1 Pro Forma Balance Sheet (in millions of dollars)

	Present (20X1)	% of Sales (20X1 Sales = $20)	Projected (20X2 Sales = $24)	
ASSETS				
Current assets	2	10	2.4	
Fixed assets	4	20	4.8	
Total assets	6		7.2	
LIABILITIES AND STOCKHOLDERS' EQUITY				
Current liabilities	2	10	2.4	
Long-term debt	2.5	n.a.	2.5	
Total liabilities	4.5		4.9	
Common stock	0.1	n.a.	0.1	
Paid-in-capital	0.2	n.a.	0.1	
Retained earnings	1.2		1.92 (a)	
Total equity	1.5		2.22	
Total liabilities and stockholders' equity	6		7.12	Total financing provided
			0.08 (b)	External financing needed
			7.2	Total

(a) 20X2 retained earnings = 20X1 retained earnings + projected net income − cash dividends paid
  = $1.2 + 5% ($24) − 40% [5% ($24)]
  = $1.2 + $1.2 − $0.48
  = $2.4 − $0.48
  = $1.92
(b) External financing need = project total assets − (projected total liabilities + projected equity)
  = $7.2 − ($4.9 + $2.22)
  = $7.2 − $7.12
  = $0.08

The steps for the computations are outlined as follows:

Step 1.   Express those balance sheet items that vary directly with sales as a percentage of sales. Any item such as long-term debt that does not vary directly with sales is designated "n.a.," or "not applicable."

Step 2.   Multiply these percentages by the 20X2 projected sales = $24 to obtain the projected amounts as shown in the last column.

Step 3.   Simply insert figures for long-term debt, common stock, and paid-in-capital from the 20X1 balance sheet.

Step 4.   Compute 20X2 retained earnings as shown in (b).

Step 5.   Sum the asset accounts, obtaining total projected assets of $7.2, and also add the projected liabilities and equity to obtain $7.12, the total financing provided. Since liabilities and equity must total $7.2, but only $7.12 is projected, we have a shortfall of $0.08 "external financing needed."

Although the forecast of additional funds required can be made by setting up pro forma balance sheets as described above, it is often easier to use the following formula:

External		Required		Spontaneous		Increase in
funds needed	=	increase	−	increase in	−	retained
(EFN)		in assets		liabilities		earnings
EFN	=	$(A/S) \Delta S$	−	$(L/S) \Delta S$	−	$(PM)(PS)(1 - d)$

where

A/S = Assets that increase spontaneously with sales as a percentage of sales.

L/S = Liabilities that increase spontaneously with sales as a percentage of sales.

ΔS = Change in sales.

PM = Profit margin on sales.

PS = Projected sales

d = Dividend payout ratio.

Example 2. In Example 1,

$A/S = \$6/\$20 = 30\%$
$L/S = \$2/\$20 = 10\%$
$\Delta S = (\$24 - \$20) = \$4$

PM = 5% on sales
PS = $24
d = 40%

Plugging these figures into the formula yields:

$$
\begin{aligned}
\text{EFN} &= 0.3(\$4) - 0.1(\$4) - (0.05)(\$24)(1 - 0.4) \\
&= \$1.2 - \$0.4 - \$0.72 = \$0.08
\end{aligned}
$$

Thus, the amount of external financing needed is $800,000, which can be raised by issuing notes payable, bonds, stocks, or any combination of these financing sources.

The major advantage of the percent-of-sales method of financial forecasting is that it is simple and inexpensive to use. One important assumption behind the use of the method is that the firm is operating at full capacity. This means that the company has no sufficient productive capacity to absorb a projected increase in sales and thus requires additional investment in assets. Therefore, the method must be used with extreme caution if excess capacity exists in certain asset accounts.

To obtain a more precise projection of the firm's future financing needs, however, the preparation of a cash budget may be required.

THE CPA'S INVOLVEMENT AND RESPONSIBILITY WITH PROSPECTIVE FINANCIAL STATEMENTS

The American Institute of Certified Public Accountants (AICPA) in Statement of Position 45-4 provides guidelines for business enterprises which publish financial forecasts. Improved financial forecasting should be of concern to the AICPA and the Securities and Exchange Commission as a basis for financial decision making and security analysis, and in affecting the future market value of securities through investor expectations. Figure 2 presents an excerpt from the 1983 Annual Report of Masco Corporation which contains (1) a five-year cash flow forecast, (2) forecasts of a five-year growth rate for sales, and (3) key assumptions used in the forecasts.

There are three types of functions that CPAs can perform with respect to prospective financial statements that will be relied upon by third parties: examination, compilation, and application of agreed-upon procedures. CPAs must prepare prospective financial statements according to AICPA standards. There must be disclosure of the underlying assumptions.

Prospective financial statements may be for general use or limited use. General use is for those not directly dealing with the client. The general user

Figure 2 Management Forecast Disclosure by Masco Corporation

FIVE-YEAR FORECAST

We have included in the annual report a sales forecast for each of our major product lines and operating groups for 1988.

While we recognize that long-term forecasts are subject to many variables and uncertainties, our experience has been that our success is determined more by our own activities than by the performance of any industry or the economy in general. In addition, the balance and diversity of our products and markets have been such that a shortfall in expected performance in one area has been largely offset by higher than expected growth in another.

Although variations may occur in the forecast for any individual product line, we have a relatively high level of confidence that our overall five-year growth forecast is achievable.

ASSUMPTIONS USED IN FORECAST

1. Average 2-3 percent annual real growth in GNP.
2. Average inflation 5-7 percent.
3. Present tax structure to continue.
4. No change in currency exchange rates.
5. No acquisitions.
6. No additional financing.
7. Dividend payout ratio 20 percent.
8. Four percent after-tax return on investment of excess cash.
9. No exercise of stock options.

FIVE-YEAR CASH-FLOW FORECAST

(In thousands)	1984-1988
Net Income	$ 850,000
Depreciation	280,000
	1,130,000
	(230,000)
	(280,000)
	(260,000)
	(170,000)
Net Cash Change	190,000
Beginning Cash, 1-84	210,000
Cash, 12-31-88	$ 400,000

SALES GROWTH BY PRODUCTS

	Sales Forecast		Actual Sales		(In thousands)
	5-Year Growth Rate 1984-1988	1988	5-Year Growth Rate 1979-1983	1983	1978
Products for the Home and Family	14%	$1,225,000	16%	$ 638,000	$308,000
Products for Industry	16%	875,000	9%	421,000	278,000
Total Sales	15%	$2,100,000	13%	$1,059,000	$585,000

SALES GROWTH BY SPECIFIC MARKETS AND PRODUCTS [1] [2]

	Forecast		Actual		(In thousands)
	5-Year Growth Rate 1984-1988	1988	5-Year Growth Rate 1979-1983	1983	1978
Masco Faucet Sales [3]	15%	$490,000	9%	$243,000	$155,000
Faucet Industry Sales-Units	7%	35,000	(5)%	25,000	32,000
Masco Market Share-Units	2%	38%	5%	34%	27%
Housing Completions	4%	1,700	(4)%	1,400	1,700
Independent Cold Extrusion Industry Sales	13%	$580,000	1%	$310,000	$290,000
Masco Cold Extrusion Sales [3]	14%	$170,000	5%	$ 88,000	$ 70,000
Truck Production	7%	3,400	(8)%	2,400	3,700
Auto Production	4%	8,200	(6)%	6,800	92,00
Masco Auto Parts Sales	13%	$210,000	8%	$113,000	$ 76,000

(1) Excludes foreign sales.   (2) Industry data Masco estimates.   (3) Includes foreign sales.

Source: 1983 Annual Report of Masco Corporation, p. 42.

may take the deal or leave it. Limited use is for those having a direct relationship with the client.

Prospective financial statements may be presented as a complete set of financial statements (balance sheet, income statement, and statement of cash flows). However, in most cases, it is more practical to present them in summarized or condensed form. At a minimum, the financial statement items to be presented are:

- Sales
- Gross margin
- Nonrecurring items
- Taxes
- Income from continuing operations
- Income from discontinued operations
- Net income
- Primary and fully diluted earnings per share
- Material changes in financial position

Not considered prospective financial statements are proforma financial statements and partial presentations.

The American Institute of CPA's Code of Professional Ethics includes the following guidelines regarding prospective financial statements:

- Cannot vouch for the achievability of prospective results.
- Must disclose assumptions.
- Accountant's report must state the nature of the work performed and the degree of responsibility assumed.

CPAs are not permitted to furnish services on prospective financial statements if the statements are solely appropriate for limited use but are distributed to parties not involved directly with the issuing company. They are not allowed to use plain-paper services on prospective financial statements for third-party use.

A prospective financial statement may be classified as either a forecast or a projection.

Financial Forecast

A financial forecast presents management's expectations, and there is an expectation that all assumptions will take place. *Note:* A financial forecast encompasses a presentation that management expects to occur but that is not necessarily most probable. A financial forecast may be most useful to general users, since it presents the client's expectations. A financial forecast and not a financial projection may be issued to passive users, or those not negotiating directly with the client.

A financial forecast may be given a single monetary amount based on the best estimate, or as a reasonable range. *Caution:* This range must not be chosen in a misleading manner.

Irrespective of the accountant's involvement, management alone has responsibility for the presentation because only management knows how it plans to run the business and accomplish its plans.

Financial Projection

A financial projection presents a "what-if" scenario that management does not necessarily expect to occur. However, a given assumption may actually occur if management moves in that direction. A financial projection may be most beneficial for limited users, since they may seek answers to hypothetical questions based on varying assumptions. These users may wish to alter their scenarios based on anticipated changing situations. A financial projection, like a forecast, may contain a range.

A financial projection may be presented to general users only when it supplements a financial forecast. Financial projections are not permitted in tax shelter offerings and other general-use documents.

Types of Engagements

The following five types of engagements may be performed by the CPA in connection with prospective financial statements:

Plain Paper. The CPA's name is not associated with the prospective statements. This service can only be conducted if all of the following conditions are satisfied:

- The CPA is not reporting on the presentation.
- The prospective statements are on paper not identifying the accountant.
- The prospective financial statements are not shown with historical financial statements that have been audited, reviewed, or compiled by the CPA.

Internal Use. The prospective financial statements are only assembled, meaning mathematical and clerical functions are performed. Assembling financial data is permitted if the following two criteria exist:

- Third parties will not use the statements.
- The CPA's name is associated with the statement.

Note that assembling prospective financial statements is limited only to internal use. Appropriate language on the statements might be "For Internal Use Only."

Compilation. This is the lowest level of service performed for prospective financial statements directed for third parties. The compilation engagement involves:

- Assembling prospective data.
- The conduct of procedures to ascertain whether the presentation and assumptions are appropriate.
- Preparation of a compilation report.

With a compilation, no assurance is given regarding the presentation or assumptions, but rather it serves to identify obvious matters to be investigated further. Working papers have to be prepared to show there was proper planning and supervision of the work, as well as compliance with required compilation procedures. The CPA must also obtain a management letter from the client regarding representations given to him.
Warning: A compilation should not be made when the forecasted financial statements exclude disclosure of the significant assumptions or when the financial projections exclude the hypothetical assumptions.

Agreed-Upon Procedures. This relates to applying procedures agreed to or requested by specific users, and issuing a report. The report identifies the procedures undertaken, gives the accountant's findings, and restricts distribution of the report to the particular parties. The specified users have to participate in establishing the nature and procedures. Also, the procedures undertaken must be more than just reading the prospective data.

Examination. The CPA appraises the preparation underlying the supporting assumptions and the presentation of prospective financial information in accordance with AICPA standards. A report is then issued on whether AICPA guidelines have been adhered to and whether the assumptions are reasonable. It is the highest level of assurance. An adverse opinion must be given if there is a failure to disclose a material assumption or if disclosed assumptions are unreasonable. For example, there may be not reasonable expectation that the actual figure will fall within the range of assumptions presented in a forecast having a range. A disclaimer opinion is necessary in the event of a scope limitation, such as when a required examination procedure cannot be performed because of client restrictions or inappropriate circumstances.

EARNINGS FORECAST

For many years, financial analysts have predicted earnings per share and stock price performance. Considerable emphasis has been placed on such forecasts in order to provide guidance to investors. Recently, management forecast disclosures in financial statements have placed greater emphasis on the development of forecasting methodology in this area. The accuracy of these earnings forecasts has been given much attention recently, primarily due to the SEC's position on financial forecasts and issuance of a Statement of Position by the AICPA.

Security Analysts versus Time-Series Models

Forecasts of earnings per share for business firms are published by both management and security analysts. Unfortunately, however, the accuracy of EPS forecasts by security analysts has been shown to be little if any better than that produced by some "naive" models such as extrapolating the past trend of earnings. Indeed, it increasingly appears that the change in EPS may be a random variable.

Projections of EPS are frequently made by independent security analysts. Examples of forecast sources include (1) Value Line Investment Survey, (2) Lynch, Jones and Ryan's Institutional Brokers Estimate System (IBES), (3) Standard & Poor's The Earnings Forecaster, and (4) Zacks Investment Research's Icarus Service. Figure 3 presents an excerpt from the monthly report from Lynch, Jones, and Ryan's IBES Service which contains various earnings forecasts by individual security analysts.

Figure 3 Extract from Monthly Summary Report of the IBES Service

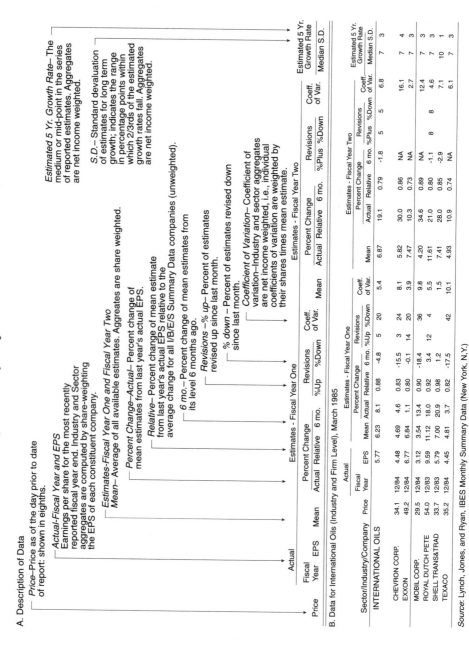

A. Description of Data

Price–Price as of the day prior to date of report: shown in eighths.

Actual–Fiscal Year and EPS
Earnings per share for the most recently reported fiscal year end. Industry and Sector aggregates are computed by share-weighting the EPS of each constituent company.

Estimates–Fiscal Year One and Fiscal Year Two
Mean– Average of all available estimates. Aggregates are share weighted.

Percent Change–Actual– Percent change of mean estimates from last year's actual EPS.

Relative– Percent change of mean estimate from last year's actual EPS relative to the average change for all I/B/E/S Summary Data companies (unweighted).

6 mo.– Percent change of mean estimates from its level 6 months ago.

Revisions –% up– Percent of estimates revised up since last month.

% down – Percent of estimates revised down since last month.

Coefficient of Variation– Coefficient of variation–Industry and sector aggregates are net income weighted, i.e., individual coefficients of variation are weighted by their shares times mean estimate.

Estimated 5 Yr. Growth Rate– The medium or mid-point in the series of reported estimates. Aggregates are net income weighted.

S.D.– Standard devaluation of estimates for long term growth; indicates the range in percentage points within which 2/3rds of the estimated growth rates fall. Aggregates are net income weighted.

B. Data for International Oils (Industry and Firm Level), March 1985

Sector/Industry/Company	Price	Actual Fiscal Year	Actual EPS	FY1 Mean	FY1 Pct Chg Actual	FY1 Pct Chg Relative	FY1 6 mo.	FY1 Rev %Up	FY1 Rev %Down	FY1 Coeff. of Var.	FY2 Mean	FY2 Pct Chg Actual	FY2 Pct Chg Relative	FY2 6 mo.	FY2 Rev %Plus	FY2 Rev %Down	FY2 Coeff. of Var.	Est 5 Yr Growth Rate Median	Est 5 Yr Growth Rate S.D.
INTERNATIONAL OILS			5.77	6.23	8.1	0.88	-4.8	5	20	5.4	6.87	19.1	0.79	-1.8	5	5	6.8	7	3
CHEVRON CORP.	34.1	12/84	4.48	4.69	4.6	0.83	-15.5	3	24	8.1	5.82	30.0	0.86	NA	NA		16.1	7	4
EXXON	49.2	12/84	6.77	6.84	1.1	0.80	-0.1	14	20	3.9	7.47	10.3	0.73	NA	NA		2.7	7	3
MOBIL CORP.	29.5	12/84	3.12	3.54	13.4	0.90	-18.4		36	9.8	4.20	34.6	0.89	NA	NA		12.4	7	3
ROYAL DUTCH PETE	54.0	12/83	9.59	11.12	18.0	0.92	3.4	12	4	5.5	11.61	21.0	0.80	-1.1	8	8	4.6	7	3
SHELL TRANS&TRAD	33.7	12/83	5.79	7.00	20.9	0.98	1.2			1.5	7.41	28.0	0.85	-2.9			7.1	10	1
TEXACO	35.2	12/84	4.45	4.81	3.7	0.82	-17.5		42	10.1	4.93	10.9	0.74	NA	NA		6.1	7	3

Source: Lynch, Jones, and Ryan, IBES Monthly Summary Data (New York, N.Y.)

Figure 4 summarizes the pros and cons of both approaches.

Figure 4 Pros and Cons of Security Analyst and Univariate Time-Series Model Approaches to Forecasting

Security Analysts Approach to Forecasting

Pros

1. Ability to incorporate information from many sources.
2. Ability to adjust to structural change immediately.
3. Ability to update continually as new information becomes available.

Cons

1. High initial setup cost and high ongoing cost to monitor numerous variables, make company visits, and so on.
2. Heavy dependence on the skills of a single individual.
3. Analyst may have an incentive not to provide an unbiased forecast (e.g., due to pressure to conform to consensus forecasts).
4. Analyst may be manipulated by company officials (at least in the short run).

Univariate Time-Series Model Approach to Forecasting

Pros

1. Ability to detect and exploit systematic patterns in the past series.
2. Relatively low degree of subjectivity in the forecasting (especially given the availability of computer algorithms to identify and estimate models).
3. Low cost and ease of updating.
4. Ability to compute confidence intervals around the forecasts.

Cons

1. Limited number of observations available for newly formed firms, firms with structural change, and so on.
2. Financial statement data may not satisfy distributional assumptions of time-series model used.
3. Inability to update forecasts between successive interim or annual earnings releases.
4. Difficulty of communicating approach to clients (especially the statistical methodology used in identifying and estimating univariate models).

Source: Foster, George, *Financial Statement Analysis,* 2nd ed., Prentice Hall, Englewood Cliffs, NJ, 1986, p. 278.

Table 1 shows sources of earnings forecasting data preferred by financial analysts.

Table 1   What Are Your Present Sources of Earnings Forecasting Data?

	Rank	1	2	3	4	5
Company contacts		56	28	24	8	9
Own research		55	15	5	1	
Industry statistics		19	14	14	7	
Other analysis		12	17	2	8	11
Historical financial data		8	12	8	5	4
Economic forecasts		7	7	10	3	
Competition		1	7	2	6	1
Computer simulation						2
Field trips			1			
Government agencies				2		
Industry & trade sources		1	7	17	3	5
Public relations of a promotional nature						1
Retired directors						1
Rumor						2
Wall Street sources		1	4	9	3	4

Rank   1 = most preferred
       5 = least preferred

Source: Carper, Brent W., Barton Jr., Frank M., Wunder Haroldene, F. "The Future of Forecasting." *Management Accounting.* August, 1997, pp. 27–31.

This section compares various forecasting methods using a sample drawn from the Standard and Poor's 400. It also examines the ability of financial analysts to forecast earnings per share performance based on the relationship of past forecasts of future earnings by financial analysts and through the use of recent univariate time-series models.

Our sample of Earnings per Share (EPS) was drawn from the 1984 through 1988 time period using the quarterly *Compustat Industrial* data tapes available from S&P. Included in our sample are 30 firms randomly selected from the Standard & Poor's 400 index for manufacturing firms over the period January 1984 to July 1988, using monthly data as reported to the public security markets. To collect data on financial analyst forecasts, we have selected the *Value Line Forecasting Survey,* which is one of several reporting agencies that employ financial analysts and report their forecasts on a weekly basis.

In order to compare the forecasting ability of financial analysts with extrapolative models, seven time-series models were used to forecast earnings per share. The popular computer forecasting software RATS was used to estimate the models.

Data for the resulting sample of firms were used over the five-year time period studied (i.e., January 1984–June 1987) to estimate the models. This period was a relatively short time period to avoid the possibility of structural changes in the economy affecting the results of the study.

Next, forecasts were derived from July 1987 to June 1988 using monthly data. The accuracy of the forecasts from each of the models for the period was evaluated using two measures: (1) MAPE (mean absolute percentage error) and (2) MSE (mean square error).

Forecasting Methodology

In this section, we present each forecasting model. These models relate to various models proposed by earnings forecasters in the accounting, finance, and forecasting literature. They are the following:

1. Exponential Smoothing Model with Additive Seasonal Effect.
2. Single Exponential Smoothing Model.
3. Exponential Smoothing Model with Linear Trend and Seasonal Additive Effects.
4. Exponential Smoothing Model with Exponential Trend and Seasonal Additive Effects.
5. Box-Jenkins Analysis SARIMA(1,0,0) (0,1,0) s = 12

   A seasonal autoregressive integrated moving average (SARIMA) model is identified with first-order autoregressive parameters and a 12-month seasonal adjustment.
6. Box-Jenkins Analysis SARIMA(1,0,0) (0,1,1) s = 12

   A seasonal autoregressive integrated moving average (SARIMA) model is identified with first-order autoregressive parameters and a 12-month seasonal adjustment. It also contains a seasonal moving average.
7. Linear Trend Analysis
8. Value Line Forecast

Forecasting Accuracy

In Table 2, the Sample Average Forecast Error was estimated for each of 12 months, based on earlier data. From July 1997 through June 1998, the monthly forecast errors are presented using the MAPE measure. From this analysis, there is some variation in forecasting accuracy. The exponential forecasting methods performed well for methods 1, 2, and 3. The Box-Jenkins approaches for methods 5 and 6 and the linear trend analysis for method 7 were reasonably successful. Overall, however, the monthly Value Line forecast resulted in the largest forecast errors.

Table 2 Sample Average Forecast Errors from 30 Companies Mean Absolute Percentage Error (MAPE)

Method	1	2	3	4	5	6	7	8
1997:7	0.28	0.30	0.39	1.54	0.42	0.64	0.57	1.77
1997:8	0.24	0.23	0.29	1.51	0.72	0.95	0.58	1.39
1997:9	0.19	0.22	0.16	1.51	1.00	1.23	0.56	0.70
1997:10	0.19	0.22	0.16	1.55	1.28	1.54	0.56	0.70
1997:11	0.24	0.43	0.46	1.48	1.72	1.98	0.56	1.73
1997:12	0.27	0.71	0.71	1.48	2.09	2.35	0.69	4.28
1998:1	0.42	0.83	1.11	1.46	2.47	2.60	0.55	4.97
1998:2	0.42	0.83	1.11	1.46	2.47	2.60	0.55	4.97
1998:3	0.67	2.15	2.10	2.00	3.31	3.45	0.73	6.01
1998:4	0.78	3.17	1.48	1.72	3.53	3.65	0.73	9.00
1998:5	0.81	1.44	1.44	1.80	0.86	0.99	0.68	8.62
1998:6	0.81	1.44	1.44	1.80	0.86	0.99	0.68	8.62

Table 2 presents the MSE results. Generally, the mean square error reflected similar conclusions (see Table 3).

Table 3 Sample Average Forecast Errors from 30 Companies Mean Square Error (MSE)

Method 1		2	3	4	5	6	7	8
1997:7	0.42	0.34	0.39	6.27	0.12	0.12	1.21	1.59
1997:8	0.31	0.23	0.40	6.17	0.13	0.13	1.26	1.63
1997:9	0.31	0.23	0.33	5.93	0.14	0.14	1.31	1.69
1997:10	0.31	0.21	0.33	5.93	0.14	0.14	1.31	1.69
1997:11	0.32	0.64	0.76	6.22	0.48	0.47	1.47	2.19
1997:12	0.34	0.78	0.87	5.93	0.55	0.53	1.62	2.39
1998:1	0.71	1.32	1.38	5.91	0.97	0.95	1.45	0.99
1998:2	0.71	1.32	1.38	5.91	0.97	0.95	1.45	0.99
1998:3	1.40	5.48	1.81	5.68	3.89	3.86	2.28	0.85
1998:4	1.20	6.10	1.40	5.33	3.45	3.43	1.95	0.82
1998:5	1.21	7.29	1.41	5.21	3.35	3.34	2.03	0.74
1998:6	1.21	7.29	1.41	5.21	3.35	3.34	2.03	0.74

CONCLUSION

Financial forecasting, an essential element of planning, is a vital function of financial managers. It is needed where the future financing needs are being estimated. Basically, forecasts of future sales and their related expenses provide the firm with the information needed to project its financing requirements. Furthermore, financial forecasting involves earnings forecasts which provide useful information concerning the expectations of a firm's future total market return. This is of interest to security analysts and investors. Different forecasting methods of earnings were compared in terms of their accuracy. Also presented was a CPA's involvement with prospective financial statements.

CASH FLOW FORECASTING

A forecast of cash collections and potential writeoffs of accounts receivable is essential in *cash budgeting* and in judging the appropriateness of current credit and discount policies. The critical step in making such a forecast is estimating the cash collection and bad debt percentages to be applied to sales or accounts receivable balances. This chapter discusses several methods of estimating *cash collection rates* (or *payment proportions*) and illustrates how these rates are used for cash budgeting purposes.

The first approach, which is based on the *Markov model,* involves the use of a probability matrix based on the estimates of what are referred to as transition probabilities. This method is described on a step-by-step basis using an illustrative example. The second approach involves a simple average. The third approach offers a more pragmatic method of estimating collection and bad debt percentages by relating credit sales and collection data. This method employs regression analysis. By using these approaches, a financial planner should be able to:

- Estimate future cash collections from accounts receivable.
- Establish an allowance for doubtful accounts.
- Provide a valuable insight into better methods of managing accounts receivable.

MARKOV APPROACH

The Markov (probability matrix) approach has been around for a long time. This approach has been successfully applied by Cyert and others to accounts receivable analysis, specifically to the estimation of that portion of the accounts receivable that will eventually become uncollectible. The method requires classification of outstanding accounts receivable according to age categories that reflect the stage of account delinquency, e.g., current accounts, accounts one month past due, accounts two months past due, and so forth. Consider the following example: XYZ department store divides its accounts receivable into two classifications: 0 to 60 days old and 61 to 120 days old. Accounts that are more than 120 days old are declared uncollectible by XYZ. XYZ currently has $10,000 in accounts receivable: $7,000 from the 0-60-day-old category and $3,000 from the 61-120-day-old category. Based on an analysis of its past records, it provides us with what is known as the matrix of transition probabilities. The matrix is given as shown in Table 1.

Table 1 Probability Matrix

From To	Collected	Uncollectible	0-60 Days Old	61-120 Days Old
Collected	(1)	0	0	0
Uncollectible	0	(1)	0	0
0-60 days old	.3	0	.5	.2
61-120 days old	.5	.1	.3	.1

Transition probabilities are nothing more than the probability that an account receivable moves from one age stage category to another. We note three basic features of this matrix. First, notice the squared element, 0 in the matrix. This indicates that $1 in the 0-60-day-old category cannot become a bad debt in one month's time. Now look at the two circled elements. Each of these is 1, indicating that, in time, all the accounts receivable dollars will either be paid or become uncollectible. Eventually, all the dollars do wind up either as collected or uncollectible, but XYZ would be interested in knowing the probability that a dollar of a 0-60-day-old or a 61-120-day-old receivable would eventually find its way into either paid bills or bad debts. It is convenient to partition the matrix of transition probabilities into four submatrices, as follows:

$$\begin{bmatrix} I & O \\ R & Q \end{bmatrix}$$

so that

$$I = \begin{bmatrix} 1 & 0 \\ 0 & 1 \end{bmatrix} \qquad O = \begin{bmatrix} 0 & 0 \\ 0 & 0 \end{bmatrix}$$

$$R = \begin{bmatrix} .3 & 0 \\ .5 & .1 \end{bmatrix} \qquad Q = \begin{bmatrix} .5 & .2 \\ .3 & .1 \end{bmatrix}$$

Now we are in a position to illustrate the procedure used to determine:

- Estimated collection and bad debt percentages by age category
- Estimated allowance for doubtful accounts

Step-by-step, the procedure is as follows:

Step 1. Set up the matrix $[I - Q]$.

$$[I - Q] = \begin{bmatrix} 1 & 0 \\ 0 & 1 \end{bmatrix} - \begin{bmatrix} .5 & .2 \\ .3 & .1 \end{bmatrix} = \begin{bmatrix} .5 & -.2 \\ -.3 & .9 \end{bmatrix}$$

Step 2. Find the inverse of this matrix, denoted by N.

$$N = [I - Q]^{-1} = \begin{bmatrix} 2.31 & .51 \\ .77 & 1.28 \end{bmatrix}$$

Note: The inverse of a matrix can be readily performed by spreadsheet programs such as Microsoft's Excel, Lotus 1-2-3, or Quattro Pro.

Step 3. Multiply this inverse by matrix R.

$$NR = \begin{bmatrix} 2.31 & .51 \\ .77 & 1.28 \end{bmatrix} \begin{bmatrix} .3 & 0 \\ .5 & .1 \end{bmatrix} = \begin{bmatrix} .95 & .05 \\ .87 & .13 \end{bmatrix}$$

NR gives us the probability that an account will eventually be collected or become a bad debt. Specifically, the top row in the answer is the probability that $1 of XYZ's accounts receivable in the 0-60-day-old category will end up in the collected and bad debt category will be paid, and a .05 probability that it will eventually become a bad debt. Turning to the second row, the two entries represent the probability that $1 now in the 61-120-day-old category will end up in the collected and bad debt categories. We can see from this row that there is a .87 probability that $1 currently in the 61-120-day-category will be collected and a .13 probability that it will eventually become uncollectible.

If XYZ wants to estimate the future of its $10,000 accounts receivable ($7,000 in the 0-60 day category and $3,000 in the 61-120 day category), it must set up the following matrix multiplication:

$$[7,000 \quad 3,000] \begin{bmatrix} .95 & .05 \\ .87 & .13 \end{bmatrix} = [9,260 \quad 740]$$

Hence, of its $10,000 in accounts receivable, XYZ expects to collect $9,260 and to lose $740 to bad debts. Therefore, the estimated allowance for the collectible accounts is $740.

The variance of each component is equal to

$$A = be \, (cNR - (cNR)_{sq})$$

where $c_i = b_i / \sum_{i=1}^{2} b_i$ and e is the unit vector.

In our example, b = (7,000 3,000), c = (.7 .3). Therefore,

$$A = [7{,}000 \quad 3{,}000] \begin{bmatrix} 1 \\ 1 \end{bmatrix} \left\{ [.7 \;\; .3] \begin{bmatrix} .95 & .05 \\ .87 & .13 \end{bmatrix} - [.7 \;\; .3] \begin{bmatrix} .95 & .05 \\ .87 & .13 \end{bmatrix}_{sq} \right\}$$

$$= 10{,}000 \, [\, [.926 \quad .074] - [.857476 \quad .005476] \,]$$

$$= [685.24 \quad 685.24]$$

which makes the standard deviation equal to $26.18 ($\sqrt{\$685.24}$). If we want to be 95 percent confident about our estimate of collections, we would set the interval estimate at $9,260 + 2(26.18), or $9,207.64 -$9,312.36, assuming t = 2 as a rule of thumb. We would also be able to set the allowance to cover the bad debts at $740 + 2(26.18), or $792.36.

SIMPLE AVERAGE

The most straightforward way to estimate collection percentages is to compute the average value realized from past data, i.e.,

$$P'_i = AVE \, (C_{t+i}/S_t)$$

$$= \frac{1}{N} \sum_{t=1}^{N} \frac{C_{t+i}}{S_t}, \quad i = 0,1,2 \ldots$$

where

P'_i = an empirical estimate of collection percentages,

C_{t+i} = cash collection in month t+i from credit sales in month t,

S_t = credit sales in month t, and

N = the number of months of past data to compute the average.

LAGGED REGRESSION APPROACH

A more scientific approach to estimating cash collection percentages (or payment proportions) is to utilize *multiple regression*. We know that there is typically a time lag between the point of a credit sale and realization of cash. More specifically, the lagged effect of credit sales and cash inflows is distributed over a number of periods, as follows:

$$C_t = b_1 S_{t-1} + b_2 S_{t-2} + \ldots b_i S_{t-i}$$

where

C_t = cash collection in month t,
S_t = credit sales made in period t,
$b_1, b_2, \ldots b_i$ = collection percentages (the same as P'_i,), and
i = number of periods lagged.

By using the regression method discussed previously, we will be able to estimate these collection rates. We can utilize "Regression" of Excel or special packages such as SPSS, MicroTSP, SAS, or Minitab.

It should be noted that the cash collection percentages $(b_1, b_2, \ldots, b_i)$ may not add up to 100 percent because of the possibility of bad debts. Once we estimate these percentages by using the regression method, we should be able to compute the bad debt percentage with no difficulty.

Table 2 shows the regression results using actual monthly data on credit sales and cash inflows for a real company. Equation I can be written as follows:

$$C_t = 60.6\%(S_{t-1}) + 24.3\%(S_{t-2}) + 8.8\%(S_{t-3})$$

This result indicates that the receivables generated by the credit sales are collected at the following rates: first month after sale, 60.6 percent; second month after sale, 24.3 percent; and third month after sale, 8.8 percent. The bad debt percentage is computed as 6.3 percent (100 – 93.7%).

It is important to note, however, that these collection and bad debt percentages are probabilistic variables; that is, variables whose values cannot be known with precision. However, the standard error of the regression coefficient and the 5-value permit us to assess the probability that the true percentage is between specified limits. The confidence interval takes the following form:

$$b \pm t\, S_b$$

where S_b = standard error of the coefficient.

Table 2 Regression Results for Cash Collection (C_t)

Independent Variables	Equation I	Equation II
S_{t-1}	0.606[a]	0.596[a]
	(0.062)[b]	(0.097)
S_{t-2}	0.243[a]	0.142
	(0.085)	(0.120)
S_{t-3}	0.088	0.043
	(0.157)	(0.191)
S_{t-4}		0.136
		(0.800)
R^2	0.754	0.753
Durbin-Watson	2.52[c]	2.48[c]
Standard Error of the estimate(S_e)	11.63	16.05
Number of monthly observations	21	20
Bad debt percentages	0.063	0.083

[a]Statistically significant at the 5% significance level.
[b]This figure in parentheses is the standard error of the e estimate for the coefficient (S_b).
[c]No autocorrelation present at the 5% significance level.

Example 1. To illustrate, assuming $t = 2$ as rule of thumb at the 95 percent confidence level, the true collection percentage from the prior month's sales will be:

$$60.6\% \pm 2(6.2\%) = 60.6\% \pm 12.4\%$$

Turning to the estimation of cash collections and allowance for doubtful accounts, the following values are used for illustrative purposes:

$S_{t-1} = \$77.6$, $S_{t-2} = \$58.5$, $S_{t-3} = \$76.4$, and forecast average monthly net credit sales = $\$75.2$

Then, (a) the forecast cash collection for period t would be

$$C_t = 60.6\%(77.6) + 19.3\%(58.5) + 8.8\%(76.4) = \$65.04$$

If the financial manager wants to be 95 percent confident about this forecast value, then the interval would be set as follows:

$$C_t \pm t\, S_e$$

where S_e = standard error of the estimate.
To illustrate, using $t = 2$ as a rule of thumb at the 95 percent confidence level, the true value for cash collections in period t will be

$$\$65.04 \pm 2(11.63) = \$65.04 \pm 23.26$$

(b) the estimated allowance for uncollectible accounts for period t will be

6.3% ($75.2) = $4.74

By using the limits discussed so far, financial planners can develop flexible (or probabilistic) cash budgets, where the lower and upper limits can be interpreted as pessimistic and optimistic outcomes, respectively. They can also simulate a cash budget in an attempt to determine both the expected change in cash collections for each period and the variation in this value.

In preparing a conventional cash inflow budget, the financial manager considers the various sources of cash, including cash on account, sale of assets, incurrence of debt, and so on. Cash collections from customers are emphasized, since that is the greatest problem in this type of budget.

Example 2. The following data are given for Erich Stores:

	September Actual	October Actual	November Estimated	December Estimated
Cash sales	$ 7,000	$ 6,000	$ 8,000	$ 6,000
Credit sales	50,000	48,000	62,000	80,000
Total sales	$57,000	$54,000	$70,000	$86,000

Past experience indicates net collections normally occur in the following pattern:

- No collections are made in the month of sale.
- 80% of the sales of any month are collected in the following month.
- 19% of sales are collected in the second following month.
- 1% of sales are uncollectible.

We can project total cash receipts for November and December as follows:

	November	December
Cash receipts		
Cash sales	$ 8,000	$ 6,000
Cash collections		
September sales		

50,000 (19%)	9,500	
October sales		
48,000 (80%)	38,400	
48,000 (19%)		9,120
November sales		
62,000 (80%)		49,600
Total cash receipts	$55,900	$64,720

CONCLUSION

Two methods of estimating the expected collectible and uncollectible patterns were presented. One advantage of the Markov model is that the expected value and standard deviation of these percentages can be determined, thereby making it possible to specify probabilistic statements about these figures. We have to be careful about these results, however, since the model makes some strong assumptions. A serious assumption is that the matrix of transition probabilities is constant over time. We do not expect this to be perfectly true. Updating of the matrix may have to be done, perhaps through the use of such techniques as exponential smoothing and time series analysis.

The regression approach is relatively inexpensive to use in the sense that it does not require a lot of data. All it requires is data on cash collections and credit sales. Furthermore, credit sales values are all predetermined; we use previous months' credit sales to forecast cash collections—that is, there is no need to forecast credit sales. The model also allows you to make all kinds of statistical inferences about the cash collection percentages and forecast values.

Extensions of these models can be made toward setting credit and discount policies. Corresponding to a given set of policies, there is an associated transition matrix in the Markov model, and associated collection percentages in the regression model. By computing long-term collections and bad debts for each policy, an optimal policy can be chosen that maximizes expected long-run profits per period.

INTEREST RATE FORECASTING

While there have been a number of efforts devoted to evaluating the accuracy of forecasts of sales and earnings per share, there has been little attention given to the reliability of interest forecasts. Noting that interest rates and earnings are more closely linked than ever before, interest rates need to be forecast accurately.

Furthermore, many corporate financial decisions, such as the timing of a bond refunding, are dependent on anticipated changes in interest rates. Especially for financial institutions, a change in the level of interest rates can be one of the most important variables determining the success of the enterprise since both lending and investing decisions are influenced heavily by anticipated movements in interest rates. Clearly, the accuracy of interest rate forecasts is important from the perspective of the producer and the consumer of such forecasts.

Whether refinancing a mortgage, changing the mix of investment portfolios, or completing a multimillion-dollar acquisition, the future direction of interest rates is a key factor. It is important to develop a tracking and forecasting system that considers not only economic factors but also psychological and political forces.

INTEREST RATE FUNDAMENTALS

Today's supply of and demand for credit determines today's short-term interest rate. Expectations about the future supply of and demand for credit determine the long-term interest rate. Therefore, it is safe to say that short- and long-term interest rates are affected by similar factors.

Then what are the specific factors that determine interest rates? The business cycle is one factor. The cycle tends to dictate credit demands by the government and businesses. Economic growth is "credit and liquidity driven" in our economy. As the demand for funds strengthens during an expansion, there is an upward pressure on interest rates. The reverse would occur during a business contraction.

Although the demand side is stressed in this explanation of the cyclical effect on interest rates, the supply side of credit and liquidity should not be ignored. For example, foreign credit supply is certainly an important factor these days. The larger the trade deficit, the larger will be the trade deficit of foreign capital into the U.S.—which, all things being equal, helps lower interest rates.

Any gap between the demand and supply will be accentuated by monetary policy. The Federal Reserve is supposed to "lean against the wind." Thus, the Fed's net addition to liquidity (growth of the monetary aggregates) will tend to raise interest rates near cyclical peaks and diminish them at cyclical troughs.

In addition, inflation affects short- and long-term interest rates. One key factor is compensation for anticipated inflation, which would otherwise erode the purchasing power of principal and interest and hence ruin the supply of savings.

The stage is set for interest rate forecasting. Interest rates are the dependent variable within a multiple regression framework in which the state of the business cycle, monetary policy, and inflation anticipation are the right-hand explanatory variables.

The difficulty, however, is that the correct measurement of the explanatory factors is hard to find. For example, how do you represent the business cycle? It can be characterized by a multitude of business conditions and their statistical representations. The Fed's monetary policy is another example. Finding the right "proxies" would be a burdensome task.

Furthermore, the interest rate as the dependent variable is also hard to define since there are short-term rates, intermediate-term rates, and long-term rates. Table 1 presents a guide to selecting the dependent variable and conceivable independent variables. This table is by no means an exhaustive list and is only a suggested guide, based on a review of past efforts at forecasting interest rates.

Table 2 provides a list of variables that emerged from some selected prior empirical testing by interest rate experts.

STATISTICAL METHODOLOGY AND A SAMPLE MODEL

Despite many difficulties, statistical forecasts of interest rates are commonly attempted by business economists and are frequently structured along the lines of the sample equation shown in Table 3. Multiple regression analysis appears to be the dominant approach to building the model for interest rate forecasting.

Table 1 Commonly Used Variables in Interest Rate Forecasting

Dependent Variables

1. *Short-Term Rates*

   U.S. Treasury bill rates (notably three-month)

   Federal funds rate

   Prime rate

2. *Long-Term Rates*

   New AA utility bond yields

   20-year U.S. Treasury bond yields

   30-year U.S. Treasury bond yields

   10-year U.S. Treasury bond yields

   Commercial mortgage rates

   Residential mortgage rates

Independent Variables

1. *Real Economic Activity*

   Real GDP

   Change in real GDP

   Change in non-agricultural payroll employment

   Confidence index

   Leading economic indicators

2. *Capacity Utilization*

   Rate of growth in productivity

   Vendor performance

   New capacity utilization estimates

   Manufacturers' capacity utilization

   Operating rates to preferred rates

   Utilization rate ... Manufacturing

   Capacity utilization ... Primary materials

   Capacity utilization ... Advanced processing

   Buying policy

   Business equipment/consumer goods

   Help wanted/unemployment

   Number of initial jobless claims

   Change in unfilled orders

   Output/capacity

3. *Credit Demands by Government and Businesses*
   Income velocity (GDP/M-1)
   Federal budget deficit/GDP
   Change in mortgage debt
   Change in bank loans to business
   Change in installment debt
4. *Inflation Rate*
   Change in CPI (Consumer Price Index)
   Change in PPI (Producer Price Index)
5. *Monetary Aggregates*
   Change in money supply (M-1)
   Change in money supply (M-2)
   Real money base—Money supply in constant dollars (M-1)
6. *Liquidity*
   Money supply (M-1)/GDP
   Money supply (M-2)/GDP
7. *Banking*
   Member bank borrowing
   Loans/deposits . . . Commercial banks
   Loans/investments . . . Commercial banks
8. *Households*
   Change in household net worth (flow of funds)
9. *Corporations*
   Internal cash flow/business capital spending
10. *Foreign Credit Supplies and Foreign Influences*
    Size of current account (i.e., foreign trade) deficit/GDP
    Foreign interest rates
11. *Expectational-type Variables*
    Moving average of prior years of actual inflation
    Moving average of the change in the 3-month T-bill yield
    Polynomial distributed lag of the percentage change in the CPI

In Table 3, we show the 20-year U.S. Treasury bond yield as a function of the unemployment rate, the growth in money supply, a weighted average of past inflation, and volatility in the three-month Treasury bill.

Table 2   Key Variables in Interest Rate Forecasting Found in the Literature

Dependent Variable	Independent (Explanatory) Variables
1. *Roger Williams*[1]	
Federal fund rate	Vendor performance
	Change in money supply M-1 or M-2
	Rate of change in the CPI
New AA utility bond yields	Vendor performance
	Rate of change in the CPI lagged one period
	Ratio of bank loans to investments lagged one period
2. *The Prudential*[2]	
10-year Treasury bond yields	Government deficits/GDP
	Foreign trade/GDP
	Rate of growth in productivity
	Moving average of the five prior years of actual inflation
	Lagged change in GDP
	Foreign interest rates
	Variance and momentum indexes
3. *Schott*[3]	
20-year Treasury bond yields	Log (unemployment rate)
	Percentage change in M-1
	Polynomial distributed lag of the percentage change in the CPI
	Volatility = moving average of the change in the three-month T-bill.
4. *Horan*[4]	
New AA utility bond yield	Income volatility (GDP/M-1)
	Moving average of CPI change
	Commercial paper rate
	RHO (autoregressive error term)

[1]Roger Williams, "Forecasting Interest Rates and Inflation," *Business Economics,* January 1979, pp. 57-60.
[2]The Prudential, "Understanding Long-Term Interest Rates," *Economic Review,* July 1991, pp. 1-8.
[3]Francis H. Scott, "Forecasting Interest Rates: Methods and Application," *Journal of Business Forecasting,* Fall 1986, pp. 11-19.
[4]Lawrence J. Horan, "Forecasting Long-Term Interest Rates—A New Method," *Business Economics,* September 1978, pp. 5-8.

Table 3   Model and Values of Parameters

Model

20-Year T-Bond Yield =

$b_0 + b_1 \times$ log (Unemployment Rate) $+ b_2 \times$ % Change in M-1
$+ b_3 \times$ Change in CPI, Annualized $+ b_4 \times$ Volatility

Value of Parameters

Independent Variable	Coefficient	t-Value*
1. Constant	11.137	4.36
2. Log (unemployment rate)	−3.297	−3.65
3. Percentage change in M-1	−0.026	−2.16
4. Polynomial distributed lag of the percentage change in the CPI annualized; lag of 4 quarters, 2nd degree polynomial	−0.24	2.73
5. Volatility; 4-year moving average of the absolute value of the change in the 3-month T-bill	1.726	2.05

n   = 47
S_e = 0.4709
R^2 = 0.975
Durbin-Watson = 1.64**

---

*Statistically significant at the 5 percent significance level.
**No autocorrelation (serial correlation) at the 1 percent level.
Source: Schott, Francis H., "Forecasting Interest Rates: Methods and Application," *Journal of Business Forecasting,* Fall 1986, p. 18.

CHECKLIST FOR SCREENING OUT EXPLANATORY FACTORS

In order to pick the best regression equation for interest rate forecasting, you should pretty much follow the same criteria as in Multiple Regression Analysis:

1. Many independent variables listed in Table 2 tend to be highly correlated with each other (*muticollinearity*). This will help lead to the elimination of a number of overlapping series.

2. Variables cannot be retained unless the positive or negative signs of regression coefficients are consistent with theoretical expectations.

3. Traditional yardsticks such as R^2, t-test, F-test, and Durbin-Watson test must be used to select preliminary equations.

4. The predictive performance of the preliminary models needs to be tested based on *ex ante* and *ex post* forecasts.

   a. It is usually measured by such metrics as MPE, RSME, MSE, MAD, and/or Henry Theil U Coefficient.

   b. Compare the forecasts with some "naive" (but much less costly) approach, such as assuming that rates in the future will be the same as today.

   c. Compare quantitative approaches such as econometric forecasting with judgmental forecasts. Judgment can be the overriding factor in interest rate forecasting.

   d. In addition to these evaluations, a separate evaluation of *turning point errors* needs to be made. A turning point error takes place either when you project an increase in interest levels but rates declined or when you anticipated its decline but rates increased. It is often argued that the ability of forecasters to anticipate reversals of interest rate trends is more important than the precise accuracy of the forecast. Substantial gains or losses may arise from a change from generally upward-moving rates to downward rate trends (or vice versa), but gains or losses from incorrectly predicting the extent of a continued increase or decrease in rates may be much more limited.

A WORD OF CAUTION

No reasonable business planners should rely solely on statistical methods such as multiple regression. Other quantitative methods need to be attempted. It is important to realize that differences among forecasting methods and assumptions and in a choice of proxies regarding the explanatory variables can yield vastly different results from analyst to analyst. Judgments and expert opinions can help determine the future direction of interest rates. The right marriage between a quantitative evaluation and expert judgments is a must. Consensus forecasts such as those of the National Association of Business Economists (NABE), which receive wide coverage in the financial press, and econometric forecasts made by consulting firms such as The Wharton Econometric Associates, Chase Econometrics, and DRI/McGraw-Hill, should be consulted as well.

The cost of errors in interest rate forecasting can be as severe as that of exchange rate forecasting mistakes. Schott at Equitable Life suggests that businesses use specific strategies and policies to reduce their exposure to interest rate forecasting mistakes (e.g., asset/liability maturity matching and hedging with futures).

CONCLUSION

Interest rate forecasting is as treacherous as other economic forecasting, such as the prediction of corporate earnings and foreign exchange rates. The chapter briefly touched upon fundamentals: business cycles, the outlook for the demand and supply of credits, monetary policy, and the inflation rate. It also presented a sample model that reflects on the fundamental theory. The forecasting ability of the model should also be judged in terms of its ability to anticipate major changes in the direction (or turning point) of rates.

FORECASTING FOREIGN EXCHANGE RATES*

This chapter addresses the problem of forecasting foreign exchange rates. It explores the need for managers to forecast the exchange rates. It then establishes a framework of the international exchange markets and explores the relationship between exchange rates, interest rate, and inflation rate. The chapter focuses on the different types of forecasting techniques used to predict the foreign exchange rates and concludes by setting up a framework within which forecasts can be evaluated.

WHY FORECAST EXCHANGE RATES?

Frequently companies are faced with a decision regarding forecasting foreign exchange rates. Some companies choose to ignore forecasting, while others often rely on their banks for the answer. Very few companies dedicate resources to forecasting foreign exchange rate.

Many companies argue that the forecasts of international exchange rates are often inaccurate and hence invalid. Therefore, there is no need to forecast. These companies, however, fail to understand that forecasting is not an exact science but rather an art form in which quality of forecasts generally tend to improve as companies and managers gain more experience in forecasting.

In today's global environment, companies trading across national boundaries are often exposed to transaction risk, the risk that comes from fluctuation in the exchange rate between the time a contract is signed and when the payment is received. Historically, exchange rates have been fixed and there have been very few fluctuations within a short time period. However, most exchange rates today are floating and can easily vary as much as 5% within a week. Moreover, the recent crisis in the European

---

* This chapter was coauthored by Anique Qureshi, Ph.D., CPA, CIA, associate professor of accounting at Queens College, and an accounting consultant.

monetary market illustrates the need for accurate exchange rate information. There are four primary reasons why it is imperative to forecast the foreign exchange rates.

1. Hedging Decision

Multinational companies (MNCs) are constantly faced with the decision of whether or not to hedge payables and receivables in foreign currency. An exchange rate forecast can help MNCs determine if they should hedge their transactions. As an example, if forecasts determine that the Swiss franc is going to appreciate in value relative to the dollar, a company expecting payment from a Swiss partner in the future may not decide to hedge the transaction. However, if the forecasts showed that the Swiss franc is going to depreciate relative to the dollar, the U.S. partner should hedge the transaction.

2. Short-Term Financing Decision for MNC

A large corporation has several sources of capital market and several currencies in which it can borrow. Ideally, the currency it would borrow would exhibit a low interest rate and depreciate in value over the financial period. For example, A U.S. firm could borrow in German marks; during the loan period, the marks would depreciate in value; at the end of the period, the company would have to use fewer dollars to buy the same amount of marks and would benefit from the deal.

3. International Capital Budgeting Decision

Accurate cash flows are imperative in order to make a good capital budgeting decision. In case of international projects, it is not only necessary to establish accurate cash flows, but it is also necessary to convert them into an MNC's home country currency. This necessitates the use of a foreign exchange forecast to convert the cash flows and, thereafter, evaluate the decision.

4. Subsidiary Earning Assessment for MNC

When an MNC reports its earnings, international subsidiary earnings are often translated and consolidated in the MNC's home country currency. For example, when IBM makes a projection for its earnings, it needs to project its earnings in Germany, then it needs to translate these earnings from deutsche marks to dollars. A depreciation in marks would decrease a subsidiary's earnings and vice versa. Thus, it is necessary to generate an accurate forecast of marks to create a legitimate earnings assessment.

Forecasting Foreign Exchange Rates

SOME BASIC TERMS AND RELATIONSHIPS

At this point, it is necessary to address some of the basic terminology used in foreign exchange as well as the fundamental laws of international monetary economics. It is also necessary to establish a basic international monetary framework before forecasting.

Spot Rate

Spot rate can be defined as the rate that exists in today's market. Table 1 illustrates a typical listing of foreign exchange rates found in the *Wall Street Journal*. The British pound is quoted at 1.6708. This rate is the spot rate. It means you can go to the bank today and exchange $1.6708 for £1.00. For example, if you need £10,000 for a paying off an import transaction on a given day, you would ask your bank to purchase £10,000. The bank would not hand you the money, but instead it would instruct its English subsidiary to pay £10,000 to your English supplier, and it would debit you account by (10,000 × 1.6708) $16,708.

Forward Rate

Besides the spot rate, Table 1 also quotes the forward rate. The 90-day forward rate for the pound is quoted as 1.6637. In the forward market, you buy and sell currency for a future delivery date, usually one, three, or six months in advance. If you know you need to buy or sell currency in the future, you can hedge against a loss by selling in the forward market. For example, let's say you are required to pay £10,000 in 3 months to your English supplier. You can purchase £10,000 today by paying $16,637 (10,000 × 1.6637). These pounds will be delivered in 90 days. In the meantime you have protected yourself. No matter what the exchange rate of pound or U.S. dollar is in 90 days, you are assured delivery at the quoted price.

As can be seen in the example, the cost of purchasing pounds in the forward market ($16,637) is less than the price in the spot market ($16,708). This implies that the pound is selling at a forward discount relative to the dollar, so you can buy more pounds in the forward market. It could also mean that the U.S. dollar is selling at a forward premium.

Interest Rate Parity Theory

The interest rate parity theory says that interest rate differential must equal the difference between the spot and the forward rate. The validity of this theory can easily be tested by a simple example. Let's assume that the interest rate in the U.S. is 10%. An identical investment in Switzerland yields 5%.

Table 1 Sample Listing of Foreign Exchange Rates

Thursday, April 30, 1998

The New York foreign exchange selling rates below apply to trading among banks in amounts of $1 million and more, as quoted at 4 p.m. Eastern time by Dow Jones and other sources. Retail transactions provide fewer units of foreign currency per dollar.

Country	U.S. $ equiv.		Currency per U.S. $	
	Thu	Wed	Thu	Wed
Argentina (Peso)	1.0001	1.0001	.9999	.9999
Australia (Dollar)	.6500	.6494	1.5385	1.5399
Austria (Schilling)	.07911	.07913	12.640	12.638
Bahrain (Dinar)	2.6525	2.6525	.3770	.3770
Belgium (Franc)	.02698	.02698	37.065	37.060
Brazil (Real)	.8744	.8736	1.1436	1.1447
Britain (Pound)	1.6708	1.6697	.5985	.5989
1-month forward	1.6682	1.6672	.5994	.5998
3-months forward	1.6637	1.6625	.6011	.6015
6-months forward	1.6575	1.6566	.6033	.6036
Canada (Dollar)	.6988	.6959	1.4310	1.4369
1-month forward	.6993	.6964	1.4301	1.4369
3-months forward	.7001	.6971	1.4284	1.4345
6-months forward	.7012	.6981	1.4261	1.4324
Chile (Peso)	.002208	.002209	452.85	452.65
China (Renminbi)	.1208	.1208	8.2781	8.2782
Colombia (Peso)	.0007322	.0007292	1365.72	1371.35
Czech. Rep. (Koruna)	. . . .	. . . .	. . . .	. . . .
Commercial rate	.03031	.03017	32.995	33.149
Denmark (Krone)	.1460	.1460	6.8475	6.8490
Ecuador (Sucre)	. . . .	. . . .	. . . .	. . . .
Floating rate	.0001996	.0001996	5010.00	5010.00
Finland (Markka)	.1836	.1835	5.4480	5.4490
France (Franc)	.1661	.1661	6.0195	6.0200
1-month forward	1.664	1.664	6.0088	6.0092
3-months forward	1.670	1.670	5.9886	5.9888
6-months forward	1.678	1.678	5.9605	5.9594

Furthermore, the exchange rate is .7097 dollar per franc. An investor can invest $100,000 in the U.S. and earn interest of $5,000 (100,000 × .10/2) in six months. The same investor can today purchase 140,905 francs (100,000/.7097) and invest in a Swiss bank to earn 144,428 francs. Now when the investor decides to transfer his currency to the U.S., what will be the exchange rate? If the investor has sold francs in the 180-day forward market, the exchange rate should be 0.7270 and investor earnings would transfer to $105,000. If the exchange rate were lower, i.e., 0.7100, the amount would be $102,543 and no one would be interested in investing in Switzerland. All Swiss investors would want to invest in the U.S., so they would buy dollars and drive down the exchange rate until the exchange rate was 0.7270 and excess profits disappeared.

Fisher Price Effect

The Fisher Price effect states that the difference in interest rates must equal the expected difference in inflation rates. Interest rate is made up of several different components:

$$\text{Interest Rate} = K_r + K_i + K_{drp}$$

where

K_i = the inflation premium
K_{drp} = the default risk premium
K_r = the real interest rate

Fisher argued that the real interest rate remains the same for all countries. Thus the differences in exchange rate are a direct result of differences in inflation rates. (It is assumed that the investments are identical and therefore default risk would be the same.) If the real interest rates were different, that would provide an excellent opportunity for currency arbitrage and eventually, the market would make the exchange rates such that the real interest rate was identical.

Purchasing Power Parity

The law of purchasing power parity states that the expected difference in inflation rate equals the difference between the forward and the spot rate. This can be easily proven. According to the interest rate parity theory, the difference in interest rates equals the difference between the forward and spot rates. According to the Fisher Price effect, the difference between interest rates also equals the difference between inflation rates. Therefore, the difference between the inflation rates should equal the difference between the forward and spot rates.

The three previously described theories form the cornerstone of international finance. These theories are very important in that they are used in developing some fundamental forecasting models. These three models have been kept relatively simple, although real life is not this simple. Frequently these models are modified to account for real world and market imperfections.

FORECASTING TECHNIQUES

The international financial markets are very complex. Therefore, a variety of forecasting techniques are used to forecast the foreign exchange rate. A certain method of forecasting may be more suited to one particular exchange rate or scenario. There are four major ways of forecasting foreign exchange rates: fundamental forecasting, market-based forecasting, technical forecasting, and a mixture of the three.

Fundamental Forecasting

Fundamental forecasting is based on fundamental relationships between economic variables and exchange rates. Given current values of these variables along with their historical impact on a currency's value, corporations can develop exchange rate projections. In previous sections, we established a basic relationship between exchange rates, inflation rates, and interest rates. This relationship can be used to develop a simple linear forecasting model for the deutsche mark.

$$DM = a + b \,(INF) + c \,(INT)$$

where

> DM = the quarterly percentage change in the German mark
>
> INF = quarterly percentage change in inflation differential (U.S. inflation rate – German inflation rate)
>
> INT = quarterly percentage change in interest rate differential (U.S. interest rate – German interest rate)

Note: This model is relatively simple, with only two explanatory variables. In many cases, several other variables are added, but the essential methodology remains the same.

Example 1. The following example illustrates how exchange rate forecasting can be accomplished using the fundamental approach. Table 2 shows the basic input data for the ten quarters. Table 3 shows a summary of the regression output, based on the use of Microsoft Excel.

Table 2

Period	US CPI	US INF	G CPI	G INF	US INT	G INT	DM/$	INF Diff	INT Diff
Apr 95	123.7	1.56%	104.0	0.87%	9.64%	6.97%	1.8783	0.69%	2.67%
Jul 95	124.7	0.81%	104.5	0.48%	9.51%	6.87%	1.8675	0.33%	2.64%
Oct 95	125.9	0.96%	105.2	0.67%	9.92%	7.40%	1.8375	0.29%	2.52%
Jan 96	128.1	1.75%	105.9	0.67%	10.82%	8.50%	1.6800	1.08%	2.32%
Apr 96	129.4	1.01%	106.4	0.47%	11.42%	8.87%	1.6820	0.54%	2.55%
Jul 96	131.6	1.70%	107.3	0.85%	11.25%	8.93%	1.5920	0.85%	2.32%
Oct 96	133.8	1.67%	108.4	1.03%	10.83%	9.00%	1.5180	0.65%	1.83%
Jan 97	134.9	0.82%	108.7	0.28%	10.06%	9.70%	1.4835	0.55%	0.36%
Apr 97	135.7	0.59%	108.7	0.00%	10.16%	8.40%	1.7350	0.59%	1.76%
Jul 97	136.6	0.66%	109.7	0.92%	9.84%	8.60%	1.7445	−0.26%	1.24%
Oct 97	137.8	0.88%	111.8	1.91%	9.62%	8.40%	1.6750	−1.04%	1.36%
Jan 98	138.8	0.73%	1112.7	0.81%	9.36%	8.00%		−0.08%	1.36%

Period	*Quarterly % Change*		
	INF Diff.	INT Diff.	DM/$
Jul 95	−0.5231	−0.01124	−0.00575
Oct 95	−0.1074	−0.04545	−0.01606
Jan 96	2.6998	−0.07937	−0.08571
Apr 96	−0.4984	0.099138	0.00119
Jul 96	0.5742	−0.0902	−0.05351
Oct 96	−0.2431	−0.21121	−0.04648
Jan 97	−0.1565	−0.80328	−0.02273
Apr 97	0.0874	3.888889	0.169532
Jul 97	−1.4329	−0.29545	0.005476
Oct 97	3.0346	−0.01613	−0.03984
Jan 98	−0.9234	0.114754	

Source: The raw data was derived from *International Economic Conditions,* August 1998.

Table 3 Microsoft Excel Regression Output

Analysis of Variance	df	Sum of Squares	Mean Square	F	Significance F
Regression	2	0.039325	0.01966	41.317	0.00013
Residual	7	0.003331	0.00048		
Total	9	0.042656			

	Coefficients	Standard Error	t-Statistic	P-value	Lower 95%	Upper 95%
Intercept	−0.0149	0.0072502	−2.057589	0.06975	−0.0321	0.00223
INF Diff.	−0.0171	0.0050964	−3.352584	0.00849	−0.0291	−0.005
INT Diff.	0.04679	0.0055715	8.39862	15E−05	0.0336	0.05997

Regression Statistics

Multiple R	0.9602
R Square	0.9219
Adjusted R Square	0.8996
Standard Error	0.0218
Observations	10

Our forecasting model that can be used to predict the DM/$ exchange rate for the next quarter is:

$$DM = -0.0149 - 0.0171 \ (INF) + 0.0468 \ (INT)$$
$$R^2 = 92.19\%$$

Ex post predictions are summarized in Table 4 and plotted against actual values in Figure 1.

Assuming that INT = −0.9234 and INF = 0.1148 for the next quarter,

$$DM = -0.0149 - 0.0171 \ (-0.9234) + 0.0468 \ (0.1148) = 0.00623$$
$$DM/\$ = (1 + 0.00623) \times (1.6750) = 1.6854$$

According to the forecast, the exchange rate in the first quarter of 98 should be 1.6854. The actual rate was 1.6392. The error in the forecast was .0462 (1.6854 − 1.6392) and the mean percentage error (MPE) of the forecast was 2.78%.

This example presented a simple fundamental forecasting model for foreign exchange rates. This model is especially useful if the exchange rates

Forecasting Foreign Exchange Rates

Table 4

Observation	Predicted Y	Residuals	Standardized Residuals	Percentile	DM/$
1	−0.00651	0.000756	0.034667	5	−0.0857
2	−0.01521	−0.00085	−0.039159	15	−0.0535
3	−0.06476	−0.02095	−0.960496	25	−0.0465
4	−0.00176	0.002953	0.135359	35	−0.0398
5	−0.02895	−0.02456	−1.125773	45	−0.0227
6	−0.02065	−0.02584	−1.184324	55	−0.0161
7	−0.04983	0.027104	1.242462	65	−0.0057
8	0.165562	0.00397	0.181967	75	0.0012
9	−0.00426	0.009735	0.446276	85	0.0055
10	−0.06752	0.027684	1.269022	95	0.1695

Figure 1   Plot of Predicted and Actual Y Values

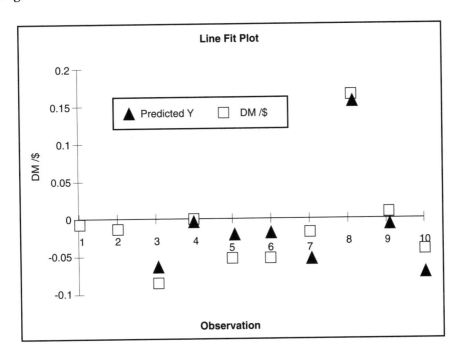

are freely floating and there is minimum government or central bank intervention in the currency market. Note that this model relies on relationships between macroeconomic variables.

However, there are certain problems with this forecasting technique. First, this technique will not be very effective with fixed exchange rates. This technique also relies on forecast to forecast. That is, one needs to project the future interest rate and the future inflation rate in order to compute the differentials that are the used to compute the exchange rate. *Note:* These estimates are frequently published in trade publications and bank reports. Second, this technique often ignores other variables that influence the foreign exchange rate.

Market-Based Forecasting

The process of developing forecasts from market indicators is known as *market-based forecasting*. This is perhaps the easiest forecasting model. While it is very simple, it is also very effective. The model relies on the spot rate and the forward rate to forecast the price. The model assumes that the spot rate reflects the foreign exchange rate in the near future. Let us suppose that the Italian lira is expected to depreciate versus the U.S. dollar. This would encourage speculators to sell lira and later purchase them back at the lower (future) price. If continued, this process would drive down the price of lira until the excess (arbitrage) profits were eliminated.

The model also suggests that the forward exchange rate equals the future spot price. Again, let us suppose that the 90-day forward rate is .987. The market forecasters believe that the exchange rate in 90 days is going to be .965. This provides an arbitrage opportunity. Markets will keep on selling the currency in the forward market until the opportunity for excess profit is eliminated.

This model, however, relies heavily on market efficiency. It assumes that capital markets and currency markets are highly efficient and that there is perfect information in the marketplace. Under these circumstances, this model can provide accurate forecasts. Indeed, many of the world currency markets such as the markets for U.S. dollar, German mark, and Japanese yen are highly efficient, and this model is well suited for such markets. However, market imperfections or lack of perfect information reduces the effectiveness of this model. In some cases, this model cannot be used.

Technical Forecasting

Technical forecasting involves the use of historical exchange rates to predict future values. It is sometimes conducted in a judgmental manner, without statistical analysis. Often, however, statistical analysis is applied in technical forecasting to detect historical trends. There are also time series models that examine moving averages. Most technical models rely on the past to predict the future. They try to identify a historical pattern that seems to repeat and then try to forecast it. The models range from a simple moving average to a complex auto-regressive integrated moving average (ARIMA). Most models try to break down the historical series. They try to identify and remove the random element. Then they try to forecast the overall trend with cyclical and seasonal variations.

A moving average is useful to remove minor random fluctuations. A trend analysis is useful to forecast a long-term linear or exponential trend. Winter's seasonal smoothing and Census XII decomposition are useful to forecast long-term cycles with additive seasonal variations. ARIMA (auto-regressive integrated moving average) is useful to predict cycles with multiplicative seasonality. Many forecasting and statistical packages such as Forecast Pro, Sibyl/Runner, Minitab, and SAS can handle these computations. An example of technical forecasting follows.

Example 2. This example uses the past six years of monthly data of the German mark (DM/$) exchange rate to forecast the DM/$ for the first 9 months in 1998. The data is given in Table 5 and plotted in Figure 2.

Table 5   Germany Currency 7-Year Monthly Closings

Month	1992	1993	1994	1995	1996	1997	1998
January	2.3892	1.8298	1.6785	1.8646	1.6805	1.4835	1.6190
February	2.2185	1.8268	1.6884	1.8296	1.6930	1.5195	1.6395
March	2.3175	1.8028	1.8219	1.8927	1.6947	1.7000	1.6445
April	2.1865	1.7985	1.6773	1.8783	1.6822	1.7350	1.6590
May	2.1327	1.8215	1.7015	1.9858	1.6913	1.7255	1.6080
June	2.1986	1.8249	1.8211	1.9535	1.6645	1.8120	1.5255
July	2.0940	1.8590	1.8810	1.8675	1.5920	1.7445	1.4778
August	2.0520	1.8145	1.8748	1.9608	1.5680	1.7425	1.4055
September	2.0207	1.8460	1.8798	1.8730	1.5650	1.6612	1.4105
October	2.0630	1.7255	1.7684	1.8353	1.5180	1.6750	
November	1.9880	1.6375	1.7354	1.7895	1.5030	1.6327	
December	1.9188	1.5713	1.7803	1.6915	1.4955	1.5175	

Source: The raw data was derived from *Business International,* December 1998.

Figure 2 Plot of 6-Year DM/$ Rate

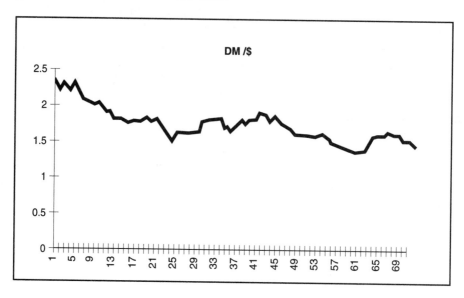

The data pattern seems to show a mild cycle with additive seasonality. Winter's seasonal smoothing is the ideal method under these situations. The data was run in Forecast Pro for Windows, a PC software package. The summary of the forecast is presented in Table 6 and plotted against actual values in Figure 3. Table 6 also summarizes the predictive performance of the model. The mean percentage error (MPE) was somewhat low (1.19%), which is generally indicative of a good forecast.

Table 6 Summary of Forecast

Forecast	Actual	Error	% Error
1.6080	1.6190	−0.0110	−0.68%
1.6507	1.6395	0.0112	0.68%
1.7248	1.6445	0.0803	4.77%
1.6593	1.6590	0.0003	0.02%
1.6079	1.6080	−0.0001	−0.01%
1.5879	1.5255	0.0624	4.01%
1.4863	1.4778	0.0085	0.57%
1.4526	1.4055	0.0471	3.30%
1.3834	1.4105	−0.0271	−1.94%
	Average:	0.0191	1.19%

Figure 3 Plot of Actual versus Smoothed Values

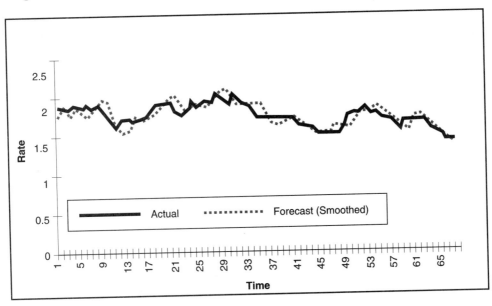

Mixed Forecasting

Mixed forecasting in not a unique technique but rather a combination of the three previously discussed methods. In some cases, a mixed forecast is nothing but a weighted average of a variety of the forecasting techniques. The techniques can be weighted arbitrarily or by assigning a higher weight to the more reliable technique. Mixed forecasting may often lead to a better result than relying on one single forecast.

A FRAMEWORK FOR EVALUATING FORECASTS

Forecasting foreign exchange is an ongoing process. Due to the dynamic nature of international markets, forecasts may not be accurate. However, the quality of a forecast does improve with a forecaster's experience. Therefore, it is necessary to set up some kind of framework within which a forecast can be evaluated.

The simplest framework would be to measure the errors in forecasting, which are discussed in detail in the next chapter ("Evaluation of Forecasts"). Several measures such as MAD, MSE, and MPE can be calculated and tracked. If more than one forecasting technique is used, or a mixed forecast is used, a company may be able to decide which technique is superior. It may then adjust the weighting scale in a mixed forecast.

A good framework makes it easy for a company to predict errors in forecasting. For example, if a forecaster is consistently forecasting the foreign exchange rate for the German mark above its actual rate, this would suggest that the forecaster needs to adjust the forecast for this bias. Furthermore, a tracking signal and the turning point error need to be systematically monitored.

CONCLUSION

In reality, currency forecasting is neglected in many multinational firms. They often argue that forecasting is useless since it does not provide an accurate estimate. They do not even have a hedging strategy. Failure to accurately forecast currency can have a disastrous impact on earnings. Moreover, it is important to realize that forecasting is often undertaken so the corporation has a general idea about the overall trend of the future and that the companies are not caught off guard. While currency forecasts are not 100 percent accurate, they do provide some advance warning of future trends.

It is also important to realize that forecasting is not an exact science. The quality of forecasts tends to improve over time as the forecaster gains more experience. One cannot ignore the value of judgment and intuition in forecasting, although evidence shows that forecasts using qualitative techniques are not as accurate as those using quantitative techniques.

Note: An experienced forecaster uses both qualitative and quantitative techniques to create a reasonable forecast.

EVALUATION OF FORECASTS

The cost of a prediction error can be substantial. Forecasters must always find ways to improve their forecasts. That means that they might want to examine some objective evaluations of alternative forecasting techniques. This chapter presents the guidelines they need. Two evaluation techniques are presented here. The first is in the form of a checklist. A forecaster could use it to evaluate either a new model he or she is in the process of developing or an existing model. The second is a statistical technique for evaluating a model.

COST OF PREDICTION ERRORS

There is always a cost involved with a failure to predict a certain variable accurately. It is important to determine the cost of the prediction error in order to minimize the potential detrimental effect on future profitability of the company. The cost of the prediction error can be substantial, depending upon the circumstances. For example, failure to make an accurate projection on sales could result in poor production planning, too much or too little purchase of labor, and so on, thereby causing potentially huge financial losses.

The cost of the prediction error is basically the contribution or profit lost on an inaccurate prediction. It can be measured in terms of lost sales, disgruntled customers, and idle machines.

Example 1. Assume that a company has been selling a toy doll having a cost of $.60 for $1.00 each. The fixed cost is $300. The company has no privilege of returning any unsold dolls. It has predicted sales of 2,000 units. However, unforeseen competition has reduced sales to 1,500 units. Then the cost of its prediction error (that is, its failure of predict demand accurately) would be calculated as follows:

1. Initial predicted sales = 2,000 units.

   Optimal decision: purchase 2,000 units.

   Expected net income = $500 [(2,000 units × $.40 contribution) – $300 fixed costs]

2. Alternative parameter value = 1,500 units.

   Optimal decision: purchase 1,500 units.

   Expected net income = $300 [(1,500 units × $.40 contribution) – $300 fixed costs]

3. Results of original decision under alternative parameter value.

   Expected net income:

   Revenue (1,500 units × $1.00) – Cost of dolls (2,000 units × $.60) – $300 fixed costs

   = $1,500 – $1,200 – $300 = $0.

4. Cost of prediction error, (2) – (3) = $300.

CHECKLIST

Two main items to be checked are the data and the model with its accompanying assumptions. The questions to be raised are the following:

1. Is the source reliable and accurate?

2. In the case when more than one source is reliable and accurate, is the source used the best one?

3. Are the data the most recent available?

4. If the answer to question 3 is yes, are the data subject to subsequent revision?

5. Is there any known systematic bias in the data that may be dealt with?

The model and its accompanying assumptions should be similarly examined. Among other things, the model has to make sense from a theoretical standpoint. The assumptions should be clearly stated and tested as well.

MEASURING ACCURACY OF FORECASTS

The performance of a forecast should be checked against its own record or against that of other forecasts. There are various statistical measures that can be used to measure performance of the model. Of course, the performance is measured in terms of forecasting error, where error is defined as the difference between a predicted value and the actual result.

$$\text{Error (e)} = \text{Actual (A)} - \text{Forecast (F)}$$

MAD, MSE, RMSE, and MAPE

The commonly used measures for summarizing historical errors include the *mean absolute deviation* (MAD), the *mean squared error* (MSE), the *root mean squared error* (RMSE), and the *mean absolute percentage error* (MAPE). The formulas used to calculate MAD, MSE, and RMSE are:

$$\text{MAD} = \Sigma \, |e| \, / \, n$$
$$\text{MSE} = \Sigma \, e^2 \, / \, (n - 1)$$
$$\text{RMSE} = \sqrt{(\Sigma \, e^2/n)}$$

Sometimes it is more useful to compute the forecasting errors in percentages rather than in amounts. The MAPE is calculated by finding the absolute error in each period, dividing this by the actual value of that period, and then averaging these absolute percentage errors, as shown here:

$$\text{MAPE} = \Sigma \, |e|/A \, / \, n$$

The following example illustrates the computation of MAD, MSE, RMSE, and MAPE.

Example 2. Sales data of a microwave oven manufacturer are given below:

Period	Actual (A)	Forecast (F)	e (A–F)	|e|	e^2	Absolute Percent Error |e|/A
1	217	215	2	2	4	.0092
2	213	216	-3	3	9	.0014
3	216	215	1	1	1	.0046
4	210	214	-4	4	16	.0190
5	213	211	2	2	4	.0094
6	219	214	5	5	25	.0023
7	216	217	-1	1	1	.0046
8	212	216	-4	4	16	.0019
			-2	22	76	.0524

Using the figures,

$$\text{MAD} \quad = \Sigma \ |e| \ /n = 22/8 = 2.75$$

$$\text{MSE} \quad = \Sigma \ e^2 \ / \ (n-1) = 76/7 = 10.86$$

$$\text{RMSE} \quad = \sqrt{\Sigma \ e^2} \ / \ n = \sqrt{76/8} = \sqrt{9.5} = 3.08$$

$$\text{MAPE} \quad = \Sigma \ |e|/A \ / \ n = .0524/8 = .0066$$

One way these measures are used is to evaluate forecasting ability of alternative forecasting methods. For example, using either MAD or MSE, a forecaster could compare the results of exponential smoothing with alphas and elect the one that performed best in terms of the lowest MAD or MSE for a given set of data. Also, it can help select the best initial forecast value for exponential smoothing.

THE U STATISTIC AND TURNING POINT ERRORS

There are still a number of statistical measures for measuring accuracy of the forecast. Two standards may be identified. First, one could compare the forecast being evaluated with a naive forecast to see if there are vast differences. The naive forecast can be anything; for instance, the same as last year, moving average, or the output of an exponential smoothing technique. In the second case, the forecast may be compared against the outcome when there is enough data to do so. The comparison may be against the actual level of the variable forecasted, or the change observed may be compared with the change forecast.

The Theil U Statistic is based upon a comparison of the predicted change with the observed change. It is calculated as:

$$U = 1/n \ \Sigma \ (F - A)^2 \ / \ (1/n)\Sigma \ F^2 + (1/n)\Sigma \ A^2$$

As can be seen, $U = 0$ is a perfect forecast, since the forecast would equal actual and $F - A = 0$ for all observations. At the other extreme, $U = 1$ would be a case of all incorrect forecasts. The smaller the value of U, the more accurate are the forecasts. If U is greater than or equal to 1, the predictive ability of the model is lower than a naive no-change extrapolation. *Note:* Many computer software packages routinely compute the U Statistic.

Still other evaluation techniques consider the number of *turning point errors,* which is based on the total number of reversals of trends. The turning point error is also known as "error in the direction of prediction." In a certain case, such as interest rate forecasts, the turning point error is more serious than the accuracy of the forecast. For example, the ability of forecasters to anticipated reversals of interest rate trends is more important—perhaps substantially more important—than the precise accuracy of the forecast. Substantial gains or losses may arise from a move from generally upward-moving rates to downward rate trends (or vice versa), but gains or losses

Evaluation of Forecasts

from incorrectly forecasting the extent of a continued increase or decrease in rates may be much more limited.

CONTROL OF FORECASTS

It is important to monitor forecast errors to insure that the forecast is performing well. If the model is performing poorly based on some criteria, the forecaster might reconsider the use of the existing model or switch to another forecasting model or technique. The forecasting control can be accomplished by comparing forecasting errors to predetermined values, or limits. Errors that fall within the limits would be judged acceptable while errors outside of the limits would signal that corrective action is desirable (see Figure 1).

Figure 1 Monitoring Forecast Errors

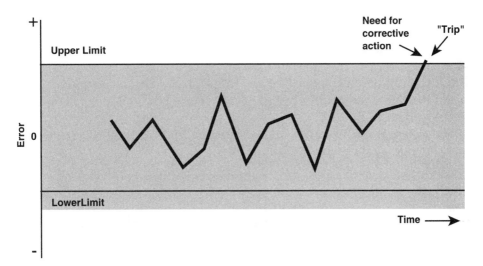

Forecasts can be monitored using either tracking signals or control charts.

Tracking Signals

A tracking signal is based on the ratio of cumulative forecast error to the corresponding value of MAD.

$$\text{Tracking signal} = \Sigma(A - F) / MAD$$

The resulting tracking signal values are compared to predetermined limits. These are based on experience and judgment and often range from plus or minus three to plus or minus eight. Values within the limits suggest that the forecast is performing adequately. By the same token, when the signal goes beyond this range, corrective action is appropriate.

Example 3. Going back to Example 2, the deviation and cumulative deviation have already been computed:

$$MAD = \Sigma \ |A - F| \ / \ n = 22 \ / \ 8 = 2.75$$
$$\text{Tracking signal} = \Sigma \ (A - F) \ / \ MAD = -2 \ / \ 2.75 = -0.73$$

A tracking signal is as low as -0.73, which is substantially below the limit $(-3$ to $-8)$. It would not suggest any action at this time.

Note: After an initial value of MAD has been computed, the estimate of the MAD can be continually updated using exponential smoothing.

$$MAD_t = \alpha(A - F) + (1 - \alpha) \ MAD_{t-1}$$

Control Charts

The control chart approach involves setting upper and lower limits for individual forecasting errors instead of cumulative errors. The limits are multiples of the estimated standard deviation of forecast, S_f, which is the square root of MSE. Frequently, control limits are set at 2 or 3 standard deviations:

$$\pm 2 \ (\text{or } 3) \ S_f$$

Note: Plot the errors and see if all errors are within the limits, so that the forecaster can visualize the process and determine if the method being used is in control.

Example 4. For the sales data below, using the naive forecast, we will determine if the forecast is in control. For illustrative purposes, we will use 2 sigma control limits.

Year	Sales	Forecasts	Error	Error²
1	320			
2	326	320	6	36
3	310	326	-16	256
4	317	310	7	49
5	315	317	-2	4
6	318	315	3	9
7	310	318	-8	64
8	316	310	6	36
9	314	316	-2	4
10	317	314	3	9
			-3	467

First, compute the standard deviation of forecast errors:

$$S_f = \sqrt{e^2 / (n-1)} = \sqrt{467/(9-1)} = 7.64$$

Two sigma limits are then plus or minus $2(7.64) = -15.28$ to $+15.28$.

Note that the forecast error for year 3 is below the lower bound, so the forecast is not in control (see Figure 2). The use of other methods such as moving average, exponential smoothing, or regression would possibly achieve a better forecast.

Figure 2   Control Chart for Forecasting Errors

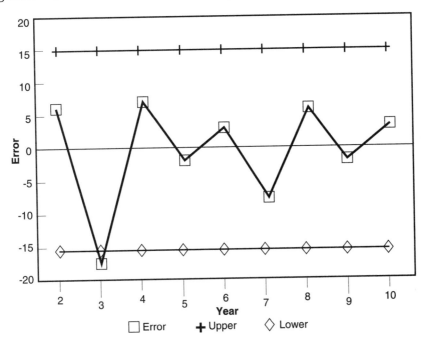

Note: A system of monitoring forecasts needs to be developed. The computer may be programmed to print a report showing the past history when the tracking signal "trips" a limit. For example, when a type of exponential smoothing is used, the system may try a different value of α (so the forecast will be more responsive) and continue forecasting.

CONCLUSION

There is always a cost associated with a failure to predict a certain variable accurately. Because all forecasts tend to be off the mark, it is important to provide a measure of accuracy for each forecast. Several measures of forecast accuracy and a measure of turning point error can be calculated.

These quite often are used to help managers evaluate the performance of a given method as well as to choose among alternative forecasting techniques. Control of forecasts involves deciding whether a forecast is performing adequately, using either a control chart or a tracking signal. Selection of a forecasting method involves choosing a technique that will serve its intended purpose at an acceptable level of cost and accuracy.

FORECASTING TOOLS AND SOFTWARE

The life cycle of a typical new product is divided into four major stages: introduction, growth, maturity, and saturation (decline). Depending upon the nature of the market, a right choice of forecasting methodology is called for. Table 1 shows life cycle effects upon forecasting methodology. Table 2 summarizes the forecasting methods that have been discussed in this book. It is organized in the following format:

1. Description
2. Accuracy
3. Identification of turning point
4. Typical application
5. Data required
6. Cost
7. Time required to develop an application and make forecasts

Furthermore, in an effort to aid forecasters in choosing the right methodology, Table 3 provides rankings of forecasting methodology by:

1. Accuracy: Why do you need the forecast?
2. Cost: How much money is involved?
3. Timing: When will the forecast be used?
4. Form: Who will use the forecast?
5. Data: How much data are available?

Table 1   Life Cycle Effects on Forecasting Methodology

Introduction

    Data: No data available; rely on qualitative methods.

    Time: Need long horizon.

    Methods: Qualitative (judgment) such as market surveys and Delphi.

Growth

    Data: Some data available for analysis.

    Time: Still need long horizon; trends and cause-effect relationships important.

    Methods: Market surveys still useful. Regression, time series, and growth models justified.

Maturity

    Data: Considerable data available.

    Time: More uses of short-term forecasts; still need long-term projections, but trends change only gradually.

    Methods: Quantitative methods more useful. Time series helpful for trend, seasonal. Regression and exponential smoothing very useful.

Decline

    Data: Abundant data.

    Time: Shorter horizon.

    Methods: Continue use of maturity methods as applicable. Judgment and market surveys may signal changes.

Table 2 Summary of Commonly Used Forecasting Methods

Summary of Commonly Used Qualitative (Judgmental) Forecasting Techniques

Technique	PERT-Derived	Sales Force Polling	Consumer Surveys
Description	Based on three estimates provided by experts: pessimistic, most likely, and optimistic.	Based on sales force opinions; tend to be too optimistic.	Based on market surveys regarding specific consumer purchases.
Accuracy:			
Short-term (0-3 mon)	Fair	Fair to good	Fair to good
Medium-term (3 mon-2 yr)	Poor	Poor	Poor
Long-term (2 yr and over)	Poor	Poor	Poor
Identification of turning point	Poor to fair	Poor to good	Poor
Typical application	Same as expert opinions.	Forecasts of short-term sales forecasts.	Forecasts of short-term sales forecasts.
Data required	Same as expert opinions.	Data by regional and product line breakdowns.	Telephone contacts, personal interviews, or questionnaires.
Cost of forecasting with a computer	Minimal	Minimal	Minimal
Time required to develop an application and make forecasts	Two weeks	Two weeks	More than a month

Continued on next page

Table 2   Summary of Commonly Used Forecasting Methods *(continued)*

Summary of Commonly Used Quantitative Forecasting Methods

Technique	PERT- Derived	Sales Force Polling	Consumer Surveys
Description	Functionally relates sales to other economic, competitive, or internal variables and estimates an equation using the least-squares technique.	A system of interdependent regression equations that describes some sector of economic sales or profit activity. The parameters of the regression equations are usually estimated simultaneously.	Models based on learned behavior: Consumers tend to repeat their past brand loyalty.
Accuracy:			
Short-term (0-3 mon)	Good to very good	Good to very good	Excellent
Medium-term (3 mon-2 yr)	Good to very good	Very good to excellent	Poor
Long-term (2 yr and over)	Poor	Good	Poor
Identification of turning point	Good	Excellent	Good
Typical application	Forecast of sales by product classes, forecasts of earnings, and other financial data.	Forecasts of sales by product classes, forecasts of earnings.	Forecasts of sales and cash collections.
Data required	At least 30 observations are recommended for acceptable results.	The same as for regression.	Data required for transaction probabilities.
Cost of forecasting with a computer	Varies with application	Expensive	Expensive
Time required to develop an application and make forecasts	Depends on ability to identify relationships	More than a month	More than a month

Continued on next page

Table 2 Summary of Commonly Used Forecasting Methods *(continued)*

Summary of Commonly Used Time Series Methods

Technique	Classical Decomposition	Box-Jenkins
Description	Decomposes a time series into seasonals, trend cycles, and irregular elements. Primarily used for detailed time-series analysis (including estimating seasonals).	Iterative procedure that produces an autoregressive, integrated moving average model, adjusts for seasonal and trend factors, estimates appropriate weighting parameters, tests the model, and repeats the cycle as appropriate.
Accuracy:		
Short-term (0-3 mon)	Very good to excellent	Very good to excellent
Medium-term (3 mon-2 yr)	Good	Poor to good
Long-term (2 yr and over)	Very poor	Very poor
Identification of turning point	Very good	Fair
Typical application	Tracking and warning, forecasts of sales and financial data.	Production and inventory control for large-volume items, forecasts of cash balances and earnings.
Data required	A minimum of three years' history to start. Thereafter, the complete history.	Production and inventory control for large-volume items, forecasts of cash balances and earnings.
Cost of forecasting with a computer	Minimal	Expensive
Time required to develop an application and make forecasts	One day	Two days

Source: Heavily adapted from Chambers, John, S. Mullick, and D. Smith, "How to Choose the Right Forecasting Technique," *Harvard Business Review,* Vol. 49, no. 4, July–August 1971.

Table 3 The Forecasting Decision Matrix

Techniques	Timing: When Will the Forecast Be Used?	Rankings
Qualitative or Judgmental	Short Lead Time ↑ ↓ Long Lead Time	Expert Opinion Consensus Opinion Sales Force Polling Market Surveys Delphi
Time Series	Short Lead Time ↑ ↓ Long Lead Time	Trend Analysis Moving Average Exponential Smoothing Classical Decomposition Box-Jenkins
Causal, Markov, and Direct	Short Lead Time ↑ ↓ Long Lead Time	Markov Regression Leading Indicator Life Cycle Analysis Surveys Econometric Input-Output Analysis

Techniques	Form: Who Will Use the Forecast?	Rankings
Qualitative or Judgmental	Precise Forecast ↑ ↓ Imprecise Forecast	Market Surveys Expert Opinion Sales Force Polling Delphi
Time Series	Precise Forecast ↕ Imprecise Forecast	All Similar, Giving Precise Forecasts
Causal, Markov, and Indirect	Precise Forecast ↕ Imprecise Forecast	All Similar, Giving Precise Forecasts

Techniques	Data: How Much Are Available?	Rankings
Qualitative or Judgmental	Considerable Data Required ↑ ↓ Little Data Required	Generally All Similar, Little Historical Data Needed
Time Series	Considerable Data Required ↕ Little Data Required	All Similar, At Least Two Years' Data Usually Required
Causal, Markov, and Indirect	Considerable Data Required ↑ ↓ Little Data Required	Input-Output Analysis Econometric Life Cycle Analysis Markov Leading Indicator Regression Surveys

FORECASTING AND STATISTICAL SOFTWARE

There are numerous computer software programs used for forecasting purposes. They are broadly divided into two major categories: forecasting software and general purpose statistical software. Some programs are stand-
alone, while others are spreadsheet add-ins. Still others are templates. A
brief summary of some popular programs follows.

1. Sales & Market Forecasting Toolkit

Sales & Market Forecasting Toolkit is a *Lotus 1-2-3 template* that produces
sales and market forecasts, even for new products with limited historical
data. It provides eight powerful methods for more accurate forecasts, and
includes spreadsheet models, complete with graphs, ready to use with your
numbers. The *Sales & Market Forecasting Toolkit* offers a variety of forecasting methods to help you generate accurate business forecasts, even in
new or changing markets with limited historical data.

The forecasting methods include:

- Customer Poll
- Whole Market Penetration
- Chain Method
- Strategic Modeling
- Moving averages, exponential smoothing, and linear regressions

The Customer Poll method helps build a forecast from the ground up,
by summing the individual components such as products, stores, or customers. Whole Market Penetration, Market Share, and Chain Method are
top-down forecasting methods used to predict sales for new products and
markets lacking sales data. The Strategic Modeling method develops a forecast by projecting the impact of changes to pricing and advertising expenditures. Statistical forecasting methods include exponential smoothing, moving averages, and linear regression.

You can use the built-in macros to enter data into your forecast automatically. For example, enter values for the first and last months of a 12-
month forecast. The compounded-growth-rate macro will automatically
compute and enter values for the other ten months.

It is available from:

Lotus Selects
P.O. Box 9172
Cambridge, MA 02139-9946
(800) 635-6887   (617) 693-3981

2. Forecast! GFX

Forecast! GFX is a *stand-alone* forecasting system that can perform five types of time-series analysis: seasonal adjustment, linear and nonlinear trend analysis, moving-average analysis, exponential smoothing, and decomposition. Trend analysis supports linear, exponential, hyperbolic, S-curve, and polynomial trends. Hyperbolic trend models are used to analyze data that indicate a decline toward a limit, such as the output of an oil well or the price of a particular model of personal computer. *Forecast! GFX* can perform multiple-regression analysis with up to 10 independent variables.

> Intex Solutions
> 35 Highland Cir.
> Needham, MA 01294
> (617) 449-6222   (617) 444-2318 (fax)

3. ForeCalc

ForeCalc, Lotus and *Symphony add-in,* features the following:

- Uses nine forecasting techniques and includes both automatic and manual modes.
- Eliminates the need to export or reenter data.

You can use it in either automatic or manual mode. In automatic mode, just highlight the historical data in your spreadsheet, such as sales, expenses, or net income; then *ForeCalc* tests several exponential-smoothing models and picks the one that best fits your data.

Forecast results can be transferred to your spreadsheet with upper and lower confidence limits. *ForeCalc* generates a line graph showing the original data, the forecasted values, and confidence limits.

ForeCalc can automatically choose the most accurate forecasting technique:

- Simple one-parameter smoothing
- Holt's two-parameter smoothing
- Winters's three-parameter smoothing
- Trendless seasonal models
- Dampened versions of Holt's and Winters's smoothing

ForeCalc's manual mode lets you select the type of trend and seasonality, yielding nine possible model combinations. You can vary the type of trend (constant, linear, or dampened), as well as the seasonality (nonseasonal, additive, or multiplicative).

Business Forecast Systems, Inc.
68 Leonard St.
Belmont, MA 02178
(617) 484-5050

4. StatPlan IV

StatPlan IV is a *stand-alone* program for those who understand how to apply statistics to business analysis. You can use it for market analysis, trend forecasting, and statistical modeling.

StatPlan IV lets you analyze data by range, mean, median, standard deviation, skewness, kurtosis, correlation analysis, one- or two-way analysis of variance (ANOVA), cross tabulations, and t-test.

The forecasting methods include multiple regression, stepwise multiple regression, polynomial regression, bivariate curve fitting, autocorrelation analysis, trend and cycle analysis, and exponential smoothing.

The data can be displayed in X-Y plots, histograms, time-series graphs, autocorrelation plots, actual vs. forecast plots, or frequency and percentile tables.

It is available from:

Lotus Selects
P.O. Box 9172
Cambridge, MA 02139-9946
(800) 635-6887   (617) 693-3981

5. Geneva Statistical Forecasting

Geneva Statistical Forecasting, a *stand-alone* program, can batch-process forecasts for thousands of data series, provided the series are all measured in the same time units (days, weeks, months, and so on). The software automatically explores as many as nine different forecasting methods, including six linear and nonlinear regressions and three exponential-smoothing techniques, before picking the one that best fits your historical data.

The program incorporates provisions that simplify and accelerate the process of reforecasting data items. Once you complete the initial forecast, you can save a data file that records the forecasting method assigned to each line item. When it is time to update the data, simply retrieve the file and reforecast, using the same methods as before.

Geneva Statistical Forecasting tries as many as nine forecasting methods for each line item.

Pizzano & Co.
800 W. Cummings Park
Woburn, MA 01801
(617) 935-7122

6. SmartForecasts

SmartForecasts, stand-alone forecasting software, does the following:

- Automatically chooses the right statistical method.
- Lets you manually adjust forecasts to reflect your business judgment.
- Produces forecast results.

SmartForecasts combines the benefits of statistical and judgmental forecasting. It can determine which statistical method will give you the most accurate forecast, and handle all the math.

Forecasts can be modified using the program's EYEBALL utility. You may need to adjust a sales forecast to reflect an anticipated increase in advertising or decrease in price. *SmartForecasts* summarizes data with descriptive statistics, plots the distribution of data values with histograms, plots variables in a scattergram, and identifies leading indicators.

You can forecast using single- and double-exponential smoothing, and simple- and linear-moving averages. It even builds seasonality into your forecasts using Winters's exponential smoothing, or you can eliminate seasonality by using time-series decomposition and seasonal adjustment.

In addition, *SmartForecasts* features simultaneous multiseries forecasting of up to 60 variables and 150 data points per variable, offers multivariate regression to let you relate business variables, and has an Undo command for correcting mistakes.

Smart Software, Inc.
4 Hill Rd.
Belmont, MA 02178
(800) 762-7899   (617) 489-2748 (fax)

7. Tomorrow

Tomorrow, a *stand-alone* forecasting program, uses an optimized combination of linear regression, single exponential smoothing, adaptive rate response single exponential smoothing, Brown's one-parameter double exponential smoothing, Holt's two-parameter exponential smoothing, Brown's one-parameter triple exponential smoothing, and Gardner's three-parameter damped trend. Some of the main features include:

- There's no need to reformat your existing spreadsheets. *Tomorrow* recognizes and forecasts formula cells (containing totals and subtotals, for example). It handles both horizontally and vertically oriented spreadsheets. It accepts historical data in up to 30 separate ranges.

- Allows you to specify seasonality manually, or calculates seasonality automatically.

- Allows you to do several forecasts of different time series (for example, sales data from different regions) at once.

- Recognizes and forecasts time-series headings (names of months, etc.).

- Forecast optionally becomes normal part of your spreadsheet.

- Undo command restores original spreadsheet.

- Browse feature allows you to look at any part of the spreadsheet (including the forecast) without leaving *Tomorrow*.

- Checks for and prevents accidental overlaying of nonempty or protected cells.

- Optional annotation mode labels forecast cells, calculates MAPE, and, when seasonality is automatically determined, describes the seasonality.

- Includes comprehensive context-sensitive online help.

Isogon Corp.
330 Seventh Ave.
New York, NY 10001
(212) 967-2424

8. Forecast Pro

Forecast Pro, stand-alone forecasting software, uses artificial intelligence. A built-in expert system examines your data. Then it guides you to exponential smoothing, Box-Jenkins, or regression, whichever method suits the data best.

Business Forecast Systems, Inc.
68 Leonard St.
Belmont, MA 02178
(617) 484-5050   (617) 484-9219

9. MicroTSP

MicroTSP is a *stand-alone* software program that provides the tools most frequently used in practical econometric and forecasting work. It covers the following:

1. Descriptive statistics.
2. A wide range of single-equation estimation techniques including ordinary least squares (multiple regression), two-stage least squares, non-linear least squares, and probit and logit.

Forecasting tools include:

1. Exponential smoothing including single exponential, double exponential, and Winters's smoothing.
2. Box-Jenkins methodology.

> Quantitative Micro Software
> 4521 Campus Drive, Suite 336
> Irvine, CA 92715
> (714) 856-3368

10. Sibyl/Runner

Sibyl/Runner is an interactive, *stand-alone* forecasting system. In addition to allowing the usage of all major forecasting methods, the package permits analysis of the data, suggests available forecasting methods, compares results, and provides several accuracy measures in such a way that it is easier for the user to select an appropriate method and forecast needed data under different economic and environmental conditions. For details, see Makridakis, Hodgsdon, and Wheelwright, "An Interactive Forecasting System," *American Statistician,* November 1974.

> Applied Decision Systems
> Lexington, MA 02173
> (614) 424-9820

11. Forecast Plus

Forecast Plus, a *stand-alone* forecasting program, uses artificial intelligence. A built-in expert system examines your data. Then it guides you to thirteen forecasting methods including exponential smoothing, Box-Jenkins, or regression, whichever method suits the data best.
The software features the following:

- A simple-to-use menu system
- High-resolution graphic capability
- Ability to choose an appropriate forecasting technique
- Ability to handle all phases of forecasting analysis

- Ability to save forecasted data
- Optimization of smoothing constants

StatPac, Inc.
3814 Lyndale Avenue South
Minneapolis, MN 55409
(612) 822-8252

12. Other Forecasting Software

There are many other forecasting software programs, such as *Autocast II* and *4 Cast* (Delphus, Inc., 103 Washington St. #348, Morristown, NJ 07960 201-267-9269) and *Trendsetter Expert Version* (Concentric Data Systems, 110 Turnpike Rd., Westborough, MA 01581 800-325-9035).

13. General Purpose Statistical Software

There are numerous statistical software programs widely in use that can be utilized in order to build a forecasting model. Some of the more popular ones include *Systat, SAS Application System, Statgraphics, SPSS, PC-90, Minitab, RATS,* and *BMD*.

CHOOSING THE RIGHT PACKAGE

Since different software packages apply different techniques for many of the same tasks, it is a good idea to select a package that explains which method it is using and why, so you can eventually learn the most appropriate technique for your specific forecasting task. Figure 1 spells out the options in choosing the right package.

CONCLUSION

Today's financial managers have some powerful tools at hand to simplify the forecasting process and increase its accuracy. Several forecasting models are available, and the automated versions of these should be considered by any manager who is regularly called upon to provide forecasts. A personal computer with a spreadsheet is a good beginning, but the stand-alone packages currently available provide the most accurate forecasts and are the easiest to use. In addition, they make several forecasting models available and can automatically select the best one for a particular data set.

Figure 1 Which Forecasting Software Is Right for You? Know Your Options

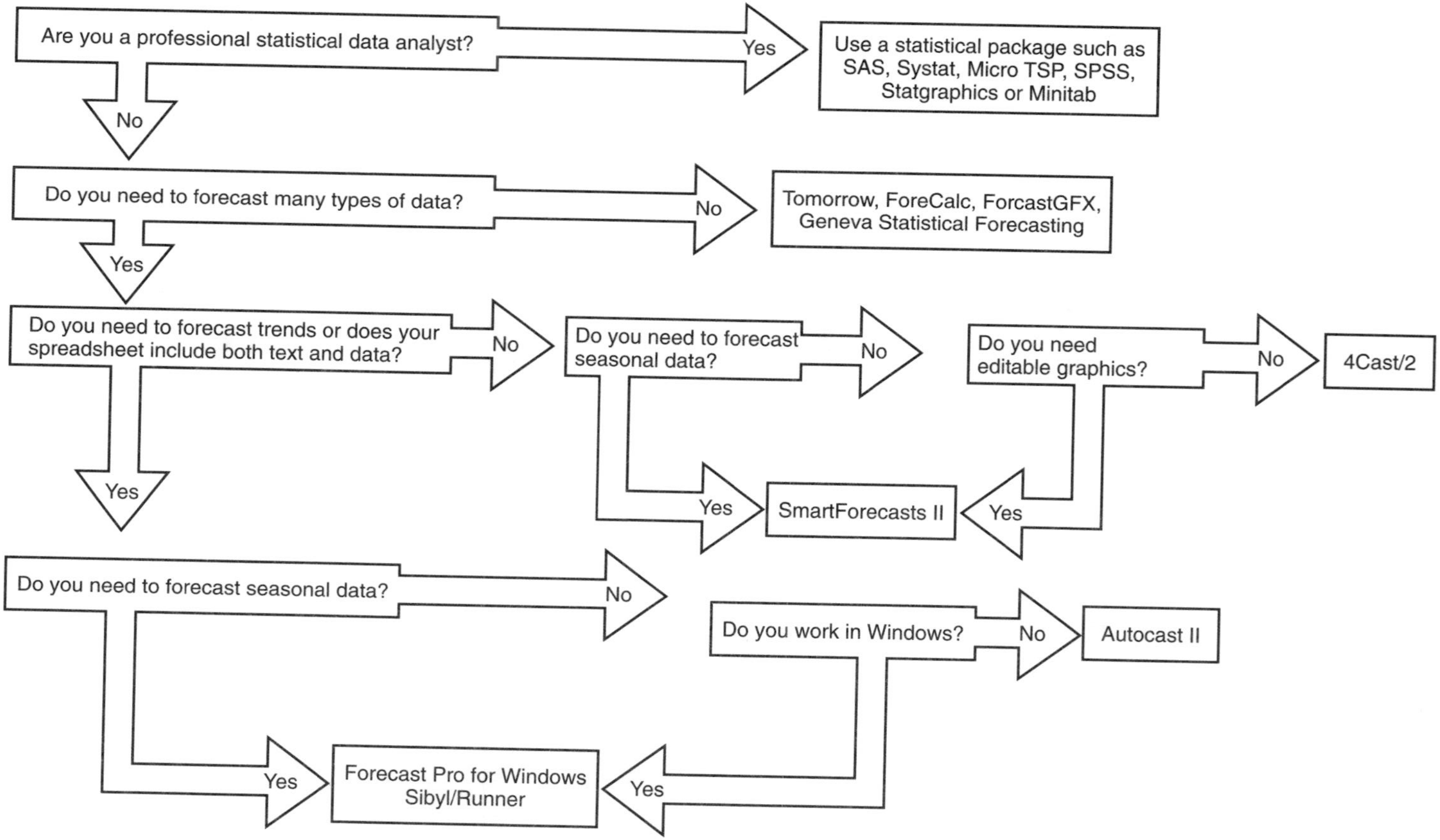

THE USE OF COMPUTER SOFTWARE IN MANAGERIAL ACCOUNTING*

Computer software is available for most areas of managerial accounting, including cost systems, activity-based costing (ABC), forecasting, budgeting and planning, inventory evaluation, material requirement appraisal, project management, capital budgeting, risk analysis, linear programming, and flow-charting. There are stand-alone packages, templates, and spreadsheet add-ins. The purpose of this chapter is to alert you to software useful in managerial accounting, including their features, applications, and suitability to meet a particular company's needs.

PLANNING AND BUDGETING

In the areas of planning and budgeting, many useful software programs exist.

Planet Corporation's *Business Maestro* generates operational and strategic business plans, while its *Budget Maestro* accounts for projects and evaluates trends in human resources and related costs.

Orange Systems' *ALCIE* provides capacity planning, purchasing, job shop control, inventory management, and distribution.

Comshare's *Commander Budget* does budgeting with the use of spreadsheets and prepares management reports. It performs multidimensional analysis, analyzes budgeted figures and their impact on the business, performs variance analysis, looks at "what-if" scenarios, performs exception

---

*This chapter was coauthored by Anique A. Qureshi, Ph.D., CPA, CIA, associate professor of accounting and information systems at Queens College.

analysis, and prepares management reports. It has application interfaces to financial databases.

Adaytum Software's *Planning* integrates budgeting links between cost centers, expense/sales, production plans, and cash flow analysis. Variance analysis is performed.

KCI Computing's *Control* is multidimensional and dynamic in handling budgets, planning models, consolidations, foreign currency translation, and cost allocations.

SAS Institute's *CFO Vision* software does costing by project, job, customer, and business segment. It performs financial consolidations, reporting, and analysis. It examines the reasons behind the figures and improves the timeliness and availability of business reporting.

Design Data Systems' *DDS Financial* integrates financial distribution, project management, and sales force modules.

TM1 software does multidimensional budgeting, forecasting, and reporting. It looks at various pricing scenarios, and evaluates the consequences of budget options.

Walker Interactive's *Business Framework Series* is used for budgeting, planning, forecasting, and analysis of cost and profitability.

Software 2000 Incorporated's *Infinium Financial Manager* performs purchase management, order processing, inventory control, quality control, and master production scheduling. It also does financial analysis, cost allocation, budgeting, specialized reporting, project management, and currency management.

M-USA Business Systems' *Pacioli 2000* has modules for inventory control, job costing, budgeting, project control, cash management, assembly control, and sales history.

Alcar is strategic planning and appraisal software for Fortune 1000 companies. Users can assess whether a plan or acquisition can be sufficiently funded by internal cash flow or outside financing.

Arbor Software's *Essbase* is a multidimensional database for business planning, evaluation, and management reporting.

Big Software's *Big Business* is a business management system integrating sales, marketing, inventory, and finance. It monitors inventory and tracks customers.

Synex Systems' *F9 Universal* software integrates budget reports.

Chief financial officers may use *CFO Spreadsheet Applications,* a spreadsheet template, for selecting optimal alternative capital investments and to manage cash flows.

Budget Express is a spreadsheet add-in facilitating "what-if" analysis, comparing current to future values based on inputted changes. It makes the preparation of budgets and forecasts easy. For instance, it automatically totals columns and rows and calculates summary information by month, quarter, and year.

Pro Plan is a template used for financial planning and reporting. It prepares such financial statements as the income statement, balance sheet, and statement of cash flows. Ratio reports are also generated.

Profit Planner is a template used to project sales, cost of sales, operating expenses, assets, liabilities, and stockholders' equity. The financial figures for a company are compared to industry averages.

What-If Solver is an optimization add-in used to solve optimization problems subject to various constraints.

SRC Software's *Advisor Series* includes decision support, planning and forecasting, currency translations, and international consolidations. It handles complex budgeting and financial reporting situations.

Microcompass Systems' *QL Financials* is a software program containing budget management, sales and purchase ordering, and inventory management. It has multicurrency features.

Social Systems' *Simplan* is used for integrated, multipurpose planning and budgeting. It can be used for revenue forecasting, econometric modeling, and time-series analysis. In projecting sales, variables to be considered include selling price, units, availability of materials, interest rates, and market share.

Comshare's *Interactive Financial Planning System (IFPS)* is a multipurpose, interactive financial modeling system aiding in constructing, solving, and asking "what-if" questions of financial models. Interrelationships of data are considered. The output is in the form of a spreadsheet. Data inputted into the model include revenue, selling price, volume, growth rate, variable cost, fixed cost, gross margin, contribution margin, net present value, internal rate of return, departmental figures, assets, working capital, and market position. Alternative options to result in a desired outcome may also be presented. Information may be summarized in final form in terms of department, geographic region, product line, service line, customer, and supplier. *IFPS* has statistical functions that may be performed such as moving average, regression, and autocorrelation. Leading and lagging variables may be considered such as estimating future cash collections based on prior credit sales. There is a sampling routine based on examining the population, considering the probability distribution. Sensitivity analysis (considering the effect on an outcome of changing a variable) is another feature of *IFPS*. There is also a goal-seeking mode. Variables are analyzed as to their overall contributions. The software has graphic capabilities.

EXPRESS is used for financial planning and analysis, including pro forma financial statements and risk analysis. There are statistical and analytical features such as percent difference, sorting, maximum–minimum, and leads and lags. Statistical functions include regression, cluster analysis, factor analysis, exponential smoothing, deseasonalization, and time series. There are graphic displays.

Ferox Microsystems' *ENCORE! PLUS* performs analytical functions and risk evaluation.

Micro Data Base's *GURU* is an expert system shell used to prepare reports, statistical analysis, and data management. The software provides managerial and financial advice for routine decisions.

Financial modeling for profit planning and budgeting can be done using powerful spreadsheet programs such as *Lotus 1-2-3, VP Planner, Javelin, Excel, SuperCalc, QuattroPro, Educom Financial Planning Model (EFPM), XSIM, Empire, Foresight, Orion,* and *Venture.*

Ernst and Young's *Prosper* performs corporate financial planning and analysis of financial data. It prepares budgets and cash flow reports along with various visual presentations. It also performs investment analysis.

Smart Shop's *Cash Wise* prepares and evaluates cash flow projected statements to meet a company's strategic planning needs. It responds to "what-if" scenarios.

FuziWare Inc.'s *FuziCalc* is a unique spreadsheet that allows the decision maker to benefit from the structure of quantitative decision analysis, without forcing the user to provide very precise numerical inputs. The spreadsheet is based on the fuzzy set theory and fuzzy logic; it takes the computational complexity out of fuzzy arithmetic. Its primary strength is in modeling under uncertainty. As a spreadsheet, *FuziCalc* offers only the very basic features. Many features that one is accustomed to in conventional spreadsheets are lacking in *FuziCalc.* Most users will probably want *FuziCalc* to supplement, rather than replace, their conventional spreadsheet. *FuziCalc* is easy to use and offers powerful features to model decision making under uncertainty.

FORECASTING AND STATISTICS

There are numerous software programs for forecasting financial and nonfinancial information. Further, a spreadsheet template can produce sales and market forecasts for new products and services based on historical data.

Spreadware's *Pro Forma* prepares and analyzes pro forma financial statements. It tracks cash inflows and outflows, and conducts "what-if" evaluation among alternatives. Variance analysis is performed.

Business Matters Incorporated's *Cashe* is a comprehensive business forecasting and modeling software product. Financial planning is made easier through built-in formulas and linked relationships, which may be adjusted with changing information. In-depth analysis is performed, including that for changes in assumptions or scenarios. External factors such as changing interest rates are taken into account when forecasting. Analysis of variances, break-even, and risk evaluations are performed. It allows for the modification of business assumptions so financial forecasts may be reviewed, updated, and compared easily.

Geneva's *Statistical Forecasting* is a stand-alone package for forecasting data series over a specified time period (e.g., monthly). It includes linear and nonlinear regressions and exponential smoothing techniques.

Tomorrow is forecasting software based on a mix of exponential smoothing and regression. Data used may be in up to 30 separate ranges. Seasonality adjustments are made. Forecasts may be made in different time series, such as revenue by different geographic areas.

Forecast! GFX is software for doing time-series analyses (adjusted for seasonality), exponential smoothing, moving average, and decomposition. Trend applications are used to appraise data moving toward a lower limit. There is a multiple regression feature for a maximum of 10 explanatory variables used to explain a dependent variable.

Forecast Pro uses artificial intelligence in forecasting data, while *Forecast Plus* uses artificial intelligence to evaluate data, and then selects an appropriate forecasting method among 13 available ones. Optimization of smoothing constants and excellent graphics features are included.

ForeCalc is an add-in forecasting program. It can take historical data in a spreadsheet and, using exponential smoothing, determine the optimal projection based on the best fit of the data. The software also provides confidence limits. Information may be graphically displayed. Seasonal factors are considered in the model.

Sibyl/Runner is an interactive, stand-alone forecasting package allowing for data appraisal. It recommends the appropriate forecasting method for the given facts, compares results, and provides various accuracy measures.

Stat Plan IV is stand-alone software using statistics to solve business problems. It is very useful in management decision making. Data may be evaluated by range, standard deviation, mean, correlation, analysis of variance, and statistical significance. The forecasting methods include regression, autocorrelation, and exponential smoothing. Data may be graphically plotted, including comparing actual to budget figures. Applications include trend depictions, financial modeling, and market appraisal.

Smart Forecasts automatically selects the best statistical technique to use based on the facts in a particular case. The approach allows for flexibility based on desired changes of the user via the program's *EYEBALL* utility. For example, the revenue projection is changed as changes are made in selling price, promotion plan, and consumers' disposable income. Forecasting may be in the form of moving averages and exponential smoothing. Seasonality can be adjusted, such as by using time-series decomposition. It considers up to 60 variables.

Micro TSP involves econometric forecasting including descriptive statistics, multiple regression, and exponential smoothing.

Infordata Systems' *INQUIRE* is a special-purpose package used for decision support. Its features include query, data retrieval, and report generation.

Pendock Mallorn's *Pro-Forma Plus* is a financial forecasting model for preparing financial projections. "What-if" analysis for alternative assumptions is provided. It does variance, ratio, and break-even analysis.

General purpose statistical software includes such packages as *Statistical Package for Social Scientists (SPSS), Systat, Statgraphics, Statistical Analysis System (SAS), Statpack,* and *Minitab.*

PROJECT PLANNING AND EVALUATION

Deltek Systems' *Costpoint* does project and activity accounting. It tracks by project costs and hours, compares estimates to actual for each task level, allocates costs, computes project revenue and profitability, tracks backlogs and purchase commitments, manages material, plans procurements, and fosters inventory control.

Concepts Dynamic's *CDI Project Control System* keeps track, manages, and reports revenue, cost, and time by major project.

Power Cerv's *INTERGY* software has features for order processing, purchasing, and project management.

Ross Systems' *The Renaissance CS Financials* monitors, projects, and controls financial results. It includes features of purchase order, currency management, inventory control, budgeting, and bid tracking.

ProSoft Corporation's *Carpe Diem* software generates electronic timesheets and cost reports.

Marsh Software Systems' *Axiom Project Manager* tracks projects, and performs job-costing functions. There is an interface to financial software.

GBA Systems' *Pedigree Software* has modules for project accounting management and for preventive maintenance control.

Design Data Systems' *DDS Work Order Management* is for order entry and project reporting.

Design Data's *SQL*TIME* is software for project scheduling including scheduling for personnel and capital resources. It also resolves scheduling conflicts.

Open Systems' *Traverse* is international accounting business software.

Proposed projects may be evaluated using the *Project Evaluation Toolkit* template. It uses various capital budgeting methods such as discounted cash flow analysis. Alternative scenarios may be appraised by changing variables such as cost or revenue projections, changes in timing of cash flows, and changes in beginning or interim dates.

CapPlans is a template for appraising a proposed project using capital budgeting techniques such as payback period, internal rate of return, and net present value. It can forecast cash flows for up to 15 years. It prepares graphs and managerial reports. Sensitivity analysis routines are also included.

Computer Associates' *CA Masterpiece* performs job and project costing, inventory control, and time recording.

JBA International's *System 21* does costing by project and job, warehousing, work order processing, production control, manufacturing routing and scheduling, capacity planning, and analysis of material requirements.

J.D. Edward's *One World* does job and project cost accounting, time recording, warehouse management, production control, master production scheduling, routing, materials requirements planning, capacity requirements planning, and manufacturing control.

Oracle's *Financials* includes applications for job and project, costing, work-order processing, production control and scheduling, bills of materials routing, plant capacity, and appraisals of materials.

FTP Software's *Group Works* enables efficient project organization, management, and execution. It performs scheduling assignments, tracks deadlines, assigns tasks, sets priorities, and monitors project status. The software also makes problem-solving suggestions.

CAPITAL BUDGETING

Worth It Software's *Worth It* does capital budgeting and analysis. It aids in the capital expenditure management process. The software is used to budget acquisitions by business units, project future operating changes, highlight negative trends, appraise alternative investment plans, and compare their relative costs.

RISK ANALYSIS

Corporate risk may be analyzed using the spreadsheet add-in *@Risk*. It examines the effect of changing circumstances on the company's profitability, competitive reaction, and market position. Sampling methods are used for "what-if" analysis. The software indicates the degree of acceptability of the particular risk and recommends ways to reduce such risk, including contingency plans.

Business Foundations' *Internal Operations Risk Analysis* appraises a company's areas of risk. It is an expert system developed around more than 150 interview questions. Based on the answers to the questions, the software prepares analytical and management reports summarizing the strengths and weaknesses in the company's operations. A risk rating (high, medium, or low) is assigned to risk categories. It recommends corrective steps for problem areas. There is an upgrade for industry-specific situations.

Pleier and Associates' *ADM Plus* performs risk management analysis.

COST ACCOUNTING SYSTEMS

Maxwell Business Systems' *Job Cost Accounting and Management Information System* (JAMIS) is a job costing system. The software keeps track of employee hours worked, distributes (allocates) labor cost to the responsible unit, keeps track of department or product costs, distinguishes between direct labor and indirect labor, and manages inventory. Job costs are broken down into 100 different transactions. Since the software tracks all costs, it can also perform activity-based accounting because the jobs can be expressed in terms of activities or tasks. The activities can further be divided into subactivities or subtasks. Costs may be broken down by operation or function (e.g., buying materials). Costs may also be identified by division or department. JAMIS can also be used to budget by cost type (e.g., labor, materials, and supplies). Costs may be tracked by project or contract for multiple years. It has time-based budgeting. It makes automated retroactive rate adjustments. The system supports contract types, cost classes, and job budgeting.

SouthWare Innovations' *Excellence Series* has features for job costing, contract management, service management, and wholesale distribution.

Manufacturing Management Systems' *Quite-A-Profit* performs competitive pricing, target costing, and earnings appraisal by product or service.

Peachtree Accounting has a module for *Job Costing* to track and report the revenue, cost, and profit for individual jobs and projects.

Macola Software's *Progression Series Accounting and Distribution Software* has modules for job costing, inventory management, and shop floor control. It prepares many management reports, including those analyzing inventory and manufacturing operations.

Lawson Software's *Activity Manager* performs activity-based management and costing. It performs multidimensional data analysis, offers "what-if" scenarios, does cost allocations, performs inventory control, and aids in warehousing.

Abacus Data Systems' *ADAMS 4GL* aids in warehousing, shop-floor control, inventory control and management, work-order management, and customer analysis.

Prosoft's Inc.'s *Contractor Cost Accounting Package* offers speed and flexibility. The system is fully integrated and each module interacts with others. It offers modules for General Ledger, Accounts Payable, Job Costing, Payroll, Accounts Receivable, and Purchase Orders. Accounts are user-defined and can be referenced and accessed by name or by number. You can customize the program and its reports to suit your needs.

3C Software's *Impact* allows you to set up the system to use any cost accounting method—ABC, Traditional, Machine-Based, Job, Direct, Japanese, JIT, or your own hybrid—so you can control how costs are calculated. It allows you to define the methodology, calculations, variables, products, processes, and reports. *Impact* contains an integrated, full-featured query and report writer that allows reports to be generated quickly and easily. Typical reports include: Product Cost Sheets, Product Pricing Sheets, Variance Reports, Inventory Valuations, Budgets and Forecasts, Profitability Reports, and other customized reports to meet cost reporting requirements.

ACTIVITY-BASED COSTING (ABC)

Activity-Based Costing (ABC) records cost based on manufacturing or service activities. Costs are assigned by activity and linked to the related products and services. Besides using spreadsheets for this purpose, there exists specialized software unique to ABC.

Price Waterhouse's *Activa* is activity-based software providing cost management for manufacturing and service companies. It does forecasting and simulation, product and service costing, activity-based budgeting, performance measurement reporting, profitability analysis, and valuing of products and processes. It can manage information across multiple periods for multiple locations. For multinational companies, it can provide information in multiple currencies.

Armstrong Laing's *Hyper ABC* provides ABC costing information. It provides multidimensional cost object analysis that allows the user to evaluate business across customers, products, services, and distribution channels. It compares budget to actual figures for variance determination. "What-if" analysis is performed such as for the effects of changing variables on volume.

Sapling Software's *Net Prophet* does activity-based costing, constraint checking, capacity planning, "what-if" evaluation, scenario playing, and process analysis. It has flexible reporting, model validation, and graphic features.

ABC Technologies' *Oros EIS with Power Play* and *Oros 3.0* provide data warehousing, target costing, and process yield. They provide a picture of activity-based information through active charts, graphs, and cross-table formats. *Oros* does analysis of profitability and performance.

ICMS Software's *CMS-PC* software has spreadsheet-style screens for activity-based product costing. There is an activity dictionary database. The project manager helps with activity interview questions.

Syspro Impact Software's *IMPACT* ABC module appraises preproduction manufacturing and sales costs. There is online cost inquiry and simulated cost recovery.

Applied Computer Services' *PROFILE* ABC software performs analysis of activity data, profitability evaluation, appraisal of staffing requirements, reengineering, and makes activity-based management decisions.

Deloitte and Touche's *Strategic Cost Management* software assigns costs to activities, operations, products, and services. It manages cross-functional processes and involves "what-if" decision making.

Com MIT Systems' *Com MIT-ABC* tracks, collects, and allocates costs based on activities and cost drivers. "What-if" alternatives are evaluated.

Lead Software's *Activity Analyzer* involves product costing by activity and process. It tracks cycle time, capacity, cost drivers, rates, and personnel.

Automatic Consulting's *Cost Accounting System for Service Organizations* (CASSO) evaluates costs at the activity, workgroup, and product levels.

There are many other software packages that may be used in activity-based costing, including KPMG Peat Marwick's *Profit Manager,* Deloitte and Touche's *TR/ACM,* Coopers and Lybrand's *AB Cost Manager,* VanDeMark Products' *Alpha Cost,* Polaris Systems' *e3 System,* ABC Technologies' *Easy ABC,* and Marcam Corporation's *Prism.*

APPRAISAL OF INVENTORY

SQL Financials International's *Purchasing Control* is used to control the purchasing processes. It provides information about purchase orders, items, vendors, receipts, invoices, and payments.

Computer Associates' *ACCPAC* is financial management software including order entry, inventory control, and job costing.

Lawson Software's *Insight Business Management System* includes supply chain and procurement, materials distribution, and audit controls.

Inventory Analyst is a template for computing economic order quantity, reorder point, and optimal inventory levels. Inventory history is depicted as a basis to predict future trends. It incorporates such forecasting techniques as moving average, exponential smoothing, and time series. Seasonal factors are incorporated.

Computron Software's *Computron Financials* does inventory stock control and time recording.

Dun & Bradstreet's *Smart Stream* does inventory stock control, warehousing, accounting for manufacturing processes, production scheduling and routing, and materials requirements planning.

Syspro Impact Software's *Impact Encore* does materials and resource planning to aid in cutting costs and improving delivery and quality. It has a purchase order system and can handle activity-based costing. It aids in tracking items through the production process.

Open Systems' *Accounting Software* inventory module features alternative costing and pricing methods including matrix pricing for customers. It can perform physical and cycle counts based on specified criteria. It also determines the level of inventory requiring a reorder. The package also has sales order functions.

Fourth Shift Corporation's *Manufacturing Software System* keeps track of inventory and manufacturing.

Best Ware's *MYOB* software's inventory module provides a listing of items, restocking information, and backorder listing.

EXECUTIVE MANAGEMENT GAMES

Computerized management games provide an excellent learning tool in making financial and managerial decisions so as to develop analytical and strategic abilities. The management game is a type of mathematical model and simulation. Simulation is designed to simulate a system and to generate a series of quantitative and financial results regarding system operations. In management games, participants make decisions at various stages in an attempt to better comprehend the external simulated environment. The games allow for a better understanding of the interrelationships of the various functions within the business and how such interactions affect overall performance. Some good management games are *PERT-SIM* for project planning and control, *Westinghouse Simulation Exercise* for distribution and logistics, *IBM Production Manpower Decision Model* for production and personnel scheduling, *MARKSIM* for marketing decision making, *X-Otol* for distribution analysis, Green and Sisson's *Materials Inventory Management Game* for inventory planning, and *FINASIM* for financial management simulation. (PERT stands for Program Evaluation and Review Technique, which refers to the sequence of steps to complete a long-term project in the minimum time.) Other executive management games are Harvard University's *Harvard Business Game*, K. Goosen's *Management Accounting Game*, R. Schrieber's *Top Management Decision Game*, Carnegie Mellon's *COGITATE*, and R. Barton's *IMAGINIT Management Game*.

LINEAR PROGRAMMING

Linear programming is the allocation of limited capital and human resources to maximize gain or minimize cost. *Linear Interactive and Discrete Optimization (LINDO)* can be used to obtain optimal solutions.

What's Best! is linear programming software that aids in determining the optimal allocation of limited capital, human, and financial resources. It considers time constraints and is ideal for management decision making. The objective of the software is to maximize revenue or minimize cost.

FLOWCHARTING

Flowcharts are diagrams that use standardized symbols, interconnected with flow lines, to visually represent complex procedures and data flow. People generally understand pictures better than words, and visual representation of data can often enhance understanding. Accountants can use flowcharts to document and understand the processing of information through the accounting system. Flowcharting software allows users to illustrate policies, processes, and procedures with diagrams. Typical flowcharting packages allow users to create diagrams for process and data flows, hierarchy charts, fishbone diagrams, structure charts, cause and effect diagrams, and organizational charts. Most packages contain templates or specialized libraries of symbols typically used by accountants and other professionals. It is also possible to create a custom library composed of frequently used shapes.

Micrografx Inc's *ABC FlowCharter* is a powerful and easy-to-use package. You can "drag and drop" hundreds of shapes from its extensive template library.

HavenTree Software Ltd.'s *EasyFlow* is a specialized drawing program. It uses the "drag and drop" approach to flowcharting. The user selects shapes from a palette and drops them into the appropriate place in the work area. *EasyFlow* comes with excellent documentation and tutorials.

Clear Software's *allCLEAR* takes a unique approach to flowcharting. To create a flowchart in *allCLEAR,* you write a script in the form of an outline. The punctuation in the script determines how the flowchart will look. The script approach makes it easy to create and modify even complicated flowcharts. However, the script approach greatly restricts the user's ability to customize flowcharts.

Patton & Patton Software Corp's *Flow Charting* is a good choice for the flowcharting beginner. It is a specialized drawing program and utilizes the "drag and drop" approach to flowcharting. It comes with an excellent tutorial.

Aldus Corp.'s *IntelliDraw* is a powerful diagramming and illustration package. It is not exclusively a flowcharting package. *IntelliDraw* is ideal if you work with many types of drawings and flowcharting is just one of your many needs.

Micrografx Inc.'s *ABC SnapGraphics* is a general purpose drawing and illustration package. It offers an easy-to-use interface and makes extensive use of "drag and drop" capabilities. It is ideal for an individual who prefers ease of use over esoteric features.

Shapeware Corp's *Visio* offers users a choice of "drag and drop" or script approach. Drawing flowcharts with *Visio* is very similar to manually drawing flowcharts. *Visio* works with computerized versions of plastic stencils that include cutouts for various symbols.

CORPORATE VALUATIONS

There are many reasons for determining the value of a company. The reason for the valuation might be for the purchase or sale of the business, mergers and acquisitions, buy-back agreements, expanding the credit line, or tax matters (see Table 1).

For buying or selling a business, a valuation might be important for establishing an asking or offering price. But what is the value of the business? Is it the value of the company's assets? Is it the value of the company's earnings? Is it the value of the company's loyal customers and good reputation? Is it something else? The answer is that it might be any of the above, or all of the above. Further, you must consider the type of business and its major activities, industry conditions, competition, marketing requirements, management possibilities, risk factors, earning potential, and financial health of the business.

Usually, *value* is determined by an interested party. Although there is usually no single value (or "worth") that can be associated with a business in all situations, there is usually a defendable value that can be assigned to a business in most situations. To be a proficient valuation analyst, a CFO requires analytical and writing skills. More specifically, one must be adept at financial analysis, economic forecasts, accounting and audit fundamentals, income taxes, and legal and economic research.

The valuation process is an art and not a science, because everyone's perception is slightly different. This chapter provides basic steps involved in valuation and various ways to determine what a business is worth. Further, various Internal Revenue Service Revenue Rulings are presented, recommending specific valuation measures, especially with regard to income tax issues.

To determine a company's value, the purpose of the valuation and an appropriate perspective must be specified. The perspective might be that

Table 1 Business Valuation Opportunities

- Buy-sell agreements
- Mergers, acquisitions, and spinoffs
- Liquidation or reorganization of a business
- Initial public offering
- Minority shareholder interests
- Employee stock ownership plans
- Financing
- Return on investment analysis
- Government actions
- Allocation of acquisition price
- Adequacy of life insurance
- Litigation
- Divorce action
- Compensatory damage cases
- Insurance claims
- Estate and gift taxes
- Incentive stock options
- Charitable contributions

Source: National Association of Certified Valuation Analysts

of a buyer, a seller, the IRS, or a court. When these are known, a business appraisal can be performed. Generally, the appraisal process determines the value of the business based on an asset, earnings (or cash flows), and/or market approach. In valuing the business, the following factors should be considered:

- History of the business
- Nature of the company
- Economic and political conditions
- Health of the industry
- Distribution channels and marketing factors
- Financial position
- Degree of risk
- Growth potential
- Trend and stability of earnings
- Competition
- Employee relationships
- Location
- Customer base

- Quality of management
- Ease of transferability of ownership

STEPS IN VALUATION

As an initial step in valuation, the key financial information must be accumulated and analyzed, including historical financial statements, projected financial statements, and tax returns. There must be familiarity with the business, including the company's strategic position in the industry. Further, the major assumptions of the valuation must be clearly spelled out. A variety of "what-if" scenarios must be investigated to reduce valuation errors. Figure 1 summarizes the basic steps in business valuations.

DEFINITIONS OF "VALUE"

Various individuals will have different ideas of how much a business is worth and how its value should be determined. Various individuals and groups might define "value" differently.

FAIR MARKET VALUE

Fair market value is generally defined as the price at which property would change hands between a willing buyer and a willing seller, when neither is compelled to act and both have a reasonable knowledge of the relevant facts. With the asset approach, assets are valued at fair (i.e., appraised) market value.

Fair market value is often an important valuation definition in estate, gift, and other federal tax-related valuations. It is a well-accepted IRS and tax court concept. Generally, these groups will consider that a company's value is equivalent to its fair market value. Accordingly, a financial manager will need to consider this definition when performing valuations that may have the IRS as an interested party.

REPLACEMENT VALUE

Replacement value is the cost of replacing something. The use of the definition might be applicable for establishing "damages" in antitrust suits, in condemnation proceedings, and in similar situations. At times, the definition could be used in a federal or state court. In some situations, replacement value might be determined to be a company's fair market value.

Figure 1 Steps in a Valuation

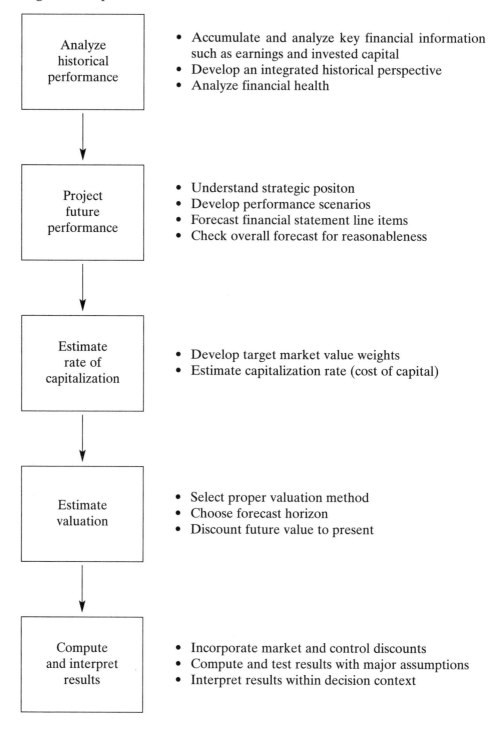

Analyze historical performance	• Accumulate and analyze key financial information such as earnings and invested capital • Develop an integrated historical perspective • Analyze financial health
Project future performance	• Understand strategic positon • Develop performance scenarios • Forecast financial statement line items • Check overall forecast for reasonableness
Estimate rate of capitalization	• Develop target market value weights • Estimate capitalization rate (cost of capital)
Estimate valuation	• Select proper valuation method • Choose forecast horizon • Discount future value to present
Compute and interpret results	• Incorporate market and control discounts • Compute and test results with major assumptions • Interpret results within decision context

LIQUIDATION VALUE

The lowest value associated with a business is its liquidation value. Liquidation value is, in effect, the value of an item (a business) sold to the highest available bidder. Typically, the seller is compelled to sell and the buyer knows of the seller's need to sell. Liquidation value is a depressed value. For a business, assets might be sold piecemeal. Usually, liquidation value is defined as the amount received by the seller after selling and administrative expenses are paid. At times, a company's liquidation value could be its fair market value.

"GOING CONCERN" VALUE

"Going concern" value is the opposite of liquidation value. Going concern value is the value of a business based on the presumption that the business will continue as an operating entity. That is, the company will not be liquidated. A company's going concern value will usually be its fair market value.

MATCHING VALUE DEFINITIONS
AND VALUATION REASONS

An initial step in the business valuation process is to match the reason and perspective of the valuation with an appropriate definition of value. Note that each definition of "value" is not mutually exclusive. In a given situation, several definitions might concurrently apply. Table 2 shows valuation reasons and value definitions that might be connected with them.

GENERAL APPROACHES TO BUSINESS VALUATION

When a company is not publicly traded, willing buyers and willing sellers capable of establishing an independent and objective value for a business won't exist at most times when the valuation is needed. Accordingly, an

Table 2 Definition of Value

Valuation Reason	FMV	Liq. Value	Repl. Value	Going Concern Value
Purchase of Business	X		X	X
Sale of Business	X			X
Shareholder Litigation	X			X
Bankruptcy, Dissolution		X		
Recapitalization	X			X

estimate of the price at which the company might change hands between a willing buyer and a willing seller must be made. To do this, one or more of three approaches to valuation might be used.

1. Market Comparison

Values of comparable companies in the industry may provide useful norms. The idea is to establish the company's value based on actual sales that are indicative of the company's current value.

A basic requirement for using prior sales of a firm's ownership interests in the appraisal of its current value is that each prior sale be indicative of the existing circumstances of the company. If prior sales were made in the too distant past, or were of a form or substance not indicative of the subject company's current situation, the use of the sale(s) may not be appropriate for establishing the company's current worth. In particular, small sales of non-controlling interests and sales between related parties might not indicate the value of the company and its related ownership interests at the time of the sale. They would not be indicative of the company's current value either.

When comparable company sales are evaluated, the requirements are greater. Comparable company sales should be used only when the sales have occurred in the recent past and are of a sufficient size to appropriately establish a supportable value. They should be in the same industry. The companies should be similar in products and services offered, competitive positions, financial structures, and historical financial performance. Unfortunately, finding comparable companies is difficult because closely held company operating performance and sale information are frequently unavailable. *Note:* Refer to Sanders, John, *Biz-Comps Business Sale Statistics,* published by BizComps (P.O. Box 711777, San Diego, CA 92171, www.bizcomps.com). This is the annual report compiling information for 1,600 businesses in many industries.

2. Earnings (or Cash Flows)

A second approach for business valuations is based on earnings. The earnings approach considers a company's value to be equivalent to its ability to create income (or cash flow). The concept is to associate the firm's income with a rate of return commensurate with the company's investment risk.

3. Assets

A third approach for establishing the value of a business is to consider the company's value to be equivalent to the value of its net tangible assets. For the dissolution of the business, the company's value might be based on the liquidated value of the company's assets. If the company is to be "duplicated," the company's value might be based on asset replacement values. If the company will continue as a going concern, the company's value might be based on the fair market value of the company's assets.

PERFORMING A GENERAL ANALYSIS OF THE COMPANY BEING VALUED

For appraisal purposes, the determination of a company's value is usually based on a market, earnings, and/or assets approach to value. There are various business valuation methods associated with each. To understand and apply the methods, one needs to understand various attributes about the company being valued. Especially, an understanding is necessary of the company's:

- industry,
- customers and markets,
- products and services,
- employees and management,
- assets, and
- historical and projected financial performance.

Each of these areas will significantly affect the valuation of the business and the use of various valuation methods.

Industry Outlook

In assessing a company's industry, a CFO should evaluate the economic outlook for the industry, barriers to entry, government controls, and similar items. If the industry is expected to grow, firms in the industry might be perceived as being increasingly valuable. Further, you will need to consider competition. In a highly competitive industry, companies might be reduced in value because of competitive pressures, price discounting, etc.

Customers and Markets

In assessing a company's customers and markets, you should evaluate the company's key customers and the strength of the customers. If the company has many customers, and none of the customers represent a significant percentage of the sales of the company, the company might be increasingly stable. The company may have a lower associated investment risk. If a company has only a few large customers, you will need to weigh carefully the implications and the likelihood of its losing the customers.

Products and Services

In evaluating a company's products and services, you should look at their quality. You should compare the company's products and services with competitive products and services. Evaluate the company's investments in research and development and historical trends in sales and expenses of important products and services. Consider the number of products and services the company offers and the extent to which the company relies on one or several products or services for most of its sales and profits. When a company has only one or a few products or services, the competitive risks associated with the products and services become a factor. Generally, diverse and stable product lines might be associated with a stable company. Limited product lines might imply an increased investment risk.

Employees and Management

Qualified management usually means that the company is stable. Qualified management might enhance the value of the company. To the extent that a firm has had significant turnover in its management (and/or employees), the company might be considered a risky investment. In general, inexperienced management and a high turnover rate are indicative of a high-risk company.

Assets

Typically, the value of a company's tangible assets is a minimum value associated with the business. For valuation purposes, judge a company's assets to ensure that the assets are indeed valuable. Scrutinize in detail such items as obsolete inventory, old fixed assets, bad debts in accounts receivable, and capitalized expenses. For some assets, specific evaluations may be necessary.

Historical and Projected Financial Performance

Evaluating a company's historical and projected financial performance can be time-consuming and complex. A CFO needs to establish the reliability of the company's historical financial statements and assess the implications of sales, expenses, and profits. Typically, for determining the value of a company, you evaluate the company's operating performance. Accordingly, you may have to remove the implications of non-typical and non-operating transactions included in the company's financial statements.

Corporate Valuations

A company's historical financial statements might include excess compensation and significant perks to owners. Frequently, the CFO will need to add excess compensation paid to owners back to the company's income to fully understand the profitability of the company. Adjustments might also be made to the financial statements to convert cash basis statements to accrual basis statements. In particular, cash basis statements might not display accounts receivable, accounts payable, and accrued liabilities.

In evaluating a company's financial performance, the CFO will want to review various expense ratios as a percent of sales, and review various sales, income, and expense trends. In particular, the CFO would assess the financial statements for purposes of making assumptions about the future profitability of the company. Evaluate various company ratios and compare them with other companies in the industry. You might also develop projected financial statements for the company for three or more years.

BUSINESS VALUATION METHODS

There are numerous ways of determining the value of the business. Further, there are many possible combinations of various methods. Nine popular valuation methods are illustrated below.

1. Adjusted Net Assets Method

The adjusted net assets valuation method presumes the value of a company is equivalent to the value of its net tangible assets. Asset values are often based on fair market values when the company is expected to continue as a going concern, on liquidated values when the company is not expected to continue as a going concern, and on replacement values when the costs of duplicating the company are being assessed.

The fair market value of the net tangible assets of the company may be based on independent appraisal. An addition is made for goodwill. An investment banking firm that handles the purchase and sale of businesses may be hired to appraise the tangible property. Usually, the fair market value of the assets exceeds their book value.

An advantage of the adjusted net assets valuation method is that it is frequently easy to determine the value of a company's tangible net assets. A disadvantage of the method is that it ignores the important implications of company's earnings. In many instances, an adjusted net assets valuation is a conservative valuation. It might be a minimum value associated with a business.

Example 1.

Net Tangible Assets (at Fair Market Value)	$12,000,000
Plus Goodwill	6,000,000
Valuation	$18,000,000

2. Gross Revenue Multiplier Method

The value of the company may be determined based on the revenue-generating capacity of the company. For example, many Internet stocks that lose money in the short run and yet have great future earnings potential tend to derive their value from their revenue-generating capacity or registered member subscriptions. The formula for this method is as follows:

Value of the Business = Revenue x Gross Revenue Multiplier

The gross revenue multiplier used is the one customary in the industry. The industry norm gross multiplier is based on the average ratio of market price to sales typical in the industry.

If reported earnings are suspect, this method may also be advisable.

Example 2.

Gross revenue	$32,500,000
x Gross revenue multiplier	.4
Valuation	$13,000,000

3. Capitalization of Earnings Method

The capitalization of earnings valuation method is in many ways the opposite of the adjusted net assets valuation method. It uses income, as opposed to assets, to value the business. A variation of the method incorporates *cash flows* as opposed to earnings.

The capitalization of earnings valuation method is based on the notion that the investors will only acquire stock in a company if they can earn a rate of return that is high enough to offset the risks associated with the investment. The trade-off is the risk of the loss of the investment with the rate of return that might be realized. In general, high-risk companies need to yield high rates of return to stimulate equity investments. Low-risk companies can produce lower rates of return and still attract equity investors.

The formula for the capitalization of earnings method follows:

Value of the Business = Earnings (or Cash Flow)/Capitalization Rate

Frequently, earnings or cash flow for this method is the current year's earnings (or cash flow), a simple average of two to five prior years, a weighted-average adjusted historical earnings, or the company's projected profit for the following year. The method presumes the earnings value used in the method is indicative of future earnings expectations on an ongoing basis. In this method, earnings can be any one of the following:

- Before-tax earnings
- After-tax earnings
- Earnings before interest and taxes (EBIT)

The capitalization rate is the rate of return an investor would expect to receive for investing in the company based on the company's perceived risk. It is typically a weighted cost of capital, weights being a target mix of different sources of financing, equity or nonequity.

Two examples for this method are presented below.

Example 3.

Earnings (Simple Average)	$1,250,000
/Capitalization rate	10%
Valuation	$12,500,000

The following example uses weighted-average historical earnings, in which more weight is given to the most recent years. This is more representative than a simple average. Using a weighted-average makes sense because current earnings reflect current prices and recent business activity. In the case of a five-year weighted average, the current year is assigned a weight of 5 while the initial year is assigned a weight of 1. The multiplier is then applied to the weighted-average five-year adjusted historical earnings to derive a valuation.

Example 4.

Year	Historical Earnings	Weight	Total
20X0	$2,780,000	5	$13,900,000
20X1	$1,670,000	4	$6,680,000
20X2	$1,350,000	3	$4,050,000
20X3	$1,780,000	2	$3,560,000
20X4	$2,100,000	1	$2,100,000
		15	$30,290,000

Corporate Valuations

Weighted average 5-year earnings:

$30,290,000/15 = $2,019,333

Weighted average 5-year earnings	$2,019,333
/Capitalization Rate (20%)	20%
Valuation	$10,096,667

4. Price–Earnings Ratio Method

For publicly traded stocks, stock trading prices are often directly proportional to earnings. Often, within industries, there is consistency between companies. The price–earnings ratio method is predicated on the notion that price–earnings ratios (P/Es) of publicly traded stocks might be indicative of a closely held company's value. The notion is this: If the closely held company were publicly traded, it would trade at a price similar to the price at which comparable companies trade.

The formula for this method is as follows:

Value of the Business = Earnings per share (EPS)/Price–Earnings Multiplier (P/E)

Typically, earnings for this method is the most recent year's earnings per share (EPS) or an average of two to five prior years. The P/E multiplier is usually an historical average based on comparable, actively traded stocks. Some use a P/E ratio based on the most current period rather than an average of prior years.

Example 5.

Earnings after taxes	$1,000,000
Outstanding shares	250,000
Earnings per share (EPS)	$4
P/E ratio	15
Estimated market price per share	$60
x Number of shares outstanding	250,000
Valuation	$15,000,000

5. Dividend Payout (or Dividend-Paying Capacity) Method

The dividend payout (or dividend-paying capacity) valuation method presumes that the "compensation" for stock ownership is dividends. The method is based on the notion that a stock's value is related to the company's ability to pay dividends and the yield investors expect.

356

The dividend payout method involves the following steps:

1. Company's Dividend-Paying Capacity = Earnings × Dividend Payout Percentage
2. Value of Business = Company's Dividend-Paying Capacity/Dividend Yield Rate

Typically, earnings for this method is an average of two to five prior years. Some use before-tax profits. Others use after-tax profits. The dividend payout percentage and dividend yield rate are established with reference to comparable publicly traded stocks. A variation of the method would establish the company's dividend-paying capacity to be monies received by the owners of the closely held company as dividends, excess compensation, and perks.

Although the method is in infrequent use, the method incorporates some of the most defendable valuation principles of all methods.

Example 6.

Earnings after taxes	$1,000,000
Dividend payout percentage	40%
Dividend-paying capacity	$400,000
/Dividend Yield Rate	4%
Valuation	$10,000,000

6. Excess Earnings Return on Assets Method

The excess earnings return on assets valuation method implies that within an industry, a given level of company assets will generate a particular level of earnings. To the extent a company has earnings above the expected level of earnings, the company is presumed to have an enhanced value. The enhanced value is attributed to goodwill (or intangible assets). The addition of the value of the goodwill and the fair market value of the net tangible assets equals the total valuation.

The excess earnings return on assets method involves the following steps:

1. Industry-Expected Earnings = Company Assets × Industry-Expected Return on Assets
2. Excess Earnings = Company Earnings – Industry-Expected Earnings
3. Goodwill (intangible assets) = Excess Earnings/Capitalization Rate
4. Value of the Business = Goodwill + Fair Market Value of Net Tangible Assets

This method has several variations. Gross assets or net assets and book values or fair market values might be used to calculate industry earnings and excess earnings.

As per IRS Revenue Ruling 59-60 (to be discussed later), the IRS recommends this method to value a business for tax purposes.

Example 7.

Year	Net Tangible Assets	Assets	Weight Total
20X0	$10,000,000	1	$10,000,000
20X1	$14,000,000	2	$28,000,000
20X2	$18,000,000	3	$54,000,000
20X3	$19,000,000	4	$76,000,000
20X4	$18,500,000	5	$92,500,000
		15	$260,500,000

Weighted Average Net Tangible Assets	
$260,500,000/15 = $17,366,667	
Weighted Average Earnings (5 years)—Assumed	$1,800,000
Minus Industry Rate of Return on Weighted Average	
Net Tangible Assets ($17,366,667 x 10%)	1,736,667
Excess Earnings	$63,333
/Capitalization Factor (20%)	0.2
Plus Goodwill (Intangibles)	$316,667
Plus Fair Market Value of Net Tangible Assets	$16,000,000
Valuation	$16,316,667

7. Excess Earnings Return on Sales Method

The excess earnings return on sales valuation method values a company based on sales, earnings, and assets. Generally, the method implies that within an industry, a given level of sales will generate a given level of earnings. When a company has earnings above the industry's expected level of earnings, the company is considered to have goodwill (or intangible assets). The value of goodwill plus the fair market value of the net tangible assets is considered to be the value of the company.

The excess earnings return on sales method involves the following steps:

1. Industry-Expected Earnings = Company Sales x Industry-Expected Return on Sales

2. Excess Earnings = Company Earnings – Industry-Expected Earnings
3. Goodwill (Intangible Assets) = Excess Earnings/Capitalization Rate
4. Value of the Business = Goodwill + Fair Market Value of Net Tangible Assets

Variations in this method include the use of the company's current year's sales or a two- to five-year average for computing the industry-expected profits.

Example 8.

Year	Sales	Weight	Total
20X0	$11,100,000	1	$11,100,000
20X1	$12,500,000	2	$25,000,000
20X2	$20,000,000	3	$60,000,000
20X3	$21,000,000	4	$84,000,000
20X4	$24,200,000	5	$121,000,000
		15	$301,100,000

Weighted Average Sales	
$301,100,000/15 = $802,933	
Weighted Average Earnings (5 years)—Assumed	$1,800,000
Minus Industry Rate of Return on Weighted Average	
Sales ($20,073,333 x 4%)	802,933
Excess Earnings	$ 997,067
/Capitalization Factor (20%)	0.2
Valuation of Goodwill (Intangibles)	$4,985,333
Plus Fair Market Value of Net Tangible Assets	$16,000,000
Valuation	$20,985,333

8. Discounted Cash Flow Method

The discounted cash flow (DCF) method equates the value of a business with the cash flows the business is expected to create.

The discounted cash flow method presumes that the purpose of a company is to generate cash flow (or earnings) and therefore, assets, distribution channels, and so on, have a value related to the cash flows they are able to create. Conceptually, the method is similar to the capitalization of earnings valuation method, except that in the discounted cash flow method, projected earnings (or cash flows) as opposed to historical earnings (or cash flows) are assessed. If the growth rate is used to project future earnings, the rate may be based on prior growth rate, future expectations, and the inflation rate. The discount rate may be based on the market interest rate of a low-risk asset investment.

The formula for the discounted cash flow method follows:

Value of the Business =

Present Value of the Earnings (or Cash Flow) Projection

+ Present Value of Terminal Value (Selling Price)

Typically, cash flows are projected for at least five years and a terminal value (or selling price) is established for the value of the business at the end of the term.

Example 9.

Year	Cash Flows (7% growth rate)	Present Value (PV) Factor at a 10% discount rate	Total PV
20X0	$500,000	0.909	$454,500
20X1	$535,000	0.826	$441,910
20X2	$572,450	0.751	$429,910
20X3	$612,522	0.683	$418,352
20X4	$655,398	0.621	$407,002
Present Value of Future Earnings			$2,151,674

If the anticipated selling price at the end of year 20X4 is $15,000,000, the valuation of the business equals:

Present value of future earnings	$2,151,674
Present value of selling price $18,000,000 × .621	$11,178,000
Valuation	$13,329,674

9. Combination Valuation Method

The combination valuation method is not really a method; it's a combination of other methods. Often, the use of a combination method establishes a more reasonable value for a business than any single method. In particular, in a combination method, earnings, assets, comparable companies, prior sales of company stock, and other important valuation concepts might be accounted for.

Further, the valuation of the company may be estimated based on a weighted-average value of several methods. The most weight should typically be placed on the earnings method and the least on the asset approaches.

Example 10.

Method	Valuation Amount	Weight	Total
Adjusted Net Assets	$18,000,000	1	$18,000,000
Excess Earnings on Rate of Return	$20,985,333	2	$41,970,666
		3	$59,970,666
Total/3 = $69,970,666/3 = $19,990,222			
Valuation			$19,990,222

Generally, before a combination method should be used, it should be established that the combination method results in a better valuation than any method individually, and that the use of each method in the combination supports the final valuation.

MARKETABILITY DISCOUNTS

Generally, a business ownership interest that can be sold quickly will be worth more than a similar ownership interest that cannot be sold quickly. In various business valuation methods, this implication may or may not be considered. When it is not, a marketability discount might be associated with the value of the ownership interest otherwise determined. A marketability discount is the reduction in the value of a company (or ownership interest) because the company (or ownership interest) might take considerable time to sell.

There are differences of opinion about marketability discounts. The IRS objects to them and will argue that the implications of marketability will have been accounted for elsewhere in the valuation process. Many believe that statistics prove there is in fact a depressed value for closely held company ownership interests, and they might assign discounts as high as 25% to 45% to account for this.

In assigning a marketability discount, some analysts compute the cost of taking the company public and deduct that amount from the value of the company otherwise determined. The presumption is that if the company is taken public, its ownership interests will be marketable.

CONTROL PREMIUMS AND DISCOUNTS

A business valuation does not have to be restricted to the valuation of an entire company. Frequently, partial ownership interests are valued for purchase or sale, divorce proceedings, estate planning, and other reasons.

When a partial ownership interest is appraised, it is not necessarily true that its value is equivalent to its ownership percentage times the value of the company. Generally, to the extent the ownership interest can control the activities of the business, the ownership interest may have an enhanced value. To the extent the ownership interest has little control over the operations of the company, the ownership interest might have a reduced value. Practitioners frequently account for this with control premiums and lack-of-control discounts.

For closely held companies, noncontrolling ownership interests can have a depressed value. The company might not be particularly marketable, and the noncontrolling interests might have an even greater lack of appeal because of their inability to influence the payment of dividends and the general operations of the company.

In developing control premiums and lack-of-control discounts, the circumstances of the ownership interests must be considered. Before a discount or premium is assigned, it should be determined that in fact an ownership interest has an increased or decreased value based on control/lack of control implications. For example, in a company in which the father is the controlling owner and two children are the noncontrolling owners, circumstances might indicate that the noncontrolling owners are in fact receiving dividends, etc., commensurate with the value of their ownership percentages. Accordingly, depending on the purpose of the valuation, the assignment of a discount to the non-controlling interests might not be appropriate. Before assigning premiums or discounts, it is very important to ensure that the control/lack of control implications were not accounted for in some other way in the valuation process.

SUMMARY

Performing a business valuation is not a simple task. Although a business valuation might seem overwhelming at first, valuation concepts are in fact very logical and intuitive. The major issue is to clearly understand the concepts of valuation and how the concepts are used by the interested party. The next step is to fully investigate the company being valued, its industry, and various implications that might affect its value. Financial forecasting, analytical reviews, sales forecasting, financial analysis, and various planning activities are important parts of the business valuation process.

REVENUE RULING 59–60

In valuing the stock of closely held corporations, or the stock of corporations where market quotations are not available, all other available financial data, as well as all relevant factors affecting the fair market value must be considered for estate tax and gift tax purposes. No general formula may be given that is applicable to the many different valuation situations arising in the valuation of such stock. However, the general approach, methods, and factors which must be considered in valuing such securities are outlined.

Section 1. Purpose

The purpose of this Revenue Ruling is to outline and review the approach, methods and factors to be considered in valuing shares of the capital stock of closely held corporations for estate tax and gift tax purposes. The methods discussed herein will apply likewise to the valuation of corporate stocks on which market quotations are either unavailable or are of such scarcity that they do not reflect the fair market value.

Section 2. Background and Definitions

01. All valuations must be made in accordance with the applicable provisions of the Internal Revenue Code of 1954 and the Federal Estate Tax & Gift Tax Regulations. Sections 2031(a), 2032 and 2512(a) of the 1954 Code (Sections 811 and 1005 of the 1939 Code) require that the property to be included in the gross estate, or made the subject of a gift, shall be taxed on the basis of the value of the property at the time of death of the decedent, the alternative date if so elected, or the date of gift.

02. Section 20.2031-1(b) of the Estate Tax Regulations (Section 81.10 of the Estate Tax Regulations 105) and Section 25.2512-1 of the Gift Tax Regulations (Section 86.19 of Gift Tax Regulations 108) define fair market value, in effect, as the price at which the property would change hands between a willing buyer and a willing seller when the former is not under any compulsion to buy and the latter is not under any compulsion to sell, both parties having reasonable knowledge of relevant facts. Court decisions frequently state in addition that the hypothetical buyer and seller are assumed to be able, as well as willing, to trade and to be well informed about the market for the property.

03. Closely held corporations are those company shares owned by a relatively limited number of stockholders. Often the entire stock issue is held by one family. The result of this situation is that little, if any, trading in the shares takes place. There is, therefore, no established market for the stock and such sales as occur at irregular intervals seldom reflect all of the elements of a representative transaction as defined by the term "fair market value."

Section 3. Approach to Valuation

01.   A determination of fair market value, being a question of fact, will depend upon the circumstances in each case. No formula can be devised that will be generally applicable to the multitude of different valuation issues arising in estate and gift tax cases. Often, an appraiser will find wide differences of opinion as to the fair market value of a particular stock. In resolving such differences, he or she should maintain a reasonable attitude in recognition of the fact that valuation is not an exact science. A sound valuation will be based upon all the relevant facts, but the elements of common sense, informed judgment, and reasonableness must enter into the process of weighing those facts and determining their aggregate significance.

02.   The fair market value of specific shares of stock will vary as general economic conditions change from "normal" to "boom" or "depression," that is, according to the degree of optimism or pessimism with which the investing public regards the future at the required date of appraisal. Uncertainty as to the stability or continuity of the future income from a property decreases its value by increasing the risk of loss of earnings and value in the future. The value of shares of stock of a company with very uncertain future prospects is highly speculative. The appraiser must exercise his judgment as to the degree of risk attaching to the business of the corporation which issued the stock, but that judgment must be related to all of the other factors affecting value.

03.   Valuation of securities is, in essence, a prophecy as to the future and must be based on facts available at the required date of appraisal. As a generalization, the prices of stocks which are traded in volume in a free and active market by informed persons best reflect the consensus of the investing public as to what the future holds for the corporations and industries represented. When a stock is closely held, is traded infrequently, or is traded in an erratic market, some other measure of value must be used. In many instances, the next best measure may be found in the prices at which the stocks of companies engaged in the same or a similar line of business are selling in a free and open market.

Section 4. Factors to Consider

01. It is advisable to emphasize that in the valuation of the stock of closely held corporations or the stock of corporations where market quotations are either lacking or too scarce to be recognized, all available financial data, as well as all relevant factors affecting the fair market value, should be considered. The following factors, although not all-inclusive, are fundamental and require careful analysis in each case:

   (a) Nature of the business and the history of the enterprise from its inception.

   (b) Economic outlook in general and the condition and outlook of the specific industry in particular.

   (c) Book value of the stock and the financial condition of the business.

   (d) Earning capacity.

   (e) Dividend-paying capacity.

   (f) Whether or not the enterprise has goodwill or other intangible value.

   (g) Sales of the stock and the size of the block of stock to be valued.

   (h) Market price of stocks of corporations engaged in the same or a similar line of business having their stocks actively traded in a free and open market, either on an exchange or over-the-counter.

02. The following is a brief discussion of each of the foregoing factors.

   (a) The history of a corporate enterprise will show its past stability or instability, its growth or lack of growth, the diversity or lack of diversity of its operations, and other facts to form an opinion of the degree of business risk. For an enterprise which changed its form of organization but carried on the same or closely similar operations of its predecessor, the history of the former enterprise should be considered. The detail considered should increase with the date of appraisal, since recent events are of greatest help in predicting the future—but a study of gross and net income, and of dividends covering a long prior period, is highly desirable. The history to be studied should include, but need not be limited to, the nature of the business, its products or services, its operating and investment assets, capital structure, plant facilities, sales records and management, all of which should be considered as of the date of the appraisal, with due regard for recent significant changes. Events of the past that are unlikely to recur in the future should be discounted, since value has a close relation to future expectancy.

(b) A sound appraisal of a closely held stock must consider current and prospective economic conditions as of the date of appraisal, both in the national economy and in the industry or industries with which the corporation is allied. It is important to know that the company is more or less successful than its competitors in the same industry, or that it is maintaining a stable position with respect to competitors. Equal or even greater significance may attach to the ability of the industry with which the company is allied to compete with other industries. Prospective competition which has not been a factor in prior years should be given careful attention. For example, high profits due to the novelty of its product and the lack of competition often lead to increasing competition. The public's appraisal of the future prospects of competitive industries or of competitors within an industry may be indicated by price trends in the markets for commodities and for securities. The loss of the manager of a so-called 'one-man' business may have a depressing effect upon the value of the stock of such business, particularly if there is a lack of trained personnel capable of succeeding to the management of the enterprise. In valuing the stock of this type of business, therefore, the effect of the loss of the manager on the future expectancy of the business and the absence of management-succession potentialities are pertinent factors to be taken into consideration. On the other hand, there may be factors which offset, in whole or in part, the loss of the manager's services. For instance, the nature of the business and of its assets may be such that they will not be impaired by the loss of the manager. Furthermore, the loss may be adequately covered by life insurance, or competent management might be employed on the basis of the consideration paid for the former manager's services. These, or other offsetting factors, if found to exist, should be carefully weighed against the loss of the manager's services in valuing the stock of the enterprise.

(c) Balance sheets should be obtained, preferably in the form of comparative annual statements for two or more years immediately preceding the date of appraisal, together with a balance sheet at the end of the month preceding that date, if corporate accounting will permit. Any balance sheet descriptions that are not self-explanatory, and balance sheet items comprehending diverse assets or liabilities, should be clarified in essential detail by supporting supplemental schedules. These statements usually will disclose to the appraiser:

- liquid position (ratio of current assets to current liabilities);
- gross and net book value of principal classes of fixed assets;
- working capital;
- long-term indebtedness;
- capital structure;
- net worth

Consideration should be given to any assets not essential to the operation of the business, such as investments in securities, real estate, etc. In general, such nonoperating assets will command a lower rate of return than do the operating assets, although in exceptional cases the reverse may be true. In computing the book value per share of stock, assets of the investment type should be revalued on the basis of their market price and the book value adjusted accordingly. Comparison of the company's balance sheets over several years may reveal, among other facts, such developments as the acquisition of additional production facilities or subsidiary companies, improvement in financial position, and details as to recapitalizations and other changes in the capital structure of the corporation. If the corporation has more than one class of stock outstanding, the charter or certificate of incorporation should be examined to ascertain the explicit rights and privileges of the various stock issues including:

- voting powers,
- preference as to dividends, and
- preference as to assets in the event of liquidation

(d) Detailed profit-and-loss statements should be obtained and considered for a representative period immediately prior to the required date of appraisal, preferably five or more years.

Such statements should show

- gross income by principal items;
- principal deductions from gross income including major prior items of operating expenses, interest and other expense on each item of long-term debt, depreciation and depletion if such deductions are made, officers' salaries, in total if they appear to be reasonable or in detail if they seem to be excessive, contributions (whether or not deductible for tax purposes) that the nature of its business and its community position require the corporation to make, and taxes by principal items, including income and excess profits taxes;
- net income available for dividends;

- rates and amounts of dividends paid on each class of stock,
- remaining amount carried to surplus; and
- adjustments to, and reconciliation with, surplus as stated on the balance sheet. With profit and loss statements of this character available, the appraiser should be able to separate recurrent from nonrecurrent items of income and expense, to distinguish between operating income and investment income, and to ascertain whether or not any line of business in which the company is engaged is operated consistently at a loss and might be abandoned with benefit to the company. The percentage of earnings retained for business expansion should be noted when dividend paying capacity is considered. Potential future income is a major factor in many valuations of closely-held stocks, and all information concerning past income which will be helpful in predicting the future should be secured. Prior earnings records usually are the most reliable guide as to the future expectancy, but resorting to arbitrary five-or-ten-year averages without regard to current trends or future prospects will not produce a realistic valuation. If, for instance, a record of progressively increasing or decreasing net income is found, then greater weight may be accorded the most recent years' profits in estimating earning power. It will be helpful, in judging risk and the extent to which a business is a marginal operator, to consider deductions from income and net income in terms of percentage of sales. Major categories of cost and expense to be so analyzed include the consumption of raw materials and supplies in the case of manufacturers, processors and fabricators; the cost of purchased merchandise in the case of merchants; utility services; insurance; taxes; depletion or depreciation; and interest

(e) Primary consideration should be given to the dividend-paying capacity of the company rather than to dividends actually paid in the past. Recognition must be given to the necessity of retaining a reasonable portion of profits in a company to meet competition. Dividend-paying capacity is a factor that must be considered in an appraisal, but dividends actually paid in the past may not have any relation to dividend-paying capacity. Specifically, the dividends paid by a closely held family company may be measured by the income needs of the stockholders or by their desire to avoid taxes on dividend receipts, instead of by the ability of the company to pay dividends. Where an actual or effective controlling interest in a corporation is to be valued, the dividend factor is not a material element, since the payment of such dividends is discretionary with the controlling stockholders. The individual or group in control can substitute salaries and bonuses for dividends, thus reducing net income and understating the dividend-paying capacity of the company. It follows, therefore, that dividends are a less reliable criteria of fair market value than other applicable factors.

(f) In the final analysis, goodwill is based upon earning capacity. The presence of goodwill and its value, therefore, rests upon the excess of net earnings over and above a fair return on the net, tangible assets. While the element of goodwill may be based primarily on earnings, such factors as the prestige and renown of the business, the ownership of a trade or brand name, and a record of success-ful operation over a prolonged period in a particular locality, also may furnish support for the inclusion of intangible value. In some instances, it may not be possible to make a separate appraisal of the tangible and intangible assets of the business. The enterprise has a value as an entity. Whatever intangible value there is, which is supportable by the facts, may be measured by the amount by which the appraised value of the tangible assets exceeds the net book value of such assets.

(g) Sales of stock of a closely held corporation should be carefully in-vestigated to determine whether they represent transactions at arm's length. Forced or distress sales do not ordinarily reflect fair market value nor do isolated sales in small amounts necessarily control as the measure of value. This is especially true in the valu-ation of a controlling interest in a corporation. Since, in the case of closely held stocks, no prevailing market prices are available, there is no basis for making an adjustment for blockage. It follows, therefore, that such stocks should be valued upon a consideration of all the evidence affecting fair market value. Although it is true that a minority interest in an unlisted corporation's stock is more difficult to sell than a similar block of listed stock, it is equally true that control of a corporation, either actual or in effect, represent-ing as it does an added element of value, may justify a higher value for a specific block of stock.

(h) Section 2031(b) of the Code states, in effect, that in valuing un-listed securities the value of stock or securities of corporations en-gaged in the same or a similar line of business which are listed on an exchange should be taken into consideration along with all other factors. An important consideration is that the corporations to be used for comparisons have capital stocks which are actively traded by the public. In accordance with Section 2031(b) of the Code, stocks listed on an exchange are to be considered first. However, if sufficient comparable companies whose stocks are listed on an exchange cannot be found, other comparable companies which have stocks actively traded on the over-the-counter market also may be used. The essential factor is that whether the stocks are sold on an exchange or over-the-counter there is evidence of an active, free public market for the stock as of the valuation date. In selecting corporations for comparative purposes, care should be taken to use only comparable companies (corporations specified in the statute have similar lines of business). However, consideration must be given to other relevant factors in order that the most valid comparison possible be obtained. For example, a corporation having one or more issues of preferred stock, bonds or debentures in addition to its common stock should not be considered to be directly comparable to one having only common stock outstanding. In like manner, a company with a declining business and decreasing markets is not comparable to one with a record of current progress and market expansion.

Section 5. Weight to Be Accorded Various Factors

The valuation of closely held corporate stock entails the consideration of all relevant factors as stated in Section 4. Depending upon the circumstances in each case, certain factors may carry more weight than others because of the nature of the company's business. To illustrate:

- Earnings may be the most important criterion of value in some cases whereas asset value will receive primary consideration in others. In general, the appraiser will accord primary consideration to earnings when valuing stocks of companies which sell products or services to the public; conversely, in the investment or holding type of company, the appraiser may accord the greater weight to the assets underlying the security to be valued.

- The value of the stock of a closely held investment or real estate holding company, whether or not family owned, is closely related to the value of the assets underlying the stock. For companies of this type the appraiser should determine the fair market values of the assets of the company. Operating expenses of such a company and the cost of liquidating it, if any, merit consideration when appraising the relative values of the stock and the underlying assets. The market values of the underlying assets give due weight to potential earnings and dividends of the particular items of property underlying the stock, capitalized at rates deemed proper by the investing public at the date of appraisal. A current appraisal by the investing public should be superior to the retrospective opinion of an individual. For these reasons, adjusted net worth should be accorded greater weight in valuing the stock of a closely held investment or real estate holding company, whether or not family owned, than any of the other customary yardsticks of appraisal, such as earnings and dividend paying capacity.

Section 6. *Capitalization Rates*

In the application of certain fundamental valuation factors, such as earnings and dividends, it is necessary to capitalize the average, or current, results at some appropriate rate. A determination of the proper capitalization rate presents one of the most difficult problems in valuation. That there is no ready or simple solution will become apparent by a cursory check of the rates of return and dividend yields in terms of the selling prices of corporate shares listed on the major exchanges of the country. Wide variations will be found even for companies in the same industry. Moreover, the ratio will fluctuate from year to year depending upon economic conditions. Thus, no standard tables of capitalization rates applicable to closely held corporations can be formulated. Among the more important factors to be taken into consideration in deciding upon a capitalization rate in a particular case are:

- Nature of the business
- Risk
- Stability or irregularity of earnings

Section 7. *Average of Factors*

Because valuations cannot be made on the basis of a prescribed formula, there is no means whereby the various applicable factors in a particular case can be assigned mathematical weights in deriving the fair market value. For this reason, no useful purpose is served by taking an average of several factors (for example, book value, capitalized earnings, and capitalized dividends) and basing the valuation on the result. Such a process excludes active consideration of other pertinent factors, and the end result cannot be supported by a realistic application of the significant facts in the case except by mere chance.

Section 8. *Restrictive Agreements*

Frequently, in the valuation of closely held stock for estate and gift tax purposes, it will be found that the stock is subject to an agreement restricting its sale or transfer. Where shares of stock were acquired by a decedent subject to an option reserved by the issuing corporation to repurchase at a certain price, the option price is usually accepted as the fair market value for estate tax purposes. See Rev. Rule. 54-76 C.B. 1954-1, 194. However, in such a case the option price is not determinative of fair market value for gift tax purposes. Where the option, or buy and sell agreement, is the result of voluntary action by the stockholders and is binding during the life as well as at the death of the stockholders, such agreement may or may not, depending upon the circumstances of each case, fix the value for estate tax purposes. However, such agreement is a factor to be considered, with other relevant factors, in determining fair market value. Where the stockholder is free to dispose of shares during life and the option is to become effective only upon death, the fair market value is not limited to the option price. It is always necessary to consider the relationship of the parties, the relative number of shares held by the decedent, and other material facts, to determine whether the agreement represents a bona fide business arrangement or is a device to pass the decedent's shares to the natural objects of his bounty for less than an adequate and full consideration in money or money's worth. In this connection see Rev. Rul. 157 C.B. 1953-2, 255, and Rev. Rul. 189, C.B. 1953-2, 294.

Section 9. Effect on Other Documents

Revenue Ruling 54-77, C.B. 1954-1, 187, is hereby superseded.

MANAGEMENT ANALYSIS OF OPERATIONS

This chapter discusses the analysis of a company's profit, including the revenue and cost components. Means to control costs are included. There is a discussion of the cost of quality (COQ) and the cost of prediction errors. The chapter presents performance measures, productivity concerns, monitoring of sales efforts, appraising personnel, evaluating the efficiency of space utilization, and analysis of business processes. The corporate controller must also take into account life cycles and time considerations. Divestitures may be necessary to get rid of operations draining the firm, such as those losing money or generating excessive risk levels.

ANALYSIS OF PROFIT

Profit margin (net income/net sales) measures the profitability of each sales dollar. Profitability should be determined by source (product, service, customer, including customer profiles), age group, industry segment, geographic area, channel of distribution, type of marketing effort, market segment, and responsibility center (division, plant, department, and units within the department). Profit variance analysis should be performed to identify causes for actual profit being less than expected. Problems should be immediately identified and corrected. Profit maximization strategies should be formulated. Reports should be prepared by profit-generating source (e.g., market, client). Profit planning including strategic pricing and volume plans should be undertaken.

ANALYSIS OF REVENUE

An analysis should be made of sales mix, product demand, order quantities, product obsolescence, manufacturing schedules, storage space, and competition. Appraise sales generated by different types of selling efforts (direct mail, television, newspaper). Also, compare sales and profit before and after product refinement. The amount of sales returns and allowances is a good indicator of the quality of merchandise. If returns and allowances are high relative to sales, buyer dissatisfaction exists and is having a negative effect on the company's reputation. Further, the company may have to pay the freight for returned goods.

Sales ratios include:

- Quality of sales = cash sales/total sales
- Days of sales backlog = backlog balance/sales volume divided by sales in period. This ratio helps to monitor sales status and planning.
- Sales per customer = net sales/average number of customers
- Order response rate = average number of transactions/average number of solicitations
- Sales response rate = average dollar sales/average solicitations
- Customer contact ratio = calls to customers/total calls

The ratio of sales to current debt looks at the degree to which short-term liabilities finance sales growth.

Determine the variability in volume, price, and cost of each major product or service.

Questions to be asked and answered are:

- Should products or services be more personalized?
- Which services or products are ineffective and/or excessively costly?
- How can products, services, manufacturing, or distribution be redesigned to make them more profitable?

A "close to the customer" strategy assures more useful customer information, improved sales, and lower distribution costs.

COST ANALYSIS AND CONTROL

Cost Analysis

A company's costs should be compared over the years to determine if there is a problem in cost incurrence. The reasons for unusual changes in costs should be noted and corrective steps taken when warranted.

Direct cost ratios may be used in analyzing operating costs, such as (1) direct labor/sales, (2) direct travel/sales, and (3) computer usage/sales.

Determine if costs are excessive relative to production volume. The ratio of selling expenses to net sales reflects the cost of selling the product. Is such cost excessive?

Locked-in (designed) costs will be incurred in the "future" based on decisions already made. It is difficult to reduce locked-in costs. "Cost down" is reducing product costs but still fulfilling customer expectations. Also, compare the number of project rejections due to high initial costs to total projects available.

Proper cost allocation should be made to responsibility centers, geographic areas, products, services, and customers.

Cost Control

Recommendations should be made for improving quality control. Expenses are often related to sales to determine if proper controls exist and if the expenditures are resulting in improved revenue and/or profitability. Examine the following ratios:

- Total operating expenses/net sales
- Specific expense/net sales
- Utilities expense/net sales
- Selling expenses/net sales

A cost/benefit analysis is crucial. Costs should be controlled by major type (e.g., manufacturing, selling, administrative, legal, insurance). Cost control reports should be prepared. Cost control may be evaluated by doing the following:

- Undertake a cost reduction program for projects, products, and services. Such a program may eliminate waste and inefficiency, resulting in improved profitability. However, cost reductions must make sense.
- Evaluate leased premises to reduce rental charges.
- Consider joint ventures to reduce costs.
- Eliminate duplicate facilities and activities by streamlining operations.
- Implement an energy conservation program.
- Place "caps" on expense categories (e.g., telephone, travel and entertainment). Pinpoint those responsible for excessive costs (e.g., excessive telephone calls). Authorization will be needed on a per-employee basis for amounts exceeding ceiling levels.

- Assign each employee an identification number for Xerox, fax, and computer use.
- Substitute cheaper sources of supply or self-manufacture the part.
- Undertake an engineering study to see if manufactured goods can be redesigned to save costs.
- Perform inspections at key points in the manufacturing cycle to correct problems early.
- Adjust output levels as needed.
- Contract for long-term purchase agreements.
- Obtain competitive bids and change suppliers, insurance companies, consultants, etc. when lower fees are obtained, assuming similar levels of quality.
- Redesign the delivery system to reduce fuel costs.
- Tie salary increments to increased productivity.
- Subcontract work if lower costs result.

COST OF QUALITY (COQ)

The cost of quality (COQ) is defined as any costs to correct poor quality or to enhance good quality. It takes into account the costs to "prevent" product defects (e.g., employee training, machine maintenance), appraisal costs (e.g., testing, inspecting), and the cost of the failure to control (e.g., scrap, rework, warranties). Problems must be detected and corrected in a timely fashion. There is also an opportunity cost of foregone earnings arising from customers switching to other suppliers because of the company's poor quality products or services. The following ratios may be enlightening: (1) cost of quality/total operating costs and (2) cost of quality/sales. The manager's objective is to minimize COQ subject to the constraints of corporate policy, customer requirements, and manufacturing limitations. Ultimately, the overall quality of the company's goods benefits.

COST OF PREDICTION ERRORS

The failure to accurately project sales could result in poor production planning, improper labor levels, etc., causing potentially huge financial losses. The cost of the prediction error is the profit lost because of the inaccurate prediction. It can be measured in lost sales, disgruntled customers, and idle machinery. It is important to determine the cost of the prediction error so as to minimize the potential negative affect on the business. Prediction relates to sales, expenses, and purchases.

PERFORMANCE MEASURES

Performance evaluation must consider the trend in a measure over time within the company, compared to competing companies, and compared to industry norms. Index numbers may be used to compare current-year figures to base-year (representative, typical year) figures. Revenue, cost, and profit may be tracked by division, department, product, service, process, contract, job, sales territory, and customer. Measures of performance include:

- Repeat sales to customers
- Backup of orders
- Number of skills per worker
- Number of complaints and warranty required services
- Rework costs relative to cost of goods manufactured
- Setup time relative to total manufacturing time
- Number and length of equipment breakdowns
- Number and duration of manufacturing delays
- Output per manhour
- Manufacturing costs to total costs
- Manufacturing costs to revenue
- Lead time
- Time per business process
- Time between receipt of an order and delivery
- Time between order placement and receipt
- Non-value-added cost to total cost
- Percentage of declining and developmental products to total products

"Production run size" is an optimum production run quantity which minimizes the sum of carrying and setup costs.

STUDYING PRODUCTIVITY

Productivity is enhanced by minimizing direct labor cost. Also, an attempt should be made to reduce indirect costs relative to direct labor costs. Management might consolidate facilities and equipment to achieve a more efficient productivity level. A measure of productivity is the relationship of the cost, time, and quality of an "input" to the quality and units generated for the "output." A proper input–output balance is needed. Resources should be utilized in optimum fashion.

SALES EFFORTS

An appraisal should be made of salesperson effectiveness (e.g., income generated by salesperson, cost per salesperson, salesperson incentives, call frequency, dollar value of orders obtained per hour spent), promotional and advertising effectiveness (marketing costs to sales, dollar expenditure by media compared to sales generated, media measures, comparison of profit before and after promotion), test market analysis (consumer vs. industry), and activity analysis (sales and marketing, customer support, order management). An analysis should also be made of product/service warranties and complaints.

LOOKING AT PERSONNEL

The ratio of sales to personnel represents a comparison of sales dollars and/or sales volume generated relative to the number of employees. It provides insight into levels of employee productivity. The following ratios should be computed: (1) sales/number of employees, (2) sales volume/number of employees, (3) sales/salaries expense. Other useful ratios are: (1) net income/manpower, (2) number of transactions/average number of employees, (3) total tangible assets/number of workers, (4) labor costs/total costs, (5) labor costs/sales, and (6) labor costs/net income. Another consideration as to employee efficiency and morale is employee turnover (number of employees leaving/average number of employees).

The ratio of indirect labor to direct labor monitors indirect labor planning and control. Labor planning and control are crucial at all supervisory levels to produce competitive products and/or to perform profitable services. Management uses this ratio to appraise indirect personnel requirements through the impact of these requirements on operations, earnings, and overhead costs. A declining ratio is unfavorable because it shows management has not maintained a desirable relationship.

Consider automation and up-to-date technology to decrease labor costs.

EFFICIENCY OF SPACE USE

The usefulness of space may be computed as follows:

- Revenue per square foot = net sales/square feet of space.
- Sales per square foot of machinery = net sales/square feet of space for machinery.

Management Analysis of Operations

- Production per square foot = total units produced/square feet of space for machinery.
- Profit per square foot = net income/square feet of space.
- Customer space = number of customers/square feet of space
- Employee space = square feet of space/number of employees
- Parking lot space = square feet of parking lot space/number of customers.
- Rent per square foot = rent expense/square feet of space.
- Expenses per square foot for owned property = expenses of owning property/square feet of space.

BUSINESS PROCESSES

A business process is an operation, function, or activity that crosses among divisions or departments of a company to manufacture the product or render the service. By concentrating on the process itself (rather than each department separately), operations and product/service quality may be improved, costs slashed, and processing time reduced.

By analyzing a process itself, it is easier to understand the complexities and interrelationships among units of the organization, and aid in better communication as to where each responsibility unit fits in. Concentrating on and improving the business process (as distinct from individual departments) results in greater efficiency and effectiveness. In appraising business processes, consider:

- What does the process cost and how long does it take?
- Does the process involve irrelevant and unneeded steps that can be cut?
- What is the quality associated with the process?
- What problems or bottlenecks exist?
- What is the work flow?

The financial manager should identify cases in which work performed by the client is redundant or unnecessary, or in which such work is too costly or time-consuming. Further, procedures, activities, or policies may be unjustifiably complex and can be simplified. A process needs to be revamped when its cost or time does not add value for the customer. Therefore, a customer survey may be warranted. The CPA may decide to recommend modifying, adding, or dropping a process.

The business process might be improved by doing the following: Reduce the number of employees involved or functions required, reduce cycle time, reduce the number of individuals required to approve the process or modification thereto, reorganize the procedures, eliminate illogical administrative steps, improve the sequence of the operation, prioritize strategies, cut out excessive paperwork, improve training, clarify job descriptions and instructions, upgrade equipment, and use up-to-date technology.

Cycle time should be expressed as average and maximum. An example of cycle time is how long it takes to process a bill to a customer. The efficiency with which a cycle is performed may be expressed by the ratio of total processing time divided by total processing plus non-processing time. A lower ratio is unfavorable and requires corrective action.

"A value-added evaluation" should be conducted for each operation, function, or responsibility unit. How much is the value-added? Is it sufficient to justify that activity or business segment? If not, what should be done (e.g., improvements made, disbandonment)? Work improvement teams can be used in production, material handling, shipping, and accounting. Such teams should document the process flows, layouts, etc. and find ways to reorganize the process to make it better.

A business process analysis may be undertaken as a preemptive troubleshooter and should be conducted on an ongoing basis. Examples of situations in which a business process analysis is crucial are when profit margins for a product line are shrinking, market share is dramatically declining, service quality is deteriorating, and customer response time is becoming prohibitive.

Operational audits should be performed to examine corporate policies and procedures and assure that they are functioning properly.

LIFE CYCLES

There are different types of life cycles affecting a business. "Product life cycle" is the time from the start of the R&D effort to the ending of customer support for the product. A "life cycle budget" of costs for this time period aids in formulating selling prices. Many costs occur even before production starts. The development product period may range from short to long. "Product life-cycle reporting" is not on a calendar year basis but rather tracks the revenue and costs for each product over several calendar years. Product cost analysis is done by product over each major stage in the product's life cycle (early, middle, late). There is a highlighting of cost interrelationships among major business functions. "Life-cycle costing" organizes costs based on the product or service life cycle. It monitors and computes the actual total costs of the product or service from beginning to end. Decisions are then made about the good or service based on its profile. "Customer life-cycle costs" concentrate on the total costs to a customer of buying and using a product over its life.

TIME CONSIDERATIONS

Time-based competition stresses the customer and considers product quality, timing, and cost/pricing. An example is how long it takes to design a new product model to meet customer demand. Another example is how long it takes to fill a customer's order. Such analysis strives to enhance productivity, improve market position, raise selling prices, and reduce risk. Efforts should be made to streamline operations.

The time between developing and marketing a product or service should be minimized to lower up-front costs (e.g., design, process, and promotion). Revenue must be generated as quickly as possible to recoup such costs.

DIVESTITURES

Divestitures may be made of unprofitable and/or risky business segments. Divestiture involves the complete or partial conversion, sale, or reallocation of capital or human resources as well as product/service lines. Freed resources may be used for some more productive business purpose. A business segment may qualify for divestiture if it is providing a poor rate of return, does not generate adequate cash flow, does not mesh with overall company strategy, has excessive risk (e.g., vulnerable to lawsuits), is in a state of decline, or when the pieces are worth more than the whole. The objectives of divestiture include repositioning the company in the industry, getting out of an industry, meeting market changes, obtaining needed funds, and cutting losses. Before a divestiture is made, a joint venture may be considered with another company.

Economic Feasibility Study for an Information Technology (IT) Investment

Capital budgeting is the process of making long-term planning decisions for alternative investment opportunities. There are many investment decisions that the company may have to make in order to grow. Examples of capital budgeting applications are installation of a new information system (IS), lease or purchase, new product development, product line selection, keep or sell a business segment, and which asset to invest in. A careful cost/benefit analysis must be performed to determine a project's economic feasibility as a capital expenditure project. This chapter covers:

- Types and special features of capital budgeting decisions.
- Concept of time value of money.
- Several popular capital budgeting techniques.
- Effect of Modified Accelerated Cost Recovery System (MACRS) on capital budgeting decisions.
- How to determine the cost of capital.
- How to make lease-purchase decisions.
- Economic feasibility study for a new information system.

WHAT ARE THE TYPES OF INVESTMENT PROJECTS?

There are typically two types of long-term capital expenditure decisions:

1. *Selection decisions* in terms of obtaining new facilities or expanding existing ones. Examples include:
   a. Investments in property, plant, and equipment as well as other types of assets.
   b. Resource commitments in the form of new product development, market research, introduction of an IS system, refunding of long-term debt, and so on.
   c. Mergers and acquisitions in the form of buying another company to add a new product line.
2. *Replacement decisions* in terms of replacing existing facilities with new ones. Examples include replacing an old machine with a high-tech machine.

WHAT ARE THE FEATURES OF INVESTMENT PROJECTS?

Long-term investments have three important features:

1. They typically involve a large amount of initial cash outlays, which tend to have a long-term impact on the firm's future profitability. Therefore, this initial cash outlay needs to be justified on a cost/benefit basis.
2. There are expected recurring cash inflows (for example, increased revenues, savings in cash operating expenses, etc.) over the life of the investment project. This frequently requires considering the *time value of money*.
3. Income taxes could make a difference in the accept or reject decision. Therefore, income tax factors must be taken into account in every capital budgeting decision.

UNDERSTANDING THE CONCEPT OF TIME VALUE OF MONEY

A dollar now is worth more than a dollar to be received later. This statement sums up an important principle: Money has a time value. The truth of this principle is not that inflation might make the dollar received at a later time worth less in buying power. The reason is that you could invest the dollar now and have more than a dollar at the specified later date.

Time value of money is a critical consideration in financial and investment decisions. For example, compound interest calculations are needed to determine future sums of money resulting from an investment. Discounting, or the calculation of present value, is inversely related to compounding, and is used to evaluate the future cash flow associated with capital budgeting projects. There are plenty of applications of time value of money in accounting and finance.

How Do You Calculate Future Values—How Money Grows?

A dollar in hand today is worth more than a dollar to be received tomorrow because of the interest it could earn from putting it in a savings account or placing it in an investment account. Compounding interest means that interest earns interest. For the discussion of the concepts of compounding and time value, let us define:

F_n = future value: the amount of money at the end of year n

P = principal

i = annual interest rate

n = number of years

Then,

F_1 = the amount of money at the end of year 1

= principal and interest = $P + iP = P(1 + i)$

F_2 = the amount of money at the end of year 2

= $F_1(1 + i) = P(1 + i)(1 + i) = P(1 + i)^2$

The future value of an investment compounded annually at rate i for n years is

$$F_n = P(1 + i)^n = P. T1(i,n)$$

where T1(i,n) is the compound amount of $1 and can be found in Table 1.

Table 1 Future Value of $1 = T1 (i,n)

Periods	4%	6%	8%	10%	12%	14%	20%
1	1.040	1.060	1.080	1.100	1.120	1.140	1.200
2	1.082	1.124	1.166	1.210	1.254	1.300	1.440
3	1.125	1.191	1.260	1.331	1.405	1.482	1.728
4	1.170	1.263	1.361	1.464	1.574	1.689	2.074
5	1.217	1.338	1.469	1.611	1.762	1.925	2.488
6	1.265	1.419	1.587	1.772	1.974	2.195	2.986
7	1.316	1.504	1.714	1.949	2.211	2.502	3.583
8	1.369	1.594	1.851	2.144	2.476	2.853	4.300
9	1.423	1.690	1.999	2.359	2.773	3.252	5.160
10	1.480	1.791	2.159	2.594	3.106	3.707	6.192
11	1.540	1.898	2.332	2.853	3.479	4.226	7.430
12	1.601	2.012	2.518	3.139	3.896	4.818	8.916
13	1.665	2.133	2.720	3.452	4.364	5.492	10.699
14	1.732	2.261	2.937	3.798	4.887	6.261	12.839
15	1.801	2.397	3.172	4.177	5.474	7.138	15.407
16	1.873	2.540	3.426	4.595	6.130	8.137	18.488
17	1.948	2.693	3.700	5.055	6.866	9.277	22.186
18	2.026	2.854	3.996	5.560	7.690	10.575	26.623
19	2.107	3.026	4.316	6.116	8.613	12.056	31.948
20	2.191	3.207	4.661	5.728	9.646	13.743	38.338
30	3.243	5.744	10.063	17.450	29.960	50.950	237.380
40	4.801	10.286	21.725	45.260	93.051	188.880	1469.800

Example 1. You place $1,000 in a savings account earning 8% interest compounded annually. How much money will you have in the account at the end of 4 years?

$$F_n = P(1 + i)^n$$

$$F_4 = \$1,000\ (1 + 0.08)^4 = \$1,000\ T1(8\%, 4\ \text{years})$$

From Table 1, the T1 for 4 years at 8 percent is 1.361.

Therefore, $F_4 = \$1{,}000\,(1.361) = \$1{,}361$.

Example 2. You invested a large sum of money in the stock of Delta Corporation. The company paid a $3 dividend per share. The dividend is expected to increase by 20 percent per year for the next 3 years. You wish to project the dividends for years 1 through 3.

$$F_n = P(1 + i)^n$$

$$F_1 = \$3(1 + 0.2)^1 = \$3\ T1(20\%,1) = \$3\ (1.200) = \$3.60$$

$$F_2 = \$3(1 + 0.2)^2 = \$3\ T1(20\%,2) = \$3\ (1.440) = \$4.32$$

$$F_3 = \$3(1 + 0.2)^3 = \$3\ T1(20\%,3) = \$3\ (1.728) = \$5.18$$

Future Value of an Annuity

An annuity is defined as a series of payments (or receipts) of a fixed amount for a specified number of periods. Each payment is assumed to occur at the end of the period. The future value of an annuity is a compound annuity which involves depositing or investing an equal sum of money at the end of each year for a certain number of years and allowing it to grow.

Let S_n = the future value on an n-year annuity

A = the amount of an annuity

Then we can write

$$S_n = A(1 + i)^{n-1} + A(1 + i)^{n-2} + \ldots + A(1 + i)^0$$

$$= A[(1 + i)^{n-1} + (1 + i)^{n-2} + \ldots + (1 + i)^0]$$

$$= A \cdot \sum_{t=0}^{n-1} (1 + i)^t = A\left[\frac{(1 + i)^n - 1}{i}\right] = A \cdot T2(i,n)$$

where T2(i,n) represents the future value of an annuity of $1 for n years compounded at i percent and can be found in Table 2.

Table 2   Future Value of an Annuity of $1 = T2(i,n)

Periods	4%	6%	8%	10%	12%	14%	20%
1	1.000	1.000	1.000	1.000	1.000	1.000	1.000
2	2.040	2.060	2.080	2.100	2.120	2.140	2.200
3	3.122	3.184	3.246	3.310	3.374	3.440	3.640
4	4.247	4.375	4.506	4.641	4.779	4.921	5.368
5	5.416	5.637	5.867	6.105	6.353	6.610	7.442
6	6.663	6.975	7.336	7.716	8.115	8.536	9.930
7	7.898	8.394	8.923	9.487	10.089	10.730	12.916
8	9.214	9.898	10.637	11.436	12.300	13.233	16.499
9	10.583	11.491	12.488	13.580	14.776	16.085	20.799
10	12.006	13.181	14.487	15.938	17.549	19.337	25.959
11	13.486	14.972	16.646	18.531	20.655	23.045	32.150
12	15.026	16.870	18.977	21.385	24.133	37.271	39.580
13	16.627	18.882	21.495	24.523	28.029	32.089	48.497
14	18.292	21.015	24.215	27.976	32.393	37.581	59.196
15	20.024	23.276	27.152	31.773	37.280	43.842	72.035
16	21.825	25.673	30.324	35.950	42.753	50.980	87.442
17	23.698	28.213	33.750	40.546	48.884	59.118	105.930
18	25.645	30.906	37.450	45.600	55.750	68.394	128.120
19	27.671	33.760	41.446	51.160	63.440	78.969	154.740
20	29.778	36.778	45.762	57.276	75.052	91.025	186.690
30	56.085	79.058	113.283	164.496	241.330	356.790	1181.900
40	95.026	154.762	259.057	442.597	767.090	1342.000	7343.900

*Payments (or receipts) at the *end* of each period.

Example 3. You wish to determine the sum of money you will have in a savings account at the end of 6 years by depositing $1,000 at the end of each year for the next 6 years. The annual interest rate is 8%. The T2(8%,6 years) is given in Table 2 as 7.336. Therefore,

$$S_6 = \$1,000 \ T2(8\%,6) = \$1,000 \ (7.336) = \$7,336$$

Example 4. You deposit $30,000 semiannually into a fund for ten years. The annual interest rate is 8%. The amount accumulated at the end of the tenth year is calculated as follows:

$$S_n = A. \ T2(i, n)$$

where

$$A = \$30,000$$
$$i = 8\%/2 = 4\%$$
$$n = 10 \times 2 = 20$$

Therefore,

$$S_n = \$30,000 \ T2(4\%, 20)$$
$$= \$30,000 \ (29.778) = \$893,340$$

What Is Present Value—How Much Is Money Worth Now?

Present value is the present worth of future sums of money. The process of calculating present values, or discounting, is actually the opposite of finding the compounded future value. In connection with present value calculations, the interest rate i is called the *discount rate*. The discount rate we use is more commonly called the *cost of capital*, which is the minimum rate of return required by the investor.

Recall that $F_n = P(1 + i)^n$

Therefore,

$$P = \frac{F_n}{(1+i)^n} = F_n \left[\frac{1}{(1+i)^n} \right] = F_n \cdot T3(i,n)$$

where T3(i,n) represents the present value of $1 and is given in Table 3.

Table 3   Present Value of $1 = T3(i,n)

Periods	3%	4%	5%	6%	7%	8%	10%	12%	14%
1	.9709	.9615	.9524	.9434	.9346	.9259	.9091	.8929	.8772
2	.9426	.9246	.9070	.8900	.8734	.8573	.8264	.7972	.7695
3	.9151	.8890	.8638	.8396	.8163	.7938	.7513	.7118	.6750
4	.8885	.8548	.8227	.7921	.7629	.7350	.6830	.6355	.5921
5	.8626	.8219	.7835	.7473	.7130	.6806	.6209	.5674	.5194
6	.8375	.7903	.7462	.7050	.6663	.6302	.5645	.5066	.4556
7	.8131	.7599	.7107	.6651	.6227	.5835	.5132	.4523	.3996
8	.7894	.7307	.6768	.6274	.5820	.5403	.4665	.4039	.3506
9	.7664	.7026	.6446	.5919	.5439	.5002	.4241	.3606	.3075
10	.7441	.6756	.6139	.5584	.5083	.4632	.3855	.3220	.2697
11	.7224	.6496	.5847	.5268	.4751	.4289	.3505	.2875	.2366
12	.7014	.6246	.5568	.4970	.4440	.3971	.3186	.2567	.2076
13	.6810	.6006	.5303	.4688	.4150	.3677	.2897	.2292	.1821
14	.6611	.5775	.5051	.4423	.3878	.3405	.2633	.2046	.1597
15	.6419	.5553	.4810	.4173	.3624	.3152	.2394	.1827	.1401
16	.6232	.5339	.4581	.3936	.3387	.2919	.2176	.1631	.1229
17	.6050	.5134	.4363	.3714	.3166	.2703	.1978	.1456	.1078
18	.5874	.4936	.4155	.3503	.2959	.2502	.1799	.1300	.0946
19	.5703	.4746	.3957	.3305	.2765	.2317	.1635	.1161	.0829
20	.5537	.4564	.3769	.3118	.2584	.2145	.1486	.1037	.0728
21	.5375	.4388	.3589	.2942	.2415	.1987	.1351	.0926	.0638
22	.5219	.4220	.3418	.2775	.2257	.1839	.1228	.0826	.0560
23	.5067	.4057	.3256	.2618	.2109	.1703	.1117	.0738	.0491
24	.4919	.3901	.3101	.2470	.1971	.1577	.1015	.0659	.0431
25	.4776	.3751	.2953	.2330	.1842	.1460	.0923	.0588	.0378
26	.4637	.3607	.2812	.2198	.1722	.1352	.0839	.0525	.0331
27	.4502	.3468	.2678	.2074	.1609	.1252	.0763	.0469	.0291
28	.4371	.3335	.2551	.1956	.1504	.1159	.0693	.0419	.0255
29	.4243	.3207	.2429	.1846	.1406	.1073	.0630	.0374	.0224
30	.4120	.3083	.2314	.1741	.1314	.0994	.0573	.0334	.0196
40	.3066	.2083	.1420	.0972	.0668	.0460	.0221	.0107	.0053

16%	18%	20%	22%	24%	25%	26%	28%	30%	40%
.8621	.8475	.8333	.8197	.8065	.8000	.7937	.7813	.7692	.7143
.7432	.7182	.6944	.6719	.6504	.6400	.6299	.6104	.5917	.5102
.6407	.6086	.5787	.5507	.5245	.5120	.4999	.4768	.4552	.3644
.5523	.5158	.4823	.4514	.4230	.4096	.3968	.3725	.3501	.2603
.4761	.4371	.4019	.3700	.3411	.3277	.3149	.2910	.2693	.1859
.4104	.3704	.3349	.3033	.2751	.2621	.2499	.2274	.2072	.1328
.3538	.3139	.2791	.2486	.2218	.2097	.1983	.1776	.1594	.0949
.3050	.2600	.2326	.2038	.1789	.1678	.1574	.1388	.1226	.0678
.2630	.2255	.1938	.1670	.1443	.1342	.1249	.1084	.0943	.0484
.2267	.1911	.1615	.1369	.1164	.1074	.0992	.0847	.0725	.0346
.1954	.1619	.1346	.1122	.0938	.0859	.0787	.0662	.0558	.0247
.1685	.1372	.1122	.0920	.0757	.0687	.0625	.0517	.0429	.0176
.1452	.1163	.0935	.0754	.0610	.0550	.0496	.0404	.0330	.0126
.1252	.0985	.0779	.0618	.0492	.0440	.0393	.0316	.0254	.0090
.1079	.0835	.0649	.0507	.0397	.0352	.0312	.0247	.0195	.0064
.0930	.0708	.0541	.0415	.0320	.0281	.0248	.0193	.0150	.0046
.0802	.0600	.0451	.0340	.0258	.0225	.0197	.0150	.0116	.0033
.0691	.0508	.0376	.0279	.0208	.0180	.0156	.0118	.0089	.0023
.0596	.0431	.0313	.0229	.0168	.0144	.0124	.0092	.0068	.0017
.0514	.0365	.0261	.0187	.0135	.0115	.0098	.0072	.0053	.0012
.0443	.0309	.0217	.0154	.0109	.0092	.0078	.0056	.0040	.0009
.0382	.0262	.0181	.0126	.0088	.0074	.0062	.0044	.0031	.0006
.0329	.0222	.0151	.0103	.0071	.0059	.0049	.0034	.0024	.0004
.0284	.0188	.0126	.0085	.0057	.0047	.0039	.0027	.0018	.0003
.0245	.0160	.0105	.0069	.0046	.0038	.0031	.0021	.0014	.0002
.0211	.0135	.0087	.0057	.0037	.0030	.0025	.0016	.0011	.0002
.0182	.0115	.0073	.0047	.0030	.0024	.0019	.0013	.0008	.0001
.0157	.0097	.0061	.0038	.0024	.0019	.0015	.0010	.0006	.0001
.0135	.0082	.0051	.0031	.0020	.0015	.0012	.0008	.0005	.0001
.0116	.0070	.0042	.0026	.0016	.0012	.0010	.0006	.0004	.0000
.0026	.0013	.0007	.0004	.0002	.0001	.0001	.0001	.0000	.0000

Example 5. You have been given an opportunity to receive $20,000 6 years from now. If you can earn 10% on your investments, what is the most you should pay for this opportunity? To answer this question, you must compute the present value of $20,000 to be received 6 years from now at a 10% rate of discount. F_6 is $20,000, I is 10%, and n is 6 years. T3(10%,6) from Table 3 is 0.565.

$$P = \$20,000 \left[\frac{1}{(1 + 0.1)^6} \right] = \$20,000 \text{ T3(10\%,6)} = \$20,000(0.564) = \$11,280$$

This means that you can earn 10% on your investment, and you would be indifferent to receiving $11,280 now or $20,000 6 years from today since the amounts are time-equivalent. In other words, you could invest $11,300 today at 10% and have $20,000 in 6 years.

Present Value of Mixed Streams of Cash Flows

The present value of a series of mixed payments (or receipts) is the sum of the present value of each individual payment. We know that the present value of each individual payment is the payment times the appropriate T3 value.

Example 6. You are thinking of starting a new product line that initially costs $32,000. Your annual projected cash inflows are:

    1   $10,000
    2   $20,000
    3    $5,000

If you must earn a minimum of 10% on your investment, should you undertake this new product line?
The present value of this series of mixed streams of cash inflows is calculated as follows:

Year	Cash inflows	x T3(10%, n)	Present Value
1	$10,000	0.909	$9,090
2	$20,000	0.826	$16,520
3	$5,000	0.751	$3,755
			$29,365

Since the present value of your projected cash inflows is less than the initial investment, you should not undertake this project.

Present Value of an Annuity

Interest received from bonds, pension funds, and insurance obligations involves annuities. To compare these financial instruments, we need to know the present value of each. The present value of an annuity (P_n) can be found by using the following equation:

$$P_n = A \cdot \left[\frac{1}{(1+i)^1}\right] + A \cdot \left[\frac{1}{(1+i)^2}\right] + \cdots + A \cdot \left[\frac{1}{(1+i)^n}\right]$$

$$= A \cdot \left[\frac{1}{(1+i)^1} + \frac{1}{(1+i)^2} + \cdots + \frac{1}{(1+i)^n}\right]$$

$$= A \cdot \sum_{t=1}^{n} \frac{1}{(1+i)^t} = A \cdot \frac{1}{i}\left[1 - \frac{1}{(1+i)}\right]$$

$$= A \cdot T4(i,n)$$

where T4(i,n) represents the present value of an annuity of $1 discounted at i percent for n years and is found in Table 4.

Example 7. Assume that the cash inflows in Example 6 form an annuity of $10,000 for 3 years. Then the present value is

$$P_n = A \cdot T4(i,n)$$

$$P_3 = \$10,000 \ T4(10\%, 3 \ \text{years}) = \$10,000 \ (2.487) = \$24,870$$

Use of Financial Calculators and Spreadsheet Programs

There are many financial calculators that contain preprogrammed formulas to perform many present value and future applications. They include *Hewlett-Packard 10B*, *Sharpe EL733*, and *Texas Instrument BA35*. Furthermore, spreadsheet software such as *Excel* has built-in financial functions to perform many such applications.

HOW DO YOU MEASURE INVESTMENT WORTH?

Several methods of evaluating investment projects are available:

1. Payback period
2. Net present value (NPV)
3. Internal rate of return (IRR)

The NPV method and the IRR method are called *discounted cash flow (DCF) methods*. Each of these methods is discussed below.

1. Payback Period

The payback period measures the length of time required to recover the amount of initial investment. It is computed by dividing the initial investment by the cash inflows through increased revenues or cost savings.

Example 8. Assume:

Cost of investment	$18,000
Annual after-tax cash savings	$3,000

Then, the payback period is:

$$\text{Payback period} = \frac{\text{initial investment}}{\text{cost savings}} = \frac{\$18,000}{\$3,000} = 6 \text{ years}$$

Decision rule: Choose the project with the shorter payback period. The rationale behind this choice is: The shorter the payback period, the less risky the project, and the greater the liquidity.

Example 9. Consider the two projects whose after-tax cash inflows are not even. Assume each project costs $1,000.

	Cash Inflow	
Year	A($)	B($)
1	100	500
2	200	400
3	300	300
4	400	100
5	500	
6	600	

Economic Feasibility Study for an Information Technology (IT) Investment

When cash inflows are not even, the payback period has to be found by trial and error. The payback period of project A is ($1,000 = $100 + $200 + $300 + $400) 4 years. The payback period of project B is $1,000 = $500 + $400 + $100):

$$2 \text{ years} + \frac{\$100}{\$300} = 2\,{}^{1}\!/_{3} \text{ years}$$

Project B is the project of choice in this case, since it has the shorter payback period.

The advantages of using the payback period method of evaluating an investment project are that (1) it is simple to compute and easy to understand, and (2) it handles investment risk effectively.

The shortcomings of this method are that (1) it does not recognize the time value of money, and (2) it ignores the impact of cash inflows received after the payback period; essentially, cash flows after the payback period determine profitability of an investment.

2. Net Present Value

Net present value (NPV) is the excess of the present value (PV) of cash inflows generated by the project over the amount of the initial investment (I):

$$NPV = PV - I$$

The present value of future cash flows is computed using the so-called cost of capital (or minimum required rate of return) as the discount rate. When cash inflows are uniform, the present value would be

$$PV = A.\,T4\,(i, n)$$

where A is the amount of the annuity. The value of T4 is found in Table 4.

Decision rule: If NPV is positive, accept the project. Otherwise, reject it.

Example 10. Consider the following investment:

Initial investment	$12,950
Estimated life	10 years
Annual cash inflows	$3,000
Cost of capital (minimum required rate of return)	12%

Table 4 Present Value of an Annuity of $1 = T4(i,n)

Periods	3%	4%	5%	6%	7%	8%	10%	12%	14%	16%	18%	20%	22%	24%
1	.9709	.9615	.9524	.9434	.9346	.9259	.9091	.8929	.8772	.8621	.8475	.8333	.8197	.8065
2	1.9135	1.8861	1.8594	1.8334	1.8080	1.7833	1.7355	1.6901	1.6467	1.6052	1.5656	1.5278	1.4915	1.4568
3	2.8286	2.7751	2.7232	2.6730	2.6243	2.5771	2.4869	2.4018	2.3216	2.2459	2.1743	2.1065	2.0422	1.9813
4	3.7171	3.6299	3.5460	3.4651	3.3872	3.3121	3.1699	3.0373	2.9137	2.7982	2.6901	2.5887	2.4936	2.4043
5	4.5797	4.4518	4.3295	4.2124	4.1002	3.9927	3.7908	3.6048	3.4331	3.2743	3.1272	2.9906	2.8636	2.7454
6	5.4172	5.2421	5.0757	4.9173	4.7665	4.6229	4.3553	4.1114	3.8887	3.6847	3.4976	3.3255	3.1669	3.0205
7	6.2303	6.0021	5.7864	5.5824	5.3893	5.2064	4.8684	4.5638	4.2883	4.0386	3.8115	3.6046	3.4155	3.2423
8	7.0197	6.7327	6.4632	6.2098	5.9713	5.7466	5.3349	4.9676	4.6389	4.3436	4.0776	3.8372	3.6193	3.4212
9	7.7861	7.4353	7.1078	6.8017	6.5152	6.2469	5.7590	5.3282	4.9464	4.6065	4.3030	4.0310	3.7863	3.5655
10	8.5302	8.1109	7.7217	7.3601	7.0236	6.7101	6.1446	5.6502	5.2161	4.8332	4.4941	4.1925	3.9232	3.6819
11	9.2526	8.7605	8.3064	7.8869	7.4987	7.1390	6.4951	5.9377	5.4527	5.0286	4.6560	4.3271	4.0354	3.7757
12	9.9540	9.3851	8.8633	8.3838	7.9427	7.5361	6.8137	6.1944	5.6603	5.1971	4.7932	4.4392	4.1274	3.8514
13	10.6350	9.9856	9.3936	8.8527	8.3577	7.9038	7.1034	6.4235	5.8424	5.3423	4.9095	4.5327	4.2028	3.9124
14	11.2961	10.5631	9.8986	9.2950	8.7455	8.2442	7.3667	6.6282	6.0021	5.4675	5.0081	4.6106	4.2646	3.9616
15	11.9379	11.1184	10.3797	9.7122	9.1079	8.5595	7.6061	6.8109	6.1422	5.5755	5.0916	4.6755	4.3152	4.0013
16	12.5611	11.6523	10.8378	10.1059	9.4466	8.8514	7.8237	6.9740	6.2651	5.6685	5.1624	4.7296	4.3567	4.0333
17	13.1661	12.1657	11.2741	10.4773	9.7632	9.1216	8.0216	7.1196	6.3729	5.7487	5.2223	4.7746	4.3908	4.0591
18	13.7535	12.6593	11.6896	10.8276	10.0591	9.3719	8.2014	7.2497	6.4674	5.8178	5.2732	4.8122	4.4187	4.0799
19	14.3238	13.1339	12.0853	11.1581	10.3356	9.6036	8.3649	7.3658	6.5504	5.8775	5.3162	4.8435	4.4415	4.0967
20	14.8775	13.5903	12.4622	11.4699	10.5940	9.8181	8.5136	7.4694	6.6231	5.9288	5.3527	4.8696	4.4603	4.1103
21	15.4150	14.0292	12.8212	11.7641	10.8355	10.0168	8.6487	7.5620	6.6870	5.9731	5.3837	4.8913	4.4756	4.1212
22	15.9369	14.4511	13.1630	12.0416	11.0612	10.2007	8.7715	7.6446	6.7429	6.0113	5.4099	4.9094	4.4882	4.1300
23	16.4436	14.8568	13.4886	12.3034	11.2722	10.3711	8.8832	7.7184	6.7921	6.0442	5.4321	4.9245	4.4985	4.1371
24	16.9355	15.2470	13.7986	12.5504	11.4693	10.5288	8.9847	7.7843	6.8351	6.0726	5.4509	4.9371	4.5070	4.1428
25	17.4131	15.6221	14.0939	12.7834	11.6536	10.6748	9.0770	7.8431	6.8729	6.0971	5.4669	4.9476	4.5139	4.1474
26	17.8768	15.9828	14.3752	13.0032	11.8258	10.8100	9.1609	7.8957	6.9061	6.1182	5.4804	4.9563	4.5196	4.1511
27	18.3270	16.3296	14.6430	13.2105	11.9867	10.9352	9.2372	7.9426	6.9352	6.1364	5.4919	4.9636	4.5243	4.1542
28	18.7641	16.6631	14.8981	13.4062	12.1371	11.0511	9.3066	7.9844	6.9607	6.1520	5.5016	4.9697	4.5281	4.1566
29	19.1885	16.9837	15.1411	13.5907	12.2777	11.1584	9.3696	8.0218	6.9830	6.1656	5.5098	4.9747	4.5312	4.1585
30	19.6004	17.2920	15.3725	13.7648	12.4090	11.2578	9.4269	8.0552	7.0027	6.1772	5.5168	4.9789	4.5338	4.1601
40	23.1148	19.7928	17.1591	15.0463	13.3317	11.9246	9.7791	8.2438	7.1050	6.2335	5.5482	4.9966	4.5439	4.1659

Present value of the cash inflows is:

$$\begin{aligned}
PV &= A.T4(i,n) \\
&= \$3,000.\ T4(12\%, 10\ years) \\
&= \$3,000\ (5.650) \qquad\qquad \$16,950
\end{aligned}$$

Initial investment (I) $\qquad\qquad\qquad\qquad\quad$ 12,950

Net present value (NPV = PV − I) $\qquad\quad$ $\$4,000$

Since the NPV of the investment is positive, the investment should be accepted.

The advantages of the NPV method are that it obviously recognizes the time value of money and it is easy to compute whether the cash flows form an annuity or vary from period to period.

3. Internal Rate of Return

Internal rate of return (IRR), also called *time adjusted rate of return*, is defined as the rate of interest that equates I with the PV of future cash inflows. In other words,

at IRR I = PV or NPV = 0

Decision rule: Accept the project if the IRR exceeds the cost of capital. Otherwise, reject it.

Example 11. Assume the same data given in Example 10, and set the following equality (I = PV):

$$\$12,950 = \$3,000.\ T4(i, 10\ years)$$

$$T4(i, 10\ years) = \frac{\$12,950}{\$3,000} = 4.317$$

which stands somewhere between 18% and 20% in the 10-year line of Table 4. The interpolation follows:

PV of an Annuity of $1 Factor

	T4(i, 10 years)	
18%	4.494	4.494
IRR	4.317	
20%		4.192
Difference	0.177	0.302

Therefore,

$$IRR = 18\% + \frac{0.177}{0.302}(20\% - 18\%)$$

$$= 18\% + 0.586(2\%) = 18\% + 1.17\% = 19.17\%$$

Since the IRR of the investment is greater than the cost of capital (12%), accept the project.

The advantage of using the IRR method is that it does consider the time value of money and, therefore, is more exact and realistic than the ARR method.

The shortcomings of this method are that (1) it is time-consuming to compute, especially when the cash inflows are not even, although most financial calculators and PCs have a key to calculate IRR, and (2) it fails to recognize the varying sizes of investment in competing projects.

Can a Computer Help?

Spreadsheet programs can be used in making IRR calculations. For example, *Excel* has a function IRR(values, guess). *Excel* considers negative numbers as cash outflows such as the initial investment, and positive numbers as cash inflows. Many financial calculators have similar features. As in Example 11, suppose you want to calculate the IRR of a $12,950 investment (the value –12950 entered in year 0 that is followed by 10 monthly cash inflows of $3,000). Using a guess of 12% (the value of 0.12), which is in effect the cost of capital, your formula would be @IRR(values, 0.12) and *Excel* would return 19.15%, as shown below.

Year 0	1	2	3	4	5	6	7	8	9	10
$(12,950)	3,000	3,000	3,000	3,000	3,000	3,000	3,000	3,000	3,000	3,000

IRR = 19.15%

NPV = $4,000.67

Note: The *Excel* formula for NPV is NPV (discount rate, cash inflow values) + I, where I is given as a negative number.

HOW DO INCOME TAXES AFFECT INVESTMENT DECISIONS?

Income taxes make a difference in many capital budgeting decisions. The project that is attractive on a before-tax basis may have to be rejected on an after-tax basis, and vice versa. Income taxes typically affect both the amount and the timing of cash flows. Since net income, not cash inflows, is subject to tax, after-tax cash inflows are not usually the same as after-tax net income.

How to Calculate After-Tax Cash Flows

Let us define:

S = Sales
E = Cash operating expenses
d = Depreciation
t = Tax rate

Then, before-tax cash inflows (or cash savings) = $S - E$ and net income = $S - E - d$

By definition,

After-tax cash inflows = Before-tax cash inflows – Taxes =
$(S - E) - (S - E - d)(t)$

Rearranging gives the short-cut formula:

After-tax cash inflows = $(S - E)(1 - t) + (d)(t)$ or
$= (S - E - d)(1 - t) + d$

The deductibility of depreciation from sales in arriving at taxable net income reduces income tax payments and thus serves as a *tax shield*.

Tax shield = Tax savings on depreciation = $(d)(t)$

Example 12. Assume:

S = $12,000$
E = $10,000$
d = 500 per year using the straight-line method
t = 30%

Then,

$$\text{After-tax cash inflow} = (\$12{,}000 - \$10{,}000)\,(1 - .3) + (\$500)(.3)$$
$$= (\$2{,}000)(.7) + (\$500)(.3)$$
$$= \$1{,}400 + \$150 = \$1{,}550$$

$$\text{Note that a tax shield} = \text{tax savings on depreciation} = (d)(t)$$
$$= (\$500)(.3) = \$150$$

Since the tax shield is dt, the higher the depreciation deduction, the higher the tax savings on depreciation. Therefore, an accelerated depreciation method (such as double-declining balance) produces higher tax savings than the straight-line method. Accelerated methods produce higher present values for the tax savings, which may make a given investment more attractive.

Example 13. The Navistar Company estimates that it can save $2,500 a year in cash operating costs for the next ten years if it buys a special-purpose machine at a cost of $10,000. No residual value is expected. Depreciation is by straight-line. Assume that the income tax rate is 30%, and the after-tax cost of capital (minimum required rate of return) is 10%. After-tax cash savings can be calculated as follows:

Depreciation by straight-line is $10,000/10 = $1,000 per year.

Thus,

$$\text{After-tax cash savings} = (S - E)\,(1 - t) + (d)(t)$$
$$= \$2{,}500(1 - .3) + \$1{,}000(.3)$$
$$= \$1{,}750 + \$300 = \$2{,}050$$

To see if this machine should be purchased, the net present value can be calculated.

$$PV = \$2{,}050 \; T4(10\%,\ 10\ \text{years}) = \$2{,}050\ (6.145) = \$12{,}597.25$$

Thus,

$$NPV = PV - I = \$12{,}597.25 - \$10{,}000 = \$2{,}597.25$$

Since NPV is positive, the machine should be bought.

Example 14. Shalimar Corporation has provided its revenues and cash operating costs (excluding depreciation) for the old and the new machine, as follows:

	Revenue	Annual Cash Operating Costs	Net Profit Before Depreciation and Taxes
Old machine	$150,000	$70,000	$80,000
New machine	$180,000	$60,000	$120,000

Assume that the annual depreciation of the old machine and the new machine will be $30,000 and $50,000, respectively. Assume further that the tax rate is 46%.

To arrive at net profit after taxes, we first have to deduct depreciation expense from the net profit before depreciation and taxes, as follows:

	Net Profits after Taxes	Add Depreciation	After-Tax Cash Inflows
Old machine	($80,000 – $30,000)(1 – 0.46) = $27,000	$30,000	$57,000
New machine	($120,000 – $50,000)(1 – 0.46) = $37,800	$50,000	$87,800

Subtracting the after-tax cash inflows of the old machine from the cash inflows of the new machine results in the relevant, or incremental, cash inflows for each year.

Therefore, in this example, the relevant or incremental cash inflows for each year are $87,800 – $57,000 = $30,800.

Alternatively, the incremental cash inflows after taxes can be computed, using the following simple formula:

After-tax incremental cash inflows = (increase in revenues)(1-tax rate)
 – (increase in cash charges)(1-tax rate)
 + (increase in depreciation expenses) (tax rate)

Example 15. Using the data in Example 14, after-tax incremental cash inflows for each year are:

	Increase in revenue × (1 − tax rate): ($180,000 − $150,000)(1 − 0.46)	$16,200
−	Increase in cash charges × (1 − tax rate): ($60,000 − $70,000)(1 − 0.46)	(5,400)
+	Increase in depreciation expense × tax rate: ($50,000 − $30,000)(0.46)	9,200
		$30,800

HOW DOES MACRS AFFECT INVESTMENT DECISIONS?

Although the traditional depreciation methods can be used for computing depreciation for book purposes, 1981 saw a new way of computing depreciation deductions for tax purposes. The current rule is called the *Modified Accelerated Cost Recovery System* (MACRS) rule, as enacted by Congress in 1981 and then modified somewhat in 1986 under the Tax Reform Act of 1986. This rule is characterized as follows:

1. It abandons the concept of useful life and accelerates depreciation deductions by placing all depreciable assets into one of eight age property classes. It calculates deductions, based on an allowable percentage of the asset's original cost (see Tables 5 and 6).

   With a shorter asset tax life than useful life, the company would be able to deduct depreciation more quickly and save more in income taxes in the earlier years, thereby making an investment more attractive. The rationale behind the system is that in this way the government encourages the company to invest in facilities and increase its productive capacity and efficiency. (Remember that the higher d, the larger the tax shield (d)(t)).

2. Since the allowable percentages in Table 5 add up to 100%, there is no need to consider the salvage value of an asset in computing depreciation.

3. The company may elect the straight-line method. The straight-line convention must follow what is called the *half-year convention*. This means that the company can deduct only half of the regular straight-line depreciation amount in the first year.

Table 5 Modified Accelerated Cost Recovery System Classification of Assets

Year	3-year	5-year	7-year	10-year	15-year	20-year
			Property class			
1	33.3%	20.0%	14.3%	10.0%	5.0%	3.8%
2	44.5	32.0	24.5	18.0	9.5	7.2
3	14.8[a]	19.2	17.5	14.4	8.6	6.7
4	7.4	11.5[a]	12.5	11.5	7.7	6.2
5		11.5	8.9[a]	9.2	6.9	5.7
6		5.8	8.9	7.4	6.2	5.3
7			8.9	6.6[a]	5.9[a]	4.9
8			4.5	6.6	5.9	4.5[a]
9				6.5	5.9	4.5
10				6.5	5.9	4.5
11				3.3	5.9	4.5
12					5.9	4.5
13					5.9	4.5
14					5.9	4.5
15					5.9	4.5
16					3.0	4.4
17						4.4
18						4.4
19						4.4
20						4.4
21						2.2
Total	100%	100%	100%	100%	100%	100%

[a]Denotes the year of changeover to straight-line depreciation.

The reason for electing to use the MACRS optional straight-line method is that some firms may prefer to stretch out depreciation deductions using the straight-line method rather than to accelerate them. Those firms are the ones that are just starting out or have little or no income and wish to show more income on their income statements.

Table 6   MACRS Tables by Property Class

MACRS Property Class & Depreciation Method	Useful Life (ADR Midpoint Life)[a]	Examples of Assets
3-year property 200% declining balance	4 years or less	Most small tools are included; the law specifically excludes autos and light trucks from this property class.
5-year property 200% declining balance	More than 4 years to less than 10 years	Autos and light trucks, computers, typewriters, copiers, duplicating equipment, heavy general-purpose trucks, and research and experimentation equipment are included.
7-year property 200% declining balance	10 years or more to less than 16 years	Office furniture and fixtures and most items of machinery and equipment used in production are included.
10-year property 200% declining balance	16 years or more to less than 20 years	Various machinery and equipment, such as that used in petroleum distilling and refining and in the milling of grain, are included.
15-year property 150% declining balance	20 years or more to less than 25 years	Sewage treatment plants, telephone and electrical distribution facilities, and land improvements are included.
20-year property 150% declining balance	25 years or more	Service stations and other real property with an ADR midpoint life of less than 27.5 years are included.
27.5-year property straight-line	Not applicable	All residential rental property is included.
31.5-year property straight-line	Not applicable	All nonresidential property is included.

[a]The term ADR midpoint life means the "useful life" of an asset in a business sense; the appropriate ADR midpoint lives for assets are designated in the tax Regulations.

Example 16. Assume that a machine falls under a 3-year property class and costs $3,000 initially. The straight-line option under MACRS differs from the traditional straight-line method in that under this method, the company would deduct only $500 depreciation in the first year and the fourth year ($3,000/3 years = $1,000; $1,000/2 = $500). The table below compares the straight-line with half-year convention with the MACRS.

Year	Straight line (half-year) Depreciation	Cost		MACRS %	MACRS Deduction
1	$500	$3,000	×	33.3%	$999
2	1,000	3,000	×	44.5	1,335
3	1,000	3,000	×	14.8	444
4	500	3,000	×	7.4	222
	$3,000				$3,000

Example 17. A machine costs $10,000. Annual cash inflows are expected to be $5,000. The machine will be depreciated using the MACRS rule and will fall under the 3-year property class. The cost of capital after taxes is 10%. The estimated life of the machine is 4 years. The salvage value of the machine at the end of the fourth year is expected to be $1,200. The tax rate is 30%.

The formula for computation of after-tax cash inflows $(S - E)(1 - t) + (d)(t)$ needs to be computed separately. The NPV analysis can be performed as follows:

	Present value factor @ 10%	Present value
Initial investment: $10,000	1.000	$(10,000.00)
$(S - E)(1 - t)$:$5,000 $(1 - .3)$ = $3,500 for 4 years	3.170[a]	$11,095.00

[a]T4(10%, 4 years) = 3.170 (from Table 4).

(d)(t):

Year	Cost		MACRS %	d	(d)(t)	Present value factor @ 10%	Present value
1	$10,000	×	33.3%	$3,330	$999	.909[b]	908.09
2	$10,000	×	44.5	4,450	1,335	.826[b]	1,102.71
3	$10,000	×	14.8	1,480	444	.751[b]	333.44
4	$10,000	×	7.4	740	222	.683[b]	151.63

Salvage value:

$1,200 in year 4: $1,200 (1 − .3) = $840[c]   .683[b]   573.72

Net present value (NPV) $4,164.59

[b]T3 values obtained from Table 3.

[c]Any salvage value received under the MACRS rules is a *taxable gain* (the excess of the selling price over book value, $1,200 in this example), since the book value will be zero at the end of the life of the machine.

Since NPV = PV − I = $4,164.59 is positive, the machine should be bought.

WHAT TO KNOW ABOUT THE COST OF CAPITAL

The cost of capital is defined as the rate of return that is necessary to maintain the market value of the firm (or price of the firm's stock). Project managers must know whether the cost of capital, often called the *minimum required rate of return*, was used either as a discount rate under the NPV method or as a hurdle rate under the IRR method. The cost of capital is computed as a weighted average of the various capital components, which are items on the right-hand side of the balance sheet such as debt, preferred stock, common stock, and retained earnings.

Cost of Debt

The cost of debt is stated on an after-tax basis, since the interest on the debt is tax deductible. However, the cost of preferred stock is the stated annual dividend rate. This rate is not adjusted for income taxes because the preferred dividend, unlike debt interest, is not a deductible expense in computing corporate income taxes.

Example 18. Assume that the Hume Company issues a $1,000, 8%, 20-year bond whose net proceeds are $940. The tax rate is 40%. Then, the after-tax cost of debt is:

$$8.00\% \ (1 - 0.4) = 4.8\%$$

Example 19. Suppose that the Hume company has preferred stock that pays a $12 dividend per share and sells for $100 per share in the market. Then the cost of preferred stock is:

$$\frac{\text{Dividend per share}}{\text{Price per share}} = \frac{\$12}{\$100} = 12\%$$

Cost of Common Stock

The cost of common stock is generally viewed as the rate of return investors require on a firm's common stock. One way to measure the cost of common stock is to use the *Gordon's growth model.* The model is

$$P_o = \frac{D_1}{r - g}$$

where P_o = value (or market price) of common stock

D_1 = dividend to be received in 1 year

r = investor's required rate of return

g = rate of growth (assumed to be constant over time)

Solving the model for r results in the formula for the cost of common stock:

$$r = \frac{D_1}{P_o} + g$$

Example 20. Assume that the market price of the Hume Company's stock is $40. The dividend to be paid at the end of the coming year is $4 per share and is expected to grow at a constant annual rate of 6%. Then the cost of this common stock is:

$$\frac{D_1}{P_o} + g = \frac{\$4}{\$40} + 6\% = 16\%$$

Cost of Retained Earnings

The cost of retained earnings is closely related to the cost of existing common stock, since the cost of equity obtained by retained earnings is the same as the rate of return investors require on the firm's common stock.

Measuring the Overall Cost of Capital

The firm's overall cost of capital is the weighted average of the individual capital costs, with the weights being the proportions of each type of capital used.

Σ (percentage of the total capital structure supplied by each source of capital × cost of capital for each source)

The computation of overall cost of capital is illustrated in the following example.

Example 21. Assume that the capital structure at the latest statement date is indicative of the proportions of financing that the company intends to use over time:

		Cost
Mortgage bonds ($1,000 par)	$20,000,000	4.80% (from Example 17)
Preferred stock ($100 par)	5,000,000	12.00% (from Example 18)
Common stock ($40 par)	20,000,000	16.00% (from Example 19)
Retained earnings	5,000,000	16.00
Total	$50,000,000	

These proportions would be applied to the assumed individual explicit after-tax costs below:

Source	Weights	Cost	Weighted Cost
Debt	40%[a]	4.80%	1.92%[b]
Preferred stock	10	12.00%	1.20
Common stock	40	16.00%	6.40
Retained earnings	10	16.00%	1.60
	100%		11.12%

[a]$20,000,000/$50,000,000 = .40 = 40%
[b]4.80% × 40% = 1.92%

Overall cost of capital is 11.12%

By computing a company's cost of capital, we can determine its minimum rate of return, which is used as the discount rate in present value calculations. A company's cost of capital is also an indicator of risk. For example, if your company's cost of financing increases, it is being viewed as more risky by investors and creditors, who are demanding a higher return on their investments in the form of higher dividend and interest rates.

Lease-Purchase Decision

The lease-purchase decision is one commonly confronting firms considering the acquisition of new assets. It is a hybrid capital budgeting decision that forces a company to compare the leasing and financing (purchasing) alternatives.

There are tax benefits of leasing equipment rather than financing it with a term loan. Depending upon your needs and the nature of your business, the entire lease payment may be fully deductible as a business expense, thereby reducing your taxable income. With a loan, only the interest and depreciation can be used for deductions. Another benefit a lease offers is 100% financing plus an additional 10% of the equipment's costs to cover soft costs, such as taxes, shipping, and installation. Some term loans offer 100% financing but, typically, they cover the cost of equipment only.

A lease can help you manage your cash flow. The payments are usually lower than for a term loan. Since a lease payment requires no down payment or deposit, you can get the equipment you need without depleting your reserve capital. The types of business that most often lease equipment to generate revenue are manufacturing, transportation, printing, and professional corporations, such as medical, law, or accounting firms. Leasing works well for such companies since they can keep their equipment current without having to dip into capital to do it. Since the business capital is not being used for equipment, they can use it for business development and expansion.

A loan is your best choice, however, if you wish to keep the equipment and build equity quickly. Loans can be structured so you can own the equipment outright at the end of the term *Note*: If you are sure you want to retain your equipment beyond the lease term and prefer to know the full cost of the financing up front, you may choose a Lease Purchase option. As its name implies, this option requires no additional payment to own the equipment at the end of the lease.

To make an intelligent financial decision on a lease-purchase, an after-tax, cash outflow, *present value* comparison is needed. There are special steps to take when making this comparison. When considering a lease, take the following steps:

1. Find the annual lease payment. Since the annual lease payment is typically made in advance, the formula used is:

$$\text{Amount of lease} = A + A.T4(i, n - 1) \text{ or } A = \frac{\text{Amount of lease}}{1 + T4\ (i, n - 1)}$$

Notice we use n – 1 rather than n.

2. Find the after-tax cash outflows.
3. Find the present value of the after-tax cash outflows.

When considering a purchase, take the following steps:

1. Find the annual loan amortization by using:

$$A = \frac{\text{Amount of loan for the purchase}}{T4\ (i, n - 1)}$$

This step may not be necessary, since this amount is usually available.

2. Calculate the interest. The interest is segregated from the principal in each of the annual loan payments, because only the interest is tax-deductible.
3. Find the cash outflows by adding interest and depreciation (plus any maintenance costs), and then compute the after-tax outflows.
4. Find the present value of the after-tax cash outflows, using Table 3.

Example 22. A firm has decided to acquire a computer system costing $100,000 that has an expected life of 5 years, after which the system is not expected to have any residual value. The system can be purchased by borrowing or it can be leased. If leasing is used, the lessor requires a 12% return. As is customary, lease payments are made in advance, that is, at the end of the year prior to each of the 10 years. The tax rate is 50% and the firm's cost of capital, or after-tax cost of borrowing, is 8%.

First compute the present value of the after-tax cash outflows associated with the leasing alternative.

1. Find the annual lease payment:

$$A = \frac{\text{Amount of lease}}{1 + T4\ (i, n - 1)}$$

$$= \frac{\$100,000}{1 + T4\ (12\%, 4\ \text{years})} = \frac{\$100,000}{1 + 3.3073} = \frac{\$100,000}{4.3073} = \frac{\$23,216}{\text{(rounded)}}$$

Steps 2 and 3 can be done in the same schedule, as follows:

Year	(1) Lease Payment($)	(2) Tax Savings($)	(3)=(1)–(2) After-Tax Cash Outflow($)	(4) PV at 8%	(5)=(3)×(4) PV of Cash Out-flow($,Rounded)
0	23,216		23,216	1.000	23,216
1–4	23,216	11,608[a]	11,608	3.3121[b]	38,447
5		11,608	(11,608)	0.6806[a]	(7,900)
					53,763

[a]$23,216 × 50%
[b]From Table 4.
[c]From Table 3.

If the asset is purchased, the firm is assumed to finance it entirely with a 10% unsecured term loan. Straight-line depreciation is used with no salvage value. Therefore, the annual depreciation is $20,000 ($100,000/5 years). In this alternative, first find the annual loan payment by using:

$$A = \frac{\text{Amount of loan}}{T4\ (i,n)}$$

$$A = \frac{\$100,000}{T4(10\%, 5\ years)} = \frac{\$100,000}{3.7906} = \$26,381\ (rounded)$$

2. Calculate the interest by setting up a loan amortization schedule.

Yr	(1) Loan Payment($)	(2) Beginning-of-Yr Principal($)	(3)=(2)(10%) Interest($)	(4)=(1)–(3) Principal($)	(5)=(2)–(4) End-of-Yr Principal
1	26,381	100,000	10,000	16,381	83,619
2	26,381	83,619	8,362	18,019	65,600
3	26,381	65,600	6,560	19,821	45,779
4	26,381	45,779	4,578	21,803	23,976
5	26,381	23,976[a]	2,398	23,983[a]	

[a]Because of rounding errors, there is a slight difference between (2) and (4).

Steps 3 (cash outflows) and 4 (present values of those outflows) can be calculate as shown in Table 7.

Table 7 Lease versus Purchase Evaluation Report

	Leasing		Purchase/Borrow					Discounted Cash Flow	
Year	Lease Payments	Net After-Tax Cash Flow	Loan Payments	Interest Expense	Depreciation Expense	Net After-Tax Cash Flow	Present Value Factor	Leasing	Purchase
0	$23,216	$23,216					1	$23,216	$23,216
1	23,216	11,608	$26,381	$10,000	$20,000	$11,381	0.9259	10,748	10,538
2	23,216	11,608	26,381	8,362	20,000	12,200	0.8573	9,952	10,459
3	23,216	11,608	26,381	6,560	20,000	13,101	0.7938	9,214	10,400
4	23,216	11,608	26,381	4,578	20,000	14,092	0.735	8,532	10,358
5		(11,608)	26,381	2,398	20,000	15,182	0.6806	(7,900)	10,333
	$92,864	$58,040	$131,905	$31,898	$100,000	$65,956		$53,761	$52,087

	Lease Proposal	Purchase Proposal
Cost of machine	$100,000	$100,000
Terms of payment	5 years	5 years
Interest rate	12%	10%
Downpayment		
Monthly lease payment at the end of the year	$23,216	
Monthly loan payment		$26,381
Depreciation		Straight-line
Residual purchase price	0%	0
Corporate tax bracket	50%	50%
After-tax cost of capital	8%	8%

The sum of the present values of the cash outflows for leasing and purchasing by borrowing shows that purchasing is preferable because the PV of borrowing is less than the PV of leasing ($52,008 versus $53,763). The incremental savings is $1,675.

ECONOMIC FEASIBILITY STUDY FOR A NEW INFORMATION SYSTEM

Determining economic feasibility requires a careful investigation of the costs and benefits of a proposed information system. The basic framework for feasibility analysis is the *capital budgeting* model in which cost savings and other benefits, as well as initial outlay costs, operating costs, and other cash outflows, are translated into dollar estimates.

The estimated benefits are compared with the costs to determine whether the system is cost-beneficial. Where possible, benefits and costs that are not easily quantifiable should be estimated and included in the feasibility analysis. If they cannot be accurately estimated, they should be listed and the likelihood of their occurring and the expected impact on the organization evaluated. Some of the tangible and intangible benefits a company might obtain from a new system are cost savings; improved customer service, productivity, decision making, and data processing; better management control; and increased job satisfaction and employee morale.

Equipment costs are an initial outlay cost if the system is purchased and an operating cost if rented or leased. Equipment costs vary from a few thousands for microcomputer systems to millions of dollars for enormous mainframes. Equipment costs are usually less than the cost of acquiring software and maintaining, supporting, and operating the system. Software acquisition costs include the purchase price of software as well as the time and effort required to design, program, test, and document software. The personnel costs associated with hiring, training, and relocating staff can be substantial. Site preparation costs may be incurred for large computer systems. There are costs involved in installing the new system and converting files to the appropriate format and storage media.

The primary operating cost is maintaining the system. There may be significant annual cash outflows for equipment replacement and expansion and software updates. Human resource costs include the salaries of systems analysts, programmers, operators, data entry operators, and management. Costs are also incurred for supplies, overhead, and other operating costs. Initial cash outlay and operating costs are summarized in Table 8.

During systems design, several alternative approaches to meeting system requirements are developed. Various feasibility measures such as

Table 8 Initial Cash Outlay and Operating Costs

Hardware	Site preparation
Central processing unit	Air conditioning, humidity, and dust controls
Peripherals	
Special input/output devices	Physical security (access)
Communications hardware	Fire and water protection
Upgrade and expansion costs	Cabling, wiring, and outlets
Software	Furnishing and fixtures
Application, system, general purpose, utility, and communications software	Staff
	Supervisors
	Analysts and programmers
Updated versions of software	Computer operators
Application software design, programming, modification, and testing	Input (data conversion) personnel
	Recruitment and staff training
Installation	Maintenance/backup
Freight and delivery charges	Hardware/software maintenance
Setup and connection fees	Backup and recovery operations
Conversion	Power supply protection
Systems testing	Supplies and overhead
File and data conversions	Preprinted forms
Parallel operations	Data storage devices
	Supplies (paper, ribbons, toner)
Documentation	Utilities and power
Systems documentation	Others
Training program documentation	Legal and consulting fees
Operating standards and procedures	Insurance

technical, operational, legal, and scheduling feasibility are then used to narrow the list of alternatives. Economic feasibility and capital budgeting techniques, which were discussed earlier, are used to evaluate the benefit-cost aspects of the alternatives.

Example 23. Sophie, an information systems (IS) project manager for the MYK chain of discount stores, is contemplating installation of a new IS system that is flexible, efficient, timely, and responsive to user and customer needs. The new system aims at improving the company's business processes. After the analysis, Sophie's IS project team decided they wanted the corporate office to gather daily sales data from each store. Analyzing the prior day's sales will help the company adapt quickly to customer needs. Providing sales data to suppliers will help avoid stockouts and overstocking.

Coordinating buying at the corporate office will help MYK to minimize inventory levels and negotiate lower wholesale prices. Stores will send orders electronically the day they are prepared. Based on store orders, the previous day's sales figures, and warehouse inventory, MYK will send purchase orders to suppliers. Suppliers will process orders and ship goods to regional warehouses or directly to the stores the day orders are received. Each store will have the flexibility to respond to local sales trends and conditions by placing local orders. Accounts payable will be centralized so the firm can make payments electronically.

Sophie's team conducted an economic feasibility study and determined that the project makes excellent use of funds. As shown in Table 9, they estimated that initial outlay costs for the system are $4.32 million (initial systems design and new hardware $1.8 million each, software $375,000, and training, site preparation, and conversion $250,000 each).

The team estimated what it would cost to operate the system for its estimated six-year life, as well as what the system would save the company. The following recurring costs were identified: hardware expansion, additional software and software updates, systems maintenance, added personnel to operate the system, communication charges, and overhead. The system will also save the company money by eliminating clerical jobs, generating working capital savings, increasing sales and profits, and decreasing warehouse costs. The costs and savings for years 1 through 6, which are expected to rise from year to year, are shown in Table 9.

Sophie calculated the annual savings minus the recurring additional costs and then calculated the annual after-tax cash savings under the MACRS tax rule. The $4.66 million system can be depreciated over the six-year period. For example, the depreciation in year 1 of $932,000 reduces net income by that amount. Since the company does not have to pay taxes on the $1 million, at its tax rate of 34% it ends up saving an additional $316,880 in year 1. Finally, Sophie calculated the net savings for each year.

Sophie used MYK's cost of capital of 10% to calculate the net present value (NPV) of the investment, which is over $3 million. The internal rate of return (IRR) is a respectable 26%. Sophie realized how advantageous it would be for the company to borrow the money (at 10% interest rates) in order to produce a 26% return on that borrowed money. In addition, payback (the point at which the initial cost is recovered) occurs in the fourth year. NPV and IRR are calculated as shown in Table 9.

Sophie presented the system and its cost/benefit calculations to top management. Challenges to her estimates (various "what-if" scenarios) were plugged into the Excel model so that management could see the effect of the changed assumptions. This spreadsheet analysis was intended to ensure a positive return from the new system under future uncertainty.

Economic Feasibility Study for an Information Technology (IT) Investment   **415**

Table 9   Economic Feasibility Study for a New Information System

	Initial Outlay 0	1	2	3	4	5	6
Initial outlay costs (I)							
Initial system design	$ 1,800,000						
Hardware	1,800,000						
Software	375,000						
Training	185,000						
Site preparation	250,000						
Conversion	250,000						
Total	$ 4,660,000						
Recurring costs							
Hardware expansion			$ 420,000	490,000	560,000	600,000	640,000
Software		310,000	250,000	290,000	330,000	370,000	390,000
Systems maintenance			160,000	210,000	230,000	245,000	260,000
Personnel costs		$ 70,000	120,000	130,000	140,000	150,000	160,000
Communication charges		485,000	800,000	900,000	1,000,000	1,100,000	1,300,000
Overhead		99,000	160,000	180,000	200,000	220,000	250,000
Total		$ 964,000	1,910,000	2,200,000	2,460,000	2,685,000	3,000,000
Cash savings							
Clerical cost savings		$ 500,000	$ 1,110,000	$ 1,350,000	$ 1,500,000	$ 1,700,000	1,950,000
Working capital savings		1,000,000	1,200,000	1,500,000	1,500,000	1,500,000	1,500,000
Increased sales and profits			500,000	900,000	1,200,000	1,500,000	1,800,000
Reduced warehouse costs			400,000	800,000	1,200,000	1,600,000	2,000,000
Total		$ 1,500,000	$ 3,210,000	$ 4,550,000	$ 5,400,000	$ 6,300,000	$ 7,250,000
Cash savings minus recurring costs		536,000	1,300,000	2,350,000	2,940,000	3,615,000	4,250,000
Less income taxes (34%)	34%	(182,240)	(442,000)	(799,000)	(999,600)	(1,229,100)	(1,445,000)
Cash savings (net of tax)		$ 353,760	858,000	$ 1,551,000	1,940,400	$ 2,385,900	2,805,000
Tax shield from depreciation		316,880	507,008	304,205	182,206	182,206	91,895
Net cash inflows (net savings) after taxes	$ (4,660,000)	$ 670,640	$ 1,365,008	$ 1,855,205	$ 2,122,606	$ 2,568,106	$ 2,896,895

Tax savings from depreciation deduction

Year	MACRS	Depreciation	Tax savings
1	20.00%	$ 932,000	$ 316,880
2	32.00%	1,491,200	507,008
3	19.20%	894,720	304,205
4	11.50%	535,900	182,206
5	11.50%	535,900	182,206
6	5.80%	270,280	91,895

Net present value calculations @ a cost of capital of 10%

Year	Net savings	PV factor	PV
0	$ (4,660,000)	1.0000	$ (4,660,000)
1	670,640	0.9091	609,679
2	1,365,008	0.8265	1,128,179
3	1,855,205	0.7513	1,393,815
4	2,122,606	0.6830	1,449,740
5	2,568,106	0.6209	1,594,537
6	2,896,895	0.5645	1,635,297
	NPV		$ 3,151,248
	IRR		26.26%

SUMMARY

We have examined the process of evaluating capital expenditure projects. We have also discussed several commonly used criteria for evaluating capital budgeting projects, including the NPV and IRR methods. Since income taxes could make a difference in the accept or reject decision, tax factors must be taken into account in every decision. Although the traditional depreciation methods can still be used for computing depreciation for book purposes, 1981 saw a new way of computing depreciation deductions for tax purposes. The rule is called the Modified Accelerated Cost Recovery System (MACRS). It was enacted by Congress in 1981 and then modified somewhat in 1986 under the Tax Reform Act of 1986. Lease-purchase decisions were also treated on an after-tax basis. Also presented is an example economic feasibility study for a new information system.

LEGAL AND REGULATORY ENVIRONMENT OF THE FIRM

An important element of the competitive environment is the growing importance of government involvement in the market economy. Recent changes in the method and scope of government regulation, including moves toward deregulation, affect the entire spectrum of economic activity, from industrials, to financial institutions (banks, savings and loans, insurance, etc.), to power and transportation utilities. Both state and federal regulation and antitrust policy constitute important constraints on many managerial decisions. As a result, their analysis constitutes an important aspect of managerial economics. This chapter presents the role of government in the market economy, including:

(a) economic and political rationale for regulation,

(b) direct regulation of firms possessing substantial market power,

(c) antitrust policy designed to maintain a "workable" level of competition in the economy, and

(d) public expenditure decisions and cost/benefit analysis.

THE RATIONALE FOR REGULATION

Government regulation is sometimes justified on the basis of its ability to correct various market imperfections or market failures that lead to inefficiency and waste. Most often, market failure is thought to be caused by:

(a) Structural problems: too few buyers or sellers.

(b) Incentive problems: externalities such as pollution.

Government regulation is sometimes justified on the basis of political considerations. Primary among such considerations are desires to:

(a) Preserve consumer choice: A wide variety of production enhances personal freedom.

(b) Limit economic and political power: Unchecked economic and political power could threaten basic liberties.

ANTITRUST POLICY: GOVERNMENT REGULATION OF MARKET CONDUCT AND STRUCTURE

Antitrust policy is a set of legislation aimed at prohibiting monopolies, restraints of trade, price fixing and discrimination, exorbitant quantity discounts to large buyers, and conspiracies to suppress competition. Federal statutes include the Sherman Antitrust Act, Clayton Antitrust Act, Robinson-Patman Act, and Celler-Kefauver Act.

Sherman Antitrust Act (1890)

The cornerstone of U.S. antitrust policy is contained in Sections 1 and 2 of the *Sherman Antitrust Act* of 1890:

Section 1: Every contract, combination in the form of trust or otherwise, or conspiracy, in restraint of trade or commerce among the several states, or with foreign nations, is hereby declared to be illegal. Every person who shall make any such contract or engage in any such combination or conspiracy shall be deemed guilty of a felony, and, on conviction thereof shall be punished by a fine not exceeding five thousand dollars (one million dollars if a corporation, or, if any other person, one hundred thousand dollars) or by imprisonment not exceeding one (three) years, or by both said punishments, in the discretion of the court.

Section 2: Every person who shall monopolize, or attempt to monopolize, or combine or conspire with any person or persons, to monopolize any part of the trade or commerce among the several States, or with foreign nations, shall be deemed guilty of a felony, and, on conviction thereof, shall be punished by a fine not exceeding five thousand dollars (one million dollars if a corporation, or, if any other person, one hundred thousand dollars) or by imprisonment not exceeding one (three) years, or by both said punishments, in the discretion of the court.

Clayton Act (1914)

The Clayton Act was designed to overcome some of the ambiguity of the Sherman Act by explicitly prohibiting certain behavior. The Clayton Antitrust Act is one of three major antitrust laws passed as amendments to the Sherman Antitrust Act in 1914. The Act listed four illegal practices in restraint of competition. It outlawed price discrimination, tying contracts and exclusive dealerships, and horizontal mergers. It also outlawed *interlocking directorates* (the practice of having the same people serve as directors of two or more competing firms).

> *Section 2:* Forbade price discrimination between firms which tended to lessen competition. This section was later amended by the Robinson-Patman Act (1936). It is important to remember that price discrimination between consumers, such as senior citizen discounts for bus service, is legal.
>
> *Section 3:* Made leases or any sales contracts that lessened competition illegal. This provision was aimed at so-called tying contracts.
>
> *Section 7:* Forbade stock mergers for monopoly purposes.

Robinson-Patman Act (1936)

The *Robinson Patman Act* (1936) is an amendment to strengthen Section 2 of the Clayton Act regarding price discrimination. For example, Section 2(a) of the Robinson Patman Act amends Section 2 of the Clayton Act and makes price discrimination illegal if it is designed to lessen competition or create a monopoly:

> *Section 2(a):* That it shall be unlawful for any person engaged in commerce, in the course of such commerce, either directly or indirectly, to discriminate in price between different purchasers of commodities of like grade and quality, . . . where such discrimination may be substantially to lessen competition or tend to create a monopoly in line of commerce, or to injure, destroy, or prevent competition.

Price discrimination that arises because of cost or quality differences is permitted under the act, as is price discrimination when it is necessary to meet a competitor's price in a market. Still, there is considerable ambiguity regarding whether a particular type of price discrimination is illegal under the law.

Celler-Kefauver Act (1950)

The *Celler-Kefauver Act* (1950) strengthened Section 7 of the Clayton Act by making it more difficult for firms to engage in mergers and acquisitions without violating the law:

> *Section 7:* That no corporation engaged in commerce shall acquire, directly or indirectly, the whole or any part of the stock or other share capital and no corporation subject to the jurisdiction of the Federal Trade Commission shall acquire the whole or any part of the assets of another corporation engaged also in commerce, where in any line of commerce in any section of the country, the effect of such acquisition may be substantially to lessen competition, or to tend to create a monopoly.

Enforcement

The *Antitrust Division of the Department of Justice (DOJ)* and the *Federal Trade Commission (FTC)* are charged with the task of enforcing antitrust regulations. The FTC has limited judicial power; taking violators to court falls almost exclusively on the Antitrust Division of the DOJ. Instead, the FTC issues cease-and-desist orders based on information gathered in a specific case. If the cease-and-desist order is not followed, the FTC may levy a fine of up to $10,000 on the guilty party. If further noncompliance occurs, the FTC usually enjoins the DOJ for further prosecution.

RESOURCE ALLOCATION AND THE SUPPLY OF PUBLIC GOODS

The resource allocation question applies both to privately produced goods and to public sector output. In theory, the amount of any good that should be supplied at a point in time is that quantity which equates the marginal social cost (MSC) of the good with its marginal social benefit (MSB).

First, the marginal *private* economic cost of a good includes all explicit and implicit costs of its production that are borne by the producer. A product's marginal *social* cost differs from its marginal private cost by the amount of external costs (third-party costs) that accompany the production of an incremental unit of output. This cost includes the value to consumers of any alternative product or products whose production is reduced or eliminated.

In a similar fashion, we can define marginal social benefit as the sum of marginal private benefits and marginal external, or third-party, benefits. The private benefits accrue to those who directly pay a price for the good, while the external benefits are enjoyed by either the purchaser or the nonpurchasers but are not accounted for in the product's market price.

A good should be provided up to the quantity where MSC = MSB. A theoretically optimal allocation of society's resources exists when for all goods the condition that MSB = MSC is attained.

Example 1. Assume a two-good case, where a and b are the goods, where both costs and benefits are measured in dollars, and where initially we have

$$MSB_a = MSC_a = 20$$
$$MSB_b = MSC_b = 40$$

Thus, the social cost of producing the marginal or last unit of a is $20, while that of producing the marginal unit of b is $40. Obviously, it is also true that

$$\frac{MSB_a}{MSC_a} = \frac{MSB_b}{MSC_b} = 1$$

First, for a given income distribution, efficient resource allocation will take place when, for n goods,

$$\frac{MSB_a}{MSC_a} = \frac{MSB_b}{MSC_b} = \ldots \ldots \frac{MSB_n}{MSC_n} = 1$$

This condition simply means that a dollar's worth of social benefit is received for an additional dollar spent on the production of each good. Any deviation from this condition would result in a situation where too much of some good (or goods) and too little of some other good (or goods) is produced.

PUBLIC PROJECT ANALYSIS AND COST/BENEFIT ANALYSIS

In public project analysis, we seek to evaluate investments from the point of view of society as a whole. This means that we need to determine social benefits deriving from public projects and social costs incurred to launch those projects. A social benefit is any gain in utility and a social cost is any loss of utility as measured by the opportunity cost of the project.

We use *cost/benefit analysis,* which is simply the extension of capital project analysis to public sector microeconomic decisions. The steps taken in the construction of a cost/benefit analysis for a public-sector undertaking are as follows:

1. Specify objectives and identify constraints.
2. Formulate alternative means of meeting objectives.
3. Estimate costs of each alternative.
4. Estimate benefits attributable to each alternative.
5. Select the best alternative.

The *benefit to cost (B/C) ratio* or *profitability index* is widely used for public expenditure decisions.

CLASSIFICATION OF GOODS

Most goods originate with private sectors. They are categorized as private goods, and those that are governmental in origin are public goods. Public goods are *nonrival* and nonexclusionary in consumption and therefore benefit persons other than those who buy the goods. A good is *nonrival* in consumption if the consumption of the good by one person does not preclude other people from also consuming the good. A good is *nonexclusionary* if, once provided, no one can be excluded from consuming it. Examples of public goods are radio signals, lighthouses, national defense, and clean air.

In order to determine which public goods or projects are worthwhile, and their optimal magnitude, we have to quantify the expected stream of costs and the value of the benefits, and whether revenues can be collected or not. Since any public project involves expected future flows of costs and benefits, we need to deal with the issue of appropriate discounting. What is a proper *social discount rate?*

SOCIAL GOODS AND EXTERNALITIES

When goods are public or social goods, there are always nonmarket interactions in which people are forced to provide resources to others while receiving full compensation or in which people receive benefits without having to make appropriate payments. These nonmarket flows of burdens and benefits are known as *externalities*. Externalities are the positive (beneficial) or negative (harmful) effects that market exchanges have on people who do not participate directly in those exchanges. Externalities are third-party *spillover,* or *neighborhood,* effects. Positive externalities include the social benefits conferred by a firm in training workers who become available to work for other firms that incur no training costs. Negative externalities include traffic congestion and environmental pollution created by a manufacturing plant. The term *technological* externalities is often used and is distinguished from *pecuniary* externalities. Quantifying these externalities and

Legal and Regulatory Environment of the Firm

including them in estimates of social benefits and social costs may not be an easy task.

Example 2. State Senator Dan Smith has proposed a new state-supported convention facility in the state's capitol. The convention facility would provide the state with annual social benefits of $500,000 (in lease receipts and in positive externalities) and would cost $4,000,000. The project has a 15-year life. The state planning board normally uses a 9% discount rate when evaluating capital projects. To determine if the state legislature should adopt Smith's proposal, we can calculate the benefit to cost (B/C) ratio. The present value of the benefit is: $500,000 at 9% for 15 years = $500,000 x 8.061= $4,030,500. B/C = 4,030,500/4,000,000 = 1.008, thus the state should accept Smith's proposal because it has a B/C ratio greater than 1.

MANAGEMENT OF ACCOUNTS RECEIVABLE

CASH DISBURSEMENT

The disbursement of cash is improved if based on controlled disbursement when the amount of money to be deposited on a daily basis to pay checks clearing that day is determined. Other effective means to disburse cash are using a positive pay service to reduce the incidence of fraud, and using an accounts receivable reconcilement service.

Export receivables and foreign risk may be managed better by taking out export credit insurance coverage to assure payment for shipped goods. Credit coverage may be obtained via the U.S. Export-Import Bank or a letter of credit from a U.S. or foreign bank. Even though a letter of credit guards against customer default, it needs to be secured before each export transaction. In emerging markets, the multinational company should consider the following as part of its accounts receivable management program:

- Stability of the foreign country's banking system.
- Variability in foreign exchange rates.
- Variance in foreign payment schedules.
- Stability of political, economic and financial conditions.
- Astuteness of financial management by the country's trade representatives and other government officials.

FINANCIAL DERIVATIVE PRODUCTS AND FINANCIAL ENGINEERING

FINANCIAL DERIVATIVES

A derivative is simply a transaction, or contract, whose value depends on (or, as the name implies, derives from) the value of underlying assets such as stocks, bonds, mortgages, market indexes, or foreign currencies. One party with exposure to unwanted risk can pass some or all of that risk to a second party. The first party can assume a different risk from the second party, pay the second party to assume the risk, or, as is often the case, create a combination.

The participants in derivatives activity can be divided into two broad types—dealers and end-users. Dealers, few in numbers, include investment banks, commercial banks, merchant banks, and independent brokers. In contrast, the number of end-users is large and growing as more organizations are involved in international financial transactions. End-users include businesses, banks, securities firms, insurance companies, governmental units at the local, state, and federal levels, "supernational" organizations such as the World Bank, mutual funds, and both private and public pension funds.

The objectives of end-users may vary. A common reason to use derivatives is so that the risk of financial operations can be controlled. Derivatives can be used to manage foreign exchange exposure, especially unfavorable exchange rate movements. Speculators and arbitrageurs can seek profits from general price changes or simultaneous price differences in different markets, respectively. Others use derivatives to *hedge* their position; that is, to set up two financial assets so that any unfavorable price movement in one asset is offset by favorable price movement in the other asset.

There are five common types of derivatives: options, futures, forward contracts, asset swaps, and hybrid. The general characteristics of each are summarized in Figure 1, although only two most common types—options and futures—are covered in detail in this chapter.

An important feature of derivatives is that the types of risk are not unique to derivatives and can be found in many other financial activities. The risks for derivatives are especially difficult to manage for two principal reasons: (1) The derivative products are complex, and (2) there are very real difficulties in measuring the risks associated with derivatives. It is imperative for financial officers of a firm to know how to manage the risks from the use of derivatives.

Figure 1   General Characteristics of Major Types of Financial Derivatives

Type	Market	Contract	Definition
Option	OTC or Organized Exchange	Custom* or Standard	Gives the buyer the right but *not* obligation to buy or sell a specific amount at a specified price within a specified period.
Futures	Organized Exchange	Standard	*Obligates* the holder to buy or sell at a specified price on a specified date.
Forward	OTC	Custom	Same as futures
Swap	OTC	Custom	Agreement between the parties to make periodic payments to each other during the swap period.
Hybrid	OTC	Custom	Incorporates various provisions of other types of derivatives.

*Custom contracts vary and are negotiated between the parties with respect to their value, period, and other terms.

OPTIONS

An option is a contract to give the investor the right—but *not an obligation*—to buy or sell something. It has three main features. It allows you, as an investor to "lock in":

1. a specified number of shares of stock,
2. at a fixed price per share, called strike or exercise price,
3. for a limited length of time.

For example, if you have purchased an option on a stock, you have the right to "exercise" the option at any time during the life of the option. This means that, regardless of the current market price of the stock, you have the right to buy or sell a specified number of shares of the stock at the strike price (rather than the current market price).

Options possess their own inherent value and are traded in *secondary markets.* You may want to acquire an option so that you can take advantage of an expected rise in the price of the underlying stock. Option prices are directly related to the prices of the common stock they apply to. Investing in options is very risky and requires specialized knowledge.

KINDS OF OPTIONS

All options are divided into two broad categories: calls and puts. A call option gives you the right (but not the obligation) to buy:

1. 100 shares of a specific stock,
2. at a fixed price per share, called the "strike or exercise price,"
3. for up to 9 months, depending on the expiration date of the option.

When you purchase a call, you are buying the right to purchase stock at a set price. You expect price appreciation to occur. You can make a sizable gain from a minimal investment, but you may lose all your money if stock price does not go up.

Example 1. You purchase a 3-month call option on Dow Chemical stock for $4 1/2 at an exercise price of $50 when the stock price is $53.

On the other hand, a single put option gives you the right (but not the obligation) to sell:

1. 100 shares of a specific stock,
2. at a fixed price, the strike price,
3. for up to 9 months, depending on the expiration date of the option.

Purchasing a put gives you the right to sell stock at a set price. You buy a put if you expect a stock price to fall. You have the chance to earn a considerable gain from a minimal investment, but you lose the whole investment if price depreciation does not materialize.

The buyer of the contract (called the "holder") pays the seller (called the "writer") a premium for the contract. In return for the premium, the buyer obtains the right to buy securities from the writer or sell securities to the writer at a fixed price over a stated period of time.

Option Holder = Option Buyer = Long Position

Option Writer = Option Seller = Short Position

	Call Option	*Put Option*
Buy (long)	The right to call (buy) from the writer	The right to put (sell) from the writer
Sell (short)	Known as *writing a call,* being obligated to sell if called	Known as *writing a put,* if the stock or contract is put

Calls and puts are typically for widely held and actively traded securities on organized exchanges. With calls there are no voting privileges, ownership interest, or dividend income. However, option contracts are adjusted for stock splits and stock dividends.

Calls and puts are not issued by the company with the common stock but rather by option makers or option writers. The maker of the option receives the price paid for the call or put minus commission costs. The option trades on the open market. Calls and puts are written and can be acquired through brokers and dealers. The writer is required to purchase or deliver the stock when requested.

Holders of calls and puts do not have to exercise them to earn a return. They can trade them in the secondary market for whatever their value is. The value of a call increases as the underlying common stock goes up in price. The call can be sold on the market before its expiration date.

WHY INVESTORS USE OPTIONS

Why use options? Reasons can vary from the conservative to the speculative. The most common reasons are:

1. You can earn large profits with *leverage,* that is, without having to tie up a lot of your own money. The leverage you can have with options typically runs 20:1 (each investor dollar controls the profit on twenty dollars of stock) as contrasted with the 2:1 leverage with stocks bought on margin or the 1:1 leverage with stocks bought outright with cash. *Note:* Leverage is a two-edged sword. It works both ways. You can lose a lot, too. That is why using leverage is risky.

2. Options may be purchased as "insurance or hedge" against large price drops in underlying stocks already held by the investor.

3. If you are neutral or slightly bullish in the short term on stocks you own, you can sell (or write) options on those stocks and realize extra profit.

4. Options offer a range of strategies that cannot be obtained with stocks. Thus, options are a flexible and complementary investment vehicle to stocks and bonds.

HOW OPTIONS ARE TRADED

Options are traded on listed option exchanges (secondary markets) such as the *Chicago Board Options Exchange, American Stock Exchange, Philadelphia Stock Exchange,* and *Pacific Stock Exchange.* They may also be exchanged in the *over-the counter (OTC)* market. Option exchanges are only for buying and selling call and put options. Listed options are traded on organized exchanges. Conventional options are traded in the OTC market.

The *Options Clearing Corporation (OCC)* acts as principal in every options transaction for listed options contracts. As principal it issues all listed options, guarantees the contracts, and is the legal entity on the other side of every transaction. Orders are placed with this corporation, which then issues the calls or closes the positions. Since certificates are not issued for options, a brokerage account is required. An investor who exercises a call goes through the Clearing Corporation, which randomly selects a writer from a member list. A call writer is obligated to sell 100 shares at the exercise price.

Exchanges permit general orders (i.e., limit) and orders applicable only to the option (i.e., spread order).

TERMS OF AN OPTION

There are three key terms you need to be familiar with in connection with options: the exercise or strike price, expiration date, and option premium. The *exercise price* is the price per share for 100 shares, which you may buy at (call). For a put, it is the price at which the stock may be sold. The purchase or sale of the stock is to the writer of the option. The striking price is set for the life of the option on the options exchange. When stock price changes, new exercise prices are introduced for trading purposes, reflecting the new value.

In case of conventional calls, restrictions do not exist on what the striking price should be. However, it is usually close to the market price of the stock it relates to. In the case of listed calls, stocks having a price lower than $50 a share must have striking prices in $5 increments. Stocks between $50 and $100 have striking prices in $20 increments. Striking prices are adjusted for material stock splits and stock dividends.

The *expiration date* of an option is the last day it can be exercised. For conventional options, the expiration date can be any business day; for a listed option there is a standardized expiration date.

The cost of an option is referred to as a *premium*. It is the price the buyer of the call or put has to pay the seller (writer). In other words, the option premium is what an option costs to you as a buyer. *Note:* With other securities, the premium is the excess of the purchase price over a determined theoretical value.

USING PROFIT DIAGRAMS

In order to understand the risks and rewards associated with various option strategies, it is very helpful to understand how the profit diagram works. In fact, it is essential to understanding how an option works. The profit diagram is a visual portrayal of your profit in relation to the price of a stock at a single point in time.

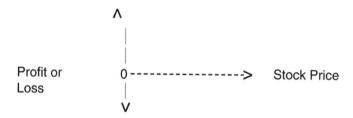

Example 2.

IBM Stock Price in 3 months	Profit (Loss)
$ 60	−$2000
$ 70	−$1000
$ 80	$ 0
$ 90	$1000
$ 100	$2000

The following shows the profit diagram for 100 shares of IBM stock if you bought them today at $80 per share and sold them in 3 months. (Commissions are ignored in this example.)

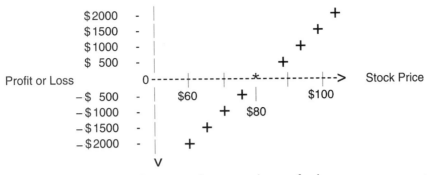

Note that all stocks have the same shape on the profit diagram at any point in the future. You will later see that this is *not* the case with options.

Example 3. Assume that on April 7, you become convinced that IBM stock, which is trading at $80 a share, will move considerably higher in the next few months. So, you buy one call option on IBM stock with a premium of $2 a share. Since the call option involves a block of 100 shares of stock, it costs you a total of $2 times 100 shares or $200. Assume further that this call option has a striking price of $85 and an expiration date near the end of September. What this means is that for $200 you have the right to buy:

1. 100 shares of IBM stock
2. at $85 a share
3. until near the end of September.

This may not sound like you're getting much for $200, but if IBM stock goes up to $95 a share by the end of September, you'd have the right to purchase 100 shares of IBM stock for $8500 ($85 times 100 shares) and to turn right around and sell them for $9500, keeping the difference of $1000, an $800 profit. That works out to 400% profit in less than five months.

However, if you are wrong and IBM stock goes down in price, the most you could lose would be the price of the option, $200. The following displays the profit table for this example.

If the IBM stock price in September turns out to be:		The value of the call option would be:		And your profit would be:
$ 75	---->	$ 0	---->	-$ 200
$ 80		$ 0		⁻$ 200
$ 85		$ 0		⁻$ 200
$ 87		$ 200		⁻$ 0
$ 90		$ 500		$ 300
$ 95		$1000		$ 800

The profit diagram will look like this:

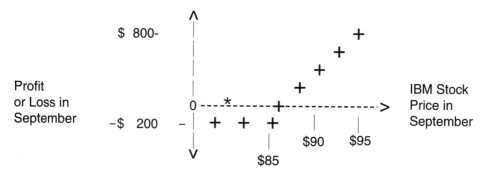

You are "long 1 IBM Sep 85 call" option.

Notice where the profit line bends—at $85, unlike stocks that have the same shape on the profit diagram at any point in the future. This is not the case with options. You start making money after the price of IBM stock goes higher than the $85 striking price of the call option. When this happens, the option is called "in-the-money."

On the other hand, the profit diagram for a put option looks like this:

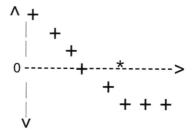

So, a put is typically used by an investor who is bearish on that particular stock. The put option can also be used as "insurance" against price drops for the investor with a long stock position.

OPTION COSTS

The premium for an option (or cost of an option) depends primarily on:

- Fluctuation in price of the underlying security. (A higher variability means a higher premium because of the greater speculative appeal of the option.)

- Time period remaining before the option's expiration. (The more time there is until the expiration, the greater the premium you must pay the seller.)

- Price spread between the stock price and the option's strike price. (A wider difference translates to a higher price.)

Example 4. ABC stock is selling at $32 a share today. Consider two options:

1. Option X gives you the right to buy the stock at $25 per share.
2. Option Y gives you the right to buy the stock at $40 per share.

Since you would rather have an option to pay $25 for a $32 stock instead of $32, Option X is more valuable than Option Y. Thus, it will cost you more to buy Option X than to buy Option Y.

Other factors that determine the cost of an option are:

- The dividend trend of the underlying security
- The volume of trading in the option
- The exchange the option is listed on
- "Going" interest rates
- The market price of the underlying stock

In-the-Money and Out-of-the-Money Call Options

Options may or may not be exercised, depending on the difference between the market price of the stock and the exercise price.

Let P = the price of the underlying stock

and S   = the exercise price

There are three possible situations:

1. If $P > X$ or $P - X > 0$, then the call option is said to be *in the money*. (By exercising the call option, you, as a holder, realize a positive profit, P–X.)

The value of the call in this case is:

$$\text{Value of call} = (\text{market price of stock} - \text{exercise price of call}) \times 100$$

Example 5. Assume that the market price of a stock is $90, with a strike price of $80. The call has a value of $1,000.

2. If $P - X = 0$, then the option is said to be *at the money*.

3. If $P - X < 0$, then the option is said to be *out of the money*. It is unprofitable. The option holder can purchase the stock at the cheaper price in the market rather than exercising the option, and thus the option is thrown away. Out-of-the-money call options have no intrinsic value.

If the total premium (option price) of an option is $14 and the intrinsic value is $6, there is an additional premium of $8 arising from other factors.

Total premium is comprised of the intrinsic value and speculative premium (time value) based on variables like risk, expected future prices, maturity, leverage, dividend, and fluctuation in price.

Total premium = intrinsic value + speculative premium (time value)

1. Intrinsic value = In the money option
i.e., P - S > 0 for a call and S - P > 0 for a put option.
2. Time value—For in-the-money options, time value is the difference between premium and intrinsic value. For other options, all value is time value.

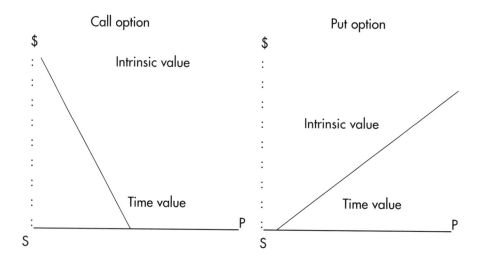

In-the-Money and Out-of-the-Money Put Options

A put option on a common stock allows the holder of the option to sell ("put") a share of the underlying stock at an exercise price until an expiration date. The definition of in-the-money and out-of-the-money are different for puts since the owner may sell stock at the strike price. For a put option, the option is in the money if $P - X < 0$.

Its value is determined as follows:

Value of put = (exercise price of put – market price of stock) × 100

The option is out of the money when $P - X > 0$ and has no value.

Example 6. Assume a stock has a market price of $100 and a strike price of the put is $116. The value of the put is $1,600.

If market price of stock exceeds strike price, an out-of-the money put exists. Because a stock owner can sell it for a greater amount in the market relative to exercising the put, no intrinsic value exists for the out-of-money put.

	ABC Calls at 60 Strike Price Stock Price	ABC Puts at 60 Strike Price Stock Price
In-the-money	Over 60	Under 60
At-the-money	60	60
Out-of-the-money	Under 60	Over 60

The theoretical value for calls and puts reflects the price at which the options should be traded. But usually they are traded at prices exceeding true value when options have a long period to go. This difference is referred to as investment premium.

$$\text{Investment premium} = \frac{\text{option premium} - \text{option value}}{\text{option value}}$$

Example 7. Assume a put with a theoretical value of $2,500 and a price of $3,000. It is therefore traded at an investment premium of 20% [($3,000 − $2,500)/$2,500].

THE RISKS AND REWARDS OF OPTIONS

Your risk in buying options is limited to the premium you paid. That is the downside risk for option investing. For example, assume you own a two-month call option to acquire 500 shares of ABC Company at $20 per share. Within that time period, you exercise the option when the market price is $38. You make a gain of $9,000 ($18 × 500 shares) except for the brokerage commission. Of course, the higher the stock's price goes, the more you can profit. However, if the market price had declined from $20, you would not have exercised the call option, and you would have lost the cost of the option. *Note:* If you owned the stock whose price fell $10 per share, you would have lost $10 a share. But if you had an option to buy that stock, you could have lost only the cost (premium) of that option, no matter how far the stock price fell.

How Do Calls Work?

By buying a call you can own common stock for a low percentage of the cost of buying regular shares. Leverage is obtained since a small change in common stock price can magnify a major move in the call option's price. An element of the percentage gain in the price of the call is the speculative premium related to the remaining time left on the call. Calls can also be viewed as a way of controlling 100 shares of stock without a large monetary commitment.

Example 8. Assume that a security has a present market price of $70. A call can be bought for $600 permitting the purchase of 100 shares at $70 per share. If the stock price goes up, the call increases in value. Assume the stock goes to $95 at the call's expiration date. The profit is $25 per share in the call, or a total of $2,500 on an investment of $600. There is a return of 417%. When you exercise the call for 100 shares at $70 each, you can immediately sell them at $95 per share.

Note: You could have earned the same amount by investing directly in the common stock. However, you would have needed to invest $7,000, resulting in a much lower return rate.

How Do Puts Work?

The put holder may sell 100 shares at the exercise price for a specified time period to a put writer. A put is bought when a price decline is expected. Like a call option, the entire premium cost (investment) would be lost if the price does not drop.

Example 9. Assume that a stock has a market price of $80. You buy a put to sell 100 shares of stock at $80 per share. The put cost is $500. At the exercise date, the price of the stock goes to $70 a share. The profit is $10 per share, or $1,000. You just buy on the market 100 shares at $70 each and then sell them to the writer of the put for $80 each. The net gain is $500 ($1,000 – $500).

The following tables summarize payoffs, risks, and break-even stock prices for various option participants.

Option Payoffs and Risks

	Call buyer	*Call seller (writer)*
Payoff	$-c + (P - S)$ where c = the call premium For a break-even, $-c + (P - S) = 0$ or $P = S + c$.	$+c - (P - S)$
Risk	Maximum risk is to lose the premium because investor	No risk limit as the stock price rises above

| | throws away the out-of-the-money option | the exercise price—uncovered (naked) option |
| | | To be covered, investor should own the underlying stock or hold a long call on the same stock |

	Put buyer	*Put seller (writer)*
Payoff	$-c + (S - P)$ where c = the put premium	$+c - (S - P)$
	For a break-even, $-c + (S - P) = 0$ or $P = S - c$	
Risk	Maximum risk is to lose the premium	Maximum risk is the strike price when the stock price is zero—uncovered (naked) option
		To be covered, investor should sell the underlying stock short or hold a long put on the same stock

Break-Even Points for Option Parties

Option parties	*Break-even market price*
A call holder	the strike price + the premium
A put holder	the strike price – the premium
A call writer	the strike price + the premium
A put writer	the strike price – the premium
A covered call writer	the original cost of the security – the premium
A covered put writer	the strike price + the premium (short the stock)

CALL AND PUT INVESTMENT STRATEGIES YOU MAY USE

Investment possibilities with calls and puts include (1) hedging, (2) speculation, (3) straddles, and (4) spreads. If you own call and put options, you can *hedge* by holding two or more securities to reduce risk and earn a profit. You may purchase a stock and subsequently buy an option on it. For instance, you may buy a stock and write a call on it. Further, if you own a stock that has appreciated, you may buy a put to insulate from downside risk.

Example 10. You bought 100 shares of XYZ at $52 per share and a put for $300 on the 100 shares at an exercise price of $52. If the stock does not move, you lose $300 on the put. If the price falls, your loss offsets your gain on the put. If stock price goes up, you have a capital gain on the stock but lose your investment in the put. To obtain the advantage of a hedge, you incur a loss on the put. Note that at the expiration date, you have a loss with no hedge any longer.

You may employ calls and puts to *speculate*. You may buy options when you believe you will make a higher return compared to investing in the underlying stock. You can earn a higher return at lower risk with out-of-the-money options. However, with such an option, the price is composed of just the investment premium, which may be lost if the stock does not increase in price.

Here is an example of this kind of speculation.

Example 11. You speculate by buying an option contract to purchase 100 shares at $55 a share. The option costs $250. The stock price increases to $63 a share. You exercise the option and sell the shares in the market, recognizing a gain of $550 ($63 – $55 – $2.50 = $5.50 × 100 shares). You, as a speculator, can sell the option and earn a profit due to the appreciated value. But if the stock price drops, your loss is limited to $250 (the option's cost). Obviously, there will also be commissions. In sum, this call option allowed you to buy 100 shares worth $5,500 for $250 up to the option's expiration date.

Straddling combines a put and call on the identical security with the same strike price and expiration date. It allows you to trade on both sides of the market. You hope for a substantial change in stock price either way so as to earn a gain exceeding the cost of both options. If the price change does materialize, the loss is the cost of both options. You may increase risk and earning potential by closing one option prior to the other.

Example 12. You buy a call and a put for $8 each on October 31 when the stock price is $82. There is a three-month expiration date. Your investment is $16, or $1,600 in total. If the stock increases to $150 at expiration of the options, the call generates a profit of $60 ($68 – $8) and the loss on the put is $8. Your net gain is $52, or $5,200 in total.

In a *spread*, you buy a call option (long position) and write a call option (short position) in the identical stock. A sophisticated investor may write many spreads to profit from the spread in option premiums. There is substantial return potential but high risk. Different kinds of spreads exist such as a *bull call spread* (two calls having the same expiration date) and a *horizontal spread* (initiated with either two call options or two put options on the identical underlying stock). These two options must be with the same strike price but different expiration dates.

You may purchase straddles and spreads to maximize return or reduce risk. You may buy them through dealers belonging to the *Put and Call Brokers and Dealers Association.*

HOW OPTION WRITING WORKS

The writer of a call contracts to sell shares at the strike price for the price incurred for the call option. Call option writers do the opposite of buyers. Investors write options expecting price appreciation in the stock to be less than what the call buyer anticipates. They may even anticipate the price of the stock to be stable or to decrease. Option writers receive the option premium less applied transaction costs. If the option is not exercised, the writer earns the price he paid for it. If the option is exercised, the writer incurs a loss, possibly significant.

If the writer of an option elects to sell, he must give the stock at the contracted price if the option is exercised. In either instance, the option writer receives income from the premium. (Shares are in denominations of 100.) An investor typically sells an option when he anticipates it not to be exercised. The risk of option writing is that the writer, if uncovered, must purchase stock or, if covered, loses the gain. As the writer, you can purchase back an option to end your exposure.

Example 13. Assume a strike price of $50 and a premium for the call option of $7. If the stock is below $50, the call would not be exercised, and you earn the $7 premium. If the stock is above $50, the call may be exercised, and you must furnish 100 shares at $50. But the call writer loses money if the stock price is above $57.

SELLING AN OPTION ON SOMETHING YOU DON'T OWN

Naked (uncovered) and *covered* options exist. Naked options are on stock the writer does not own. There is much risk because you have to buy the stock and then immediately sell it to the option buyer on demand, irrespective of how much you lose. The investor writes the call or put for the premium and will retain it if the price change is beneficial to him or insignificant. The writer has unlimited loss possibilities.

To eliminate this risk, you may write *covered options* (options written on stocks you own). For instance, a call can be written for stock the writer owns or a put can be written for stock sold short. This is a conservative strategy to generate positive returns. The objective is to write an out-of-the-money option, retain the premium paid, and have the stock price equal but not exceed the option exercise price. The writing of a covered call option is like hedging a position, because if the stock price drops, the writer's loss on the security is partly offset against the option premium.

OPTION STRATEGIES

Currently, about 90% of the option strategies implemented by investors are long calls and long puts only. These are the most basic strategies and are the easiest to implement. However, they are usually the riskiest in terms of a traditional measure of risk: variability (uncertainty) of outcomes. A variety of other strategies can offer better returns at less risk.

(1) *Long Call*
    This strategy is implemented simply by purchasing a call option on a stock. This strategy is good for a very bullish stock assessment.

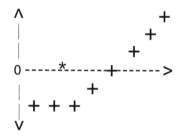

(2) *Bull Call Spread*
    This strategy requires two calls, both with the same expiration date. It is good for a mildly bullish assessment of the underlying stock.

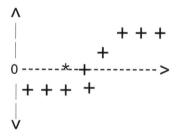

(3) *Naked Put Write*
    This strategy is implemented by writing a put and is appropriate for a neutral or mildly bullish projection on the underlying stock.

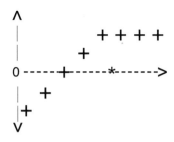

(4) *Covered Call Write*

This strategy is equivalent to the *naked put write.* This strategy is good for a neutral or mildly bullish assessment of the underlying stock.

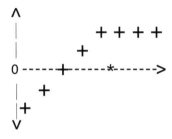

(5) *Straddle*

This strategy is implemented by purchasing both a call and a put option on the same underlying stock. This strategy is good when the underlying stock is likely to make a big move but there is uncertainty as to its direction.

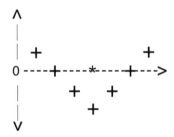

(6) *Inverse Straddle*

This strategy is implemented by writing both a call and a put on the same underlying stock. This strategy is appropriate for a neutral assessment of the underlying stock. A substantial amount of collateral is required for this strategy due to the open-ended risk should the underlying stock make a big move.

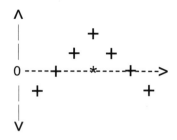

(7) Horizontal Spread

This strategy is implemented with either two call options or two put options on the same underlying stock. These two options must have the same striking price but have different expiration dates.

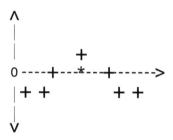

(8) Naked Call Write

This strategy is implemented by writing a call and is appropriate for a neutral or mildly bearish assessment on the underlying stock. A substantial amount of collateral is required for this strategy due to the open-ended risk should the underlying stock rise in value.

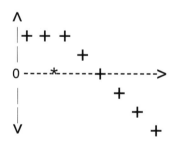

(9) Bear Put Spread

This strategy is the opposite of the bull call spread. It is implemented with two puts, both with the same expiration date. This strategy is appropriate for a mildly bearish assessment of the underlying stock.

Financial Derivative Products and Financial Engineering

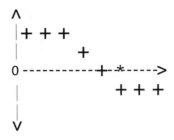

(10) *Long Put*

This strategy is implemented simply by purchasing a put option on a stock. It is good for a very bearish stock assessment.

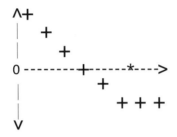

Note: Computer software such as *OptionVue* plots profit tables and diagrams and helps you evaluate large numbers of options for minimum risk and maximum reward.

HOW TO CHOOSE AN OPTION STRATEGY

The key question remains: Which option strategy should you choose? What factors should you consider? What would be a typical decision process? There are three major steps in the decision process:

(1) *Select the underlying stock*

First, you should decide which stock to consider and do a thorough analysis on the stock, including the effects of current market trends.

(2) *Choose the strategy*

You then determine the risk involved in the stock based on its volatility. Computer software can be of great help. Based on the assessment on the stock (bullish or bearish) and its volatility, a strategy is chosen. For example, a strongly bullish, high volatility stock would indicate a long call strategy, since the underlying stock is likely to rise a substantial amount.

The ranking of strategies so far discussed, from bullish to bearish, is as follows:

Bullish	• Long Call • Bull Call Spread • Naked Put Write (Covered Call Write)
Neutral	• Straddle • Inverse Straddle • Horizontal Spread
Bearish	• Naked Call Write • Bear Put Spread • Long Put

Note: The key to choosing the specific option contracts to implement a strategy is to accurately forecast both the price of the underlying stock and the amount of time it will take to get to that price. This will facilitate choosing the striking price and expiration date of the options to be used.

(3) *Assess the risk*

Option strategies have some interesting risk/reward trade-offs. Some strategies have a small chance of a very large profit while other strategies have a large chance of making a small profit.

You have to decide exactly how much to risk for how much reward.

INDEX OPTIONS

Options on stock indexes rather than on individual stocks have been popular among investors. Index options include ones on S&P 100, S&P OTC 250, S&P 500, Gold/Silver Index, and Computer Technology Index.

Index options offer advantages over stock options in several ways:

1. There is greater stability in a stock index due to *diversification.* Since an index is a composite of stocks, the effects of mergers, announcements, and reports are much milder in an index than on an individual stock.

2. Index options provide a wider selection of striking prices and expiration dates than stock options.

3. It appears easier to predict the behavior of the market than an individual stock.

4. More liquidity exists with index options. Due to the high volume of activity, it is easier to buy and sell index options for the price you want. This is especially helpful for far out-of-the-money or deep in-the-money options.

5. Index options are always settled in cash, never in shares of the underlying stock. This settlement is automatic at expiration and the cash settlement prevents unintended stock assignment.

A disadvantage of index options is that no covered writing is possible on index options.

SOFTWARE FOR OPTIONS ANALYSIS

The Value Line Options Survey (800-535-9643 ext. 2854, Dept. 414M10) recommends the few dozen buying and covered writing candidates (out of more than 10,000 options listed on the several exchanges), based on their computerized model.

The following is a list of popular options software:

Stock Option Analysis Program and Stock Options Scanner (DOS)
H&H Scientific, (301) 292-2958

An Option Valuator/An Option Writer (DOS)
Revenge Software, (516) 271-9556

Strategist (DOS)
Iotinomics Corp., (800) 255-3374 or (801) 466-2111

Advanced Stock Option Analyzer (DOS, Mac)
Option-80, (508) 369-1589

Optionvue IV (DOS)
Optionvue Systems International, Inc.
(800) 733-6610 or (708) 816-6610

Option Pro (Windows)
Essex Trading Co., (800) 726-2140 or (708) 416-3530

Options and Arbitrage Software Package (DOS)
Programmed Press, (516) 599-6527

THE BLACK-SCHOLES OPTION PRICING MODEL (OPM)

The model provides the relationship between call option value and the five factors that determine the premium of an option's market value over its expiration value:

1. **Time to maturity.** The longer the option period, the greater the value of the option.
2. **Stock price volatility.** The greater the volatility of the underlying stock's price, the greater its value.
3. **Exercise price.** The lower the exercise price, the greater the value.
4. **Stock price.** The higher the price of the underlying stock, the greater the value.
5. **Risk-free rate.** The higher the risk-free rate, the higher the value.

The formula is:

$$V = P[N(d_1)] - Xe^{-rt}[N(d_2)]$$

where

V = current value of a call option

P = current price of the underlying stock

$N(d)$ = cumulative normal probability density function = probability that a deviation less than d will occur in a standard normal distribution.

X = exercise or strike price of the option

t = time to exercise date (For example, 3 months means $t = 3/12 = 1/4 = 0.25$)

r = (continuously compounded) risk-free rate of interest

e = 2.71828

$$d_1 = \frac{\ln(P/X) + [r + s^2/2]t}{s\sqrt{t}}$$

$$d_2 = \frac{\ln(P/X) + [r + s^2/2]t}{s\sqrt{t}} \text{ or } = d_1 - s\sqrt{t}$$

s^2 = variance per period of (continuously compounded) rate of return on the stock

The formula, while somewhat imposing, actually requires readily available input data, with the exception of s^2, or volatility. P, X, r, and t are easily obtained. The implications of the option model are the following:

1. The value of the option increases with the level of stock price relative to the exercise price (P/X), the time to expiration times the interest rate (rt), and the time to expiration times the stock's variability (s^2t).
2. Other properties:

a. The option price is always less than the stock price.

b. The optional price never falls below the payoff to immediate exercise (P – EX or zero, whichever is larger).

c. If the stock is worthless, the option is worthless.

d. As the stock price becomes very large, the option price approaches the stock price less the present value of the exercise price.

Example 14. You are evaluating a call option that has a $20 exercise price and sells for $1.60. It has three months to expiration. The underlying stock price is also $20 and its variance is 0.16. The risk-free rate is 12%. The option's value is:

First, calculate d_1 and d_2:

$$d_1 = \frac{\ln(P/X) + [r + s^2/2]t}{s\sqrt{t}}$$

$$= \frac{\ln(\$20/\$20) + [0.12 + (0.16/2)](0.25)}{(0.40)\sqrt{0.25}}$$

$$= \frac{0 + 0.05}{0.20} = 0.25$$

$$d_2 = d_1 - s\sqrt{t} = 0.25 - 0.20 = 0.05$$

Next, look up the values for $N(d_1)$ and $N(d_2)$:

$$N(d_1) = N(0.25) = 1 - 0.4013 = 0.5987$$
$$N(d_2) = N(0.05) = 1 - 0.4801 = 0.5199$$

Finally, use those values to find the option's value:

$$V = P[N(d_1)] - Xe^{-rt}[N(d_2)]$$
$$= \$20[0.5987] - \$20e^{(-0.12)(0.25)}[0.5199]$$
$$= \$11.97 - \$19.41(0.5199)$$
$$= \$11.97 - \$10.09 = \$1.88$$

At $1.60, the option is undervalued according to the Black-Scholes model. The rational investor would buy one option and sell .5987 shares of stock short.

Note: Under FASB Statement No. 123, *Accounting for Stock-Based Compensation*, companies are required to provide new footnote disclosures about employee stock options based on their fair value at the date of the grant. Since options granted to employees generally are not traded on an organized exchange, Statement No. 123 requires companies to use recognized option pricing models such as the Black-Scholes model to estimate the fair values.

FUTURES CONTRACTS

Futures are another form of derivative instrument. A futures is a contract to purchase or sell a given amount of an item for a given price by a certain date in the future (thus the name "futures market"). The seller of a futures contract agrees to deliver the item to the buyer of the contract, who agrees to purchase the item. The contract specifies the amount, valuation, method, quality, month, and means of delivery, and exchange to be traded in. The month of delivery is the expiration date; in other words, the date on which the commodity or financial instrument must be delivered.

Commodity contracts are guarantees by a seller to deliver a commodity (e.g., cocoa or cotton). Financial contracts are commitments by the seller to deliver a financial instrument (e.g., a Treasury bill) or a specific amount of foreign currency.

What Is the Difference between a Long and Short Position?

A long position is the purchase of a contract expecting the price to increase. A short position is selling expecting the price to decrease. The position may be terminated by reversing the transaction. For example, the long buyer can subsequently engage in a short position of the commodity or financial instrument. Mostly all futures are offset (canceled out) prior to delivery. It is unusual for delivery to settle the futures contract.

How Are Futures Contracts Traded?

A futures contract is traded in the futures market. Trading is performed by specialized brokers. Some commodity firms deal exclusively in futures. The fee for a futures contract is tied to the amount of the contract and the item's price. Commissions vary depending on the amount and nature of the contract. The trading in futures is basically the same as with stocks, except the investor needs a commodity trading account. However, the margin buying and the types of orders are the same. You buy or sell contracts with desired terms.

FUTURES TRADING AND RISK

Futures trading may assist an investor handling inflation, but is specialized and has much risk. Your loss may be magnified due to *leverage*. Leverage (using of other people's money) means with a minimal down payment you control something of much greater value. For instance, you can put down $2,000 to control a futures contract valued at $40,000. Each time the price of a commodity increases $1, you could earn or lose $20. With an *option,* you lose just the money invested. With a futures contract, you lose a lot more. Further, futures contract prices may be very unstable. However, many exchanges place per-day price limits on each contract trading, to insulate traders from huge losses.

COMMODITIES FUTURES

A commodity contract involves a seller who contracts to deliver a commodity by a specified date at a set price. The contract stipulates the item, price, expiration date, and standardized unit to be traded (e.g., 100,000 pounds). Commodity contracts may last up to one year. You must always appraise the impact of market activity on the contract's value.

Assume that you purchase a futures contract for the delivery of 2,000 units of a commodity six months from now at $5.00 per unit. The seller of the contract does not have to have physical custody of the item, and the contract buyer does not have to take possession of the commodity at the "deliver" date. Commodity contracts are typically reversed, or terminated, before consummation. For example, as the initial buyer of 5,000 bushels of wheat, you may engage in a similar contract to sell the same amount, in effect closing your position.

You may enter into commodity trading to achieve high return rates and hedge inflation. In times of increasing prices, commodities react favorably because they are tied to economic trends. However, there is high risk and uncertainty since commodity prices fluctuate and there is a lot of low-margin investing. You need a lot of cash in case of a margin call to cover losses. To minimize risk, hold a diversified portfolio. Futures contracts are only for knowledgeable and experienced investors.

The buyer of a commodity can opt to terminate the contract or continue holding on expectation of higher profits. Conversely, the investor may use the earnings to furnish margin on another futures contract (called an inverse pyramid in a futures contract).

Commodity futures enable buyers and sellers to negotiate cash (spot) prices. Cash is paid to immediately obtain custody of a commodity. Prices in the cash market depend partly upon prices in the futures market. There may be higher prices for the commodity over time, taking into account carrying costs and expected inflation.

Commodity futures are traded in the *Chicago Board of Trade (CBOT),* the largest exchange. There are other exchanges specializing in particular commodities such as the *New York Cotton Exchange (NCTN)*, *Chicago Mercantile Exchange (CME)*, and *Kansas City Board of Trade (KBOT)*. Because of the possibility of substantial gains and losses in commodities, exchanges have caps on the highest daily price changes for a commodity. The *Federal Commodity Futures Trading Commission* regulates commodities exchanges. Commodity futures trading is accomplished through open outcry auction.

RETURNS AND RISKS FOR FUTURES CONTRACTS

The return on a futures contract stems from capital appreciation (selling price less acquisition cost) because no current income is earned. Significant capital gain may arise from price fluctuation in the commodity and the impact of leverage due to low margin. If things go against you, much of your investment may be lost. The return on investment in commodities (a long or short position) equals:

$$\text{Return on investment} = \frac{\text{Selling price} - \text{purchase price}}{\text{Margin deposit}}$$

Example 15. Assume you buy a contract on a commodity for $80,000, with a deposit of $10,000. Subsequently, you sell the contract for $85,000. The return is:

$$\frac{\$85,000 - \$80,000}{\$10,000} = 50\%$$

The margin requirement for commodity contracts is small, typically from 3% to 6% of the contract's value. (For stocks, recall that the margin requirement is 50%.) Because in commodities trading there is no loan involved, there is no interest.

An *initial margin deposit* must be made on a futures contract so as to cover a drop in market price on the contract. Such deposit varies with the type of contract and the particular commodity exchange.

A *maintenance deposit* may also be required, which is lower than the initial deposit. It furnishes the minimum margin that must be kept in the account. It is typically about 80% of the initial margin.

Example 16. On September 1, you contract to purchase 50,000 pounds of sugar at $2 a pound to be delivered by December 31. The value of the total contract is $100,000. The initial margin requirement is 15%, or $15,000. The margin maintenance requirement is 80%, or $12,000. Assuming a contract loss of $2,500, you must pay $2,500 to cover the margin position. If not, the contract will be terminated with the ensuing loss.

WHO USES FUTURES?

Trading in futures is performed by hedgers and speculators. Investors employ hedging to protect their positions in a commodity. For instance, a farmer (the seller) may hedge to obtain a higher price for goods while a processor (or buyer) of the product will hedge to get a lower price. By hedging you reduce the risk of loss but forego earning a sizable profit.

Example 17. A commodity is presently selling at $160 a pound. The potential buyer (assume a manufacturer) anticipates the price to increase. To protect against higher prices, the purchaser buys a futures contract selling at $175 a pound. Five months later, the commodity price is $225. The futures contract price will similarly increase, say to $250. The buyer's profit is $75 a pound. If 10,000 pounds are involved, the total profit is $750,000. However, the cost on the market rose by only $65 pound, or $650,000. The producer has hedged the position, deriving a profit of $100,000, and has put a tip on the rising commodity costs.

Commodities may also be used for speculation in the market. Speculators engage in futures contracts to obtain capital gain on price increases of the commodity, currency, or financial instrument.

Example 18. You buy a September futures contract for 20,000 pounds of wheat at $2 a pound. If the price rises to $2.20, you'll gain $.20 a pound for a total gain of $4,000. The percent gain, assuming an initial margin requirement of 5%, is 200% ($.2/$.1). Assuming transactions occur over a three-month period, the annual gain would be 800% (200% × 12 months/3 months). This resulted from a mere 10% ($.2/$2.00) gain in the price of a pound of wheat.

HOW TO MINIMIZE RISKS

Spreading capitalizes on wide swings in price and at the same time limits loss exposure. Spreading is like stock option trading. You engage in at least two contracts to earn some profit while capping loss potential. You buy one contract and sell the other, expecting to achieve a reasonable profit. If the worst occurs, the spread aids in minimizing the investor's loss.

Example 19. You buy Contract A for 20,000 pounds of commodity T at $300 a pound. Simultaneously, you sell short Contract B for 20,000 pounds of the identical commodity at $325 per pound. Later, you sell Contract A for $325 a pound and buy Contract B for $345 a pound. Contract A earns a profit of $25 a pound while Contract B has a loss of $20 a pound. The net effect is a profit of $5 a pound, or a total gain of $100,000.

FINANCIAL FUTURES

Financial futures include: (1) interest rate; (2) foreign currency; and (3) stock index. Financial futures trading is similar to commodity trading. It represents about 70 percent of all contracts. Due to fluctuation in interest and exchange rates, financial futures can be used as a hedge. They may also be used to speculate, having potential for wide price swings. Financial futures have a *lower* margin requirement than commodities do. For instance, the margin on a U.S. Treasury bill might be as low as 2%.

Financial futures are traded in the *New York Futures Exchange, Amex Commodities Exchange, International Monetary Market* (part of *Chicago Mercantile Exchange*), and the *Chicago Board of Trade*.

How Do Interest Rate Futures Work?

An interest rate futures contract gives the holder the right to a specified amount of the underlying debt security at a later date (typically not exceeding three years). They may be in such forms as Treasury bills, notes, and bonds, paper, "Ginnie Mae (GNMA)" certificates, CRB Index, Eurodollars, and U.S. Dollar Index.

Interest rate futures are expressed as a percentage of the face value of the applicable debt security. The value of interest rate futures contracts is linked to interest rates. For instance, as interest rates drop, the contract's value rises. If the price or quote of the contract increases, the buyer gains but the seller loses. A change of one basis point in interest rates causes a price change. A basis point equals 1/100 of 1%.

Those trading in interest rate futures do not typically take custody of the financial instrument. The contract is employed either to hedge or to speculate on future interest rates and security prices.

How Do Currency Futures Work?

A *currency futures contract* provides the right to a stipulated amount of foreign currency at a later date. The contracts are standardized, and secondary markets exist. Currency futures are stated in dollars per unit of the underlying foreign currency. They usually have a delivery date not exceeding one year.

Currency futures may be used either to hedge or speculate. Hedging in a currency may lock you into the best possible money exchange.

WHAT IS A STOCK INDEX FUTURE?

A *stock index futures contract* is linked to a stock market index (e.g., the *S & P 500 Stock Index, New York Stock Exchange Composite Stock Index*). But smaller investors can use the *S & P 100* futures contract, which has a lower margin deposit. Stock index futures allow you to participate in the overall stock market. You can buy and sell the "market as a whole" instead of one security. If you expect a bull market but are not certain which stock will increase, you should purchase (long position) a stock index future. Since there is a lot of risk, trade in stock index futures only to hedge.

TRANSACTING IN FUTURES

You may invest directly in a commodity or indirectly through a *mutual fund*. A third way is to buy a *limited partnership* involved with commodity investments. The mutual fund and partnership approaches are more conservative, because risk is spread and there is professional management.

Futures may be directly invested in as follows:

1. *Commodity pools.* Professional traders manage a pool. A filing is made with the *Commodity Futures Trading Commission (CFTC).*
2. *Full-service brokers.* They may recommend something, when attractive.
3. *Discount brokers.* You must decide on your own when and if to trade.
4. *Managed futures.* You deposit funds in an individual managed account and choose a *commodity trading advisor (CTA)* to trade it.

To obtain information on managed futures, refer to:

1. *ATA Research Inc.* provides information on trading advisors and manages individuals accounts via private pools and funds.
2. *Barclay Trading Group* publishes quarterly reports on trading advisers.
3. *CMA Reports* monitors the performance of trading advisers and private pools.
4. *Management Account Reports,* monthly newsletters, track the funds and furnish information on their fees and track records.
5. *Trading Advisor* follows more than 100 trading advisers.

There are several drawbacks to managed futures, including:

1. High cost of a futures program, ranging from 15 to 20 percent of the funds invested.

2. Substantial risk and inconsistent performance of fund advisors. *Note:* Despite its recent popularity, management futures is still a risky choice and should not be done apart from a well-diversified portfolio.

PRINTED CHART SERVICES AND SOFTWARE FOR FUTURES

There are many printed chart services such as *Future Charts* (Commodity Trend Service, (800) 331-1069 or (407) 694-0960). Also, there are many computer software programs for futures analysis and charting services, including:

Strategist (DOS)
Iotinomics Corp., (800) 255-3374 or (801) 466-2111

Futures Pro (Windows)
Essex Trading Co., (800) 726-2140 or (708) 416-3530

Futures Markets Analyzer (DOS)
Investment Tools, Inc., (702) 851-1157

Commodities and Futures Software Package, Foreign Exchange
Software Package (DOS)
Programmed Press, (516) 599-6527

FINANCIAL ENGINEERING

Closely related to the use of financial derivatives for risk management is *financial engineering*. Financial engineering, an obscure term in finance and investments, is based on financial economics, or the application of economic principles to the dynamics of securities markets, especially for the purpose of structuring, pricing, and managing the risk of financial contracts. In designing a risk-management strategy, the financial engineer, like the civil engineer designing a bridge, works within budgetary and physical restrictions. How much will it cost? How will it perform under present and future tax and accounting regulations and rules? Will it survive a financial earthquake, such as an opposite party's default? Will the strategy perform even if the market moves abruptly and severely? Basically, to be successful, the financial engineer must seek optimal solutions within many diverse and often conflicting constraints.

These varied restrictions lead to different solutions. Financial engineers can design different types of financial instruments or strategies to produce a desired outcome. Robert C. Merton has presented a concrete example of the financial engineer's ability to develop alternative routes to the same end, all basically similar but each with its pros and cons (*Journal of Banking and Finance,* June 1995). For instance, assume a corporate investor wishes to take a leveraged position in the S&P 500 basket of American stocks. Merton lists and dwells on eleven ways of accomplishing that goal. The first three are conventional ways: borrowing to buy stocks.

1. Buying each stock individually on the margin.
2. Borrowing to buy shares in a S&P 500 index fund.
3. Borrowing to purchase a basket of stocks such as AMEX's SPDR product.

The next three are products in which traditional financial intermediaries act as principals and offer payoffs that closely emulate the leveraged stock position; the actual products are structured as bank CDs, indexed notes, or variable rate annuities. The last five categories of alternatives deal with buying so-called financial derivatives, such as futures, forwards, swaps, or one of two options on the S&P index. They are so called in that their payoffs are a function (or are derived from) the value of an underlying index.

Each of the eleven instruments or strategies can give the investor exposure to the stock market, and each produces functionally similar payoffs. The multitude of solutions exists due to the differing constraints facing the financial engineer. It is important to realize that as bridges often collapse, financial engineered products can fail, and examining their wreckage to determine culpability is equally difficult.

Nevertheless, financial managers need to benchmark and keep abreast of their rivals' successful uses of financial engineering. CPAs need to be familiar with financial derivative products. The issuance of FASB 123, *Accounting for Stock-Based Compensation,* means CPAs who prepare and audit the financial statements of the companies that issue employee stock options will need to become familiar with option pricing models—including the Black-Scholes model. The new standard says the fair value of options at the date of the grant must be disclosed in a footnote.

Option theory has many applications addressed to CFOs and other financial officers. Besides the Black-Scholes solution for a relatively simple option, many capital budgeting projects have option components: Corporate debt is callable or convertible, a decision may be made to prepay a mortgage, labor contracts may endow options on workers (e.g., the choice of early retirement), real estate leases can be renewed, a mine can be opened or closed, and bank lines of credit often contain contingent elements. The correct valuations of so many interest-rate-contingent securities depend on a satisfactory dynamic model of the interest rate process.

FORENSIC ACCOUNTING*

Forensic accounting is a science (i.e., a department of systemized knowledge) dealing with the application of accounting facts gathered through auditing methods and procedures to resolve legal problems. Forensic accounting is much different from traditional auditing. The main purpose of a traditional audit is to examine the financial statements of an organization and express an opinion on the fairness of the financial statements. In other words, auditors give an opinion whether the financial statements have been prepared in accordance with generally accepted accounting principles. Auditors employ limited procedures and use extensive testing and sampling techniques. Audits are performed by independent accountants and are not conducted with a view to presenting the evidence in a judicial forum. An audit is not an investigation; its main objective is not to uncover fraud.

Forensic accounting, on the other hand, is for investigation of an allegation with the assumption that the forensic accountant will have to present the evidence in a judicial forum. A forensic accountant often employs specialists in other areas as part of a team to gather evidence. In order to present the evidence in court, there must be absolute assurance; thus testing and sampling methods are usually not employed as part of the evidence-gathering procedures. The scope of the investigation is limited because it is determined by the client.

Forensic accounting, therefore, is a specialty requiring the integration of investigative, accounting, and auditing skills. The forensic accountant looks at documents and financial and other data in a critical manner in order to draw conclusions and to calculate values, and to identify irregular patterns and/or suspicious transactions. A forensic accountant understands the fraud risk areas and has extensive fraud knowledge. A forensic accountant does not merely look at the numbers but rather, looks *behind* the numbers.

---

*This chapter is contributed by Frank Grippo, Dean, School of Business, William Paterson University.

One can extend this definition to say that forensic accounting is a discipline consisting of two areas of specialization; namely, litigation support specialists and investigation or fraud accountants. Litigation support specialists concern themselves with business valuation, testimony as expert witnesses, future earnings evaluation, and income and expense analysis. On the other hand, fraud accountants apply their skills to investigate areas of alleged criminal misconduct in order to support or dispel damages. These fields overlap: A forensic accountant may do litigation support work on one engagement and act as a fraud accountant on another. Both of these engagements could result in expert testimony by the forensic accountant. Thus, forensic accounting can be defined in a more generic way: It is merely a discipline whereby auditing, accounting, and investigative skills are used to assist in disputes involving financial issues and data, and where there is suspicion or allegation of fraud. The expertise of the forensic accountant may be used to support a plaintiff who is trying to establish a claim, or to support a defendant in order to minimize the impact of a claim against him or her. Usually such investigations involve litigation; sometimes, however, such disputes are settled by negotiation. In either case, persuasive and authoritative evidence resulting from the financial and investigative skills of the forensic accountant is imperative. Therefore, the forensic accountant must be a good businessperson and be aware of statutory law, common law, and the laws of evidence and procedure.

Usually the forensic accountant's findings are based on facts, not opinions. Facts can be investigated, and the forensic accountant can prepare a definitive report on these facts. Nevertheless, there are situations in which the forensic accountant may rely on professional judgment and present findings using an opinion-type report. Needless to say, the reports based on facts usually do not present problems in court cases because they are supported by underlying documentation. Opinion reports, on the other hand, are subjective and require the forensic accountant to demonstrate competency and to provide adequate logic for the stated opinion.

Two points are often overlooked when one is involved in a case as a forensic accountant; namely, (1) the other side usually employs a forensic accountant as well, and (2) the credibility of a forensic accountant is extremely important. Thus the forensic accountant must have high professional standards and ethics.

WHY IS FORENSIC ACCOUNTING NECESSARY?

Business and criminal activities have become so complex that lawyers and criminal investigators often do not have the expertise necessary to discharge their responsibilities. This fact plus the marked increase in white-collar crime, marital and business disputes, and other claims have created the need for the new industry of forensic accounting. Although this specialty is not limited to fraud issues, nevertheless, the reality of forensic accounting is that most of the work does involve fraud investigations. In the case of fraud, the work of a forensic accounting team is crucial, as the survival of the business may rest on the outcome. Good businesspeople must realize that fraud is a permanent risk in any and all businesses. Thus company leaders must devise ways to prevent fraud rather than trying to manage the consequences of fraud. The instances of fraud have increased because of lack of government commitment, more sophisticated criminals, inefficiency of the judicial system, more complex technology, lack of adequate penalties and deterrents, and old-fashioned greed and arrogance. Studies have shown that fraud will continue to increase. Currently, about 75% of fraud results from employees; other sources of fraud include customers, management, suppliers, and service providers. In addition, about 55% of fraud is discovered as a result of strong internal controls. Other methods of discovery include whistle-blowers, customers, internal auditors, and accidental or formal investigation.

WHEN DOES ONE EMPLOY A FORENSIC ACCOUNTANT?

Clients retain forensic accountants when they are interested in either litigation support or investigations.

Litigation Support

This is a situation in which the forensic accountant is asked to give an opinion either on known facts or facts yet uncovered. The forensic accountant is an integral part of the legal team, helping to substantiate allegations, analyze facts, dispute claims, and develop motives. The amount of involvement and the point at which the forensic accountant gets involved vary from case to case. Sometimes the forensic accountant is called upon from the beginning of the case; at other times the forensic accountant is summoned before the case is scheduled to go to court and after out-of-court settlements have failed. Thus, in litigation support, the forensic accountant assists in obtaining documentation to support or dispel a claim, reviewing documentation to give an assessment of the case to the legal team, and/or identifying areas where loss occurred. Moreover, the forensic accountant may be asked to get involved during the discovery stage to help formulate questions, and may be asked to review the opposing expert's witness report to give an evaluation of its strengths and weaknesses. During trial, the forensic accountant may serve as an expert witness, help to provide questions for cross-examination, and assist with settlement discussions after the trial.

Investigations

Investigations most often involve fraud and are associated with criminal matters. Typically, an investigative accounting assignment would result from a client's suspicion that there is employee fraud. Other parties, such as regulatory agencies, police forces, and attorneys, may retain a forensic accountant to investigate securities fraud, kickbacks, insurance fraud, money-laundering schemes, and asset search and analysis.

WHERE IS A FORENSIC ACCOUNTANT USED?

A forensic accountant is used in a number of situations, including, but not limited to the following:

- *Business valuations:* A forensic accountant evaluates the current value of a business for various personal or legal matters.

- *Personal injury and fatal accident claims:* A forensic accountant may help to establish lost earnings (i.e., those earnings that the plaintiff would have accrued except for the actions of the defendant) by gathering and analyzing a variety of information and then issuing a report based on the outcome of the analyses.

- *Professional negligence:* A forensic accountant helps to determine if a breach of professional ethics or other standards of professional practice has occurred (e.g., failure to apply generally accepted auditing standards by a CPA when performing an audit). In addition, the forensic accountant may help to quantify the loss.

- *Insurance claims evaluations:* A forensic accountant may prepare financial analyses for an insurance company of claims, business income and losses, expenses, and disability, liability, or worker's compensation insurance losses.

- *Arbitration:* A forensic accountant is sometimes retained to assist with alternative dispute resolution (ADR) by acting as a mediator to allow individuals and businesses to resolve disputes in a timely manner with a minimum of disruption.

- *Partnership and corporation disputes:* A forensic accountant may be asked to help settle disputes between partners or shareholders. Detailed analyses are often necessary of many records spanning a number of years. Most of these disputes relate to compensation and benefit issues.

- *Civil and criminal actions concerning fraud and financial irregularities:* These investigations are usually performed by the forensic accountant for police forces. A report is prepared to assist the prosecutor's office.

- *Fraud and white-collar crime investigations:* These types of investigations can be prepared on behalf of police forces as well as for private businesses. They usually result from such activities as purchasing/kickback schemes, computer fraud, labor fraud, and falsification of inventory. The investigation by the forensic accountant often involves fund tracing, asset identification, and recovery.

HOW DOES A FORENSIC ACCOUNTANT WORK?

Although each case is distinct and requires accounting and auditing procedures unique to the assignment, many forensic accounting assignments would include the following steps:

- *Meet with the client:* The forensic accountant should meet with the client to determine the scope of the engagement. In addition, it is advisable to obtain an engagement letter specifying the terms of the engagement.
- *Determine independence:* It is understood that a CPA should be independent when performing an audit or other attest services for clients. It is mandatory as well that the forensic accountant be independent, otherwise the credibility of the forensic accountant will be questioned if the engagement results in a legal case.
- *Plan the engagement:* Proper advance planning is essential to any type of engagement. The plan should be similar to an audit program, detailing objectives and procedures in a form that addresses the scope of the engagement so that some type of conclusion can be reached.
- *Gather evidence and perform analyses:* The forensic accountant should match the auditing, accounting, or investigative technique employed with the type of evidence to be obtained. A specific technique may satisfy more than one objective. When the forensic accountant, for example, performs an audit technique for a particular account, evidence for other accounts may be discovered based on the double-entry system of accounting. Forensic accountants use a variety of techniques including inquiry, confirmation, physical examination, observation, inspection, reconciliation, tracing, vouching, reperformance, and analytical procedures.
- *Arrive at a conclusion and prepare the report:* The forensic accountant should write the final report in a manner that clearly explains the nature of the assignment and the scope of the work. It should indicate the approach used for discovery of information, and detail findings and/or opinions.

A CASE IN FORENSIC ACCOUNTING

The following is an actual case involving the purchase of a business. The plaintiff alleges that the records shown to him were not accurate and that the lawyer who handled the closing for him was negligent.

MAGYAR, INC.

A Case Study in Fraud

"Since I was a little boy, I wanted to own a business. I never wanted to work for anyone else," Omar Saleem said to his wife, Sylvia.

Omar Saleem was 50 years old, came to the United States 30 years ago, and has worked for a large furniture manufacturer for 28 years. One day, he was reading the classified advertisements of the newspaper and noticed an office business for sale in the next town. He discussed the idea with his wife and she approved. So he contacted the seller and made an appointment.

Three days later Omar met with Rahman Magyar, the sole owner of Magyar, Inc. Rahman was an engaging individual, very smooth and personable. Omar was very impressed with Rahman's knowledge of the business and with his self-confidence. Rahman told Omar that he was selling the business because he was bored with it. He had built the company from nothing into a very successful business and now wanted to try something else. Omar believed everything that Rahman said. Rahman said he would be glad to open his books to Omar, but would require a good-faith, refundable deposit of $1,000. Omar agreed and made another appointment for the following week.

Omar met with Rahman and gave the $1,000 good-faith deposit. Rahman in turn showed Omar his equipment and inventory and explained more about the business. Specifically he told him that he averages about $120,000 per year in office supplies and equipment sales, and about $30,000 in services. The latter is a mail service whereby he prepares and mails packages for customers. Rahman produced a fee schedule and claimed that this end of the business had been very lucrative. After showing Omar the inventory, Rahman flashed some papers and tax returns in front of Omar to show him the growth since he opened the business in February 1994. Rahman said that the business had averaged about 20% growth each year. Omar looked at the papers, but actually didn't know what he was looking at. Furthermore, Rahman assured him that the paperwork was in order since his brother-in-law prepared it. He said his brother-in-law, Raj Kupar, was a CPA and that everything was in order. Rahman said that he would sell the business for $160,000, which is less than the normal selling price for this type of business. He said that the selling price is usually one times annual sales. He further said that "since you and I are from the same country, I will help you out. I prefer to sell to you over someone else."

He convinced Omar that he could easily make $75,000 from the business. Furthermore, he suggested that Omar move fast as there were a number of people interested in the business. Omar said that he would have to get an attorney. He promised to get back to Rahman in a week or so. Rahman even suggested an attorney.

Omar was quite excited and couldn't wait to get home to tell his wife. His wife was very supportive. Therefore, Omar asked his good friend, Stanley, if he knew an attorney. Stanley referred him to Neil Klavin, an attorney in town. On the following Monday, Omar called the attorney and made an appointment for Friday of that week. Before the meeting, Omar called Rahman and asked if he would accept $150,000 for the business. Rahman said that he would, but he wanted cash and that he would not want to finance the business. Omar said that he had $110,000 in cash, but would require a loan of $40,000. Rahman surprisingly agreed to finance $40,000, but wanted 8% interest. They verbally agreed. Omar said that he was going to see an attorney on Friday to explain the deal. Rahman said that was great.

On Friday, Omar went to the attorney, Neil Klavin, with his wife. Omar and the attorney discussed the business deal at length. Klavin said that he would be happy to represent Omar and would gladly review the contract drawn up by Rahman's attorney. Omar told the attorney that he had seen some documentation regarding income and expenses including the tax returns. Omar told the Klavin that he would like him to review the documentation as well. The attorney said fine. Omar left the office and then contacted Rahman. He gave Rahman his attorney's name and told him to have his lawyers draw up the paperwork. Omar's wife asked if he was moving a little too fast. Omar said that he had to move fast as it was a good deal and Rahman had other interested buyers. He felt comfortable that his attorney would say it was a good deal after the attorney reviewed the numbers.

About two weeks later, Neil Klavin received the financial information from Rahman's attorney along with a contract of sale and promissory note for $40,000 at 8% interest. Neil reviewed the information and appeared to find everything in order. Although he did not understand the financials and tax returns that well, he did not suggest to Omar that anything was improper. Nor did he suggest soliciting the help of an expert. For example, he did not suggest contacting a CPA to review the books, financials, and tax returns. The closing was scheduled for December 27, 1996. Rahman and Omar appeared at the closing with their wives. The contract and promissory note were signed. Omar was to start on the following Monday. Rahman agreed to stay around for a month to train both Omar and his wife. Since this was a family business (husband and wife), they only had the need for occasional casual labor. Rahman never had a payroll.

Omar showed up on January 2, 1997 eager to learn all about the business. He met Rahman, who turned over the keys to the store. Rahman was very gracious and patient as he explained things to Omar and his wife. This went on for the whole month as agreed upon at closing. During the month, Omar and his wife discussed the relative inactivity. They even mentioned this to Rahman, who replied that January is always slow because it is after the holidays. Rahman said don't worry as December more than makes up for January. Omar and his wife didn't think too much about it.

Omar was now on his own. He and his wife worked diligently at the business each day. His wife prepared advertisements for the newspaper and ran a number of specials. They methodically kept track of daily revenues and expenses. It became apparent after seven months that the volume was nothing like Rahman had said. They both wondered what they were doing wrong. They were somewhat in denial and did not want to think that they may have been misled and/or tricked. They talked between themselves and decided to talk to an attorney, but not Neil Klavin. Instead they discussed the matter with one of their customers, an attorney named Ted Rich. Ted often came into the store to buy supplies and do special mailings of packages. He took a personal interest in both Omar and his wife, Sylvia. Therefore, he suggested that they make an appointment and discuss the matter further.

Omar and Sylvia talked more about the problem. Another two months went by without any appreciable increase in sales numbers. Finally they made an appointment with Ted Rich. Omar did most of the talking. He also brought copies of all the paperwork that he had, including any financial information that he received from Rahman. He also included summaries of his revenues and expenses for the last nine months. They discussed alternatives. Ted asked a number of pertinent questions including whether Omar had an accountant, preferably a CPA, to review the financial information that he received from Rahman. Omar said that he hadn't. He said that he gave all the information to his attorney to review. Omar made it clear to Ted that he depended on his attorney, Neil Klavin, for advice. Ted was not in the business of suing other attorneys, however, he was upset that Klavin was so sloppy with the closing. He knew that Omar and his wife were naïve. Nevertheless, that was no excuse for not following due diligence procedures. He believed that Klavin should have realized this and looked out for the welfare of his client. Not wanting to make an immediate decision, Ted told Omar that he would review the information and get back to him in a couple of weeks.

A few days later, Ted reviewed the file and decided that the best way to handle the case was to get an accountant to review the financial information, including the tax returns for 1994, 1995, and 1996. Ted called Omar to ask for approval to retain an accountant. Omar agreed.

The next day Ted called George Spyros, a CPA and CFE (certified fraud examiner). George had a small forensic practice and had done work for Ted in the past. Ted and George met for about an hour the following day.

George looked at the financial statements and tax returns. The first thing George did was check to see if Rahman's brother-in-law was indeed a CPA. He was not. The reason he did that first was because his cursory review of the tax returns revealed gross preparation errors. It took George only about eight hours to do a detailed review of the paperwork. George then prepared a report for Ted (Exhibit A).

Ted reviewed the report prepared by Spyros and Company. Based on the report and his discussions with George Spyros, he decided to take the case and pursue suing Neil Klavin. Over the next few months, Ted diligently worked on the case, including obtaining interrogatories from a number of individuals including Omar and his wife, Rahman Magyar, and Neil Klavin.

Ted knew that the case was not solid. Therefore, he asked for the opinion of another attorney, Richard Darius of Darius and Spivack. He also asked for a second opinion from Edward Caruso. Both of these attorneys had experience suing other attorneys. Their opinions can be found in Exhibit B and Exhibit C, respectively.

Since the two attorneys had different opinions, Ted thought that it would be in the best interest of his client to try to settle out of court.

Exhibit A

SPYROS AND COMPANY

CERTIFIED PUBLIC ACCOUNTANTS
447 PEARL STREET
WOODBRIDGE, NEW JERSEY 07095

Mr. Theodore R. Rich
400 Pearl Street
Woodbridge, New Jersey 07095

Dear Mr. Rich,

In accordance with your request, we have reviewed the Federal income tax returns (Form 1120) of Magyar, Inc. for the eleven months ended December 31, 1994, and the years ended December 31, 1995 and 1996. The purpose of our review was to obtain reasonable assurance about whether the tax returns are free of material misstatement. Our review included examining the propriety of the amounts presented on the returns based on analytical procedures. Specifically, we have determined that:

(1) The company employed the accrual basis of accounting (see box checked on page 2 of the 1994 return). Since the balance sheets each year do not show any accounts receivable or accounts payable, one can logically conclude that all revenues and expenses were for cash.

(2) Based on the conclusion reached in (1) above, the cash balances reflected on the balance sheets on page 4 of the 1995 and 1996 tax returns are not reasonable. This fact can be supported by the following reconciliation:

Increase (decrease) in cash—

Cash balance at inception	$—
Issuance of stock in 1994	7,536
Loans in 1994	29,438
Equipment	(16,251)
Sales	101,792
Cost of sales	(118,326)
Expenses (excluding depreciation of $638)	(25,812)
Cash balance on December 31, 1994 should be	$(21,623)
Cash balance on December 31, 1994 per tax return	$250

Comments: It is unreasonable for cost of sales to be more than sales. Cash is misstated by $21,873.

Recalculated cash balance on January 1, 1995	$(21,623)
Additional issuance of stock in 1995	23,960
Payoff of loans	(29,438)
Sales	141,158
Cost of sales	(139,617)
Expenses (excluding depreciation of $638)	(38,102)
Cash balance on December 31, 1995 should be	$(63,662)
Cash balance on December 31, 1995 per tax return	$250

Comments: It is unreasonable for cost of sales to be 99% of sales. Cash is misstated cumulatively by $63,912.

Recalculated cash balance on January 1, 1996	$(63,662)
Sales	157,572
Cost of sales	(145,710)
Expenses (excluding depreciation of $638)	(24,417)
Cash balance on December 31, 1996 should be	$(76,217)
Cash balance on December 31, 1996 per tax return	$295

Comments: it is unreasonable for cost of sales to be 93% of sales. Cash is misstated cumulatively by $76,512.

We also compared the tax returns to the internal financial statements prepared by Raj Kupar, who we understand is a CPA and brother-in-law of the prior owner of the business, Rahman Magyar. Please be advised that we could not find a relationship between the financial statements and the tax returns. The tax returns were materially different from the internal financial statements. Revenues on the internal financials were approximately $15,000 higher in 1994, $18,000 lower in 1995 and $30,000 higher in 1996. There appeared to be only a partial listing of expenses, such that 1994 showed a profit of $70,000, 1995 a profit of $65,000 and 1996 a profit of $74,000. The costs and expenses were substantially less than those shown on the tax returns. In addition, the tax returns reflected substantial losses each year. Finally, the internal financial statements were not prepared in accordance with generally accepted accounting principles.

You also asked us to check whether or not Mr. Kupar is a practicing CPA in New Jersey. We did check with the New Jersey State Board of Public Accountants. He is neither a licensed CPA or licensed public accountant.

Thank you for the opportunity of serving you. If you have any questions about this report, please contact us directly.

Woodbridge, New Jersey
July 24, 1998

Exhibit B

DARIUS AND SPIVACK
One Main Street
Hackensack, NJ 07601

March 25, 1999

Theodore R. Rich, Esq.
100 Pearl Street
Woodbridge, New Jersey 07095

Re: Saleem v. Klavin

Dear Mr. Rich:

This report relates to an action for legal malpractice brought by your clients, **Omar and Sylvia Saleem against Neil Klavin,** a member of the New Jersey Bar. It derives from your request for my opinion as to whether third-party defendant Klavin breached any duty to his former clients, the third-party plaintiffs herein, when he undertook to represent them in July, 1996, with respect to the purchase of a certain office supply and mail box business, known as Magyar, Inc., located at 189 Princeton Road, Woodbridge, New Jersey.

For purposes of this report, I have read, analyzed and relied upon multiple documents contained in all your litigation files, including the February, 9, 1998 depositions of Omar Saleem, Sylvia Saleem and Rahman Magyar; the December 27, 1996 Contract of Sale between Magyar, Inc., and Omar and Sylvia Saleem; the January 4, 1997 addendum to closing statement; the January 2, 1997 Lease between Magyar, Inc. and Marjama Company; Rahman Magyar's answers to interrogatories; the December 27, 1996 note from Omar and Sylvia Saleem to Rahman Magyar; correspondence between attorneys D'Orio (for seller) and Klavin (for buyer) dated respectively October 14, 1996 and November 2, 1996 and December 3, 1996. Kindly note that the documents listed above do not include all the materials examined by me, such as all correspondence between and among the parties, all pleadings, all discovery, and the like. Most especially did I review and analyze the July 24, 1998 expert report of Spyros and Company, Certified Public Accountants, rendered on behalf of Omar and Sylvia Saleem.

STATEMENT OF FACTS

In early 1996, Omar Saleem, a native of Syria, but living and working in the United States since 1966, expressed interest in buying a small business. He read about a business for sale in the local newspaper. He answered the advertisement and soon met one Rahman Magyar, the owner of Magyar, Inc., a company engaged in the office supply and mail service business. Later, at a meeting held in the Rahman Magyar's office, Omar verbally said that he was interested in purchasing the business. About a week later Saleem called Magyar. The two agreed on a price of $150,000 including a $40,000 promissory note to Magyar. During the course of the preliminary negotiations, Magyar had assured the Saleems that the business was a very simple operation which they would have no problem understanding and that he would agree to work a month in the business free of charge to train both Omar and his wife. For whatever reason, Magyar never offered the Saleems an opportunity to examine the books and records of the Company, or to have them examined by an outside accountant. However, he did show them some tax returns and financial statements prepared by his brother-in-law, whom he alleged was a CPA. After the closing, Magyar did provide on-the-job training, but it was hurried and did not afford the Saleems hardly any opportunity to understand the economics of the business.

The essential complaint of the Saleems is that their attorney Klavin failed to provide them with appropriate legal advice and counsel in connection with the actual purchase of the business. In this regard the Saleems contend that Klavin failed to incorporate certain conditions and contingencies in the December 27, 1997 contract which would have made the sale subject to a review of all books, records, income tax returns, and the like, by a Certified Public Accountant acting on behalf of the buyers. Thus, instead of advising the Saleems not to sign the contract and make any substantial deposit until the Saleems had all the books and records examined by their accountant; and having, alternatively, failed to incorporate such protective contingencies and conditions in the contract, Klavin put his clients on the horns of a dilemma faced, as they unfortunately were, with either losing their $1,000 deposit or purchasing the business in total ignorance of its monthly income and expenses.

CONCLUSIONS OF LAW

The matter of attorney negligence arising out of this matter, must, of course, be evaluated and judged in accordance with the standard of care applicable in legal malpractice actions. In this regard, it is settled that an attorney is obligated to exercise on behalf of his client the knowledge, skill and ability ordinarily possessed and exercised by members of the legal profession similarly situated, and to employ reasonable care and prudence in connection therewith. *McCullough v. Sullivan,* 102 N.J.L. 381, 384 (E. & A. 1926); *Sullivan v. Stoudt,* 120 N.J.L. 304, 308 (E. &A. 1938; *Taylor v. Shepard,* 136 NJ Super. 85,90 (App. Div. 1982); *Saint Pius X House of Retreats v. Camden Diocese,* 88 N.J. 571, 588, (1982). Perhaps the most quoted statement of the rule of care applicable to attorney negligence suits is found in *Hodges v. Carter,* 239 N.C. 517, 80 S.E. 2nd 144 (1954):

Ordinarily when an attorney engages in the practice of the law and contracts to prosecute an action in behalf of his client, he impliedly represents that (1) he possesses the requisite degree of learning, skill and ability necessary to the practice of his profession and which others similarly situated ordinarily possess; (2) he will exercise his best judgment in the prosecution of the litigation entrusted to him; and (3) he will exercise reasonable and ordinary care and diligence in the use of his skill and in the application of his knowledge to his client's cause (Id. at 519, 80 S.E. 2nd at 145146).

What constitutes a reasonable degree of care is not to be considered in a vacuum. On the contrary, it must be the facts and circumstances of each specific case, and the type of service the attorney undertakes therein. With this in mind, I now proceed to examine the conduct of the subject defendant attorney in connection with his professional duties and conduct in the management of the above matter.

The record shows an egregious failure on the part of attorney Klavin to safeguard and protect the interests of his clients when he undertook to represent them in the purchase of Magyar, Inc. This conclusion is based upon the fact that defendant Klavin made no attempt to follow the standard and elementary procedures mandated for any attorney representing a buyer in the acquisition of a corporation. Thus, if Klavin had truly represented the interests of the Saleems, he would not only have examined all Magyar Inc.'s Federal and State tax returns, he would also, as a part of that investigation, have conducted a lien search in every place that Magyar conducted its business; would have obtained from Magyar an up-to-date financial statement in order to understand the economic aspects of the deal; would have obtained an independent audit of that financial statement; would have checked the terms, acceleration clauses and restrictions on any notes or mortgages or other indebtedness of the corporation; would have examined all insurance policies to discover what unknown liabilities existed; would have examined the viability and collectability of all accounts receivable; would have made a complete physical inventory of all corporate assets, together with a current market evaluation of same; would have examined the important contracts of Magyar and its customers, which constituted the lifeblood of that corporation; and would have performed other common-sense duties, such as talking to the main customers of Magyar, all for the overall purpose of insuring that the interests of his clients, the Saleems, were fully protected and safeguarded.

It is my opinion that if Klavin had conducted this type of basic and common-sense investigation, as he was bound to do in accordance with his duties as an attorney of this state, the Saleems would not have undertaken to purchase Magyar, and would thereby have escaped all the financial damage, loss of time, mental stress and anguish which they unfortunately suffered as a result of this purchase. Indeed, we now know that as a direct result of his negligence, Klavin caused his clients to lose at least $110,000 due to the misrepresentations made by the seller. In short, I find on the facts and the law that defendant Klavin, in his attorney–client relationship with the Saleems, fell below the standard of care and prudence exercised by ordinary members of the New Jersey Bar. Otherwise put, attorney Klavin, in his relationship with the Saleems, deviated substantially from the standard of care expected of New Jersey attorneys.

But it remains basic to the Saleems' cause of action for legal malpractice that the wrongful conduct or failures of attorney Klavin are a proximate cause of their injuries. In order to establish causation, the burden is clearly upon the Saleems to prove that the negligence of Klavin was more likely than not a substantial factor in causing the unfavorable result. *Lecral Malpractice, Mallen & Levit,* at pg. 502; and also see *Lieberman v. Employers Ins. of Wassau, 85* N.J. 325, 341 (1980); *Hoppe v. Ranzini,* 58 N.J. Super. 233, 238239 (App. Div. 1975), certif. den. 70 N.J. 144 (1976); *Lamb v. Barbour,* 188 N.J. Super. 6, 12 (App. Div. 1982); and as to the test of proximate cause see *State v. Jersey Central Power & Light Co.,* 69 N.J. 102, 100(1976); *Ettin v. Ava Truck Leasing Inc.,* 153 N.J. 463,483(1969). And plaintiff is obliged to carry this burden of proof by the presentation of competent, credible evidence, which proves material facts; and not conjecture, surmise or suspicion. *Lang v. Landy,* 35 N.J. 44, 54 (1961); *Modla v. United States, 15* F. Supp. 198, 201, (D.N.J. 1957). Otherwise stated, third-party plaintiffs herein must establish a chain of causation between their damages and the negligence or other wrongful conduct on the part of defendant Klavin. *Catto v. Schnepp,* 21 N.J. supra. 506, 511 (App. Div.) affld o.b. 62 N.J. 20 (1972).

Based upon the facts presented to me, and the applicable law, it is my view that the inexplicable failure of defendant Klavin to inspect or provide for the inspection of all Magyar, Inc. tax returns and corporate books and records, were the immediate factors that caused the Saleems to sustain heavy losses. It follows, therefore, that third-party defendant Klavin is liable to the third-party plaintiffs Saleems for legal malpractice and all causally related damages.

Very truly yours,

Richard M. Darius

Exhibit C

EDWARD J. CARUSO

Counselor at Law
300 Broad Street
Newark, New Jersey 07104

June 8, 1999

Theodore R. Rich, Esq.
100 Pearl Street
Woodbridge, New Jersey 07095

Re: Saleem v. Klavin

Dear Mr. Rich:

Please be advised that this opinion relates to an action for legal malpractice brought by your clients, Omar and Sylvia Saleem against Neil Klavin, a member of the New Jersey Bar. It derives from your request for my opinion as to whether third-party defendant Klavin breached any duty to his former clients, the third-party plaintiffs herein, when he undertook to represent them in July, 1996, with respect to the purchase of a certain office supply and mail box business, known as Magyar, Inc., located at 189 Princeton Road, Woodbridge, New Jersey.

For purposes of this report, I have read, analyzed and relied upon the following documents contained in all your litigation files:

- February, 9, 1998 depositions of Omar Saleem, Sylvia Saleem and Rahman Magyar;
- December 27, 1996 Contract of Sale between Magyar, Inc., and Omar and Sylvia Saleem;
- January 4, 1997 addendum to closing statement;
- January 2, 1997 Lease between Magyar, Inc. and Marjama Company;
- Rahman Magyar answers to interrogatories;
- December 27, 1996 note from Omar and Sylvia to Rahman Magyar;
- correspondence between attorneys D'Orio (for seller) and Klavin (for buyer) dated respectively October 14, 1996 and November 2, 1996 and December 3, 1996.
- July 24, 1998 expert report prepared by the CPA firm of Spyros and Company; and
- March 25, 1999 expert opinion of Darius and Spivack

Also please note that the documents listed above do not include all the materials examined by me, such as all correspondence between and among the parties, all pleadings, all discovery, and the like.

I have reviewed the documents referred to above in order to provide you with my opinion as to whether Neil Klavin deviated from the standard of care, which would be applicable in this transaction. Based on my review of all the documents set forth above, I am of the opinion that Mr. Klavin did not deviate from the standard of care for the reasons set forth below.

The transaction that is the subject of the litigation and this report involved the purchase of a business known as Magyar, Inc. The plaintiffs, Omar and Sylvia Saleem, executed a contract to purchase the aforesaid business from Magyar, Inc. In connection with the original negotiations relative to the business, the plaintiffs received a document showing projection of income and return on equity in connection with the business. This document was reviewed by the plaintiffs prior to the execution of the contract. The document was, in fact, executed by both of the plaintiffs, namely Omar and Sylvia Saleern.

After the parties agreed on all relevant terms for the transaction, the seller's attorney, Louis D'Orio, prepared a contract of sale. Ultimately, the contract was taken to Mr. Klavin by Omar Saleem. After reviewing the contract, Klavin prepared a review letter dated November 2, 1996. The review letter set forth a number of contingencies including, but not limited to, the following:

1. Review and approval of the existing lease . . .
2. A requirement that the buyer be permitted to review the books of the seller . . . and
3. Inclusion in the contract of a more detailed listing of scheduled assets.

The response to Mr. Klavin's letter was Mr. D'Orio's letter dated December 3, 1996. In that letter Mr. D'Orio advised Mr. Klavin that a lease contingency was not necessary since the lease had already been reviewed and approved by Mr. Klavin's clients. Mr. Klavin did question his clients in connection with the aforesaid lease and ultimately was satisfied that his clients read, understood, and were willing to accept same.

The next item discussed in Mr. D'Orio's letter was Mr. Klavin's request that his clients be permitted access to the books and records of the selling corporation. Mr. D'Orio requested that the review period be limited to five days and that there be some ascertainable standard as to whether or not the review was acceptable or unacceptable. In the last section of his letter, Mr. D'Orio provides Mr. Klavin with a more detailed schedule of assets.

It is obvious that the contents of Mr. D'Orio's letter were reviewed by Mr. Klavin and further reviewed by Mr. Klavin with his clients. I note that Mr. D'Orio requested that Mr. Klavin and/or his clients execute the letter so same could be incorporated as a part of the contract. I further note that Mr. Klavin, in fact, had his clients execute the letter after he reviewed same with him.

It is interesting that when Mr. Klavin forwarded the December 3, 1996 letter, which was executed by his clients, he included a cover letter in an effort to resolve the issue relative to a satisfactory review of the books and records. In that letter, Mr. Klavin indicates that his clients review of the books would be acceptable provided the books and records indicate gross receipts in excess of $175,000. I believe it is unequivocally clear that Mr. Klavin was sensitive to his clients' needs to review the books and records and furthermore had a discussion with his clients in connection with same. Stated another way, Mr. Klavin had placed his clients in a position where they were able to have access to the books and records before performing the contract.

In addition, the other elements of the transaction, including lease review, etc., were all properly handled by Mr. Klavin. All of the critical issues in connection with the purchase of a business were considered and reviewed with the client and were also the subject of informed consent.

In the opinion letter of Darius and Spivak. Mr. Darius suggests that "Klavin failed to incorporate certain conditions and contingencies in the December 27, 1996 contract, which would have made the sale subject to a review of all books . . ." This obviously is inapposite to the existing fact pattern, since the letter of December 3, 1996 clearly incorporates that contingency. Mr. Darius goes on to indicate that Mr. Klavin should have advised the Saleems not to sign the contract and make a deposit until the Saleems had all the books and records examined by their accountant. This simply flies in the face of the normal business practice in connection with the sale of a business. Having conducted numerous business closings over my 31 years of practice, it is my opinion that it would be extremely unusual to be involved in a transaction where a seller would let a buyer review books on any basis unless a substantial good faith deposit was made and a contract was executed by the parties.

Finally, Mr. Darius suggests that Mr. Klavin put his clients on the horns of a dilemma, which resulted in their being faced with either losing a deposit or purchasing a business in total ignorance of the monthly income. This dilemma was not created by Klavin. Mr. Klavin clearly gave his clients the opportunity to have the books and records reviewed. He received representations from his clients that they were reviewed and understood. If Mr. Klavin's clients had, in fact, performed their due diligence and reviewed the books and were unsatisfied with the result of their review, the contract could have been voided provided the review occurred within the contractual period. It was only at the day of the closing that the plaintiffs first indicated that they had not an opportunity to review the books and records of the corporation.

At that point, Mr. Klavin properly advised his clients that in the event they refused to consummate the transaction, they faced a possible loss of their deposit, and possibly other damages for breach of contract, since they did not avail themselves of the accounting contingency within the time period set forth in the contract.

I note that Mr. Darius states in his report that if Klavin had truly represented the interest of the Saleems, he would not only have examined all Magyar's Federal and State tax returns; he would also, as part of the investigation, have conducted a lien search . . . It appears that Mr. Darius is suggesting that Mr. Klavin should fulfill the role of an accountant and examine the books and records of the corporation. This is simply not an accurate statement, nor an accurate reflection of the duty of a closing attorney. Insofar as the lien search is concerned, same was, in fact, conducted by Mr. Klavin who ordered what is the normal and customary business search in connection with the proposed closing.

Mr. Darius goes on to indicate in his letter various undertakings that should have been performed by Mr. Klavin. Many of the undertakings set forth in Mr. Darius letter do not fall in the ambit of a lawyer's duty to his client. Many of the functions would be performed by an accountant or other professional and are not within the scope of a duty owed by an attorney to his client.

In the case at bar, I believe it is clear from the deposition transcript and the correspondence referred to above, that Mr. Klavin adequately performed these duties.

Very truly yours,

Edward J. Caruso

INTERNATIONAL FINANCE

FOREIGN CURRENCY FUTURES

A futures contract specifies the delivery of a specified amount of foreign currency by some given future date. Foreign currency futures differ from forward contracts in a number of significant ways, although both are used for trading, hedging, and speculative purposes. Participants include multinational corporations (MNCs) with assets and liabilities denominated in foreign currency, exporters and importers, speculators, and banks. Foreign currency futures are contracts for future delivery of a specific quantity of a given currency, with the exchange rate fixed at the time the contract is entered. Futures contracts are similar to forward contracts except that they are traded on organized futures exchanges and the gains and losses on the contracts are settled each day. Like forward contracts, a foreign currency futures contract is an agreement calling for future delivery of a standard amount of foreign exchange at a fixed time, place, and price. It is similar to futures contracts that exist for commodities (hogs, cattle, lumber, etc.), for interest-bearing deposits, and for gold. Unlike forward contracts, futures are traded on organized exchanges with specific rules about the terms of the contracts and with an active secondary market.

Futures Markets

In the United States, the most important marketplace for foreign currency futures is the International Monetary Market (IMM) of Chicago, which was organized in 1972 as a division of the Chicago Mercantile Exchange. Since 1985, contracts traded on the IMM have been interchangeable with those traded on the Singapore International Monetary Exchange (SIMEX). Most major money centers have established foreign currency futures markets during the past decade, notably in New York (New York Futures Exchange, a subsidiary of the New York Stock Exchange), London (London International Financial Futures Exchange), Canada, Australia, and Singapore. So far, however, none of these rivals have come close to duplicating the trading volume of the IMM.

Contract Specifications

Contract specifications are defined by the exchange on which they are traded. Here are the major features that must be standardized:

A Specific-Sized Contract. A German mark contract is for DM125,000. Consequently trading can be done only in multiples of DM125,000.

A Standard Method of Stating Exchange Rates. American terms are used; that is, quotations are the dollar cost of foreign currency units.

A Standard Maturity Date. Contracts mature on the third Wednesday of January, March, April, June, July, September, October, or December. However, not all of these maturities are available for all currencies at any given time. "Spot month" contracts are also traded. These are not spot contracts as that term is used in the interbank foreign exchange market, but are rather short-term futures contracts that mature on the next following third Wednesday, that is, on the next following standard maturity date.

A Specified Last Trading Day. Contracts may be traded through the second business day prior to the Wednesday on which they mature. Therefore, unless holidays interfere, the last trading day is the Monday preceding the maturity date.

Collateral. The purchaser must deposit a sum as an *initial margin* or collateral. This is similar to requiring a *performance bond* and can be met by a letter of credit from a bank, Treasury bills, or cash. In addition, *maintenance margin* is required. The value of the contract is *marked to market* daily, and all changes in value are paid in cash daily. The amount to be paid is called the *variation margin*.

Example 1. The initial margin on a £62,500 contract may be US$3,000, and the maintenance margin US$2,400. The initial US$3,000 margin is the initial equity in your account. The buyer's equity increases (decreases) when prices rise (fall). As long as the investor's losses do not exceed US$600 (that is, as long as the investor's equity does not fall below the maintenance margin, US$2,400), no margin call will be issued. If equity, however, falls below US$2,400, the investor must add variation margin that restores equity to US$3,000 by the next morning.

Settlement. Only about 5% of all futures contracts are settled by the physical delivery of foreign exchange between the buyer and seller. Most often, buyers and sellers offset their original positions prior to delivery date by taking an opposite position. That is, if one had bought a futures contract, that position would be closed out by selling a futures contract for the same delivery date. The complete buy/sell or sell/buy is called a *round turn*.

Commissions. Customers pay a commission to their broker to execute a round turn and only a single price is quoted. This practice differs from that of the interbank market, where dealers quote a bid and an offer and do not charge a commission.

Clearinghouse As Counterparty. All contracts are agreements between the client and the exchange clearinghouse, rather than between the two clients. Consequently clients need not worry that a specific counterparty in the market will fail to honor an agreement.

Currency futures contracts are currently available in over 10 currencies including the British pound, Canadian dollar, deutsche mark, Swiss franc, Japanese yen, and Australian dollar. The IMM is continually experimenting with new contracts. Those that meet the minimum volume requirements are added and those that don't are dropped. The number of contracts outstanding at any one time is called the *open interest*. Contract sizes are standardized according to amount of foreign currency—for example, £62,500, C$100,000, SFr 125,000. Exhibit 1 shows contract specifications. Leverage is high; margin requirements average less than 2% of the value of the futures contract. The leverage assures that investors' fortunes will be decided by tiny swings in exchange rates. The contracts have minimum price moves, which generally translate into about $10 to $12 per contract. At the same time, most exchanges set daily price limits on their contracts that restrict the maximum daily price move. When these limits are reached, additional margin requirements are imposed and trading may be halted for a short time. Instead of using the bid–ask spreads found in the interbank market, traders charge commissions. Though commissions will vary, a *round trip*—that is, one buy and one sell—costs as little as $15. The low cost, coupled with the high degree of leverage, has provided a major incentive for speculators to participate in the market.

Exhibit 1 Chicago Mercantile Exchange Foreign Currency Futures Specifications

	Austrian Dollar	British Pound	Canadian Dollar	Deutsche Mark	Swiss Franc	French Franc	Japanese Yen
Symbol	AD	BP	CD	DM	SF	FR	JY
Contract size	A$100,000	£62,500	C$100,000	DM125,000	SFr125,000	FF500,000	¥12,500,000
Margin requirements							
Initial	$1,148	$1,485	$608	$1,755	$2,565	$1,755	$4,590
Maintenance	$850	$1,100	$450	$1,300	$1,900	$1,300	$3,400
Minimum price change	0.00001 (1 pt.)	0.0002 (2 pts.)	0.0001 (1 pt.)	0.0001 (1 pt.)	0.0001 (1 pt.)	0.00002 (2 pts.)	0.000001 (1 pt.)
Value of 1 point	$10.00	$6.25	$10.00	$12.50	$12.50	$12.50	$10.00
Months traded	January, March, April, June, July, September, October, December, and spot month						
Last day of trading	The second business day immediately preceding the third Wednesday of the delivery month						
Trading hours	7:20 A.M.–2:00 P.M. (Central Time)						

Note: Contract specifications are also available for currencies such as the Brazilian real, Mexican peso, Russian ruble, and New Zealand dollar.

Source: Adapted from *Contract Specifications for Currency Futures and Options, Chicago Mercantile Exchange,* May, 2000 (http://www.cme.com/clearing/spex/cscurrency.htm).

Futures Contracts on Euros

The Chicago Mercantile Exchange (CME) has developed futures contracts on euros so that MNCs can easily hedge their positions in euros, as shown in Exhibit 2. The U.S.-based MNCs commonly consider the use of the futures contract on the euro with respect to the dollar (column 2). However, there are also futures contracts available on cross-rates between the euro and the British pound (column 3), the euro and the Japanese yen (column 4), and the euro and the Swiss franc (column 5). Settlement dates on all of these contracts are available in March, June, September, and December. The futures contracts on cross-rates allow for easy hedging by foreign subsidiaries that wish to exchange euros for widely used currencies other than the dollar.

Exhibit 2   Futures Contracts on Euros

	Euro/U.S. $	Euro/Pound	Euro/Yen	Euro/Swiss franc
Ticker symbol	EC	RP	RY	RF
Trading unit	125,000 euros	125,000 euros	125,000 euros	125,000 euros
Quotation	$ per euro	Pounds per euro	Yen per euro	SF per euro
Last day of trading	Second business day before third Wednesday of the contract month	Second business day before third Wednesday of the contract month	Second business day before third Wednesday of the contract month	Second business day before third Wednesday of the contract month

Reading Newspaper Quotations

Futures trading on the IMM in Japanese yen for a Tuesday was reported as shown in Exhibit 3. The head "JAPAN YEN" shows the size of the contract (12.5M yen) and states that the prices are stated in US$ cents. The June 2000 contract had expired more than a month before, so the three contracts being traded on July 29, 2000 are the September and December 2000 contracts and the March 2001 contract. Detailed descriptions of the quotations follow.

1. In each row, the first four prices relate to trading on Thursday, July 29—the price at the start of trading (open), the highest and lowest transaction price during the day, and the settlement price ("Settle"), which is representative of the transaction prices around the close. The settlement (or closing) price is the basis of marking to market.

Exhibit 3 Foreign Currency Futures Quotations

	Open	High	Low	Settle	Change	Lifetime High	Middle or Center	Open Interest
JAPAN YEN (CME)—12.5 million yen; $ per yen (.00)								
Sept	.9458	.9466	.9386	.9389	–.0046	.9540	.7945	73,221
Dec	.9425	.9470	.9393	.9396	–.0049	.9529	.7970	3,455
Mr	. ..	. ...	.... .	.9417	–.0051	.9490	.8700	318
	Est vol 28,844; vol Wed 36,595; open int 77,028, + 1.820							

2. The column "Change" contains the change of today's settlement price relative to yesterday. For instance, on Thursday, July 29, the settlement price of the September contract dropped by 0.0046 cents, implying that a holder of a purchase contract has lost 12.5m × (0.0046/100) = US$575 per contract and that a seller has made US$575 per contract.

3. The next two columns show the extreme (highest and lowest) prices that have been observed over its trading life. For the March contract, the high–low range is narrower than for the older contracts, since the March contract has been trading for little more than a month.

4. "Open interest" refers to the number of contracts still in effect at the end of the previous day's trading session. Each unit represents a buyer and a seller who still have a contract position. Notice how most of the trading is in the nearest-maturity contract. Open interest in the March '01 contract is minimal, and there has not even been any trading that day. (There are no open, high, and low data.) The settlement price for the March '01 contract has been set by the CME on the basis of bid–ask quotes.

5. The line below the price information gives an estimate of the volume traded that day and the previous day (Wednesday). Also shown are the total open interest (the total of the right column) across the three contracts, and the change in open interest from the prior trading day.

Currency Futures Quotations Reported Online

Exhibit 4 displays a currency quotation from Commodities, Charts & Quotes—Free (http://www.tfc-charts.w2d.com):

Exhibit 4

Commodity Futures Price Quotes For

(2) **CME Australian Dollar** (1)

(Price quotes for this commodity delayed at least 10 minutes as per exchange requirements)

Click here to refresh data

(3)

Month Click for chart	(4) Open	High	Low	(5) Session Last	Time	(6) Sett	(7) Chg	Prior Day Sett	Vol	O.Int	Options
Dec 99	6362	6410	6350	DN 6386	15:09	6388	+8	6378	82	22197	Call Put
Mar 00	6375	6412	6370	UP 6375	08:31	6398	-13	6388	1	112	Call Put
Jun 00	-	-	-	UC 6398	12:43	6408	-	6398	2	11	Call Put
Sep 00	-	-	-	UC 6408	09:28	6418	-	6408	-	1	Call Put

Explanatory Notes:

(1) The name of the currency, Australian dollar.

(2) The name of the exchange, the Chicago Mercantile Exchange.

(3) The delivery date (closing date for the contract).

(4) The opening, high, and low prices for the trading day. The trading unit is 100,000 Australian dollars. The price is $10 per point. Therefore, the settlement price for the trading unit is $63,620, and each Australian dollar being delivered in December is worth $.6362.

(5) The last price at which the contract traded.

(6) The "official" daily closing price of a futures contract, set by the exchange for the purpose of settling margin accounts.

(7) The change in the price from the prior settlement price to the last price quoted.

Foreign Currency Futures versus Forward Contracts

Foreign currency futures contracts differ from forward contracts in a number of important ways. Nevertheless, both futures and forward contracts are used for the same commercial and speculative purposes. Exhibit 5 compares major features and characteristics of the two instruments. Example 2 illustrates how currency futures contracts are used for hedging purposes, how they compare with currency options, and how gains and losses are calculated.

Exhibit 5 Basic Differences between Foreign Currency Futures and
Forward Contracts

Characteristics	Foreign Currency Futures	Forward Contracts
Trading and location	In an organized exchange	By telecommunications networks
Parties involved	Unknown to each other	In direct contact with each other in setting contract specifications
Size of contract	Standardized	Any size individually tailored
Maturity	Fixed	Delivery on any date
Quotes	In American terms	In European terms
Pricing	Open outcry process	By bid and offer quotes
Settlement	Made daily via exchanges' clearinghouses; rarely delivered	Normally delivered on the date agreed
Commissions	Brokerage fees for buy and sell (round-trip)	Based on bid–ask spread
Collateral and margin	Initial margin required	No explicit margin specified
Regulation	Highly regulated	Self-regulating
Liquidity and volume	Liquid but low volume	Liquid but large volume
Credit risk	Low risk due to the exchange clearinghouse involved	Borne by each party

Example 2. TDQ Corporation must pay its Japanese supplier ¥125 million in three months. The firm is contemplating two alternatives:

1. Buying 20 yen call options (contract size is ¥6.25 million) at a strike price of $0.00900 in order to protect against the risk of rising yen. The premium is $0.00015 per yen.
2. Buying 10 three-month yen futures contracts (contract size is ¥12.5 million) at a price of $0.00840 per yen. The current spot rate is $0.008823/¥. The firm's CFO believes that the most likely rate for the yen is $0.008900, but the yen could go as high as $0.009400 or as low as $0.008500.

Note: In all calculations, the current spot rate, $0.008823/¥, is irrelevant.

1. For the call options, TDQ must pay a call premium of $0.00015 × 125,000,000 = $18,750. If the yen settles at its minimum value, the firm will not exercise the option and it loses the entire call premium. But if the

International Finance

yen settles at its maximum value of $0.009400, the firm will exercise at $0.009000 and earn $0.0004/¥ for a total gain of $0.0004 × 125,000,000 = $50,000. TDQ's net gain will be $50,000 − $18,750 = $31,250.

2. By using a futures contract, TDQ will lock in a price of $0.008940/¥ for a total cost of $0.008940 × 125,000,000 = $992,500. If the yen settles at its minimum value, the firm will lose $0.008940 − $0.008500 = $0.000440/¥ (remember, the firm is buying yen at $0.008940, when the spot price is only $0.008500), for a total loss on the futures contract of $0.000440 × 125,000,000 = $55,000. But if the yen settles at its maximum value of $0.009400, the firm will earn $0.009400 − $0.008940 = $0.000460/¥, for a total gain of $0.000460 × 125,000,000 = $57,500.

Exhibits 6 and 7 present profit and loss calculations on both alternatives and their corresponding graphs.

Exhibit 6   Profit or Loss on TDQ's Options and Futures Positions

Contract size:				125,000,000	Yen
Expiration date:				3.0	months
Exercise, or strike price:				0.00900	$/Yen
Premium, or option price:				0.00015	$/Yen

(1) CALL OPTION

Ending Spot Rate ($/Yen)	0.00850	0.00894	0.00915	0.00940	0.00960
Payments:					
Premium	(18,750)	(18,750)	(18,750)	(18,750)	(18,750)
Exercise cost	0	0	(1,125,000)	(1,125,000)	(1,125,000)
Receipts:					
Spot sale of Yen	0	0	1,143,750	1,175,000	1,200,000
Net ($):	(18,750)	(18,750)	0	31,250	56,250

(2) FUTURES   Lock-in price = 0.008940 $/yen

Receipts	1,062,500	1,117,500	1,143,750	1,175,000	1,200,000
Payments	(1,117,500)	(1,117,500)	(1,117,500)	(1,117,500)	(1,117,500)
Net ($):	(55,000)	0	26,250	57,500	82,500

Exhibit 7 TDQ's Profit (Loss) on Options and Futures Positions

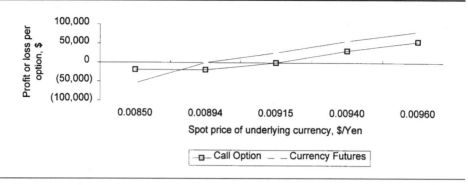

Exhibit 8 provides a comparison between a futures contract and an option contract.

Exhibit 8 Currency Futures versus Currency Options

Futures	Options
1. A futures contract is most valuable when the quantity of foreign currency being hedged is known.	1. An option contract is most valuable when the quantity of foreign currency is unknown.
2. Futures provide a two-sided hedge against currency movements.	2. Options enable the hedging of one-sided risk either with a call or with a put.
3. A buyer of a currency futures contract must take delivery.	3. A buyer of a currency options contract has the right (not the obligation) to complete the contract.

CURRENCY OPTION

Foreign currency options are financial contracts that give the buyer the right, but not the obligation, to buy (or sell) a specified number of units of foreign currency from the option seller at a fixed dollar price, up to the option's expiration date. In return for this right, the buyer pays a premium to the seller of the option. These options are similar to foreign currency futures in that the contracts are for fixed quantities of currency to be exchanged at a fixed price in the future. The key difference is that the maturity date for an option is only the last day to carry out the currency exchange; the option may be "exercised," that is, presented for currency exchange, at any time between its issuance and the maturity date, or not at all. Currency options are used as a hedging tool and for speculative purposes.

Example 3. The buyer of a call option on British pounds obtains the right to buy £50,000 at a fixed dollar price (i.e., the exercise price) at any time during the (typically) three-month life of the option. The seller of the same option faces a contingent liability in that the seller will have to deliver the British pounds at any time, if the buyer chooses to exercise the option. The market value of an option depends on its exercise price, the remaining time to its expiration, the exchange rate in the spot market, and expectations about the future exchange rate. An option may sell for a price near zero, for thousands of dollars, or anywhere in between. Notice that the buyer of a call option on British pounds may pay a small price to obtain the option but does not have to exercise the option if the actual exchange rate moves favorably. Thus, an option is superior to a forward contract having the same maturity and exercise price because it need not be used—and the cost is just its purchase price. However, the price of the option is generally greater than the expected cost of the forward contract; so the user of the option pays for the flexibility of the instrument.

Currency Option Terminology

Foreign currency option definitions are as follows:

1. The *amount* is how much of the underlying foreign currency is involved.
2. The seller of the option is referred to as the *writer* or *grantor.*
3. A *call* is an option to buy foreign currency, and a *put* is an option to sell foreign currency.
4. The *exercise* or *strike* price is the specified exchange rate for the underlying currency at which the option can be exercised.
    *   *At the money*—exercise price equal to the spot price of the underlying currency.
    *   *In the money*—exercise price below the current spot price of the underlying currency, while in-the-money puts have an exercise price above the current spot price of the underlying currency. An option that would be profitable if exercised immediately is said to be *in the money.*
    *   *Out of the money*—exercise price above the current spot price of the underlying currency, while out-of-the-money puts have an exercise price below the current spot price of the underlying currency. An option that would not be profitable if exercised immediately is referred to as *out of the money.*
5. *Types of option.* There are broadly two types of option. *American options* can be exercised at any time between the date of writing and the expiration or maturity date. *European options* can be exercised only on their expiration date, not before.

6. The *premium* or *option price* is the cost of the option, usually paid in advance by the buyer to the seller. In the over-the-counter market, premiums are quoted as a percentage of the transaction amount. Premiums on exchange-traded options are quoted as a dollar (domestic currency) amount per unit of foreign currency.

Foreign Currency Options Markets

Foreign currency options can be purchased or sold in three different types of markets:

1. Options on the physical currency, purchased on the over-the-counter (interbank) market.
2. Options on the physical currency, purchased on an organized exchange such as the Philadelphia Stock Exchange.
3. Options on futures contracts, purchased on the International Monetary Market (IMM).

Options on the Over-the-Counter Market. Over-the-counter (OTC) options are most frequently written by banks for U.S. dollars against British pounds, German marks, Swiss francs, Japanese yen, and Canadian dollars. They are usually written in round lots of $85 to $100 million in New York and $2 to $83 million in London. The main advantage of over-the-counter options is that they are tailored to the specific needs of the firm. Financial institutions are willing to write or buy options that vary by amount (notional principal), strike price, and maturity. Although the over-the-counter markets were relatively illiquid in the early years, the market has grown to such proportions that liquidity is now considered quite good. On the other hand, the buyer must assess the writing bank's ability to fulfill the option contract. Termed *counterparty risk,* the financial risk associated with the counterparty is an increasing issue in international markets. Exchange-traded options are more the sphere of the financial institutions themselves. A firm wishing to purchase an option in the over-the-counter market normally places a call to the currency option desk of a major money center bank, specifies the currencies, maturity, and strike rate(s), and asks for an *indication,* a bid–offer quote.

Options on Organized Exchanges. Options on the physical (underlying) currency are traded on a number of organized exchanges worldwide, including the Philadelphia Stock Exchange (PHLX) and the London International Financial Futures Exchange (LIFFE). Exchange-traded options are settled through a clearinghouse, so that buyers do not deal directly with sellers. The clearinghouse is the counterparty to every option contract and it guarantees fulfillment. Clearinghouse obligations are in turn the obligation of all members of the exchange, including a large number of banks.

In the case of the Philadelphia Stock Exchange, clearinghouse services are provided by the Options Clearing Corporation (OCC). The Philadelphia Exchange has long been the innovator in exchange-traded options, and has in recent years added a number of unique features to its United Currency Options Market (UCOM), which now makes exchange-traded options much more flexible—and more competitive—in meeting the needs of corporate clients. UCOM offers a variety of option products with standardized currency options on eight major currencies and two cross-rate pairs (non-U.S. dollar), with either American- or European-style pricing. The exchange also offers *customized currency options,* in which the user may choose exercise price, expiration date (up to two years), and premium quotation form (units of currency or percentage of underlying value). Cross-rate options are also available for the DM/¥ and £/DM. By taking the U.S. dollar out of the equation, cross-rate options allow one to hedge directly the currency risk that arises in dealing with nondollar currencies. Contract specifications are shown in Exhibit 9. The PHLX trades both American-style and European-style currency options. It also trades month-end options (listed as EOM, or end of month), which ensures the availability of a short-term (at most, a two- or sometimes three-week) currency option at all times, and long-term options, which extends the available expiration months on PHLX dollar-based and cross-rate contracts—providing for 18- and 24-month European-style options. In 1994, the PHLX introduced a new option contract, called the virtual currency option, which is settled in U.S. dollars rather than in the underlying currency.

Currency Option Quotations and Prices

Some recent currency option prices from the Philadelphia Stock Exchange are presented in Exhibit 10. Quotations are usually available for more combinations of strike prices and expiration dates than were actually traded and thus reported in newspapers such as the *Wall Street Journal.* Exhibit 9 illustrates the three different prices that characterize any foreign currency option. *Note:* Currency option strike prices and premiums on the U.S. dollar are quoted here as direct quotations ($/DM, $/¥, etc.) as opposed to the more common usage of indirect quotations used throughout the book. This approach is standard practice with option prices as quoted on major option exchanges like the Philadelphia Stock Exchange.

The three prices that characterize an "August 48 1/2 call option" are the spot rate, exercise price, and premium.

Exhibit 9 Philadelphia Stock Exchange Currency Option Specifications

	Austrian Dollar	British Pound	Canadian Dollar	Deutsche Mark	Swiss Franc	Euro	Japanese Yen
Symbol							
American	XAD	XBP	XCD	XDM	SXF	XEU	XJY
European	CAD	CBP	CCD	CDM	CSF	ECU	CJY
Contract size	A$50,000	£31,250	C$50,000	DM 62,500	SFr 62,500	62,500	¥6,250,000
Exercise price intervals	1¢	2.5¢	0.5¢	$1¢^1$	$1¢^1$	2¢	$0.01¢^1$
Premium quotations	Cents per unit	Cents per unit	Cents per unit	Cents per unit	Cents per unit	Cents per unit	Hundredths of a cent per unit
Minimum price change	$0.(00)01	$0.(00)01	$0.(00)01	$0.(00)01	$0.(00)01	$0.(00)02	$0.(00)01
Minimum contract price change	$5.00	$3.125	$5.00	$6.25	$6.25	$6.25	$6.25
Expiration months	March, June, September, and December + two near-term months						
Exercise notice	No automatic exercise of in-the-money options						
Expiration date	Friday before third Wednesday of the month (Friday is also the last trading day)						

Expiration settlement date	Third Wednesday of month
Daily price limits	None
Issuer and guarantor	Options Clearing Corporation (OCC)
Margin for uncovered writer	Option premium plus 4% of the underlying contract value less out-of-money amount, if any, to a minimum of the option premium plus 3/4% of the underlying contract value. Contract value equals spot price times unit of currency per contract.
Position and exercise limits	100,000 contracts
Trading hours	2:30 A.M.–2:30 P.M. Philadelphia time, Monday through Friday[2]
Taxation	Any gain or loss: 60% long-term/40% short-term

[1]Half-point strike prices (0.5¢), SFr (0.5¢), and ¥ (0.005¢) in the three near-term months only.

[2]Trading hours for the Canadian dollar are 7:00 A.M.–2:30 P.M. Philadelphia time, Monday through Friday.

Source: Adapted from *Standardized Currency Options Specifications*, Philadelphia Stock Exchange, May 2000 (http://www.phlx.com/products/standard.html).

Exhibit 10 Foreign Currency Option Quotations
(Philadelphia Stock Exchange)

Option and Underlying	Strike Price	Calls—Last			Puts—Last		
		Aug.	Sept.	Dec.	Aug.	Sept.	Dec.
62,500 German marks–cents per unit							
48.51	46	-	-	2.76	0.04	0.22	1.16
48.51	46 1/2	-	-	-	0.06	0.30	-
48.51	47	1.13	-	1.74	0.10	0.38	1.27
48.51	47 1/2	0.75	-	-	0.17	0.55	-
48.51	48	0.71	1.05	1.28	0.27	0.89	1.81
48.51	48 1/2	0.50	-	-	0.50	0.99	-
48.51	49	0.30	0.66	1.21	0.90	1.36	-
48.51	49 1/2	0.15	0.40	-	2.32	-	-
48.51	50	-	0.31	-	2.32	2.62	3.30

Spot Rate. In Exhibit 10, "option and underlying" means that 48.51 cents, or $0.4851, is the spot dollar price of one German mark at the close of trading on the preceding day.

Exercise Price. The exercise price or "strike price" listed in Exhibit 10 means the price per mark that must be paid if the option is exercised. The August call option on marks of 48 1/2 means $0.4850/DM. Exhibit 10 lists nine strike prices, ranging from $0.4600/DM to $0.6000/DM, although more were available on that date than are listed here.

Premium. The premium is the cost or price of the option. The price of the August 48 1/2 call option on German marks is 0.50 U.S. cents per mark, or $0.0050/DM. There was no trading of the September and December 48 1/2 call on that day. The premium is the market value of the option. The terms *premium, cost, price,* and *value* are all interchangeable when referring to an option. All option premiums are expressed in cents per unit of foreign currency on the Philadelphia Stock Exchange except for the French franc, which is expressed in tenths of a cent per franc, and the Japanese yen, which is expressed in hundredths of a cent per yen.

The August 48 1/2 call option premium is 0.50 cents per mark, and in this case, the August 48 1/2 put's premium is also 0.50 cents per mark. As one option contract on the Philadelphia Stock Exchange consists of 62,500 marks, the total cost of one option contract for the call (or put in this case) is DM 62,500 × $0.0050/DM = $312.50.

Speculating in Option Markets

Options differ from all other types of financial instruments in the patterns of risk they produce. The option owner has the choice of exercising the option or allowing it to expire unused. The owner will exercise it only when exercising is profitable, which means when the option is in the money. In the case of a call option, as the spot price of the underlying currency moves up, the holder has the possibility of unlimited profit. On the downside, however, the holder can abandon the option and walk away with a loss never greater than the premium paid.

Buyer of a Call

To see how currency options might be used, consider a U.S. importer, called MYK Corporation, with a DM 62,500 payment to make to a German exporter in two months. MYK could purchase a European call option to have the DMs delivered to it at a specified exchange rate (the exercise price) on the due date. Assume that the option premium is $0.005/DM, and the strike price is 48 1/2 ($0.4850/DM). MYK has paid $312.50 for a DM 48 1/2 call option, which gives it the right to buy DM 62,500 at a price of $0.4850 per mark at the end of two months. Exhibit 11 illustrates the importer's gains and losses on the call option. The vertical axis measures profit or loss for the option buyer, at each of several different spot prices for the markup to the time of maturity.

At all spot rates *below* the strike price of $0.485, MYK would choose not to exercise its option (out-of-the-money). This decision is obvious, since at a spot rate of $0.485, for example, MYK would prefer to buy a German mark for $0.480 on the spot market rather than exercise the option to buy a mark at $0.485. If the spot rate remained below $0.480 until August when the option expired, it would not exercise the option. Its total loss would be limited to only what was paid for the option, the $0.005/DM purchase price. At any lower price for the mark, the loss would similarly be limited to the original $0.005/DM cost.

Alternatively, at all spot rates *above* the strike price of $0.485, MYK would exercise the option (in-the-money), paying only the strike price for each German mark. For example, if the spot rate were $0.495 cents per mark at maturity, MYK would exercise the call option, buying German marks for $0.485 each instead of purchasing them on the spot market at $0.495 each. The German marks could be sold immediately in the spot market for $0.495

Exhibit 11   Profit or Loss for Buyer and Seller of a Call Option

Contract size:		62,500	DM
Expiration date:		2	months
Exercise, or strike price:		0.4850	$/DM
Premium, or option price:		0.0050	$/DM

PROFIT OR LOSS FOR BUYER OF A CALL OPTION

Ending spot rate ($/DM)	0.475	0.480	0.485	0.490	0.495	0.500
Payments:						
Premium	(313)	(313)	(313)	(313)	(313)	(313)
Exercise cost	0	0	0	(30,313)	(30,313)	(30,313)
Receipts:						
Spot sale of DM	0	0	0	30,625	30,938	31,250
Net ($):	(313)	(313)	(313)	0	313	625

PROFIT OR LOSS FOR SELLER OF A CALL OPTION

The writer of an option profits when the buyer of the option suffers losses
(i.e., it is a zero-sum game). The net position of the writer is therefore the negative
of the position of the holder.

Net ($):	313	313	313	0	(313)	(625)

each, with MYK pocketing a gross profit of $0.0010/DM, or a net profit of
$0.005/DM after deducting the original cost of the option of $0.005/DM for
a total profit of $312.50 ($0.005/DM × 62,500 DM). The profit to MYK, if the
spot rate is greater than the strike price, with a strike price of $0.485, a pre-
mium of $0.005, and a spot rate of $0.495, is

$$\text{Profit} = \text{Spot Rate} - (\text{Strike Price} + \text{Premium})$$
$$= \$0.495/\text{DM} - (\$0.485/\text{DM} + \$0.005/\text{DM})$$
$$= \$0.005/\text{DM or a total of } \$312.50 \ (\$0.005/\text{DM} \times 62{,}500 \ \text{DM})$$

More likely, MYK would realize the profit by executing an offsetting contract on the options exchange rather than taking delivery of the currency.
Because the dollar price of a mark could rise to an infinite level (off the upper right-hand side of the page in Exhibit 9), maximum profit is unlimited.
The buyer of a call option thus possesses an attractive combination of outcomes: limited loss and unlimited profit potential.

The *break-even price*—the price at which the gain on the option just equals the option premium—is $0.490/DM. The premium cost of $0.005, combined with the cost of exercising the option of $0.485, is exactly equal to the proceeds from selling the marks in the spot market at $0.490. Note that MYK will still exercise the call option at the break-even price. By exercising it, MYK at least recovers the premium paid for the option. At any spot price above the exercise price but below the break-even price, the gross profit earned on exercising the option and selling the underlying currency covers part (but not all) of the premium cost.

Writer of a Call

The position of the writer (seller) of the same call option is illustrated in the bottom half of Exhibit 11. Because this is a zero-sum game, the profit from selling a call, shown in Exhibit 12, is the mirror image of the profit from buying the call. If the option expires when the spot price of the underlying currency is below the exercise price of $0.485, the holder does not exercise the option. What the holder loses, the writer gains. The writer keeps as profit the entire premium paid of $0.005/DM. Above the exercise price of $0.485, the writer of the call must deliver the underlying currency for $0.485/DM at a time when the value of the mark is above $0.485. If the writer wrote the option naked—that is, without owning the currency—that seller will now have to buy the currency at spot and take the loss. The amount of such a loss is unlimited and increases as the price of the underlying currency rises. Once again, what the holder gains, the writer loses, and vice versa. Even if the writer already owns the currency, the writer will

Exhibit 12   German Mark Call Option (Profit or Loss per Option)

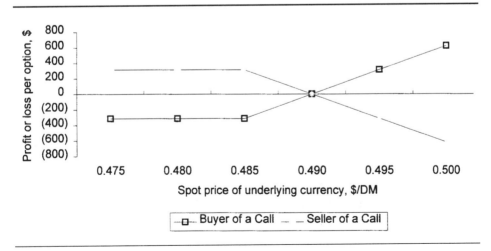

experience an opportunity loss, surrendering against the option the same currency that could have been sold for more in the open market.

For example, the loss to the writer of a call option with a strike price of $0.485, a premium of $0.005, and a spot rate of $0495/DM is:

$$\text{Profit} = \text{Premium} - (\text{Spot Rate} - \text{Strike Price})$$
$$= \$0.005/\text{DM} - (\$0.495/\text{DM} - \$0.485/\text{DM})$$
$$= -\$0.005/\text{DM} \text{ or a total of } -\$312.50$$
$$(-\$0.005/\text{DM} \times 62,500 \text{ DM})$$

This is true only if the spot rate is greater than or equal to the strike rate. At spot rates less than the strike price, the option will expire worthless and the writer of the call option will keep the premium earned. The maximum profit that the writer of the call option can make is limited to the premium. The writer of a call option would have a rather unattractive combination of potential outcomes: limited profit potential and unlimited loss potential. Such losses can be limited through other techniques.

Buyer of a Put

The position of MYK as buyer of a put is illustrated in Exhibit 13. The basic terms of this put are similar to those just used to illustrate a call. The buyer of a put option, however, wants to be able to sell the underlying currency at the exercise price when the market price of that currency drops (not rises as in the case of a call option). If the spot price of a mark drops to, say, $0.475/DM, MYK will deliver marks to the writer and receive $0.485/DM. Because the marks can now be purchased on the spot market for $0.475 each and the cost of the option was $0.005/DM, MYK will have a net gain of $0.005/DM. Explicitly, the profit to the holder of a put option if the spot rate is less than the strike price, with a strike price of $0.485/DM, a premium of $0.005/DM, and a spot rate of $0.475/DM is:

$$\text{Profit} = \text{Strike Price} - (\text{Spot Rate} + \text{Premium})$$
$$= \$0.485/\text{DM} - (\$0.475/\text{DM} + \$0.005/\text{DM})$$
$$= \$0.005/\text{DM} \text{ or a total of } \$312.50 \; (\$0.005/\text{DM} \times 62,500 \text{ DM})$$

The break-even price for the put option is the strike price less the premium, or $0.480/DM in this case. As the spot rate falls further below the strike price, the profit potential increases, and MYK's profit is unlimited (up to a maximum of $0.480/DM, if the price of a DM is zero). At any exchange rate above the strike price of $0.485, MYK would not exercise the option, and so would have lost only the $0.005/DM premium paid for the put option. The buyer of a put option has an almost unlimited profit potential with a limited loss potential. Like the buyer of a call, the buyer of a put can never lose more than the premium paid up front.

498

Exhibit 13   Profit or Loss for Buyer and Seller of a Put Option

Contract size:	62,500 DM
Expiration date:	2 months
Exercise, or strike price:	0.4850 $/DM
Premium, or option price:	0.0050 $/DM

PROFIT OR LOSS FOR BUYER OF A PUT OPTION

Ending spot rate ($/DM)	0.470	0.475	0.480	0.485	0.490	0.495	0.500
Payments:							
Premium	(313)	(313)	(313)	(313)	(313)	(313)	(313)
Spot purchase of DM	(29,375)	(29,688)	(30,000)	0	0	0	0
Receipts:							
Exercise of option	30,313	30,313	30,313	0	0	0	0
Net ($):	625	313	0	(313)	(313)	(313)	(313)

PROFIT OR LOSS FOR SELLER OF A PUT OPTION

The writer of an option profits when the holder of the option suffers losses (i.e., it's a zero-sum game). The net position of the writer is therefore the negative of the position of the holder.

Net ($):	(625)	(313)	0	313	313	313	313

Writer of a Put

The position of the writer of the put sold to MYK is shown in the lower half of Exhibit 14. Note the symmetry of profit/loss, strike price, and break-even prices between the buyer and the writer of the put, as was the case of the call option. If the spot price of marks drops below $0.485 per mark, the option will be exercised by MYK. Below a price of $0.480 per mark, the writer will lose more than the premium received from writing the option ($0.005/DM), falling below break-even. Between $0.480/DM and $0.485/DM, the writer will lose part, but not all, of the premium received. If the spot price is above $0.485/DM, the option will not be exercised, and the option writer pockets the entire premium of $0.005/DM. The loss earned by the writer of a $0.485 strike price put, premium $0.005, at a spot rate of $0.475, is:

Exhibit 14   German Mark Put Option (Profit or Loss per Option)

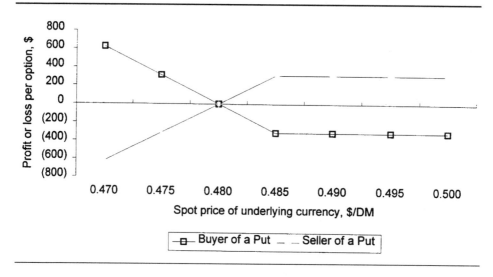

Profit Premium − (Strike Price − Spot Rate)

= $0.005/DM − ($0.0485/DM − $0.475/DM) = −$0.005/DM

= −$0.005/DM or a total of −$312.50 (−$0.005/DM × 62,500 DM)

This is true only for spot rates that are less than or equal to the strike price. At spot rates that are greater than the strike price, the option expires out-of-the-money and the writer keeps the premium earned up front. The writer of the put option has the same basic combination of outcomes available to the writer of a call: limited profit potential and unlimited loss potential up to a maximum of $0.480/DM.

Option Pricing and Valuation

Exhibit 15 illustrates the profit/loss profile of a European-style call option on British pounds. The call option allows the holder to buy British pounds (£) at a strike price of $1.70/£. The value of this call option is actually the sum of two components:

Total value (premium) = Intrinsic value + Time value

Intrinsic value is the financial gain if the option is exercised immediately. It is shown by the solid line in Exhibit 16, which is zero until reaching the strike price, and then rises linearly (1 cent for each 1-cent increase in the spot rate). Intrinsic value will be zero when the option is out-of-the-money—that is, when the strike price is above the market price—as no gain can be derived

International Finance

Exhibit 15 Intrinsic Value, Time Value, and Total Value of a Call Option on British Pounds

Spot($/£) (1)	Strike price (2)	Intrinsic Value of Option (1)–(2)=(3)	Time Value of Option (4)	Total Value (3) + (4) =(5)
1.65	1.70	0.00	1.37	1.37
1.66	1.70	0.00	1.67	1.67
1.67	1.70	0.00	2.01	2.01
1.68	1.70	0.00	2.39	2.39
1.69	1.70	0.00	2.82	2.82
1.70	1.70	0.00	3.30	3.30
1.71	1.70	1.00	2.82	3.82
1.72	1.70	2.00	2.39	4.39
1.73	1.70	3.00	2.01	5.01
1.74	1.70	4.00	1.67	5.67
1.75	1.70	5.00	1.37	6.37

Exhibit 16 Intrinsic Value, Time Value, and Total Value of a Call Option on British Pounds

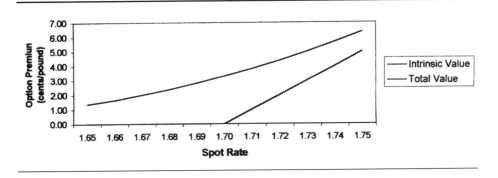

from exercising the option. When the spot price rises above the strike price, the intrinsic value becomes positive because the option is always worth at least this value if exercised. The time value of an option exists since the price of the underlying currency, the spot rate, can potentially move further in-the-money between the present time and the option's expiration date.

Currency Option Pricing

Based on the work of Black and Scholes as well as others, the model yields the option premium. The basic theoretical model for the pricing of a European call option is:

$$V = e^{-r_f t} S[N(d_1)] - e^{-r_d t} E[N(d_2)]$$

where V = Premium on a European call
e = 2.71828
S = Spot exchange rate (in direct quote)
E = Exercise or strike rate
r_f = Foreign interest rate
r_d = Domestic interest rate
t = Number of time periods until the expiration date (for example, 90 days means $t = 90/365 = 0.25$)

$N(d)$ = probability that the normally distributed random variable Z is less than or equal to d
= Standard deviation per period of (continuously compounded) rate of return

The two density functions, d_1 and d_2, and the formula are determined as follows:

$$V = [FN(d_1)] - E[N(d_2)] \, e^{-r_d t}$$

$$d_1 = \ln[F/E]/\sqrt{t} + \sqrt{t}/2$$

$$d_2 = d_1 - \sqrt{t}$$

Note: In the final derivations, the spot rate (S) and foreign interest rate (r_f) have been replaced with the forward rate (F).

The premium for a European put option is similarly derived:

$$V = \{F[N(d_1) - 1] - E[N(d_2) - 1]\} \, e^{-r_d t}$$

Example 4. Given the following data on basic exchange rate and interest rate values:

Data	Symbols	Numerical values
Spot rate	S	\$1.7/£
90-day forward	F	\$1.7/£
Exercise or strike rate	E	\$1.7/£
U.S. interest rate	r_d	0.08 = 8%
British pound interest rate	r_f	0.08 = 8%
Time	t	90/365
Standard deviation	σ	0.01 = 10%

$$d_1 = \ln[F/E]/\sqrt{t} + \sqrt{t}/2$$

$$d_1 = \ln[1.7/1.7]/(\sqrt{90/365}) + (.1)\sqrt{90/365}\,/2$$

$$= 0.025$$

$$d_2 = d_1 - \sqrt{t}$$

$$= 0.025 - (.1)\sqrt{90/365} = -0.025$$

The values of d_1 and d_2 are found from the cumulative normal probability table (Exhibit 17).

$$N(d_1) = 0.51; \; N(d_2) = 0.49$$

Substituting these values into the option premium formula yields:

$$V = [FN(d_1) - E[N(d_2)]\,e^{-r_d t}$$
$$= [(1.7)(0.51) - (1.7)(0.49)]2.71827^{-0.08(90/365)} = \$0.033/\pounds$$

Currency Option Pricing Sensitivity

If currency options are to be used effectively for hedging or speculative purposes, it is important to know how option prices (values or premiums) react to their various components. Four key variables that impact option pricing are (1) changing spot rates, (2) time to maturity, (3) changing volatility, and (4) changing interest differentials.

The corresponding measures of sensitivity are:

1. *Delta,* the sensitivity of an option premium to a small change in the spot exchange rate.
2. *Theta,* the sensitivity of an option premium with respect to the time to expiration.
3. *Lambda,* the sensitivity of an option premium with respect to volatility.
4. *Rho* and *phi,* the sensitivity of an option premium with respect to the interest rate differentials.

Exhibit 18 describes how these sensitivity measures are interpreted.

Factors Influencing Transfer Price Determination

MNCs typically have a variety of objectives. Maximizing global after-tax profits is a major goal. Other goals often include increasing market share, maintaining employment stability and harmony, and being considered the

Exhibit 17 Cumulative Normal Probability Tables

The probability that a drawing from a unit normal distribution will produce a value less than the constant d is:

$$\text{Prob}\ (\tilde{z} < d) = \int_{-\infty}^{d} \frac{1}{\sqrt{2\pi}}\ e^{-z^2/2} dz = N(d)$$

Range of d: −2.49 ≤ d ≤ 0.00

d	−0.00	−0.01	−0.02	−0.03	−0.04	−0.05	−0.06	−0.07	−0.08	−0.09
−2.40	0.00820	0.00798	0.00776	0.00755	0.00734	0.00714	0.00695	0.00676	0.00657	0.00639
−2.30	0.01072	0.01044	0.01017	0.00990	0.00964	0.00939	0.00914	0.00889	0.00866	0.00842
−2.20	0.01390	0.01355	0.01321	0.01287	0.01255	0.01222	0.01191	C.01160	0.01130	0.01101
−2.10	0.01786	0.01743	0.01700	0.01659	0.01618	0.01578	0.01539	0.01500	0.01463	0.01426
−2.00	0.02275	0.02222	0.02169	0.02118	0.02068	0.02018	0.01970	0.01923	0.01876	0.01831
−1.90	0.02872	0.02807	0.02743	0.02680	0.02619	0.02559	0.02500	0.02442	0.02385	0.02330
−1.80	0.03593	0.03515	0.03438	0.03362	0.03288	0.03216	0.03144	0.03074	0.03005	0.02938
−1.70	0.04457	0.04363	0.04272	0.04182	0.04093	0.04006	0.03920	0.03836	0.03754	0.03673
−1.60	0.05480	0.05370	0.05262	0.05155	0.05050	0.04947	0.04846	0.04746	0.04648	0.04551
−1.50	0.06681	0.06552	0.06426	0.06301	0.06178	0.06057	0.05938	0.05821	0.05705	0.05592
−1.40	0.08076	0.07927	0.07780	0.07636	0.07493	0.07353	0.07215	0.07078	0.06944	0.06811
−1.30	0.09680	0.09510	0.09342	0.09176	0.09012	0.08851	0.08691	0.08534	0.08379	0.08226
−1.20	0.11507	0.11314	0.11123	0.10935	0.10749	0.10565	0.10383	0.10204	0.10027	0.09853
−1.10	0.13567	0.13350	0.13136	0.12924	0.12714	0.12507	0.12302	0.12100	0.11900	0.11702
−1.00	0.15866	0.15625	0.15386	0.15150	0.14917	0.14686	0.14457	0.14231	0.14007	0.13786
−0.90	0.18406	0.18141	0.17879	0.17619	0.17361	0.17106	0.16853	0.16602	0.16354	0.16109
−0.80	0.21186	0.20897	0.20611	0.20327	0.20045	0.19766	0.19489	0.19215	0.18943	0.18673
−0.70	0.24196	0.23885	0.23576	0.23270	0.22965	0.22663	0.22363	0.22065	0.21770	0.21476
−0.60	0.27425	0.27093	0.26763	0.26435	0.26109	0.25785	0.25463	0.25143	0.24825	0.24510
−0.50	0.30854	0.30503	0.30153	0.29806	0.29460	0.29116	0.28774	0.28434	0.28096	0.27760
−0.40	0.34458	0.34090	0.33724	0.33360	0.32997	0.32636	0.32276	0.31918	0.31561	0.31207
−0.30	0.38209	0.37828	0.37448	0.37070	0.36693	0.36317	0.35942	0.35569	0.35197	0.34827
−0.20	0.42074	0.41683	0.41294	0.40905	0.40517	0.40129	0.39743	0.39358	0.38974	0.38591
−0.10	0.46017	0.45620	0.45224	0.44828	0.44433	0.44038	0.43644	0.43251	0.42858	0.42465
0.00	0.50000	0.49601	0.49202	0.48803	0.48405	0.48006	0.47608	0.47210	0.46812	0.46414

Exhibit 17 *Continued*

Range of d: 0.00 ≤ d ≤ 2.49

d	0.00	0.01	0.02	0.03	0.04	0.05	0.06	0.07	0.08	0.09
0.00	0.50000	0.50399	0.50798	0.51197	0.51595	0.51994	0.52392	0.52790	0.53188	0.53586
0.01	0.53983	0.54380	0.54776	0.55172	0.55567	0.55962	0.56356	0.56749	0.57142	0.57535
0.20	0.57926	0.58317	0.58706	0.59095	0.59483	0.59871	0.60257	0.60642	0.61026	0.61409
0.30	0.61791	0.62172	0.62552	0.62930	0.63307	0.63683	0.64058	0.64431	0.64803	0.65173
0.40	0.65542	0.65910	0.66276	0.66640	0.67003	0.67364	0.67724	0.68082	0.68439	0.68793
0.50	0.69146	0.69497	0.69847	0.70194	0.70540	0.70884	0.71226	0.71566	0.71904	0.72240
0.60	0.72575	0.72907	0.73237	0.73565	0.73891	0.74215	0.74537	0.74857	0.75175	0.75490
0.70	0.75804	0.76115	0.76424	0.76730	0.77035	0.77337	0.77637	0.77935	0.78230	0.78524
0.80	0.78814	0.79103	0.79389	0.79673	0.79955	0.80234	0.80511	0.80785	0.81057	0.81327
0.90	0.81594	0.81859	0.82121	0.82381	0.82639	0.82894	0.83147	0.83398	0.83646	0.83891
1.00	0.84134	0.84375	0.84614	0.84850	0.85083	0.85314	0.85543	0.85769	0.85993	0.86214
1.10	0.86433	0.86650	0.86864	0.87076	0.87286	0.87493	0.87698	0.87900	0.88100	0.88298
1.20	0.88493	0.88686	0.88877	0.89065	0.89251	0.89435	0.89617	0.89796	0.89973	0.90147
1.30	0.90320	0.90490	0.90658	0.90824	0.90988	0.91149	0.91309	0.91466	0.91621	0.91774
1.40	0.91924	0.92073	0.92220	0.92364	0.92507	0.92647	0.92785	0.92922	0.93056	0.93189
1.50	0.93319	0.93448	0.93574	0.93699	0.93822	0.93943	0.94062	0.94179	0.94295	0.94408
1.60	0.94520	0.94630	0.94738	0.94845	0.94950	0.95053	0.95154	0.95254	0.95352	0.95449
1.70	0.95543	0.95637	0.95728	0.95818	0.95907	0.95994	0.96080	0.96164	0.96246	0.96327
1.80	0.96407	0.96485	0.96562	0.96637	0.96712	0.96784	0.96856	0.96926	0.96995	0.97062
1.90	0.97128	0.97193	0.97257	0.97320	0.97381	0.97441	0.97500	0.97558	0.97615	0.97670
2.00	0.97725	0.97778	0.97831	0.97882	0.97932	0.97982	0.98030	0.98077	0.98124	0.98169
2.10	0.98214	0.98257	0.98300	0.98341	0.98382	0.98422	0.98461	0.98500	0.98537	0.98574
2.20	0.98610	0.98645	0.98679	0.98713	0.98745	0.98778	0.98809	0.98840	0.98870	0.98899
2.30	0.98928	0.98956	0.98983	0.99010	0.99036	0.99061	0.99086	0.99111	0.99134	0.99158
2.40	0.99180	0.99202	0.99224	0.99245	0.99266	0.99286	0.99305	0.99324	0.99343	0.99361

Exhibit 18   Interpretations of Option Pricing Sensitivity Measures

Sensitivity Measures	Interpretation	Reasoning
Delta	The higher the delta, the greater the chance of the option expiring in-the-money.	Deltas of .7 or up are considered high.
Theta	Premiums are relatively insensitive until the last 30 or so days.	Longer maturity options are more highly valued. This gives a trader the ability to alter an option position without incurring significant time value deterioration.
Lambda	Premiums rise with increases in volatility.	Low volatility may cause options to sell. A trader is hoping to buy back for a profit immediately after volatility falls, causing option premiums to drop.
Rho	Increases in home interest rates cause call option premiums to increase.	A trader is willing to buy a call option on foreign currency before the home interest rate rises (interest rate for the home currency), which will allow the trader to buy the option before its price increases.
Phi	Increases in foreign interest rates cause call option premiums to decrease.	A trader is willing to sell a call option on foreign currency before the foreign interest rate rises (interest rate for the foreign currency), which will allow the trader to sell the option before its price decreases.

best firm in the industry. However, not all of these goals are mutually compatible or collectively achievable. In addition, all MNCs face governmental and other constraints that influence their ability to achieve their objectives in the manner they would prefer.

In determining international intercorporate transfers and their prices, an MNC must consider both its objectives and the constraints it faces. An MNC can also achieve further tax savings by manipulating its transfer prices to and from its subsidiaries. In effect, it can transfer taxable income out of a high-tax country into a lower-tax country. This tax scheme can be particu-

International Finance

larly profitable for MNCs based in a country that taxes only income earned in that country but does not tax income earned outside the country. But even if a country taxes the global income of its corporations, often income earned abroad is not taxable by the country of the corporate parent until it is remitted to the parent.

If penetrating a foreign market is a company's goal, that company can underprice goods sold to foreign affiliates, and the affiliates can then sell them at prices that their local competitors cannot match. And if antidumping laws exist on final products, a company can underprice components and semifinished products to its affiliates. The affiliates can then assemble or finish the final products at prices that would have been classified as dumping prices had they been imported directly into the country rather than produced inside.

Transfer prices can be used in a similar manner to reduce the impact of tariffs. Although no company can do much to change a tariff, the effect of tariffs can be lessened if the selling company underprices the goods it exports to the buying company. The underpricing of intercorporate transfers can also be used to get more products into a country that is rationing its currency or otherwise limiting the value of goods that can be imported. A subsidiary can import twice as many products if they can be bought at half price. Artificially high transfer prices can be used to circumvent or lessen significantly the impact of national controls.

A government prohibition on dividend remittances to foreign owners can restrict the ability of a firm to transfer income out of a country. However, overpricing the goods shipped to a subsidiary in such a country makes it possible for funds to be taken out. High transfer prices can also be considerable when a parent wishes to lower the profitability of its subsidiary. This may be because of demands by the subsidiary's workers for higher wages or participation in company profits, because of political pressures to expropriate high-profit foreign-owned operations, or because of the possibility that new competitors will be lured into the industry by high profits. High transfer prices may be desired when increases from existing price controls in the subsidiary's country are based on production costs. Transfer pricing can also be used to minimize losses from foreign currency fluctuations, or shift losses to particular affiliates. By dictating the specific currency used for payment, the parent determines whether the buying or the selling unit has the exchange risk. Altering the terms and timing of payments and the volume of shipments causes transfer pricing to affect the net foreign exchange exposure of the firm.

International transfer pricing has grown in importance with international business expansion. It remains a powerful tool with which multinational companies can achieve a wide variety of corporate objectives. At the same time, international transfer pricing can cause relations to deteriorate between multinationals and governments because some of the objectives achievable through transfer price manipulation are at odds with government objectives. Complex manipulated transfer pricing systems can also make the evaluation of subsidiary performance difficult and can take up substantial amounts of costly, high-level management time. In spite of these problems, the advantages of transfer price manipulation remain considerable. These advantages keep international transfer pricing high on the list of important decision areas for multinational firms. Usually, multinational companies should use more consideration than domestic companies when setting transfer prices since they have to cope with different sets of laws, different competitive markets, and different cultures. Thus, it is not surprising that determining prices for international sales is very difficult, especially for internal transactions among the segments.

When planning an internal sales price (transfer pricing) strategy, a corporation should be concerned about subsidiaries' contributions and competitive positions as well as the whole corporation's profitability. The reason is that subsidiaries' contributions do not always increase overall company profit. High income means more tax. For instance, the parent company wants to show losses and pass income to its segments in low-tax-rate areas. The other reason is that transfer pricing should benefit both sides: seller and buyer. Otherwise, inappropriate transfer pricing may cause company conflicts, even lower profits. For example, if the transfer price of the parent company is too high, the subsidiaries may buy from outside parties even though buying from the parent company may be better for the organization as a whole. On the contrary, if the subsidiaries want to buy at very low prices, the parent company may not make deals with them at such a low price because it could get more money elsewhere. Thus, deciding how to set appropriate transfer prices is not easy. Multinational companies should know transfer price methods very well. They should focus on transfer price considerations, such as tax rates, competition, custom duties, currencies, and government legislation.

INTERNATIONAL TRANSFER PRICING

A transfer price is defined as the price charged by a selling department, division, or subsidiary of a multinational company (MNC) for a product or service supplied to a buying department, division, or subsidiary of the same MNC (in a different country). A major goal of transfer pricing is to enable divisions that exchange goods or services to act as independent businesses. It also encompasses the determination of interest rates for loans, charges for rentals, fees for services, and the methods of payments. International transfer pricing is an important issue for several reasons. First, raw materials not available or in short supply for an MNC unit in one country can be imported for sale or further processing by another unit of the MNC located in a different country. Second, some stages of an MNC's production process can be conducted more efficiently in countries other than that where the MNC has its headquarters. Third, many MNCs operate sales offices in some countries but do no manufacturing there. To sell their products, the sales offices or subsidiaries must import products from manufacturing affiliates in other countries. Fourth, many services for MNC units are rendered by MNC headquarters or other affiliates of an MNC. Finally, there are many international financial flows between units of an MNC. Some are payments related to goods or services provided by other units; some are loans or loan repayments; some are dividends; and some are designed to lessen taxes or financial risks. Since the transfer price for a product has an important effect on performance of individual foreign subsidiary managers, their motivation, divisional profitability, and global profits, top management of MNCs should devote special attention to designing international transfer pricing policies.

Transfer Price Structure

The four types of transfer prices used for management accounting purposes are cost-based transfer price, market-based transfer price, negotiated transfer price, and dictated transfer price.

The *cost-based transfer price* is based on full or variable cost. It is simple for companies to apply, and it is a useful method to strengthen compatibility. The major disadvantages of a transfer price at cost are that it lacks incentives to control costs by selling divisions, and it is unable to provide information for companies to evaluate performance by the return on investment (ROI) formula. In order to increase the efficiency of cost control, companies should use standard costs rather than actual costs. Also, since many tax agencies require international firms to present transfer prices fairly, the use of the cost-based method may be deemed an unfair transfer price.

The *market-based transfer price* is the one charged for products or services based on market value. It is the best approach to solve the transfer pricing problem. It connects costs with profits for managers to make the best decisions and provides an excellent basis for evaluating management performance. However, setting market-based transfer prices should meet two conditions: (1) a competitive market condition must exist, and (2) divisions must be autonomous from each other for decision making.

A *negotiated transfer price* is set by the managers of the buying and selling divisions with an agreement. A major advantage of this transfer pricing is that both sides are satisfied. But, it has some disadvantages. The division whose manager is a good negotiator may get more profits than those whose manager is a poor negotiator. Also, managers may spend a lot of time and costs in the negotiations. Usually, companies use negotiated transfer prices in those situations where no intermediate market prices are available.

Dictated transfer prices are determined by top managers. They set the price in order to optimize profit for the organization as a whole. The disadvantage is that the dictated transfer price may conflict with the decisions that division managers make.

Transfer Price Considerations

In order to be successful in business, companies must consider any policy very carefully, and transfer pricing is no exception. Income taxes and the various degrees of competition are very important considerations. Custom duties, exchange controls, inflation, and currency exchange rates are usually considered. Moreover, a multinational company should think over the whole company's profits when it sets transfer prices. On the other hand, transfer pricing strategies by parent companies should not injure subsidiaries' interests. For example, take an American firm with a subsidiary in a country with high tax rates. In order to minimize the subsidiary's tax liability and draw more money out of the host country, the parent company sets high transfer prices on products shipped to the subsidiary, and sets low transfer prices on those imported from the subsidiary. However, this procedure may cause the subsidiary to have high duties, or may increase its product cost and reduce its competitive position. Therefore, multinational companies should weigh the importance of each factor when planning transfer pricing strategies.

Many firms tend to hold the "overall profit" concept as the basic idea for transfer pricing strategies. Also, a lot of companies think of other considerations, such as differentials in income tax rates and income tax legislation among countries and, for another example, the competitive position of foreign subsidiaries.

Tax Purposes

The basic idea of transfer pricing for tax purposes is to maneuver profit out of high-tax-rate countries to lower ones. The foreign subsidiary can sell at or below cost to other family members in lower-tax-rate areas, thereby showing a loss in its local market, but contributing to the profit of buying members.

However, inappropriate transfer prices may cause companies to be exposed to tax penalties. For example, a parent company in the United States thinks that the U.S. tax rates are lower than its segment pays in a foreign country with high tax rates. The parent firm does not want to comply with the tax law of that foreign country. The company sets a high transfer price for its subsidiary so that profit of the subsidiary can be shifted to the parent company. But if the transfer price does not comply with the foreign country's tax law, the profit shifted may be lost due to a tax penalty.

In addition, revenue flights become significant as countries compete for international tax income. This stimulates national treasuries to strengthen their power to control transfer pricing practices. The United States and its major trading partners have revised transfer pricing regulations or introduced new rules.

Recent Changes in Transfer Pricing Regulations

Section 482 of the U.S. Internal Revenue Code authorizes the IRS to allocate gross income, deductions, credits, or allowances among controlled taxpayers if such allocation is necessary to prevent evasion of taxes.

Another provision in this section defines intangibles to include (1) patents, (2) copyrights, (3) know-how, (4) trademarks and brand names, (5) franchises, and (6) customer lists. Guided by this rule, the IRS can collect royalties commensurate with the economic values of intangibles, and can prevent many U.S. parent companies from transferring intangibles to related foreign subsidiaries at less than their value.

In the end of 1990, the IRS issued the proposed regulations. Under the proposed regulations, the U.S. subsidiaries owned by a foreign multinational company should submit the detailed records that reflect the profit or loss of each material industry segment. Noncompliance with the regulations may cause financial penalties.

In addition, other countries, such as Canada and Japan, enforced new transfer pricing regulations. In June 1990, the European Community countries reached agreements for the harmonization of direct taxes in Europe. They made a draft on transfer pricing arbitration to resolve transfer pricing disputes between member countries.

The Tax Implementation Problems Faced by MNCs

All of these changes put high pressure on managers and create high costs to firms seeking to maintain appropriate income allocation. First, traditional management transfer pricing methods are based on marginal revenue and marginal cost. These techniques do not satisfy the documentation and verification rules for tax purposes. Thus, managers must find appropriate transfer pricing methods to comply with tax complication requirements. Second, recent tax rules require that the transfer price methods should meet comparability and unrelated party standards. Following these tax codes will increase a global company's information costs. For example, multinational companies should submit various data and documents for different tax compliance requirements. They may even hire tax consultants to prepare all the necessary documents. Third, a manager must carefully analyze all the potential economic considerations of transfer pricing; otherwise, failure to follow tax compliance requirements may cause heavy penalties.

Transfer Pricing Methods for Tax Purposes

When the transfer price does not satisfy tax requirements, the firm can reset its transfer pricing systems. However, this approach requires companies to apply multiple transfer pricing methods fluently. Usually, there are six transfer pricing methods for tax purposes. Exhibit 19 summarizes these six transfer pricing methods.

Comparable Uncontrolled Price. This price is based on comparable prices through transactions with unrelated parties. The company that focuses on a market-based organization uses this method. In a market-based structure, the company's segments are autonomic and are independent from each other. The managers can decide to make transactions with unrelated parties if the prices offered by other members in the company are not reasonable.

Here is an example to illustrate how to use a comparable uncontrolled method. A parent company sells fiber to its foreign segment and to other parties in its domestic market. On the other hand, its foreign segment buys fiber from the parent company as well as from other manufacturers in the local market. Thus, under a comparable uncontrolled method, the parent company can set a transfer price according to both selling and buying comparable prices resulting from transactions with unrelated parties.

However, comparable uncontrolled prices are acceptable only for those global companies that make internal transactions among their segments and whose segments do not compete with each other in their backyards.

Resale Price Method. This method is the best for intermediate distributions, such as wholesalers and retailers. It also applies to market-based organizations. Usually these companies add little or no value to goods and do not have a significant manufacturing process. The formula for this method is:

$$\text{Transfer Price} = \text{Resale Price to Unrelated Party} - (\text{Gross Profit Ratio} \times \text{Resale Price})$$

Note: Computing the gross profit ratio is based on information on the profit ratios in the same product categories used by unrelated parties.

However, the information on profit ratios set by competitors is not readily obtainable and may be costly for global companies.

Exhibit 19 Transfer Pricing Methods for Tax Purposes: Tangible Property

Method Description	Comparable Uncontrolled Price	Resale Price	Cost-Plus	Comparable Profits	Profits Split	Other
Comparable Factors	Comparable sales between unrelated parties	Price to unrelated party less related gross profit; nonmanu-facturing	Production costs plus gross profit on unrelated sales	Priced to yield gross profits comparable to those for other firms	Split of combined operating profits of controlled parties	Gross profit reasonable for facts and circumstances
Comparability and Reliability Standards	Similarity of property; underlying circumstance	Comparable gross profit relative to comparable unrelated transfer	Gross profit from same type of goods in unrelated resale	Gross profit within range of profits for broadly similar product line	Allocation of combined profits of controlled parties	As appropriate
Measures of Comparability	Functional diversity; product category; terms in financing and sales; discounts	Functional diversity; product category; terms in financing and sales; intangibles	Functional diversity; accounting principles; direct vs. indirect costing	Business segment; functional diversity; different product categories acceptable if in the same industry	Profits split by unrelated parties or splits from transfers to unrelated parties	Fair allocation of profits relative to unrelated party sales

Continued

Exhibit 19 *Continued*

Method	Comparable Uncontrolled Price	Resale Price	Cost-Plus	Comparable Profits	Profits Split	Other
Description						
Same Geographic Market	Required	Required	Required	Required	Required, but some flexibility	Required, but some flexibility
Comments	Deemed the best method for all firms; minor accounting adjustments allowed to qualify as "substantially the same"	The best method for distribution operations; only used where little or no value added and no significant processing	Internal gross profit ratio is acceptable if there are both purchases from and sales to unrelated parties	Not if seller has unique technologies or intangibles because resale price is fixed; adjust the transfer price from seller	Controlled transaction allocations compared to profits split in uncontrolled transactions	Least reliable; uncertainty and costs of being wrong are severe

The Cost-Plus Method. This method is adaptable to manufacturing companies. Under this method the amount of company product cost is adjusted for gross profit ratios. The ratio can be the internal gross profit ratio if both sides in the company purchase from and sell to unrelated parties and have comparable price standards, or the ratio can be matched based on a comparable company's profit ratios for the same broad product category. The formula for the cost-plus method is:

$$\text{Transfer Price} = \text{Production Cost} + (\text{Gross Profit Ratio} \times \text{Sales Price to Unrelated Parties})$$

Comparable Profit Method. This is a profit markup method. The gross profit part of the transfer price should be compared to those within a range of profits for broadly similar product lines. The profit ratio should be based on some internal profit indicators, such as rate of return. However, if the product or process involved is unique in the market, setting transfer prices under this method is unacceptable.

Profits-Split Method. Under this method, MNCs allocate the combined profits of subsidiaries that are involved in internal transactions. Parent companies compute the combined profits after these goods to customers are sold outside of the group. Also, the profit for each member involved in intercompany transactions is comparable to unit profits where unrelated parties participate in similar activities with comparable products. The profits-split method requires companies to obtain reliable detailed data for comparable products. Usually, it is not difficult for the company to get aggregate profit data for the whole product line, but there is not enough detailed data to provide for analysis and comparison. Thus, appropriate profits-split pricing relies on whether the information on profits is reliable.

Other methods. The five transfer pricing methods cannot be adopted all the time. For example, say an MNC trades products only among its members. Each member does not purchase from or sell to unrelated parties because those products are unique and no company outside uses them. Under this situation, when the parent company sets transfer prices, there are no reliability and comparability standards to match because no comparable products in the markets exist. Therefore, the company cannot use any transfer pricing method just mentioned. When none of the five specific methods can be applied reasonably, the company may choose another method. The method should be reasonable given the facts and circumstances, and should fairly allocate profits relative to unrelated party sales. However, there are no objective guidelines under this approach. The company may face challenges by tax agencies that could result in high costs of noncompliance. To minimize the risk of penalties, companies should have the documents to justify why a method was chosen.

Competitive Position

For an MNC, its overall international competitive position is its major consideration in determining prices. It may adjust internal transfer prices to increase its segment competition so as to increase the whole company's profitability. Companies that use cost-based pricing methods especially present this approach. Under cost-based pricing, companies calculate cost on different bases, such as full cost, variable cost, and marginal cost. These cost bases allow the parent company to change its internal transfer price accordingly. For example, when a subsidiary faces serious competition in its local market, the parent company can charge the subsidiary at a reduced price based on full cost or only variable cost. In this way, the subsidiary can decrease its sale prices quickly to maintain its market share. On the other hand, in order to increase the subsidiary's competition, the parent company may raise transfer prices that it pays to its subsidiary so that the parent company can help its division make a high profit. In this way, the parent company can improve its division's ability to get loans from local banks. As a result, the subsidiary can be supported by significant financing to defeat its local competitors. Therefore, through various transfer pricing strategies, multinational corporations create good conditions for their subsidiaries to improve divisional contributions to the profitability and competitive position of the overall corporation.

The Influence of Governments

As many governments become more sensitive to their loss of tax revenues and/or to the negative effects of competition suffered by purely local producers, they revise or even create laws to control transfer pricing practices. Therefore, multinational companies should focus on the "fairness" of the transfer price and on regulations specifying market prices. Also, multinational companies should improve their long-term relationships with various governments.

The Influence of Currency Changes

Typically in many foreign countries, particularly in Latin America, the value of the local currency depreciates quite rapidly relative to the U.S. dollar. Among American corporations having subsidiaries in those areas, the parent companies may charge them high transfer prices for exported products, or may pay them low transfer prices for imported products. By so doing, the parent companies can draw divisional profit out of the host countries and minimize the exchange risk.

Custom Duties

In the 2000s, rates of custom duties and customs legislation are important factors when MNCs plan international transfer pricing strategies. If there is a high custom rate in a divisional country, the parent company may offer a low transfer price to its subsidiary for parts shipped to the division. Thus, the parent company reduces the custom duty payments, and helps the subsidiary compete in foreign markets by keeping costs low.

ANALYSIS OF FOREIGN INVESTMENTS

Also called *international capital budgeting*, foreign investment decisions are basically capital budgeting decisions at the international level. Capital budgeting analysis for foreign as compared to domestic projects introduces the following complications:

1. Cash flows to a project and to the parent must be differentiated.
2. National differences in tax systems, financial institutions, financial norms, and constraints on financial flows must be recognized.
3. Different inflation rates can affect profitability and the competitive position of an affiliate.
4. Foreign exchange rate changes can alter the competitive position of a foreign affiliate and the value of cash flows between the affiliate and the parent.
5. Segmented capital markets create opportunities for financial gains or they may cause additional costs.
6. Political risk can significantly change the value of a foreign investment.

   The foreign investment decision requires two major components:

- *The estimation of the relevant future cash flows.* Cash flows are the dividends and possible future sales price of the investment. The estimation depends on the sales forecast, the effects on exchange rate changes, the risk in cash flows, and the actions of foreign governments.
- *The choice of the proper discount rate (cost of capital).* The cost of capital in foreign investment projects is higher due to the increased risks of:
    - Currency risk (or foreign exchange risk). This risk of changes in exchange rates may adversely affect sales by making competing imported goods cheaper.

- *Political risk (or sovereignty risk).*The possibility of nationalization or other restrictions with net losses to the parent company.

The methods of evaluating multinational capital budgeting decisions include net present value (NPV), adjusted present value (APV), and internal rate of return (IRR).

Example 5. Here we will illustrate a case of multinational capital budgeting. We analyze a hypothetical foreign investment project by a U.S. manufacturing firm in Korea. The analysis is based on the following data gathered by a project team.

Product. The company (to be called Ko-tel hereafter) is expected to be a wholly owned Korean manufacturer of customized integrated circuits (ICs) for use in computers, automobiles, and robots. Ko-tel's products would be sold primarily in Korea, and all sales would be denominated in Korean won.

Sales. Sales in the first year are forecasted to be won 26,000 million. Sales are expected to grow at 10% per annum for the foreseeable future.

Working capital. Ko-tel needs gross working capital (that is, cash, receivables, and inventory) equal to 25% of sales. Half of gross working capital can be financed by local payables, but the other half must be financed by Ko-tel or Am-tel.

Parent-supplied components. Components sold to Ko-tel by Am-tel have a direct cost to Am-tel equal to 95% of their sales price. The margin is therefore 5%.

Depreciation. Plant and equipment will be depreciated on a straight-line basis for both accounting and tax purposes over an expected life of 10 years. No salvage value is anticipated.

License fees. Ko-tel will pay a license fee of 2.5% of sales revenue to Am-tel. This fee is tax-deductible in Korea but provides taxable income to Am-tel.

Taxes. The Korean corporate income tax rate is 35%, and the U.S. rate is 38%. Korea has no withholding tax on dividends, interest, or fees paid to foreign residents.

Cost of capital. The cost of capital (or minimum required return) used in Korea by companies of comparable risk is 22%. Am-tel also uses 22% as a discount rate for its investments.

Inflation. Prices are expected to increase as follows.

Korean general price level:	9% per annum
Ko-tel average sales price:	9% per annum
Korean raw material costs:	3% per annum
Korean labor costs:	12% per annum
U.S. general price level:	5% per annum

Exchange rates. In the year in which the initial investment takes place, the exchange rate is won 1,100 to the dollar. Am-tel forecasts the won to depreciate relative to the dollar at 2% per annum.

Dividend policy. Ko-tel will pay 70% of accounting net income to Am-tel as an annual cash dividend. Ko-tel and Am-tel estimate that over a five-year period the other 30% of net income must be reinvested to finance working capital growth.

Financing. Ko-tel will be financed by Am-tel with a $11,000,000 purchase of won 8,250,000,000 common stock, all to be owned by Am-tel.

In order to develop the normal cash flow projections, Am-tel has made the following assumptions:

1. Sales revenue in the first year of operations is expected to be won 26,000 million. Won sales revenue will increase annually at 10% because of physical growth and at an additional 9% because of price increases. Consequently, sales revenue will grow at $(1.1)(1.09) = 1.20$, or 20% per annum.

2. Korean raw material costs in the first year are budgeted at won 4,000 million. Korean raw material costs are expected to increase at 10% per annum because of physical growth and at an additional 3% because of price increases. Consequently, raw material cost will grow at $(1.1)(1.03) = 1.13$, or 13% per annum.

3. Parent-supplied component costs in the first year are budgeted at won 9,000 million. Parent-supplied component costs are expected to increase annually at 10% because of physical growth, plus an additional 5% because of U.S. inflation, plus another 4% in won terms because of the expected deterioration of the won relative to the dollar. Consequently, the won cost of parent-supplied imports will increase at $(1.1)(1.05)(1.04) = 1.20$ or 20% per annum.

4. Direct labor costs and overhead in the first year are budgeted at won 5,000 million. Korean direct labor costs and overhead are expected to increase at 10% per annum because of physical growth, and at an additional 12% because of an increase in Korean wage rates. Consequently, Korean direct labor and overhead will increase at $(1.1)(1.12) = 1.232$ or 12.32% per annum.

5. Marketing and general and administrative expenses are budgeted at won 4,000 million, fixed, plus 4% of sales.

6. As for liquidation value, at the end of five years, the project (including working capital) is expected to be sold on a going-concern basis to Korean investors for won 9,000 million, equal to $7,045.1 at the expected exchange rate of won 1,277.49/$. This sales price is free of all Korean and U.S. taxes, and will be used as a terminal value.

Exhibit 20 Beginning Balance Sheet

Assets	Millions of Won	Thousands of Dollars
1 Cash balance	650	619
2 Accounts receivable	0	0
3 Inventory	1,050	1,000
4 Net plant and equipment	7,000	6,667
5 Total	8,700	8,286
Liabilities and Net Worth		
6 Accounts payable	700	667
7 Common stock equity	8,000	7,619
8 Total	8,700	8,286

Exhibit 21 Sales and Cost Data

Item	1	2	3	4	5
1 Total sales revenue	26,000	31,174	37,378	44,816	53,734
2 Korean raw material	4,000	4,532	5,135	5,818	6,591
3 Components purchases from Am-tel	9,000	10,811	12,986	15,599	18,737
4 Korean labor and overhead	5,000	6,160	7,589	9,350	11,519
5 Depreciation	700	700	700	700	700
6 Cost of sales [(2)+(3)+(4)+(5)]	18,700	22,203	26,410	31,467	37,547
7 Gross margin [(1)−(6)]	7,300	8,971	10,968	13,349	16,187
8 License fee [2.5% of (1)]	650	779	934	1,120	1,343
9 Marketing and general & administrative	5,040	5,247	5,495	5,793	6,149
10 EBIT* [(7)−(8)−(9)]	1,610	2,945	4,538	6,436	8,694
11 Korean income taxes (35%)	564	1,031	1,588	2,253	3,043
12 Net income after Korean taxes [(10)−(11)]	1,047	1,914	2,950	4,183	5,651
13 Cash dividend [70% of (12)]	733	1,340	2,065	2,929	3,956

* EBIT = earnings before interest and taxes

Given the facts and stated assumptions, the beginning balance sheet is presented in Exhibit 20. Exhibit 21 shows revenue and cost projections for Ko-tel over the expected five-year life of the project.

Exhibit 22 shows how the annual increase in working capital investment is calculated. According to the facts, half of gross working capital must be financed by Ko-tel or Am-tel. Therefore, half of any annual increase in working capital would represent an additional required capital investment.

Exhibit 23 forecasts project cash flows from the viewpoint of Ko-tel. Thanks to healthy liquidation value, the project has a positive NPV and an IRR greater than the 22% local (Korean) cost of capital for projects of similar risk. Therefore Ko-tel passes the first of the two tests of required rate of return.

Does Ko-tel also pass the second test? That is, does it show at least a 22% required rate of return from the viewpoint of Am-tel? Exhibit 24 shows the calculation for expected after-tax dividends from Ko-tel to be received by Am-tel. For purposes of this example, note that Am-tel must pay regular U.S. corporate income taxes (38% rate) on dividends received from Ko-tel. However, the U.S. tax law allows Am-tel to claim a tax credit for income taxes paid to Korea on the Korean income that generated the dividend. The process of calculating the regional income. in Korea is called "grossing up" and is illustrated in Exhibit 24, lines 1, 2, and 3.

This imputed Korean won income is converted from won to dollars in lines (4) and (5). Then the U.S. income tax is calculated at 38% in line (6). A tax

Exhibit 22 Working Capital Calculation

		Year			
Item	*1*	*2*	*3*	*4*	*5*
1 Total revenue	26,000	31,174	37,378	44,816	53,734
2 Net working capital needs at year-end [25% of (1)]	6,500	7,794	9,344	11,204	13,434
3 Less year-beginning working capital	1,700	6,500	7,794	9,344	11,204
4 Required addition to working capital	4,800	1,294	1,551	1,860	2,230
5 Less working capital financed in Korean by payables	2,400	647	775	930	1,115
6 Net new investment in working capital	2,400	647	776	930	1,115

Exhibit 23 Cash Flow Projection—NPV and IRR for KO-TEL

Item		0	1	2	3	4	5
1	EBIT [Exhibit 21, (10)]		1,610	2,945	4,538	6,436	8,694
2	Korean income taxes (35%)		564	1,031	1,588	2,253	3,043
3	Net income, all equity basis		1,047	1,914	2,950	4,183	5,651
4	Depreciation		700	700	700	700	700
5	Liquidation value						9,000
6	Half of addition to working capital		2,400	647	775	930	1,115
7	Cost of project	−8,000					
8	Net cash flow	−8,000	−654	1,967	2,874	3,954	14,236
9	IRR	0.26765 = 26.77%					
10	NPV = PV (at 22%) − I	$1,421.37					

credit is given for the Korean income taxes paid, as calculated in line (7). Line (8) then shows the net additional U.S. tax due, and line (10) shows the net dividend received by Am-tel after the additional U.S. tax is paid. Finally, Exhibit 25 calculates the rate of return on cash flows from Ko-tel from the viewpoint of Am-tel. However, Ko-tel fails to pass the test because it has a negative NPV and an IRR below the 22% rate of return required by Am-tel.

What-If Analysis

So far the project investigation team has used a set of "most likely" assumptions to forecast rates of return. It is now time to subject the most likely outcome to sensitivity analyses. The many probabilistic techniques are available to test the sensitivity of results to political and foreign exchange risks as are used to test sensitivity to business and financial risks. But it is more

Exhibit 24 After-Tax Dividend Received by AM-TEL

Item	0	1	2	3	4	5
				Year		

Item	0	1	2	3	4	5
In millions of won						
1 Cash dividend paid [Exhibit 21, (13)]		733	1,340	2,065	2,929	3,956
2 70% of Korean income tax [Exhibit 21, 11)]		394	721	1,112	1,577	2,130
3 Grossed-up dividend [(1)+(2)]		1,127	2,061	3,177	4,506	6,086
4 Exchange rate (won/$)	1,050.00	1,075.20	1,101.00	1,127.43	1,154.49	1,182.19
In thousands of dollars						
5 Grossed-up dividend [(3)/(4)×1000]		1,048.2	1,872.3	2,817.7	3,902.7	5,147.8
6 U.S. tax (38%)		398.3	711.5	1,070.7	1,483.0	1,956.2
7 Credit for Korean taxes [(2)/(4)×1000]		366.9	655.3	986.2	1,365.9	1,801.7
8 Additional U.S. tax due [(6)−(7), if (6) is larger]		31.4	56.2	84.5	117.1	154.4
9 Excess U.S. tax credit [(7)−(6), if (7) is larger]		0.0	0.0	0.0	0.0	0.0
10 Dividend received by Am-tel after all taxes [(1)/(4)×1,000−(8)]		649.9	1,160.8	1,747.0	2,419.7	3,191.6

common to test sensitivity to political and foreign exchange risk by simulating what would happen to net present value and earnings under a variety of what-if scenarios. Spreadsheet programs such as Excel can be utilized to test various scenarios (see Exhibit 26).

Exhibit 27 depicts an NPV graph of various scenarios.

Exhibit 25 NPV and IRR for AM-TEL

Item	0	1	2	3	4	5
				Year		
In millions of won						
1 License fee from Ko-tel (2.5%) [Exhibit 21, (7)]		650	779	934	1,120	1,343
2 Margin on exports to Ko-tel [5% of (3) in Exhibit 21]		450	541	649	780	937
3 Total receipts		1,100	1,320	1,584	1,900	2,280
4 Exchange rate (won/$)	1,050.00	1,092.00	1,135.68	1,181.11	1,228.35	1,277.49
In thousands of dollars						
5 Pretax receipts [(3)/(4) × 1000]		1,007.3	1,162.2	1,340.9	1,547.1	1,784.9
6 U.S. taxes (38%)		382.8	441.6	509.5	587.9	678.3
7 License fees and export profits, after tax		624.5	720.6	831.4	959.2	1,106.7
8 After-tax dividend [Exhibit 24, (10)]		649.9	1,160.8	1,747.0	2,419.7	3,191.6
9 Project cost	−11,000.0					
10 Liquidation value						7,045.1
11 Net cash flow	−11,000.0	1,274.4	1,881.4	2,578.3	3,378.8	11,343.4
12 IRR	0.1714 = 17.14%					
13 NPV = PV (at 22%) − I	($1,549.20)					

Exhibit 26 NPV Profiles for KO-TEL and AM-TEL—Sensitivity Analysis

Discount rate (%)	0	4	8	12	16
Project pt of view (Ko-Tel)	$14,378.57	10,827.01	7,958.71	5,621.75	3,702.09
Parent pt of view (Parent)	$9,456.37	6,468.67	4,043.44	2,056.77	415.48

20	22	24	28	32	36	40
$2,113.17	1,421.37	788.65	(322.83)	(1,261.35)	(2,058.46)	(2,739.20)
$(951.26)	(1,549.20)	(2,097.87)	(3,066.53)	(3,890.23)	(4,594.99)	(5,201.51)

Exhibit 27   NPV Profiles for KO-TEL and AM-TEL Sensitivity Analysis

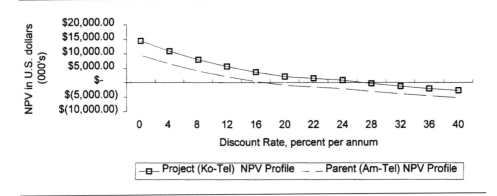

BALANCE OF PAYMENTS

The balance of payments (BOP) is a systematic record of a country's receipts from, or payments to, other countries. In a way, it is like the balance sheets for businesses, only on a national level. The reference you see in the media to the *balance of trade* usually refers to goods within the goods-and-services category of the current account. It is also known as *merchandise* or *visible trade* because it consists of tangibles such as foodstuffs, manufactured goods, and raw materials. Services, the other part of the category, is known as *invisible trade* and consists of intangibles such as interest or dividends, technology transfers, and others (such as insurance, transportation, financial). When the net result of both the current account and the capital account yields more credits than debits, the country is said to have a surplus in its balance of payments. When there are more debits than credits, the country has a deficit in the balance of payments. Exhibit 28 presents the components of each and their interrelationships. Data are collected by the U.S. Customs Service. Figures are reported in seasonally adjusted volumes and dollar amounts. It is the only nonsurvey, nonjudgmental report produced by the U.S. Department of Commerce. The balance of payments appears in *Survey of Current Business*.

The balance of payments (BOP) statement is based on a double-entry bookkeeping system that is used to record transactions. Every transaction is recorded as if it consisted of an exchange of something for something else— that is, both as a debit and as a credit. As a general rule, currency inflows are recorded as *credits*, and outflows are recorded as *debits*. Exports of goods and services are recorded as a credit. In the case of imports, goods and services are normally acquired for money or debt. Hence, they are recorded as a debit. When items are given rather than exchanged, special types of counterpart entries are made in order to furnish the required offsets. Just as in accounting, the words *debits* and *credits* have no value-laden meaning such as

Exhibit 28   Balance of Payments Accounts

Sources	Uses	Balance Account (Sources minus Uses)
1. Current Transactions		
• Exports of goods	• Imports of goods	• Trade balance
• Exports of services	• Imports of services	• Invisible balance
Inward unilateral transfers	Outward unilateral transfers	• Net inward transfers
• Private	• Private	
• Public	• Public	
		CA = Current account balance = Net inflow from current transactions
2. Capital transactions		
• Classified as private versus government		
• or classified by type of transaction:		
• Inward portfolio investment	• Outward portfolio investment	• Net inward investment
• Short-term	• Short-term	
• Long-term	• Long-term	
• Inward direct investment	• Outward direct investment	• Net inward investment
		KA = Capital account balance = Net inflow from capital transactions
3. Settling Items		
3A. Central bank transactions		
• Decreases in foreign reserves	• Increases in foreign reserves	• Net decreases in foreign reserves $(-)\Delta$RFX
3B. Errors and Omissions		
• Unrecorded inflows	• Unrecorded outflows	• Errors, omissions (E&O)
	Grand total of BOP	$0 = \text{CA} + \text{KA} - \Delta\text{RFX} + \text{E\&O}$

good or *bad*. They are merely rules or conventions; they are not economic truths. Under the conventions of double-entry bookkeeping, an increase in the assets of an entity is always recorded as a debit; an increase in liabilities is always recorded as a credit. Thus a debit records (1) the import of goods and services, (2) an increase in assets, or (3) reductions in liabilities. A credit

International Finance

records (1) the export of goods and services, (2) a decrease in assets, or (3) increases in liabilities.

The balance of payments statement is traditionally divided into three major groups of accounts: (1) current accounts, (2) capital accounts, and (3) official reserves accounts. We will define these accounts and illustrate them with some transactions. The double-entry system used in the preparation of the balance of payments allows us to see how each transaction is financed and how international transactions usually affect more than one type of account in the balance of payments. The illustrative transactions presented here are for the United States in the year 2001.

Current Accounts

The current accounts record the trade in goods and services and the exchange of gifts among countries. The trade in goods is composed of exports and imports. A country increases its exports when it sells merchandise to foreigners. This is a source of funds and a decrease in real assets. A country increases its imports when it buys merchandise from foreigners. This is a use of funds and an acquisition of real assets.

Example 6. A U.S. manufacturer exports $5,000 in goods to a customer in Greece. According to the sales terms, this account will be paid in 90 days. In this case two things happen. The merchandise export, a reduction in real assets, provides the manufacturer with an increase in external purchasing power—a credit entry. But the exporter is financing the transaction for 90 days—that is, the exporter's accounts receivable have increased by $5,000. It has made a short-term investment abroad. This acquisition of a short-term asset or claim represents a use of the country's external purchasing power—a debit entry. Here is how this transaction will appear in the U.S. balance of payments accounts:

	Debit	Credit
Increase in short-term claims on foreigners (the account receivable)	$5,000	
Exports		$5,000

The *trade in services* includes interest and dividends, travel expenses, and financial and shipping charges. Interest and dividends received measures the services that the country's capital has rendered abroad. Payments received from tourists (travel expenses) measures the services that the country's hotels and shops provided to visitors from other countries. Financial and shipping charges to foreigners measures the fees that the financial community and ship owners charged to foreigners for the special services they rendered. In these cases the nation gave the service of assets it possessed (for example, a hotel) to foreigners. Thus, these transactions are a source of external purchasing power. In contrast to the preceding cases, when the country's residents are the recipients of the services from foreign-owned assets, then the given country loses purchasing power to the rest of the world.

Example 7. A Japanese resident visits the United States. Upon his arrival, he converts his $2,500 worth of yen into dollars at the airport bank. When the visitor departs, he has no dollars left. In this case, the United States provided services (such as hotel rooms and meals) to foreigners amounting to $2,500. In exchange for these services, U.S. banks now have $2,500 worth of yen. The willingness of U.S. banks to hold the yen balances (a liability of the Japanese government) provided the required financing for the Japanese tourist. The services that the United States provided to the Japanese are clearly a source of purchasing power for the U.S.—a credit entry. However, the accumulation of yen in U.S. banks is an increase in U.S. holdings of foreign financial obligations (a use of purchasing power) and thus a debit entry. Here is how this transaction will appear in the U.S. balance of payments:

	Debit	Credit
Increase in short-term claims on foreigners (the yen holdings)	$2,500	
Receipts for travel services to foreigners		$2,500

The exchange of gifts among countries is recorded in the *unilateral transfers account*. This account is also labeled *remittances* or *unrequited transfers*. A typical entry in this account is the money that emigrants send home. Another example is a gift that one country makes to another. When a country makes a gift, it can be said that it is acquiring an asset that we may call *goodwill*. As with any other asset acquisition, the gift represents a use of external purchasing power.

Example 8. A U.S. resident who left his family in Hungary sends a $1,000 check to his wife back home. The gift that the U.S. resident sent is a unilateral or unrequited transfer. For accounting purposes it can be treated as a purchase of goodwill that reduces U.S. purchasing power—a debit entry. However, this gift was made possible by the credit or financing that the Hungarians extended to the United States when it accepted a financial obligation (a check) in U.S. dollars from a U.S. resident. This latter part of the transaction, an increase in liabilities to foreigners, is a source of external purchasing power—a credit entry. Here is the entry for this transaction in the U.S. balance of payments:

	Debit	Credit
Gifts to foreigners	$1,000	
Increase in short-term liabilities to foreigners (the check)		$1,000

Capital Accounts

The *capital accounts* record the changes in the levels of international financial assets and liabilities. The various classifications within the capital account are based on the original term to maturity of the financial instrument and on the extent of the involvement of the owner of the financial asset in the activities of the security's issuer. Accordingly, the capital accounts are subdivided into *direct investment*, *portfolio investment*, and *private short-term capital flows*. Direct investment and portfolio investment involve financial instruments that had a maturity of more than one year when issued initially. The distinction between direct investment and portfolio investment is made on the basis of the degree of management involvement. Considerable management involvement is presumed to exist in the case of direct investment (usually a minimum of 10% ownership in a firm) but not in the case of portfolio investment.

Example 9. A U.S. resident buys a $3,000 bond newly issued by a German company. The payment is made with a check drawn on a U.S. bank account. As a result the U.S. resident now owns a German bond, and the German company owns U.S. dollar deposits. The U.S. acquisition of the German bond (a financial asset) implies a decrease in U.S. external purchasing power; the account long-term investments or claims on foreigners must be debited. However, the dollar balances that the German company now owns represent an increase in U.S. liabilities to foreigners, which increases U.S. foreign purchasing power; the account short-term liabilities to foreigners must be credited. Two interpretations are possible here. We can say that the purchase of the German bond was financed with short-term liabilities issued by the United States, or we can say that the purchase of short-term dollar instruments by the Germans was financed by their issuing a long-term bond. Here is how this transaction will appear in the U.S. balance of payments:

	Debit	Credit
Increase in long-term claims on foreigners (the German bond)	$3,000	
Increase in short-term liabilities to foreigners (the dollar deposits)		$3,000

Short-term capital movements involve financial paper with an original maturity of less than one year. In the previous examples, payment or financing of various transactions was made with either currency or a short-term financial note (except for the alternative interpretation of the financing of Example 9). Payments in U.S. dollars were called changes in U.S. short-term liabilities to foreigners. Payments in foreign currency were called changes in U.S. short-term claims on foreigners. These accounts are part of the short-term capital accounts. The examples produced a net increase in short-term claims on foreigners (a debit) of $7,500, and a net increase in short-term liabilities to foreigners (a credit) of $4,000. A different type of entry in these accounts is presented in the next example.

Example 10. A Swiss bank buys $6,000 worth of U.S. Treasury bills. It pays by drawing on its dollar account with a U.S. bank. The sale of Treasury bills to a foreigner is equivalent to the U.S. borrowing external purchasing power from foreigners, an increase in liabilities to foreigners (a credit entry). However, the purchase is paid by reducing another debt that the United States had to foreigners (U.S. dollars in the hands of foreigners). This reduction in U.S. liabilities is a use of funds (a debit) entry. Here is how the transactions will be entered in the U.S. balance of payments:

	Debit	Credit
Decrease in short-term liabilities to foreigners (the dollar account)	$6,000	
Increase in short-term liabilities to foreigners (the Treasury bill)		$6,000

Official Reserve Accounts

Official reserve accounts measure the changes in international reserves owned by the country's monetary authorities, usually the central bank, during the given period. International reserves are composed mainly of gold and convertible foreign exchange. Foreign exchange reserves are financial assets denominated in currencies such as the U.S. dollar that are freely and easily convertible into other currencies, but not in such currencies as the Indian rupee, because the Indian government does not guarantee the free conversion of its currency into others and not much of an exchange market exists for it. An increase in any of these financial assets constitutes a use of funds, while a decrease in reserve assets implies a source of funds. In some situations, this fact seems to run against intuitive interpretations, as when we say that an increase in gold holdings is a use of funds (signified by a minus sign or debit in the U.S. balance of payments). However, an increase in gold holdings is a use of funds in the sense that the United States might have chosen to purchase an alternative asset such as a bond issued by a foreign government. In order to be considered part of official reserves, the financial asset must be owned by the monetary authorities. The same asset in private hands is not considered part of official reserves. In addition, the country's own currency cannot be considered part of its reserve assets; a country's currency is a liability of its monetary authorities. Changes in these liabilities are reported in the short-term capital account, as illustrated previously.

Example 11. An exchange trader is worried about a recent economic forecast anticipating an increased rate of inflation in the United States. As a result, she sells $4,700 of U.S. dollars against marks (she buys marks). The transaction is done with the U.S. central bank. One reason the central bank may have wanted to be a party to this transaction is to support the exchange rate of the U.S. dollar—that is, to prevent the possible decline in the value of the U.S. dollar that could result from the sale of the dollars by the trader. When the central bank purchases the dollars, there is a decrease in U.S. liabilities to foreigners—a debit entry. The central bank pays for these dollars with marks it maintained as part of the country's foreign exchange reserves. The central bank is financing the support of the exchange rate with its reserves. The decrease in the level of reserves (a financial asset) represents a credit entry. Here is how this transaction will appear in the U.S. balance of payments:

	Debit	Credit
Decrease in short-term liabilities to foreigners (the dollars)	$4,700	
Decrease in official exchange reserves (the marks)		$4,700

The Balance of Payments Statement

Exhibit 29 summarizes the transactions discussed in the examples of this section, together with some additional transactions, in a balance of payments statement for the United States. This is also the format followed by the International Monetary Fund in its analytic presentation of balance of payments tables which appears in *The Balance of Payments Yearbook*. Here are the additional transactions:

1. A foreign car, priced at $4,000 equivalent, is purchased. Payment is made with foreign currency held by the importer in the U.S.

2. A foreigner's fully owned subsidiary in the U.S. earns $2,000 in profits after taxes. These profits are kept as part of retained earnings in the subsidiary.

3. A U.S. resident receives a $500 check in guilders as a gift from a cousin who lives abroad.

4. A U.S. company purchases 30 percent of a foreign candy store for $4,500. Payment is made in U.S. dollars.

5. A U.S. resident sells a $5,000 bond issued by a U.S. company to a French investor. Payment is made in U.S. dollars.

6. The U.S. central bank purchases $5,000 worth of gold to be kept as part of foreign reserves. Payment is made in U.S. dollars.

Exhibit 29   Balance of Payments for U.S. for the Year 2000

(+: Sources of funds; –: Uses of funds)

Current accounts

Merchandise account

Exports	$5,000	
Imports	–4,000	
Balance in merchandise trade		1,000

Service account

Receipts for interest and dividends, travel, and financial charges	2,500	
Payments for interest and dividends, travel, and financial charges	2,000	
Balance in invisibles (services)		500
Balance of trade in goods and services			1,500

Unilateral transfers

Gifts received from foreigners	500	
Gifts to foreigners	–1,000	
Balance in unilateral transfers		–500
Current accounts balance		1,000

Capital accounts

Long-term capital flows

Direct investment

U.S. investment abroad (+: decrease; –: increase)	–4,500		
Foreigners' investment in U.S. (+: increase; –: decrease)	2,000	–2,500	

Portfolio investment

U.S. claims on foreigners (–: decrease; –: increase)	–3,000		
U.S. liabilities to foreigners (+: increase; –: decrease)	5,000	2,000	
Balance in long-term capital			–500
Basic balance			500

Private short-term capital flows

U.S. claims on foreigners (+: decrease; –: increase)	–4,000		
U.S. liabilities to foreigners (+: increase; –: decrease)	3,800		
Balance in short-term private capital			–200
Overall balance			300

Official reserves accounts

Gold exports less imports (–)	–5,000
Decrease or increase (–) in foreign exchange	4,700
Balance in official reserves	$–300

Each of the tables shown in a balance of payments represents the total of the transactions affecting the given account during the reporting period. However, these totals are not calculated from entries such as the ones we have discussed. In our examples, we recorded a debit and a credit for each international transaction. In practice, the data reported in the balance of payments are gathered from sources that often are concerned with only a portion of the transactions just discussed. For example, the data presented in the import account are often collected from customs declarations, while the financing of these transactions appears largely among the data for changes in foreign assets and liabilities reported by financial institutions. That is why we often find an additional account in the balance of payments statement: *errors and omissions.*

The accounts in the balance of payments are often presented in a format similar to the one shown in Exhibit 29. Entries appear under the three major groupings of accounts discussed in the preceding section: current accounts, capital accounts, and official reserve accounts. The statement often supplies totals for these major groups of accounts, as well as for some of their components. In addition, as one reads from top to bottom, the typical presentation of the balance of payments provides cumulative running subtotals, usually called *balances.*

In Exhibit 29 the *balance of trade in goods and services* shows a positive balance of $1,500. The sources of external purchasing power exceeded the uses of the trade accounts by $1,500. This balance is composed of a positive balance in trade in merchandise of $1,000 and a positive balance in trade in services of $500. When we add the negative balance of $500 in unilateral transfers to the balance of trade in goods and services, we obtain the *balance in the current accounts.* In the U.S., the current accounts balance is a surplus of $1,000.

In the long-term capital account, the U.S. had a deficit in direct investments. While foreigners invested $2,000 in the U.S. (the U.S. increased its liabilities to foreigners—a source of funds for the U.S.), the U.S. made direct investments in foreign countries in the amount of $4,500. (The U.S. acquired financial assets—a use of funds for the U.S.) Many of these investments involved acquiring whole ventures in other countries. Although in some cases the ownership had to be shared with others, the direct investor retained a substantial share (at least 10%) of the total ownership and, presumably, management. The deficit in the direct investment accounts of the U.S. was somewhat compensated for by the surplus in the portfolio accounts. Foreigners bought $2,000 more of long-term financial instruments from the U.S. than the U.S. bought from other countries. When the balance in the long-term capital accounts is added to the current accounts balance, the result is called the *basic balance.* The U.S. basic balance is a positive $500. In the private short-term capital accounts, foreigners bought $3,800 worth of short-term securities issued by the U.S., while the U.S. invested $4,000 in short-term securities issued by foreign countries. The sum of the private short-term capital accounts and the basic balance produces another subtotal, often referred to as the *overall balance*. In the U.S. the overall balance produces a surplus of $300—a net source of external purchasing power for the U.S.

By definition, the net change in official reserves must be equal to the overall balance. Given the double-entry system of accounting in the balance of payments, the net of the accounts included in any balance must equal the net of the remaining accounts. In the U.S. the surplus in the overall balance of $300 equals the increase in official reserves (a debit or minus entry) of $300. Alternatively, we can say that the total of all the entries in the U.S. balance of payments is 0.

SUPPLEMENT TO CHAPTER 43

PAYROLL TAXES

EMPLOYMENT ELIGIBILITY VERIFICATION

All employees must submit a completed Form I-9, Employment Eligibility Verification, at the time of hire. The purpose of Form I-9 is to ensure that employees are legally entitled to work in the United States. Form I-9 must be retained by the employer rather than submitted to Immigration and Naturalization Service.

SOCIAL SECURITY AND MEDICARE TAXES

For 2001, social security tax must be withheld from the first $80,400 of employee wages. Accordingly, the maximum amount that can be withheld from an employee's wages during 2001 is $4,984.80

TAX DEPOSITS

With respect to federal payroll tax deposits, as discussed on page 925 of the main text, effective for the quarter beginning January 1, 2001, if an employer accumulates less than a $2,500 tax liability during a calendar quarter, no deposits are required and the liability may be paid with the tax return for the period.

SAMPLE FILLED-IN TAX FORM

Presented below is Woody Corporation's Payroll summary for the quarter ended March 31, 2000. Woody Corporation's sole employee is John Zurg, who lives in Tennessee, a state that does not impose an income tax. In this example, Woody Corporation is a monthly depositer.

Pay Date	Gross Wages	FICA Withheld	Medicare Tax Withheld	Federal Tax Withheld	Net Pay
1/7	$1,955.18	$121.22	$28.35	$480.00	$1,325.61
1/21	1,826.21	113.23	26.48	460.00	1,226.50
2/4	1,955.18	121.22	28.35	480.00	1,325.61
2/18	1,632.87	101.24	23.68	440.00	1,067.95
3/3	1,550.00	96.10	22.48	430.00	1,001.42
3/17	1,985.82	123.12	28.79	490.00	1,343.91
3/31	1,755.00	108.81	25.45	450.00	1,170.74
Total	$12,660.26	$784.94	$183.58	$3,230.00	$8,461.74

Woody Corporation made the following federal tax deposits for the quarter ended March 31, 2001:

2/15	$1,518.56
3/15	1,468.98
4/15	2,179.50
Total	$5,167.04

Presented on the next page is Woody Corporation's filled-in Form 941 for the quarter ended March 31, 2001.

Payroll Taxes

Form **941**
(Rev. January 2001)
Department of the Treasury
Internal Revenue Service

Employer's Quarterly Federal Tax Return
▶ See separate instructions for information on completing this return.
Please type or print.

Enter state code for state in which deposits were made **only** if different from state in address to the right ▶ ☐ (see page 2 of instructions).

WOODY CORPORATION   03/31/2001

99-9999999

123 SPRINGFIELD STREET
ANY CITY   TN   11111

OMB No. 1545-0029

T	
FF	
FD	
FP	
I	
T	

If address is different from prior return, check here ▶ ☐

IRS Use

1 1 1 1 1 1 1 1	2	3 3 3 3 3 3 3	4 4 4	5 5 5
8 7 8 8 8 8 8 8		9 9 9 9	10 10 10 10 10 10 10 10 10	

If you do not have to file returns in the future, check here ▶ ☐ and enter date final wages paid . . ▶
If you are a seasonal employer, see **Seasonal employers** on page 1 of the instructions and check here . . ▶ ☐

1	Number of employees in the pay period that includes March 12th. ▶	1	1
2	Total wages and tips, plus other compensation	2	12660.26
3	Total income tax withheld from wages, tips, and sick pay	3	3230.00
4	Adjustment of withheld income tax for preceding quarters of calendar year . . .	4	
5	Adjusted total of income tax withheld (line 3 as adjusted by line 4 - see instructions)	5	3230.00
6	Taxable social security wages . . . . . **6a** 12660.26 x 12.4% (.124) =	6b	1569.87
	Taxable social security tips . . . . . **6c** x 12.4% (.124) =	6d	0.00
7	Taxable Medicare wages and tips . . . . **7a** 12660.26 x 2.9% (.029) =	7b	367.15
8	Total social security and Medicare taxes (add lines 6b, 6d, and 7b). Check here if wages are not subject to social security and/or Medicare tax . . . . ▶ ☐	8	1937.02
9	Adjustment of social security and Medicare taxes (see instructions for required explanation) Sick Pay $_____ +/- Fractions of Cents $ 0.02 +/- Other $_____ =	9	0.02
10	Adjusted total of social security and Medicare taxes (line 8 as adjusted by line 9 - see instructions)	10	1937.04
11	**Total taxes** (add lines 5 and 10)	11	5167.04
12	Advance earned income credit (EIC) payments made to employees	12	
13	Net taxes (subtract line 12 from line 11). **If $2,500 or more, this must equal line 17, column (d) below (or line D of Schedule B (Form 941))**	13	5167.04
14	Total deposits for quarter, including overpayment applied from a prior quarter	14	5167.04
15	**Balance due** (subtract line 14 from line 13). See instructions. . . . . . ▶	15	0.00
16	**Overpayment.** If line 14 is more than line 13, enter excess here . . ▶ $_____ and check if to be: ☐ Applied to next return **or** ☐ Refunded.		

- **All filers:** If line 13 is less than $2,500, you need not complete line 17 or Schedule B (Form 941).
- **Semiweekly schedule depositors:** Complete Schedule B (Form 941) and check here . . . . ▶ ☐
- **Monthly schedule depositors:** Complete line 17, columns (a) through (d) and check here . . . . ▶ ☒

17	Monthly Summary of Federal Tax Liability. Do not complete if you were a semiweekly schedule depositor.			
	(a) First month liability	(b) Second month liability	(c) Third month liability	(d) Total liability for quarter
	1518.56	1468.98	2179.50	5167.04

Sign Here
Under penalties of perjury, I declare that I have examined this return, including accompanying schedules and statements, and to the best of my knowledge and belief, it is true, correct, and complete.

Signature ▶   Print Your Name and Title ▶   Date ▶

For Privacy Act and Paperwork Reduction Act Notice, see back of Payment Voucher.   Form **941** (Rev. 1-2001)

ELECTRONIC FEDERAL TAX PAYMENT SYSTEM

With respect to EFTPS, as discussed on page 926 of the main text, the Treasury has raised the deposit threshold from $50,000 to $200,000. Further, non-employment taxes (e.g., corporate income taxes) will have to be included in the determination of whether the $200,000 threshold has been reached.

DIVESTITURE

APB OPINION NUMBER 29

According to APB Opinion Number 29, a gain or loss cannot be recorded on a corporate divestiture. However, footnote disclosure should be provided of the nature and provisions of the divestiture.

If there is an exchange of stock held by a parent in a subsidiary for stock of the parent company itself held by stockholders in the parent, there is a non-pro-rata split-off of the business segment because a reorganization is recorded at fair value. However, if there is a split-off of a targeted company distributed on a proportionate basis to the one holding the applicable targeted stock, it should be recorded at historical cost provided the targeted stock did not arise in contemplation of the later split-off. If the contemplated situation did in fact exist, then the transaction is recorded at fair value. In a split-off, there is a distribution of shares being exchanged on a proportionate basis for the shares of the new entity. In a split-off, the transaction is in effect the acquisition of treasury stock. Retained earnings is not charged.

In a spin-off, there is a distribution of the segment's shares to the investor's shareholders without the holders surrendering their shares.

In some instances, a split-off or spin-off may be treated as a discontinued operation of a business segment.

In a split-up, there is a transfer of the operations of the original entity to at least two new entities.

INDEX

Index   545

Index   549

Index

Investment worth, measuring, **S394–398**
internal rate of return (IRR), **S397–398**
net present value (NPV), **S395–397**
payback period, **S394–395**
Investments, 11–12
in balance sheet analysis, 645–46
Investor's Business Daily (IBD), **S53, S54**
Invoicing in accounting package software, **S34**
Involuntary conversion, fixed assets, 94
Involuntary petition, **S100–101**
Irrevocable contract, **S80**

JAMIS, **S35**
Javelin, **S334**
Job Cost Accounting and Management Information System (JAMIS), **S338**
Job Costing, **S338**
Job cost sheet, 219
Job costing in accounting software package, **S35**
Job order costing, 219–20, 236
and standard costing, 392
Joint costs, 213
Joint products:
allocation of costs to, 237–39
comparing methods of, 239–40
manufacturing in different proportions, 245–46
multiple split-off points, 244–45
physical measure and net realizable value, 241–43
processing vs. selling at split-off point decision, 246–48
unit cost method, 240–41
weighted-average unit cost method, 240–41
Journal of Banking and Finance, 419
Judgmental approach to forecasting, **S257–260**
Junior mortgages, 826
Junk bonds, 780
Just-in-time manufacturing, 497–506, **S227**
benefits of, 501–2
costing, 503–5
and cost management, 497–98, 503–5
definition of, 498–99
implementation examples, in U.S. 502–3
traditional manufacturing compared with, 499–501
cost management, 501
decentralization of services, 501
manufacturing cells and multi-function labor, 499–500
reduced inventories, 499

total quality control (TQC), 500

Kanban system, 498–99
Kansas City Board of Trade (KBOT), **S454**
Kerberos server, **S3**
KEYBEROS software, **S29**
Knowledge discovery, **S9**

Label checks, 36
Labor market conditions, indices of, 713
Labor performance report, 369
Labor time standards, 366
Labor variances, 366–68
Lagged model structure, 335–37
Lagged regression approach to cash flow forecasting, **S283–286**
Lagging indicators, 716
Lambda Index, 1012, 1018–19
Land improvements, fixed assets, 90
LANS, **S18**
Leap file, **S2**
Leapfrog financing, 862
Learning curve, 10, 525–28
Lease-purchase decision, 821, **S409–413**
Leases, 162–71, **S141–143**
advantages of leasing, 819
business combinations, **S143**
drawbacks to leasing, 820–21
financial leases, 819
lease-purchase decision, 821, **S409–413**
lessee, 162–65
capital lease, 163–65
operating lease, 162
lessor, 165–69
direct financing method, 165–67
operating method, 165
sales-type method, 167–69
leveraged leases, 170–71, 819
money-over-money leases, **S142–143**
operation (service) leases, 818
related parties, **S142**
sale and leaseback, 169, 819
subleases, 169–70
transfer of lease receivable, **S141–142**
Least-squares method (regression analysis), 260–61
Ledger, general, **S33**
Legal analysis, 1012
Legal considerations, 703–4, **S419–425**
Legal and regulatory environment of firm, **S419–425**
antitrust policy, government regulation and, **S420–422**
Cellar-Kefauver Act of 1950, **S422**
Clayton Antitrust Act, **S421**

enforcement, **S422**
interlocking directorates, **S421**
Robinson-Patman Act of 1936, **S421**
Sherman Antitrust Act of 1890, **S420–421**
cost-benefit analysis, **S375, S423–424**
goods, classification of, **S424**
public project analysis, **S423–424**
rationale for, **S419–420**
resource allocation and supply of public goods, **S422–423**
marginal social benefit, **S422–423**
social good and externalities, **S424–425**
Legality as element of contract, **S80–81**
Lessee, 162–65
Lessor, 165–69
Letter of credit, 801
Leverage, 282–83, **S432, S452–453**
advantages of, 941
disadvantages of, 941–42
financial, 282–83
operating, 282
total, 283
Leveraged buyouts, characteristics conducive to, 942
Leveraged leases, 170–71, 819
Liabilities, 97–106
in balance sheet analysis, 652–54
of NPOs, **S198**
bonds payable, 98–101
compensated absences, accounting for, 103–4
disclosure of long-term purchase obligations, 105–6
early extinguishment of debt, 101–2
estimated liabilities (contingencies), 102–3
obligations callable by the creditor, 105
refinancing short-term debt to long-term debt, 104–5
special termination benefits to employees, accounting for, 104
Librarian, EDP department, 34
Life cycles, management analysis of, **S380–381**
Life insurance, 703
Limit tests, 36
Linear Interactive and Disaster Optimization (LINDO), **S341**
Linear programming, 10, **S341–342**
computer software for, **S341–342**
drawback of, 517–18
and optimal budget, 512–17
Linear regression, estimating beta using, 524–25
Line of credit, 800–801
Link analysis, **S9**

Maximum efficiency standards, 357

Maximum practical capacity, 231

Mean absolute deviation (MAD), **S293, S307, S311–312**

Mean absolute percentage error (MAPE), **S276, S311–312, S327**

Mean squared error (MSE), **S277, S293, S311–312, S314**

Measures of overall economic performance, 711–12
  Gross Domestic Product (GDP), 711
  housing starts, 712
  industrial production, 711
  personal income, 711
  retail sales, 712
  unemployment rate, 712

Mechanic's lien, **S93**

Medical and catastrophic coverage, 702

Medicare tax, **S535**

Memory-based reasoning (MBR), **S10**

Merchandise trade, **S525**

Merger analysis, 1011

Mergers, 932–34, **S98–99**
  advantages of, 933
  conglomerate mergers, 932
  disadvantages of, 934
  earnings per share, effect on, 944–46
  financing, 939–44
    giving assets, 940–41
    giving stock, 940
    leverage, 941–42
  horizontal mergers, 932
  market price per share, effect on, 944–46
  vertical mergers, 932
  (*see also* Acquisitions; Business combinations)

Mergers and acquisitions, 12

Merton, Robert C., **S459**

MicroFCS, **S67**

Microeconomics, 705–7
  definition of, 705
  demand, supply, and market equilibrium, 706
  profit maximization, 707

Meta-data integration software, **S7–8**

Microsoft Excel, **S55, S281, S302–304, S334, S335, S393, S398**

MicroTSP, **S283, S327–328**

Middleware, **S17**

Minimum required rate of return, **S406**

Minitab, 59, **S305, S329, S336**

Mixed cost analysis, 10

Mixed costs, 213, 256
  analysis of, 257–67
    contribution income statement, 264
    high-low method, 258–60

least-squares method (regression analysis), 260–61
  multiple regression, 264
  regression statistics, 262–64
  using spreadsheet program for regression, 264

Mixed forecasting, **S307**

Mix variances, unfavorable, probable causes of, 379

Mix and yield variances, 379

Model specification, financial modeling:
  behavioral equations, 333
  decision rules, 334–35
  definitional equations, 333
  lagged model structure, 335–37
  model structure, 333–34

Modeling languages, financial, **S67**

Modified accelerated cost recovery system (MACRS), 910, **S183–189, S402–406, S417**
  half-year convention, **S402**
  by property class, **S404**

Modified return on investment (ROI), 481–83

Monetary indicators, 717–23
  balance of payments, 722
  federal deficit, 721–22
  inflation, 720–21
  interest rates, 718–19
  money supply, 718
  productivity and units labor costs, 721
  recession, 721
  strong dollar/weak dollar, 722–23

Monetary policy, 708–9

Money and credit market indicators, 714

Money market funds, 790

Money market preferred stock (MMPS), 794

Money-over-money lease, **S84–S85**

Money supply, as monetary indicator, 718

Monthly Economic Letter, **S53**

Monitoring accounts receivable, 743–45

Monthly material variance report, 366

Mortgage-backed securities, 775, 787–88

Mortgage bonds, 778, 828, 831

MPE, **S293**

MSE (mean squared error), **S277, S293, S307, S311–312, S314**

Multicollinearity, **S292**

Multidimensional database, **S6**

Multiemployer pension plans, **S144**

Multimedia database, **S6**

Multinational corporation, 887–888, **S151–162, S295–308**
  financial goals of, 888
  financial management of, 887
  foreign operations, types of, 888, **S151–162**

Multinational operations, accounting for, **S151–162**

accounting dimensions of international business, **S151–152**

"accounting nationalism," **S151–152**

accounting standards, harmonization of, **S160–162**
  European Economic Community (EEC), **S161**
  International Accounting Standards Committee (IASC), **S160–161**
  International Federation of Accountants (IFAC), **S161**
  International Organization of Securities Commissions (IOSCO), **S161**

dimensions, **S151–152**
  financial statements, translation of, **S155, S156–157, S158**
  foreign currency exchange rates, **S152–153**
  for foreign currency transactions, **S153–155**
  remeasurement procedures, **S155, S157, S159**
  denominated in foreign currency, **S153–155**
  denominated in U.S. currency, **S153**
  and environmental risks, **S238**
  functional currency, **S156–157**
  interpretation of foreign financial statements, **S160**
  Generally Accepted Accounting Principles (GAAP), **S160**
  spot rates, **S152–153**

Multiple conflicting goals:
  examples of, 518–20
  and goal programming, 517–20

Multiple cost pools, Hewlett-Packard illustration of, 494–97

Multiple discriminant analysis (MDA), 1012, **S62**

Multiple-employer pension plans, **S144–145**

Multiple regression, 264, **S279, S283–286, S288**

Multistage sampling, 628–29

Muticollinearity, **S292**

Mutual fund, **S457**

MYOB, **S341**

Naked call write, **S446**

Naked (uncovered) options, **S443–444**

Naked put write, **S444**

National Association of Accountants (NAA), 209

National Association of Business Economists (NABE), **S293**

National capital markets, 901–2

National Council on Compensation Insurance (NCCI) Inc., **S244**

National Environmental Policy Act (NEPA), **S102**

National Labor Act, 704
National money markets, 901–2
Negative externalities, **S424–425**
Negative good will, **S147**
Negotiated transfer price, **S509–510**
Neighborhood effects, **S424**
Net operating loss deductions, 909
Net present value (NPV), 422–26, **S395–397**
Net Prophet, **S339**
Network administrator, EDP department, 34
Net working capital per share, 935
Neural networks, **S13–14, S25–30**
 feed-forward networks, **S13–14**
Neuro Shell Trader, **S27**
New York Cotton Exchange (NCTN), **S454**
New York Futures Exchange, **S456, S479–480**
New York Stock Exchange (NYSE), **S480**
 Composite Stock Index, **S457**
 reporting to, 31
90-day Treasury bills, 719
Noise Control Act, **S103**
Noncompensatory stock option plans, **S129–130**
Noncontrollable costs, 216
Nondiscretionary projects, 432
Nonexclusionary goods, **S424**
Nonmanufacturing costs, 211
Nonprofit organizations:
 and capital budgeting, 437
 and cost-volume-revenue analysis, 277–78
Nonprofit organizations, management accounting for, **S191–222**
 break-even and cost volume- revenue analysis for, **S163–178**
 financial ratios, key, and metrics, **S191–222**
  acid-test (quick) ratio, **S194–195**
  accounts receivable ratios, **S195**
  activities statement, **S199–200**
  asset utilization, **S197**
  audit reliability, **S207**
  balance sheet, analysis of, **S193–197**
  bankruptcy, potential, spotting, **S207–210**
  capital structure, appraisal of, **S199**
  case study, **S210–222**
  contributions, **S205**
  costs, **S200–201**
  current ratio, **S194**
  disclosures, **S202**
  endowments, **S205–206**
  failure, potential, alertness to, **S207–210**
  financial flexibility, **S197**
  fixed assets, analysis of, **S198**
  fund balance, appraisal of, **S199**
  fund raising ability, **S204**

 grants, **S206**
 lawsuits against, **S202**
 liabilities, analysis of, **S198**
 liquidity analysis, **S193–197**
 operating capital maintenance, **S199**
 performance metrics, **S202–204**
 pledges, analysis of, **S204**
 pledges receivable and turnover, **S196**
 procedure, **S192**
 profitability, **S201–202**
 restricted access, **S194**
 revenue, **S200**
 risk/return analysis, **S206–207**
 software, **S207**
 solvency, **S199**
 Statement of Functional Expenses, **S201**
 trend analysis, **S192–193**
 working capital, **S193**
Nonrival goods, **S424**
Nonstatistical sampling, 632–33
Nonvested stock, **S130**
Non-volume-related overhead costs, 489–90
Normal capacity, 232
Normal selling price, accepting orders below, 289–90
Notes receivable, sample audit program for, 607–9

Occupational Safety and Health Act (OSHA), 703, **S84–85**
One World, **S337**
Online analytical processing (OLAP), **S14–15**
Online transaction processing (OLTP), **S15**
Open interest, **S481, S484**
Operating budget, 315–16
Operating exposure, 892, 896
Operating lease, 162
Operating leverage, 282
Operating method, leases, 165
Operating section, Statement of Cash Flows, 120–21
Operating (service) leases, 818
Operational auditing, 550
Operations, management analysis of, **S373–381**
 of business processes, **S379–380**
 cost analysis and control, **S374–376**
 "cost down," **S375**
 cost of quality (COQ), **S373, S376**
 divestitures, **S381**
 life cycles, **S380–381**
 performance measures, **S377**
 of personnel, **S378**
 prediction errors, cost of, **S376**
 productivity, studying, **S377**
 of profit, **S373**
 of revenue, **S374**
 of sales efforts, **S378**
 of space use, **S378–379**

 time considerations, **S381**
 value-added evaluation, **S380**
Opinion/recommendations, internal audit reports, 549
Opportunity costs, 217
Optimal budget, and linear programming, 512–17
Optimism Index, 717
Option contract, **S80**
Option price, **S490**
Option Pro, **S449**
An Option Valuator/ An Option Writer, **S449**
OptionVue, **S447**
Options, 775, **S430–451** (*see also* Financial derivatives)
Options and Arbitrage Software Package, **S449**
Option writing, **S443**
Options Clearing Corp. (OCC), **S433, S491**
Order paper, **S95**
Ordinary repairs, fixed assets, 90
Organization costs, **S118–119**
 amortization of, 909
Orion, **S334**
Oros EIS with Power Play, **S339**
Oros 3.0, **S339**
Out-of-pocket costs, 217
Out-of-the-money options, **S489**
Outsourcing, **S245, S249–250**
Output controls, 36
Overhead costing, 485–90
 multiple-product situation, 486–90
  costing accuracy problems, 488–89
  departmental rates, 488
  failure of volume-related cost drivers, 489–90
  plant-wide overhead rate, 487–88
 single-product situation, 485–86
Overhead variances, 368–77
 fixed, 370–71
 total overhead, variances for, 371–77
 variable, 369–70
Overseas Private Investment Corporation (OPIC), 901
Overstated liabilities, in balance sheet analysis, 654

Pabblo and Paccasso, **S242–243**
Pacific Stock Exchange, **S433**
Pacioli 2000, **S332**
Par value method, treasury stock, 109
Parol Evidence Rule, **S82**
Patents, **S125**
Payback:
 advantages of, 419–20
 deficiencies of, 420
Payback period, 419–20, **S394–395**
Payback reciprocal, 421
Pay-in-kind (PIK) preferred stock, 194

Index   **561**

Risk management and analysis,
  (cont.)
 risk analysis and management
    software, **S239–240**
  Intranet, **S240**
  RMIS (risk management infor-
    mation system), **S239**
  testing laboratory, **S244**
 risk control, **S240**
 risk modeling software applica-
    tions, **S243–244**
 software packages and prod-
    ucts, **S240–243, S244**
 terrorism, **S239**
 types of risk, **S238–239**
RISK MASTER/WIN, **S242**
Risk software, **S239–243**
Risk management database services,
  online, **S240–243, S244**
Risk management information sys-
  tems (RMIS), **S239, S244**
Risk modeling software applica-
  tions, **S243–244**
Risk/return analysis of NPO,
  S206–207
RMSE (root mean squared error),
  S293, S311–312
Robinson-Patman Act (1936), **S421**
Root mean squared error (RMSE),
  S293, S311–312
Round trip, **S481**
Round turn, **S481**

S corporations, 917–22, **S96**
Safety Compliance Assistant, **S243**
Sale and leaseback, 169–189
Sales, management analysis of, **S378**
Sales accounting, **S82–83**
 buyer, breach by, **S83**
 "cover," remedy of, **S83**
 seller, breach by, **S83**
Sales & Market Forecasting Toolkit,
  S323
Sales budget, 316–18
Sales efforts, management analysis
  of, **S378**
Sales force polling, in forecasting,
  S258
Sales forecasts, **S253**
 and managerial functions, **S252**
Sales mix analysis, 275–77
Sales-type method, leases, 167–69
Sales variances, 358–59
Sample audit program:
 for accounts payable, 615–17
 for cash in bank, 605–7
 for expense items, 621–22
 for fixed assets, 612–14
 for inventory, 609–12
 for prepaid expenses and deferred
    charges, 614–15
 for sales and other types of
    income, 619–20
 for stockholders' equity, 617–19
 for trade accounts and notes
    receivable, 607–9

Sampling:
 attribute, 625–26
 classical variables, 629
 discovery, 626–28
 multistage, 628–29
 nonstatistical, 632–33
 random, 623–26
SARIMA, **S275**
SAS (Statistical Analysis System), 59,
  S275, S283,S305, S329, S336
Scenario analysis in reengineering,
  S248
Scope, internal audit reports, 548
 basis of stock, 920
 computing taxable income, 918–19
 converting C corporations to,
    921–22
  built-in gains tax, 921
  passive investment income tax,
    921
  termination/revocation, 921–22
 distributions to shareholders, 919
 election, 917–18
 shareholder/employee benefits,
    920
 tax year, 920–21
Screening decisions, 413
SEC Compliance, 23
SEC filing requirements, 939–50
SEC reporting, 15–24
 Basic Information Package (BIP),
    16
 EDGAR system, 23
 Form 8-K, 22
 Form 10-K, 21–22
 Form 10-Q, 22–23
 Form S–1, 16–17
 Form S–2, 17
 Form S–3, 17–18
 Form S–4, 18
 Form S–8, 18
 Form S–18, 18
 integrated disclosure system, 16
 management discussion/analysis,
    18–19
 Regulation S-B, 21
 Regulation S-K, 20–21
 Regulation S-X, 19–20
 Secondary markets, **S341**
 Securities Act of 1933, 15
 Securities Exchange Act of 1934,
    16, **S24**
 takeover regulation, 23
Secured loans, 800
Secured-loan value, 960
Secured transactions, **S88–91**
 collateral, four types of, **S89**
 definitions, **S88**
 "floating lien," **S89**
 perfection, **S88–90**
 purchase money security interest
    (PSI), **S88, S89–90**
 requirements, **S88**
 rights of parties upon default,
    S32–S33
 types, two, **S31**
Securities, 775

Securities Act of 1933, 15
Securities Act of 1934, 16
Securities and Exchange
  Commission, **S138, S266**,
Security analyzer tool for analyzing
  networks (SATAN), **S20**
Security investments, 155–62
 equity method, 157–60
 held-to-maturity bond invest-
    ments, 161–62
 market value adjusted, 155–57
Segmental disclosures, **S133–136**
Segmental performance, 451–74
 cost center, 454–58
 investment center, 466–74
 manager performance, 452–53
 profit center, 458–61
 responsibility center, 453
 revenue center, 453–54
Segmental reporting, 200–205
 consolidation aspects, 204
 disclosure requirements, 203–5
 for mission centers, **S172–S76**
 reportable segments, determina-
    tion of, 201
 reporting requirements, 201–3
Self-constructed assets, 89
Self tender, 951
Selling and administrative expense
  budget, 322
Selling price, accepting orders
  below, 289–90
Semidirect costs, 295
Semivariable costs, *See* Mixed costs
Semivariance, 443
Senior management, special reports
  to, 28–29
Senior mortgages, 826
Sensitivity analysis, 443, **S2**
Serial bonds, 828
Service level, 765–68
Service sales revenue, **S109–111**
Shadow prices, 10
Shareholder value:
 cash flow from operations, 1004–5
 cost of capital, 1005–6
 creation of, 1007–9
 estimating, 1001–3
 limitations, 1009–10
 residual value, 1006–7
 value drivers, impact of, 1009
Shareholder value analysis, (SVA),
  999, 1009–10
Sharpe EL733, **S393**
"Shell," AI, **S21**
Sherman Antitrust Act (1890),
  S420–421
Short-form merger of corporations,
  S98–99
Short-term debt, refinancing to
  long-term debt, 104–5
Short-term debt securities, 775
Short-term financing, 797–813
 bank loans, 799–804
 commercial finance loan, 804
 commercial paper, issuance of,
    804–5

Index   567